Aqua Expeditions
Volume II

Great Global Hot Spots
For
Scuba Diving and Snorkeling

Wendy Canning Church

Books by Wendy Canning Church:

NON FICTION
*Aqua Expeditions: A Global Travel Guide for the Scuba
Diver and Snorkeler Volume I*

FICTION
An African Affair

Dedication

With many warm thanks, I again dedicate Aqua Expeditions to each writer and photographer that gave so generously and freely of their time, experience and talents to create this compendium. I speak for all of us in commending the scuba facilities, live-aboards and their professional staffs which uphold high safety standards. We laud the resorts that ensure qualitative lodging and service whether they be five-star or simple.

Wendy Canning Church

Forward

We do not add superfluous filler to our guides. We do include completed Scuba/Snorkeling Facilities Questionnaires that enable the traveler to plan with bonifide knowledge of their trip location.

We do not rate dive/snorkel sites. Knowledge gathered diving worldwide has proven to us time and time again that water and weather conditions can change not only day by day but also hourly or even at a moment's notice. This can make a dive site rated for even the most experienced undiveable. We do describe the underwater terrain, its flora, fauna and fishlife.

We do not recommend divers/snorkels going off on their own at an unfamiliar location no matter how great their experience We do urge you to dive /snorkel with a reliable facility who will guide you to and from a site, point out critters, corals, the underwater vegetation and assist in an emergency.

We do not completely rely on medical assistance at a destination but do carry a first aid kit, medical insurance card, DAN insurance (1 800 446 2671 or 919-684-2948 Fax 919 490 6630) and prescriptions with refills.

Before planning our vacations, we do check with our travel clinic for necessary shots and prophylactic pills (i.e. malaria to be taken before, during and after the trip).

We do not drink the water anywhere unless it is certified potable. We do drink bottled water. We do not buy food from street vendors. We do dine in recommended restaurants.

We do pack everything needed for the trip; (sun block, insect repellent, and a wide brim hat) lock our luggage and use nametags. We do not pack expensive items but carry them on board. In case of lost luggage, take on board a bathing suit and a lightweight change of clothing. Leave jewelry at home. We do not carry a great deal of cash. We do take fifty U.S. one dollar bills for tipping, luggage carts etc. We do make a duplicate list of traveler's checks and leave it with a friend.

We do arrive at the airport two hours ahead of time for international destinations. We do carry two forms of picture identification (passport and visa if necessary). We do not put our film through the x-ray machine but do hand it to security. We do double the amount of film we think we will use.

We do not rely completely on the media for information on political situations but we do check with the U.S. State Department Travel Advisory Section (202 647 5226). We do advise our global readers to check with their Consulates.

We do not rely on a whistle to attract the dive boat in high seas. We do use a Dive Alert that generates a blast of sound that can be heard a mile away. This is easily installed on your BC (800 275 4332 or fax 206 285 6897). We carry a Com2Me bright orange safety sausage which can be inflated in emergancies in our BC pocket. We do recommend that you have your equipment serviced before you depart and pack a redive kit. We do not rely on local facilities for repairs or spare parts.

We do dress accordingly, respecting the dress code of other countries.

We do suggest that you be in good condition before diving. We make an effort to keep fit with a regular regime at our local fitness center and spa. We have used their guidelines to find similar facilities and have included a number of highly qualified first rate hotels/resorts that have Spas and Scuba.

We hope you enjoy Volume II and wish you memorable travels!!!

We do a safety stop after every dive and do not ever dive or snorkel alone.

For more information on Aqua Expeditions Volume I contact:
Wendy Canning Church
92 Mount Vernon Street, Boston, MA 02108
Fax: (617) 227-8145

TABLE OF CONTENTS

Spas with Scuba

"The world is a book, and those who do not travel read only a page."

— *St. Augustine*

AFRICA

Kenya East
Steve Curtis

Kenya's coastline is comprised of 300 kms of white, palm fringed beaches, dotted with small islands, some seemingly held back in time, with donkeys the only transport amongst the ancient Arab buildings.

Kenya, located on the East Coast of Africa and divided by the equator is a land of great diversity and friendly people. North and Northeast Kenya are hot and arid, while the Highland areas of the South are cool and lush, with Mount Kenya, Africa's second highest mountain, towering over the fertile land of central Kenya.

The National Parks of Kenya are great tracts of rich savannas, arid deserts, lakes, forests, towering rock formations and hills, set aside for the preservation of the unique flora and fauna of the country.

Scorpion Fish by Carol Boone

THE DIVING

Aqua Venture, a PADI training facility, is situated halfway up the coastline at the friendly **Ocean Sports Hotel** on Watamu Beach (100 kms north of the main port of Mombassa). Here you can experience Kenya's underwater world at its finest. Aqua Ventures is able to cater all those interested in the sport of Scuba Diving, from those wishing to learn how to dive, to the more experienced who wish to renew their acquaintance with the underwater world. If you bring your own equipment, you must have buoyancy control device with auto inflator, a regulator with alternate air source, depth and pressure gauge. Wet suits are advised although the water is very warm. They recognize any diving qualification, i.e., PADI, NAUI, BSAC, VDST, VIT, VDTL and SAA.

The use of spear guns is absolutely forbidden. There is to be no collecting of or molesting of marine life whatsoever. Apart from charges at the various dive centers, there is a Marine Park fee.

You can fit in two dives a day in order to experience all the Indian Ocean has to offer a diver. Whether exploring the *Mida* wreck, visiting the underwater caves, or exploring the reef, you'll see it all!

WATAMU MARINE PARK

Watamu Marine Park boasts some of the finest diving off the coast of Kenya. **The diving grounds, which lie in the Marine Reserve, are unspoiled with a wide variety of both soft and hard corals as well as many varieties of fish.** Though Watamu cannot boast of the immense drop-offs and permanent gin clear waters of the Red Sea and The Great Barrier Reef, it can show divers unspoiled dive sites with abundant and varied coral and marine life which divers return to explore time and time again.

There are 12 sites, all of which are no more than a 20-minute boat ride away. The sites are all buoyed in order to prevent any coral damage due to anchors being thrown. The sites are generally 30 feet, dropping off to about 80 feet in depth with visibility sometimes exceeding 100 feet. There is also the possibility to dive on a nearby ship wreck or some caves where one might be lucky enough to see the giant rock cod.

The variety of colorful and interesting fish, as well as the beautiful and extensive coral "gardens" will dazzle you. It is truly a photographer's paradise, and all under the protection of the Marine Parks of Kenya.

CANYON

Descending, perhaps onto the aptly named **Canyon** dive site, the diver first notices the reef top, at about 30 feet, layered with an amazing variety of soft and hard corals. Beautiful butterfly and angelfish dance over the formations, whilst the occasional turtle glides by. Not far off lies the drop off, its edges decorated with orange, purple and white soft corals, the prominent walls home to a colorful variety of fish. Swimming over the edge, one immediately notices a large arch filled with shoals of iridescent glassfish, whilst up squadrons of jacks can often been seen patrolling the drop.

Crossing over the narrow, sandy "gully" (at about 80 feet) that separates the two reefs, the diver can observe snapper, sweet lips, various rock cod, and schools of fusiliers and banner fish, all the time keeping an eye out for the lurking shapes of the reef and whale shark that frequent these waters.

At the end of the dive, it is worth spending some time near the buoy line studying the small or more camouflaged treasures of the reef such as the gently swaying anemones and their companions, the "clown fish" and the vividly colored nudibranch or **the strange looking crocodile fish.**

On the return boat journey you may be lucky enough to encounter the playful dolphins and they do not mind stopping whilst you don mask, snorkel and fins and jump into the water and watch these beautiful creatures more closely.

BRAIN CORAL

At the end of one of the reefs stands a piece of rose coral approximately 3 meters high by 4 meters diameter. **This large piece of coral is often a favorite spot for large rock cod and at the right time of year, manta rays.**

One side of the coral slopes directly to the sand in which the diver often finds blue spotted rays resting. There is also a resident, very striking clown triggerfish. The other side of the coral is joined to the top of the reef, which is covered in a large variety of corals and home to a plentiful cross-section of the Indian Ocean marine life.

MORAY REEF

Buoyed slightly back from the drop off, this dive site means a short swim to visit the star of the show who lives halfway down the drop off, **"George, the tame Moray!"** George is a large brown moray (about 4 feet long) who is willing to be touched and has endless patience in posing for the photographer, often leaving his hole for a closer look at all the activity. The diver may be lucky enough to also spot what must be George's grandfather, as he is at least twice the size of George!

MIDA WRECK AND CAVES

These dive sites are a slightly longer boat ride (30 minutes) and can only be scheduled at certain tides. The wreck is approximately 7 years old and is an old steel hull shrimp boat (about 60 feet in length). It is home to many an octopus, moray, crocodile fish and rock cod, while keeping a close eye on the divers **are large schools of batfish!**

SCUBA AND SNORKELING FACILITIES QUESTIONNAIRE

NAME **Aqua Ventures Ltd./Steve Curtis**
ADDRESS **P.O. Box 275, Watamu**
Kenya, East Africa

TELEPHONE **(0122) 32420/32008**   FAX **(0122) 32266/32256**   TELEX
CAPITOL: **Nairobi**   GOVERNMENT: **Corrupt**
POPULATION: **25 Million**   LANGUAGE: **English/Swahili**
CURRENCY: **Kenya Schilling/Cents**   ELECTRICITY: **220v**
AIRLINES: **Kenya Airways**   DEPARTURE TAX? **U.S. $20**
NEED VISA/PASSPORT?   YES x   NO   PROOF OF CITIZENSHIP? YES   NO x

YOUR FACILITY IS CLASSIFIED AS: SCUBA CENTER x   RESORT
BUSINESS HOURS: **07:30 - 17:30**
CERTIFYING AGENCIES: **PADI, BSAC, CMAS**
LOG BOOK REQUIRED? YES x   NO
EQUIPMENT: SALES   RENTALS x   AIR FILLS
PRIMARY LINE OF EQUIPMENT: **Spirotechnique/Sea Quest**
PHOTOGRAPHIC EQUIPMENT: SALES   RENTALS   LAB

CHARTER/DIVE BOAT AVAILABLE? YES x   NO   DIVER CAPACITY **10-14-14**
COAST GUARD APPROVED? YES x   NO   CAPTAIN LICENSED? YES   NO
SHIP TO SHORE? YES x   NO LORAN?   YES NO x   RADAR? YES NO x
DIVE MASTER/INSTRUCTOR ABOARD? YES   NO   BOTH x

DIVING & SNORKELING: SALT x   FRESH
TYPE OF DIVING/SNORKELING IN AREA: WALL   BEACH x WRECK x   REEF x   CAVE x   ICE
DIVING/SNORKELING IN YOUR AREA IS BEST SUITED FOR: BEGINNER x INTERMEDIATE x ADVANCED x
BEST TIME OF YEAR FOR DIVING/SNORKELING: **N.B. Mid April-Mid August - Center closed**
TEMPERATURE: NOV-APRIL   **84F**   MAY-OCT: **78F conditions unpredictable**
VISIBILITY: DIVING: 30-80 FT   SNORKELING: 30-80FT

PACKAGES AVAILABLE: DIVE x   DIVE STAY x   SNORKEL   SNORKEL-STAY
ACCOMMODATIONS NEARBY: HOTEL x   MOTEL   HOME RENTALS
ACCOMMODATION RATES: EXPENSIVE x MODERATE x   INEXPENSIVE x
RESTAURANTS NEARBY: EXPENSIVE x MODERATE x   INEXPENSIVE x
YOUR AREA IS   REMOTE   QUIET WITH ACTIVITIES x   LIVELY
LOCAL ACTIVITY/NIGHTLIFE: **Casino/nightclubs 20 minutes drive away**
CAR NEEDED TO EXPLORE AREA? YES x   NO **(Also bicycles available for hire)**
DUTY FREE SHOPPING?   YES x   NO **(At airport)**

LOCAL EMERGENCY SERVICES   NEAREST HYPERBARIC TREATMENT FACILITY
COASTGUARD **None**   AUTHORITY: **Kenya Navy**
TELEPHONE: LOCATION: **Mombasa Harbour**
CALLSIGNS: TELEPHONE: **011-3468**

LOCAL DIVING DOCTOR:
NAME: **Dr. Bakara**
LOCATION: **Kenya Navy/Mombasa Harbour**
TELEPHONE: **011-451201 ext. 3401/3463**

The Caves are only in 6 meters of water and house some very large rock cod and are also teeming with sweet lips and red snappers. **White tip shark and barracuda are often spotted cruising by the caves.**

Kenya West

Safari in Masai Mara

Wendy Canning Church

AFTER DIVING KENYA

When we landed early in the morning, a member of Micato Safaris met us. We were greeted with the warmest of smiles, which we found ever pleasant on our four-day Safari. He took care of even the smallest detail, spoiling us outrageously. We were definitely "happy campers" throughout the trip.

In Nairobi we stayed at the Hilton before our safari, and the Nairobi Safari Club after. Both are quality properties, which have recently undergone extensive renovations. The newly built Grand Regency is ultra deluxe, while our favorite hotels were the in-town Norfolk Hotel and the Windsor Golf and Country Club located 25 minutes outside the city.

We flew out of Nairobi the next morning via Kenya Airways and landed in the Masai Mara Reserve. **The Reserve encompasses 750 square miles and borders southwestern Tanzania.** Our home for the next four days was the lovely **Mara Sopa Lodge,** tucked high in the lush green hills of the Reserve. The Lodge has all the comforts of a first class hotel and the true blessing of no telephone, television or radio in the guest rooms. The Lodge can accommodate 200 guests in small bungalows that have a spacious bedroom and bath. The public rooms are large and there is a pool and a boutique on the premises.

After unpacking and lunch, we embarked on our first game run. Game runs are scheduled for early in the morning and late in the afternoon, because the animals take shelter from the heat at midday. The Reserve allows no vans out after 6:00 PM to give the animals privacy. **We set out, donned in our safari hats (a gift from Minato Safaris), anxious to spot the "big five," i.e. elephant, lion, rhino, leopard, and water buffalo.**

Our guide and our driver had a warm manner, sense of humor, patience and eagle eyes, which made our Safari a very special one. The vans that Micato Safaris use carry only six guests although there are nine seats. This way everyone is assured a window seat for spotting game. Binoculars are provided to each guest and the guide's makes sure that the cooler in the van is always filled with cold soft drinks to quench the thirst from the heat and the dust. The roof shelters the passengers from the sun, but it "pops-up" so one can stand to take photographs. **No request for a photo shot was ever denied.** The guide would wait as long as it took for each of the photographers to get their shot, and always positioned the van so that the sun was in back of us to get the best possible picture... not always an easy feat.

Herds of buffalo grazed lazily before our eyes. Elephants moved gracefully, despite their size, out of the bush and into the morning's haze. Families of lions played and ate together, while rhinos romped in the river. On our last day we saw the remains of an impala, which a leopard had killed and carried high into a tree so that no other predators could move in on his catch.

The myriad of animal life was breathtaking. **We saw families of zebra, giraffe, waterbuck, cheetah, dik-dik impala, marabou stork, jackal, ostrich, monkey, brown llama, vulture, crocodile and even warthog.** The warthogs mate at the Reserve and then go across the border to Tanzania from February until April to have their babies. In August and September when they return you will see thousands of them in the Reserve.

The vegetation at the Reserve is sparse, as it is the main staple of the animals. **Each** elephant alone eats up to 250 kilograms a day and the hippo another 125 kilograms each day. The topography consists of flat plains stretching to hilly terrain and to the mountains beyond. One finds sausage trees, candelabra trees and palm trees within the grounds. The baby lion cubs especially favor the shade of the palm trees.

The days slipped by quickly with so much to see and delight the eye. Early mornings were spent on game runs, followed by lunch, then a dip in the pool or a siesta. In the afternoons we set off again on another game run.

Masai Mara National Reserve by Wendy Canning Church

There are two optional tours that one may take, a hot air balloon ride and a visit to a Masai village. The hot air balloon drifts high above the Reserve so that one can see and photograph the animals in the bush and roaming the plains. The ride is followed by a champagne breakfast.

The Masai people live both in and outside the Reserve. The tribe is one of the 42 that dwell in Kenya. Each tribe speaks its own language, but many speak Kiswahili as well so the tribes are able to communicate. The Masai are a nomadic tribe, moving every two years in search of grazing pasture and water, but they never move more than ten miles from their existing village.

They dwell in huts that are made of groups of sticks tied together and then the groupings are held together with mud. There is one large room in the hut with a small partition off the bedroom to house the husband when he comes to visit. As you enter the house there is a small alcove where the animals are kept. A small fire burns day and night for cooking. The tribe spends most of the day outdoors.

The clothing worn during the day serves as blankets at night. Their diet consists of meat and milk mixed with animal blood. There is a school nearby and while village elders encourage education, attendance is not mandatory and often irregular.

The boys are considered to be more important than the girls, as they can carry on the family line. Young men go out of the village to find brides at the age of 18. The bride will be 14. The men live a polygamous life, taking as many wives as they can afford, usually having to pay 10 cows for each bride. If the wife is unable to produce children, he is free to divorce her. Each wife has her own hut. Husbands who wish to visit a wife send a stool to the house with a boy child signaling that he will be having dinner at her hut and spending the night. A man who wishes to spend the night with another man's wife, whose husband is within the same age group as the prospective visitor, merely needs to place a spear in front of the woman's hut. This is interpreted as a "do not disturb" sign. There is no jealousy as this has been the custom for generations.

The Masai tribe values its cows highly, both for dowry purposes, and as a sacrifice to their God, Engai. If there are heavy rains, they will rejoice by sacrificing a cow.

Their spiritual leader, Laibon, communicates with Engai if there are problems. Duties are delegated and are different for the male and the female. The wives build the huts, make jewelry, fetch water and firewood and milk the cows. After circumcision at the age of 14, the men are called Moran warriors and take care of the village and graze the cows. At age 25 the men become Junior Elders. At age 40 they are Senior Elders and become part of the Counsel of Elders that resolves disputes. They are also responsible for seeking out new areas to live when it is time to move.

The average age at death is 50 for the males and 55 for the females. Healthcare is a problem. There are no inoculations in the village, so the village can suffer yellow fever, cholera and malaria.

Nevertheless, the Masai are a happy lot. **A visit to their village is truly educational and an important step in the understanding of Kenya and its culture.** There is a fee to visit the village which is paid directly to the Head Elder. **You may photograph the village and its people, as well as purchase their crafts, which include lovely colorful beaded jewelry, masks and spears.**

How can one describe all this – adventurous? Perhaps, " truly mystical". To see animals in their natural habitat roaming free, caring for their young, quenching their thirst at the watering holes, sleeping peacefully under shade of a tree and witnessing a kill. One is reminded of the laws of the jungle and the ways of survival.

At the end of the day, the path to your room is lit by millions of stars for both the Southern and Northern constellations are visible. You slip into your bed and discover the hot water bottle tucked under the covers to help ward off the cool night air. The aroma of the many beautiful plantings is carried on the breeze and fills your room. The sound of no sound and the thoughts of tomorrow's adventure lull you to sleep in this perfect unspoiled environment.

Airlines servicing Nairobi from the U.S. include Lufthansa, KLM, Swissair, Air France, Alitalia and British Airways.

Micato Safari
15 West 26th
New York, NY 10010
1-800-MICATO-1 (P)
212-545-8297 (F)

Editors note: After our safari we returned to Narobi where a dinner invitation from the Pintos, who own and operate Micato Safaris, awaited us. What a fitting ending to a perfect experience to share it with those who have so professionally and lovingly arranged these tours for more than thirty years along with their son Dennis who is liaison in the U.S. office in New York.

This is one of the true treasures of traveling.

Mozambique
Inhaca

A Hint Of African Adventures Past

Al J. Ventor

The Indian Ocean coast provides tourists with the kind of African quasi-Colonial experience that an older generation still speaks of with nostalgia. Indeed, the variety of people and places improves the farther north into the tropics you travel and applies especially to Mozambique.

Right now there is a corner of that huge country that was once known as Portuguese

East Africa, is bigger than Texas and twice as interesting, that is immediately accessible and capable of giving visitors a memorable experience. **That is Inhaca, the island with a coastline of about 100 kilometers at the entrance to Delogoa Bay.**

Mozambique is always an unusual experience, but perhaps even more now during this heady period of transformation in southern African relations when new forms of political dispensation are slowly taking shape.

Some enter from South Africa by road from Swaziland through numerous roadblocks past the rusting vehicles. Across the line of fire of the Russian 54/55 burnt-out hulks of hundreds of tanks on the hill near the border post (it rarely moves because there is no petrol) and you will encounter a new and sometimes disturbing aspect of travel overland in Africa. **We suggest that you fly directly to Maputo,** the experience is a little more sedate. The uniforms are all there and the Kafkaesque bureaucracy has barely slackened.

Mozambique today is cheap (unless you are staying in five star accommodations) easily accessible and, as we always used to say in the old days, "you ain't going to be disappointed."

Soon there will be Portuguese, Colonial style Laurentina beer again. The prawns and chicken peri-peri are as excellent as always, and most importantly, the natives are friendly.

Even the revolutionary fervor of the two decades has flagged. There are major thoroughfares named after the likes of Ho Chi Minh, Che Guevara, Lenin, Marx, Stalin, Tito, Mao Tse Tung and a host of others. Foreign visitors tend to gather along **Julius Nearer Avenue** on which the **Hotel Polana** is located, as are many of the better restaurants and bars. The **Pilli Pilli** offers an excellent meal and they sometimes have draught beer.

Not even the historical archives in Lisbon provide a clue as to when the Portuguese first discovered Inhaca. In 1502 there was a map showing the Baie de Lagoa and its three rivers. That veteran navigator of the East, Masco Da Gamma, is likely to have sheltered in the lee of the island on his voyage hugging the contours of the coast, though the Arabs of Sofa, farther up the coast would have told him about the place when he reached them.

The days' catch by Wendy Canning Church

The explorer, Loren Marques (also Portuguese), after whom the port was named was sent there in 1545 to survey the trading possibilities of the bay and he reported enormous quantities of Ivory. This was the beginning of a long period of Lisbon's sailors being commercially active here. What is today known as Portuguese Island was the official trading station; it was then, appropriately known as Elephant Island.

In time, Inhaca also became a haven for shipwrecked Portuguese sailors who made their way northwards up the coast to places like the Transco's Wild Coast. Among these were the survivors of the wrecks of the *Sao Tome* (1589) and the *Sao Jo* (1552) which went ashore in South Africa near the Umzimvubu River where Port St. John's now stands. There were also the *Sao Joao Baptista* (1622), the *Santissimo Sacramento* and the *Nossa Senhora de Atalaya do Pinheiro* (both 1647).

In 1587 three English vessels arrived off Ithaca to trade, a year later came the Dutch on board the *Nora* for the specific purpose of accurately charting Delagoa Bay. They established themselves in a fort near the present city of Maputo in 1721, but left nine years later declaring the region "unprofitable". Uninhabitable would have been more appropriate because of the mosquitoes and fever.

Before the Portuguese took control again, both the English and the Austrians had been active in and around Inhaca and consequently, the area is steeped in the early history of European expansion in Africa.

THE DIVING

Inhaca offers a week-long seafari that incorporates scuba diving, two or three days of overland hiking with beachside camps and big-game fishing with catches that may include marlin, shark, sailfish, tuna, dorado, kingfish and barracuda.

During our stay two large sailfish were hooked off the adjacent Portuguese Island, Ponta do Ouro, barely a kilometer away and well within sight of where we were staying, the **Inhaca Protea Hotel.**

The most interesting experience for people keen on scuba diving is the scatter of ship wrecks that line the entrance to what was once one of Portugal's most important imperial possessions on the sea route to India. There are many of them dating from the 1939 - 1945 war.

One of these, on the **Bassas Denae** - a large reef about 12 kilometers out to sea, offers a wealth of marine life. It was apparently torpedoed on its way out of Lourenco Marques harbor during World War II.

No one could tell me the name of the ship, but she lies on the reef, totally broken up and covering an area of about three or four football fields. All that remains of the wreck that is identifiable are the boilers; we counted four of them, all sheltering a wide variety of fish: rock cod, grouper, the occasional shoal of barracuda, shark, morays, Moorish idols and other reef fish. The visibility, so far out in the Mozambique current, was excellent.

On both mornings when we dived off Bassas Denae there were several shoals of whale with their calves frolicking off the deep water drop off a few hundred meters from where we entered the water. Every few minutes one of them would breech and fall back in a cascade of white water with a clap of thunder that could be heard miles away. **Divers have approached them in the past, though this is not recommended when they are with their young.**

Several wrecks can be dived much closer inshore. One of these, discovered in the spring of 1992, has not yet been properly explored or identified.

There are other diving attractions, one of them quite startling. **The "airport"** lies to the north of the island and is **so named because of the number of ragged tooth sharks that can be found lounging on the "runways".** It is of course not to be confused with the airstrip that brings visitors to Inhaca in small aircraft from Maputo airport on the mainland.

This is always an exciting dive, better in certain respects than Aliwal Shoal. Most of the local inhabitants are ragged tooth sharks, but here are also Zambezi tiger, and according to some reports, **great white sharks are to be found off Inhaca all year round.**

Other excellent dive sites are situated to the south off Cape Santa Maria, Ponte Torres, and, farther down the mainland coast all the way to the Natal border with South Africa.

While spear fishing is permitted on the offshore reefs, as there is nothing the authorities can do about it. It is prohibited in the immediate vicinity of Inhaca, which has now been declared a national park. The park's staff is active and by comparison with most African standards, dedicated to their task. While we were there two South Africans spear fishing in the area of the Reserve were arrested escorted to Maputo and deported, sans gear.

One of the greatest attractions of Inhaca is that conditions in the inshore areas are excellent for novices. While the visibility may not be as good as on the offshore reefs, marine life is plentiful. The best dives take place at the turn of high tide. You can catch the tide on the way out and drift a kilometer along the reef.

To the south, near the Saco da Inhaca, there are coral gardens with more marine life than any other inshore reefs that I have seen. These reefs are abundant in varieties of fish and shells.

AREAS OF INTEREST

The Inhaca Protea Hotel has its own transport and they will take parties of up to eight to any location of your choice. Other activities include water skiing, wind surfing, and hobie cats, and less pleasant is a 20 percent tourist charge on all facilities. It is as well that you know this beforehand.

A series of two or three day trips form an important adjunct to outdoor activities on Inhaca. Whether these are booked through **Gone Fishin' Safaris** at the **Hotel Polana** (Tel; 092581 491001 Fax; 092581 491480) or simply on your own, with tent, camping equipment and fishing gear on your back, all paths lead to and from the water.

A feature of hiking trails is the **Mangrove swamps**, which cover much of the interior, and provide a fascinating array of above-and-below water aquatic life. The tidal flats to the north and south are an experience. The shell life alone will make the trip worthwhile. There are flamingoes, as well as a huge variety of African bird life at several locations and it is all quite safe for visitors.

Sand dunes provide another dimension. In keeping with African East Coast topography, the seaward side of Inhaca consists of huge railing dunes abutting the sea with sand surfing a possibility. What is nice is that you are guaranteed not to have to dodge a single beach buggy or motorcycle.

Enjoy the island, a quite magnificent ocean experience, and the people and seafood dishes that have lost none of the old Lusitanian gastronomic appeal.

For those who cannot afford many of the facilities mentioned, pack a pup tent, gather together your fishing gear and diving equipment, take the ferry *Maputo* to Inhaca (its schedule is frustratingly erratic) and head for one of the quiet little coves on the south of the island.

You can fish or snorkel for a week or year. The sea will provide most of your needs and you can always arrange for a passing canoe to bring you a few additional beers, or a carafe of cheap Portuguese vine tint, paraffin for your lamps, a basketful of fruit or a clutch of those delightfully delicious white clams or mussels that many of the island women spend time in the mud flats searching for at low tide. Make sure they are fresh though; use your nose for that litmus test.

RESERVATIONS

Further south on Ponta do Ouro virgin diving is offered at simple accommodations by Motels do Mer and Scuba Adventure Mozambique. Scuba Center at Motel do Mer: (011483-39778). You cross the border from South Africa at Kwangwanse near Kosi Bay. The motel picks you up at the border. You can leave your car on the South Africa side. Entry requirements are passport and visa from the Mozambique Consulate

Editors note: **You would be remiss not to spend a weekend at the elegant Hotel Polana. General Manager David Ankers oversees this historic beauty, filled with panache and elan. The accommodations and amenities are superb.**

MALARIA

A serious word of warning, Inhaca, as with the rest of East Africa, falls within the malaria belt

It is essential that every member of your party regularly take anti-malarial pills. Also, if you are not under air conditioning, mosquito nets and a good insect repellent like Tabard of Peaceful Sleep as well as mosquito coils are important considerations.

What is vital is the need to recognize the earliest signs of malaria, which are not unlike flu -headaches, coughing, hot flashes and eventually fever. If you have not been taking a prophylatic it might be too late.

Raggie Shark by Reimund Van Heerden

South Africa

Kwazula/Natal

Aliwal Shoal and Sodwana

Andy Cobb

ALIWAL SHOAL

The coast of southern Africa supports thousands of different types of plants and animals from virtually every major marine group. Although some of these species occur all around the coast, many are restricted to particular regions.

Three distinct coastal regions are recognized in southern Africa. The East Coast, incorporating Natal and Tanskei, is bathed by the warm, southerly flowing Agulhas current. Although this region lies well outside the tropics, it is colonized mainly by warm water species of tropical origin.

By contrast, the cold, northerly flowing waters of the Benguela system on the west coast from Cape Point northwards, are occupied by a quite distinct group of cold water species which only give way to more tropical forms near the Angolan border.

Along the Cape south coast is an intermediate Temperate Zone which, because of its isolation from other temperate regions of the world, contains a high proportion of species that are unique to southern Africa.

The Aliwal Shoal is 48 miles south of Durban, the harbor city of Natal and four miles offshore. The Aliwal Shoal is a fossilized sand dune formed 80,000 years ago. It is half a mile wide and one and a half miles long.

The sandstone has eroded over the years to form caves, overhangs and gullies. **These form an ideal habitat for the Spotted Ragged Toothed Shark to rest in during the day.** Most of their feeding activity is at night. **Tiger, Blacktip and Hammerhead Shark come through in large number as well.**

The Shoal itself has a mixture of warm and cold water reef fish and the water temperatures vary from 60 degrees F to 80 degrees F in summer. **The colder water brings a lot of activity to the reef. We have Whales coming through, notably the Humpback Whale and the small Toothed Whales, three species of Dolphins, and three species of Turtle.** It has some exceptionally hard corals on it, and a variety of Bryzoan lace corals. The soft corals and sponges are notable.

Whales seen most often here are the Humpback. However, Sperm, Pygmy Sperm and Minke whales do pass through. The most noticeable Dolphins are the Indian Ocean Bottle Nose, Common and Spinner dolphins. There are no porpoises off South Africa on its Indian Ocean coastline.

The most commonly seen Rays are Manta, Short Tail, Honeycomb, Devil, Marbled Electric, Butterfly, Blue Spotted and Round Ribbontail Rays.

The most seen and enjoyed sharks are the Ragged Toothed. Those commonly seen are the Hammerhead, Zambezi, Blacktip, Spinner and Hound Shark. Others seen are the Thrasher, Blue Pointer, Tiger and Bronze Whaler sharks.

The Shoal and *The Produce* have the Harlequin Goldie, which is peculiar to the area. There are many of the Coral fish. A haven for Dagga Salmon, Gerrick, Barracuda (all seasonal) and the resident shoals of Slinger and Tassle fish. The largest fish in the ocean, again seasonal, the Whale Shark is a magic experience to see and ride. Anemone fish are scarce. The wrecks will host the Brindle Bass.

You will also see the Spiny Lobster, of which there is the Red Rock lobster and Blue Mozambique lobster, the little Squill fish, Crabs, Hermit crabs, Cleaner shrimp and Manits shrimp. A wide selection of nudibranchs is also seen on the Shoal.

I had an association with a 180lb Potato Bass called Clive from 1984 to 1992. He added a special magic to my life and would respond to my call underwater. Clive was shot by a spearfishermen, which tipped the scale in my being a very active conservationist and outspoken lobbyist. I have campaigned that the Aliwal Shoal should be a protected area and succeeded, with the teamwork of Grant Trebble of "Second Nature", in getting a workshop held. The result of which has been to form a management committee called the Aliwal Forum to create a management plan for a multi-user marine reserve. **Under South Africa environmental law the area can be proclaimed a protected "Sea-scape."**

Diving off South Africa is not typical resort diving, other than at Sodwana Bay. Our coastline is wild and hence resort courses cannot be offered in Natal. Resort courses are limited to 30 feet maximum depth. There is no safe, enjoyable diving at 30 feet along the Natal coast as there are no protective barrier reefs.

Environmental diving can be done all the year round on Aliwal Shoal or at Sodwana. The minimum qualification is Scuba Diver (O.W.I).

We use boats that are semi-rigid inflatables with skilled, competent, qualified skippers and oxygen and first aid on board. Through my association with **Sea Fever Lodge and Dive Centre**, I offer a professional charter boat to and from Aliwal Shoal. All launches are through the surf. **For group packages I will be with the group above and below the water. The cage dives are in hard-hull boats with a launch via the river through the surf.**

For all of the three below mentioned specialty subjects, I can run a course to comply with the NAUI C.E.U. course standards. Have a holiday, enjoy some good adventure diving and end up with a diving qualification. I have a fully equipped Scuba School with a 4-meter deep solar heated swimming pool for training.

BOAT DIVING

The launch site is from a coastal town called **Umkomaas**. This is a Zulu word named by the Zulu king Shaka meaning the "Place of Whales".

THE PINNACLES

The Pinnacles are best dived when there is little to very slight surge and the current is not too strong. There are many caves, overhangs, holes, craters, tunnels and gullies to explore.

MANTA POINT

The eastern shoulder of the Southern Pinnacle is a point at 16 meters with overhangs on the southern edge and a cave and a blowhole on the northern edge.

NORTH SANDS

This large overhang with a back door is on the southeast of North Sands and has its own residents and is a rest house for Raggies when they are passing through. Hound Sharks have plenty of refuge in the area but are very shy.

STRIKE I

The first strike can be found at the back of the cave by the Outer Anvil Rock. This cave has a back door that can be dived through if there is no swell. The hole in that area and the Raggie Cave are good for Angler/Frog fish. You have to be very observant.

STRIKE II

The *Aimee Lykes* on her maiden voyage struck the Shoal twice. Evidence of this can be seen by giant pieces of swarf lying nearby to the Pinnacle cave. The amount of metal removed was amazing, but apparently only from the outer skin. The *Aimee Lykes* was returned to Durban for repairs.

LION FISH HOLE

This is a crater in the Southern Pinnacle, which for the last 10 years has always had a lionfish residing there.

OUTER ANVIL ROCK

From the eastern side this rock looks like an anvil. It is a collecting point for Raggie, when they are around, and a good pointer for Raggie Cave.

RAGGIE CAVE & SHARK ALLEY

From July to December this area is not only in demand to see the Raggies, but is an excellent area for all flora and fauna.

SOUTH SANDS

This is a good area for sighting the Giant Guitarfish, Stingrays, and Skates.

TIGER COVE

This area was a Tiger Cowry colony and is very different to its outside edge, but with some large tunnels and caves.

CATHEDRAL

A 28-meter dive to an outer edge reef hole, one will see large Stingrays, Moray Eel and Sharks.

SHARK DIVING

Since 1984 I have been recording shark data for the Natal Sharks Board and have over 700 logged hours with shark. Diving with shark has been an incredible facet of my life and maintains a special freshness to diving.

Sharks are to be respected and avoided especially in the following instances: Diving in a sardine run; diving in low visibility water where the shark cannot see you clearly; diving when injured and bleeding; do not splash and make noise on the surface; do not react but stay calm and in a group. Sharks are hazardous when not respected or basic rules not followed. GET OUT OF THE WATER IF SHARKS ARE DISTURBED.

Advanced Shark diving can be done on the Protea Banks. This reef is 4 1/4 miles off shore and we dive with the Bull Shark, Dusty, Spinner, and three types of Hammerhead, Copper shark, Spotted Ragged Toothed shark and Tiger shark.

Sometimes the shoaling fish can be particularly spectacular. This is specialized diving with no cage. Our Cage diving is off Mtunzini, north of Durban in Kwazula/Natal. Here there is a lot of activity with Hammerhead, Bull shark and Mako. **The Great White is also seen in the area.**

Shark diving is from mid-July to December on Aliwal Shoal and the minimum qualification is Advanced Scuba Diver (O.W.II). This includes a shark dissection on a shark embryo I get from the Natal Shark Board.

WRECK DIVING

The two wrecks we dive on the Shoal are *The Produce* and *The Nebo*.

THE PRODUCE

This was a molasses freighter that hit the Shoal and the skipper tried to beach the ship. However, it sunk 3 kms off shore. The wreck is badly broken up and very dangerous to enter. The marine life is well established.

THE NEBO

This was a small coastal steam freighter that was carrying bridge structures and was pooped and sunk on the 20th of May 1884. The wreck has collapsed, apart from a section that holds a large Brindle Bass. *The Nebo* lies at an average depth of 24 meters and at the prop, 26 meters.

SODWANA

During the Boer War, before the turn of the century, the Boer army received its munitions from this area in their fight against the English.

At Sodwana one gets the nearest that South Africa can be to resort diving. The reefs are the southern most coral reefs of the African continent. The main ocean current, the Aghulus pulls down the warm water from the Mozambique current. The corals are predominantly soft coral. Soft corals emit a toxin, which makes their habitat unfriendly to the hard corals; however, there are many types of hard corals as well.

The best time for diving Sodwana is midweek to avoid all the local divers in their numbers who have the weekends to catch up on their diving.

I specialize in taking divers for adventure diving options on Aliwal, through the game parks and onto Sodwana for some environmental diving. I have a four-wheel drive passenger-carrying vehicle, which tows a large trailer with entire diving gear and clients' luggage. The vehicle is high and ideal for game viewing.

Sodwana is relatively gentle diving with all the pretty, colorful reef fish. The water conditions are relatively mild. Other options should there be no diving would be **birdwatching on Lake Sabaya** and as the area is remote, there are no city or town options. Some of the sand dune water birdwatching can also be of interest.

The Mozambique coast and the water of the Greater St. Lucia are the hatcheries for many of the fish species off the Natal coast. The warm water reef fish found on the Aliwal Shoal are spawned from this area.

The high water mark is off limits, as the Greater St. Lucia area is a prime turtle breeding beach for the leather back, green, loggerhead and hawksbill turtles. The Natal Parks Board will take people to watch the egg laying process during the turtle egg-laying season. Egg lying is done at night. **A word of warning — turtles do not have eyelids and flashlights can crack the cornea and blind them.** Turtles always return to the beach they were hatched from, but as there is a lot of human activity in the Sodwana Bay area, the turtles normally go south or north of the Bay.

There is comfortable, rustic accommodation at the **Sodwana Bay Lodge**, which is fully appointed. Air conditioning is impossible due to the rustic nature of the buildings, however they do have fans. The lodge will transport divers down to the beach for the dives and back to the lodge. All hire gear is available at the dive resort operation based at the lodge. A very pleasant and relaxing ambience is achieved. The lodge is away from the sea front.

BOAT DIVES

A rocky outcrop called **Jesser Point** protects the launch site. The launches are all through the surf, but the point protects the bay and provides calm water. The skippers can warm up their boat engines, get the boats up on the plane for momentum and judge the sets for a safe exit. The Natal Parks Board controls the launch site, as Sodwana is part of the Greater St. Lucia Nature Reserve.

The reef formations are all fossilized sand dunes formed 180,000 years ago, the same time period as the Aliwal Shoal and the Protea Banks were formed. The reef names are unimaginative, but named after the linear distance from the launch site, such as 2 mile, 3 mile, 5 mile, 7 mile, and 9 mile. **There are many reefs south of Sodwana that are in pristine condition as they are fully protected from any form of human incursion.**

The types of dives are best suited to the reef selected. The boats used by the charter operator for the lodge is hard-hulled catamarans designed for surf launches. Diving on 5, 7, and 9 Mile is normally very early in the morning or when the sea is flat. Two-Mile Reef is ideally suited for night dives, weather and sea conditions permitting.

2 MILE

This reef is close and easily accessible. The points on the reef are normally associated with the old marker buoys that boats used to tie up on. **Nowadays, all the diving is drift diving and profiles range from 40 feet to 75 feet.**

Sponge Reef is a deeper dive on 2 Mile as this section is flat and shelving down as part of the fossilized beach. The ecosystem is out on display and the invertebrate life easily found and enjoyed. Each protrusion from the fossilized beach is also a refuge and there is a profusion of fish. Dive profiles range from 60 feet to 110 feet.

3 MILE

Not dived on much as it is a small reef covered in staghorn coral but full of fish. Dive profiles range from 60 feet to 75 feet.

5 MILE

This reef is like a tabletop sand dune with interesting faults. Dive profiles range from 60 feet to 80 feet. On this reef I have found parts of a steel wreck. The wreck I believe is from a munition ship, which exploded in the Boer War period.

7 MILE

This is my favorite reef and I prefer it to 9 Mile. The drop-offs are from 40 feet to 70 feet. However, a good dive profile for the added time is an 18 metier on the drop-offs. There are caves and gullies on this reef.

9 MILE

Very similar to 7 Mile but a longer boat ride.

SNORKELING

Snorkeling is possible by going out with the divers and snorkeling on 2 Mile alongside the divers boat. This is necessary to protect the snorkeler from boat traffic. However, at low tide with only a mask and snorkel, the pools around Jesser Point are full of juvenile reef fish.

The sun is beguilingly cruel to fair skin and when snorkeling it is best to have a shirt on and a factor 15 sun screen cream protection well applied to the back of legs and necks.

MALARIA

Sodwana is a malaria area and a prophylactic protection is required. Staying in the lodge there are mosquito nets for the night. But also before the sun goes down, ensure that legs, ankles and knees are covered. Exposed flesh can be covered in an insect

SCUBA AND SNORKELING FACILITIES QUESTIONNAIRE

NAME **Sodwana Bay Lodge & Hotel Resort**
ADDRESS **P.O. Box 5478,**
Durban 4000
CONTACT **Bev Engelbrecht**
TITLE **Reservations Manager**
TELEPHONE **(031) 3045977**   FAX **(031) 3048817**   TELEX
CAPITOL: GOVERNMENT: **Gov. of National Unity**
POPULATION: LANGUAGE: **English**
CURRENCY: ELECTRICITY: **Yes & Gas**
AIRLINES: **Airunk: JHB to Hluhluwe**   DEPARTURE TAX? **Yes**
NEED VISA/PASSPORT? YES **x** NO   PROOF OF CITIZENSHIP?   YES   NO **x**

YOUR FACILITY IS CLASSIFIED AS: SCUBA CENTER   RESORT **x**
BUSINESS HOURS: **Durban Office: 0800Hrs - 1700Hrs**
CERTIFYING AGENCIES:
LOG BOOK REQUIRED?   YES **x**   NO
EQUIPMENT: SALES **x** RENTALS **x**   AIR FILLS **x**

CHARTER/DIVE BOAT AVAILABLE? YES **x** NO   DIVER CAPACITY **10-11 divers**
COAST GUARD APPROVED?   YES **x** NO   CAPTAIN LICENSED? YES **x** NO
SHIP TO SHORE? YES NO **x** LORAN? YES NO **x**   RADAR? YES **x** NO
DIVE MASTER/INSTRUCTOR ABOARD? YES **x** NO   BOTH **x Depends on #'s**

DIVING & SNORKELING: SALT **x** FRESH
TYPE OF DIVING/SNORKELING IN AREA: WALL BEACH **x** WRECK REEF **x** CAVE **x** ICE
DIVING/SNORKELING IN YOUR AREA IS BEST SUITED FOR: BEGINNER **x** INTERMEDIATE **x** ADVANCED **x**
BEST TIME OF YEAR FOR DIVING/SNORKELING: **Year round**
TEMPERATURE: NOV-APRIL   **120-130F**   MAY-OCT: **92-97F**
VISIBILITY: DIVING: **+50FT**   SNORKELING: **50FT**

PACKAGES AVAILABLE: DIVE **x**   DIVE STAY **x**   SNORKEL   SNORKEL-STAY **x**
ACCOMMODATIONS NEARBY: HOTEL **x**   TENTED CAMPS **x**   HOME RENTALS **x**
ACCOMMODATION RATES: EXPENSIVE   MODERATE   INEXPENSIVE **x**
RESTAURANTS NEARBY: EXPENSIVE   MODERATE **x**   INEXPENSIVE
YOUR AREA IS: REMOTE **x**   QUIET WITH ACTIVITIES **x** LIVELY
LOCAL ACTIVITY/NIGHTLIFE: **Quiet - Pool Bar**
CAR NEEDED TO EXPLORE AREA?   YES **x**   NO **Excursions also available**
DUTY FREE SHOPPING?   YES   NO **x**

LOCAL EMERGENCY SERVICES   NEAREST HYPERBARIC TREATMENT FACILITY
COASTGUARD **N.R.S.I. - Durban**   AUTHORITY: **Durban**
TELEPHONE: **031-37220 - Durban**   LOCATION:
CALLSIGNS: **Radio**   TELEPHONE:

LOCAL DIVING DOCTOR:
NAME: **M.R.I.**
LOCATION: **Natal Parks Board - Sodwana**
TELEPHONE: **035-571-0051**

repellent cream. The malaria prophylactic is normally required to be started before a holiday and continued after the holiday is complete.

Prophylactics hide the malaria symptoms and if you are not feeling well 10 days after being first in a malaria area and you are back home, have treatment for malaria.

South Africa
Kwazula/Natal
Protea Banks
Andy Cobb

The Red Eye Sardines follow the east coast of South Africa in shoals up to 1 1/2 kilometers long or in small pockets and are seen in June and July each year off the Kwazula/Natal coast. This sardine run which takes place each year has an eternal time clock. The sharks know their calendar and will congregate on the Protea Banks waiting for the sardine run.

The Protea Banks is a game-fisherman's paradise situated 7 kilometers off the shore of Shelly Beach which is south of Port Shepstone and north of Margate on the Kwazula/Natal south coast.

The Protea Banks are part of the same formation of fossilized sandbanks as that of Aliwal Shoal and the reefs off Sodwana. This is a deep reef, with the shallow belly of the reef at 38 meters and the deeper belly at 42 meters, dropping off to 50 meters plus. The shallowest part of the reef is the northern and southern pinnacles, which rise to 28 meters. The reef is a magnet for all the pelagic shoaling fishes i.e. Kaakop, Yellowtail, and Bonito of which there are types three, Kingfish, Tuna, and Kuta. Hence the Protea Banks attract large quantities of shark. The shark activity is related to the shoaling activity.

The common sharks seen are Spinner, Dusky, Copper, Blacktip, Tiger, Java, Zambezi and all three types of Hammerhead. The difference between a Java and a Zambezi can only be determined by a tooth count and measuring the first dorsal and second dorsal fin heights. The higher divided ratio and the extra tooth each side of the jaw is a Java shark.

My first dive on the Protea was as a divemaster for a group who had organized a charter boat. Our charter boat was called *Sensational* and our skipper must be one of the most colorful charter boat skippers on the Natal coast, Denise Milton. This fiery blond is definitely in control and is a very professional skipper with a very well appointed and maintained boat. She thought we were all mad and after our first experience on the Protea I could see why.

Diving in such shark infested water there is no hot tubing or pre-grouping on the surface. One - two - three - go, and all backward roll and drop 1.2 meters from the side of the boat into the water, and meet up again at 5 meters below the surface.

On this first occasion, 20 Zambezi very quickly herded us. Some were circling below, others above and the rest around us. Visibility was about 8 meters and their attention was intense for 5 to 8 minutes, after which we were left alone and only had the odd shark come and check us out on and off throughout the dive.

Denise is quite a character and after my introduction to her with subsequent groups, she would embark on her shark stories, one of, which was how a Zambezi with a head one-meter wide, would come to her boat and nudge their boat.

For game fishing, the fishing charter boats "chum the sea" - which is throwing bait into the water to attract game fish. Sharks have a learned pattern of behavior and it was found that the Zambezi would soon reorganize themselves and swim under the hull of the boat. As soon as they heard a strike as the fishing reel latches scream, they would duck out from their cover and relieve the fisherman of his catch. Zambezi would also recognize certain boat engines and automatically come under the boat. This is why the shark attention is so quick when divers enter the water, as they are already there.

With subsequent groups of divers I organized to dive on the Protea Banks I call Advanced Shark Diving. Denise was not allowed to talk to my divers before a dive and get them hyped up with her stories.

Karen Tredger, a NAUI Diving Instructor, was on one of my early groups to the Protea Banks. Denise told me after one of the dives when we had all backwards rolled into the sea, the next moment out of the water and back onto the boat was Karen, with all her gear on. This was a Herculean effort as the side of the boat is at least 1.2 meters off the water. Karen reckoned she had landed on a shark and had plenty of incentive to get back onto the boat.

Corcodile Fish by Lynn Funkhouser

Having a professional Sheely Beach diving charter boat operation has opened up the Protea Banks and I have had some superb dives with African Dive Adventures. They also have their resident Potato Bass friends to show. The southern pinnacle used to have a 6-meter Tiger shark. Alas, this shark was eventually hooked and is no more. But we did see a 4-meter Tiger in a 2-knot current and the group just held onto the sandstone reef in order to stay and enjoy this grand creature. Tiger Shark are ferocious feeders, more so than the Great White. They come past the Natal coastline in great numbers, but scuba divers rarely see them.

On one dive, I had a 3-meter Zambezi taking undue interest in me, so I felt it was time to take issue and swam at the shark full speed. This challenge was met early, and the Zambezi with a powerful tail flick retreated and left me alone.

The prime necessity in diving with sharks is not to trigger the wrong response and divers must be relaxed and enjoy seeing the shark. They should concentrate on its features to identify and also understand their behavior pattern. Should the shark start feeding on the game fish coming through, then it is time to get out of the water and go up as a group just as one went down as a group.

The Zambezi are the most visible shark, and I have seen them react to a group of divers with an unusual display. There is a distinct change from the normal swimming pattern and they click into a very exaggerated, but flowing motion, as if they were roller-skating on their pectoral which are fully horizontal. This in contrast to the aggressive display that is very distinct, with tail pressed hard over to one side, pectorals pulled in and back arched as they swim with short jerky movements.

Shark being cartilaginous fish can throw out their bottom jaw, which is pivoted on the top jaw to the cartilaginous skull, into their biting mode. This movement pushes the nose up, to give a gummy look, at the same time for shark with hinged teeth the front row of teeth stands up for action. Sharks will yawn by thrusting their jaw forward into what I call their biting mode. This is a fascinating movement to watch, so long as the body language is not matching and aggressive.

One dive group on the Protea Banks had a large Zambezi swim up to the group and yawn. This was too much for the group who spent no time getting back on the boat.

There is a recent story of a fisherman who caught a Hammerhead on the Protea Banks in the presence of divers and after an extensive fight, the fisherman cut the line. The same divers, who watched it sinking with feeble stressed movements, observed the exhausted shark. The next moment, a very large Zambezi bit the Hammerhead in half. What an incredible sight to witness. The hammerhead was signaling its distress and paid the penalty.

Possibly the best dive I have ever had was in 1994 when, with my advanced shark diving group, on our descent to the southern pinnacles, we met up with 30-40 fully grown Ragged Toothed Shark of 1.8 to 2.1 meters long (add a meter for the tail). These sharks were not resting but in their pack hunting mode and active. I took the group down the middle of the group of shark and was concentrating on trying to record and identify certain individuals from their natural distinguishing marks, which I do on every Spotted Ragged Toothed Shark for the Natal Sharks Board. The next thing, I had sudden "engine failure" and could not fin. I discovered the whole group was sitting on my fins, hence, my immobility. With over 700 hours underwater watching shark only, I had forgotten the possible impact on my divers by swimming through a large group of 30-40 shark.

The Porte is an incredible venue, however; man's greed is threatening the reef fish. The local fishing rules are that no one bottom fishes the Porte Banks. However there remains an element that continued to bottom fish and their sinkers fill each swirl hole on the reef. These areas should be preserved for game fishing and scuba diving. Unfortunately, effluent from Plenty Saiccor at Umkomaas reaches the Protea Banks. The fishermen refer to this as black water. Fish have to see as well. When this black water reaches the Protea Banks, there is no fishing.

The Shelly Beach Launch facilities are superb and meet the standards that overseas tourists would expect. The launch site is controlled and is a N.S.R.I. base. Diving on the Protea Banks is for advanced divers with good water skills, and the dives on Protea Banks will be ones that will never be forgotten. If it is not shark it will be the shoaling hordes of pelagic game fish.

SCUBA AND SNORKELING FACILITIES QUESTIONNAIREPRIVATE

NAME	**Andy Cobb Eco Diving**
ADDRESS	**10 Marion Rd., St. Winifreds, P.O. Box 386, Winklespruit, South Africa**
CONTACT	**Andy Cobb**
TITLE	**NAUI Instructor**

TELEPHONE **(031)964239**   FAX **(031)964239**   TELEX

CAPITOL: **Durban**   GOVERNMENT: **South African, A.N.C., NP & I.F.P.**

POPULATION: **(1991) 720,000**   LANGUAGE: **English**

CURRENCY: **Rands**   ELECTRICITY: **Yes**

AIRLINES: **South African Airways**   DEPARTURE TAX? **No**

NEED VISA/PASSPORT?   YES **x**   NO   PROOF OF CITIZENSHIP?   YES **x**   NO

YOUR FACILITY IS CLASSIFIED AS: **Scuba Center, Dive Tour Operator, Adventure Diving**

BUSINESS HOURS: **07H00 - 17H00**

CERTIFYING AGENCIES: **NAUI, S.A. Diving Assn., S.A. Tourist Assn.**

LOG BOOK REQUIRED?   YES **x**   NO

EQUIPMENT: SALES **x**   RENTALS **x**   AIR FILLS **x**

PRIMARY LINE OF EQUIPMENT: **Full range: Sea Fever Dive Centre (sales)**

PHOTOGRAPHIC EQUIPMENT: SALES   RENTALS   LAB **x**

CHARTER/DIVE BOAT AVAILABLE?   YES **x**   NO   DIVER CAPACITY **Max. 10 divers/boat**

DEPT. TRANSPORT APPROVED?   YES **x**   NO   CAPTAIN LICENSED?   YES **x**   NO

SHIP TO SHORE?   YES **x**   NO   LORAN?   YES **x**   NO

RADAR?   YES   NO **x**

DIVE MASTER/INSTRUCTOR ABOARD?   YES **x** NO   BOTH **x Always**

DIVING: SALT **x**   **Not suitable for snorkeling**

TYPE OF DIVING IN AREA: WALL   BEACH   WRECK **x**   REEF **x**   BOAT **x**   ICE

DIVING IN YOUR AREA IS BEST SUITED FOR: BEGINNER **x** INTERMEDIATE **x** ADVANCED **x**

BEST TIME OF YEAR FOR DIVING/SNORKELING: **July - December for shark**

TEMPERATURE: NOV-APRIL   **92-96F**   MAY-OCT: **97-105F Variable**

VISIBILITY: DIVING: **20-100FT**

PACKAGES AVAILABLE: DIVE   DIVE STAY **x Alternative available for non-divers**

ACCOMMODATIONS NEARBY: HOTEL **x**   LODGE **x**   CHALETS **x**

ACCOMMODATION RATES: EXPENSIVE   MODERATE **x**   INEXPENSIVE

RESTAURANTS NEARBY: EXPENSIVE   MODERATE **x**   INEXPENSIVE

YOUR AREA IS: REMOTE   QUIET WITH ACTIVITIES **x**   LIVELY

LOCAL ACTIVITY/NIGHTLIFE: **Durban 60 kms away or 30 minutes away**

CAR NEEDED TO EXPLORE AREA?   YES **x**   NO

DUTY FREE SHOPPING?   YES **x Airport only**

LOCAL EMERGENCY SERVICES   NEAREST HYPERBARIC TREATMENT FACILITY

COASTGUARD **N.S.R.I. Durban**   AUTHORITY: **S.A. Navy**

TELEPHONE: **(031) 37-2011**   LOCATION: **Salsbury Island, Durban**

CALLSIGNS: **(031) 304-0602**   TELEPHONE: **(031) 466-1130**

                                   For all emergencies: Central Emergency Control

LOCAL DIVING DOCTOR: **Telephone: 10177**

NAME: **Dr. L. Grevenstein**

LOCATION: **Umkomaas**

TELEPHONE: **(0323) 31336**

AUSTRALIA

Port Douglas
The Great Barrier Reef
Raymond Elman

There are many ways to get close to Australia's Great Barrier Reef - live-aboard dive boats, island resorts, the large resort town of Cairns (pronounced "cans"), but the best choice is Port Douglas. Port Douglas offers a plethora of non-diving activities - hikes through ancient rain forests containing flora from the dinosaur age, bungee jumping, hang gliding, tennis, golf, great beaches, outstanding restaurants - plus the closest mainland access to the Reef.

GETTING THERE

I traveled from Boston to New Zealand and Australia. There is an old expression, "Getting there is half the fun." In this case, not true. We were given this bit of advice by one experienced Pacific Rim traveler: "Throw away your watch."

The first stop in Australia was Sydney. August is a winter month in Sydney, but the temperatures still hover around a pleasant sixty degrees, and lush exotic tropical plants bloomed everywhere. Although there are places to dive around Sydney, we preferred sightseeing and eating (a plethora of great restaurants offering choices not available in the US), saving diving for the Great Barrier Reef.

August is considered one of the best months to visit the Reef, located in the tropical northern part of Australia (Queensland), for much the same reason that people in our hemisphere want to visit the Caribbean during our winter. **There is one other compelling reason to visit the Reef during Australia's winter - the lethal box jellyfish. The most venomous creature alive, box jellyfish make their appearance around the shores of Queensland only during the hot summer months.**

We flew north from Sydney to Cairns on Quantas Airlines and discovered another quirk of travel in Australia - domestic flights do not take reservations, it's strictly first-come-first-served. The flight takes about 3-4 hours. From Cairns it was a one-hour, 45-mile, drive up a beautiful coastal highway to Port Douglas. On the right side of our vehicle we had an expansive view of the Coral Sea, and on our left the view alternated between fields of sugarcane, mango trees and mountainous rain forest.

PORT DOUGLAS

Port Douglas is on a neck of land between three bodies of water - the Coral Sea on the east, bay on the west, and a backwater estuary replete with crocodiles and fresh water fish. Port Douglas has managed to avoid the type of garish over-development that plagues many mainland resort areas in Australia. There are no high rise buildings, and there are no buildings at all on gorgeous Seven-Mile Beach - a broad crescent-shaped ocean beach, fringed by wild rain forest flora and fauna. The town itself boasts one main street, Macrossan Street; three other streets with shops and restaurants, Owen, Grant, and Wharf; and a large shopping and boating complex called Marina Mirage, where all of the dive boats dock. There are about 20 restaurants and at least one of everything one might need a grocery store, pharmacy, video store, and bank. Almost all of the shops and restaurants are interesting and tasteful.

DIVING THE GREAT BARRIER REEF

There are two main ways to get out to the reef from Port Douglas - gargantuan ocean catamarans that can accommodate 300 people, and more modest 40 to 60-foot vessels.

Weather-wise our week in Queensland was not ideal. The wind had been blowing 20-25 knots every day, and continued almost unabated during our stay. The natives claimed it was most unusual. The result was unusually rough seas that caused the cancellation of all dive trips during our first few days at Port Douglas.

On our fifth day in Port Douglas, the winds diminished enough for the dive boats to visit the Reef. Since it was blowing so hard for so long, it was hard for me to believe that we would find calm waters. So I decided that the largest boat would prove gentlest and selected the gigantic *Quick Silver* as my first ferry to the Reef.

The *Quick Silver* catamaran is a huge, gleaming silver ship that holds 300 people. The interiors are plush compared to most boats I have been on. Still, when the boat left the protection of the harbor, the choppy seas had their anticipated impact.

During the ride to the reef, a marine biologist studying the reef gave a slide presentation on what we would see. He emphasized coral types rather than fish life. He also poo-poo-ed the idea of shark attacks. The two highly publicized deaths that had occurred

Many Petaled Nudibranch by Lynn Funkhouser

in the past year - a mother of five and a honeymooning husband - happened during the summer south of Brisbane.

Getting out to the reef was as smooth as possible under the weather conditions. By the time we docked at their permanent pontoon on the outer reef, the sun had come out.

I donned a wetsuit with legs and sleeves over my full set of skins. All of my prior diving experiences had been in warm Caribbean waters, so I was a little surprised to find that the reef waters were colder than the Caribbean at that time of year.

The passengers were efficiently separated into snorkelers, novice divers, and certified divers. Of the more than 100 people that boarded the *Quick Silver*, only about 12 were certified divers. The certifieds were led onto an open-sided motorized dive platform and whisked away to our first dive site - **Two Rock.**

I was partnered with a young Cathay Pacific pilot (based in Hong Kong but bred in the UK). He turned out to be a great partner - very precise and confident.

As soon as I hit the water, I realized that this was the coldest water of my diving experience. I later learned that the water doesn't get any colder.

Our first dive was mainly an exploration of different coral types along a ribbon reef. We didn't see as many fish as I usually see on healthy reef—probably due to the turbulent waters. The coral far surpassed anything I had ever seen. There was a staggering variety, and the colors were a breathtaking palette of pastels and neon/fluorescence. They referred to the open dive boat as a "wet" boat, and recommended against bringing anything aboard that might be ruined if wet. There was a 25-knot wind howling when we exited the water and with the boat providing no protection from the wind, teeth were soon chattering. So after we changed tanks, all the divers sat shivering and shaking as the boat headed toward the second dive site - **The Wreck.**

As soon as we moored at **The Wreck,** Ben, the local dive pet - a 200 pound Maori Wrasser—swam onto the boat's dive platform for a little fondling and a piece of fish. Ben accompanied us throughout our dive, and I was able to pet him, and even stick my hand in his mouth.

The other highlight of this dive was seeing giant clams. Despite their tremendous size (five to eight feet across the top); they open and close rather quickly.

We returned to the ship by 2:15 PM, where a sumptuous feast awaited us. As soon as I dried off, I tossed down a cup of hot coffee and devoured a lunch of prawns and many salads. On the ride back to Port Douglas, we alternately dozed off and chatted with the crew.

The next day I made another journey out to the Reef, aboard the *Outer Edge,* for a three-tank dive. Though the *Outer Edge* is a fast 60 foot catamaran, I was worried that a much smaller boat would not do very well in rough seas - and we were told that the forecast was for winds gusting to 30 knots. As it turned out, the trip to the Reef was bumpy, but manageable. Once anchored on the Reef, the boat was very stable.

We dove three reefs: **Undine, Swallow,** and **Rudder.** Each one offered a different configuration of coral, though no unusual fish - the most unusual thing I saw was an octopus.

However, the Outer Edge dive masters were very attuned to touching, so we touched a lot of non-fishy things - huge sea cucumbers, anemone, giant clams.

I liked the *Outer Edge.* The crew was crisp and thorough. They served food after each dive. We were not left to shiver in the wind. As soon as we dried off from a dive, we were ushered to their carpeted salon - out of the wind, for hot coffee and biscuits. All and all it was a very pleasurable experience.

ACCOMMODATIONS

Unquestionably, the grand dame of Port Douglas varied accommodations is the **ITT Sheraton Mirage.** It has been my experience that Sheraton resorts outside of the United States tend to be of higher quality than the Sheraton facilities within our borders. And the Port Douglas Sheraton is one of the best. Near the beach, but well hidden, we came upon many lovely villas. The landscaping is gorgeous. Following a winding path, we reached the main complex. There are two huge swimming pools, a "lagoon" with small sand "beach" and a conventional pool. The interior of the main complex seemed like any large resort.

We opted to stay at **Reef Terraces Resorts (RTR).** We were provided a two-story town house with two bedrooms and two bathrooms. Included was a full kitchen with microwave oven and dishwasher and full laundry room. It was spacious, and painted white throughout. The townhouse included a small patio and terrace with views of the golf course. Every so often an exotic bird would come pecking around our patio.

The Reef Terraces' pool is a beautiful stone free form affair with lush landscaping and a waterfall. We dined outside in the garden surrounding the pool. It was very comfortable - no bugs, gentle breeze, pleasant temperature.

The Reef Terraces shares all facilities with the **Radisson,** which is next door. This includes tennis courts, golf course, and an all day and night free kids club.

DINING

Most of the restaurants offer indoor and outdoor dining. The two best restaurants we dined at in Port Douglas (based on our non-scientific taste-testing odyssey), are listed below in order of preference.

Nautilus is widely regarded as Port Douglas' best restaurant. Nautilus is approached by a hike up a torch lit pounded earth path - straight up from Macrossan Street. The trick is not to appear out-of-breath when you reach the Maitre 'de.

Nautilus' ambiance is fabulous. There are several dining areas, all outdoors. Some of the areas are covered to protect diners during the rainy summer season. We sat in a large open patio, surrounded by tall royal palms. The plants were beautifully lit to full atmospheric effect. Sprinkled about the area are tall freestanding candelabras, showing evidence of many melted candles.

The food is as good as the ambiance. Tuna tartar with finely chopped sweet chili peppers, sweet basil, and onions - topped by a raw quail egg yolk. Coral Sea Trout in a mild Thai chili sauce, with extremely thin sweet potato chips, and a delicious slaw-like salad. Nautilus is unsurpassed for a delicious romantic dining adventure.

Danny's is another highly regarded restaurant specializing in seafood. Once again we opted for al fresco dining in a courtyard garden. The large portioned appetizers were among our best taste treats in Australia - charbroiled Morton Bay Bugs in a light chili sauce, and sautéed calamari in a sauce of garlic, soy, oyster sauce, and white wine. For an interesting entree, order the locally famous Mud Crabs in chili sauce. The crabs are very large. Although they are good, the shells are hard to crack.

AREAS OF INTEREST

We rented a Moke, the cheapest form of car rental. Mokes are open sided jeep-like cars stripped of all amenities - no trunk, no glove box. However, there are seat belts, which distinguishes mokes from Mexican jeeps. Driving the moke is definitely an adventure. Mokes cost $35 Aus per day, closed in cars are at least twice as much. You don't really need a car on a daily basis in Port Douglas. Most things are pretty close at hand (within a 15-20 minute walk), and there are shuttle buses and taxis. However, it is worthwhile to drive up to the **Kuranda Rain Forest**, and it is also worthwhile to drive around the outer edges of Port Douglas.

Behind **Macrossan Street** is the only hill in town, which is layered with beautiful houses and apartments featuring stunning vistas. From a couple of vantage points we had 360-degree views of the Port Douglas peninsula. The older residential areas near the beach contain crumbling non-descript houses - probably leftovers from the sleepy fishing village days. **Our other discovery was a fruit, vegetable and health food store at the far end of Four-Mile Beach, which was by far the most interesting and best quality food store in town.**

DAINTREE RAIN FOREST

Even the drive to the Daintree Rain Forest is a worthwhile experience. We drove up the coastal road to Mossman. The road passes through endless sugar cane fields edged by mountains covered by rain forest on the west and the Coral Sea to the east. It's breathtakingly beautiful.

Except for the paths we were about to take, the Rain Forest is impenetrable to all but Aborigines and highly experienced jungle hikers. **The Daintree is full of poisonous animals and plants, and is the rarest repository of plant forms that existed during the time of the dinosaurs.** Approximately 130 million years ago Australia, Antarctica, South America, India, Africa, Madagascar, New Caledonia, New Guinea and New Zealand were joined in a massive supercontinent called Gondwanaland. At this time, the world's climate was warm enough that moist tropical rain forest covered much of Gondwanaland's surface. But then the landmasses began to split up, each beginning to take up its present position, and climatic conditions began altering swiftly. As a result, most of the original Gondwanaland flora became extinct - with the exception of a few isolated rain forests in Australia like Daintree. As conditions worldwide cooled, heralding the beginning of the Ice Ages, Australia was rafting northwards to the tropics.

The circular trail through Daintree Rain Forest is about 4 km; a combination of hard packed mud and climbing rocks. Huge tangles of gigantic trees, massive undulating root systems, cable-like jungle vines suitable for a Tarzan swing, and loud rushing rapids dominate the senses. Everything is dripping wet. The place smelled green - like entering an intense greenhouse or botanical garden.

On the way back from a roaring-rapids-through-a-gorge viewing spot, we had an encounter with a very large bird with a bright red head, a bright yellow collar and a black body. The bird had feet like a chicken, and bobbed along in a chicken-like manner. He ran up and down our path a few times, and eventually darted off into the jungle. This would be our only unusual wildlife sighting. (I bought a bird book the next day - it was a bush turkey).

DO IT IN A DINGY

During one of the windy days when none of the dive boats were leaving the harbor, we stumbled upon an operation called "Do It In a Dingy." They rent small motorized dinghies for fishing in or exploring a fresh water estuary that flows right past Marina Mirage. They advertise that they offer calm waters on windy days. We decided to try a little guided fishing.

Our fishing guide, Louie, looked like he was sent by central casting - muddy bare feet, dirty khaki Bermuda shorts, a faded maroon T-shirt, a one or two day unshaven face, topped by a wool plaid baseball cap. As soon as we started to motor up the estuary we were protected by dense jungle growth from the 30-knot winds. It only took 15 minutes to get to Louie's favorite fishing hole. We spin cast live bait: small bream-like fish called finger marks (for the dark spot behind their eyes), and interrogated Louie - who was reluctant to talk about himself.

It turned out that opposed to the grizzled guide that Louie appeared to be, he was actually a grizzled Spanish chef from Melbourne who had organized a guide-gig as a type of working vacation.

Although we didn't catch a boatload of fish, we did have a great time, and the fish we hooked were terrific fighters. All in all it was a great thing to do on a windy day.

KURANDA RAIN FOREST

Kuranda, the Aboriginal word for "meeting place of the Spirits" is an Aborigine village tucked away in the rain forest. **The Kuranda Mountain Train, which attracts more than 100,000 passengers per year, winds its way up from Cairns through some of the most breathtaking scenery in North Queensland.** Passing over spidery trestles no wider than the train and hundreds of feet off the mountain, the trip to Kuranda is marked by clouded peaks, cascading mountainsides spilling over with lush foliage and dramatic views of the Barron River with spectacular waterfalls.

The village is filled with quaint shops, an outdoor market featuring stalls of local artists, craftsman and farmers, restaurants, and the charming Kuranda Inn. Not to be missed are the **Australian Butterfly Sanctuary**, the **Wildlife Noctarium**, and the **Tjapukai Aboriginal Dance Troupe**.

AUSTRALIAN EMBASSY
1601 MASSACHUSETTS AVENUE
WASHINGTON,D.C. 20009
TEL 202 939 6400

BAHAMAS

Bahama Live-Aboards
Bruce Hastings

When you go on a "Dive Vacation", you obviously want to do as much diving as possible during your stay. You obviously want to see the most fish, the most beautiful walls, and the most unusual coral reefs and formations. Most importantly, as far as I am concerned, you do not want to be one of a hundred other divers all in the same area.

Well, you have two choices. First, buy a boat, outfit it for diving, and then travel the world in search of THE SPOT to dive. What? Don't have the time or patience for such a Cousteau-like undertaking? Well then your second choice is to go on a live-aboard dive cruise.

Live-Aboards offer the diver the advantage of having all your diving arranged and planned as well as greater range then the average day tripper. More "out of the way"dive destinations are made available to you during your vacation.

Live-Aboards come in all shapes, sizes, and price ranges. Two live-aboard dive cruises that I have had the pleasure to vacation on are **Blackbeard's Cruises** and **Nekton Dive Cruises**. Both are based in Southern Florida and operate in the Bahamas. Both offer six day trips, are staffed by a very professional crew and dive staff, and are **an exceptional value for your travel dollar.**

Blue Holes by Lynn Funkhouser

BLACKBEARD'S CRUISES
Blackbeard's Cruises operate three 65-foot sailboats that can take up to 24 guests and a crew of 6. A stay onboard is typical of living onboard a sailboat, meaning that private space is scarce. Guest sleeping quarters are divided into three areas: one in the main cabin and two others forward in the bow, which are in bunks or "rakes". The toilets are the mechanical pump-type, and showers are salt water, with a limit of only 30 seconds of fresh water to rinse. Most of your time will be spent on deck as the cabin areas can become cramped.

For more than twice the price of a Blackbeard's Cruise, you can enjoy the Nekton Pilot. At first glance one will wonder what this odd floating vessel is. It might remind you of a converted mini oil-drilling rig. She has a 78-ft long by 40-ft wide rectangular hull, which sits up out of the water on two large pontoons called SWATH. The idea is that the pontoons run in the calmer waters just below the choppy surface and give the boat a much smoother ride than a V-hulled boat of comparable size. A further advantage is that all the engines, generators, compressors, water purifiers, and other noisemakers are housed in the pontoons making for a quieter boat overall and freeing the three upper decks for more living space. There are 16 individual guest cabins with two single or (when pushed together) a queen-sized bed and each room has its own private bath with a shower and unlimited hot water.

I joined Blackbeard's for a cruise onboard the *Sea Explorer*, the oldest of their three boats. I was the first to arrive that Saturday, so the rest of the afternoon was spent reading on deck, enjoying the sun, and meeting the others on the cruise. The Blackbeard's crew served a barbecue lunch and once everyone was aboard and organized, the crew held a pre-cruise briefing and soon we were underway, heading east toward Bimini. The six-hour crossing of the Gulf Stream turned out to be the worst part of the entire trip. This "landlubber" had difficulty dealing with sailing in 3 ft to 5-ft seas. It was good to set foot on land in Alycetown on Bimini later that night.

On Sunday morning, our divemaster, "Jimbo", gave the assembled eager divers a briefing about diving from a 65-ft sailboat. The deck space is limited and he explained the relatively simple procedure. Once the boat is moored at the dive site, each diver takes a tank from the storage bin, mounts his/her BC and regulator and sets it on the deck by the stern. When you and your dive buddy are suited up and ready, you walk to the stern area, a crewmember helps you on with your gear, and a giant stride off the side and you're doing it. It's a system that works very well for Blackbeard's and never during the week with 23 other divers was there too much congestion or confusion.

Most of the diving is done in the Bimini Islands area. Blackbeard's dive itinerary calls for three different dives at three different dive sites each day with a night dive after dinner. After the night dive, the crew would sail to the leeward side of a local island to anchor for the night. Occasionally the boat would be sailed over to a small island for an opportunity to have lunch on shore and walk the beach. Blackbeard's crew has been sailing and diving these waters and knows all the great sites. I found the timing and selection of the dives (i.e. depth of dive, time to next dive site, length surface interval, etc.) such that they "fit" into the dive tables very well, I was never faced with having to delay or skip a dive because of the tables. Divemaster Jimbo confided that the itinerary is planned that way.

Meals served on board were very good, "home cooking" served buffet style. Breakfasts consisted of cereal, fruit, toast, muffins, and such. Lunches were usually soup and sandwiches and dinners were hot tasty and very welcomed after a long day of diving. The last night of the cruise (Wednesday) is usually spent back in Alycetown for a delicious steak barbecue and local nightlife. Thursday is the last day of the cruise with three dives scheduled and the crossing back to Florida with a late night arrival in Miami. After clearing customs and farewells it was off to the airport for the flight home.

THE NEKTON DIVING CRUISES

A year later, I once again chose a live-aboard dive vacation, only this time on one that promised more comfort, conveniences, and less of a risk of seasickness. The Nekton Diving Cruises went back to some of the same areas that I had dived the previous year with Blackbeard's but with a few new areas that possibly Blackbeard's sailboats would not find accessible.

Upon arrival at Nekton's dock in Miami, we were informed that we had been invited to attend a wedding ceremony onboard for a couple who planned to use the cruise as their honeymoon. After the ceremony, a few toasts of champagne, a pre-cruise briefing, and crew introductions, we were off to West End, Grand Bahama Island.

The Nekton Pilot sails with a large crew. The ship is always active. At night the ship is moved from one dive area to the next, a full crew must be on "watch" at all times. Two Captains, two First Mates, two Ship's Engineers, etc. can equate to a large crew.

Each day of diving includes visiting two sites, the first for the morning dive(s) and the second site, usually only a couple miles from the first, for the afternoon and evening dives. At each dive site, a thorough briefing is given which includes a drawing of the reef site, depths compass directions, possible current concerns, and a description of the marine and plant life in the area. Just about all the crewmembers are Divemasters and very knowledgeable. After the briefing, the "pool" is declared open and you and your buddy are free to dive as you feel fit. *The Nekton Pilot* has a very spacious and organized dive platform so suiting up and entry into the water is easy and convenient. A divemaster is stationed on the sundeck watching the water for bubbles, keeping track of dive groups, and watching for possible distress signals. At least one divemaster, if not two, are on the rear platform assisting divers in and out of the water. For the photographers among us, large fresh water barrels are located on the platform for cameras or camcorders, and the crewmembers on the platform are familiar with how to handle these items. The between dive times were spent on the sundeck reading, working on tans, or swapping stories about what each saw on this reef and planning your next dive.

The "Bahama Adventure" cruise called for two days of diving in the Grand Bahama Island area then off to a remote site called the **Gingerbread Grounds,** an area of pristine coral reefs and then back toward Bimini for the remainder of the week. Unfortunately the winds picked up and the seas got high and the decision was made to head south towards Bimini a day early, thus skipping the Ginger-bread Grounds. The fortunate part was that we would be diving a reef called simply "**The Strip**". This small reef, just off Bimini Island, in only 35-40 feet, offered some of the best photo opportunities. The highlight was when an eight foot green moray emerged from its hole and swam after my buddy's fin.

These rough seas also gave us a chance to check Nekton's claim of "the world's most stable and comfortable liveaboard". Well, *The Nekton Pilot* is not rock steady and smooth, but it is not far from it. The boat still rocks and rolls in the high seas (5 to 7 feet) but the motion is damped to a slower more deliberate motion. I was told that because of the construction of *The Nekton Pilot*, a large, square, very upright hull, it actually gets blown around as much as the seas pitch and roll it. Last spring, the engineers made changes to the submerged hulls to improve the ballasting and the boat's comfort.

Meals on board *The Nekton Pilot* are superb. The boat is equipped with a full galley and Chef Wade is a master with his cuisine. For breakfast, cereals, muffins, bagels, juice and coffee are served first with pancakes, French toast, waffles, and other hot items prepared a little later. Lunches were usually salads with chicken or meat, soup, or just sandwiches (Wednesday was taco day!). Dinners vary from fresh seafood to Italian to meat and potatoes. Wade is willing and able to create special meals for anyone with special dietary needs. All meals are served buffet style and there is plenty of room in the dining area for all to sit and relax.

Here are just two examples of live-aboard diving cruises to choose from. Blackbreard's Cruises and Nekton Dive Cruises are two excellent choices run by professional staffs and manned by able crews. But as the old axiom goes, "you get what you pay for". **For the budget minded diver, Blackbeard's Cruises are an excellent choice, the bottom-time-for-the-buck can not be beat.** The accommodations are limited and space can be cramped. **For just over twice the price, Nekton Diving Cruises offer comfort, luxury, and more room than most.**

The choice is yours, Enjoy!

BERMUDA

"Seductive and Serene"
Wendy Canning Church

Lying alone in the Atlantic, this seductive and serene island is a favorite of world travelers whether traveling from distant destinations or on a short two-hour flight via American Airlines from Boston or New York.

My remembrance of Bermuda was of a picture perfect island of pastel-colored houses stretching to the sea, crystal clear waters in different hues of aquamarine, and a setting reminiscent of an early 19th century English novel. On this, my fourth visit, little has changed.

Shaped like a boot, Bermuda is not one island, but rather some 140 large and small islands connected by bridges that sit on a submerged volcano. The Royal Navy referred to Bermuda as the "Isles of Devils," because of its network of uncharted and treacherous reefs that surround these islands. It is these reefs, along with a history of hurricanes, storms, strong currents, piracy and privateers, that has left a legacy for both the scuba diver and snorkeler to explore.

One cannot speak of Bermuda without discussing her hundreds of shipwrecks. Although a Spanish mariner, Juan de Bermudez, discovered Bermuda in 1503, an English shipwreck, The Sea Venture commanded by Sir George Somens, led to the first permanent settlement in 1609.

It is believed that only a *handful* of the total number of wrecks has been discovered and that countless numbers sleep silently beneath the shifting sands. Even today, yachtsmen refer to Bermuda as a "ship trap." The separate islands are fraught with reefs and shoals, with only one deep-water channel running through the maze. Sailors beware! Charts must be followed with exact precision or your yacht may become the next artificial reef.

This meticulously clean island is divided into nine parishes of 1,250 acres each. The capital is Hamilton, a British colony with the Governor representing the crown and the Premier elected by its citizens. Its moderate climate makes it a year round vacationland. It's population of 40% white and 60% African descendants have honed a unique culture giving the world Bermuda Shorts and the Bermuda Onion. Intermingled are the age-old British customs of Boxing Day, afternoon tea, and cricket.

Bermuda is the third richest country in the world. There is no unemployment, the per capita income is $34,000 and there is no income tax. A 20-mph speed limit is strictly enforced. One drives on the left. Only property owners may own cars (one and one half per household). Other transportation is by motor bike, taxi, bus, or ferry.

Where else would you find all clocks set five minutes fast so that one might not miss transportation or be late for an appointment? We feel very comfortable recommending Bermuda as a dive destination for those who are seeking a beautiful, crime free, clean island with warm and friendly natives and an elegant international flavor.

SCUBA DIVING & SNORKELING

Most of the dive and snorkel sites are relatively shallow. Depths range from 25 ft to 80 ft with the average depth of about 30-45 ft. The Bermuda climate is sub tropical: 85 degrees Fahrenheit in summer, 65 degrees Fahrenheit in winter. **This makes March to November the ideal time to dive.**

Diving and snorkeling are suitable for all levels from beginners to experienced professionals. **The best snorkeling on the South Shore is at Church Bay.** The reef goes straight out. Take Middle Road to Church Bay Park. As long as it is not rough, **another South Shore spot is Clear Water Beach Park at the Sonesta Beach Hotel.**

Tucked away at the far end of the beach is **South Side Scuba and Watersports. South Side ranks up there with the most safety conscious operations.** They truly care that the diver has both a safe and enjoyable experience.

Certification cards are a requirement. Those without them will have a checkout in the pool or on the boat line, as do those who have been "out of the water for a while".

Their new dive boat is 40 feet long. It is Coast Guard approved, has VHF radio, oxygen, and first aid equipment. She can comfortably haul 30 divers, has a canopy, head and ample room for guests.

WRECK DIVING

Bermuda has the northern-most living coral reef in the world and has proven to be an excellent wreck catcher. **Most of the wrecks are in the 30-50 foot depth range with the deepest around 80 feet giving Bermuda some of the worlds finest shallow-water wreck diving.** In places as many as three wrecks from different time periods came to grief on the same site!

Marie Celestia - 1864 - Confederate side-paddle steamer wrecked in route to Delaware with a cargo of rifles and canned beef. Lying in a sand gully surrounded by coral caves at 60 feet.

Minnie Breslaur - 1873 - A British steamer sunk on her maiden voyage while bound for New York with a cargo of lead, dried fruit, and cork. She lies in 50 feet of water and is badly broken up.

The Hermes - 1985 - A fully intact, 165-foot long freighter, scuttled by the Bermuda Diving Association, she sits upright on a sandy bottom. Ringed by reefs, she is picture perfect at 80 feet.

The King - A former U.S. Army tug, was used for treasure hunting. *The King* is now treasure for the diver to behold with the coral formations that have taken hold. South Side Scuba sank the tug on January 17, 1984, to form an artificial reef. She is situated in the National Park waters and

Silversides by Lois Hatcher

is protected by the Bermuda government. In 65 feet of water, the diver has 40 minutes to explore her and the reef beyond. She is completely intact, but penetration is limited to the bridge. There is also a compressor on the back and an L-shaped mailbox similar to the one Mel Fisher used to vacuum up the mother lode from the *Atocha*.

SPECIAL REEF DIVES
Southwest Breakers

You descend 25 feet to the sandy bottom and began to investigate the crevices, and glide down gullies and look into caves with a backdrop of sea fans and coral in a variety of different colors. The beauty of this dive is that it is never the same. Being at the breakwater with constantly changing sea conditions reveal new and interesting sea life each dive. It is a shallow dive, so you get lots of bottom time.

That evening we made a second trip to this site for a night dive. **Night dives are spectacular in Bermuda.** The coral change color, the fish that are active during the day are found sleeping, and the critters that hide in the daytime come out at night. We entered the water around eight under a bright, full moon that offered excellent visibility. As our eyes became adjusted to the dark and lights became brighter, we were able to investigate a far different group of sea life than we had during our day dives.

Middle Breakers
This is also a shallow dive. There was a myriad of reef fish, but the most interesting aspect of the dive was the different size arches one could swim through.

Hang Over Reef
This is a spectacular reef with numerous beautiful crevices and caves to be investigated.

BEACHES
Bermuda beaches are a lovely cast of pink. There are numerous well-hidden coves and overhangs. Some feel **Horseshoe Bay**, Southampton Parish, is the comeliest, but visit others, each has their own aura. The **Bermuda Visitors Bureau** will give you a list and description of each. They are located at 43 Church Street, Hamilton 5-24, Bermuda. U.S Tel 800 223 6106

OTHER ACTIVITIES
There are probably more golf courses along these twenty-three miles than anywhere else in the world. There is also the Bermuda Golf Academy in Southampton Parish for lessons.

Tennis can be played at the major hotels.

Horseback Riding can be arranged at the Warwick - Spicelands Riding Center - 238-8212

ACCOMMODATIONS
The Sonesta Beach Resort, located in Southampton Parish, rises up from the reefs on the ocean's edge. It is a comfortable modern hotel with majestic sea views situated on 25 acres of landscaped grounds that surround three natural bays.

The Sonesta is a complete resort within itself, offering 400 guestrooms. It is in every way a full service resort offering six tennis courts, outdoor and indoor pools, three beaches, scuba diving, snorkeling, sailboats, fishing from shore and moped rentals. There is croquet and miniature golf on the grounds. Golf can be arranged at the Port Royal Course (10 minutes), Belmont Golf Course (15 minutes) or Riddler Bay (10 minutes). In the lobby are branches of Bermuda's finer stores. Supervised children's program is available from June 15th until Labor Day.

MAP guests can choose from the many restaurants: **Lillian's** serves Northern Italian food: The **Boat Bay Club** has American cuisine and the **Sea Grape Bar, Oceanside** for a romantic dinner. All the restaurants are very good and live up to their measure, but my favorite was Lillian's.

Each room has a terrace facing the ocean or the pool. This is a perfect place to sun or begin your day with breakfast, or just to inhale the intoxicating ocean breeze. Looking out to sea, a diver cannot help but ponder what awaits them on the 9 am dive.

Sonesta Beach Hotel
P.O. Box HM1070
Hamilton, HMEX, Bermuda.
Telephone (809) 238-8122 or (800) 342-7170

On our previous visit to Bermuda we toured and dived at **Cambridge Beaches** and vowed to stay there on our next visit. **We spent a delightful week and dived with Fantasea Divers. Please see Honeymoon and Anniversary Section for Cambridge Beaches and Fantasea Divers.**

DINING
- For good food at reasonable prices, try **Paw Paws** located on the South Shore, serving local cuisine and specializing in fresh fish.

SCUBA AND SNORKELING FACILITIES QUESTIONNAIRE

NAME: **South Side Scuba LTD.**
ADDRESS: **P.O. Box PG38**
Paget PGBX Bermuda
CONTACT: **Robert Limes**
TITLE: **Owner**
TELEPHONE: **441 236 0394**   FAX: **441 236 0394**
CAPITAL: **Hamilton**   GOVERNMENT: **Westminster Parlamentary**
POPULATION: **56,000**   LANGUAGE: **English**
CURRENCY: **BDA dollar on par U.S.**   ELECTRICITY: I **10 AC**
AIRLINES: **All Major Carriers**   DEPARTURE TAX? **20**
NEED VISA/PASSPORT? **No**   PROOF OF CITIZENSHIP? **Yes**

YOUR FACILITY IS QUALIFIED AS: **Resort**
BUISINESS HOURS: **8:00 - 5:00**
CERTIFYING AGENCIES: **PADI**
LOG BOOK REQUIRED? **No (encouraged)**
EQUIPMENT: **Rentals, Air Fills**
PRIMARY LINE OF EQUIPMENT: **Sherwood, Dacor**
PHOTOGRAPHIC EQUIPMENT:

CHARTER/DIVE BOAT AVAILABLE? **Yes**   DIVER CAPACITY **24**
COAST GUARD APPROVED? **Yes**   CAPTAIN LICENSE? Yes
SHIP TO SHORE? **Yes**   LORAN ?   RADAR   ?
DIVE MASTER/INSTRUCTOR ABOARD? **Yes (all guides licensed instructors)**

DIVING & SNORKELING: **Salt**
TYPE OF DIVING/SNORKELING IN AREA? **Beach, Wreck, Reef**
DIVING/SNORKELING IN YOUR AREA IS BEST SUITED FOR: BEGINNER **X** INTERMEDIATE **X** ADVANCED **X**
BEST TIME OF YEAR FOR DIVING/SNORKELING: April 1 - December 1
TEMPERATURE: NOV-APRIL **63 F**   MAY-OCT: **70 - 85 F**
VISIBILITY: DIVING **60 - 80 FT**   SNORKELING:

PACKAGES AVAILABLE: **Dive**
ACCOMMODATIONS NEARBY: **Hotel, Guest Houses**
ACCOMMODATIONS RATES: **Expensive, Moderate**
RESTAURANTS NEARBY: **Expensive, Moderate**
YOUR AREA IS: **Expensive, Moderate**
CAR NEEDED TO EXPLORE AREA? **No**
DUTY FREE SHOPPING? **Yes**

LOCAL EMERGENCY SERVICES: **911**   NEAREST HYPERBARIC TREATMENT FACILITY:
COASTGUARD: **Bermuda Harbor Radio**   AUTHORITY: **King Edward VII Memorial Hospital**
TELEPHONE: **441 297 1010**   LOCATION: **Paget Bermuda**
CALLSIGNS: **CH 16 VHF**   TELEPHONE: **441 236 2345**

LOCAL DIVING DOCTOR:
NAME: **Dr. Edward Schultz**
LOCATION: **King Edward Memorial Hospital**
TELEPHONE: **441 236 2345**

f you have a craving for Chinese food, **Chopsticks** is the spot.

he **Lighthouse Tea Room** near the Sonesta, serves all day. Their high tea is ie best on the island. Terry Pryer of South Side Scuba and his wife are irt owners.

- In Hamilton, **Tuscany** is a favorite for Italian food as is **Portifino** for Bermudian food.
- **Rosas Cantina** on Front Street serves Mexican food.
- Indian food is served at the **Bombay Bicycle Club.**
- Other good choices on Front Street are **The Porch** and **The Cock and Feather**.
- At **The Club** on Bermuda Road, you will find a lively crowd of natives and visitors enjoying dancing until the wee hours.

Red Rope Sponges and Blue Chromis by Lois Hatcher

AREAS OF INTEREST

The old **Navy Dockyard** has undergone a 20 million-dollar renovation. Located in Somerset Parish, it is a 30-minute ferry ride from Hamilton or a 45-minute bus ride. Here you will find the **Maritime Museum, Arts Center, Snorkel Park**, 29 shops and 4 restaurants. Our favorite is the **Frog and Onion Pub** across from the Maritime Museum.

Hamilton, the Capitol, offers duty free shopping. Look for special buys on Irish linens and cashmere sweaters.

CARRIBBEAN

Aruba
"A Sure Bet"

Raymond Elman

The year-round temperature in Aruba is consistently between 80-85 degrees; in fact, they don't even bother to provide weather reports in Aruba. It is situated less than 50 miles off the coast of Venezuela, or four hours from New York on Air Aruba. Aruba is out of the hurricane path; and is a desert island with only 16.8 inches of annua fall, so you don't have to worry about your vacation dollar being wasted o ⌐ weather.

In addition, Aruba has several qualities that make it **one of the world's most desirable destinations:** (a) there is 0.05% unemployment - only the physically infirm are unemployed - thus there are strong middle and working classes and very little crime. We never experienced a nano-second of fear for our safety. (b) We dined at many excellent restaurants - definitely some of the best food we've ever tasted in the Caribbean. The cuisine comes in many forms: French, Aruban, Argentinean, Italian, and Continental, just to name a few. (c) There are lodging accommodation of every description: high rise resort complexes, low rise resort complexes, all-inclusive, apartments and time share suites, cottages and private homes. (d) The diving is decent, varied and very well documented. I tried three different dive operations, which covered a spectrum from excellent to good. (e) Aruba offers a high level of convenience: the US dollar is accepted everywhere, everyone speaks English, and most of the dive sites are less than 20 minutes from the hotels.

BOAT DIVING

One of the great things about diving in Aruba is the convenient proximity of dive operators to hotels and dive sites. The three dive operators I tried were located on Palm Beach, right in front of many of Aruba's major hotels, and most of the dive sites were less than a 30 minute boat ride from Palm Beach. **So on a two-tank dive I spent the majority of my time diving instead of traveling.**

Red Sail Sports has four locations on Aruba. The one we used is between the Hyatt and the Americana. I must say that Red Sail Sports is the best organized, most buttoned up dive shop I have experienced in the Caribbean.

The premises are neat and air-conditioned. There is a locker room for changing clothes and storing unnecessaries. There is an abundance of personnel to help clients choose dive trips and fill out information forms.

HARBOUR REEF & SONESTA AIRPLANES

We sailed on their comfortable boat *Aventura*. The first dive was at **Harbour Reef** (40-90 Ft) where we saw a rare "frog fish," a little red fish that sits on the bottom and sort of hops on its little fins. The next interesting sighting was two huge light green moray eels that have taken up residence in the hull of a sunken pilot boat at 40 to 90 feet. The morays are 6-8 feet in length and 18 inches in diameter. I was glad that they don't seem to favor exiting their abode. All around us were the usual assortment of Caribbean reef fish. We saw a peacock flounder, which is covered with beautiful spots, and has what appears to be a bird-like plume sticking up from the middle of its back.

The second dive was at **Sonesta Airplanes**, a Convair 400 and Beach 18 sunken in 40-60 feet of water just off Sonesta Island. Everything was pretty much straight forward.

Red Sail Sports
J.E. Irausquin Boulevard #83
P.O. Box 218
Oranjestad, Aruba
1-800- 255-6425

MALMOK AIRPLANES

Unique Water Sports was a step down in quality of both the diving equipment, the boat, and the personnel seemed less buttoned-up - more like the jovial types I usually encounter at dive operations. So, naturally, I had much more fun with Unique - go figure.

The first dive at Malmok Airplanes (also known as Arashi Airplanes) was fun. We only went down 45 feet, so the view was brightly lit. We glided over large well-preserved brain coral, stag horns, sea fans, and anemone. Lots of reef fish swam along with us. The dive bonus was prodding a decent size octopus to scoot from one hiding place to another, and finding a four-foot moray eel under a ledge. As advertised, there are a couple of airplanes and parts strewed around down there, but they were not the featured attraction.

Unique Water Sports
J.E. Irausquin Boulevard #74
Oranjestad, Aruba
Telephone: 011-2478-60096

THE ANTILLA

My third dive trip was to the wreck of the *Antilla* with the **Scuba Aruba** crew. It seemed like I was on a slide - each dive crew and boat got cheesier. This time the boat was only slightly more sea worthy than a slab of plywood on pontoons. The dive master was a guy named Dan, who sported a half-dozen tattoos and had a John Belushi-like flair for the edge of sanity. The 400-foot *Antilla* is a great wreck dive - better than the **R.M.S. Rhone** near Tortolla. Dan and I were off on our own, and Dan treated the *Antilla* like a gigantic personal jungle gym. He led me in and out of various compartments and passageways, which became increasingly narrower, until we could barely squeeze through some of the openings. This included wriggling between the ocean floor and a narrow rusted opening where the hull had settled on the bottom. **The bottom line is that the dive was fun and so was Dan, even though the boat was basic, and Dan, who was the first dive master of my experience to shun skins or a wet suit, was a great playmate.**

Scuba Aruba
P.O. Box 4100
Noord, Aruba
Telephone: 011-2478-66690/75797

SHORE DIVES & SNORKELING

I filled my days in-between boat dives with shore dives and snorkeling. **There are several interesting areas for snorkeling and shore dives.** The most luxurious spots are in front of the private island that is part of the **Aruba Sonesta Resort** at Seaport Village complex. The small island has two beaches each of which makes a semicircle around turquoise lagoons, and a nature trail through a small mangrove swamp. Reefs that eventually lead to the Sonesta Airplanes site front both beaches. The reefs begin in about 20 feet of water and gradually descend to 110 feet at the far end of the airplanes. I call this a "luxurious" shore dive because the island hosts a Red Sail Sports shop, and the Sonesta resort provides beach lounge chairs, a restaurant and a bar. In addition, a designated topless beach caters to the European sensibility.

Another interesting snorkeling and dive spot starts on a stretch of Malmok Beach at the western tip of Route 1, just in front of the private residences of Malmok, the Beverly Hills of Aruba. This area is not crowded with people, but teeming with reef fish. The ambitious strong swimmer could swim out to the wreck of the *Antilla.*

ACCOMMODATIONS

Aruba offers accommodations of every description:

HYATT REGENCY ARUBA BEACH RESORT AND CASINO
J.E. Irausquin Blvd. 85
Telephone: (2978) 61234

There is no question that the Hyatt is the high priestess of the beach. The decor is very tasteful and Caribbean breezy. The hotel offers a variety of dining experiences.

RADISSON ARUBA CARIBBEAN BEACH RESORT & CASINO
J.E. IrauSquin Blvd. 81
Telephone: (2978) 67700

Our junior suite was spacious, well appointed with a terrace ocean view. The Radisson has the largest stretch of beach, though the grounds are not as well conceived as the

Hyatt. Bistro 81 is far and away the best restaurant at the Radisson. The Radisson offers a lively casino.

ARUBA SONESTA RESORT & CASINO AT SEAPORT VILLAGE
L.G. Smith Blvd. 82
Telephone: (2978) 36000

The Sonesta is different from the other resorts. It is located right in the middle of Oranjestad, not on the beach. Beach access is gained by catching a launch that leaves every 15 minutes from a canal that snakes its way into the middle of the hotel complex, and traveling out to the Sonesta's private island

Costa Linda Beach Resort
J.E. Irausquin Blvd. 59
Telephone: (2978) 38000

This is where the Queen of the Netherlands stays when she is in Aruba: Costa Linda is a lovely, "low rise," upscale timeshare resort located on Manchebo Beach.

BUSHIRI BEACH HOTEL
L.G. Smith Blvd. 55-B
Telephone: (2978) 31100

The Bushiri is the first all-inclusive hotel on Aruba and may be of interest to bargain hunters. The grounds are pretty and well maintained. The rooms are a little small and a bit tired, but the food is abundant, and comparable to all other all-inclusives I have visited. We experienced the liveliest nightlife at the Bushiri when a large group of South Americans danced the night away on the seaside terrace to the motivational rhythms of a local band.

DINING
I can't say enough good things about the restaurants on Aruba.

Generally, I don't expect much when I dine out in the Caribbean. So usually I seek out Caribbean restaurants that provide something I can't find in New York or Boston - namely, seaside ambiance: open air restaurants on the edge of gently lapping turquoise waters. In Aruba, the seaside ambiance comes with something extra special - great food.

CHEZ MATHILDE
Haenstraat 23
Oranjestad

Chez Mathilde, a classic French restaurant is housed in one of Aruba's oldest homes. For over a century the same family has kept the house in its original state. The atmosphere is formal, though dress is not. The menu is adventurous, which to me means unusual combinations of interesting ingredients. Chez Mathilde has a large and interesting selection of wines.

LA TRATTORIA EL FARO BLANCO
Tierra del Sol

At El Faro Blanco you don't have to have much of an imagination to feel like you are dining al fresco at a gorgeous Italian villa overlooking the Mediterranean. The restaurant is perched on a hilltop near the California Lighthouse, overlooking the sea and the southern coast of Aruba. The best way to appreciate the restaurant and the view is to come just before sunset. Have a drink and maybe some appetizers while you watch the sun sink into the sea and hope for the mythic "green flash." Then dine outdoors on the terrace as the stars begin to shine and the lights of the Malmok and Palm Beach areas twinkle on. The food is outstanding.

GASPARITO
Gasparito 3

Gasparito is located in what is called a "typical- style" house, the early colonial housing of Aruba. The space is intimate and service is warm, as though you were a guest in their home. I am a major fan of fresh conch, so whenever I'm in the Caribbean I eat conch in every format available. Gasparito's conch stew is as good as it gets.

BISTRO 81
J.E. Irausquin Blvd. 81
Radisson Resort & Casino

Bistro 81 is decorated to appear like a French bistro and has excellent food at a reasonable price. The presentation of their dishes was an up-to-the-minute-hip-trendy- architectural feast for the eyes.

EL GAUCHO
Wilhelminastraat 80

El Gaucho has warm cozy ambiance. The cuisine is Argentinean. I devoured one of the best-sautéed squid dishes I have ever tasted.

CHARLIE'S BAR
Zeppenfeldstraat 56
San Nicolas

Iam not sure if Charlie's should be listed as a restaurant or an activity. Charlie's, which has been around since 1941, is one of those places you run into from time to time that are uniquely defined by the memorabilia on display, the attitude of the staff, and decades of stories that have become legendary. The menu itself is an event. Try the grilled "scampi," fish soup, Creole "calamari," and steak fries.

AREAS OF INTEREST

We rented a car and made a five-hour circumnavigation of the island. We started with a drive down hotel row, first the low rises, and then the high rises. Then we drove up Route 1 through **Malmok**, the Beverly Hills of Aruba, where houses are valued from $1-4 million. Our first stop was the **California Light House**, which is perched high on a hill overlooking the South coast.

From there we went to the **Tierra del Sol** golf development which is gorgeous. **Golf aficionados rejoice! Tierra del Sol is an eighteen-hole championship golf course designed by Robert Trent Jones II. Tierra del Sol challenges golfers of all skill levels with four sets of tees and approach angles on every hole.** Each hole also features a panoramic Caribbean view. The main clubhouse has a strong Spanish influence, yet still modern (neoclassical), with extraordinary views and a swimming pool, Pro Shop, and restaurant, Ventanas del Mar.

Our next stop was the lovely little **Alto Vista Chapel**, sitting all alone on a wild north coast hillside overlooking the ocean. Then we motored over to the mysterious **Casibari Rock Formations** and **Indian drawings** - huge boulders piled up without explanation.

We then drove over some dusty dirt roads, through a barren landscape, to the **Natural Bridge**, a natural rock formation spanning a small inlet through which the ocean surges. At that point lunch seemed like a good idea, so we drove to **San Nicolas** and had lunch at **Charlie's Bar**. After an entertaining lunch, we drove around the **Coastal Oil Refinery**, explored the old Exxon housing compound, cruised **Baby Beach** at the southeastern tip of Aruba, and drove up to **Seroe Colorado** for a magnificent vista of the whole island.

There are many things to do in Aruba, **para-sailing** ("You can see the whole island from up there"), **fishing, sailing, golfing, snorkeling, scuba diving, sightseeing, and horseback riding** across the arid north side of the island to the **Natural Pool**. However, **the most popular non-athletic activities seem to shopping and gambling at the hotels' casinos.**

Ministry of Tourism
L.G. Smith Boulevard
Oranjestad
Aruba, Dutch Caribbean
TEL 011 2978 39035

Barbados

"Little England"

Wendy Canning Church

Barbados has gained its nickname "Little England" from visitors because of the influence that English settlers brought to the island. This influence still prevails in every aspect of its culture, from architecture to the school system. Yet along with this aura of British formality, there is a proud African culture, 90% literate. They have taken their place beside the white population.

Barbados is the most easterly and one of the most developed of the Caribbean islands. It is 21 miles long and 14 miles wide. The calm, serene waters of the Caribbean are found on its leeward side, and the thunderous, tumultuous Atlantic waters on its windward side, at one point within eight miles or one-half hour by car of each other.

There is no landmass for approximately 3,000 miles between Barbados and Africa thus Barbados is assured fresh breezes and clean waters. June through November brings the rainy season, but not to worry, these showers disappear as suddenly as they appear. Visitors can quickly return to water sports and tanning.

According to the history of Barbados, the first settlers were the Arawak Indians from South American, but recent archaeological digs have begun to disprove this. It is now thought that the earliest visitors to the island could have been the Egyptians or the Phoenicians who took advantage of the calm currents to make the crossing in their boats of reeds and wood.

The Arawak Indians, a gentle and peace loving tribe, settled on Barbados around 300 BC. The Carib Indians captured, tortured, raped, and even practiced cannibalism on their victims eventually obliterating them.

The Portuguese landed in 1536 naming the island Los Barbados (the Bearded Ones) after the fig trees whose roots resemble beards. The Spanish came later, but neither of these visitors ever established a permanent settlement.

British Captain John Powell landed in Holetown in 1625 claiming this 166 square mile island in the name of James I, King of England. Captain Powell returned to Barbados on February 17, 1627 with 80 settlers and slaves, establishing a permanent settlement near Holetown and laying a cornerstone for prosperity by the planting of cotton, tobacco and yams.

In 1637, a Dutchman, Peter Blower, brought the first sugar cane plants to Barbados. Sugar was in high demand in Europe and remained Barbados' main crop for 300 years leading to the lucrative rum industry.

In 1639, the first legislature was established, the oldest in the Caribbean.

Slaves were needed to till the fields and by the 1600's slaves outnumbered the white settlers by 3 to 1. This created unrest and the landowners went to great lengths to keep them under control.

Slavery was finally abolished in 1838, but it was not until the depression and the riots of 1937 that Barbados' black leaders emerged and began to rule the island with the white landowners.

In 1966, Barbados became a fully independent nation within the British Commonwealth.

The greatest legacy of the English settlers is the school system, which to this day is the finest in the Caribbean.

DIVING AND SNORKELING SITES

Each morning the van from **Hightide Watersports** would fetch us at **Coral Reef Club** and deliver us to the Watersport Center five minutes away. **Hightide will pick up and deliver divers from anywhere on the West Coast free of charge.**

We boarded the 32-foot custom built boat fully equipped with oxygen, first aid, VHF radio, canopy, fresh water showers, camera table, dry storage and comfortable seating. At a speed of 20 knots we were quickly transported to one of 20 dive sites offered.

The calm Caribbean water on the west and south coast area is where scuba diving and snorkeling takes place.

Our first dive was in the National Park at Dottin's Reef. Beginners, intermediate and advanced divers will enjoy this lovely reef with sea rod, common Venus fan, barrel and brightly colored mustard sponges.

A diminutive sand eel came out to greet us and our divemaster found a beautiful large spotted undulating moray eel. The fish are Lilliputian, but teem around the reef

Wreck of S.S. Stavronikita by Willie Hewitt

and since this is not a deep dive, the diver has sufficient bottom time to swim along with them. **This also is a good snorkeling spot.**

So much of the underwater world has been fished out that Barbados has become known more for its wreck diving. I had dived every wreck available on my last trip, but *The Pamir*.

The wreck of *The Pamir* is a good distance from most of the dive centers, so it remains a fairly virgin dive site. Maximum depth is 67 feet to the propeller, and topside she is 30 feet–**thus she also makes a good snorkeling site.**

Divers descend the mooring line and drop to her bow. From there you can investigate the beautiful soft and hard corals resplendent in every hue imaginable on her bones. One can penetrate her stern near the engine section.

After investigating *The Pamir* we swam to a nearby reef, quite intact, ablaze in color and rife with reef fish.

Other wrecks to dive while in Barbados:

SS Stavronikita lies in 130 feet of water off the West Coast. Unlike most wrecks, the *SS Stavronikita* is intact and can be penetrated. She is also well marked by a buoy.

A Greek cargo ship 356 feet long, she was on her way from Ireland to Barbados carrying cement, but caught fire on August 26, 1976 in the open sea. An attempt was made to tow her remains closer to the shores of Barbados but while in transit the lines broke due to the weight of the 101,000 bags of cement.

She lay at bay for two years until 1978 when the Barbados government purchased her with the intent to sink her closer to shore in order to clear the shipping lane and establish an underwater park. Hence the *SS Stavronikita* is now under the auspices of the Barbados Marine Reserve. As a result, the ship and the marine life that inhabit her are protected by strict laws.

The *SS Stavronikita* is a deep dive and should only be attempted by an experienced diver with wreck diving experience. Bottom time and air consumption should be monitored carefully.

The Bremen is located in Carlisle Bay. It is 50 feet in length, a French navy tug that sunk in 1919. Her top deck lies in 10 feet of water and her bottom is at 25 feet. Time and the tides have taken their toll on her hull, but it is a delightful dive due to the polychromatic fish that teem and call her home, such as the parrotfish, blue tang butterfly fish and the red tipped blenny. **She makes a good dive for the beginner or the snorkeler and can be accessed by shore or by boat.**

Located just to the north of *The Bremen*, *The Miriam Bell Wolfe* sank in a hurricane in September of 1955. She is a wooden boat, which has largely broken up. Similar to *The Bremen* the interesting thing about this dive is the swarm of fish that have flocked to her remains.

The Granny lies north of *The Miriam Bell Wolfe* in 45 feet of water. Turtles frequent Carlisle Bay and *The Granny* seems to attract them. Therefore, she is sometimes referred to as the "Turtle Wreck". Like *The Miriam Bell Wolfe*, there is very little left of her structure, but a swarm of fish can still be found swimming about.

Willie Hewitt and the staff of Hightide spoiled us by setting up, breaking down and washing our gear, introduced us to some lovely dive sites, and upheld the highest safety standards.

ACCOMMODATIONS

Visitors from all over the world call **Cobblers Cove** their home while in Barbados. One can understand why the property is lovely to the eye, set on its sweeping private white beach, cuisine is gourmet, wine list superb, and an array of activities are offered.

Cobbler's Cove is located on the West Coast and is the only member of Relais and Chateaux in Barbados. **Hamish Watson, the General Manager,** presides over his castle as a Duke would his over his manor house and houseguests. He has newly added another Camelot suite perfect for that special occasion

Cobblers Cove
St. Peters, Barbados, West Indies
Tel: 246-422-2291
Fax: 246-422-1460

Other divers highly recommended **Almond Beach Hotel, an all-inclusive resort (except scuba).** I had toured and visited this property on my last visit. I thought it presented a good value for the dollar.

Please see Honeymoon and Anniversary Section for the Coral Reef Club.

AREAS OF INTEREST

First of all rent a Moke or a motor scooter from **Fun Seekers** to get around and really see this beautiful island. You will need to procure a temporary diver's license and you can do this when you arrive at the airport, at the rental Car Company, or at the police station.

The Barbados Wildlife Reserve, St. Peter. Call (246) 499-8826 for more information.

The Mount Gay Rum Distillery, St. Andrews.

The Atlantis Submarine - a one-hour underwater adventure. Call (246) 436-8929 for more information.

The *Jolly Roger*, a replica of an old pirate ship, cruises along the West Coast with both day and evening cruises. Chose from steak, chicken or flying fish for lunch. Each is served with cold salads. Calypso music plays throughout the cruise and there is even a dance floor on the top deck. Rum punch is free so watch out! After lunch they pull into a cove where you can rent water skis, jet skis, walk the plank or go ashore for tanning and snorkeling. This is truly an adventure for the entire family. We have gone each time we go back to Barbados and it never ceases to be a great time. For more information call (246) 436-6424.

The **Barbados Museum** is the showplace of Barbadian natural history and artifacts. It is located at Garrison, St. Michael.

The **Flower Forest** is a 50-acre site 850 feet above sea level and located at Richmond Plantation. It is being developed into a unique garden interspersed with a wide variety of fruit trees and banana groves, which is near the western edge of Scotland District, the most picturesque and scenic area of Barbados - a photographer's paradise.

Sugar Cane Wagons by Wendy Canning Church

The **George Washington House** is a modest house at the junction of Bay Street and Chelsea Road. It once housed the first president of the United States. At the time he was visiting Barbados with his brother, and suffered an attack of small pox while on the island. It is thought that Barbados is the only place outside of the United States ever visited by George Washington.

The **Chase Vault** is famous because of the unsolved moving coffins mystery. Situated in the cemetery of Christ Church Parish Church on the cliff above Oistins, visitors can still see the vault where, during the 19th century, coffins were discovered to have moved from the positions in which they were placed.

Harrison's Cave is acclaimed as one of the unique Cave Systems in the Western world. The Cave has large chambers, stalagmites and stalactites, lakes, streams and waterfalls. The Cave was officially opened 1981 and has proven to be of great educational and scientific interest, as well as a major tourist attraction.

BEACHES
There are ten miles of coastline beaches in Barbados. Each offers different activity depending upon the condition of the sea they lie off.

WEST COAST
The waters are calm and best for scuba diving and snorkeling.

Folkstone Park in St. James Parish is an underwater park with a marked underwater trail. A little barge sits in twenty feet of water about 200 yards off shore. Picnic tables and a small beach makes this a pleasant spot for a days outing. **This a conservation area for snorkelers.** Here you will also find the Martin Museum.

Mullins Beach - The water is clear. There is shade. **This is a good snorkeling area.**

Church Point - Near the Colony Club, this beach offers good swimming, very scenic and beverages available at the Colony Club.

Paynes Bay offers **good snorkeling** and water sports.

SCUBA AND SNORKELING FACILITIES QUESTIONNAIRE

NAME: **Hightide Watersports**
ADDRESS: **Sandy Lane Hotel**
St. James, Barbados
CONTACT **Willie Hewitt**
TITLE: **General Manager**
TELEPHONE: **(246) 432-0931**   FAX: **(246) 432-0931**
CAPITOL: **Bridgetown**   GOVERNMENT: **Democratic**
POPULATION: **275,000**   LANGUAGE: **English**
CURRENCY: **Barbadien Dollar**   ELECTRICITY: **110**
AIRLINES: DEPARTURE TAX?
NEED VISA/PASSPORT? **Yes**   PROOF OF CITIZENSHIP?

YOUR FACILITY IS QUALIFIED AS: **Resort**
BUISINESS HOURS: **5 7 days**
CERTIFYING AGENCIES: **PADI**
LOG BOOK REQUIRED?   **Yes (or C Card)**
EQUIPMENT: **Sales,   Rentals,   Airfills**
PRIMARY LINE OF EQUIPMENT:
PHOTOGRAPHIC EQUIPMENT: **Rentals**

CHARTER/DIVE BOAT AVAILABLE? **Yes**   DIVER CAPACITY: **12**
COAST GUARD APPROVED? **Yes**   CAPTAIN LICENSE? **Yes**
SHIP TO SHORE? **Yes**   LORAN ? **No**   RADAR   ? **No**
DIVE MASTER/INSTRUCTOR ABOARD? **Yes**
DIVING & SNORKELING: **Salt**
TYPE OF DIVING/SNORKELING IN AREA? **Wreck, Reef**
DIVING/SNORKELING IN YOUR AREA IS BEST SUITED FOR: BEGINNER **X** INTERMEDIATE **X** ADVANCED **X**
BEST TIME OF YEAR FOR DIVING/SNORKELING:
TEMPERATURE: NOV-APRIL   **78 F**   MAY-OCT: **84 F**
VISIBILITY: DIVING   **60 - 80 FT**   SNORKELING: **60 - 100 FT**
PACKAGES AVAILABLE: **Dive, Dive Stay**
ACCOMMODATIONS NEARBY: **Hotel**
ACCOMMODATIONS RATES:
RESTAURANTS NEARBY:
YOUR AREA IS: **Quiet with Activities**
LOCAL ACTIVITY/NIGHTLIFE:
CAR NEEDED TO EXPLORE AREA?   **No**
DUTY FREE SHOPPING?   **Yes**

LOCAL EMERGENCY SERVICES: NEAREST HYPERBARIC TREATMENT FACILITY:
COASTGUARD: **Barbados**   AUTHORITY: **Barbados Defense Force**
TELEPHONE: LOCATION: **St. Annís**
CALLSIGNS: **VHF CH 16**   TELEPHONE: **436-6185**

LOCAL DIVING DOCTOR:
NAME: **Michael Brown**
LOCATION:
TELEPHONE: **436-6215**

SOUTH COAST

You will find small to medium waves.

Accra Beach offers plenty of activity, food, drink, and rentals. **A good place to body surf.**

Sandy Beach - This is a perfect beach for families. The waters are shallow and calm and there is a picturesque lagoon. Food and drink are available.

Casuarena Beach - **This is a good beach for the windsurfer.** Food and drink are sold.

Silver Sands Beach - A scenic beach with fine white sand. Here you will find the more experienced windsurfers.

The best windsurfing is at Club Mistral.

SOUTH EAST COAST

The surf is high with large waves.

Foul Bay - A picturesque bay with many fishing boats. There are no food or beverages available.

Crane Beach - A spectacular beach with large sand dunes and pink sand. There is good body surfing. Food and beverages are available at **Crane Beach Hotel.**

EAST COAST

The East Coast has the biggest surf. The Atlantic stretches as far as the eye can see. Surfing is superb but swimming is definitely not recommended, so check out these points of interest while you're there:

West of Bridgetown - Trafalgar Square, Queen Anne's Park, Government House, Barbados Museum, St. Anne's Fort.

Atlantic Sights - Sam Lord's Castle, Villa Nova, Andromeda Gardens, Flower Forest.

West Coast - Bridgetown, St. James Church, Speightstown, Animal Flower Cave, Farley Hill, Nicholas Abbey, Harrison's Cave.

DINING OUT

The five star hotels have a reciprocal dine- around arrangement.

Brown Sugar Restaurant serves Creole cuisine. It is located in St. Michael on the West Coast. 246 426 7684

The Royal Pavilion Hotel Dining Room is as romantic as you can get. Seaside dinning in an exquisite setting. Food and service are perfection.

Secrets is located in St. Lawrence gap in the Bagshot House It offers simply delicious cuisine. 246 422 4447

The Inn On The Beach serves simple but delicious fresh seafood. 246 435 6956

On the West Coast you can also get your fix of fried chicken, pizza, and take out at the super market in Holetown.

BARBADOS TOURISM AUTHORITY
800 SECOND AVENUE
NEW YORK, NY 10017
TEL 800 221 9831

Bonaire

"An Eco-Tourist Fairyland"

Wendy Canning Church

Bonaire is unpolluted, unhurried, uncrowded and crime free, making it an eco-tourism Fairyland, that replenishes the body, mind and soul.

Bonaire was discovered in 1499 by Amerigo Vespucci, it had been inhabited for centuries by Arawak Indians. Spain attempted to colonize the island between 1527 and 1633, but in 1634 the Dutch claimed Bonaire and established a military stronghold on the island.

The British occupied Bonaire briefly during the early 1800's, and the island suffered from the raids of French and British pirates. However, the Dutch regained control in 1816 and established a government plantation system based on commercial crops.

By the 1950's international tourism began to spur Bonaire's economy. It was at this time that the salt pans were modified to use solar energy and they became the most successful in the world.

Bonaire is part of the Netherlands Antilles, which also consists of Curacao, St. Eustatius, St. Martin, Saba, and Aruba. The Queen of the Netherlands appoints the Governor, and the locally elected legislature has three island commissioners. The capital is Kralendijk.

The official language is Dutch but the native tongue is PaPiamento. At age twelve English and Spanish are required courses in the schools. However, it is not uncommon to find an islander who speaks four or five languages, which is an added attraction for worldwide travelers.

Shaped like a boomerang, Bonaire, the most eastern of the Leeward Islands, is located 50 miles off the coast of Venezuela, or two hours and forty five minutes by Air Aruba from Miami, Florida.

Packed into its total land area of 112 square miles are enough plentiful pristine delights and varied activities both above and beneath its waters, natural and man made, to please a visitor of any age. Its population of 13,500 intends to keep it this way by strict enforcement of environmental safeguards. Determined to protect their natural resources, **Bonaire was the first of the Antilles to enact strict environmental legislation on land and sea, reserve a sanctuary, National Park, and safeguard flamingos in a wildlife reserve.**

A pragmatic philosophy is prevalent between the government, the tourist industry and developers. The only changes that will be made are those guaranteeing the protection of the islands natural habitat. Any homogenization of Bonaire culture or destruction of its natural wonders will not be tolerated.

Located out of the hurricane belt, with an average daily air and water temperature of 82 degrees F and annual rainfall of 22 inches, **one is almost guaranteed 365 days of sunshine.** There is cycling, bird watching, sea kayaking, deep-sea fishing, golf, tennis, hiking, windsurfing, horseback riding, touring, **snorkeling and scuba diving.**

The island has established **"Family Month"** during August. Resorts, restaurants and tour operators offer special packages.

The Bonaire economy is based primarily on tourism, salt harvesting, oil and transshipment, apparel manufacturing and construction. The currency is the Netherlands Antilles Florin or Guilder. US dollars are widely accepted.

Rental cars, jeeps and vans are available from a number of agencies. Valid US driver's licenses are accepted. Driving is on the right, and no traffic lights make driving around the island easy and unhurried. Taxis and small bus service is also available.

Drinking water is potable, distilled from purified seawater.

The Tourist Department, located in Kralendijk, has brochures and maps. The personnel are welcoming, professional, and pleased to help visitors with the slightest request.

**BONAIRE GOVERNMENT TOURISM BOARD
10 ROCKEFELLER PLAZA, SUITE 900
NEW YORK, NY 10020**

DIVING

As a result of submarine volcanic eruptions that occurred millions of years ago, Bonaire is at the peak of a submerged mountain, with deep sloping reefs close to shore. The reefs are some of the healthiest in the world, and underwater visibility is over 100 feet year-round. **All of the waters surrounding Bonaire and the uninhabited Klein Bonaire, "Little Bonaire", are designated as a Marine Park where spearfishing and collecting anything living or dead is prohibited.**

Bonaire offers diving and snorkeling 24 hours a day at an assortment of over 85 marked and protected sites. Starlet, brain, Elkhorn and yellow pencil are just a few types of coral which can be seen along with a menagerie of **over 200 species of fish life** including parrotfish, queen triggerfish and spotted moray eel.

The best reefs are found within the protected lee of the island; the North and East Coasts are quite rough. The West Coast and Klein Bonaire reefs have a narrow, sloping terrace and extend seaward with a drop-off at 33 feet, followed by a slope varying from 30 feet to a vertical wall of 100 to 200 feet deep.

Accessible by boat is **Alice in Wonderland,** a double reef complex, separated by a sand channel and extending from Pt. Vierkant south toward Salt Pier. There are a number of good dive sites within this reef system. **Buoys mark all dive and snorkel sites. Angel City,** one of the most popular, is home to 1,000-ton freighter *Hilma Hooker,* Bonaire's most notorious shipwreck. Less than a mile off the south coast is the uninhabited Klein Bonaire (Little Bonaire) which acts like a barrier reef, creating calm, leeward waters. Here **24 marked reef sites** with depths of 20-130 ft are accessible by boat or from shore. Some of my favorites were **Carl's Hill, Serenity** and **Forest.**

The automobile license plates on Bonaire read "A Diver's Paradise," and there is no disputing the accuracy of this slogan.

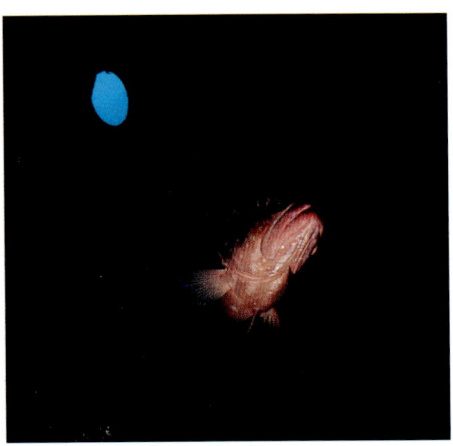

Nassua Grouper by Lois Hatcher

SNORKELING

All of the attributes that make Bonaire a haven for divers apply to snorkeling. Snorkelers can wade from the shore to the reefs and view an array of coral, including elkhorn, barrier, fire and leaf corals, and a range of colorful, fish such as redlip blennies, jewfish and parrotfish.

The reefs just off Klein Bonaire and Washington Slagbaai Park receive rave reviews from snorkelers. Yellow stones along the roadside designate shore dive and snorkeling sites.

All dive shops on the island rent snorkeling equipment and can provide instruction. In addition, there is a reef preservation program offers visiting divers free advanced and photo buoyancy control workshops through all island dive shops. As a result of these efforts, divers and snorkelers find the reefs virtually untouched, with lush coral growth and an abundant fish population.

OTHER ACTIVITIES

Fishing: The catch in Bonaire varies by season; November through February is best for Marlin and Sailfish; February, March and April is Dorado, March to late June is Wahoo and Amber Jack; June through September is Yellowfin and Bonito.

Sea Kayaking: The calm water surrounding most of Bonaire makes for wonderful kayaking.

Cycling/Mountain Biking: There are over 300 kilometers of trails on Bonaire. Local bike shops offer rentals, sales, repairs and guided tours.

Horseback Riding: Bonaire's best known area for riding is the Warahama Ranch, a wonderful retreat tucked away in the wilderness.

ACCOMMODATIONS

Sand Dollar Condominium Resort is adjacent to the Sand Dollar Dive & Photo Shop and the Green Parrot Restaurant. Ten minutes from the airport, this two story complex has 73 accommodations all with terrace and balcony, air-conditioning, cable TV, and well equipped kitchens. Sand Dollar would be a good spot for those seeking a self-catering holiday. On property, there are tennis courts, an Olympic size pool, a drive-through bank, car rental, grocery store and ice cream parlor.

We toured a sampling of condominiums and found them all well kept, equipped and tastefully furnished. **We recommend the following: B14, a 3B / 3B with large kitchen.** Especially appealing is the wraparound terrace overlooking Klein Bonaire. C11 is a 1-bedroom condo, D16 has 2 bedrooms, 73 is a studio with Murphy bed.

Open daily, **Sand Dollar Dive and Photo Shop** is a full PADI 5 star facility that offers all phases of diving instruction and certification. The state-of-the-art underwater photography shop has equipment sales and rental, film processing and slide viewing room, plus underwater photo/video instructions.

FOR KIDS ONLY!

Sand Penny Club is a complimentary program for the children ages 3-6. **Sand Tiger Club** gears activities for youngsters ages 6-15. **The Jr. Sand Diver Club** is a program for ages 12-15 and offers PADI junior open water certification with a 25% discount.

Oceans Classroom is a discovery-based program, which combines snorkeling with hands-on learning about the ocean and its inhabitants. Optional Snorkeling Certification is available at an additional cost.

For reservations at the Sand Dollar Condominium Resort contact:

Aqua Expeditions
92 Mt. Vernon Street
Boston, MA 02108 USA
Tel: 617-723-7134
Fax: 617-227-8145
email: aquax@msn.com

OTHER ACCOMMODATIONS

Harbour Village Beach Resort: Please see Honeymoon and Anniversary Section for more information on this elegant five-star resort.

The Blue Iguana B&B has seven rooms and is conveniently situated downtown. It is cozy and friendly. (P) 599-7-6855

The Great Escape is situated on the South Side of the island. This small, but charming, B&B has ten rooms. (P) 599-7-7488

AREAS OF INTEREST

Kralendijk, the capital of Bonaire is a quiet town of colorful, well preserved buildings. Sightseeing highlights are Fort Oranje, Queen Wilhemina Park, Government House and the miniature Greek temple-style fruit and vegetable market. Krelendijk's numerous bars and restaurants offer authentic local seafood dishes and Amstel beer (brewed at neighboring Curacao) at reasonable prices. Open-air cafes overlook the waterfront.

North—Gotomeer is a favored flamingo spot located inland. **Rincon** is the islands oldest village and just beyond its borders are 500-year-old Arawak Indian inscriptions.

South—The enormous **salt flats** are the island's largest flamingo nesting ground. **Primitive huts,** which were once homes to slaves and the nearby 30 foot obelisks, were built in 1838 to help mariners locate their anchorages. Further down the coast is the island's oldest lighthouse, **Willemstoren,** built in 1837. The landlocked **Lac Bay** offers excellent windsurfing.

Washington-Slagbaai National Park covers the northwest corner of the island, an area of 13,500 acres. An exploring and bird watching haven, **the park is home to 189 species of birds and endless cliffs, valleys, beaches and cacti-lined pathways.**

DINING

- Honeymoon or anniversary diners should book **Kasa Coral** at Harbour Village Beach Resort.
- Enjoy a sunset sail on an authentic **Siamese Junk, the** *Samur.* The ship, which sails daily, offers cocktails, dinner, snacks and incredible sunsets.
- Grab a seaside table at the **Green Parrot Restaurant** serving the best hamburgers on Bonaire and watch for the green flash at sunset.
- For haute Italian cuisine, **Capriccio** is your best bet.
- The locals suggest **Richardo's Waterfront** for seafood and steak.
- Have a pizza at **The Leeward Inn.**
- Eat some of the Caribbean's best homemade ice cream at **Prisca** in Rincon.
- Lose your shirt—or win a jackpot—gambling at **Divi Flamingo Beach Hotel's** "barefoot" casino.
- Check out the colorful fish at **Karel's Bar** on the wharf in Kralendijk. The bar often features local bands, which draw a happy dancing crowd.
- If you are ready for more action, head for the **Tipsy Seagull** and dance till dawn.
- Dance the night away at the new and improved **E Wowo "the eye"**, located in the center of Kralendijk, or try another new addition to nightlife on Bonaire at the **Fantasy Disco.**

British Virgin Islands

Wendy Canning Church

If you have heard that this destination is serene and unspoiled, a haven for yachts-men as well as divers, offering crystal clear water and sheltered anchorage, then you have heard correctly.

The British Virgin Islands fondly known as the BVIs are comprised of 45 islands, islets and cays, many of which are uninhabited. Actually the entire area is part of the archipelago, along with the U.S. Virgin Islands, that stretches for some sixty miles east of Puerto Rico and lies between the Atlantic Ocean and the Caribbean Sea.

Their position within the belt of the trade winds allows for a semi-tropical climate with 75-85F temperatures year around with winds of 10 to 20 knots. The exception is Christmas week when the winds are stronger. This makes for an ideal vacation destination.

You will not find Kentucky Fried Chicken, casinos, glitzy nightclubs or large resort complexes in the BVIs. What you will find are restaurants, some small and intimate, friendly with an island flavor, guest accommodations to fit any pocketbook, local entertainment and beautiful scenery, both above and beneath the sea.

It is rumored that when Christopher Columbus discovered the islands in 1493, he was told not to land because of the fierce cannibal tribe. In fact the Arawak Indians who were driven away by the fierce and treacherous Caribs who raped, pillaged and practiced cannibalism first settled these islands. The Caribs were hated and feared throughout the Caribbean.

Pirates holed up in the protected caves of Sopers Hole in the 1800's. The Dutch were the first settlers from Europe and were soon followed by the English who were the first to gain an economic stronghold.

Because of economic hardships, the 19th century was a time when most of the Europeans returned home, leaving their plantations to become overrun and turned to ruin.

A small percentage of Europeans remained and to this day work hand in hand with the former slaves. One would never question that there is still a strong legacy of English culture flourishing.

Tortola

Spanish for Turtle Dove

You can reach Tortola either by American Eagle from Puerto Rico landing on Beef Island or by a ferry from St. Thomas (USVI).

Tortola is the largest island in the chain, being twelve miles long and three miles wide. The highest point on the island is 1710 feet above sea level in Sage National Park. We drove past this point on our way to the hotel through the beautiful spiral mountain range that runs through the island.

The Prospect Reef Resort is located one mile from Road Town, the capital. It sits on the water edge and offers a variety of services and accommodations to fit any pocketbook. It has 131 rooms, suites, and two, 2-bedroom villas on 40 tropical acres. Many rooms have kitchenettes, and the villas have full kitchens as well as a living room and dining room. They have a nice little beach and a natural pool enclosed by huge boulders.

Since our last visit the hotel has a new owner. Sadly, General Manager, Graham Sedgewick, and his staff who could not have been more friendly and helpful have been replaced.

Cats at Sunset by Wendy Canning Church

Editors Note: The hotel was undergoing complete renovation when we stayed there both before and after our trip to Virgin Gorda.

Prospect Reef Resort Ltd.
P.O. Box 104
Road Town,
Tortola, British Virgin Islands
Tel: (284) 494-3311, Fax: (284) 494-5595
Reservations (From USA): (800) 356-8937
(From Canada): (800) 463-3608

THE SCUBA DIVING AND SNORKELING

We chose to dive with Underwater Safaris (18 years in business). They had been recommended to us numerous times for their safety standards, terrific dive sites, the attitude of the staff and the warm and generous interest shown to each diver. They are undoubtedly one of the most organized dive operations we have ever seen.

Rendezvous Tours was created by Underwater Safaris more than 18 years ago. This unique concept enables cruising yachtsmen to call and arrange for a "Rendezvous" for the crew and guest to dive the local sites from the convenience of their anchorage. The divers can be picked up at one location and dropped at another, if the skipper wishes to move the boat.

They give full service support from two bases. Safari's base is located in Road Harbor at The Moorings; Safari Cay is their shop at Cooper Island adjacent to The Beach Club. Both locations are open daily and monitor Channels, 16 and 09 which enables you to

Piece of Paradise by Wendy Canning Church

make dive bookings when you are in range. You may also call them collect via Tortola Radio.

A Dozen Best Dive Sites. They know and dive most sites throughout the year: **The Indians, Angelfish Reef, Carrot Shoal, Dead Chest West, Santa Monica Rock, The Steps, Spyglass Wall, Blonde Rock, Painted Walls, Vanishing Rock, Alice in Wonderland, and The Wreck of the *R.M.S. Rhone*.**

They provide dive service to local hotels and to the majority of the bareboat and crewed yacht companies. Dive-stay packages are available with **Treasure Isle Hotel,** set on the hillside overlooking Road Harbor and the Sir Francis Drake Channel which is run by The Moorings. It has more than 40 luxurious rooms, all air conditioned, with an open-air restaurant and bar adjacent to the scenic freshwater pool.

Tortola Maria's by the Sea is located right on the waterfront in Road Town, just a few walking minutes from the dock. For those who look for some nightlife, Maria's provides quick access to Town as well as it is own restaurant, bar and freshwater pool. The **Cooper Island Beach Club** is a small resort located at Manchioneel Bay on Cooper Island, approximately six miles across the Sir Francis Drake Channel from Road Town.

The first morning we were off to **Spyglass,** a mini wall dive off Norman's Island. In earlier times, pirates living on Norman's Island took advantage of the bight running past it. Ships making passage to St. Thomas would misconstrue the pirates' signals thinking that they would bring them through the bight and into St. Thomas. As a result they ended up floundering on Norman's rocks and beaches.

It is a beautiful island. For those interested, the price is $7 million dollars. The only drawback is that there is no anchorage.

We rolled over into the water and followed our guide. Working our way southeast, looking out for the pelagics who like these waters because of the bight. **We saw a number of stingrays and good size nurse shark. As we swam further along a beautiful spotted drum came into view.** There were stovepipe sponges and a few elephant ear as well as shrimp living among the anemones.

We ascended, stopping at 15 feet for 3 minutes even though the wall dive was not a decompression dive. The practice is one that is done on every dive with Underwater Safaris which I believe is a good one and exhibits high safety standards.

Our second dive was a shallow one exploring the north section of the wall. There were beautiful purple sponges, brown and black coral, lobster, trumpetfish, brain coral, schools of yellowhead, a spotted moray eel, parrot fish, squirrelfish, blue hamlet, butterfly fish, sergeant major, and black durgeon. **As you move along the wall look out to the left and you are likely to see rays and larger pelagics.**

Unfortunately our time was up but we had dived with this wonderful group when we stopped at Cooper Island.

Underwater Safaris
1 800 537 7032

SCUBA AND SNORKELING QUESTIONNAIRE

NAME: **Underwater Safaris Ltd.**
ADDRESS: **P.O. Box 139**
Road Town, Tortola, BVI
CONTACT: **Tony Green**
TITLE: **Managing Director**
TELEPHONE: **284-494-3235**   FAX **284-494-5322**   EMAIL: **undsaf@caribsurf.com**
CAPITOL: **Road Town**   GOVERNMENT: **British Dependent**
POPULATION: **17,000**   LANGUAGE: **English**
CURRENCY: **US Dollars**   ELECTRICITY: **110V**
AIRLINES: **AA, LIAT**   DEPARTURE TAX? **Yes, $10**
NEED VISA/PASSPORT   YES   NO x
PROOF OF CITIZENSHIP?   YES x   NO

YOUR FACILITY IS CLASSIFIED AS: SCUBA CENTER x   RESORT
BUSINESS HOURS: **8:00AM - 7:00PM**
CERTIFYING AGENCIES: **PADI**
LOG BOOK REQUIRED?   YES   NO x
EQUIPMENT: SALES X   RENTALS x   AIR FILLS x
PRIMARY LINE OF EQUIPMENT?   SHERWOOD
PHOTOGRAPHIC EQUIPMENT: SALES   RENTALS x   LAB

CHARTER/DIVE BOAT AVAILABLE?   YES x   NO   DIVER CAPACITY 12, 12, 18
COAST GUARD APPROVED?   YES   NO x CAPTAIN LICENSED?   YES   NO x
SHIP TO SHORE?   YES x   NO   LORAN?   YES   NO x   RADAR?   YES   NO x
DIVE MASTER/INSTRUCTOR ABOARD? YES x   NO   BOTH
DIVING AND SNORKELING: SALT x   FRESH
TYPE OF DIVING/SNORKELING IN AREA: WALL   BEACH   WRECK x   REEF x   CAVE   ICE
DIVING/SNORKELING IN YOUR AREA IS BEST SUITED FOR: BEGINNER x   INTERMEDIATE x   ADVANCED x
BEST TIME OF YEAR FOR DIVING/SNORKELING:
TEMPERATURE: NOV-APRIL: **78F**   MAY-OCT.   **84F**
VISIBILITY: DIVING: **60 - 80Ft.** SNORKELING **40Ft.**

PACKAGES AVAILABLE: DIVE x   DIVE STAY x   SNORKEL   SNORKEL STAY
ACCOMMODATIONS NEARBY: HOTEL x   MOTEL   HOME RENTALS
ACCOMMODATION RATES: EXPENSIVE   MODERATE x   INEXPENSIVE
RESTAURANTS NEARBY: EXPENSIVE   MODERATE x   INEXPENSIVE
YOUR AREA IS: REMOTE   QUIET WITH ACTIVITIES   x   LIVELY
LOCAL ACTIVITY/NIGHTLIFE:
CAR NEEDED TO EXPLORE AREA: YES x   NO
DUTY FREE SHOPPING: YES   NO x

LOCAL EMERGENCY SERVICES: NEAREST HYPERBARIC TREATMENT FACILITY:
COAST GUARD: AUTHORITY:
TELEPHONE: LOCATION: **St. Thomas**
CALLSIGNS: TELEPHONE:

LOCAL DIVING DOCTOR:
NAME: **Dr. Vanterpool**
LOCATION: **Road Town**
TELEPHONE: **809-494-2346**

ACTIVITIES

When not underwater, take time to explore Tortola. We rented a Jeep and drove the entire island, stopping here and there to investigate other hotels, beaches and restaurants.

Cane Garden Bay is one of the most popular beaches and has wonderful snorkeling. Brewers Bay is secluded with tranquil estates and a campground. Long Bay is on the western side but does not have a very good beach. Sugar Mill Hotel, which is a little further on has its own beach and is a wonderful place for windsurfing and snorkeling. On the eastern side of Tortola you will find Josiah's Bay and Lambert Bay. These beaches are beautiful with good snorkeling and swimming.

DINING

We dined out each night in Road Town and found a number of good restaurants, both funky and elegant. You will find a **Pussers Rum Company Store and Pub** where you get a good variety of pub food and a broad selection of beer and ale. Tel. 4-2467.

If you get a craving for Chinese food go to **Chopsticks**. Tel. 4-3616.

The **Fort Burt Restaurant** is a short walk from Prospect Harbour. The food is excellent and served in a pleasant setting overlooking the harbor. The fort was built in the 17th century by the Dutch and is a wonderful piece of island history. Tel. 4-2587.

The **Paradise Pub** is situated on the water and is also a short walk from the Prospect Reef. The food is simple but very good. Casual dress is acceptable. It has a happy hour and some form of entertainment nightly. It is a fun spot. Tel. 4-2608.

On the west end of the island you will find the **Sugar Mill Hotel** and its wonderful restaurant. Tel 5-4355. Jeff and Jinx Morgan are hosts and owners. Do dress for a four-course dinner in this enchanting location. The food and ambiance are a treat and a must for one great dining experience on Tortola.

Editor's note: On our earlier visit to Tortola we found it a quite seductive island. Now even in the quiet off-season we found it a bustling little Mecca. Tortola has been "discovered".

BRITISH VIRIGIN ISLANDS TOURIST BOARD
P.O. BOX 134 ROAD TOWN, TORTOLA, BVI
TEL: 284 494 3134
FAX: 284 494 3866

British Virgin Islands

Virgin Gorda

North Sound

Wendy Canning Church

If coming from North America, fly to San Juan, Puerto Rico, or to St. Thomas USVI. If arriving from Europe or South America, American Airlines flies directly to San Juan or Antigua. Reliable commuter airlines will take you – in less than an hour to Tortola's Beef Island Airport. At the nearby harbor you can connect with the scheduled ferry that will deliver you directly to North Sound. Or, if you advise the resort of your arrival, a launch will pick you up for an unforgettable half-hour boat-trip.

Virgin Gorda, with a population of 1400 spread over 15 square miles of mountains, boulders, and beaches, has become one of the international travelers most popular vacation destinations.

Measuring just eight-and-a-half miles long, Virgin Gorda is the third largest in the island chain. Dramatic slopes plunge from Gorda Peak, at 1,500 feet, to the crystalline bays and inlets far below. Not many islands offer the range of exclusive resorts, most with panache, elan and unbridled elegance. The option of restaurants will gratify the most discriminating palate. Whether you stop for breakfast, lunch or dinner, you're surely find yourself lingering longer than you expected. Virgin Gorda has that effect on visitors.

A year round temperate climate allows the guest to enjoy a myriad of delights both above and beneath its waters, fulfilling the dream of the perfect getaway. There are few places left in the world that have developed comfort while sacrificing nothing to God's palette of unfettered nature.

The pace of life is slow on Virgin Gorda, but if you don't want to spend the day on a beach, there are plenty of other activities. You can explore **The Baths, where huge boulders seem to have been arranged by a playful giant to provide a myriad of rock pools, secret beaches and trails. Visit the Copper Mine standing guard against the blue Atlantic.** Or just spend the morning on a hillside cooled by gentle breezes while you watch the ferries cross the North Sound. Book a Boston Whaler with a picnic and pass the day at a deserted bay.

Cactus Point provides some of the best snorkeling in North Sound; it is not the place to be walking around. The water surrounding Cactus Point is almost always calm and **makes snorkeling from a Boston Whaler easy.** Tropical fish are always near and some of the most colorful corals can be seen there. Just south of Cactus Point there is a nice beach where you can bring your Boston Whaler and rest with lunch or refreshers.

On the north side of **Prickly Pear Island** there are two very nice beaches, both have beautiful white sand and provide **great snorkeling.** Normally the water is calm inside this protected area.

The West Side of Eustatia Island is a very good spot for snorkeling and is also fairly private. This is a beautiful anchorage with a very nice beach and wonderful sea life. This area is not as protected as others and may present a challenge when snorkeling.

The beach at **Oil Nut Bay** is about a half mile long with beautiful white sand and blue water. Take a picnic lunch and spend a day enjoying the beach and Oil Nut Bay Reef. **This is a good spot for snorkeling** as many colorful fish play on and near the reef. If looking for shells, they may be found in the grassy areas, as this is where they feed. If you do find a shell, please be sure there is not a living animal inside.

Eustatia Reef is ten miles long and **is famous for its snorkeling.** Eustatia Reef is the home of many different types of coral (brain coral, staghorn, fan and finger coral, etc.) and fish. Blue tang; parrot fish and French grunts are just a few types seen. Often you may see octopus, squid and sea turtles.

Drakes Anchorage. If you are interested in a short hike, take your Boston Whaler over to Drake's Anchorage and leave it at the dinghy dock. A short walk over the hill to Honeymoon Beach adds a new element to North Sound. **Honeymoon Beach is very small, private and offers stunning blue water with magnificent snorkeling.**

Nearby sights are Fallen Jerusalem, Little Fort National Park, The Baths, and the Copper Mine. Parks include Gorda Peak National Park (a hiker paradise) and Spring Bay National Park. Also good hiking can be found on the North Sound trails.

Yachtsmen will find safe anchorage at The Dogs and the Virgin Gorda Baths. Boat or jeep can reach both.

Other beaches to explore nearby are Big Trunk Bay, Devil's Bay, Handsome Bay, Long Bay, Tahoe Bay, Savannah Bay, Spring Bay, and The Baths.

Editor's note: When using a Boston Whaler always check water/weather as conditions can change. Be sure and advise your hotel of your destination and time of return.

Please see Honeymoon and Anniversary Section for Biras Creek and Bitter End Yacht Club.

SCUBA AND SNORKELING QUESTIONNAIRE

NAME: **Kilbrides Sunchaser Scuba Ltd.**
ADDRESS: **P.O. Box 46**
Virgin Gorda, BVI
TITLE: **Staff**
TELEPHONE: **284-495-9638, 800-932-4286**   FAX **284-495-7549**
CAPITOL: **Spanish Town**   GOVERNMENT:
POPULATION: 1500   LANGUAGE: **English**
CURRENCY: **US**   ELECTRICITY: **120 watt**
AIRLINES: **AA, LIAT**   DEPARTURE TAX? **$10**
NEED VISA/PASSPORT   YES **x**   NO   PROOF OF CITIZENSHIP? YES **x** NO
YOUR FACILITY IS CLASSIFIED AS: SCUBA CENTER **x**   RESORT
BUSINESS HOURS: **7:45AM - 5:00PM**
CERTIFYING AGENCIES: **PADI/NAUI**
LOGBOOK REQUIRED?   YES   NO **x**
EQUIPMENT: SALES   RENTALS **x**   AIR FILLS X
PRIMARY LINE OF EQUIPMENT?   SHERWOOD/SEAQUEST
PHOTOGRAPHIC EQUIPMENT: VIDEO SALES **x**   RENTALS   LAB

CHARTER/DIVE BOAT AVAILABLE?   YES **x**   NO   DIVER CAPACITY **23**
COAST GUARD APPROVED?   YES **x**   NO   CAPTAIN LICENSED? YES **x**   NO
SHIP TO SHORE?   YES **x**   NO   LORAN? YES **x**   NO   RADAR?   YES   NO **x**
DIVE MASTER/INSTRUCTOR ABOARD?   YES **x**   NO   BOTH
DIVING AND SNORKELING: SALT **x**   FRESH
TYPE OF DIVING/SNORKELING IN AREA: WALL   BEACH   WRECK **x**   REEF **x**   CAVE   ICE
DIVING/SNORKELING IN YOUR AREA IS BEST SUITED FOR: BEGINNER **x** INTERMEDIATE **x** ADVANCED **x**
BEST TIME OF YEAR FOR DIVING/SNORKELING: **Year round**
TEMPERATURE: NOV-APRIL: **77F**   MAY-OCT.   **81F**
VISIBILITY: DIVING: **60-100Ft.** SNORKELING **60-100Ft.**

PACKAGES AVAILABLE: DIVE **x**   DIVE STAY **x**   SNORKEL   SNORKEL STAY
ACCOMMODATIONS NEARBY: RESORT **x** MOTEL   HOME RENTALS **x**
ACCOMMODATION RATES: EXPENSIVE **x**   MODERATE **x**   INEXPENSIVE
RESTAURANTS NEARBY: EXPENSIVE **x**   MODERATE **x**   INEXPENSIVE **x**
YOUR AREA IS: REMOTE   QUIET WITH ACTIVITIES **x**   LIVELY
LOCAL ACTIVITY/NIGHTLIFE: DINING/DANCING
CAR NEEDED TO EXPLORE AREA: YES   NO **x**
DUTY FREE SHOPPING: YES   NO **x**

LOCAL EMERGENCY SERVICES: NEAREST HYPERBARIC TREATMENT FACILITY:
COAST GUARD: **St. Thomas, USVI**   AUTHORITY: **Dr. David Boaz**
TELEPHONE: **809-774-1911**   LOCATION: **St. Thomas General Hospital**
CALLSIGNS: **VISAR**   TELEPHONE:

LOCAL DIVING DOCTOR:
NAME: **Jana Downing, MD**
LOCATION: **Road Town, Tortola, BVI**
TELEPHONE: **284-494-2763**

The Cayman Islands

Wendy Canning Church

The Cayman Islands lie 480 miles south of Miami, Florida in the Western Caribbean. They consist of three islands, Grand Cayman, Cayman Brac and Little Cayman. Cayman Brac and Little Cayman are referred to as "sister islands", since a channel separates them that is only seven miles long. All three islands are situated on a coral reef that is eight miles long, descending to six thousand feet.

The population of all three islands is 27,000 with the majority on Grand Cayman. The people are mainly of English, Irish, Scottish, Welsh and African descent. English is the official language. Georgetown, on Grand Cayman is the capital. Columbus landed on May 10, 1503, naming the islands Las Tortugas after the large sea turtles that frequent the waters. The Spanish never established a permanent settlement. Pirates used the hidden caves and inlets for safe anchorage to repair their ships and hide their treasure.

The islands were renamed the Caymans from the Carib word for crocodile. In 1670 the "Treaty of Madrid" made the Caymans British property.

Twenty-five years ago there was not a paved road on Grand Cayman. Today, it ranks as the fifth largest financial center in the world with over six hundred branches of global banks.

Passports are not required for U.S. or Canadian citizens but you must have a return ticket and proof of citizenship.

THE CAYMAN ISLAND WATER SPORTS ASSOCIATION

The Cayman Island Water Sports Association (30 members) meets frequently and sets rules for its members, prices, safety standards, maximum depth for diving (100 feet), ratio of dive masters to divers and what equipment must be carried aboard a boat. All members adhere to these rules.

This is to be commended for they realize though in competition for business, the safety of the diver, the well-being of the sea life, the coral reef, and the fragile ecosystem depend upon a combined effort.

The Association has established 200 permanent moorings. The use of spear guns is forbidden. Divers cannot wear gloves. Marine Park zones have been set where no one can take any kind of sea creature, living or dead. "Take only pictures, leave only bubbles" is their motto.

GRAND CAYMAN

Grand Cayman is 28 miles long and 7 miles wide. The high season is December through April; most of the rainfall comes in May through October.

Grand Cayman has been discovered! You will find 4 and 5 star hotels, luxurious waterfront homes, apartments/ condos, American franchise take out, very expensive restaurants and $8.00 drinks. Grand Cayman has the reputation as the most expensive island in the Caribbean.

DIVING

On an acre of land, a half mile south of downtown Georgetown you will find **Parrots Landing**. I chose to dive with Parrots Landing because it had been highly recommended. Seldom have I witnessed an operation that was so organized, its boats comfortable and shipshape, its staff professional and safety conscious and genuinely helpful and friendly.

Parrots Landing opened in February 1988 with something different in mind for divers and non-divers coming to Grand Cayman. They offer hassle-free diving and snorkeling, small to medium boat capacity, a little extra freedom and a different dive-site each day. They operate six boats that go to remote and virgin dive sites along the North, South, East and West walls. They have a full-service shop on-site that sells, repairs, and rents dive equipment. There is also a photo lab and school operated by Lois Hatcher.

For the advanced-computer diver they offer a boat that departs at 8:30 a.m. This boat is limited to six divers and ventures to diver selected sites. This non-guided buddy team type dive requires each diver to monitor his or her dive with a computer. Multi-level diving and the use of a computer allow for more accurate and efficient bottom time. The 100-foot maximum depth limits remain in effect.

There were six of us on *The Macaw* bound for **Lemon Drop** at the North Wall. *The Macaw* is 23 feet long with 220 horsepower engines, roomy enough for gear and divers with a nice comfortable cabin and head. This is a dive at 100 feet maximum. With giant stride entry we descended down the mooring line and made our way to the wall. There was spectacular light from above, so we had excellent visibility to explore at that depth.

Sponge Growth at Orange Canyon by Lois Hatcher

Our first glimpse was of a ray lying partially buried in the sand. He darted away at the sight of divers. There is a small channel so you can catch a glimpse of eagle rays while checking out the wall. There are three large pinnacles separated by canyons and sand chutes. The black coral and gorgonias are beautiful.

We came upon a large array of plate coral. At 50 feet we encountered all variety of reef fish. This is an impressive dive and not one to be missed.

Orange Canyon is made up of two wide ravines. Reaching our maximum depth of 100 feet schools of large tarpon, barra-cuda, and an abundance of brain, barrel and plate coral made this an interesting site. As we ascended there were angelfish, trumpetfish, orange sponges and brilliant pink coral.

Tarpon Alley North Wall is comprised of three canyons, one leads to a drop off, the others to open sand. Schools of tarpon appeared before our eyes, their silver bodies shimmering in the light from above.

The Stingray City dive and snorkel excursion is available everyday of the week. Rumor has it that "Stingray City" is the most dived and snorkeled site in the world. There are many photographic opportunities as you feed squid to over 25 friendly southern stingrays. Divers and non-divers alike will certainly want to sail the *Cockatoo* from North Sound and set anchor at Stingray City. Squid is provided for snorkelers to hand feed the stingrays.

For more information contact:
Parrots Landing Watersports Park
P.O. Box 1995
Georgetown
Grand Cayman, Cayman Islands, BWI

ACCOMMODATIONS

"There's a place where the Caribbean is still gracious, the way it used to be" is The Caribbean Club motto. Jerry Payne built the Club twenty-seven years ago when beach front property prices on Seven-Mile Beach were not prohibitive and density was not a problem. **This is a little jewel of a resort and my choice for lodging on Grand Cayman.**

The 18 privately owned one and two bedroom villas are all individually decorated in taste. Each is centrally air-conditioned with color TV and a kitchen. Tennis is available on the premises. **Lantanas Restaurant** is on the property and serves cuisine in a warm, unobtrusive and tony atmosphere. Tel: 809-947-5595, Fax: 809-947-5653.

SCUBA AND SNORKELING FACILITIES QUESTIONNAIRE

NAME **Parrots Landing Watersports Park**
ADDRESS **P.O. Box 1995 Georgetown**
Grand Cayman, Cayman Islands, BWI
CONTACT **Larry Leonard**
TITLE **Reservations Manager**
TELEPHONE **800-448-8128**   TELEX
CAPITOL: GEORGETOWN   GOVERNMENT: BRITISH COMMONWEALTH
POPULATION: LANGUAGE: ENGLISH
CURRENCY: **Cayman Islands Currency**   ELECTRICITY:
AIRLINES: **Cayman Airways, United**   DEPARTURE TAX? **$7.50 U.S.**
NEED VISA/PASSPORT?   YES   NO x   PROOF OF CITIZENSHIP?   YES x   NO

YOUR FACILITY IS CLASSIFIED AS: SCUBA CENTER x   RESORT
BUSINESS HOURS: **8 a.m. - 6:00 p.m.**
CERTIFYING AGENCIES: **PADI, NAUI, SSI**
LOG BOOK REQUIRED?   YES   NO x **C-card required**
EQUIPMENT: SALES X   RENTALS x   AIR FILLS x
PRIMARY LINE OF EQUIPMENT: **Dive Gear**
PHOTOGRAPHIC EQUIPMENT: SALES   RENTALS x   LAB x

CHARTER/DIVE BOAT AVAILABLE?   YES x   NO   DIVER CAPACITY SEE ATTACHED
COAST GUARD APPROVED? CAYMAN GOVT. YES x   NO   CAPTAIN LICENSED?   YES x   NO
SHIP TO SHORE?   YES x   NO   LORAN?   YES   NO   RADAR?   YES   NO
DIVE MASTER/INSTRUCTOR ABOARD? YES x   NO   BOTH x
DIVING & SNORKELING: SALT x   FRESH
TYPE OF DIVING/SNORKELING IN AREA: WALL x   BEACH x   WRECK x   REEF x   CAVERN x   ICE
DIVING/SNORKELING IN YOUR AREA IS BEST SUITED FOR: BEGINNER x   INTERMEDIATE x   ADVANCED x
BEST TIME OF YEAR FOR DIVING/SNORKELING: **All year round**
TEMPERATURE: NOV-APRIL   **81-82F**   MAY-OCT: **82-85F**
VISIBILITY: DIVING: **100FT**   SNORKELING: **100FT**

PACKAGES AVAILABLE: DIVE x   DIVE STAY x   SNORKEL   SNORKEL-STAY X
ACCOMMODATIONS NEARBY: HOTEL x   MOTEL x   HOME RENTALS CONDOS
ACCOMMODATION RATES: EXPENSIVE x   MODERATE x   INEXPENSIVE x
RESTAURANTS NEARBY: EXPENSIVE x   MODERATE x   INEXPENSIVE x
YOUR AREA IS: REMOTE   QUIET WITH ACTIVITIES x   LIVELY x
LOCAL ACTIVITY/NIGHTLIFE: **Bars, restaurants, movie theater**
CAR NEEDED TO EXPLORE AREA?   YES   NO
DUTY FREE SHOPPING?   YES   NO

LOCAL EMERGENCY SERVICES   NEAREST HYPERBARIC TREATMENT FACILITY
COASTGUARD **Cayman Islands**   AUTHORITY:
Port of Authority   LOCATION: **Georgetown Hospital**
TELEPHONE: **949-2228**   TELEPHONE: **555 in an emergency**
CALLSIGNS: **Channel 16 on VHF radio**

LOCAL DIVING DOCTOR:
NAME: **Dr. Hetley**
LOCATION: **Crewe Road**
TELEPHONE: **949-7400**

The Caribbean Club is something of an anomaly in the modern world. The beach is pristine and the staff remains amenable and welcoming which may explain why many of the guests return year after year.

WHEN YOU COME UP FOR AIR

- Definitely schedule a voyage on the **Atlantis Submarine**. One can view the impressive variety of fish through their own porthole in an air-conditioned seat.
- Enter the **Million Dollar Month International Fishing Tournament** that takes place each June.
- Visit the Cayman Islands Turtle Farm.
- Play golf on a course designed by Jack Nicklaus and use the famous Cayman ball.
- Visit Pedro Castle which was built in 1780 . It is Cayman's oldest structure.
- Shop in downtown Georgetown for duty-free bargains. Jewelry, perfume, crystal, and many other gifts can all be purchased here.
- Visit the Cayman Islands National Museum.
- Go to Hell! Ironshore rock formations more than one and a half million years old look that look like the remains of hellfire. You can send a postcard from Hell!
- Ride Research Submersibles Ltd., a two-passenger sub that reaches depths of 800 feet.

CAYMAN BRAC & LITTLE CAYMAN

Grand Cayman gives a hint of what lies ahead for the worldwide diver seeking virgin diving. Cayman Brac brings one closer to that quest. Little Cayman does not disappoint the diver who has traveled far to find one of the last untouched areas. The quest is worth the effort.

Please refer to Honeymoon and Anniversary Section for more information on Pirates Point on Little Cayman.

CAYMAN ISLANDS DEPARTMENT OF TOURISM
420 LEXINGTON AVENUE # 2733
NEW YORK, N.Y. 10170
TEL 212 682 5582

CURACAO

"Undiscovered Dive Opportunities!"

Mike Innis

Down off the coast of Venezuela, riding the gentle currents of the Caribbean and hiding below the hurricane zone sit 3 jewels: Aruba, Bonaire, and Curacao also know as the "ABCs". I've dived Bonaire for years; I've sampled the underwater sights of Aruba a couple of times; but for some reason, I'd never gotten to Curacao. Conventional wisdom had always said, "If you want to dive, go to Bonaire; if you want to party, Curacao is the place!"

I'm glad to report that, once again, conventional wisdom was only half-right. Curacao offers both partying and excellent diving. Add to that the fact that the island has a rich cultural history and an interesting topside topography, and you've got yourself a fascinating vacation destination.

The history of Curacao is rich and varied. From the Spanish in the 1500's, down through the Dutch, the English, and the Dutch again, the island has been a major Caribbean seaport for 300 years, dealing in everything from the sad cargoes of slaves to supertankers full of petroleum products. A large population of Jews, trying to escape persecution in Europe, came to the island and for many years had a major influence on the building of modern Curacaon commerce. Each culture has left its mark and made its influence felt. A walking tour of Willemstad, combined with a driving island tour will help give you the full flavor of this fascinating place.

Dive sites that have gone relatively unnoticed for years surround Curacao. As a result, the reefs, walls and underwater flora are in pristine shape, just waiting for you to discover them. Like all islands, there is windward, rougher side and a kinder, gentler leeward side. On those rare few days each year when the wind conditions are right, the diving goes from excellent to spectacular because you can dive on the wild side. Ask the local dive guides -when the wind drops, they head out, en masse, for the windward side! Water temperatures do not vary much throughout the year, ranging from the low 80's to the low 90's. Visibility is a consistent 80-100 feet, since there's only 20 inches of rain per year and consequently very little runoff. The "rainy" season is November and December, but doesn't pack an umbrella even if you visit the island during these months; they rarely get what we might call a "rain event."

I recommend that you put Curacao down on your list of dive destinations that you should visit. It's got it all. Well, almost all; the ski lift is broken, and the ice diving classes have been canceled due to lack of ice, but...

DIVING & SNORKELING WITH HABITAT CURACAO

I was fortunate enough to stay in two places: the brand new **Habitat Curacao** (800-327-6709), and the older, established **Lions Dive Hotel** (888-546-73483 toll free). Rates will vary widely throughout the year, depending upon whether or not the resort is having a special. Some will occasionally include airfare from major cities, or throw in a buffet breakfast. Also, non-diver packages are considerably cheaper, so if you're traveling with a person who doesn't dive, make sure the reservations agent understands. (Then get the non-diver to take a resort course while they're there; it's a great place to learn SCUBA!) Call and shop carefully for the best price at the time of year you intend to visit.

Nestled away from the madding crowd on the sparsely developed southwest coast, everything at Habitat was just as you would expect for a resort that opened in late 1996. Brightly painted, squeaky clean, all new rental dive equipment and a fast new PRO42 dive boat that hustles you out to and back from the dive sites in fine style. I stayed in one of the Junior Suites, of which there are 54. Each is air-conditioned, has a small refrigerator and electric stove in it, and faces west overlooking the Caribbean so you'll not miss out on those tropical sunsets. The infrastructure in place to support the divers is what reminds you of the Habitat's Bonaire heritage. "Dive Freedom" they proclaim; and dive freedom is what they provide. **Anytime of the day or night that you get**

The Tugboat by Mike B. Innis

the urge, you can bolt on a fresh tank, walk to the end of the dive pier, and drop in on the local underwater inhabitants.

Shore diving is excellent, just a few fin strokes away from the pier. A healthy, active reef awaits you at 30 feet, then dropping off to a gentle slope at about 100 feet. After the gentle slope, a vertical drop to depths far beyond the recommended sport diver limits provides a cobalt blue backdrop for your dives. **Snorkelers will be happy with Habitat, since they can explore hundreds of yards of shoreline on either side of the resort.** I certainly took advantage of the dive boat, but I made 5 shore dives on the house reef, and was never bored or disappointed.

My two favorite boat dive sites were **Mushroom Forest** and **San Juan**. Mushroom Forest was a maze of star coral mounds that look like they'd never had a fin kicked over them. The dive is ended at Mushroom Cave. Really a cavern that extends back 80 feet or so, it is fun to surface inside the cave and look out at the bright sunshine and gorgeous water. San Juan is another keeper, right off a beautiful sandy beach. Elkhorn and shingle coral in profusion provide lots of hiding places for spotted drum, soldier fish, clouds of wrasse, and groups of banded coral shrimp.

ACTIVITIES

Since Habitat is somewhat isolated, the resort does an excellent job of providing the guests with opportunities to get out and about during surface intervals. You can rent a 4WD Toyota pickup truck, complete with tank racks, and get out and explore other shore diving sites. If you simply must have some "action," buses run into **Willemstad** twice a day. Just let the front desk know and they'll set it up for you. There is no charge for this shuttle service. Options for eating out are somewhat limited unless you rent a vehicle, in which case there are several restaurants within easy driving distance of the property. I elected to take all my meals at the resort's restaurant, the **Rum Runner**. The food and service were quite good, and each evening they added a couple of specials, not on the menu, to add some variety.

DIVING & SNORKELING WITH LIONS DIVE HOTEL

From the splendid isolation of Habitat, I moved through the bustling capital and took up residence at Lions Dive Hotel. The rooms here were clean, air conditioned, and most of them have a sea view. This long established hotel is busy. The locals use it for dining and as a gathering place in the evening after work. It's a fun and lively place in which to stay.

The dive business side of Lions Dive, **Underwater Curacao**, is attached to the hotel property, and is an efficient, professionally run operation. The two-dive boats run morning and afternoon one tank trips every day. The schedule is posted a week ahead of time, and divers use sign-up sheets to book their spots on the boats.

Most of the sites can be reached within 20 minutes of clearing the breakwater. Top sites are the wrecks of the *Superior Producer* and the *Tugboat*. The *Producer* accidentally sank in 1987 with a full cargo of clothing and alcoholic beverages. She sits in 100 feet of water, perfectly upright, and provides divers with safe swim-throughs, lots of wildlife, and even a chance to pick up an artifact that has been overlooked. One of our divers found a perfectly folded, short sleeved sports shirt, after almost ten years of submergence and who knows how many visits by divers!

The *Tugboat* sank in only 15 feet of water, and is excellent for both diving and snorkeling. The tug sits close to a drop off, so divers can work their way down the wall for a while, then come back up and do their safety stop while exploring the remains of the boat.

Shore diving and snorkeling from Underwater Curacao is OK, but I have a couple of concerns about these activities. Firstly, it is a good, 100-yard surface swim, through the little harbor and out the breakwater. Divers must have a dive flag with them, and must keep a sharp eye out for boat traffic inbound and outbound from the marina.

Secondly, once outside the breakwater, there is a great deal of Jet Ski traffic. The jet skiers stay fairly close to shore, run the machines quite fast, and I'm not too sure they know what a dive flag is. I tried it, and there is good diving from the shore; but the risk of getting run down or over needs to be considered, especially in light of the fact that you can jump on a dive boat and get to some really nice, safer places with no effort at all.

ACTIVITIES
One of the unique things about Lions Dive is the fact that, as a registered guest, you have a free pass, anytime you want, to visit the Seaquarium, which is right next door. The collection of sealife is nothing short of spectacular. People visiting the Caribbean for the first time who'd really like to know what that "orange colored fish with the big eyes" is called can run from the dive boat to the Seaquarium and find out! It's like having the world's largest, animated fish identification card at your disposal.

The restaurant at Lions Dive, **Rumors**, will keep you fed in fine style during your stay. The resort is close enough to town that a cab ride won't break the bank, so you can motor into town for the evening and have your pick of anything from Chinese, Italian, Texan, French or local Curacaon food. The fast food places have established themselves as well, so you can grab a Burger King, a Mac or a Pizza Hut meal if you feel your cholesterol level is dropping too low. The hotel also offers free shuttles into town a couple of times each day.

CURACAO TOURIST BOARD
475 PARK AVENUE SOUTH, SUITE 2000
NEW YORK, N.Y. 10016
TEL 212 682 5582

Dominica

"Adventure Diving"

Martha Watkins Gilkes

I have made at least a dozen trips to Dominica, and I keep returning, even after diving nearly every island in the Caribbean. The underwater scenery of Dominica is as spectacular as the scenery on land, with rugged mountains continuing into the sea. Shallow coral reefs lead out to dramatic drop-offs and sheer wall covered with tremendous black coral trees and huge barrel and tube sponges. The volcanic action has formed arches and caves, now heavily encrusted with marine life.

Not found on many other islands, there is also a sub-aquatic hot freshwater spring just offshore in only 10-20 feet of water known as "Champagne." Freshwater bubbles drift slowly through the black sand towards the surface appearing like liquid crystal glistening in the sunlight. This is the perfect ending to a night dive as I ascended from the nearby reef to the hot bubbles to experience nature's sauna. On every night dive I have done at "Champagne", I have been greeted by schools of squid.

Some of the more popular dive sites are:

Scotts Head Drop-off is a 20-foot ledge with a dramatic drop-off to over 120 feet. The walls are covered in large tube sponges and georgians and occasional black coral trees.

The **Soufriere Pinnacle** rises out of Soufriere Bay from around 150 feet to within 5 feet of the surface. The pinnacle is covered with soft and hard corals and a variety of tropical reef fish.

The **La Bim Wall** is an extensive 1.5-mile wall that drops off from a 20-foot ledge to over 800 feet in some places. Large schools of blue and brown chromis fish mass among the pillar and boulder coral on the 20-foot ledge.

Point Guignard drops from 15 feet to 110 feet along the cliff face of blackbar soldier fish. I repeatedly dove one cave, which made a safe shallow dive. The cave is large enough for divers to enter, penetrating the rock wall about 40 feet. A mass of blackbar soldier fish parted ranks as I entered and lobster often inhabits the roof.

More advanced dive sites are on the Atlantic side of the island. These include King David's Throne, Mountain Top, The Village and The Condo. Boat entry and exit is difficult due to wave action and the site availability is limited. However, the visibility is generally excellent and the marine life is prolific. You often see massive sting rays, occasional nurse sharks, large school of Margate, snappers and pelagic fish. **Although I know there are numerous other exciting dives, I repeatedly return to this area!** The large rock formations offer a network of three intertwining caves filled with soft corals, brightly colored sponges, and large schools of blackbar soldier fish and assorted reef fish that gently part as divers swim through.

On all four sites, there are enormous coral overhangs providing shelter for a large variety of colorful reef fish and marine growths. Massive stingrays frolic on the nearby sand bottom and are easily approached if a diver is quiet. The northern end of Dominica does not provide the sheer spectacular drop-offs but offers some magnificent diving.

Grand Savanna, Trumpet Fish Reef, Point Roande, and Bertie's Dream are a few of the more popular sites. Some have permanent moorings installed to protect the coral reef against anchor damage.

Wreck diving does not feature prominently, although there are a number of known wreck sites. One dive shop frequents *The Barge*, a shallow site in 40 feet used mainly as a night dive due to numerous basket star fish.

The *Canefield Tug* is a 55-foot tug lying in 90 feet of water. She is home for schools of reef fish and features wire coral and hydroids, black margate, large barracuda, jacks and mackerel also cruise around. The location is near the mouth of the river and the run-off can cause very low visibility so the site is not always diveable.

The newest wreck on Dominica, intentionally sunk as a diving site in July 1990 is not completely intact. This 80 foot steel hull freighter plied the waters between the islands carrying produce. She now lies in 60 feet of water.

Are there any disadvantages to diving in Dominica? Well, Dominica sometimes experiences heavy rains and the run-offs

Green Gold by Wendy Canning Church

from the numerous rivers can cause clouding of the sea near to the shore. The protected leeward side of the island suffers a lack of fish life, as the traditional way of fishing with wire fish pots has taken a toll on the small reef fish. Attention is being focused on this issue in the hope of finding a solution. However, the spectacular drop-offs encrusted with the huge sponges and black coral trees still provide breathtaking underwater scenery.

The Dominica dive shops are well organized and equipped. The longest established scuba diving shop on the island, **Dive Dominica**, is a NAUI Dream resort and SSI Resort Member. Well-known diver Derek Perryman, the first qualified diving instructor on the island and his attractive wife Ginette run it.

1-888-262-6611
FAX 809-448-6088

SCUBA AND SNORKELING FACILITIES QUESTIONNAIRE PRIVATE

NAME: **Underwater Curacao**
ADDRESS: **Baper Kibra**

CONTACT: **Ewant Van Walbeek**
TITLE: **Dive Instructor**
TELEPHONE: **618581 / 618100**   FAX: **618501**

CAPITOL: **Willemstad**   GOVERNMENT: **Democracy**
POPULATION: LANGUAGE: **Dutch**
CURRENCY: **Antillian Guilder**   ELECTRICITY: **220v /110v**
AIRLINES: **KLM / ALM**   DEPARTURE TAX:
VISA/PASSPORT: **yes**   PROOF OF CITIZENSHIP: **yes**

YOUR FACILITY IS QUALIFIED AS: **resort**
BUISINESS HOURS: **8:00 - 17:00**
CERTIFYING AGENCIES: **Padi / SSI**
LOG BOOK REQUIRED:
EQUIPMENT: **Sales, Rentals, Air Fills**
PRIMARY LINE OF EQUIPMENT: **Mares**
PHOTOGRAPHIC EQUIPMENT: **Rentals**

CHARTER/DIVE BOAT AVAILABLE: **Yes**   DIVER CAPACITY: **21 Per Boat**
COAST GUARD APPROVED: **Yes**   CAPTAIN LICENSED: **YES**
SHIP TO SHORE: **Yes**   LORAN: **No**   RADAR: **No**
DIVE MASTER/INSTRUCTOR ABOARD: **Instructor**

DIVING & SNORKELING: **Salt**
TYPE OF DIVING/SNORKELING IN AREA: **Wall, Beach, Wreck, Reef**
DIVING/SNORKELING IN YOUR AREA IS BEST SUITED FOR: **Beginner, Intermediate, and Advanced**
BEST TIME OF YEAR FOR DIVING/SNORKELING: ALL YEAR
TEMPERATURE: NOV-APRIL **90-100**   MAY-OCT: **90**
VISIBILITY: DIVING **89+ Feet**   SNORKELING: **80+ feet**

PACKAGES AVAILABLE: **Dive, Dive Stay, Snorkel, Snorkel Stay**
ACCOMMODATIONS NEARBY: **Hotel**
ACCOMMODATIONS RATES: **MODERATE**
RESTAURANTS NEARBY: **MODERATE**
YOUR AREA IS: **QUIET WITH ACTIVITIES**
LOCAL ACTIVITY/NIGHTLIFE: SEAQUARIUM, BARS ON THE BEACH, BAR WITH SEAVIEWS
CAR NEEDED TO EXPLORE AREA: YES
DUTY FREE SHOPPING: YES

LOCAL EMERGENCY SERVICES: NEAREST HYPERBARIC TREATMENT FACILITY:
COASTGUARD: CELL PHONE HO   AUTHORITY:
TELEPHONE: 561 1913   LOCATION: ST. ELIZABETH HOSPITAL
CALLSIGNS: TELEPHONE: 624900
LOCAL DIVING DOCTOR:

NAME: DR. DAVEL AAR
LOCATION: DR W. P. MAALWEG 22
TELEPHONE: 617142

Dive Dominica is operated in conjunction with **Castle Comfort Diving Lodge** (ten cozy rooms) with is run by Derek's mother. Located by the dive shop the decor is marine-related.

Castaway's Water Sports is located at Castaways Hotel on the waterfront. The operation is geared towards a European market with equipment being metric and certifications offered being CMAS or VDTL, a German qualification. In addition to scuba diving certificates, full training courses are given in windsurfing and sunfish sailing.

Not everyone wants to visit a Caribbean island that has few white sand beaches, no casinos, no duty-free shops and no glittering nightlife. Dominica appeals to people who want to immerse themselves in its lush mountain jungle -botanists, bird-watchers, nature-lovers, hikers and climbers. Adventuresome scuba divers come to seek unknown diving destinations. **Dominica draws explorers who know there aren't too many places like this one left on earth!**

Dominica does not depend on super-highways, casinos and towering hotels. The lack of such "improvements" is why the reef life still abounds, especially when compared to nearby islands. The rush of rivers still drowns out traffic noise on the island roads, and the scent of fresh pungent lime is still stronger than exhaust fumes!

The Dominicans, a warm friendly people are filled with pride for their beautiful island. They know they have something special that has slipped away from many of the other surrounding islands, and they are happy and proud to share it with their visitors. These things help keep this island the choice for the adventure diver who wants to escape the "realities" of tourism a while longer and explore the unexplored.

DOMINICA CONSULATE
820 SECOND AVENUE 9TH FLOOR
NEW YORK, NY 10017
TEL 212 599 8478

Grenada

"The Isle of Spice"

Wendy Canning Church

The democratic nation state of Grenada is the southern most of the Windward Islands. It is comprised of Grenada (population 100,000+), Carriacou (population 8,000), and Petit Martinique (population 800). St. George's, in Grenada, is the Capital.

It is known to many, as the "Isle of Spice" for more spices are grown here per square mile than anywhere else in the world. The aroma of spice in the open-air markets envelops the shopper. The visitor is immersed in a melange of nutmeg (Grenada's leading export, providing a third of the world's supply), along with mace, cinnamon, cloves, bay leaves, pepper, ginger and capsicum (a hot spice used in chili). The spices are not only used in their cuisine, but you'll also find nutmeg on top off your rum punch.

In earlier times a witch's cauldron was never without a good dose of spices. Some natives wore a mixture of spices around their neck to ward off illness. Many even still use the spices as aphrodisiacs.

A strong English influence is prevalent and everyone speaks English. French African patois may be heard between conversing natives.

The dry season is January-May with intermittent showers the rest of the year.

One drives on the left. Rental cars are for hire and they have a good public transportation system of buses or taxis. Do tour this idyllic island. It is one that will become a favorite. The 100,000 natives could not be more hospitable and crime is almost non-existent.

The currency is Eastern Caribbean. A passport is needed for entry. **American Airlines was our carrier from North America.**

A forest clad central mountain range rises to almost 2,000 feet dividing its 120 miles of luxuriant beauty.

ACCOMMODATIONS

We chose to stay at **La Source, the first all-inclusive resort on the island.** It is situated on its southwestern tip not more than minutes from Point Salines International Airport. The entire complex of whitewashed buildings with melon tiled roofs reminds you more of the Mediterranean than the Caribbean. The resort sits on a long stretch of soft sand beach aptly named Pink Gin Beach.

There is a solitary "au natural" beach for those who want an all over tan. It is reached by leaving the main gate and taking a short walk down the hill to the sea.

The 100 guestrooms and suites are quaint. Both the bedrooms and the bathrooms are large. The four-poster beds, white marble floors, Caliste artwork and native woven carpets remind one of a bygone era. All rooms have a balcony, telephone and radio clocks, but blissfully no TV. A mini-fridge is handy for cool drinks. Robes are provided for those many trips to the spa.

Guests take breakfast and dinner in an attractive dining room on an upper level of the Great House, which takes advantage of the cool ocean breezes. Arrive before 7:30 p.m. so you can secure a table on the terrace and watch the town of St. George, dressed like a Christmas tree twinkle back at you across the waters.

The food is plentiful, delicious and beautifully presented. You can put on 10 pounds or take off a few. The menu is that varied.

When it comes to entertainment, I don't think anyone will be bored. La Source offers Caribbean specialties such as limbo and dancing to steel band music.

The water sports facilities include snorkeling, scuba diving, water skiing, windsurfing, sunfish sailing and swimming. Included in the land and sports facilities are tennis,

Bianca C 1961 Ablaze in St. George's Harbor

fencing, archery, volleyball, weight training, jogging, hiking, aerobics, stretch classes and golf (9-hole, par 3).

Guest facilities include all service charges and government taxes at the resort, transfers to and from the airport, gratuities and safety deposit box. Not included in the guest facilities are: car hire service, arrangement of trips and tours, long distance phone calls, drug store purchases, flower arrangements, or house doctor or nurse visits.

There is a well-stocked boutique with all sorts of goodies from the daily paper to designer bathing suits and wraps.

THE SPA

Susan Swift runs the spa with an iron fist in a velvet glove. From 9 a.m. until 6 p.m. she graciously handles all guest requests (these were numerous during my stay with every guest in the hotel taking advantage of the **Oasis plan**).

The relaxing Oasis treatments include massage, aromatherapy, seaweed wrap, hair treatment, facial, foot massage, salt and oil loofah rub, sauna, meditation, yoga, stress management and massage for two. Manicure, pedicures, hair and beauty services, waxing and reflexology are available at an extra cost.

This is the perfect place for those who have never experienced spa treatments. The all-inclusive price makes it even more attractive.

THE SCUBA DIVING & SNORKELING

Water temperatures and sea conditions vary from 76F - 84F, 30 - 100 foot visibility and seas from 2-4 feet depending on the time of year. The summer months are best for scuba diving and snorkeling.

The all-inclusive package at La Source includes either a "Discover Scuba" course for those who wish to learn how to dive or one tank dives in the morning and afternoon for certified divers.

Be sure you sign up immediately upon arrival for the days you wish to dive or you might find yourself our of luck because the dive boat, which holds 8 guests, may be booked.

There are a variety of courses offered at an extra charge. PADI is the only certification given, but student referrals from other agencies are accepted and one can complete their course.

I was astounded when I walked into the dive center to check in and saw written in bold letters on the wall: "Welcome to LaSource Scuba. We want your dive experience to be the best possible. Your safety is our most important concern. We adhere strictly to all PADI standards. Open water divers are limited to 60 ft. (18 meters). Advanced open water divers may dive to 100 ft. (30 meters). Advanced open water divers with deep diver specialty training or extensive logged experience may dive to 130 ft. (40 meters). There is no diving below 130 feet (40 meters) at LaSource."

Translated this means that Open Water I divers, no matter what their experience level may be, can not dive below 60 feet. Of course one can take an advanced course and then dive deeper. At this writing that would cost an extra $250.

Their boat is a 32 foot island fast boat. It accommodates 8 guests comfortably. Those wishing to make the all day trip to the North Shore are urged to use plenty of sunscreen, wear hats and cover up since there is no canopy on the boat.

To board, the diver swims from shore in equipment, removes gear then climbs a standard boat ladder. All divers use back roll entries. It is not suitable for very obese or handicapped divers.

The reefs offer a wide assortment of sponges, corals, and invertebrates. You will see an abundance of juvenile fish, a wide selection of parrotfish, wrasse, butterfly, blinnie and goby. Most other Caribbean fish are also represented. No shark population has been observed to date on their regular dive sites. Large game fish however, are represented seasonally. Most waters are fished locally hence the small fish sizes.

There is snorkeling off the beach. Since there are currents it is best to begin at the far right side of the beach facing the water so that you drift down with the currents.

ROSE REEF

Rose Reef is part of the extensive reef that runs from St. George's to Point Salinis. It is a short ten-minute boat ride from LaSource. Her maximum depth is at 60 feet and it is here that you begin to investigate large areas of layered plate coral. If luck is with you, curious turtles and large, shimmering barracuda will be sighted.

As you move into the shallows, finger, brain, elliptical, star, flower and ribbon corals are viewed in abundance along with brightly hued sponges and pastel colored fans. Here is where you will also spot the small reef fish. **There were shoals of neon blue, dusky colored brown chromis and Sergeant major.**

At a number of cleaning stations frisky wrasse stood on their heads while smaller cleaner wrasse gleaned a meal from them. A little further on, we spotted a cleaning station where tiny electric blue shrimp were lunching.

This is a nice dive for viewing the smaller fish and interesting variety of marine invertebrates.

HAPPY HILL

Happy Hill is located off Grand Mole about a 20-minute ride from LaSource. This is a fringe or wall/reef dive. The wall/reef tops at 80 feet and ends at 40.

Descending to our maximum depth, we swam towards the wall. Here a huge crab splayed its body against the coral. An elongated spotted moray eel, good-sized lobsters and a large multi-colored parrotfish were also sighted.

As we ascended the reef, the abundance of coral, hard and soft sponges resembled a landscape painting. The smaller reef fish, tiny shrimp, transparent gobies, and pufferfish sashayed in and out of the cavern.

I am sure with better visibility this would make a very good dive site for this is one of the best reefs on the Caribbean side.

WIBBLE REEF

Wibble Reef, a ten minute boat ride from LaSource, is off the wreck of the *Bianca C*. Wibble is one of the most pristine reefs on Grenada since it is in depths too deep for boats to anchor and damage it. On its ocean side there are substantial drop offs to 160 feet; on the landside, she bottoms at 80 feet. Currents are swift; thus a drift dive is in order.

One is apt to spot pelagics, jacks and tunas. Rays, blacktail, large grouper, and barracuda call this home as well as a number of lobsters and moray eels.

Currents bring in oxygen and nutrients; therefore you see schools of fish, particularly creole wrasse and brown chromis. We swam through a school of at least 500 blue chromis who danced by above and below us.

Two handsome Queen angelfish darted in and out of the large variety of hard and soft corals. Especially lovely were the pastel purple vase fans.

Swift currents and fair visibility limited the true beauty of the dive but I would put this site on the <u>must</u> be dived list.

BIANCA C

The Bianca C, a 600 foot, 18,000 ton luxury liner owned by the Costa Cruise line lay quietly in outer St. George's Harbor, her passengers in slumber on October 21, 1961, scheduled to set sail early the following morning. On board were 400 voyagers, 300 crew, and a handful of Grenadians who planned to sail aboard her to England. She was well known to all on the island, as Grenada was a frequent port of call.

Early Sunday morning, October 22, 1961, Captain Francisco Crevaco hoisted a distress flag that was quickly seen by members of the Grenada Yacht Club on the East Side of the island. All forces were marshaled. Every type of vessel came to her rescue, dinghies, fishing boats, yachts and, yes, even some rowed.

It is believed a fire had begun in her engine room. How had this happened? Was it sabotage? Were explosives smuggled aboard or did it occur when her engines were started to begin taking their marine beauty to sea again?

Explosions continued in the ship and fire spread throughout.

Alas, the ship was not to be saved, but all of her passengers and crew were, except for one crewmember, the Second Mate.

The island opened its heart and homes to passengers and crew; but the question still remained as to what to do with *The Bianca C* which was creating a navigational hazard in the shipping channel and would have to be towed to sea.

The Captain was adamant that the ship first be inspected for the cause of the blaze. All agreed, but then she would have to be moved. After the inspection was completed, the *H.M.S. Londonderry*, a British warship towed her out to sea, but just before she reached her designated grave site she began to slip beneath the sea exactly at high noon off Pink Gin Beach.

At her deepest she is in 170 feet of water with her swimming pool at 128 feet, where divers still pick up tiles as souvenirs and her top decks are in 100 feet.

We dived her with a negative entry. (Meaning divers rolled over the side at the same

moment and descended head first, contrary to all certifying rules), then made a rapid descent, so the strong currents would not carry us past her. This gives a diver little chance to equalize their ears.

It is a tricky entry and should only to be attempted by those experienced divers who have dived not only deep, but also in swift currents. A head first entry can cause mask squeeze and even vertigo, which is exactly what happened to one of our party. She aborted the dive with excessive serious sinus squeeze that resulted in blood in her mask, over her face, and in her hair.

All of us who reached the wreck had little time to examine her. Fleetingly, what I saw was a ship whose bones had spectacular soft and hard corals, fans and a forest of black coral living on her. Unfortunately, we only had moments to view the copious sea life. Moving left to her south was a nearby reef at 70 feet. We proceeded in gassing off in a multi-level dive and then for 5 minutes at 15 feet.

Having logged more dives than I can count all over the world, some in very tricky waters, **I have mixed emotions about diving the *Bianca C.***

I'm told that in calm seas the visibility is good with slight current and the munificent sea life that has called her home can fully be appreciated and there is a good possibility you will see jacks, barracuda, large grouper, spotted eagle rays and shark. When I asked what time of year that would be, the answer was "No one ever knows what the conditions will be until you are beneath the water."

There are many who feel that the Titanic should never have been penetrated once found, but left untouched in respect to those who perished. **Perhaps the *Bianca C* should be left to rest in her watery grave, not because of those who perished on her but for those who might.**

AREAS OF INTEREST

The shops in **Georgetown** carry a variety of duty free goods from cashmere to perfume. Visit the lively **open-air market** for straw goods and, of course, spices.

Two-mile **Grand Anse Beach** has a spot for every sunworshipper.

At Gouyave (formerly Charlotte Town), you will find the **Spice Factory.**

Dougaldston Estate is where the visitor will experience firsthand knowledge of a working plantation that is one of the main growers and exporters of nutmeg and cocoa.

Grenville, the second largest town in Grenada, has its own **Spice Factory** and an **outdoor market.**

In the north are **Sauteurs** and nearby **Morne des Sauteurs** (Leaper's Hill). Rumor has it that the Caribs plunged to their death from here rather than succumb to French occupation.

East of Sauteurs is **Levera Bay**, an idyllic spot to swim. It was here that Columbus suposedly sighted the island in 1498.

The inland road back to St. George's from Levera Bay is spectacular. Beware of the many hairpin turns in the road. You will pass **Grand Etang National Park and its extinct volcano**, 549 meters (1,800 feet) high, that cradles a beautiful lake of 5 hectares (13 acres).

For more information contact:

La Source
Pink Gin Beach
P.O. Box 852
St. George's
Grenada, West Indies

Guadeloupe

"Land of Pretty Waters"

Wendy Canning Church

Guadeloupe, an archipelago in the Caribbean Sea, lies some 1,845 miles from New York, 4,360 miles from Paris, and 310 miles from San Juan. The major two islands, Basse-Terre Island and Grande-Terre (Great Island), it's volcano rising 1,467 meters high, are separated in the south by a channel crossed by a bridge. The smaller, outlying islands are Marie Galante, Le Desirade and Les Saintes.

Guadeloupe has a land area of 330 square miles. It actually is "one" island in two: Basse-Terre, with the capital city of the same name, and Grande-Terre, site of most of the hotels. Basse-Terre, which translates as lowland, is in reality a very mountainous island. Lest this seem paradoxically French, a word of explanation: "Basse" and "Grande" describe not the terrain, but rather the low and high winds that blow over them.

The peaceful Arawaks were the first settler's 2,000 years ago. Christopher Columbus discovered Marie Galante and Guadeloupe on November 4, 1493 and christened it Santa Maria la Guadalupe da Estremadura.

The warring Carib Indians drove out the Spaniards who arrived after Columbus and named it Karkukea (Land of Pretty Waters). First settled by the French in 1635 under a grant from Cardinal Richelieu, and except for two invasions by the English, the French flag has flown over Guadeloupe until this day.

In 1650 Governor Charles Houel introduced sugar cane to Guadeloupe. Almost 30,000 slaves were brought from Africa to cultivate this lucrative crop, build sugar mills, and construct Pointe-a-Pitre.

On February 10, 1763 a treaty was signed between the French and English. In return for Guadeloupe, the English were given Antigua, Montserrat, Dominica, Barbados, Grenada, and the Grenadines.

During the French Revolution slavery was abolished, but the slave owners would not live up to the decree and a "Reign of Terror" took place. The economy faltered and in 1798 slavery was re-instated by Napoleon. The slaves revolted. The English invaded again. Landowners abandoned their plantations and foreign investors took over the lucrative sugar trade.

In 1848, slavery was abolished. The same man, Victor Schoelcher, who had led the movement to free 72,000 slaves on Martinique, later to become governor there, led the move to liberate 87,500 slaves. Hindu and Chinese laborers were then imported to till the sugar fields.

It became an Overseas Department of France in 1946, a status identical to the departments of metropolitan France. In 1974, it was given further status of Region. Today it is divided into 34 communes and 36 canton. Guadeloupe has two locally elected legislative bodies, the Conseil General and the Conseil Regional, as well as a consultative body called the Economic and Social Committee. Guadeloupe is represented in the French Parliament in Paris by two senators and four deputies, as well as by two members of the Economic Council.

The entire current population of all the islands is 400,000. 60% are under twenty. 77% are black, 16% are Hindu, and 5% are white. Catholicism is the main religion. The principal city is Pointe-a-Pitre (referred to as PaP), busy during the day, but very quiet at night. Most people live in the suburbs.

French and Creole are the official languages. English is spoken in most hotels but some knowledge of French is indeed useful along with a pocket dictionary.

The economy is based on agriculture. Bananas, pineapple, coffee and cocoa beans are exported to France. Tourism is second, travelers visiting mostly on cruise ships. Since there are few retirees, one finds young adults living at home, sometimes until the age of 28, due to lack of employment. The unemployment rate is 20-25%. Those employed

Hat Market by Wendy Canning Church

are paid four times the wages on other islands; therefore, one finds the cost of living here quite high.

DIVING IN PETITE TERRE

On my first day on the island, I booked a day trip to Petite Terre aboard the *Awak* Catamaran. The decision to visit **Petite Terre** was an excellent one and should not be missed, but choosing the much publicized *Awak* Catamaran was a disaster.

I found the *Awak* to be overcrowded and its employees' attitude abrupt and purely dollar-oriented. They seemed to have more interest in pushing their T-shirts and resort courses (not included in the cruise fare) than in their guests' comfort. Not only that, but I was told that the *Awak* offered scuba diving, but when I arrived onboard with all my gear the management informed me that they only offer resort courses.

The final straw, and particularly disconcerting, was their instructors' judgment in conducting resort courses when seas were high and currents so strong that students had to hang onto a rope under the boat. In my opinion this shows a total disregard for safety standards.

Returning to my hotel, **Le Hamak**, I told the owner, Monsieur Rozen (who was a pioneer in the area), about my experience. He smiled knowingly and recommended I contact **Paradoxe Croisieres** instead.

Paradoxe Croisieres is conveniently located at the marina in St. Francois. They offer both scuba diving and snorkeling. After 2 hours of an enjoyable cruise you arrive at Petite Terre where you will enjoy a relaxing day of sandy beaches and coconut trees.

Here is the paradise of iguanas, stone crabs and sea birds. Here you will also get a fantastic view over **La Desirade** and **Marie Galante**. There is a protected lagoon where we went diving and snorkeling. The lagoon offers a wide range of fish and lots of lobster. After the dive, there is a B.B.Q. on the beach, with Planter's rum, salad, fish or meat, cheese, French wine and fresh water. After a nap under the coconut trees and a last swim in the blue lagoon we headed back to St. Francois.

Paradoxe Croisieres also offers cruises to the islands of Marie Galante and Les Saintes. If you wish, you can cruise to these islands on your own and charter a boat with or without a crew. **Be sure to call Paradoxe Croisieres and make a reservation for a truly enjoyable day.**

Paradoxe Croisieres
Marina Avenue de l'Europe, Saint Francois
Tel: 19-590-884173
Fax: 19-590-88-79-52

The next day I drove to the charming seaside town of Le Moule, the former capital, to dive with the **Plongee Club de L'autre Board** at the **Tropical Club Hotel**. Jean and Emmanuelle Michel who are instructors own the center.

Not far offshore Le Moule's fine white sand beaches a coral barrier reef stretches for 3 kilometers. The seas were very high that day so there was no diving but I spent an hour visiting with affable owner, Jean, and had a tour of the center. When I dived in Malendure some days later I was told the diving in Le Moule was quite interesting with entirely different underwater topography than in Malendure.

ACCOMMODATIONS IN PETITE TERRE

There are accommodations to fit every pocketbook from four and five-star hotels to "Relais Creole," small family-run inns which number over 200.

We stayed in St. Francois at Le Hamak Hotel. Please see Honeymoon and Anniversary section for complete details.

The two-star **Tropical Club Hotel** in Le Mole is located across the street from Le Plunge and has 96 bedrooms with kitchenettes and private beach. Units are comprised of studios with either one double bed, 2 twin beds, or two 1 person beds above each other (maximum 4 people in a room).

All studios have a private bathroom with a shower, an equipped kitchenette, air-conditioning, phone, television and an individual balcony or terrace with a sea view. There is a restaurant, snack grill, 2 bars, a swimming pool in front of the beach, scuba diving, snorkeling and sailboarding, as well as an animation program (day and night). There is also a fitness center in-house and tennis courts one-half a mile away. Scooters and mountain bikes can be rented at the hotel.

Tropical Club Hotel
L'autre bord
97160 Le Moule
Tel: 19-590-23.78.38
Fax: 19-590-23.78.39

Across the road from the Tropical Club Hotel overlooking the sea, is the 3-star **Cottage Hotel** operated by the same owner. Very attractively furnished, it has 24 air-conditioned duplex apartments with kitchenettes, bath and showers, TV, and a phone on the second level. Two couches in the living room can easily accommodate extra guests.

Careful attention has been given to all the details of these roomy apartments. For example, the kitchenettes and dining area are situated on the terrace overlooking the sea – a very nice touch. One will find a true French country ambiance and upscale accommodations at a good price.

Stingrays by Lois Hatcher

On the first level of the hotel, is a traditional restaurant, pizzeria-bar (open until 2 a.m.), saladerie-grilladerie, supermarket, House Agent (Tourist Rent), post office, hairdresser-beauty center, pharmacy, surf wear shop, newsagent, souvenirs, tobacco and a rental car company.

Cottage Hotel
Plage des Alizes
97160 Le Moule
Guadeloupe
Tel 19 (590) 23.78.38
Fax: 19 (590) 23.78.39

DIVING IN BASSE TERRE

On my fourth day I departed Le Hamak Hotel to drive to **Malendure** on the West Coast. Driving north, crossing the Pone de la Gabare drawbridge over the Sale River, the road takes one through the **National Parc**, comprising 1/5 of Guadeloupe.

Les Heures Saines is a first rate center staffed with safety conscious and friendly staff having a love of sea and play. Open every day, they offer 15 different dive sites for all levels. **Their specialty is first dives for children and adults.**

They carry a complete line of equipment, regulators with pressure gauge, and direct system B.C. Bring your own skin or wet suit.

One of two roomy boats with a capacity for either 10 or 22 divers and snorkelers with onboard airfills will ferry guests to an underwater kingdom.

My two days diving with the club were cut short by hurricane warnings, but those dives that I made introduced me to a healthy terrain abundant with sea life. Normally, the visibility here is between 60 and 120 feet.

If I had to choose my favorite site, it would be my very last with this qualitative center, and was aptly named **The Swimming Pool.** GiGi, who spoke wonderful English, was my guide. She was giving another lady a lesson toward her certification and I joined them since they would be diving shallow and I could get more bottom time.

The 55 minutes we spent beneath the beautiful big blue were filled with an encyclopedia of tropical reef fish, some in pairs, but most in teeming shoals dressed in shades of electric blue, velvet black, and honey almond, all harmonized against a thriving underwater garden. I knew we were close to Pigeon Island, rumored to be one of the world's top dive spots, and suspected I was getting just a small sample of what lay ahead for me.

We were no sooner backs at the dock then a hurricane warning came over the radio. The boat was to be taken to a safe cove. Alas, my diving was over.

For more information contact:

Les Heures Saines
Telephone: (590) 98.86.63
Fax: (590) 98.77.76

Because of hurricane warnings, all ferries were cancelled to **Terri de Haut**, where I planned to dive with **Diving Notice** and spend two nights at their hotel adjacent to the Center…next trip!

ACCOMMODATIONS IN BASSE TERRE

I booked three days at a "Relais Creole Inn," **The Paradis Creole**, whose owners also operate the diving and snorkeling center **Les Heures Saines**.

The Paradis Creole is charming, situated in lush green surroundings with an exceptional view of the Caribbean, to Pigeon Island and the tropical forest. It has 10 air-conditioned rooms with a terrace (2 of which are bungalows). They are small and simple but adequate. There is a small bar adjacent to the pool and dining area. The daily rate includes breakfast of juice, coffee or tea, and French bread.

Paradis Creole
Poirier Pigeon
97132 Bouillante GPE
Tel: (590) 98.71.62
Fax: (590) 98.77.76

DINING IN BASSE TERRE

There are many small restaurants in town. I found even the simplest expensive. For lunch I recommend stopping at the local well-stocked supermarket and purchasing items for a picnic.

The only exception worth your money is **La Rocher de Malendure**, a few steps from the dive center. This split-level restaurant is set in a beautiful tropical garden with a lovely view of the sea. The specialties are smoked swordfish, "souchy" Antillian Tahitian, Lobster-Fishermen's plate, local shrimp and conch, and coconut flan. Its seafood is outstanding! Telephone: (590) 98.70.84.

GOSSIER

I spent three days at the 4-star **Auberge de La Vielle Tour** in Gossier waiting out the hurricane. The Sofitel Group recently purchased this 160-room hotel, which opened in December 1995.

My room overlooked the large pool with the sea beyond. There was a patio for reading and relaxing. The roomy air-conditioned accommodations are tastefully furnished with TV, direct dial phones, mini bar, a large bathroom, and lots of closet space. **Be sure to request room 324.**

The price of your room includes a buffet breakfast that consists of fruit, juices, cereal, eggs, meats, and cheese. **The gourmet restaurant has been a legend for years** but was closed for renovation during my stay.

Even though most of the staff speak only French, somehow they manage to fulfill your requests.

The beach is small with little palm-fringed umbrellas to shade you from the intense sun. It's very enjoyable to walk the long strip of beach where there are at least another dozen hotels, all attractive and in varying price ranges.

The **AquaFari Scuba Center** is situated minutes away on foot from La Vielle Tour.

For a few francs you can catch a boat from the small dock on the beach which takes you to the delightful **Islet Gosier**, minutes from shore. The island is uninhabited; the only structure a lighthouse. Take a picnic and while away the day on its silver sand beaches. Be sure to take the boat round-trip or you will end up paying two full fares.

AREAS OF INTEREST

If one really wants to get to know the island it is necessary to rent a car or hire a driver. A valid driver's license is needed to rent a car and an international driver's permit must be obtained. Book ahead and pick up your car at the airport in Pointe-a-Pitre upon arrival.

The 1,225 miles of road are some of the best in the Caribbean. The shape of Guadeloupe is often likened to that of a butterfly, a correct analogy, particularly when seen from the air. Basse-Terre is the western wing, separated from Grande-Terre by the Salee River and connected by a bridge. Grande-Terre, the eastern wing, is low-lying, has a pastoral terrain, and is edged with powdery beaches and coral cliffs. Raizet Airport and most tourist facilities are located here.

The highest point on Basse-Terre is **La Soufriere Volcano** which rises 4,813 feet to crown the majestic **Parc National**, a 74,100 acre wonderland of waterfalls, lakes, flowers and rain forests that is verdant and unspoiled. Hailed by ecologists, this remarkable preserve rewards wildlife enthusiasts, nature lovers and just plain tourists. The Parc offers the visitor waterfalls, a pond to swim in and walking tours of the Zoological and Botanical Parc. Parc exhibition huts are devoted to the volcano and forest, to water, coffee, and sugar.

The marina in St. Francois has a variety of small cafes and boutiques. A well-stocked supermarket is located there.

Before you go, or when you arrive, contact the Guadeloupe Tourist Office located in downtown Pointe-a-Pitre. Their maps, brochures, ferry schedules and price list for hotels and Relais Creole were essential in making my visit such a superb one.

I especially want to thank Luigy Sosse and Guy Claude Germain. These gentlemen and their staff (many of whom speak English) were very helpful.

Guadeloupe Tourist Office
5 Square de la Banque
97181 Pointe-a-Pitre
Guadeloupe
Tel: (590) 82.09.30
Fax: (590) 83.89.22

You'll need a valid passport to enter. Cats and dogs over 3 months old in good health with anti rabies shots may enter, but check to make sure they are allowed at your hotel.

American Airlines was our carrier from North America. There are no arrival or departure taxes except for charter flights.

I found Guadeloupe and its people warm and charming. While modern amenities abound for the visitor, the inhabitants have not given up to gentrification. Their culture is still deeply embedded in their lifestyle -a melange of old and new. Karkukea, this "Land of Pretty Waters", will no doubt inveigle you to return and perhaps even to remain.

Jamaica

"Out of One, Many People"

Wendy Canning Church

Jamaica lies 590 miles from Miami. The third largest Northern Caribbean island: 146 miles long, 51 miles wide, and 4,441 square miles in total. The topography is comely, veiled in dense vegetation, with lofty mountain ranges reaching 7,000 feet and fertile sweeping valleys spilling into the shimmering sea.

Its history is similar to the other islands. The Arawak Indians arrived in 600 AD and established a settlement, naming their new home Xaymaca, (land of wood and water) which was later changed to Jamaica.

The Spanish, under Christopher Columbus, landed in the 1600's and obliterated the Arawaks through means of murder, overwork and the diseases they had brought with them.

Pirates and buccaneers plied the Jamaican waters. The most notorious of these was Henry Morgan who plundered the Spanish Fleet. Spain lost interest in Jamaica due to its lack of silver and gold.

The English landed in 1665 and found the island to their liking. They established permanent settlements and laid the foundation for the lucrative sugar and rum trade. Slaves were brought from Africa to tend both the plantation houses and the fields. Many of them ran away (the Maroons) and went into the Blue Mountains to live an independent existence. The English granted slaves their freedom in 1838.

In 1865, Jamaica became a Crown colony. Independence was achieved in 1944, and Jamaica joined the Commonwealth of Nations in 1962. Today, Jamaica's population of 2,300,000 is made up of a variety of different nationalities. Hence the motto: "Out of many, one people". English is the official language, but you will hear the natives speak patois, a combination of Creole and English.

The currency is the Jamaican dollar. A passport is needed to enter. American Airlines was our chosen carrier.

Visitors to Jamaica will not find a sleepy little island where quaint customs abound.

Rather, they will find an island with a level of energy and comfort to fit any budget and taste–from the quiet of a fully staffed private villa on its own beach, to the small guest house in a village where the sounds of reggae and Bob Marley hang on the breeze.

For information on Half Moon Golf and Tennis Club please see the Honeymoon and Anniversary Section.

JAMAICA TOURIST BOARD
801 SECOND AVENUE,20TH FLOOR
NEW YORK, NY 10017
TEL 212 856 9727

Sans Souci Lido

Wendy Canning Church

The Sans Souci Lido is an all-inclusive property located in Ocho Rios on Jamaica's North Shore about 70 miles from Montego Bay (less than 2 hours by car). This elegant beach resort evokes a bygone era that catered to the landed gentry. Positioned on the tranquil Caribbean, it advertises itself as an all-inclusive resort with a European-style spa.

The grounds and public areas are meticulously maintained and work is continually being done to bring this beauty back to the gem it once was. Its graceful colonial architecture is awash in Sans Souci pink and no one can change the color due to restrictions in the architectural contract. Within this esthetic well-composed setting guests will find natural bubbling springs in hidden grottos amongst verdant scented gardens.

The all-inclusive package includes: accommodations, meals, snacks and drinks, spa treatments, use of all land and water sports facilities with equipment and instruction, entertainment, recreational activities, wedding ceremony (if applicable), hotel taxes and airport transfers with absolutely no tipping allowed.

Whether they be couples, singles or guests over 16 years of age they can choose one of the 97 suites, eight deluxe rooms, or six penthouse suites, many with panoramic views and terraces. The interiors boast king-size and twin beds, separate living areas, air-conditioning, satellite color television, hairdryers, direct dial telephones, mini refrigerators, in-room coffee/tea service and some rooms are even equipped with whirlpool tubs.

There are land sports and sea sports to suit every interest. Guests can consult the resident tennis pro and practice on two courts lighted for night play or test their skills at table tennis, basketball, volleyball, shuffleboard, bocci, darts or croquet. You can also opt to explore the property on bicycle or on one of the walking trails. In addition, greens fees and transportation to and from the Runaway Bay Golf Club are included. Exercise enthusiasts will enjoy the complete fitness center with stationary bicycles, stairclimbing machines and treadmill equipment, as well as aerobics, aqua aerobics and reggae dance classes.

Seaside activities include windsurfing, sunfish sailing, snorkeling, kayaking, glass bottom boat rides, scuba with resort certification, Hobie cats, two swimming pools, mineral whirlpool tub and a natural mineral spring pool.

Delightful diversions include resting in a secluded hammock while observing Jamaica's most colorful native residents in the bird sanctuary, tickling the mind in the game room, feeding Charlie the giant sea turtle or browsing in the boutiques. Additionally, Sans Souci Lido offers excursions to Dunn's River Falls and Ocho Rios for shopping.

The food is delicious, beautifully prepared and served by a staff that sincerely aims to please each guest. Breakfast and lunch buffets are served either indoors or out. Guests can dine in the casual Ristorante Palazzina, or in the Casanova Restaurant (jackets recommended and reservations required). Casually dining under the stars at the La Terrazza is complete with strolling musicians or try the Beach Grill which serves grilled favorites and traditional Jamaican specialties throughout the day. Snacks, 24-

hour room service and a delightful afternoon tea is served on the terrace at 4 o'clock. A wonderful touch.

Live nightly entertainment showcases Jamaican cabaret artists, musicians and cultural shows. Guests can take spirits in one of four bars, while listening to a piano and saxophonist. Weekly theme gala parties include the Caribbean Carnival barbecue, a torch-lit beach fiesta and the Gala Buffet when the beachside lawns are transformed into a twinkling fairyland.

Tasteful, romantic and beautiful weddings feature all arrangements for the ceremony (which can take place in a gazebo overlooking the alluring waters, or in luxuriant gardens, on the beach, or anywhere the bride and groom choose), marriage license, minister, witnesses, tropical flowers, live music, champagne and a traditional Jamaican wedding cake. The background is unmatched with the multi-colored waters beyond.

Treatment Retreat by Wendy Canning Church

THE SPA

Sans Souci Lido has a wonderful locally staffed Spa facility that overlooks the sea. These ladies sweetly banish tension through 1/2 hour massage, body scrubs, reflexology, facials, manicures, and pedicures as the frangence of oleander are carried to your treatment room by the soft sea breee.

Sauna is also available, as well as a mineral spring pool. The natural mineral springs, renowned for their therapeutic— and romantic value, have been noted in Jamaican history books since the 1700's. According to the legend, the Admiral of an English warship and a Spanish maiden shared a forbidden love and would secretly meet at the mineral spring grottos. It is believed that by dipping into these mineral waters one's heart will be filled with the power of the couple's forbidden, passionate love.

THE SCUBA DIVING & SNORKELING

There is a snorkeling boat that takes guests to a nearby reef where one can view the multicolored diminutive reef fish. The snorkeling boat leaves twice a day.

Sea Dive Jamaica, Ltd. services divers at Hotel Shaw-Park. Guests are ferried by the Sans Souci boat, a five minute boat ride.

The management of Sans Souci is planning to bring the scuba diving on-property and have it supervised by their very capable Watersports Director.

For more information contact:

Sans Souci Lido
P.O. Box 103, Ocho Rios, Jamaica, W.I.
Telephone: 809-974-2353 or 1-800-203-7456
Fax: 809-974-2544

Swept Away Resort by Wendy Canning Church

Swept Away, Negril, Jamaica

"Everything is included, but the crowds" is the aphorism for Swept Away. They even include the cost of your wedding which includes a ministers fee, marriage license, tropical bouquets, wedding cake and champagne. The all inclusive vacation is becoming more of a rule than an exception for travelers.

Located on the northern most tip of Jamaica in Negril,which is 60 miles from the Montego Bay Airport (90 minutes by car). Swept Away is a 20 acre world of tranquillity and relaxation. Ten of these acres are beach front on Long Bay, the other ten across the street, allow the resort to possess the most comprehensive sports complex in the Caribbean.

This "couples only" hideaway has 134 suites, each with its own verandah. One can choose a view of the gardens, the atrium, or the beach. The large verandahs are a perfect place to have a continental breakfast, read or just lay back and take in the breathtaking views.

We chose a suite that overlooked the atrium, which put us close enough to the "action" yet far enough away to ensure peace and quiet. It was a delight to view the towering palms, sunsplashed in the early morning reaching skyward from the center of our home away from home. In the evening as we climbed the stairs, the palms and surrounding plantings were illuminated by both spot lights and the stars overhead. After dinner, as we drifted off to sleep, the scent of these plantings would mix with that of the sea and were carried on a gentle breeze that filled our room.

Being scuba divers, we are early risers and on the way to breakfast each morning found that the only other people up were those in charge of maintaining the grounds. They had already been up for hours raking the beach and tending the grounds. The same attention to detail applies to the entire staff at Swept Away. They are genuinely friendly and always eager to assist you in anyway they can. The complex as a whole has the feeling of a private estate rather than a public resort. **The owner of this "private estate", Lee Issa, is frequently on the premises, making Swept Away a "hands on" establishment. He introduces himself to the guests and can be seen everywhere.**

One never needs to leave the compound with all there is to offer at Swept Away. The open air dining room serves breakfast, lunch and dinner. This is where you will find the evening's entertainment presented by the resident staff. Most nights they have a theme dinner and accompanying cabaret.

Above the dining room is an open air verandah where one can sit on very comfortable couches and chairs, read or play backgammon, checkers or billiards. There is also a television room as well as a piano bar. There are four full-service bars that also offer non-alcoholic fruit concoctions. Tea is served everyday at five.

The "veggie bar" located on the beach, serves fresh fruit and vegetable juice, sandwiches, fresh vegetables and other light snacks. Pizzas are made on request at the Sports Bar. "Feathers",Swept Away's gourmet restaurant, is located across the way at the Sports Complex. The cuisine is not only delicious but beautifully presented. Reservations are a must and please dress for the occasion.

I defy even the most athletic to be bored at the Sports Complex. There are ten tennis courts - five clay and five hard courts, all lighted for night play. There are squash and racquetball courts and a half mile running track. One will also find a basketball court and a lap pool. The gym has a variety of weights and exercise equipment along with aerobics classes, yoga classes, Jacuzzis, a sauna and steam baths.

Massages are offered at an extra charge - treat yourself to one. Be sure to request Oya Ozcan, a delightful, highly skilled woman. She has a degree in physical therapy and massage. You will also find a nurse on the premises at the Sports Complex. She is on duty from 9:00 a.m. until midnight. A doctor is on call 24 hours a day at an additional charge.

On the ocean side one can choose to splash in the freshwater pool or enjoy a ride in one of the glass bottom boats. They also offer sunfish sailing, water skiing, kayaking, windsurfing, snorkeling and scuba diving. Parasailing is available at an additional charge.

A sample of the tours one can take if they wish to get off the premises and discover the rest of Jamaica (see the Tour Desk to arrange for all tours):

Great Eagle "Catamaran Cruise Party" - The most popular tour. Includes snorkeling at Negril's largest reef (all gear and life jackets on-board), scenic cruise up the West End along the caves and cliffs, open bar and snacks, live reggae musicians, limbo dancing, bamboo dancing, and a stop at "Joseph's Cave" where the movie *2000 Leagues Under the Sea* was filmed. Videos are taken of the cruise which can be viewed (and purchased) at the Tour Desk.

Black River Safari Boat Tour - A beautiful taxi ride takes you to this boat trip (1 and 1/2 hours long). You will see native and migratory birds, crocodiles basking in the sun, the longest river in Jamaica and the gorgeous Mangrove swamps. A Jamaican lunch is included. After lunch the boat takes you to the fabulous falls. Take a plunge into the cool waters or just marvel at the quiet charm of the countryside and the foliage. The tour finishes up with a tour along Bamboo Avenue which you have probably seen in the "Come back to Jamaica" commercials.

Horseback Riding at Babo's Stable - Ride on some of Negril's best horses (not only in good condition, but these horses are loved.) Only a 10 minute drive from Swept Away (round-trip taxi included) takes you into the spectacular hills of Negril where the Rastafarians live. The guides are wonderful. This trip is a must for the experienced rider. For the beginners the guides will take pictures of and for you - just ask.

Deep Sea Fishing - In Negril they catch Blue Marlin, Bonita, Barracuda, King Fish, Tuna, and Dolphin (not Porpoise). The trip is four hours long and the boats can take up to 7 people. Bar and snacks included as well as all bait and tackle.

Cuba - One day trip - Special visas are obtained, nothing is stamped in your passport. You will learn about the people, culture and history of this exciting and beautiful country. Visit the Morro Castle with its breath-taking vistas of the Sierra de Maestra Mountains and its Museum of Piracy. Tour the oldest rum distillery in the world - now called Caney - formerly Bacardi. Shop for world famous Cuban cigars, rum and souvenirs. Air-conditioned bus tour of Santiago de Cuba, the second largest city in Cuba. You get an English-speaking guide. Head downtown to Carlos de Caspedes Square and marvel at the gorgeous architecture of pre-Castro Cuba. Lunch at the beautiful El Morro restaurant and much, much more. Cameras welcome.

Night-time glass bottom boat - Take a ride up the West End on the *Sundowner* and check out the sunset (comfortable sunset deck on-board). Includes open bar, snacks and reggae music. Marvel at Negril's rocky cliffs and caves. When the sun goes down they put the lights on the glass bottom. The marine life you will see in the evening is totally different from the daytime. Educational, comfortable, exciting, a knowledgeable crew - all the ingredients for a great time!

Belvedere Estate - A beautiful 1 hour drive through Jamaica's countryside brings you to the magnificent Belvedere Estate. The lush gardens possess a tremendous variety of flowers, plants and trees. Taste pineapple and orange juice from their groves. Charming guides take you through this absolutely lovely Living Museum. They have reproduced a working Jamaican village from the 1800's. Lunch is served in the reproduction "Cook House". Visit the sugar mill and factory that actual works. See and taste the cane juice as it is made into white and brown sugar. Learn coffee, pimento and cocoa drying techniques. A rastafarian herbalist explains the use of a wide variety of tropical herbs and spices. View two gorgeous waterfalls and the blacksmith, bakery and the village souvenir shop.

Mountain Valley Bamboo Rafting - Take a romantic ride through incredible countryside on your Bamboo Raft (comfortable and dry). Complimentary drinks and lunch are included. Then onto "Rhea's World" for a tour of their Banana plantation and "zoo," where you will find a large variety of exquisite tropical birds, a Jamaican snake, beehives, rabbits, and a lovely liquor tasting of a number of different Jamaican drink delicacies.

Swept Away has the most able and safety conscious diving and snorkeling staff. They check your C Card and ask you to fill out a rather extensive medical form. Everyone, and I mean everyone, is checked out in the pool before they are allowed to dive. This might upset some of you experienced divers, but it is for your own protection and the safety of those diving with you. No one in Jamaica is allowed to get their tanks filled unless they are diving with a qualified guide.

The center itself is well maintained and carries an up to date list of equipment - no

"O.K" by Wendy Canning Church

need to bring your own! Gear is set up for you before the dive and is broken down and rinsed after the dive.

Your inclusive package with Swept Away covers two one tank dives daily. There are a myriad of dive sites to explore - most of them only 10 to 20 minutes from shore. The boat can handle 23, but we never had more than 10. It is a spacious and comfortable boat that is run by Captain Hanes, who was a member of the Jamaican Olympic Boxing Team, and his assistant Junior. My only suggestion is that they add a canopy to the boat to protect you from the sun.

Advanced divers are scheduled for 9:00 a.m. and 1:30 p.m. beginners, resort courses or those taking a Discover Scuba introduction go out at 11:00 a.m. However, some days there was a combination of divers on the 11:00 a.m. trip. There are two shallow reefs and we quite enjoyed them; it gave us more bottom time as well. In addition, it is always a delight to see people experience their first dive; their faces filled with awe at the new and magical world they have discovered.

A sample of the diving - most of which are drift dives you ascend and descend with your buddy and there is always a lead guide and a trailer.

Shark's Club - Entry by giant stride. Requires safety stop at 15 feet for 3 minutes. A great first dive! Here you will discover many tunnels and arches along the reef. We did not sight any sharks, but we did spot a grouper that weighed nearly 100 pounds. We also saw schools of blue chromis, creole wrasse, angelfish, and both white and Spanish grunts. Water temperature was 82F. and the visibility was 150 feet.

Fish Pond - This is a shallow reef dive that is scheduled for Monday, Wednesday and Friday for the people taking the Resort Course and for the beginners. My buddy and I went each day we enjoyed it so much. One descends to the sandy bottom at 30 feet and then swims towards the reef where all types of reef fish abound: moray eels, trumpet fish, four eyed butterfly fish, yellow tail, snapper, and baby squid. I also spotted a puffer fish in a barrel sponge on my descent. He was obviously agitated because it had already swallowed 10 times its weight in water.

Deep Plane - This dive site is only 10 minutes from shore. Descending down to 80 feet one comes upon an airplane wreck along a healthy reef that is home to many a barracuda and trigger fish.

Discovery Reef - This dive is located some 50 minutes from shore. It is a reef dive with a maximum depth of 90 feet. Hard and soft corals cover the reef in a rainbow of colors. The formations are very diverse and unique to these waters. This is a truly beautiful dive.

The Throne Room - Only 15 minutes from shore, this dive was my favorite. The throne room is located in 38 feet of water. On the way down into the cavern you will pass along a reef covered with a multitude of soft and hard corals. Once through the tunnel you are free to sit on a giant orange sponge in the shape of a throne! It is quite a kick to see each diver take his turn sitting on the throne.

There is a special boat for snorkeling which takes guests to a number of sites. It is remarkable the variety of fish one sees. Not only will you see small reef fish, but larger ones as well, such as stingrays. I suggest that even the scuba divers make at least one snorkeling trip.

The topography is breathtaking. The lace like purple and pink corals that one sees in the shapes of bowls and vases are simply magnificent. Jamaica is a perfect location for those who want to try scuba diving via a Resort Course. I would recommend it to anyone who wants to take the full course in order to receive their certification (this is offered at an extra charge). Many dive sites are perfect for those that have done their pool and classroom work at home and need only to complete their open water dives for certification.

I have been diving all over the world and to me the diving at Swept Away offered a relaxing and beautiful experience. I do not want to dive deep on every dive, nor do I need to see pelagics on every dive. The underwater world as a whole is a gift that I always enjoy.

Swept Away has recently added a complete spa which we plan to cover in Volume III. You can get married 24 hours after arriving in Jamaica if you have applied for your marriage license and submitted proof of status. You will need proof of citizenship (certified copy of birth certificate, signed by a notary public, which includes your father's name); parent's written consent if under 21 years of age; proof of divorce if applicable (certified copy or original certificate of divorce); copy of death certificate for widow or widower. You do not need a blood test.

Many airline carriers serve the Montego Bay airport. We booked a charter flight from Boston through Sunburst Holidays that was operated by Capitol Air. We were quite pleased with the service we received. They operated on time and were on par with any other airline. They have offices in New York, Los Angeles, Baltimore, Atlanta and Montego Bay. Sunburst Holidays has been in operation since 1973 and they are the "Jamaican Specialist." Departure taxes are included in your airfare. Your transfer to Swept Away is provided in the Swept Away package. You will need proof of citizenship.

Sunburst Holidays in the United States 1-800-666-8346

SCUBA AND SNORKELING FACILITIES QUESTIONNAIRE

NAME   **Resort Divers - Swept Away**
ADDRESS   **P.O. Box 77, Negril, Shop #6**
              Island Plaza, Ochio Rios, Jamaica
CONTACT   **Angela Sham or Courtney Brown**
TITLE   **OWSI, MSDI**
TELEPHONE   **957-4061**   FAX **957-4060**

CAPITAL: **Kingston**   GOVERNMENT: **Democratic**
POPULATION: LANGUAGE: **English**
CURRENCY: **Jamaican Dollar**   ELECTRICITY: **110v/50 cycles**
AIRLINES: **American**   DEPARTURE TAX? **Yes**
NEED VISA/PASSPORT?   YES **x**   NO   PROOF OF CITIZENSHIP?   YES NO **Passport**

YOUR FACILITY IS CLASSIFIED AS: SCUBA CENTER   RESORT **x**
BUSINESS HOURS: **8:30 a.m. to 4:00 p.m.**
CERTIFYING AGENCIES: **PADI**
LOG BOOK REQUIRED?   YES **x**   NO
EQUIPMENT: SALES **x**   RENTALS **x**   AIR FILLS **x**
PRIMARY LINE OF EQUIPMENT: **Sherwood**
PHOTOGRAPHIC EQUIPMENT: SALES   RENTALS   LAB

CHARTER/DIVE BOAT AVAILABLE?   YES **x**   NO   DIVER CAPACITY   **24**
COAST GUARD APPROVED?   YES **x**   NO   CAPTAIN LICENSED? YES **x**   NO
SHIP TO SHORE?   YES **x** NO   LORAN YES   NO   RADAR? YES **x**   NO
DIVE MASTER/INSTRUCTOR ABOARD?   YES   NO   BOTH **x**

DIVING & SNORKELING: SALT **x**   FRESH
TYPE OF DIVING/SNORKELING IN AREA: WALL   BEACH   WRECK **x**   REEF **x**   CAVE   ICE
DIVING/SNORKELING IN YOUR AREA IS BEST SUITED FOR: BEGINNER **x**   INTERMEDIATE **x** ADVANCED **x**
BEST TIME OF YEAR FOR DIVING/SNORKELING:
TEMPERATURE: **NOV-APRIL:**   73 F   **MAY-OCT:**   85 F
VISIBILITY: **DIVING:**   100+ FT   **SNORKELING:** 100+ FT

PACKAGES AVAILABLE: **Included with stay at Swept Away x**   SNORKEL   SNORKEL-STAY
ACCOMMODATIONS NEARBY: **Located at Swept Away Resort x**   MOTEL   HOME RENTALS
ACCOMMODATION RATES: EXPENSIVE **x**   MODERATE **x**   INEXPENSIVE
RESTAURANTS NEARBY: EXPENSIVE **x**   MODERATE **x**   INEXPENSIVE **x**
YOUR AREA IS: REMOTE   QUIET WITH ACTIVITIES   LIVELY **x**
LOCAL ACTIVITY/NIGHTLIFE:
CAR NEEDED TO EXPLORE AREA?   YES **x**   NO
DUTY FREE SHOPPING?   YES **x**   NO

LOCAL EMERGENCY SERVICES   NEAREST HYPERBARIC TREATMENT FACILITY
COASTGUARD: AUTHORITY: **Peter Gayle**
TELEPHONE: LOCATION: **Discovery Bay Marine Lab**
CALLSIGNS: **Channel 16 Marine**   TELEPHONE: **973-2241**

LOCAL DIVING DOCTOR:
NAME: **Dr. Kellerman, Bruhn**
LOCATION: **Mile Clinic**
TELEPHONE: **57-4888**

Martinique

"The Isle of Flowers"

Wendy Canning Church

Martinique is 1,965 miles from New York, 1,470 miles from Miami, 425 miles from San Juan, and 4,261 miles from Paris. The island covers 425 square miles, is 50 miles long and 22 miles wide and is part of the Lesser Antilles, making it the largest in the Windwards. In the east the waters of the Atlantic Ocean, and in the west washed by the Caribbean. Mountainous in the north, it has a rich and fertile central plain and becomes hilly toward the south.

Covered with tropical rain forests, rolling plains and grazing lands, it owes its delightful climate to the soft breezes of the Trade Winds.

Its 360,000 inhabitants are 85% black, 10% Hindu, and 5% white. 60% are Catholics, others Baptist and Hindu. Of these 360,000 people, 120,000 live in the sprawling, bustling city of Fort-de-France teeming with duty-free shops and open-air markets with vendors selling everything from food to madras.

French and Creole are the official languages. Is it necessary for you to parlez Francais in order to play? The answer is both yes and no. **One does not need to be fluent in order to visit this exquisite island in the French West Indies, but certainly the following are a must: Bonjour, s'il vous plait, and merci. Take along a small pocket dictionary.**

American Airways was our carrier from North America. You will need a passport to enter. The currency is the French Franc. There are no arrival or departure taxes except for private charters.

Best buys are rum, perfume, French silk scarves, straw items, and the creole doll (poupee martiniquaise) dressed in madras. Fort-de-France shopping streets spread from Savane to the River Levassor. Luxury items can be found at Roger Albert. There are also duty-free items at the airport.

A traveler will immediately realize that this island is as French as pate de foie gras. Under French rule since its colonization, archeological findings prove that the peace loving Arawak Indians were the first settlers 2,000 years ago, driven out 1,000 years later by the fierce and savage Caribs.

Columbus came upon Martinique in 1494, but was prevented from coming ashore by the Caribs. He later returned and landed in 1502 at Le Carbet, a small town on the south coast, calling it "the best, the most fertile, most delightful and the most charming land in the world".

In 1635, a nobleman from Normandy, Pierre Belain d'Esnombuc, arrived from France with 100 settlers landing at the seaside town of St. Pierre, establishing the first colony on the island for France.

Sugar, pineapple and bananas were introduced and cultivated. Export to France from the lucrative plantations made French landowners rich and powerful. To till the land, slaves were brought from Africa in 1636.

Britain and France fought over the island for 100 years. In the 18th century (1762) with the Treaty of Paris, France gave Britain land in Canada in exchange for Martinique and Guadeloupe.

Slavery was abolished in 1848, but Empress Josephine (born on Martinique in La Pagerie in 1763 at Trois Islets) convinced Emperor Napoleon to rescind the order for Josephine's family, owned a lucrative sugar cane plantation which needed inexpensive labor to till the crops. Thus, slavery continued for another 75 years.

Victor Schoelcher, a white native, fought for abolishing slavery and won against the

Sea Anemones with Goldies by C. Cauezzaue

objections of other white plantation owners. There was much bloodshed with masters killing their slaves, but Schoelcher won out and was later elected Governor. Old wounds do not heal quickly. Even today landowners' ancestors are referred to as "Be-Ke" to distinguish them from other white French. When a native speaks the name "Be-Ke", one can sense the lingering bitterness.

Saint Pierre, the northern Caribbean city known as the "Paris of the Antilles", was the capitol until the eruption of the 4,700-foot Mt. Pelee on May 8, 1902. At the same time a tidal wave struck and 30,000 people died within 3 minutes. The entire city was destroyed, along with its history, leaving only ruins. Today, it is a quiet fishing village with gray volcanic sand beaches, a souvenir of Pelee. From that time, Fort-de-France became the capitol.

In 1946, Martinique became an Overseas Department of France, a status identical to the departments of metropolitan France. In 1974, it was given the further status of Region. A Prefect is appointed by the French Minister of the Interior.

The electorate sends four Deputies and two Senators to the French Parliament. A legislative body, the Conseil General, is elected by the citizens of Martinique and has 45 representatives. The Conseil Regional, also elected by the citizens of Martinique, has 41 members. Each town has its own mayor.

Martinique is an island to be explored. Mountainous landscapes covered with lush forests, ringed by alternating cliffs and light sandy beaches. A car is not necessary, but will enhance your trip. To rent a car, one must have a valid driver's license and be 21. Book ahead and pick up at the airport or in Fort-de-France.

Since it was my first visit to Martinique, I decided to hire a driver/taxi. The fates were with me. I could not have had a more cheerful or knowledgeable lady than Bernadette. Together we toured the island. She was full of all the "little bits" of knowledge about Martinique that one does not read in a guidebook, i.e. when I asked her about the percentage of crime on the island she replied, "Oh, the crimes here are ones of passion. You see, there are seven men for every woman."

As we passed the sugar cane fields, Bernadette told me that the sugar cane industry employs workers year round. The harvesting lasts from January to July with workers cutting the cane round the clock. The roots stay in the ground and will grow back for six years when they are dug up and new ones are planted. Passing the banana trees, she noted, "Banana trees are like babies. They take nine months to mature. After every fourth crop you must root them over again."

We drove along the Atlantic coast, passing through the small, quaint towns of **Sainte-Luce** and **Sainte-Anne**. In Sainte-Anne we walked the **Plage des Salines**, resembling a wedding cake with its miles of sugar white sand. Its tall coconut trees shaded us from the blazing sun.

Not far from Sainte-Anne in Le Francois is the colonial style **Habitation Clement**, the only Creole property that is completely open to the public. It was here that President Bush and Mitterand met for talks and luncheon after the Gulf War on March 14, 1991. Built on a hilltop, the 18th century property sits above the distillery and sugar cane plantation, on an emerald landscape cooled by the Trade Winds. Furnishings are from the 18th and 19th century in the Indies Company style of beautiful mahogany.

A visit to **the distillery**, still in operation, and the storehouse with casks holding 100,000 gallons of maturing rum will enlighten the visitor as to how sugar cane is processed. A store on premises offers free rum, tasting sessions, and a variety of different vintages for sale.

Another day we set off traveling north along the Caribbean coast to **St. Pierre**. This is fishermen's country.

We stopped along the way at **Le Carbet** and the cove where Columbus landed in 1502. The **Gauguin Museum** is quite near on Turin Cove. Gauguin lived and painted here for five months in 1887, living in a home built in the shadows of an old viaduct. A museum was erected on this spot and one can view reproductions of the work he painted while in Martinique.

The enchanting **Butterfly Farm** is just minutes up the road from the museum.

It is a scenographic drive with the many gommiers (fishermen's boats) which are carved from the trunk of gum trees, vividly painted and humorously named, viewed out at sea culling their daily catch.

We had luncheon at **Le Fromanger Restaurant** built into the jungle clad hills overlooking the shores below with pictorial views of St. Pierre. Our meal began with a delicious local appetizer of boiled green bananas and salted fish in a special spiced sauce presented on a banana leaf. Our second course was fresh fish with cream sauce, rice and vegetables. It's one of St. Pierre's best restaurants in a handsome setting along with a bit of history. There is an exquisite tree on the grounds that was one of the few pieces of nature that survived the eruption in 1902.

A new attraction in St. Pierre, the **Mobilis Submarine** (Tel: 596.78.28.28), takes passengers on a tour of the harbor to view the ships that went down in that fateful three minute eruption.

Wreck of the Nahoon by Elise Negrel

Homeward bound, we drove inland through the fertile tropical **rain forest**. There are also guided tours for hikers and waterfalls to swim under. Every day is a rainy day here with an accumulation of 300 inches a year. The road and forest beyond gives forth a profusion of lime, banana, and breadfruit trees along with a mosaic of color from the hibiscus, frangipani, bougainvillea, anthuriums, magnolia and oleander. The air is intoxicating with this variegation.

The Botanical Gardens, a rainbow of flora, is further along on the same road.

One comes to the **Route de Balata**. There is a delightful surprise in store around a bend in the road—the imposing structure—a miniature version of the famous Sacre-Coeur Basillica of Montmartre in Paris.

To explore Martinique and discover her many delights and charms is tantamount to discovering a unique perfume that compresses a blend of different flowers, enticing one's senses. Martinique, "The Isle of Flowers", is a blend of different sensations and scents, and as a great perfume, your memories of her will be subtle, enticing and lingering.

To arrange to have Bernadette as your driver you can contact her at:

Bernadette
Ti-Marie A4
Place d'Armes
97232 Lamentin, Martinique
Tel & Fax: (596) 51.31.87
Taxi No. 528 YT 972

Write or call her before arrival. She will pick you up at any hour at the airport and drive you throughout your stay.

Another must is a visit to the **Board of Tourism in Fort-de-France**. They will supply you with brochures and maps. I spent many an hour with Duteil who speaks fluent English. She sincerely wanted to give me all the help I needed to gain knowledge of the island and its culture.

Office Departemental du Tourisme
(Martinique Tourist Office)
Blvd. Alfassa (Bord de Mer)
97206 Ford-de-France
Martinique, F.W.I.
Tel: (596) 63.79.60
Fax: (596) 73.66.93

THE DIVING

Most centers you dive or snorkel with in Martinique will be referred to as "a club". All "clubs" are strictly monitored by the Coast Guard, who can stop their boats any time and check to see if they meet all safety standards and if every diver on board is cer-tified (those taking a resort course and snorkelers excluded).

My first dive was with the **Centre De Plongee Meriden** that serves the Hotel Bakoua at the Meriden Hotel, a short walk along the beach.

This particular center operates like a private club. It is a plus if you speak French. They frown on any other certification but CMAS and make no bones about telling you. They do include equipment in the price of the dive.

The following day, I set out early for a dive with **Diamant Novotel Club** on the Caribbean's south coast located at the Hotel Diamant in Pointe de la Chery near Sainte-Anne. This is a particularly scenic area for its natural attractions are sugar cane, banana and pineapple plantations that stretch as far as the eye can see.

The Diamant Novotel Club is well equipped, organized, and friendly. Our first dive site was the **Rocher du Diamont**, the famous diamond rock rising 600 feet from the sea. It was used by the British in 1804 as a sloop of war, manning it for 17 months but sur-rendered, legend says, only when the wily French invaded first with barrels of rum to bait them and when that failed, with battalions. True or not, to this day it is known as H.M.S. Diamond Rock.

DIAMOND ROCK

The site, just minutes away from the center, is suited to all levels of experience. Divers were separated into groups according to these levels. I chose to dive shallow to get more bottom time. We plunged into the azure waters and descended to 58 feet swimming through a large dramatic arch followed by a web of alleyways and swim throughs. Ablaze with dazzling bright sponges and barrel corals, its ecosystem is supported by hundreds of species of reef fish. The dive proved pure and perfect and was over much too quickly.

On the other side there is a large cave. At 8 meters you can put your head into a hole and take your regulator out of your mouth and converse with your buddy. This site is also a captivating spot for snorkelers welcomed on the boat. I would certainly return to this center and dive other sites on their roster and surely return to the underwater world of Rocher du Diamant.

LA SURPRISE

I did this dive with Tropicasub Plongee, owned by Lionel LaFont and located in St. Pierre. This dive goes to a maximum depth of 84 feet. There was a healthy current so Lionel asked the group to stay close.

Lionel, a guide with keen eyes, pointed out ever so many critters hiding in the crevices of the reef, bluish lobster and cream colored crabs with faded red rouge tenacles, spotted brown and white, and grass green moray eels along with a Merlin snake slithering in and out of the vegetation.

Lionel is a gentleman I would definitely like to spend a great deal more time diving with. He and his wife run a safe, organized and friendly operation.

Many of his sites include the wrecks from the eruption of Mt. Pelee in 1902. Before these dives he gives a 20-30 minute history lesson on each.

On my return trip to Martinique I would split my diving between this facility and Diamant Novotel Club.

ACCOMMODATIONS

There are hotels to fit every budget. Breakfast is included with the price of your hotel room. A typical lunch can run $20, dinner $30-45 for one. Those on a budget can choose accommodations with kitchenette or one of the many campgrounds and cut costs by picnicking and dining in. The supermarkets are well stocked.

Knowing that I had a very full itinerary, I decided to book my entire stay at one hotel, the four star **Bakoua Hotel** and use that as my base for touring the island, diving and inspecting other hotels. **Please see Honeymoon and Anniversary section for the Bakoua Hotel.**

I did have luncheon at the **Hotel Novelette Diamond**. The attractive terrace had a fetching setting with a view of our dive site. The food was wonderful, the fish and salad fresh and delicious. I believe this picturesque hotel would make a good spot for visitors wishing to stay on this side of the island.

The rooms are air-conditioned and fitted with a loggia, bathroom, hairdryer, direct dial phone, individual safe, radio, television and video channel.

Along with scuba diving, water skiing and windsurfing, the hotel also features 2 tennis courts, a golf driving range, volleyball and horseback riding school. The "Le Pirate" club is open for children aged 6 to 12 during the French school holidays.

The pool snack bar "Le Grenadine" serves cocktails, sandwiches and cool drinks. The "Aliases" restaurant serves the freshest of grilled fish. At sunset, taste the delicious punches at the "Planter" bar and try "Le Flamboyant" restaurant for evenings with live folk entertainment, theme dinners and a la carte dining. The restaurant "La Cabana de Peachier" serves West Indian specialties in a magical setting.

SCUBA AND SNORKELING FACILITIES QUESTIONNAIRE

NAME **Sub Diamond Rock**
ADDRESS **Pointe de la Cherry, 97223 Diamant**
Martinique
CONTACT **Claude Caverrale**
TITLE **Gerant**
TELEPHONE **19 (596) 76.25.80** FAX **(repondeur)**

CAPITAL: **Fort de France** GOVERNMENT: **French**
POPULATION: **350,000** LANGUAGE: **French**
CURRENCY: ELECTRICITY: **220v**
AIRLINES: DEPARTURE TAX?
VISA/PASSPORT? **No** PROOF OF CITIZENSHIP? **Yes**
BUSINESS HOURS: **8:30am - 4:30pm**
CERTIFYING AGENCIES:
LOG BOOK REQUIRED? **Yes**
EQUIPMENT:

CHARTER/DIVE BOAT AVAILABLE? DIVER CAPACITY **15**
COAST GUARD APPROVED? **Yes** CAPTAIN LICENSE? **Yes**
SHIP TO SHORE? LORAN? **Yes** RADAR? **No**
DIVE MASTER/INSTRUCTOR ABOARD? **Yes, Both**

DIVING & SNORKELING:
TYPE OF DIVING/SNORKELING IN AREA? **Reef**
DIVING/SNORKELING IN YOUR AREA IS BEST SUITED FOR: **Beginner, Intermediate & Advanced**
BEST TIME OF YEAR FOR DIVING/SNORKELING:
TEMPERATURE: NOV-APRIL MAY-OCT:
VISIBILITY: DIVING **30 M** SNORKELING:

PACKAGES AVAILABLE: **Dive, Divestay**
LOCAL ACTIVITY/NIGHTLIFE: .
CAR NEEDED TO EXPLORE AREA?
DUTY FREE SHOPPING? **No**

LOCAL EMERGENCY SERVICES: NEAREST HYPERBARIC TREATMENT FACILITY:
COASTGUARD AUTHORITY:
TELEPHONE: LOCATION: **JL. Gadung No. 1 Surabaya**
CALLSIGNS: TELEPHONE:

LOCAL DIVING DOCTOR:
NAME: **Armand Flamen**
LOCATION:
TELEPHONE: **596. 46 4612**

SCUBA AND SNORKELING FACILITIES QUESTIONNAIRE

NAME   **Tropicasub Plongee**
ADDRESS   **La Guinguette Quartier Mouillage**
                  97 & 50 St. Pierre
CONTACT   **Monsieur Lionel LaFont**
TITLE   **Director**
TELEPHONE   **19 596. 78.38.03**   FAX **19.596.52.46.82**   TELEX

CAPITOL: **Fort-de-France**   GOVERNMENT: **French**
POPULATION: **360,000**   LANGUAGE: **French, English, German**
CURRENCY: **French Franc**   ELECTRICITY: **220v**
AIRLINES: **American**   DEPARTURE TAX? **No**
NEED VISA/PASSPORT?   YES x   NO   PROOF OF CITIZENSHIP?   YES   NO

YOUR FACILITY IS CLASSIFIED AS: SCUBA CENTER x   RESORT
BUSINESS HOURS: **9H30 - 5H00 (departures) except Monday**
LOG BOOK REQUIRED?   YES x   NO
EQUIPMENT: SALES   RENTALS X   AIR FILLS x
PRIMARY LINE OF EQUIPMENT: **Spirotechnique**
PHOTOGRAPHIC EQUIPMENT: SALES   RENTALS   LAB x

CHARTER/DIVE BOAT AVAILABLE?   YES x   NO   DIVER CAPACITY **10 people**
COAST GUARD APPROVED?   YES x   NO   CAPTAIN LICENSED?   YES x   NO
SHIP TO SHORE?   YES   NO x   LORAN? YES   NO x   VHF   YES x   NO
DIVE MASTER/INSTRUCTOR ABOARD? YES   NO   BOTH x
DIVING & SNORKELING: SALT   FRESH x
TYPE OF DIVING/SNORKELING IN AREA: WALL x   BEACH   WRECK x   REEF x   CAVE x   ICE
DIVING/SNORKELING IN YOUR AREA IS BEST SUITED FOR: BEGINNER x INTERMEDIATE x ADVANCED x
TEMPERATURE: NOV-APRIL   **28C**   MAY-OCT: **28C**

PACKAGES AVAILABLE: DIVE x   DIVE STAY x   SNORKEL x   SNORKEL-STAY x
ACCOMMODATIONS NEARBY: HOTEL x   MOTEL x   HOME RENTALS x
ACCOMMODATION RATES: EXPENSIVE   MODERATE   INEXPENSIVE
RESTAURANTS NEARBY: EXPENSIVE x MODERATE x   INEXPENSIVE x
YOUR AREA IS: REMOTE   QUIET WITH ACTIVITIES   LIVELY
LOCAL ACTIVITY/NIGHTLIFE: **Quiet**
CAR NEEDED TO EXPLORE AREA?   YES   NO
DUTY FREE SHOPPING?   YES x   NO

COASTGUARD   AUTHORITY: **Fort-de-France Hospital**

LOCAL DIVING DOCTOR:
NAME: **Dr. Samu**
LOCATION: **Hospital La Meynard, Fort-de-France (with helicopter)**
TELEPHONE: **75.15.75**

For more information contact:

Novelette Diamond
Pointe de la Cheery
97223 Le Diamant
Tel: (596) 73.66.15/76.42.42

If camping is more your style, the beach at Point du Marian is another seductive setting for swimming and picnicking. Bernadette and her family often camp here in **Saint-Anne at the Vivre Et Camper.** You can bring your tent and all your goodies, or come without anything but your clothing and they will rent everything. Caravans are also available.

For more information contact:

Vivre Et Camper a Saint Anne
P.O. 897227
Saint Anne

MARTINIQUE PROMOTION BUREAU
C/O FRENCH GOVERNMENT TOURIST OFFICE
444 MADISION AVENUE
NEW YORK, NY 10022
TEL 212 838 7800

Saba

Jeffrey R. Noordhoek

In *Aqua Expeditions Volume I* Joan Bourque's article hit the nail right on the head in her description of the quaint, sparsely populated, majestic island of Saba. This little known spot has everything to offer the diver who is looking for an off the beaten track spot with beautiful aquatic life and few people.

Everything on this small island is small scale, therefore very friendly. **Sea Saba** arranges dive packages with **Julianas** or **Captain's Quarters**, each ten rooms surrounded by colorful tropical gardens. A unique way to enjoy Saba's hillside views is from the veranda or your own private cottage, buy fresh lobster or fish and have a great barbecue.

Saba's quaint villages are nestled into the side of her lush green Mt. Scenery at 1200 feet above sea level, which means no mosquitoes, breathtaking views and cool nights - summer or winter. Restaurants and gift shops are a tropical 5-minute stroll away. Taxis and transportation are easily arranged. If you want something special, just ask.

The **Saba Marine Park** has 30 permanent moorings in place, which translates to no anchor, diving, or fishing damage. The dive sites are as varied as they are rich in marine life. The most praised sites are the underwater pinnacles; seamounts that rise up to 80 feet below the surface from over a thousand-foot depth only a half-mile offshore. A lot of drama only a stone's throw away. These habitats are far enough out to be fed by healthy open ocean currents. Not only delicate brilliant corals but awesome pelagic life.

The personnel working for Sea Saba are friendly, knowledgeable and safety conscious. The dive leader in charge of my adventures on Saba was Gordon McCulloch. Gordon has been diving for twelve years and instructing for the last nine.

My day of diving around Saba entailed two dives with a snorkeling stop in-between. Our first dive was a deep dive (110 ft.) at a spot named Third Encounter. The main attraction to the area was a huge needle (pinnacle) rising from the ocean floor 1,000 feet below which had a plateau at around 90 feet. The pinnacle was swarming with marine life and was adorned with bright sponges and coral.

Following the first dive we moored the boat in a little bay named Torrent Point. **This spot provided the snorkelers on the boat the perfect opportunity to get a view of the exciting underwater activity around the island.** The highlight of Torrent Point was a sea

Black Coral by Joan Bourque

cave that snorkelers could safely traverse which produced dramatic views of shallow water fish and crustaceans.

The second dive spot was **Tent Reef** which is home to a wall that drops off to 100 feet and contains a myriad of crevices and rock overhangs to explore. Although we ventured around Tent Reef in the early afternoon, I was told it makes an excellent spot for a night dive. The highlight is a quiet eel garden at the top of the reef.

My single regret about diving Saba was that it was only one day, and not more!

St. Barths

Coleman F. Church 3rd

A petite Cote d'Azur barely visible on the map, Saint Barthelemy awaits with panache and perfection. The island is only 6 miles long from Pointe a Toiny to Pointe a Colombier, but the irregular coastline boasts over twenty white sand beaches on which the sun shines 350 days a year.

St. Barthelemy (St. Barths) sits apart from other Caribbean Islands as the hilly topography did not allow sugar cane production and greatly limited slavery. Today, its population of 3,050 is predominantly white and of French origin. It was discovered by Columbus in 1496 and throughout its history has been controlled by the French, the English and the Swedes who handed it back to France in 1878. The culture is definitely more French than West Indian.

International jet-setters began vacationing on St. Barths in the 1950's and gave it the reputation for being ultra chic, and as a result, expensive. Dress is casually elegent with cotton and linen the recommended attire.

The language is primarily French but most residents speak English. Currency is the French Franc, but many prices are quoted in American dollars.

No major airlines fly directly to St. Barths. You make connections in St. Maarten, St. Thomas, or Guadeloupe. We highly recommend **Air Barths** for its safe, reliable and efficient service.

THE DIVING

St. Barths offers ideal conditions for long and successive dives as the maximum depth is 90 feet. Visibility is usually 60 to 90 feet and water temperature is 80 degrees F. Given the limited depth and white sand bottom, it is a photographers dream, as the sun reflects off the sand increasing the light to above average levels.

We were pleasantly pleased with the **St. Barth Plongee** dive operation operated by Bertrand Caizergues.

They never take more than eight people at a time. There is quick access to dive sites (3 to 20 minutes) on a 25-foot boat with twin 115 HP engines. A divemaster is backup remaining onboard when the divers are down.

There are 25 different dive sites ranging from 9 to 90 feet.

Our first dive was **Small Island**, a reef dive for intermediate and advanced divers. The water temperature was about 80F and the visibility 50 feet. The site is less than fifteen minutes from the dock. It is a good size reef with sloping sides down to a sand bottom at 70 feet. We saw a number of lobster, French angel fish, small spotted rays, occasional bottles, large barrel sponges, a small green moray, trunkfish and a six foot nurse shark.

Our second dive was at **Sugar Brood**, a reef/wreck dive at 60 feet with excellent visibility. On the wreck were two sleeping shark, a 20 pound lobster, spider crabs galore, colorful sponges, and a ciguateras which is toxic if eaten.

Our third dive was **L'ane Rouge**, a wall dive with medium visibility yet, a nice wall dive - good sponge colors - many French angel fish, spotted eels, queen angel fish, yellow tail snapper and lovely barrel sponges.

Each year from the end of March through early April, the Saint Barth Plongee dive operation, in cooperation with organizers of the Underwater Film Festival of Antibes/Juan les Pins, presents a week-long series of events highlighted by 15 prize-winning short-subject nautical movies narrated in French or English.

Saint Bath Plongee also sponsors two underwater photo contests: one for professionals and one for amateurs. There is a contest for drawings of underwater subjects, and several exhibits of sea related paintings, photos and posters.

For more information contact: M. Bertrand Caizerguea, Saint Barth Plongee, P.O. Box 46, St. Barthelemy Cedex, French West Indies, Tel/Fax: (590) 27.54.44.

ACCOMMODATIONS

We stayed at the **Carl Gustav**, perched high on the hillside above Gustavia, offering splendid views of the harbor and the sea, and the **Hotel Filao Beach.**
(Please see Honeymoon and Anniversary Section for the Carl Gustav).
FILAO BEACH HOTEL

The Filao Beach Hotel is the only deluxe hotel located on the famous **St. Jean Beach.** It is an ideal beach for parents and children and a great spot for windsurfing and other watersports.

The hotel affords leisure lovers a haven of peace and delight. Filao Beach has 30 spacious individual bungalows with bath, telephone, private safe, air conditioning, color television and a private terrace. All rooms overlook the sea or the tropical gardens. The rooms are tastefully furnished in bamboo and light tropical fabrics. Each bungalow is named after a famous French Chateaux.

Filao Beach is a member of the highly acclaimed Relais and Chateaux group. **Pierre Verdier, the general manager, was raised in a Relais and Chateaux hotel in France that is owned by his parents.** He learned service and guest satisfaction early on and infused his staff with his knowledge and high standards.

The bungalows are set in a semi-circle among the lovely gardens with a centerpiece seaside building that contains the bar, swimming pool and restaurant. There is a large wood deck that overlooks the white sand of St. Jean beach and the watersports shop that offers scuba diving, snorkeling, windsurfing, para-sailing and pedal boating.

Breakfast is served on your patio or in the restaurant. Luncheon is open to the public and gathers a number of restaurateurs who come to sample the salads, cheeses and daily specials from the sea. The restaurant is closed for dinner to insure quiet and privacy for the hotel guests. There are many good French and Creole restaurants in the area.

There are very few hotels in the Caribbean that can provide the service and most pleasant atmosphere created by Pierre Verdier and his charming capable staff.

For more information contact:

Hotel Filao Beach
P.O. Box 167
Saint Barthelemy
97133 Antilles Francaises-FWI
Tel: (590) 27 64 84
Fax: (590) 27 62 24

EDEN ROCK

Visitors to Saint Barths in the 1950's found only one tourist hotel on the island: the 6-room Eden Rock perched atop a promontory bisecting beautiful **Saint Jean Beach**. Since that time, the original hotel has gone through a number of changes, but it still maintains its perch.

Eden Rock has recently been reopened by an English couple, David and Jane Matthews, who have not only restored it, but greatly improved on the comforts and attractiveness, including an excellent new restaurant with chef Quadric Caplet, formerly of Cassettes.

DINING

St. Barths offers a vast selection of restaurants, from open-air waterfront cafes to romantic hillside dining rooms. **St. Barths has the best French cuisine in the West Indies.** Each spring they host the *Festival Gastronomique*, which features wines and menus from the major regions of France.

The delis have all the necessary ingredients for great picnic lunches to take along to the beaches or touring. Our favorites were **Rotisserie** in St. Jean and **Fauchon** in Gustavia. Do not leave the island without trying the pate at the Rotisserie! There is also a well-stocked supermarket and liquor

French Angel Fish by Lois Hatcher

store at the airport and in Gustavia on the waterfront. Don't count on the open-air markets for they are extremely overpriced.

For luncheon, the **Marigot Bay Club** with a seaside setting is a "don't miss" as is **La Gajac**, the intimate restaurant at **La Toiny**. Both are located in Anse de Toiny. We can also highly recommend luncheon at the **Filao Beach Hotel**. A more casual lunch choice is **La Saladerie** in Gustavia (27 52 48).

For dinner, **Ines's Ghetto** (27 53 20) downtown features moderately priced Creole cuisine that includes conch baked in pastry and excellent meat dishes served with fruit sauces.

For sushi try the **L'Iguane** in Gustavia.

The upscale **Eddy's** is around the corner, but has no signage. It is treated as somewhat of a secret. The entrance is down the alleyway that leads to the Roots Boutique in Gustavia (27 53 20). They serve excellent food in an open-air setting.

Le Ti St. Barth in Pointe Milou (27 97 71) specialty is barbeque. The décor is casual, but romantic with lots of different French fabrics, hammocks, candles and pictures decorating the walls. Go early because they run out of barbeque and their other specials early. Moderately priced.

Don't be fooled by the long dirt road that runs along the cemetery to **Maya's** in Gustavia. This is one of the best restaurants on the island. Again, very romantic, and pricey, but well worth it for the food, the wine list and the atmosphere. Be sure to make reservations (27 75 73).

The food at the Carl Gustav is definitely "fit for a king" (See Honeymoon and Anniversary section for more information on the Hotel Carl Gustav).

AREAS OF INTEREST

Gustavia is the Capitol of St. Barths and wraps itself like a horseshoe around the harbor. When you walk the narrow streets of Gustavia, you will notice that every thoroughfare has two nameplates, one with its Swedish name and one with its official French name. Wooden and stone buildings are home to expensive boutiques and restaurants.

The 15 square mile island has 22 beaches each with its distinct character. There is no rainy season and water is considered very precious. A rental car is needed to reach beaches or other recreational facilities and there is a shortage of taxis.

We rented an Australian Moke from Budget. It is a great car for touring, as it has no doors making it very easy for photographing. It is great fun to drive along the rocky coastline and see the variety of caves and beaches. Car rentals can be booked ahead. Most are located at the airport. Remember there are only two gas stations on the island - one at the airport and the other at L'Orient.

A short drive over the hills from Gustavia you will find **Corosol** which is one of the oldest villages on the island. The **Inter Oceans Museum** is located here. It has over 3500 different seashells, corals and crustaceans from all over the world.

The **Wall House** Museum is located at La Pointe in Gustavia, a restored Swedish building with French/Swedish historical information on the first floor and library on the second level.

On the windward side you will find the **Grand Fond Valley** resembling Normandy's green pastures. Further along low stone walls and hillsides covered with dry glens remind one of Ireland.

For horseback riding, visit the **Plaza** on Baiede St. Jean owned by Stephanie Zedle.

There are two quasi-boutiques that have good quality and interesting merchandise. One is **Roots** in Gustavia and the second is **Toulous Marino** also in Gustavia - take a few minutes to see their interesting wares.

For French chic visit the **Mandarine** boutique in Gustavia. The owner is a transplant from Newport, RI and she has a great collection of womens clothing, hand bags, jewelry and locally produced bath oils and perfume that make a great gift for the unfortunate people who have been left at home.

If you are a cigar lover, be sure to visit **La Casa del Habano** in St. Jean. They have a wide variety of cigars and locally produced rum. Be sure to sample the passion fruit and the vanilla. We guarantee you'll want to bring some home with you.

SCUBA AND SNORKELING FACILITIES QUESTIONNAIRE

NAME: **Saint Barth Plongee**
ADDRESS: **P.O. Box 46 FWI**
97095 Saint Barthelemy Cedex
CONTACT: **Bertrand Caizergues**
TITLE: **Owner**
TELEPHONE: **(590) 27 54 44**   FAX: **(590) 27 54 44**
CAPITOL: **Gustavia**   GOVERNMENT: **Francais**
POPULATION: **5,000**   LANGUAGE: **French & English**
CURRENCY: **Francs, US accepted**   ELECTRICITY: **220 V**
AIRLINES: **Europe Paris SXM**
Londres via Antigua, American via St. John   DEPARTURE TAX? **$6.00 US**
NEED VISA/PASSPORT? **No**   PROOF OF CITIZENSHIP?

YOUR FACILITY IS QUALIFIED AS: **Scuba Center**
BUISINESS HOURS: **8am-11am , 2pm-7pm**
CERTIFYING AGENCIES: **PADI, Cedip, ANMP**
LOG BOOK REQUIRED? **No**
EQUIPMENT: **Sales**
PRIMARY LINE OF EQUIPMENT: **Scubapro BC's Regs MK 20/G 250/ R 190**
PHOTOGRAPHIC EQUIPMENT: **Sales, Rental**

CHARTER/DIVE BOAT AVAILABLE? **No** DIVER CAPACITY
COAST GUARD APPROVED?   CAPTAIN LICENSE?
SHIP TO SHORE?   LORAN ?   RADAR   ?
DIVE MASTER/INSTRUCTOR ABOARD? **Yes**

DIVING & SNORKELING: **Salt**
TYPE OF DIVING/SNORKELING IN AREA? **Wall, Wrecks, Reef Cave, Night**

DIVING/SNORKELING IN YOUR AREA IS BEST SUITED FOR: BEGINNER **X** INTERMEDIATE **X** ADVANCED **X**
BEST TIME OF YEAR FOR DIVING/SNORKELING: **Everyday**
TEMPERATURE: **NOV-APRIL 80 F MAY-OCT: 80 F**
VISIBILITY: **DIVING 120 FT**   **SNORKELING: 100 FT**

PACKAGES AVAILABLE: **Dive, Divestay, Snorkel**
ACCOMMODATIONS NEARBY: **Hotel, Home Rentals**
ACCOMMODATIONS RATES: **Expensive, Moderate**
RESTAURANTS NEARBY: **Expensive, Moderate, Inexpensive**
YOUR AREA IS: **Remote, Quiet with Activities**
LOCAL ACTIVITY/NIGHTLIFE: **Horse, Tennis, Running, Sleeping, All Sailing**
CAR NEEDED TO EXPLORE AREA? **Yes**
DUTY FREE SHOPPING? **Yes**

St. Eustatius

"Historic Gem of the Caribbean"

Wendy Canning Church

This comely, tranquil, unspoiled and almost undiscovered tropical isle of 11.8 square miles gives the visitor a feeling of what it used to be like to travel -friendly people, no locks on the doors and unchanged customs and culture. Couple this with a perfect year round climate and the traveler will have discovered a rare find.

Christopher Columbus discovered it in 1493. Known locally as "Statia," St. Eustatius lies 150 miles southeast of Puerto Rico. It is justly thought of as the **Historic Gem of the Caribbean.** During the 1700's, Statia was the largest trading center in the Caribbean. As many as 3500 ships a year brought goods of all kinds. In 1636, after the war between Holland and Spain, the Dutch took possession.

During the 17th and 18th centuries, Statia was the link between Europe and the American colonies. Statia's Capitol, Oranjestad, was a prosperous and bustling trade hub. Its docks overflowed with cases of food, arms and ammunition to keep Washington's Army fighting the War of Independence. **Trading was so lucrative that the island became known as the "Golden Rock".**

On November 16, 1776, the American Brig-of-War, the *Andrew Doria*, sailed into the harbor of Statia firing its thirteen gun salute indicating Americas long sought independence. **The eleven gun salute reply roaring from the cannons at Fort Oranje under the command of Governor Johannes de Graff established Statia as the first foreign nation to officially recognize the newly formed United States of America.**

Due to the fierce rivalry between the Dutch, English, Spanish and French, St. Eustatius changed hands no less than 22 times before 1860. Around 1830, the large merchants began leaving and lower town warehouses gradually fell into disuse and decay becoming the ruins they are today.

There are ruins from upper town down to the harbor. When a visitor closes their eyes, they can imagine the town, which was built from the brick ballast in ships bellies from all corners of the world.

Ironically, Statia is once more a trans-shipment center, now for oil and petroleum products. It is definitely an important center for tourism and can be reached by a 15-minute flight from St. Martin on Winair which arrives at Franklin Delano Roosevelt Airport.

The Statians are a proud and gentle people who will welcome you warmly. They take great pride in their island and its many activities and happily share it with you. Today,

Flying Girard by Wendy Canning Church

Statia's population of 2,100 is comprised of 16th century African descendants, Saladuids from South America who arrived in the 15th century and Dutch decendents of the original settlers. Dutch is the official language taught in schools and used by the government but all Statians speak English.

The currency is the Antillean Guilder. A valid passport or birth certificate is needed for entry.

Exellent weather prevails year-round.

THE SCUBA DIVING AND SNORKELING

The heritage of Statia provides a unique setting for divers and non-divers. For the diver, Statia's waters unlock the treasures of intriguing marine life, ballast stones, anchors, canons, warehouses, pottery shards, clay pipes, bottles and remains of old trading ships, natural and coral reefs. Snorkeling and diving Statia will take you over the remains of 17th and 18th century life on Statia. Dive sites are virgin and not yet impacted or run over by divers.

Creative and innovative Golden Rock Dive Center's motto is: "Whatever you want." Owners Glen and Michele Farer fulfill their motto: computer diving, multi level, reef, wall, 60+ feet or shallow dives. Divers and snorkelers will be introduced to an underwater world of healthy coral reefs rife with fish both macro and micro.

Over 30 dive sites are close to shore, the dive boats are fast and comfortable with ample room for equipment and divers with a canopy. Afterwards, they serve you a luncheon of fresh lobster stuffed with conch, salad, fresh bread and desert.

At Golden Rock clients are invited to explore the magic kingdom that lies under clear virgin waters. I spent a week with the crew at Golden Rock and came away with not only new friends, knowledge of Statia, but also with pieces of clay pipe, shards and fragments of the famous blue beads every visitor and local hunts for.

Golden Rock continues to find and mark new sites, here are some of my favorites:

Blue Bead Hall off Gallows Bay is a 50-ft. dive. **This is the spot to head for treasure hunting**. Even if you do not find a blue bead you are sure to spot many of the beautiful flying fish in different hues.

Barracuda Reef on the south side. This site is aptly named for the schools of silver sleek barracuda that call it home. Along with parrotfish, rockfish, stone fish, blue striped lizardfish, you will also see speckled moray eel and snakefish. One will marvel at the healthy sponges both hard and soft. As we swam along the wall, we heard the pilot whales having lengthy conversations.

Double Wreck of Fallows Bay. These ships sunk in the late 1600s when each fired upon the other because of a dispute over a business transaction. Their dispute has left us with a dive where shrimp, octopus, starfish, lobster, spotted rays, arrow crabs, trumpet fish, and a wondrous variety of sponges delight the eye. **The lucky diver might also find a 200-year-old bottle or old pipe fragments.**

Snorkelers are welcome aboard the dive boat or can jump in the water in front of the dive shop. One can snorkel through an ancient sunken city surrounded by unusual tropical fish, coral gardens and remnants of the 18th century.

Golden Rock also has a wonderful program for children of all ages which includes snorkeling, diving, fishing and archeology beach walks.

There was one other dive center in lower town when I was there. I dived with them and found that Golden Rock delivered what I wanted".

For more information contact:

Golden Rock Dive Center
St. Eustatius, The Netherlands Antilles
Telephone/Fax 011-599-38-2964
USA (Bookings Only) 1-800-311-6658

ACCOMMODATIONS

I stayed at the **Golden Era Hotel** situated on the harbor minutes from the Golden Rock Dive Center, restaurants and town. Its 20 air-conditioned rooms are simple and clean with telephones, TV, and a small refrigerator. For more information contact: Golden Era Hotel, P.O. Box 109, St. Eustatius, (phone) 599-3-82345, (fax) 599-3-82445

Other options include **La Maison Sur La Plage** located on the Atlantic side of the island on beautiful Zeelandia Beach. This ten-room beach hotel is one mile from the airport. The Gourmet French restaurant is outstanding, Relax at the pool, play a game of boule or backgammon. Each room has a private bath, terrace and a TV.

Talk of the Town Hotel Bar & Restaurant is located at the edge of town. All 18 rooms have air-conditioning, telephone, cable TV and a private bathroom. Seven rooms are located on the first floor in the main building. The deluxe room's (9) are situated around the swimming pool in cottages consisting of two or three rooms. The "efficiencies" (2) are equipped with a kitchen.

Aquaduct by Wendy Canning Church

The **Old Gin House** was an 18th century tavern. It is located two miles from the airport in historic lower town. It has twenty individually furnished rooms. Rooms have either an ocean or poolside view. There is an outdoor breakfast area, indoor dining facilities and patio bar, library and reception. During the devastating hurricane, The Old Gin House suffered severe damage. **A group of local people refurbished this historic gem whose guests have included Jackie Kennedy Onasis and Truman Capote.**

DINING

On an island of this size, the number, variety and quality of restaurants amazed me. I can highly recommend the following:

The Blue Bead Bar & Restaurant located on beautiful Gallows Bay among 18th century ruins specializes in West Indian, Continental and Indonesian cuisine (Telephone: 82873).

B's Garden is located in the courtyard of the Government's Guesthouse. B's offers delicious food in a superb atmosphere. Every night is a special night at B's. Luncheon is also pleasant dining in the cool shade of century old trees and foliage (Telephone: 82733).

The restaurant at La Maison Sur La Plage is a must. Do dress casually elegant and have a delicious and romantic ocean view dinner. Located at Zeelandia Beach, serving French cuisine in an airy trellised restaurant with a beautiful view. All major credit cards excepted (Telephone: 82256).

If you crave a hamburger, go to **Superburger** in the heart of town on the Granffweg. "Comfort food" including burgers, sandwiches, shakes and ice cream is simple and good. Take out is available. (Telephone: 82412).

AREAS OF INTEREST

With a valid driver's license, you may drive a car on Statia. You can choose from at least seven rental companies. For information inquire at your hotel or the Tourist Information Stand at the airport, or hire a taxi. **Taxi rates are fixed so be sure to check the schedule once onboard.**

St. Eustatius International Trade Center is a historical and archaeological gem which reflects the glory of Statia's past.

Take a **walking tour** of the upper town and lower town. It is one of the island's highlights and will give you an overview of its fascinating history. A brochure is available at the Historical Foundation Museum (approximately 1-1/2 hours).

The **Historical Foundation Museum** is located right in town. It is extremely interesting and well arranged, one of the finest in the Caribbean and well worth the visit.

The Quill is a perfectly formed 2,000-foot extinct volcano. A hike into its lush tropical rain forest takes approximately 2+ hours. Guides are available at the Nature Hikes Office.

For those that like hiking, try the island's **12 nature tracks**. Some easy, some tiring some a little slippery when wet. Brochures are available at the Tourist Office.

Fort Oranje is well worth a visit. The French built it in 1629. In 1636 it was enlarged and the Zeelanders renamed it. Memorials in the Fort Courtyard include Michiel Adriaanz de Ruyter: Dutch Admiral on Statia May 11-17 1665, erected in 1907; Copper plaque commemorating the salute to the Hurricane Man of War, "Andrew Doria" November 16, 1776. Presented by President Franklin D. Roosevelt on December 12, 1939; World War II memorial erected on May 4, 1957 and a centennial plaque donated by the government of the U.S. Virgin Islands.

The **Government's Guesthouse** was built in the 18th century and restored in 1992. Queen Beatrix officially opened the building with the unveiling of the plaque on November 16, 1992.

The Ruins of the Synagogue, "Honen Dalim", (she who is charitable to the poor), was built in 1739. It is the second oldest in the Western Hemisphere. One can find among the gravestones some that are richly embellished. The oldest is dated 1742, the latest 1843

BEACHES

Oranje Beach is lovely. Here you will find interesting sand colors with areas of light beige and black. Waves are lower on the leeward side of the island with no strong current, undertow, sea urchins or dangerous fish. No life guard.

Zeelandia Beach is two miles long and usually deserted with black and tan sand. It is beautiful with the exciting Atlantic surf and the fresh invigorating trade winds. **There is a dangerous undertow.** Swimming is not recommended, but it is fine for wading with a partner, sunbathing and beach hiking. No life guard.

Lynch Beach is located on the Atlantic side. It is a small beach with light brown sand. The water is shallow in spots for children at certain times of the year. Stay near shore and watch for undertow. No life guard.

Editors note: Taxi Driver Josser Daniel will give you a most comprehensive and pleasant historical tour (Telephone: 03-82358-BUSZ).

Many thanks to the St. Eustatius Tourist Board and especially to Roland Lopes, Public Relations Director, who was so helpful during my stay and for introducing me to" The Historic Gem of the Carribean."

For more information contact:

St. Eustatius Tourism Development Foundation
Oranjestad, St. Eustatius
Netherland Antilles
Tel 599-3-82433

For airline reservations contact:

WINAIR
Statia
Tel 599-3-82362
St. Maarten
Tel 599-5-54210

St. Kitts
Donna Marchetti

St. Kitts could be described as an island of moderation. It lacks the shopping frenzy of St. Thomas, yet there are duty-free shops, a batik factory and a handful of souvenir shops. It's not a gambler's haven like Aruba, but those who look hard enough will find a casino. Sugar-white sand aficionados will discover many pristine, if smaller, stretches of white powder on which to spread their towels. Though not wild like jungle-covered Dominica, St. Kitts has a rain forest of considerable size and even a volcano you can hike to the top of. Likewise, divers who come to St. Kitts looking for a Bonaire or Cozumel won't find it, but will instead find colorful, uncrowded reefs and personalized diving.

St. Kitts by Donna Marchetti

The 68-square mile island of St. Kitts lies in the Eastern Caribbean just south of St. Maarten. The first inhabitants of the island were the Arawaks, who made their way from South America 2,000 years ago. By the time Columbus passed by in 1493, the war-like Caribs had driven them out. It was more than a hundred years before the first settlers came, both English and French, to do battle with the Caribs and stake a claim to the island. Although the British achieved domination in the end, the island has been influenced by both French and English culture.

In 1983, St. Kitts became an independent country, though still a member of the British Commonwealth. Most of today's 45,000 inhabitants are descendants of African slaves and European indentured servants brought to the island for manual labor in the 17th and 18th centuries.

Unlike other Caribbean islands that depend on tourism to make a living, St. Kitts is a working island producing about 30,000 tons of sugar per year. Small gauge railroad tracks criss-cross the island, facilitating the transport of cane, molasses and crews.

SCUBA DIVING & SNORKELING

There are several dive operations on St. Kitts, all of them small and personalized:

Pro-Divers (869-465-3223; fax 869-465-0265) is located at Turtle Beach on the southern peninsula, but will bring their dive boats to the public pier in town to pick up divers staying at one of the hotels there. **In addition to dive excursions, Pro-Divers offer PADI certification, snorkeling and boat charters to Nevis.**

Kenneth's Dive Center (869-465-2620) has a small shop in Basseterre but picks up divers at the public pier. I dived with both of these operations and found them to be friendly, competent and safety-conscious.

Moray Eel and diver by Lois Hatcher

St. Kitts Scuba (869-465-1189 fax 869-465-3696), based at the Bird Rock Hotel in Basseterre, is the newest operation on St. Kitts. It is a PADI/ NAUI facility. While the rates at the three operations are about the same, Pro-Divers includes gear rental, if needed.

Most of the diving takes place off the southeastern end of the island, making either Basseterre or Turtle Beach good points of departure. Visibility varies—in two dive trips to the island I had 50-foot days and 100-foot days. The water temperature is comfortable year-round, but warmer in the summer. Currents are negligible at most sites and most dives are not deep, **making St. Kitts a good place for novice divers or those who haven't been in the water for awhile, though experienced divers will appreciate St. Kitts as well.** The reefs are colorful and alive with fish, evidence that, among other factors, the area has not been over-dived.

Monkey Shoals is a popular shallow dive just west of the southernmost point on the island. Ledges along a sandy bottom harbor blackbar soldierfish, grunts, eels and nurse sharks. The area swarms with rock beauties, wrasse, blue and brown chromis, blue tangs, fairy basslets and a host of other reef fish.

Nags Head, just east of Monkey Shoals, is a beautiful, deeper dive along a gently sloping wall covered with coral, vase sponges and sea fans. There are many reef fish, but the highlight for me was seeing three spotted eagle rays pass by in the distance.

When you're looking for dinner, **Friar's Bay Reef** is the place to go. It's not surprising to find seven to ten large lobsters within a few square yards. There are also several huge coral heads on this circular reef that sometimes goes by its nickname, Jell-O Mold.

Coconut Tree Reef, just south of Basseterre, is one of St. Kitts' largest reefs, with depths ranging from 40 to 200 feet. This colorful site is populated with surgeonfish, jacks, parrotfish and barracuda.

There are numerous wrecks around the island; two are most frequented by divers. The *River Taw* is a 144 foot freighter that sank in fifty feet of water off Frigate Bay about ten years ago. Southwest of Basseterre lies the *M. V. Talata*, which sank to its resting-place in seventy feet of water in 1985.

Snorkelers need do nothing more than drive to one of the southern beaches, hop in the water and swim out from the shore. One of the most popular places for snorkeling is Turtle Beach, located near the tip of the peninsula. In addition to good snorkeling, there's a pleasant beach and a casual restaurant, making it a good place for a daylong family outing. Rental snorkel gear is available at the **Pro-Divers** shop on the beach.

For those snorkelers who like to explore off the beaten track, at least two wrecks can be seen off White House Bay, also on the southern peninsula. Shifting sands from the 1995-96 hurricane season revealed an old wooden warship with canons in about twenty feet of water. Farther out is a larger, newer, more intact wreck that sits on a thirty-foot bottom, rising almost to the surface in places. There are many juvenile fish on the wreck, along with a large population of bristle worms—look but don't touch!

ACCOMMODATIONS

You can have it just about any way on St. Kitts—small and intimate, large and raucous, old and refined, or just plain pleasant.

Quiet, stately **Ottley's Plantation Inn** (PO Box 345, St. Kitts, W. I.; 869-465-7234 or 1-800-772-3039; fax 869-465-4760) was once the estate of a sugar plantation. It sits on 35 acres of manicured grounds at the foot of Mt. Liamuiga overlooking the water. It is not close to town—or anything else for that matter—but there is a complimentary shuttle to Basseterre and to beaches. The spacious rooms and cottages are beautifully decorated, all with air conditioning. There is a swimming pool and **perhaps the best restaurant of the island, the Royal Palm.**

The opposite extreme in atmosphere may be found at **Jack Tar Village** (PO Box 406, Frigate Bay, St. Kitts, W. I.; phone 869-465-8651 or 1-800-999-9182; fax 869-465-1031) an all-inclusive, 244-room resort and casino south of Basseterre. The facilities include a golf course, beaches, restaurants, pools, tennis courts and shops. **Baby-sitting and kids club (ages 4-12) are available.**

In town, the **Ocean Terrace Inn** (PO Box 65, Basseterre, St. Kitts, W. I. phone 869-465-2754 or 1-800-524-0512 fax 896-465-1057) is a quiet, moderately sized option. Its 53 rooms, suites and apartments have A/C and television. There are two pools, restaurants and a Jacuzzi. OTI's Fisherman's Wharf is one of the best dining values among the hotel restaurants.

Horizons Villa Resort (PO Box 1143, Frigate Bay, St. Kitts W. I.; phone 869-465-0584 or 1-800-830-9069; fax 869-465-0785) perched high on a hillside overlooking the water, has a multitude of accommodations in a quiet setting. There are **also suites and one-, two-, three- and four-bedroom condos.** The resort has a pool and a very nice restaurant, the Poolside Cafe.

There are numerous small guesthouses that offer more economical choices. For a complete listing of accommodations contact St. Kitts and Nevis Hotel and Tourism Association, PO Box 438, Liverpool Row, Basseterre, St. Kitts, W. I.; phone 869-465-5304; fax 869-465-7746.

AREAS OF INTEREST

One of the nicest things about St. Kitts is that there's plenty to do, but the pace isn't frantic. Except in Basseterre, there's not much traffic, and getting around is quite easy. For those who plan to rent a car, you must purchase a temporary St. Kitts driver's license; driving is on the left.

A tour of the island begins in **Basseterre**, the capitol city, founded in 1625 by French settlers. A few buildings from the 18th century British rule have managed to survive years of earthquakes, fire and hurricanes, though much of the architecture is Victorian. One of the most-photographed structures on the island is the **clock tower**, constructed in the late 1800s, which stands in the area known as the Circus. There are many nice shops nearby as well as **the open-air restaurant, the Ballahoo, where you can sit and watch the entire goings on in the busy town center.**

Heading west on the road that runs the perimeter of the island, you'll come to the entrance to **Romney Manor**, home of **Caribelle Batik**. Here artisans use the Indonesian method of hand dyeing cotton fabric to make beautiful island-style clothing. The surrounding gardens are lovely to walk through. Nearby are **ancient petroglyphs** carved by the Caribs into large volcanic boulders long before Europeans arrived.

The road continues west toward **Brimstone Hill Fortress National Park**, an impressive bastion built by the British over a hundred-year period beginning in the late 1600s. It was manned until the Crimean War, when its soldiers were sent off to fight in Europe. The fort fell into disrepair until the 1960s brought a new awareness of its historical value, and restoration was begun. The fort houses a small museum containing artifacts from various periods in St. Kitts' history. Perhaps one of the most memorable aspects of the fort is the panoramic view that includes the plain below, the blue sea and on a clear day the islands of Montserrat, Nevis, St. Barths, St. Eustatius, Saba and St. Maarten.

Shortly beyond the fort, the road curves around a point and heads back east along the less populated side of the island, which is dotted with a few small villages, some wide beaches and a bank of steep black rock cliffs. Just as the road comes nearly back to Basseterre, there is a cut-off that veers to the left and heads to the southern peninsula. This is the driest part of the island, and the vegetation is noticeably different. Unlike the northern end with its lush forests, the peninsula is covered mostly with scrub and cacti. There are, however, numerous monkeys, especially if you are there in the early morning or late afternoon. **Many of the island's most beautiful beaches are at the south end** and only a few people populate most of them at any given time.

Two all-day excursions are well worth the visitor's time and money. A hike to the top of **Mt. Liamuiga**, known also as Mt. Misery, offers a chance to learn about the flora of the island on the way to the crater's rim. At the top, the views are spectacular. Hikers should be in good physical condition, as the trail is demanding and the hike lasts about five hours. It is both more enjoyable and safer to go with a guide than attempt it on your own. **Greg's Safaris** (PO Box 65, Basseterre, St. Kitts, W. I.; phone 869-465-4121; fax 869-465-0707) will feed you, guide you, teach you, and even give you a well-deserved drink of local cane spirits when you've finished.

For a completely relaxed, decadently lazy day, sail to Nevis on a catamaran. The Spirit of St. Kitts and the Eagle depart from Basseterre daily, stopping at a calm inlet for snorkeling before tying up at a sandy beach for a barbecue. Swim, sleep, read or walk the shoreline for several hours, then enjoy a long, slow sail back to St. Kitts. **Leeward Island Charters** can be reached at PO Box 586, St. Kitts, W. I. phone 869-465-7474.

Note: though the U.S. Postal Service lists "St. Kitts" as "St. Christopher," hotels unanimously use "St Kitts"; that practice is adhered to throughout this article.

SCUBA AND SNORKELING FACILITIES QUESTIONNAIRE

NAME: **Pro-Divers**
ADDRESS: **P.O. Box 174, Basseterre**
St. Kitts
CONTACT: **Margot or Auston Macleod**
TITLE: **Owners**
TELEPHONE: **869-465-3223**   FAX: **869-465-0265**   TELEX
CAPITAL: **Basseterre**   GOVERNMENT: **St. Kitts-Nevis**
POPULATION: **45,000**   LANGUAGE: **English**
CURRENCY: **Eastern Caribbean, OR US $**   ELECTRICITY: **220V AND/OR 110V**
AIRLINES: **American Airlines, Liat**   DEPARTURE TAX? **$10 US OR $27 EC**
NEED VISA/PASSPORT?   **Yes**   PROOF OF CITIZENSHIP?   **Yes**

YOUR FACILITY IS CLASSIFIED AS: **Scuba Center**
BUSINESS HOURS: **9-5 pm 7 days**
CERTIFYING AGENCIES: **PADI**
LOG BOOK REQUIRED? **Preferred**
EQUIPMENT: **Rentals**
PRIMARY LINE OF EQUIPMENT: **Sherwood**
PHOTOGRAPHIC EQUIPMENT: **Rentals**
CHARTER/DIVE BOAT AVAILABLE? **yes**   DIVER CAPACITY: **#1 - 12 #2 - 14**
COAST GUARD APPROVED? **yes**   CAPTAIN LICENSED? **not required**
SHIP TO SHORE? **yes**   LORAN? **yes**   RADAR? **no**
DIVE MASTER/INSTRUCTOR ABOARD? YES BOTH
DIVING & SNORKELING: **Salt**
TYPE OF DIVING/SNORKELING IN AREA: **Wall, Beach, Wreck, Reef, Cavern**
DIVING/SNORKELING IN YOUR AREA IS BEST SUITED FOR: **Beginner, Intermediate, Advanced**
BEST TIME OF YEAR FOR DIVING/SNORKELING: **All Year**
TEMPERATURE: NOV-APRIL **78F**   MAY-OCT: **80-82F**
VISIBILITY: DIVING: **60-120 FT** SNORKELING: **100 FT**
PACKAGES AVAILABLE: **Dive, Dive Stay**
ACCOMMODATIONS NEARBY: **Hotel, Guest House, Home Rentals**
ACCOMMODATION RATES: **Expensive, Moderate, Inexpensive**
RESTAURANTS NEARBY: **Expensive, Moderate, Inexpensive**
YOUR AREA IS: **Quiet With Activities**
LOCAL ACTIVITY/NIGHTLIFE: **Pubs, Nightclubs, Music Festival in June, Casino, Fashion Shows,**
Street By, Carnival in December
CAR NEEDED TO EXPLORE AREA? **Preferred**
DUTY FREE SHOPPING? **Yes**

LOCAL EMERGENCY SERVICES   NEAREST HYPERBARIC TREATMENT FACILITY
Saba Police, Fire, Ambulance - 911   AUTHORITY: **DR. Jack Buchanan**
COASTGUARD: **ST. Kitts - Nevis Coast Guard**   LOCATION: **Saba M A**
TELEPHONE: TELEPHONE: **Call Saba Radio**
CALLSIGNS:

LOCAL DIVING DOCTOR:
NAME: **DR. Kathleen Allen-Ferdinand**
LOCATION: **Victoria Road, Basseterre**
TELEPHONE: **869-465-5348/9**

SCUBA AND SNORKELING FACILITIES QUESTIONNAIRE

NAME **Dive Nevis**
ADDRESS: **P.O. Box 494**
Newcastle, Nevis West Indies
CONTACT: **Brad Hazledine, Kim Stavroff**
TITLE: **Owners**
TELEPHONE: **(809) 469-9395** FAX: **(809) 469-9375**

CAPITOL: **Charlestown**   GOVERNMENT: **British Commenwealth**
POPULATION: **9,000**   LANGUAGE: **English**
CURRENCY: **EC $**   ELECTRICITY: **110/220**
AIRLINES: **American, Liat, Winair, Carib**   DEPARTURE TAX? **yes 10 US**
NEED VISA/PASSPORT? **No**   PROOF OF CITIZENSHIP? **Yes**

YOUR FACILITY IS QUALIFIED AS: **Scuba Center**
BUISINESS HOURS: **8am-5pm**
CERTIFYING AGENCIES: **PADI**
LOG BOOK REQUIRED? **No**
EQUIPMENT: SALES, RENTALS, **Airfills**
PRIMARY LINE OF EQUIPMENT: **Sherwood**
PHOTOGRAPHIC EQUIPMENT: **Rentals**

CHARTER/DIVE BOAT AVAILABLE? **Yes**   DIVER CAPACITY: **6**
COAST GUARD APPROVED? **Yes**   CAPTAIN LICENSE? **Yes**
SHIP TO SHORE? **Yes**   LORAN ? **Yes** RADAR? **No**
DIVE MASTER/INSTRUCTOR ABOARD? **YES**

DIVING & SNORKELING: **Salt**
TYPE OF DIVING/SNORKELING IN AREA? **Wall, Beach, Wreck, Reef**
DIVING/SNORKELING IN YOUR AREA IS BEST SUITED FOR: BEGINNER **x** INTERMEDIATE **x** ADVANCED **x**
BEST TIME OF YEAR FOR DIVING/SNORKELING: **April - December**
TEMPERATURE: NOV-APRIL **80F**   MAY-OCT: **88F**
VISIBILITY: DIVING **70 FT**   SNORKELING: **50 FT**

PACKAGES AVAILABLE: **Dive, Divestay, Snorkel, Snorkel Stay**
ACCOMMODATIONS NEARBY: **Hotel, Home Rentals**
ACCOMMODATIONS RATES: **Expensive, Moderate**
RESTAURANTS NEARBY: **Expensive, Moderate, Inexpensive**
YOUR AREA IS: **Quiet with Activities**
LOCAL ACTIVITY/NIGHTLIFE: **Nightclubs, Hotels with Entertainment, Golf, Tennis**
CAR NEEDED TO EXPLORE AREA? **Yes**
DUTY FREE SHOPPING? **No**

LOCAL EMERGENCY SERVICES: NEAREST HYPERBARIC TREATMENT FACILITY:
COASTGUARD: **St. Kittis**   AUTHORITY: **SABA**
TELEPHONE: **465-8384**   LOCATION: **Saba Marine Park**
CALLSIGNS: **Stalwart**   TELEPHONE: **(919) 684-8111**

LOCAL DIVING DOCTOR:
NAME: **Dr. Patrick Dias**
LOCATION: **Charlestown**
TELEPHONE: 469-5455

St. Martin/St. Maarten

Two Countries - One Island

Coleman F. Church 3rd

One hundred and eighty miles off the coast of Puerto Rico lies the 37 square mile island of St. Martin/St. Maarten. It is the smallest island in the world to be divided between two sovereignties. It was discovered by Christopher Columbus in 1493 on the feast day of St. Martin and so named.

Over the years the Dutch, French and Spanish clashed over control and there were 16 changes of flag from 1648 to 1816. The treaty of 1648 delineated the boundaries of the island. The Dutch received 16 square miles and the French 21 square miles. No rift exists between the peoples of the two countries. The inhabitants are justly proud of their 350 years of peaceful co-existence.

St. Maarten is part of the Northern Antilles, along with Bonaire, Aruba, Curacao, Saba and St. Eustatius. St. Martin is a territory of Guadeloupe. The population is approximately 64,000. There are no borders or customs officials between the two countries, just the two different spellings. The two capitols are Marigot and Philipsburg.

Sugar became king, and with it came not only prosperity, but also slaves from Africa to man the plantations. When slavery was abolished in 1848 on St. Martin and 1863 on St. Maarten, a recession hit both governments. An economic depression lasted until 1939 when the island was declared a free port. The island then became a Caribbean hub of trade.

The 1940's saw the building of the Princess Juliana Airport and the two cultures' identities were clearly defined. The Dutch side was developed and earmarked for tourism. Large scale resorts, cruise ships and casinos became the mainstay. The French side developed slowly catering to a more up market group, quiet, sedate and as French as pate de fois gras.

These two countries also share the Atlantic on the east coast and the Caribbean on the west. The island was hit violently by two hurricanes in the fall of 1995, but with great courage and perspicacity it has been brought back to a bustling holiday retreat. **St. Martin/St. Maarten is an exciting island if you enjoy scuba diving, dining, shopping, gambling (10 casinos), water sports, beaches and nightclubs.**

ACCOMMODATIONS

All of the hotels are back in operation including the elegant **La Samanna**, (now owned by The Oriental Express Hotel Chain). We had a marvelous luncheon there at their **Terrace Grill**. On our next visit we will definitely spend time there.

We opted to stay on the French side at **Privilege Resort & Spa** (please see Honeymoon and Anniversary chapter for more information) and to dive with **Octoplus**. There are accommodations here to fit any pocketbook from pensions to 5 star resorts to the naturalist retreat **Club Orient**. Most hotels are within a half-hour of the airport.

Purple Spotted Shrimp on Anemone by Lois Hatcher

DIVING

We dived with an extremely safety conscious and well-informed dive operation, **Octoplus**, which is located in Grand Case. It is owned and operated by Florence Cougnow and Jean-Michel Lebret, who are fluent in English, Spanish and French. **They have a full line of diving, snorkeling, and underwater camera equipment available.** Their boat *Deannafa* is a former French lobster boat, measuring 60 feet in length and 18 feet in the beam. It is a traditional vessel with great character and charm that is safe and secure.

A sampling of our favorite dive sites:

Proselyte Reef: Depth: 55 feet. Coral, reef fish, 4 wrecks. One wreck was sunk in 1801 named *The Proselyte*. The three others have been sunk in the last seven years. The *Lucie* is a cargo ship in pieces, with lots of reef fish, scorpion fish, creole wrasse. The *Minnow* is in concrete. Many little reef fish. The *Tiglano* is at 75 feet, and is a cargo ship that is 120 feet long. Here you will find lobster, soldier fish, trumpet fish, parrot fish, creole wrasse, French grunts.

One Step Beyond: Depth: 95 feet. In St. Barth Channel.

Hen & Chickens: Depth: 75 feet. Sometimes you will see shark but stone coral, pompano, jacks, triggerfish, and barracuda are usually present.

Tintamarre: Depth: 45 feet. Wreck and swim through reef. Here you'll see rays, nurse shark, dolphin, reef fish, sergeant major, parrotfish, and southern sennet.

Spanish Rock: Depth: 45 feet. Nurse shark, barracuda, many species of coral, sponges, chromis, wrasse, parrotfish, and angelfish all call this place home.

Cupecoy Reef and Wreck: Depth: 45 feet. *The Gregory*, a cargo ship, is here, as well as barrel sponges, stingray, an occasional nurse shark, reef fish, blue chromis, angelfish.

Grouper: Depth: 45-50 feet. Shark, turtles, rays and groupers, of course

Simpson Bay: Depth: 75 feet. A wreck called *The Bridge* is here where you'll find scorpion fish, and occasionally frogfish, reef fish.

Anguillita: Depth: 90 feet. Here we saw shark, turtles, reef fish, coral, and sponges.

The Creole Rock and Le Re De L'Anse Marcel: Depth: 30-40 feet. This is a shallow dive, but good for refresher and initiation. We saw lots of coral, gorgonia, worms, little reef fish, occasionally spadefish, and queen angelfish.

It was a pleasure diving with Octoplus and we highly recommend their operation.

AREAS OF INTEREST

This is a lovely island and you should book a car for the entire stay. There is a great deal to see and do.

Other than diving and dining, there is excellent shopping in the fascinating capital of **Marigot** on the French side.

Although it was tempting to spend all our time on the French side, we toured the Dutch side. In the capital of Philipsburg one finds bustling **Front Street** with shops, restaurants and casinos.

At **Little Bay** is 300-year-old **Fort Amsterdam**. From here you can view **Fort Willem**. Further out of town is **Great Bay** where visitors can participate in watersports.

BEACHES

There are 36 beaches, free of charge, on the island. Our favorites on the **Dutch side**:

LITTLE BAY BEACH

Calm water and superb snorkeling. There is a beach bar and other activities are available.

SIMPSON BAY BEACH

There are nice long sweeps of sand. It is very private. You can swim, jog or sun and quite often never see a soul.

The most beautiful and private beaches are on the French side.

GRAND CASE BEACH

In the little town of **Grand Case** you will find this lovely long white sand beach with crystal clear waters. You will also find some of the finest restaurants in the Caribbean.

SCUBA AND SNORKELING FACILITIES QUESTIONNAIRE

NAME: **Octoplus Dive Center And Diving Cruises**
ADDRESS: **15 BVD De Grand Case B P 5072**
97070 St. Martin Cedex E.W.I.

TELEPHONE: **011-(590)-87-20-62**   FAX: **011-(590)-87-20-63**
CAPITOL: **Marigot**   GOVERNMENT: **French**
POPULATION: **33,000 (St. Martin)**   LANGUAGE: **French/English**
CURRENCY: **French francs/US Dollars**   ELECTRICITY: **220 V/ 110**
AIRLINES: **A.A. & others**   DEPARTURE TAX? **$15.00 (airport on the Dutch side**
NEED VISA/PASSPORT? **Yes, Passport**   PROOF OF CITIZENSHIP?

YOUR FACILITY IS QUALIFIED AS: **Scuba Center**
BUISINESS HOURS: **8:30 am - 6:00 pm**
CERTIFYING AGENCIES:
LOG BOOK REQUIRED? **Yes**
EQUIPMENT: Rentals, Airfills
PRIMARY LINE OF EQUIPMENT: **Sherwood, Seaquest, Spirotechnique (equipment renewed regularly)**
PHOTOGRAPHIC EQUIPMENT:
CHARTER/DIVE BOAT AVAILABLE? **Yes**   DIVER CAPACITY: **12 (live aboard 8)**
COAST GUARD APPROVED? **Yes**   CAPTAIN LICENSE? **Yes**
SHIP TO SHORE?   LORAN ? **no GPS**   RADAR   ? **Yes**
DIVE MASTER/INSTRUCTOR ABOARD? **Yes, Both**
DIVING & SNORKELING: **Salt**   TYPE OF DIVING/SNORKELING IN AREA? **Wreck, Reef**
DIVING/SNORKELING IN YOUR AREA IS BEST SUITED FOR: BEGINNER **X** INTERMEDIATE **X** ADVANCED **X**
BEST TIME OF YEAR FOR DIVING/SNORKELING: **Dec - Aug**
TEMPERATURE: **NOV-APRIL   82 F** MAY-OCT: **86 F**
VISIBILITY: **DIVING   60 FT   SNORKELING: 60 FT**
PACKAGES AVAILABLE: **Dive, Divestay, Snorkel, Snorkelstay**
ACCOMMODATIONS NEARBY: **Hotel, Motel**
ACCOMMODATIONS RATES: **Expensive, Moderate**
RESTAURANTS NEARBY: **Expensive, Moderate**
YOUR AREA IS: **Quiet with Activities, Lively**
LOCAL ACTIVITY/NIGHTLIFE: **Restaurants, Village, Beach, Rock & Roll Cafe**
CAR NEEDED TO EXPLORE AREA? **Yes**
DUTY FREE SHOPPING? **Yes**
LOCAL EMERGENCY SERVICES: **Yes**
NEAREST HYPERBARIC TREATMENT FACILITY: **Saba**
Guadeloupe
COASTGUARD : **Smur DiLoriot**   AUTHORITY: **Police 87 50 04/ Gendarnerie 87 50 10**
TELEPHONE: **(011 590) 87 26 91**   LOCATION: **Marioot & Grand Case**
CALLSIGNS: **TELEPHONE:**
LOCAL DIVING DOCTOR: **Neighboring the dive center**   TELEPHONE: **011 590 87 52 33**
NAME: **Yves Taveau**
LOCATION: **Grand Case**

COCONUT GROVE

A long stretch of shaded beach; this was our very favorite. Here you walk for miles without seeing another person. **Good for snorkeling and refreshments.**

ORIENT BAY

If you are looking for action, head for this spot. There are lots of people, food, drink and watersports. **Snorkel trips are also offered.** Here one also finds **some of the best diving in the Caribbean.**

Mullet Bay is shady and very popular on the weekends **Cupecoy** is bordered by cliffs, **Anse Marcel** has calm waters and **Palm Bay** is isolated and home to a variety of birds.

DINING

The island has over two hundred restaurants. They range from very expensive, calm and intimate, refined and chic, to simple and fun.

Other than **La Sammanna**, we can recommend **L'Astrolabe** at the Esmeralda Resort. The **Miico** for breakfast and **La Louisiane** for lunch, located at Marcel Cove, and the **Fish Pot Village Cafe** in Grand Case.

For more information on the island contact Ms. Bernadette Davis, the director of the **Office of Tourism** (Port de Marigot, 957150 Saint Martin Tel. 590-87-57 21/23). She and her staff are most helpful.

St. Lucia

"The Helen of the West Indies"

Wendy Canning Church

St. Lucia is located in the Windward Islands between Martinique and St. Vincent. One can see both on a clear day. Fondly referred to as "The Helen of the West Indies" and no wonder—her comeliness is as perfect as Helen's and will be indelibly imprinted on your vignette of travel memories.

Its capitol is Castries. An almond shaped island, St. Lucia's 238 square miles are mountainous with abundant vegetation, sheltered palm fringed beaches (many accessible only by boat), and rich, fertile agricultural land surrounds the glistening coast. For sheer physical beauty, the area around the Pitons is breathtaking.

The first settlers in St. Lucia were the peace loving Arawaks who arrived from South America in 900 BC. The warring Caribs arrived in the 16th century, slaughtering most of the Arawaks, and taking their women as slaves. During this time pirates used its caves and inlets for hideaways.

Some say Columbus discovered St. Lucia on his fourth journey to the Americas while others give Juan La Cosa credit for landing in 1499 with a contingent of sailors after his ship was wrecked.

The first to colonize the island were the British landing at Vieux Fort in 1605 on the ship, *Olive Branch*. They drove the Arawaks out. France and England fought over St. Lucia and this little island changed hands 14 times during the 17th and 18th century. When Napoleon fell so did French rule to the British. St. Lucia became part of the Windward Islands governed by Barbados.

Slaves gained their freedom in 1838. In 1979 St. Lucia gained her independence, becoming a member of the British Commonwealth. Although St. Lucia is the largest English speaking island in the Windwards, you will hear many of its 150,000 natives speaking patois, a mixture of African and French. 90% are practicing Catholics.

Brought from India in the mid-1900's, bananas are a major source of revenue. Referred to as "green gold", they are scientifically classified as an herb, and account for 80% of St. Lucia's revenue with the largest importer being England.

Towing Wreck of The Lesleen M by P. Jackson

Tourism is booming and why not? With so much to offer and a year round subtropical climate cooled by the tradewinds, and accommodations in all price ranges offering a smorgasbord of activities, St. Lucia is a good choice for travelers who want to "lime" or "lyme", a local word for kickback and relax.

The currency is the East Caribbean dollar. A valid passport is needed to enter. **American Airlines is the major carrier from North America.** There is a departure tax.

Many thanks to the St. Lucia Hotel and Tourist Association that provided a wealth of information. The local number is 452-5978.

ACCOMMODATIONS

The **Wyndham Morgan Bay Resort** is located on the northeastern coast, a short drive from Vigie Airport. Her 32 acres are tucked away overlooking a chalk white sand beach on Choc Bay. **Despite its size, this all inclusive property built in 1992, resembles more a charming rambling summer resort in Maine than a Caribbean hideaway.** What gives it's West Indian origin away are muted melon buildings with rose colored doors and white lattice gazebos that lead to upper floors. The grounds, meticulously maintained, are a mélange of tropical plantings. As the visitor strolls from the fitness center or to the tennis courts, coconuts, bananas, and calabash trees come into view intermingled with hibiscus and bird of paradise plants.

Two hundred forty rooms in eight buildings each with three floors are cradled in this nature's wonderland. All rooms are air conditioned with private terraces, direct dial telephone, TV, marble bathroom replete with herbal toiletries and hairdryer. A nice touch is the coffeepot and basket of teas, sugar and cream for early risers and those taking afternoon tea.

The hotel incorporates the culture of St. Lucia not only in entertainment provided but the native vendors' market on the premises, and a lady resembling your grandmother who sits at a discreet table at luncheon selling homemade jams and jellies.

The tasteful boutique sells Sea Island Cotton wraps, designer clothing, straw hats, liquor, newspapers and sundries.

Athletic facilities include: watersports with free instruction, water skiing, windsurfing, sailing, pedal boats, scuba lessons in the pool, fitness center with free instruction, aerobics, steam room, sauna, jacuzzi, volleyball, lawn croquet, badminton, archery, horseback riding (additional charge), table tennis, swimming pool, deep sea fishing, scuba diving (additional charge) and snorkeling.

Other guest services include baby-sitting, car rental, Kid's Klub, safe deposit boxes, laundry/valet, tour desks, currency exchange and Wedding Packages.

Meals are plentiful and prepared with the freshest of fruits and vegetables, many of which are grown on the property. The diner <u>always</u> has a choice of meat, poultry, or fresh fish. The chef takes great care to present these in a delicious but nutritious manner so that guests don't feel guilty when helping themselves to a "little extra". At each meal a local dish is also included.

Their Tradewinds restaurant serves breakfast and dinner buffet style, while a live in-house Caribbean band entertains. Dress code is casual/elegant. At the Palm Grill on the beach one may take luncheon or dinner in a more casual atmosphere. The Beach Bar serves hamburgers, hot-dogs and sandwiches. Tea is served here from 3-5.

At The Sundowner next to the pool one will find the action if they are looking for mixed drinks or nightly entertainment.

Under the direction of the most capable Dermot Connelly who comes to Wyndham from Walkers Cay in the Bahamas, the entire resort is run with clockwork precision yet in a totally relaxed holiday atmosphere.

Who cultivates the exotic plantings? Who knows? Who keeps the beach pristine and the public areas immaculate? Who knows? By some strange miracle all these tasks are accomplished in an unobtrusive manner, yet when a guest needs service, a staff member is at hand ready to grant it, always with a smile as wide as the Pitons are high. Here is a resort that exceeds their motto, "The Right Way, The Wyndham Way".

The all-inclusive price includes round-trip transfers, room taxes and all gratuities, air conditioned rooms with private balconies and terraces, all meals, all beverages including premium brands, live entertainment nightly, beach and watersports.

For more information contact:

Wyndham Morgan Bay Resort
St. Lucia, WI
P.O. Box 2167 Gross Islet
Phone: 758-450-2511
Fax: 758-450-1050

Please see Honeymoon and Anniversary Section for information on the Jalousie Hilton Resort and Spa.

THE SCUBA DIVING & SNORKELING

Dive Fair Helen; is a small operation noted for their small groups, flexibility and safety. It is owned and operated by Andre St. Omer, a native of St. Lucia, with two instructors and 1 boatman.

Specializing in a wide range of scuba courses, environmental education and land and sea ecology/historical tours, **Dive Fair Helen offers excursions for passengers, snorkelers, beginning scuba and certified divers.**

Andre, a marine biologist, was with the Ministry of Agriculture and Fishing for 10 years and is responsible for the inception of the Marine Reserve Park and helping establish safety regulations for dive operators to follow in St. Lucia. He is also an underwater photographer and his newest project is making a documentary for the Grenadine region to educate those in authority to "save our seas".

Since St. Lucia is known as the "Helen of the West Indies", Andre named his operation Dive Fair Helen after Helen of Troy, because he feels that so much of her underwater remains untouched and pristine. All his staff wears green to symbolize the complete interaction of nature both above and beneath the water.

It was not just the high safety standards or first rate service or considerable empressment that kept us diving with Andre along with divers whose own hotels included

diving in their rate. It was their love of and respect for the water that Andre and each of his crew shared with us. We all came away with a deeper understanding imparted not by word but rather example of how precious and fragile the underwater world is. We are only visitors and should behave accordingly.

The following are just a sampling of dive sites they offer:

LESLEEN M

Lesleen M off Anse Couchon is a 165-foot freighter sunk in 1986 by Andre and marine biologist Keith Nicholas to create an artificial reef. She sits upright in 65 feet of calm waters on a flat sandy bottom. Divers can descend to her decks at 30 feet by a rope. Visibility ranges from 20 to 80 feet. These conditions make it a site for all levels and ideal conditions for a night dive. **An extra-added attraction is that she can be penetrated.**

It would take pages to list the myriad of marine life that teems about her exterior and interior. On her bow immense branches of flowering white telesto sway to and fro along with a profusion of black coral. Her bones are decorated with all hues of gorgonia, tunicates, rainbow colored hard and soft corals and brilliantly blazing sponges — lavender vase and vivid mustard yellow.

How Green Grows My Garden courtesy of Jalousie Hilton Resort and Spa

A resident pea green moray eel calls *The Lesleen M* home. If a visitor to his home is lucky he or she will come out of one of the many coral encrusted crevices. Undulating, it displays its elongated body. **This is a must dive.**

WEST POINT

West Point is a good site for macro photography. It is located off Anse Couchon and is a vibrant coral garden, a private comely playground for diminutive fish: blue shrimp, orange, white and black dusky squirrelfish, neon gobies, yellow and light blue honeycomb cowfish, black and yellow trunkfish, gray and black jackknife spotted drum, and the blue, gray and brown peacock flounder. The barrel sponges, each unique in coloration and configuration, look as if they had been thrown on a potter's wheel.

Snorkelers are welcomed on the boat and some joined us for our trip to Soufriere. While they snorkeled at a nearby beach we dived two sites off Rachet Point, Fairlyland and Big Reef. Our maximum depth was 60 feet but is was tempting to descend further to take in the bountiful world of sea life growing on the coral walls. Most of the reef fish could be accounted for but it was the topography that was magnificent.

VIRGIN POINT

At Virgin Point off Anse Couchon we dived shallow for 50 minutes. Aptly named, this site is a microcosm of underwater topography in St. Lucia. We drifted over for what seemed an eternity of ribbon, club finger, yellow pencil pillar, butterprint, sheet, and scroll coral, viewing them and the reef below swarming with ever so many smaller fish living in these habitats. Look for the blazing orange sponge shaped like catcher's mitts swaying among the coral as if ready to catch the third strike.

AREAS OF INTEREST

Castries, the maze-like capitol of St. Lucia, is the main port and largest city on the island. The town was founded in the 18th century by the French, and completely destroyed by fire four times, most recently in 1948. The Central Market offers shoppers local crafts, as well as a marvelous selection of fresh herbs and spices.

Gros Islet comprises not much more than a few blocks, but on Friday nights, it's the most exciting place on the island. This is the home of the "Jump Up", a weekly party, which practically everyone on the island attends.

Marigot Bay framed on three sides by steep emerald hills, and skirted by coconut palms offers one of the safest natural hurricane shelters in the Caribbean. There are Customs and Immigration facilities here. Marigot Bay is an important center for charter boats.

Morne Fortune ("Hill of Good Fortune") rises over the south side of Castries. The road winding up its slopes affords visitors many sensational vistas of the city and harbor below. There are several artists' workshops in this area that are open to the public, including the famous Bagshaw Studios and Caribelle Batik Factory.

Just south of Soufriere are the twin peaks known as The Pitons. Gros Piton rises to 2,619 feet, while Petit Piton looms 2,460 above sea level. In between lies Anse des Pitons, a breathtakingly beautiful bay, best seen from the water or by helicopter.

Located just north of Castries Harbor, Pointe Seraphine is a tourist center with duty-free shopping and an information center for visitors.

More than 10% of the island is covered by rain forest. If you'd like to visit it, full-day excursions can be arranged.

Founded in 1746, Soufriere is engagingly out of step with modern times. The fishing village is shabby in a charming way, but the approach into town from the sea could be one of the great moments in sailing. Soufriere actually sits in what was once a volcanic crater.

One of St. Lucia's leading attractions is the natural sulfur springs of Mount Soufriere, a dormant volcano near the town of Soufriere. Sulfur Springs is the only walk-in volcano in the world. The bubbling grayish-yellow mud from these springs is said to have therapeutic characteristics. Visit Diamond Falls Mineral Baths and the Botanical Gardens filled with local flora.

ST. LUCIA TOURIST BOARD
820 SECOND AVENUE
NEW YORK, NY 10017
TEL 212 867 2950

SCUBA AND SNORKELING FACILITIES QUESTIONNAIRE PRIVATE

NAME   **Dive Fair Helen**
ADDRESS   **Vigie Marina**
              P.O. Box 188, Castries, St. Lucia
CONTACT   **Andre N. St. Omer**
TITLE   **Manager/Dive Instructor**
TELEPHONE **758-450-1640**   FAX **758-453-6512**   TELEX
CAPITOL: **Castries**   GOVERNMENT: **Democratic**
POPULATION: **150,000**   LANGUAGE: **English**
CURRENCY: **EC**   ELECTRICITY: **220v 240v**
AIRLINES: **American**   DEPARTURE TAX? **Yes**
NEED VISA/PASSPORT? YES **x** NO   PROOF OF CITIZENSHIP?   YES **x** NO
YOUR FACILITY IS CLASSIFIED AS: SCUBA CENTER **x**   RESORT
BUSINESS HOURS: **8-4 Monday through Saturday**
CERTIFYING AGENCIES: **PADI**
LOG BOOK REQUIRED?   **Yes**   NO
EQUIPMENT: SALES   RENTALS   AIR FILLS
PRIMARY LINE OF EQUIPMENT: **Dacor**
PHOTOGRAPHIC EQUIPMENT: SALES   RENTALS **x**   LAB
CHARTER/DIVE BOAT AVAILABLE?   YES **x**   NO   DIVER CAPACITY **16**
COAST GUARD APPROVED?   YES **x**   NO   CAPTAIN LICENSED? YES   NO **X**
SHIP TO SHORE?   YES **x** NO   LORAN? YES NO   RADAR?   YES   NO **x**
DIVE MASTER/INSTRUCTOR ABOARD? YES   NO   BOTH **x**
DIVING & SNORKELING: SALT **x**   FRESH
TYPE OF DIVING/SNORKELING IN AREA: WALL **x** BEACH **x** WRECK **x** REEF **x** CAVE   ICE
DIVING/SNORKELING IN YOUR AREA IS BEST SUITED FOR: BEGINNER **x** INTERMEDIATE **x** ADVANCED **x**
BEST TIME OF YEAR FOR DIVING/SNORKELING: **All year round. Best time Nov-April**
TEMPERATURE: NOV-APRIL   **78+F**   MAY-OCT: **78+F**
VISIBILITY: DIVING: **150+ FT**   SNORKELING: **100+ FT**

PACKAGES AVAILABLE: DIVE **x**   DIVE STAY   SNORKEL   SNORKEL-STAY
ACCOMMODATIONS NEARBY: HOTEL **x**   MOTEL **X**   HOME RENTALS **x**
ACCOMMODATION RATES: EXPENSIVE **x** MODERATE **x** INEXPENSIVE **x**
RESTAURANTS NEARBY: EXPENSIVE **x** MODERATE **x** INEXPENSIVE **x**
YOUR AREA IS: REMOTE   QUIET WITH ACTIVITIES **x**   LIVELY
LOCAL ACTIVITY/NIGHTLIFE:
CAR NEEDED TO EXPLORE AREA?   YES **x**   NO
DUTY FREE SHOPPING?   YES **x**   NO

LOCAL EMERGENCY SERVICES   NEAREST HYPERBARIC TREATMENT FACILITY
COASTGUARD **St. Lucia Marine Police**   AUTHORITY:
TELEPHONE: **453-0770**   LOCATION: **Barbados**
CALLSIGNS: **None**
TELEPHONE:

LOCAL DIVING DOCTOR:
NAME: **Dr. Didier**
LOCATION: **Soufriere, St. Lucia**
TELEPHONE: **453-0900**

Bequia

Joan Iaconetti

Over the years, I have visited more colorful and dramatic sites and wrecks than Bequia has to offer. But while the Little Cayman and the Great Barrier Reef may be richer in aquatic life, Bequia makes up for it with professionally-run safe diving that is truly uncrowded (dive motorboats hold no more than 6 to 8 divers), and many unspoiled sites, sometimes literally just-discovered.

The Grenadines are mini-Tahiti's, everybody's fantasy of what a lush-green-tropical-paradise should be. The fact that the Grenadines are still undeveloped...few hotels bigger than two dozen rooms except for Canouan, very few tourists...is a major draw for the seasoned diver/traveler.

No matter where you stay on Bequia, you can dive with any operator. **The Bequia Beach Club** is somewhat isolated from the main drag in beachside Port Elizabeth, but the German management specializes in divers and diving. Full equipment is available here, but note that **their tanks have European fittings, and at last visit, did not fit USA regulators. However, in a pinch, US tanks can probably be rented from other dive shops.**

Visibility varies, but is never less than 50 feet and often up to 100 on a clear, calm day. During the summer, water temperature can be up to 82 F.; in winter, it is constantly 78 or 80 F. Even on cooler days, I never wear more than a T-shirt under my BC. There's just no necessity for wetsuit or even diveskin here, unless you're supersensitive to chills.

DIVE SITES
DEVIL'S TABLE

It doesn't look like much... a shallow dive, barely 40 feet, a "beginner's" dive, close by in Admiralty Bay near the fort...but it's one of the richest and most accessible sites on Bequia. Arrow crabs, giant schools of damsel fish and sergeant majors, an occasional spiny lobster (most of them are seen on your plate during season), brain and soft corals, nudibranchs, and most every fish seen on that laminated plastic card that's sold in every dive shop. Finally, when you've shown the instructor you can handle it, you'll be taken to visit an 8-foot green moray eel that lives in a sunken tugboat at 90 feet.

WEST CAY, "THE WALL"

Relatively big water makes for a sometimes heart-thumping entry, as you position yourself so that the surge can propel you through a notch in the reef...a reef that is very near the surface.

Often surrounded by swarms of needlefish, you navigate the cut and find yourself in 90 feet of water. You sink slowly along the cay, past all manner of coral hard and soft. The dive is actually a gradual circular ascent around the wall of the cay (a tiny islet, pronounced "key") that is home to numerous species of fish

Eagle Ray by Lois Hatcher

and marine life. Eagle rays, single and mating octopus, nurse sharks, small seahorses, baby squid and the more usual suspects (trumpetfish, angelfish, big-eyed reds, squirrelfish, morays, tile and trunkfish of all sizes) have been spotted regularly on this dive. **Because entry is a bit tricky, West Cay is only available in good weather and after you've already completed 2 or 3 dives with any Bequia operator.** Water is a bit cooler (maybe 75-77 F) than on calmer dives but I never bother with even a diveskin in Bequia, and even on overcast days, visibility is still more than acceptable. Getting back aboard a small dive boat ladder can be a bit challenging in big waves, but assistance is always available if you prefer to remove tank and BC before climbing aboard.

THE BOULDERS, MOONHOLE

Moonhole is a unique, private community of people who live on the south end of Bequia in stone houses with no electricity and no glass in the windows. **Despite the fact you cannot explore this area without an invitation from a resident, the community does welcome snorkelers and divers who come via boat to the bay just east of Shipstern, Bequia's whale-shaped headland.** The water is that impossibly beautiful turquoise, with brain and staghorn coral visible from the surface at 20-30 feet. All the usual Caribbean fish life noted above is present, and **the site is ideal for travel companions who snorkel but don't dive. In fact, snorkelers need only hire a water taxi and arrange to be picked up an hour or two later; it's not necessary to book a dive boat to come here.**

Unlike most snorkel sites, Moonhole is also a good dive site because of the calmness and clarity of the water. Nearby to the east is a site called the **Boulders** (40-60 feet), so named for the giant underwater rocks you can swim among. Here you're diving on Bequia's underwater ledge, and instructors know where to look to show you hiding lobsters, morays, arrow crabs, and spiky pufferfish.

THE BULLET

Often inaccessible because of rough seas or weather, The Bullet is a beachless cay that juts almost straight up, just off Bequia's northeast point. The circular dive takes half an hour to reach by speedboat, but is worth the trip: nurse sharks have been spotted, along with the occasional eagle ray (one lucky boatload even heard whale songs, but this is rare). Abundant coral of all kinds is seen on both the wall of the cay and on the sea floor, and large schools of fish are common.

ACCOMMODATIONS

The Frangipani Hotel: The "Frangi", a Caribbean institution, has five units surrounded by trees and bushes, built of stone with private verandas and bath. Four simple rooms are in the main house, only one with private bath, dive packages available, breakfast included. 11 rooms. Phone (784) 45-83255. AE, MC, V accepted. **Sunsports Dive Shop** is next door and offers packages, snorkeling, and instruction.

Friendship Bay Hotel: A main house on the hill (large terraces, sweeping views) and rooms built of coral stone closer to the beautiful, long, quiet beach. Has it's own tiny dive facility; Moderate to Expensive. 27 rooms. Phone 800-223-6764 locally, (784) 45-83222. AE, MC, V.

Bequia Beach Club: Looking for all the world like a little ski chalet on a tropical beach, the BBC is run by Germans for a mainly German clientele, but welcome others for full- service diving. Moderate. Phone (784) 45-83248. 10 units, AE accepted.

Keegan's Guest House: For those truly on a budget, Keegan's offers family-style West Indian meals, no hot water, and Salvation Army Furnishings. But it's on gorgeous Lower Bay Beach, about a mile stroll from Sunsports. Inexpensive. Phone (784) 45-83530. No credit cards; they prefer travelers checks.

Isola and Julie's GuestHouse: In Port Elizabeth on the main beachfront drag, this simple (no amenities) inn has a good restaurant and some rooms have hot water. Inexpensive to Moderate. 25 rooms. Phone (784) 45-83304, -83323, -83220. No credit cards.

DINING & OTHER ACTIVITIES

All of the restaurants along Admiralty Bay are acceptable, with the best food at **Mac's Pizzeria and Bake Shop. The Porthole** is the place to meet yachties and hard-core sailors from every country imaginable, as is the bar at the **Frangipani**. For quieter atmosphere and good local food, try **Theresa's Restaurant** and **Dawn's Creole**, both on the far end of Lower Bay.

Jump-ups (barbecue/dances) constitute island nightlife: at the **Frangi** on Thursday, and **Friendship Bay Resort** on Saturday.

Hike over to the **La Pompe** area to see Bequia's famous **"two-bow" boats**, being constructed by eye without plan. These are still used for fishing and even whaling; Bequia is one of the only areas where limited whaling, by hand-held harpoon, has Greenpeace's okay.

ST. VINCENT & THE GRENADINES
Tourist Office
801 Second Ave.
New York, NY 10017
Tel 212 687 4981

St. Vincent

"Undiscovered, Unmarred, Unruffled"

Wendy Canning Church

Whether visitors arrive on St. Vincent by plane at E.T. Joshua airport or cruise into its port of entry, Wallilabu Bay, by private yacht, each will be awed by this comely island of 144 square miles cradled in crystalline clear waters, with a topography of lush green vegetation, its hills adorned with tropical plantings. As if this were not enough for any palette, the dramatic waterfalls spilling from the highest points to meet the sea completing the pulchritudinous canvas.

The Windward Island chain, which inciiudes the Grenadines and St. Vincent, lay 1600 miles southeast of Miami.

St. Vincent's proximity to the equator blesses the traveler with a year round temperate climate. Cool months are November to February, while March to June bring dry weather and July to November is the shower season.

The Ciboneys from South America settled Hairoun, or St. Vincent as it was later named, before the Pharaohs ruled the Nile. From there on its history is similar too much of the Caribbean. The peace loving Arawaks arrived but were soon driven out by the warlike Caribs.

When the French and English first took interest in the island there were endless battles between the yellow Caribs and the black Caribs (runaway slaves; shipwreck survivors on their way to the slave markets) who were later freed or sent to Honduras or Belize.

The island changed hands between England and France. Finally the British won out and St. Vincent became a crown colony until 1969 when independence was gained.

Most air travelers reach St. Vincent either through Miami, Barbados or San Juan with a continuing flight on Mustique Airways or American Eagle. U.S. and Canadian citizens need proof of citizenship (birth certificate or passport); all other travelers must provide a valid passport. A return ticket is also required.

Kingstown is the capital where you will find banks, the post office, small shops selling native crafts, and open air markets with fresh fruits, vegtables and fish.

The currency is Eastern Caribbean. Rental cars are available. There is excellent bus service. Taxi rates are fixed. Ferryboats make trips to other nearby islands.

Dress is casually elegant. Please inquire of restaurants to see if jackets and/or ties are required when making reservations.

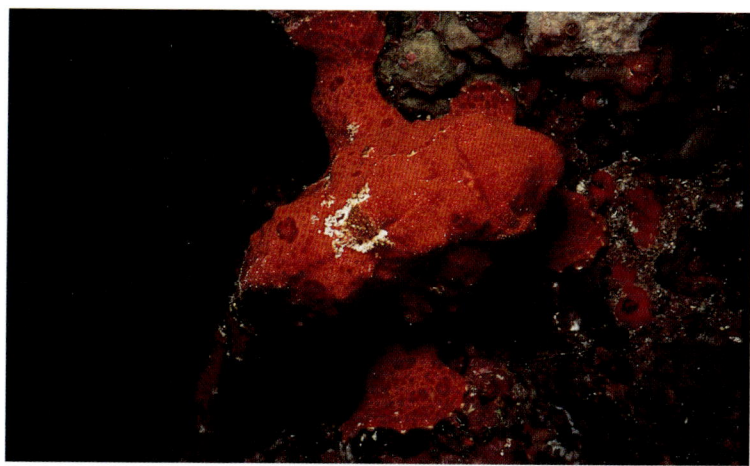

Frogfish by Lois Hatcher

THE SCUBA DIVING AND SNORKELING

There are two operations on the island **Fantasea Tours**, the first and the oldest, and **Dive St. Vincent**, which is owned and operated by Bill Tewes who has been in continuous operation for fifteen years. Many of Bill's superb underwater photographs have been published, and if you purchase postage stamps in St. Vincent you will notice that many are of his beautiful images.

Both operators dive and snorkel the same sites. The moorings are 12'-30' deep and are uasually 20 yards from shore (not always a beach), but dry land for sure. **It works nicely for snorkeling.**

This was our second trip to St. Vincent so we asked Bill and Earl to take us to their favorite dive sites.

• **New Guinea Reef** is a black coral-watcher's dream. All three types of black coral proliferate here and are interspersed with bright lemon yellow sponges...what drama. With wondrous overhangs at depths of 25 to 59 feet, a profusion of soft corals decorate the entire area. Sea horses of many colors drifrt lazily through the scene along with black shrimp.

PERFECT FOR EXPERIENCED SNORKELERS

• **Bottle Reef** is a combination of a wall and coral garden dive site, with a touch of St. Vincent history for spice. **Uncountable fish watch over a collection of antique gin and rum bottles tossed down from the English fort overlooking the site.** If you are keen eyed, you might find one.

BEAUTIFUL SITE FOR BOTH DIVERS AND SNORKELERS

• At **The Forest**, divers swim amid giant gorgonians, 6 to 10 feet tall. The effect is like drifting through a forest of trees inhabited by fish instead of birds. **You might spot an orange or yellow frogfish.**

LOVELY AREA FOR SNORKELERS

• **The Gardens** slope from 25 to 125 feet and **are** an idyllic spot where thousands of fish "grow" in every conceivable color. **A beautiful array of small corals and black coral makes the site perfect for photography.**

PERFECT FOR BEGINNING SNORKELERS – CALM AND SHELTERED

• **The Wall** starts at 20 feet and drops steeply to oblivion. Encrusted with black coral and heavily populated with fish, the area offers unlimited variety. The dive is finished up in the shallow to explore a pristine coral garden. Maximum depth is 100 feet. **Keep an eye out for the rare cherubfish. It is the smallest angelfish at only one and one half inches in length.**

ANOTHER GREAT SITE FOR ADVANCED SNORKELERS

- **The Falls of Baleine (French for whales) are a must dive/snorkel trip.** You can do one, two, or no dives on the way. It is a very popular outing, as you will see the entire leeward coast of St. Vincent, including the volcano. The sixty feet falls are about 100 yards into the rain forest at the very north end of St. Vincent. The water falls into a natural rock lined pool where you can swim. On the way home, they stop for lunch at a small restaurant in the bush, which serves excellent local food. **Fantasea's boat has a canopy to protect you from sun or rain so we suggest that you book this and other tours with them.**

There are three wrecks lying close to each other in Kingstown Bay. The *Seimstrand* collided with the *Nomad* and both sunk. The *Nomad's* top deck is in fifteen feet of water and the *Seimstrand's* in sixty. An unarmed French warship sits in 105 feet of water, a healthy swim from the others.

Upon descent one swims to her first to investigate an anchor and several cannons. Turning about, the dive continues at the *Nomad* and at the *Seimstrand* which has resplendent sponges over her entire bones.

This can be a tricky dive in heavy currents and is only recommended for experienced divers. Most snorkeling sites can only be reached by boat. The exceptions are those on the leeward side: Mount Wayene Lagoon and Barronaille Bay.

Editors note: The currents in St. Vincent can be quite strong. It is suggested that you dive only with a guide from one of the scuba centers.

ACCOMODATIONS

St. Vincent defers to other islands for glitzy resorts. In lieu of them they offer visitors accommodations to fit any pocketbook, from small boutique hotels catering to guests seeking the utmost privacy with five star service to the smaller, simpler, quality properties and guesthouses.

Camelot Inn is "exclusive and exquisite." It is aptly named, as it is a historic mansion (formerly the residence of the French governor). Nestled among almond, nutmeg and mango trees, ginger, flowering hibiscus, crontas and oleander grow. Perched high above the sea, these scents intermingle with the ocean air and the melange gives one an intoxicating sense of beaty and serenity – truly a fairyland.

Situated in Kingstown Park, overlooking the main harbor (approximately a five-minute drive to Kingstown), it is coveniently located yet far enough away to give the guest a sense of the perfect tranquil holiday haven.

Its twenty-two rooms are lovely: tastefully decorated, replete with personal amenities, fluffy bathrobes, slippers and English toiletries. They are air-conditioned, have telephones, television and wall safe. There are four categories to choose from.

Under the most able management of owner Audrey Ballantyne and her staff, the Inn runs like clockwork. The elegant public areas are welcoming. One can also find a quiet place to read, take a cool drink or enjoy the panoramic views.

The Inn is not directly on the volcanic black beach, but there is a shuttle bus. It has a swimming pool and a state of the art gym and sauna.

Dining here is a true experience no matter where you stay on the island. The cuisine is a blend of international and native and is beautifully prepared and presented. A superb wine list is available, and the service is impeccable. The architect retained the original stonework, thus the diner has a sense of history to compliment their splendid five-course dinner.

Having spent five wonderful days we agree that the **Camelot Inn exemplifies their motto "Exclusive and Exquisite."**

Editors note: Request room #104, or 102-103. They are two bedroom suites. For air reservations:

Mark Carter
Stratton Travel-Mustique Airways
RR1, Box 245
245 Valley Road
Canadensis PA 18325
1-800-526-4789
Fax 717-595-8869
Camelot Inn
P.O. Box 787
Kingstown
St. Vincent and Grenadines
Tel. 784-456-2100
Fax 784-456-2233

The Umbrella Beach Hotel is situated across form Young Island and steps from both the dive shops. The hotel's nine rooms have kitchens, private baths, telephones and patios. **This is a good bet for those on a budget** or who want proximity to the dive shops, airport and Kingstown.

Umbrella Beach Hotel
Villa Beach
St. Vincent and the Grenadines
Tel. 784-458-4651
Fax 784-457-4930

Fantasea Tours owns the **Paradise Hotel**. The accommodations are clean, simple and comfortable: telephones, air-conditioned, and balconies. They offer dive/stay packages.

Paradise Hotel
Villa Beach
Box 1286
St. Vincent and the Grenadines
Tel. 784-457-4795
Fax 784-457-4221

Rosewood Apartment Hotel has six self-catering units with air conditioning, telephone and television. They are nicely furnished and each apartment has its own patio.

Rosewood Apartment Hotel
Box 687
St. Vincent and the Grenadines
Tel/Fax 784-457-5051

Please see Honeymoon and Anniversary Section for Young Island Resort.

DINING

Young Island Resort is a must for the most romantic dinner on St. Vincent. An *African Queen* type ferry will take you across the channel to the private island. The cuisine, wine list and service are five star. Treat yourself to a Vincentian coffee made with local rum and watch the world go by. Steps from the waters edge. Expensive. 809-458-4826.

The French Restaurant has earned a four star rating. It is located directly on the sea in the villa area. This small, open air dining spot serves wonderful French cuisine. Begin with the escagot, which is perfection. Follow with the conch curry lobster flamed in aged brandy. The Bananas Foster are superb with pina colada ice cream. Expensive. 784-458-8221.

Petite Byahaut is reached by boat, as it is four miles from Kingstown harbor. It offers fresh seafood, gourmet and vegetarian cuisine. The boat pickup is at Buccament Bay, 784-457-7008. VAF 68. Moderate.

King Arthur Dining Room At Camelot Inn serves perfectly presented gourmet continental and West Indian cuisine in the dining room or on the Guineviere Terrace. In season there is entertainment on Saturday night. Moderate to expensive.

The Limen Pub is near the Young Island Dock. It serves roti and a native goat curry. Inexpensive.

Surfside Restaurant in Arnos Valle has great pizza and West Indian favorites.

KFC has two locations. One is at the corner of Melville and Greenville Streets, and the KFC uptown is at the corner of James and Bay Streets.

ACTIVITIES

One would be remiss not to hire a car or driver/guide for at least one day and tour this idyllic paradise with its varied terrain. **Your journey will take you to two distinct coastal zones, which divide the island. On the leeward (west) side you will find the palm-fringed beaches,** Cottley Hall, Mount Wynee and Reatins. Great swimming, picnicking, snorkeling and viewing of the fancifully colored underwater kingdom.

A profusion of flora, a visual odyssey is captured on the steep slopes and nature trails at Buccament Valley. It is perfect for hiking, bird watching and picnicking.

Further **among the leeward highway is La Soufriere Volcano. It is 4,049** feet above sea level. This is an arduous hike.

The windward (east) coast is copius and dramatic. The tumultuous Atlantic crashes against the jagged cliffs and on the volcanic lava beaches.

The entire journey begins in Kingstown and takes one hour which gives you time to visit sights nearby.

Kingstown has a beautiful open-air market, which esells native crafts, fruits, vegtables and fish fresh from the sea. Market days are Friday and Saturday, arrive before 10 am. **There are a number of restaurants in town where you can get a light luncheon (We suggest Basil's at the Cobblestone Inn, The Bounty, Sid's Upstairs on Backstreet or BJ's on Bay Street).**

THE BOTANIC GARDENS

Situated in the northern part of town, there are the oldest (established in 1765) botanical gardens in the Americas. Amongst the breadfruit trees (the first breadfruit tree was planted by Captain Bligh of the *HS Bounty*) you might spot the rare St. Vincent parrot.

Fort Charlotte is loacted just outside of Kingstown. It was built in 1806 by the British to fend off the warring Caribs. It is 600 feet above sea level and has views of all south St. Vincent from a Coast Guard lookout post.

The former barracks have been converted into a museum with a pictorial history of the island.

Tennis and Squash can be arranged at the Kingstown Tennis Club if not offered at your hotel.

Massage – Vanessa Layne, a native Vincentian, trained in Miami. She is skilled in all types of massage techniques and will come to your hotel. **Vanessa is highly skilled and a delight.** Tel: 784-458-4270.

Banana Tree Blossoming by Wendy Canning Church

SCUBA AND SNORKELING FACILITIES QUESTIONNAIRE

NAME: **Sunsports**
ADDRESS: **Box 1, Bequia**
St. Vincent & Grenadines
CONTACT: **Bob Monnens**
TITLE: **Owner**
TELEPHONE: **(784) 458-3577**   FAX: **(784) 457-3031**

CAPITOL: **Kingstown**   GOVERNMENT: **St. Vincent & Grenadines**
POPULATION: **105,000**   LANGUAGE: **English**
CURRENCY: **EC $ (Eastern Caribbean)**   ELECTRICITY: **220 V 50 C**
AIRLINES: **Mustique Airway**   DEPARTURE TAX? **$20 EC**
NEED VISA/PASSPORT? **No (Passport recommended)**

YOUR FACILITY IS QUALIFIED AS: **Scuba Center**
BUISINESS HOURS: **8 A.S.T.-5 A.S.T.**
CERTIFYING AGENCIES: **PADI**
LOG BOOK REQUIRED? **No**
EQUIPMENT: **Sales, Rentals, Airfills**
PRIMARY LINE OF EQUIPMENT: **ScubaPro**

CHARTER/DIVE BOAT AVAILABLE? **Yes**   DIVER CAPACITY: **2 boats/8 ea**
COAST GUARD APPROVED? **Yes**   CAPTAIN LICENSE? **No**
SHIP TO SHORE? **Yes**   LORAN? **No**   RADAR? **No**
DIVE MASTER/INSTRUCTOR ABOARD? **Yes**

DIVING & SNORKELING: **Salt**
TYPE OF DIVING/SNORKELING IN AREA? **Wall, Wreck, Reef**
DIVING/SNORKELING IN YOUR AREA IS BEST SUITED FOR: BEGINNER **x** INTERMEDIATE **x** ADVANCED **x**
BEST TIME OF YEAR FOR DIVING/SNORKELING:
TEMPERATURE: NOV-APRIL **80 F**   MAY-OCT: **82 F**
VISIBILITY: DIVING   **100 FT** SNORKELING: **20 F**

PACKAGES AVAILABLE: **Dive, Dive Stay**
ACCOMMODATIONS NEARBY: **Hotel, Home Rentals**
ACCOMMODATIONS RATES: **Expensive, Moderate, Inexpensive**
RESTAURANTS NEARBY: **Expensive, Moderate, Inexpensive**
YOUR AREA IS: **Quiet with Activities**
LOCAL ACTIVITY/NIGHTLIFE: **Local Jump ups, Walking, Day Charters**
CAR NEEDED TO EXPLORE AREA? **No**
DUTY FREE SHOPPING? **No**

LOCAL EMERGENCY SERVICES: NEAREST HYPERBARIC TREATMENT FACILITY:
COASTGUARD: **St. Vincent**   AUTHORITY:
TELEPHONE: **784-457-4578**   LOCATION: **Barbados**
CALLSIGNS: **Juliet Eight Foxtrot**   TELEPHONE: **246-436-6185**

LOCAL DIVING DOCTOR:
NAME: **Dr. Brown**
LOCATION: **Barbados**
TELEPHONE: **246-436-6215**

Our second visit to St. Vincent was more rewarding than our first because we took time out to discover the myriad of natural attractions and interesting history the island offers.

There are a few places left in the world as undiscovered, unmarred and unruffled. St. Vincent can be counted among these.

St. Vincent's/The Grenadines
Tourist Offices
P.O. Box 834, Kingstown
Tel: 784-457-1502
Fax: 784-456-2610

Turks & Caicos

Providenciales

Raymond Elman

Anyone who is well traveled is accustomed to being greeted upon arrival at a new destination by someone saying, "You should have been here 10 years ago, it used to be great." If you want to visit a place that is just about perfect right now, try Providenciales, because right now is Provo's golden era.

Provo is on the cusp of major recognition and development, but it hasn't fallen over the edge yet. What that means is that beaches are still sugar white and empty; waters are crystal clear (up to 250 feet visibility) and unpolluted; coral reefs, walls, and marine life are abundant and not fully explored; the native population is still friendly; and creature comforts and infrastructure are in place.

HISTORY

It's difficult to find a colonial bed in New England that George Washington didn't sleep in, and it's equally difficult to find a Caribbean island that Columbus didn't step upon. He stepped on Grand Turk almost five centuries ago; Lucayan Indians are believed to have been the first people to actually reside on the islands.

In the 16th and 17th centuries the islands provided "cover" for a motley assortment of pirates. Western civilization and slavery arrived in 1678 when Bermudian salt rakers claimed the islands. From 1700 to the late 1800s, Turks & Caicos were claimed by a succession of colonial adventurers - Spain, France, England, and eventually Jamaica annexed the islands. In 1972, ten years after Jamaica became independent, the Queen of England appointed a governor for Turks & Caicos, and they remain an independent crown colony.

Today Turks & Caicos are the proverbial melting pot of nationalities. There are so many Canadians residing on the islands that there have been several efforts launched in the Canadian parliament to make Turks & Caicos a Canadian protectorate.

The Turks & Caicos Islands are 575 miles southeast of Miami. The Bahamas are 30 miles to the northwest, and the Dominican Republic is 100 miles southeast. The nine major islands of Turks & Caicos are clustered in two groups separated by a 22-mile wide channel.

The eastern group is the Turks: Grand Turk and ten cays, including Salt Cay. The western group is the Caicos: North, Middle, East, South, and West Caicos, Providenciales, and 10 cays, including Pine Cay. Encircling the group of islands is a reef that extends for more than 200 miles.

There are international airports on Grand Turk, Providenciales, North Caicos, and South Caicos, and domestic airports on all the inhabited islands.

Air service to Turks & Caicos fluctuates with the rise and fall in the fortune of various airlines. Today, regularly scheduled service from Miami is provided by Ameri-

Villa Camilla

can Airlines. Air Jamaica provides service through Montego Bay, Northwest Airlines flies from Detroit to Provo every Sunday, and Lynx Air International flies in from Fort Lauderdale.

Unquestionably, the best way to get to Provo is by charter flight. We flew GWV charter from Boston (door to door in 3 1/2 hours).

ACCOMMODATIONS

Most of the hotels and condominium establishments are located on or overlooking Grace Bay, a gorgeous 13 mile stretch of white sand and turquoise waters. **At first most of the hostelries were small in size and quaint. Today, however, it is not unusual to find large chains. For example, the Ramada Turquoise Reef Resort and Casino opened to launch the nineties.**

The following hotels either have diving centers on the premises or are located within a snorkel throw of a dive shop:

Ramada Turquoise Reef Resort & Casino (800) 234-7768
Grace Bay Club (649) 946-5050
Le Deck Hotel & Beach Club (800) 223-9815
Ocean Club Condominium Resort (800) 457-8787
Turtle Cove Inn Resort (800) 887-0477

However, the best way to experience Provo is to rent one of the available houses or villas. We rented Villa Camilla, a fantastically well conceived main house and guest house compound right on Grace Bay Beach.

Villa Camilia offers a three bedroom main house with an adjacent two-unit guesthouse. Every bedroom has its own deck facing the water and custom bathroom. We rented the main house with two other couples and had all the privacy we needed. In addition, the main house has a large, comfortable, vaulted ceiling living area on the second floor, flowing around an open atrium, between the kitchen and the dinning area. There are two more decks on the second floor, one facing the sunrise, the other facing the sunset.

During the week we stayed at Villa Camilla there was never an uninvited sole sitting on our beach, and just to the south of our beach was a reef, teeming with marine life, that started in five feet of water and descended to a depth of thirty feet – perfect for both snorkeling and diving.

In fact, one beautiful full-moon-lit night, we finished our dinner, grabbed our diving gear, and climaxed a wonderful evening with a night dive on our "private" reef.

For more information contact Aqua Expeditions (617) 723-7134.

Surprisingly, a week's stay at Villa Camilla costs less than a room for two at a good resort.

DINING

Dining out in Provo has recently come of age, as evidenced by an article in *Gourmet* magazine. Nevertheless, the last time we visited Provo we managed to dine in some restaurants that were adequate, but not great. **So it is wise to select your dining spots carefully.** When we are in the Caribbean, our first criteria for a restaurant is outdoors seating. We can always get great food back home, but outdoor dining is hard to come by in February. My favorite dishes in Provo are anything using conch – I can't seem to get enough of that mollusk – and Provo is one of the few islands with a conch farming operation.

Despite the tempting island restaurants, we opted to eat most breakfasts and lunches at home, and went out to dinner every other night, mainly because we had a fully equipped contemporary kitchen at Villa Camilla (and almost everyone, in our party was capable of preparing an elegant meal).

The restaurants we enjoyed the most were inexpensive and unpretentious. The only places we returned to for more than one experience were:

BANANA BOAT RESTAURANT

A full Caribbean bar & grill overlooking the water on Turtle Cove. We especially enjoyed all of the conch dishes, though everything was well prepared. (Tel: 15706)

TIKI HUT CABANA BAR & GRILL

A great all-around indoor/outdoor restaurant serving breakfast, lunch, and dinner, featuring creative conch dishes. Also located on the water at Turtle Cove Inn. (Tel: 15341)

PUB ON THE BAY

A local favorite in Blue Hills. Order in the restaurant and sit under the tiki huts across the street, which offer great water views. The conch and other native fish dishes are the way to go. (Tel: 15309)

TASTY TEMPTATIONS

Despite the cutesy name, Tasty Temptations, located near the downtown area (Tel: 64049), is a serious French bakery and coffeehouse, managed by French Canadian expatriates. They offer the same quality croissants, breads, pastries, espresso, and cappuccino that you'll find in Montreal.

BELLA LUNA

Owned by Italians who apply Italian magic to native bounty. **They also provide a pretty good disco on weekends for dancing off the extra calories.** (Tel: 65214)

COCO BISTRO

A French owned bistro with indoor / outdoor seating in a coconut grove, featuring Mediterranean cuisine — including Moroccan dishes. (Tel: 65369)

THE DIVING AND SNORKELING

Three of the best dive operators on Provo are:

FLAMINGO DIVERS

P.O. Box 322, Providenciales
Turks & Caicos Islands, B.W.l.
Phone/Fax: (809) 946-4193

PROVO TURTLE DIVERS

Turtle Cove Marina, Providenciales
Phone: (809) 946-4232/4585
Fax: (809) 946-4326/5296

DIVE PROVO
Ramada Turquoise Reef Resort, Providenciales
Phone: (809) 946-5029/5040
Fax: (809) 946-5936
In the USA: 1-800 234-7768

Art Pickering, proprietor of Provo Turtle Divers, is commonly regarded as the God-father of Provo diving, having pioneered SCUBA diving in these waters; he rightfully bills himself as the oldest and most experienced diving operation in the Turks & Caicos Islands. **Nevertheless, during our one-week stay on Provo, we placed a higher value on friendliness and flexibility than on experience, and we found that with Flamingo Divers.**

We told the proprietors of Flamingo Divers, that we wanted to customize our dive package so that we could keep all of their gear at our Villa to enable us to make beach dives on the days that we didn't go out with them on one of their boats. While that concept was a problem for some of the dive operations, it wasn't for Flamingo Divers, and the rates they charged were very reasonable.

They were, extremely friendly and dependable. They allowed their patrons to help choose the dive sites for the week and were not married to a tight time schedule. Some of their gear was a little worn but all was serviceable. It should be noted, however, that ownership of Flamingo Divers has recently changed hands. The new owner is Roger Coon with whom we have no experience.

DIVE SITES

The best known (though by no means fully explored) dive spot in the Turks & Caicos is the West Wall or Northwest Point, which is really hundreds of dive sites along a vertical edge of the Continental Shelf. It's about a 45 minute boat ride to the wall. Some of the named dive sites are:

Black Coral Forest, which starts at 45 feet and descends to about 130 feet, where red gorgonians, elephant ear sponges and black coral trees abound. Eagle rays and sharks have been seen cruising this site.

The Crack, a steep crevice which drops from 50 feet to 100 feet. We met large friendly groupers at this spot that swam right up to our mask and stared us in the eye.

The Plateau, a home for eagle rays, sharks and manta rays in about 60 feet of water.

Closer to where you are likely to be staying on the North Shore, or Grace Bay, are several shallower dive sites, some which can be reached from shore and double as excellent snorkeling spots.

The Aquarium, located right in front of Villa Camilla, features a crescent shaped coral head that begins in about 5 feet of water and gently descends to about 25 feet. The reef hosts a plethora of reef fish, and is frequently visited by schools of barracuda. **This is an excellent dive for beginners and snorkelers, and also a good spot for a night dive.**

Another dive spot close to shore is **Smith's Reef,** which is just beyond the cut that leads to Turtle Cove. This coral head also varies in depth from 5 to 25 feet. It is home to eagle rays, turtles, and an occasional grouper, which makes it **one of Provo's most popular snorkeling spots.**

Pinnacles, which is roughly in front of the Ramada, is an interesting series of coral ridges varying in depth from 35 to 60 feet. At Pinnacles you may find grouper, turtles, eels, and reef fish.

Southwind is an 80-foot long cargo ship resting at 60 feet, which sank in 1985. Its visitors include Nassau groupers and schools of horse-eyed jacks.

WHEN YOU COME UP FOR AIR

There are **tennis** courts at several of the hotels (Ramada, Ocean Club, Turtle Cove, Erebus). The courts at Erebus are open to the public. The first **golf** course on Provo opened in late 1992.

Bill fishing and bone fishing in and around Turks & Caicos is among the best in the world. Anything that can be done with a **sail** on warm water can be done here: windsurfing, para sailing, and sailing.

Two wildlife events not to be missed are feeding iguanas on the uninhabited cays near Provo, and swimming with Jo Jo the dolphin when he makes one of his frequent excursions inside the barrier reef.

Right now is Providenciales golden moment. It has the comforts of the present, while still retaining the charms of the past, and the diving is at the top end of the spectrum.

United States Virgin Islands

"They're Your Islands"

Mike B. Innis

St. Thomas

St. Thomas is probably the most famous of the three American Virgin Islands. It is a major cruise ship port, offers a large selection of duty-free merchandise to the visitors, and is probably more like "America" than its sister islands of St. John and St. Croix.

The capital, Charlotte Amalie, is a busy, hustling, bustling city, with a pace of life more like Ft. Lauderdale than the stereotypical tropical island. I stayed at the **Bolongo Bay Beach Club and Villas.** My bayside room was very nice; clean, roomy, had a great view; and the staff were courteous and helpful.

Food and service at the Bolongo were quite good. I had breakfast and lunch there, then for dinner wandered to **Mim's,** just a short stroll down the beach from the hotel. Definitely a laid-back ambiance, yet the service was prompt and attentive, the view was good and the food was tasty.

The first morning I took a taxi to the Renaissance Grand Beach Hotel and dived with Chris Sawyer, owner of **Chris Sawyer Diving Center.** Chris and his team did a superlative job, giving us a very thorough boat orientation, as well as in depth pre-dive briefings. The boat is Coast Guard certified and has all the safety bells and whistles one could hope for to ensure a safe dive. Chris and one of his divemasters were in the water with us on both dives, while the captain monitored things from the surface.

Our first dive, on **Grass Cay,** dispelled any doubts I may have had about the health of the reefs! It was alive with representatives from the entire food chain: from the tiniest baitfish to the barracuda.

Our next dive was a drift dive at **Mingo Pass.** The current wasn't exactly ripping that day, making for a very calm drift dive, but again the health of the ecosystem was abundantly evident.

The next day I was scheduled to do another local, St. Thomas area dive, with the dive operation located at Bolongo, **St. Thomas Diving Club.** I was informed that, instead of a local dive, plans had been changed and **the dive boat was going to the wreck of the H.M.S. *Rhone*, off Salt Island in the British Virgin Islands. Having dived this world class wreck before, I was not broken hearted with the plan change. And, sure enough, the Rhone provide two good dives for us, even though she's 130 years old!**

Andre Webster, the boat captain for STDC, has been diving the Virgin Islands for 20 years, and his divemaster, Michael, is a marine biologist. These two guys handled any questions about what that "funny looking fish with the big eyes and long dorsal fin" promptly and professionally. The boat, a large, stable catamaran pushed along by a pair of 200HP outboards, zipped us around the islands in speed and safety.

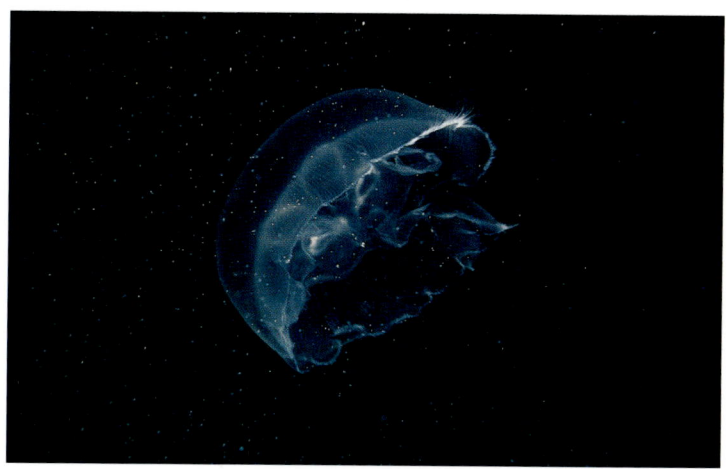

Jellyfish by Peter Jackson

St. John

On the return trip from the Rhone, I was dropped off at St. John, the next island on my itinerary, and taxied to **Gallows Point Resort**. Gallows Point is one of the nicer (more expensive) places at which to stay on St. John. The rooms are really condominiums, with full kitchens and fabulous views. The bathroom was huge; the shower could sleep six comfortably, and shower 10 good friends with no problem at all! For reservations contact:

Aqua Expeditions
92 Mt. Vernon Street
Boston, MA 02108
Fax: 617-227-8145

Dinner at the on-site 3 star restaurant was excellent, but a bit pricey; still a welcome change to the more common and less expensive eateries I had experienced. The next night I ate at a "real" Tex Mex place that had an excellent reputation with the divemasters. It was a lively, upbeat place, and, as a native Texan, I can tell you that the food was as close to Tex Mex as you're going to get outside Austin!

My dive hosts in St. John were Marcus and Patty Johnston, who own and operate **Cruz Bay Watersports**. Leaving from the National Park Service Docks, their 42 foot vessel took us comfortably to our first dive site, **Carvell Rock. This is truly a world class dive, and has been used by the National Geographic Society as a filming site.** We moored on the lee side, dropped over the side into a virtual cloud of bait fish, fought our way through their kingdom, and reached a cut through the Rock which put us onto the windward side. A series of mini-walls and the sheer face of the rock itself provided spectacular vistas and flora and fauna enough to keep the hardest of hard cores happy. We circumnavigated the Rock and surfaced, excited and very happy at the dive boat.

Our second dive took us to **Mingo Pass** again, but, like most sites, they change from day to day, even hour to hour, and the dive was super. Upon our return to St. John, Patty offered me a tour of the new Westin (old Hyatt) hotel site, which was closed down after Hurricane Marilyn in 1995. This hotel was the base site for Cruz Bay Watersports, and they are looking forward to the grand reopening, scheduled for 1998. Cruz Bay has a couple of large compressors and a well-laid out repair facility on the grounds of the new Westin.

SCUBA AND SNORKELING QUESTIONNAIRE

NAME: **St. Thomas Diving Club**
ADDRESS: **7147 Bolongo Bay**
               St. Thomas, VI 00802
CONTACT: **Bill Letts**
TITLE: **Owner**
TELEPHONE: **809-776-2381**   FAX   **809-777-3232**   TELEX

CAPITOL   CHARLOTTE AMALIE   GOVERNMENT: **US**
POPULATION: 50,000   LANGUAGE: **English**
CURRENCY: US   ELECTRICITY: **110**
AIRLINES: **AA, Delta**   DEPARTURE TAX? **No**
NEED VISA/PASSPORT   YES   NO x   PROOF OF CITIZENSHIP? YES x   NO

YOUR FACILITY IS CLASSIFIED AS: SCUBA CENTER x   RESORT
BUSINESS HOURS: **8:00am - 5:30pm**
CERTIFYING AGENCIES: **PADI**
LOG BOOK REQUIRED?   YES   NO x
EQUIPMENT: SALES x   RENTALS x AIR FILLS x
PRIMARY LINE OF EQUIPMENT?   **Sherwood**
PHOTOGRAPHIC EQUIPMENT: SALES   RENTALS x LAB

CHARTER/DIVE BOAT AVAILABLE?   YES x   NO   DIVER CAPACITY 18
COAST GUARD APPROVED?   YES x   NO   CAPTAIN LICENSED?   YES x   NO
SHIP TO SHORE?   YES x   NO   LORAN? YES NO x   RADAR?   YES   NO x
DIVE MASTER/INSTRUCTOR ABOARD? YES x   NO   BOTH

DIVING AND SNORKELING: SALT x   FRESH
TYPE OF DIVING/SNORKELING IN AREA: WALL BEACH x   WRECK x   REEF x   CAVE   ICE
DIVING/SNORKELING IN YOUR AREA IS BEST SUITED FOR: BEGINNER x INTERMEDIATE x ADVANCED x
BEST TIME OF YEAR FOR DIVING/SNORKELING:
TEMPERATURE: NOV-APRIL: **79F**   MAY-OCT.   **82F**
VISIBILITY: DIVING: **80-100Ft.** SNORKELING **80Ft.**

PACKAGES AVAILABLE: DIVE x   DIVE STAY   SNORKEL   SNORKEL STAY
ACCOMMODATIONS NEARBY: HOTEL x   MOTEL   HOME RENTALS
ACCOMMODATION RATES: EXPENSIVE MODERATE x   INEXPENSIVE
RESTAURANTS NEARBY: EXPENSIVE MODERATE x   INEXPENSIVE
YOUR AREA IS: REMOTE   QUIET WITH ACTIVITIES   x   LIVELY
LOCAL ACTIVITY/NIGHTLIFE: **Theme nights at resort/dancing/bars**
CAR NEEDED TO EXPLORE AREA: YES x   NO
DUTY FREE SHOPPING: YES x   NO

LOCAL EMERGENCY SERVICES: NEAREST HYPERBARIC TREATMENT FACILITY:
COAST GUARD: **USCG Auxiliary**   AUTHORITY: **St. Thomas Hyperbaric Chamber**
TELEPHONE: **809-774-6663**   LOCATION: **St. Thomas Hospital**
CALLSIGNS: **Monitor VHF #16**   TELEPHONE: **809-776-2686**

LOCAL DIVING DOCTOR:
NAME: **Dr. David Boaz**
LOCATION: **St. Thomas Hyperbaric Chamber**
TELEPHONE: **809-776-2686**

St. Croix

St. Croix was the final island on my itinerary, and I reached it by taking a ferry to St. Thomas and the hydrofoil from St. Thomas to St. Croix, largest of the USVI's. I'd not ridden on a hydrofoil before, and it's definitely an experience. You're encapsulated in this long, thin tube, with big windows and efficient air conditioning, and you blast out of the harbor, up onto the machine's foils, and go skimming across the water at incredible speeds. It feels almost like a roller-coaster ride; it definitely does not feel like any boat I've ever been on! An hour and a half later, you're in Croix. You need to take a ride if you've never done one.

Anow Crab by Mike Innis

On St. Croix, I stayed at the **Caravelle**, an old fashioned, downtown type of place. I was within walking distance of several restaurants and shopping areas, and the dive storage locker for **V.I. Divers, Ltd.**, had a walk through, right onto the patio area of the hotel. It could not have been more convenient.

Bright and early the next morning, I signed the obligatory releases, loaded my gear, and around 9am we got underway for the first dive site, **Salt River Wall**. Again, there was no sign of damage to the reef or wall, and we swam through the usual variety of USVI scenery.

On the next dive, a mini-wall a few hundred yards away, we did a shallow dive, but got to see a good sized green turtle that performed nicely, giving us a couple of strafing runs before heading out to sea.

Next day was designated a **"Wreck Day."** We took a fairly long boat ride (50 minutes) to the far end of the island to Butler's Bay, where several wrecks have been put down for the benefit of the divers and fishermen. The first was the wreck of the *Rosaomaira*. Sitting perfectly upright in 100 feet of water, she offered good photo opportunities and an abundance of sea life.

From there, we motored a quarter of a mile and latched onto another buoy in shallower water where a couple of ships, a barge, and the remains of an old **HydroLab** lay awaiting us.

That evening, I took a night dive with VI Divers, and could not have asked for more: a sleeping turtle, puffer fish, stone fish, octopus; I ran out of film long before I ran out of air!

The final day I dived **Scotch Wall** and **Sleeping Shark Canyon** - good dives and very short boat rides from the dock.

I ate breakfast at the hotel every day, and dinner on one evening. Lunch was normally at a place called the **Alley Galley**, which served up the largest deli sandwiches, you've ever sunk a tooth into. Dinner at **Tivoli Gardens** was quite good; one evening meal at **Styxx**, which was also excellent and moderately priced. Dinner at the **Bombay Club**, was kind of neat experience, since you're dining in an atmosphere that resembles a catacomb of some sort.

Of the three islands, I **enjoyed St. Croix the most**. And the thing I liked about Croix the most was the **variety of diving available: reefs, wrecks, and REAL WALLS!** How about a 13,200 foot wall to play around on! On the other two islands, the reefs were healthy and the fish life was abundant; but to get below 80 feet, you had to bring your own shovel and dig like mad. I sort of like the feeling of swimming out over the edge of a wall and peering down into the blue-purpleness and wondering what's down there! But certainly, **for the person looking for great diving and not wanting to take their money offshore, any of the USVI's would be excellent choices.**

SCUBA AND SNORKELING QUESTIONNAIRE

NAME: **Chris Sawyer Diving Center**
ADDRESS: **Suite 29, 6300 Frydenhij**
St. Thomas, USVI 00862-1411
CONTACT: **Marge Garcia**
TITLE: **Office Manager**
TELEPHONE: **809-775-7320** FAX **809-775-9495** TELEX

CAPITOL: **Charlotte Amalie**   GOVERNMENT: **United States**
POPULATION: **56,000**   LANGUAGE: **English**
CURRENCY: **US dollars**   ELECTRICITY: **110v**
AIRLINES: **AA, Delta**   DEPARTURE TAX? **No**
NEED VISA/PASSPORT YES NO x   PROOF OF CITIZENSHIP? YES x NO

YOUR FACILITY IS CLASSIFIED AS: SCUBA CENTER x   RESORT x
BUSINESS HOURS: **8:30am - 5:30pm**
CERTIFYING AGENCIES: **PADI, NAUI, NASDS**
LOG BOOK REQUIRED? YES x NO
EQUIPMENT: SALES x   RENTALS x AIR FILLS x
PRIMARY LINE OF EQUIPMENT? **Sherwood, US Divers, Sea Quest, Mares**
PHOTOGRAPHIC EQUIPMENT: SALES   RENTALS   LAB

CHARTER/DIVE BOAT AVAILABLE? YES x NO   DIVER CAPACITY **12**
COAST GUARD APPROVED? YES x NO   CAPTAIN LICENSED? YES x NO
SHIP TO SHORE? YES x NO   LORAN? YES NO x   RADAR? YES NO x
DIVE MASTER/INSTRUCTOR ABOARD? YES x   NO BOTH

DIVING AND SNORKELING: SALT x FRESH
TYPE OF DIVING/SNORKELING IN AREA: WALL BEACH x WRECK x REEF x CAVE x ICE
DIVING/SNORKELING IN YOUR AREA IS BEST SUITED FOR: BEGINNER X INTERMEDIATE X ADVANCED X
BEST TIME OF YEAR FOR DIVING/SNORKELING: YEAR AROUND
TEMPERATURE: NOV-APRIL: **77F**   MAY-OCT. **80F**
VISIBILITY: DIVING: **65-70Ft.** SNORKELING **65-70Ft.**

PACKAGES AVAILABLE: DIVE x   DIVE STAY x SNORKEL x   SNORKEL STAY
ACCOMMODATIONS NEARBY: HOTEL x   MOTEL   HOME RENTALS x
ACCOMMODATION RATES: EXPENSIVE x MODERATE x INEXPENSIVE x
RESTAURANTS NEARBY: EXPENSIVE x MODERATE x INEXPENSIVE x
YOUR AREA IS: REMOTE   QUIET WITH ACTIVITIES x   LIVELY
LOCAL ACTIVITY/NIGHTLIFE: **Nightclubs, restaurants**
CAR NEEDED TO EXPLORE AREA: YES   NO x
DUTY FREE SHOPPING: YES x NO

LOCAL EMERGENCY SERVICES: NEAREST HYPERBARIC TREATMENT FACILITY:
COAST GUARD: AUTHORITY:
TELEPHONE: LOCATION: **St. Thomas Hospital**
CALLSIGNS: TELEPHONE: **809-776-2686**
LOCAL DIVING DOCTOR:
NAME: **Dr. David Boaz**
LOCATION: **St. Thomas**
TELEPHONE: **809-774-8998, Chamber 776-2680**

SCUBA AND SNORKELING QUESTIONNAIRE

NAME: **Cruz Bay Watersports**
ADDRESS: **P.O. Box 252**
St. John, USVI 00831
CONTACT: **Marcus and Patty Johnston**
TITLE: **Owner/Operators**
TELEPHONE: **809-776-6234 779-4351** FAX **809-693-8720** TELEX **800-835-7730**
CAPITOL: GOVERNMENT: **US**
POPULATION: 2500 LANGUAGE: **English**
CURRENCY: **US** ELECTRICITY: **yes**
AIRLINES: **Many** DEPARTURE TAX? NO
NEED VISA/PASSPORT YES **x** NO PROOF OF CITIZENSHIP? YES **x** NO

YOUR FACILITY IS CLASSIFIED AS: SCUBA CENTER **x** RESORT **x**
BUSINESS HOURS: 8AM - 6PM
CERTIFYING AGENCIES: **PADI, NAUI**
LOG BOOK REQUIRED? **Yes but not mandatory** NO
EQUIPMENT: SALES **x** RENTALS **x** AIR FILLS **x**
PRIMARY LINE OF EQUIPMENT?
PHOTOGRAPHIC EQUIPMENT: SALES **x** RENTALS **x** LAB **x**

CHARTER/DIVE BOAT AVAILABLE? YES **x** NO DIVER CAPACITY **16**
COAST GUARD APPROVED? YES **x** NO CAPTAIN LICENSED? YES **x** NO
SHIP TO SHORE? YES **x** NO LORAN? YES NO **x** RADAR? YES NO **x**
DIVE MASTER/INSTRUCTOR ABOARD? YES **x** NO BOTH **x**
DIVING AND SNORKELING: SALT **x** FRESH
TYPE OF DIVING/SNORKELING IN AREA: WALL BEACH WRECK REEF **x** CAVE ICE
DIVING/SNORKELING IN YOUR AREA IS BEST SUITED FOR: BEGINNER **x** INTERMEDIATE **x** ADVANCED **x**
BEST TIME OF YEAR FOR DIVING/SNORKELING:
TEMPERATURE: NOV-APRIL: **85-90F** MAY-OCT. **90-95F**
VISIBILITY: DIVING: **60-89Ft.** SNORKELING **40-50Ft.**

PACKAGES AVAILABLE: DIVE **x** DIVE STAY **x** SNORKEL **x** SNORKEL STAY
ACCOMMODATIONS NEARBY: HOTEL **x** SMALL GUEST, INN **x** HOME RENTALS **x**
ACCOMMODATION RATES: EXPENSIVE **x** MODERATE **x** INEXPENSIVE **x**
RESTAURANTS NEARBY: EXPENSIVE **x** MODERATE **x** INEXPENSIVE **x**
YOUR AREA IS: REMOTE QUIET WITH ACTIVITIES **x** LIVELY **x**
LOCAL ACTIVITY/NIGHTLIFE: **Town is loaded with restaurants and small bars**
CAR NEEDED TO EXPLORE AREA: YES **x** NO
DUTY FREE SHOPPING: YES **x** NO

LOCAL EMERGENCY SERVICES: NEAREST HYPERBARIC TREATMENT FACILITY:
COAST GUARD: **St. Thomas** AUTHORITY: **Dr. Boaz**
TELEPHONE: **809-729-6770** LOCATION: **St. Thomas Hospital**
CALLSIGNS: **US Coast Guard St. Thomas** TELEPHONE: **809-776-2686**

LOCAL DIVING DOCTOR: **St. John 776-8311 ext.2226**
NAME: **Dr. Boaz**
LOCATION: **809-776-2686 St. Thomas**
TELEPHONE: **809-776-8311 St. John**

SCUBA AND SNORKELING QUESTIONNAIRE

NAME: **V.I. Divers, Ltd.**
ADDRESS: **Pan Am Pavillion**
          Christiansted, St. Croix, USVI 00820
CONTACT: **Ed Buckley**
TITLE: **Operations Manager**
TELEPHONE: **340-773-6045**   FAX   **340-773-2859**
CAPITOL: **Charlotte Amalie**   GOVERNMENT:
POPULATION: **110,000**   LANGUAGE: **English**
CURRENCY: **US Dollar**   ELECTRICITY: **110V**
AIRLINES: **AA, DL, YS**   DEPARTURE TAX? **No**
NEED VISA/PASSPORT   YES NO **x**   PROOF OF CITIZENSHIP?   YES   NO **x**

YOUR FACILITY IS CLASSIFIED AS: SCUBA CENTER **x**   RESORT
BUSINESS HOURS: **8:00am - 7:00pm Mon -Sat, 8:00am - 3:00pm Sun.**
CERTIFYING AGENCIES: **PADI, NAUI**
LOG BOOK REQUIRED?   YES   NO
EQUIPMENT: SALES **x**   RENTALS **x** AIR FILLS **x**
PRIMARY LINE OF EQUIPMENT?   SCUPA PRO
PHOTOGRAPHIC EQUIPMENT: SALES   RENTALS **x** LAB

CHARTER/DIVE BOAT AVAILABLE?   YES **x**   NO   DIVER CAPACITY **12**
COAST GUARD APPROVED?   YES **x**   NO   CAPTAIN LICENSED? YES **x** NO
SHIP TO SHORE YES **x** NO   LORAN? YES NO **x**   RADAR? YES NO **x** GPS **x**
DIVE MASTER/INSTRUCTOR ABOARD? YES **x**   NO BOTH **x**

DIVING AND SNORKELING   SALT **x**   FRESH
TYPE OF DIVING/SNORKELING IN AREA: WALL **x**   BEACH **x** WRECK **x** REEF **x**   CAVE ICE
DIVING/SNORKELING IN YOUR AREA IS BEST SUITED FOR: BEGINNER **x** INTERMEDIATE **x** ADVANCED **x**
BEST TIME OF YEAR FOR DIVING/SNORKELING:
TEMPERATURE: NOV-APRIL: **78F**   MAY-OCT.   **82F**
VISIBILITY: DIVING: **100Ft.**   SNORKELING   **80Ft.**

PACKAGES AVAILABLE: DIVE **x**   DIVE STAY **x** SNORKEL   SNORKEL STAY
ACCOMMODATIONS NEARBY: HOTEL **x**   MOTEL **x** HOME RENTALS **x**
ACCOMMODATION RATES: EXPENSIVE **x** MODERATE **x** INEXPENSIVE **x**
RESTAURANTS NEARBY: EXPENSIVE **x** MODERATE **x** INEXPENSIVE **x**
YOUR AREA IS: REMOTE   QUIET WITH ACTIVITIES **x**   LIVELY
LOCAL ACTIVITY/NIGHTLIFE: **Nightclubs and restaurants**
CAR NEEDED TO EXPLORE AREA: YES **x**   NO
DUTY FREE SHOPPING: YES **x**   NO

LOCAL EMERGENCY SERVICES: NEAREST HYPERBARIC TREATMENT FACILITY:
COAST GUARD: **San Juan**   AUTHORITY: **St. Thomas Hospital**
TELEPHONE: **787-729-6770**   LOCATION: **St. Thomas**
CALLSIGNS: **Coast Guard San Juan**   TELEPHONE: **776-2686**

LOCAL DIVING DOCTOR:
NAME: **Dr. David Boaz**
LOCATION: **St. Thomas**
TELEPHONE: **340-774-8998**

CENTRAL AMERICA

Belize
Turneffe Island Lodge
Jane and Richard Goulston

Imagine drawing close to an idyllic island dotted with palm trees and lined with sandy beaches. Sighting the island's red and black mangroves, which hug the shore, pulling up to a small dock lined with the smiling Turneffe Island Lodge staff. That describes our arrival on Turneffe Island and our introduction to a memorable dive vacation.

The 30-mile trip to the island of Caye Bokel, which is located off the Belize coast, allows you time to get acquainted with the waters encircling Turneffe Atoll. **Caye Bokel is the atoll's most southerly island and is surrounded by the second largest barrier reef in the world.** The lodge is situated on ten of the island's twelve acres.

After you exchange hellos with lodge owners Dallas and Bobbie Gay and managers Warwick and Barbara Lowe, you and your gear are transported to the lodge. Comprised of twelve bungalows, some with ceiling fans, others air conditioned, all with a view of the Caribbean. It comfortably holds 24 people.

Southern hospitality served up family style best describes Turneffe Island Lodge's warm atmosphere of service and courtesy. The home-cooked meals feature generous portions, with a typical day's menu consisting of French toast and sausage for breakfast, homemade pizza and coleslaw for lunch, and lobster tail, fresh vegetables, homemade rolls, and salad topped off by a gourmet dessert for dinner. For snacks, hungry divers need only dip their hands into the cookie jar filled with homemade treats.

A dinner bell signals seating for meals served promptly at 7:30 AM, 12:00 PM, and 7:30 PM. In keeping with the lodge's laid-back atmosphere, meals are relaxed and eaten in the company of the lodge staff. Meal times coincide with busy fishing or diving schedules, and lunch can be packed and taken for all-day diving or fishing excursions.

Rooms are simple, cleaned daily, and comfortable. Television and telephone, though not in-room amenities, can be found in the main lodge and office. Dress is casual, as you might expect. Footwear is optional, but shirts are required in the dining room. The service is consistently fine and delivered with a smile. Children over twelve and older are welcome. As on any island, fresh water should be conserved and used wisely, though there is an ample supply for drinking and showering.

While offering spectacular, unspoiled wilderness boat diving, Turneffe Island Lodge is equally outstanding as a fishing operation specializing in guided back country and flats angling for bonefish, and tarpon. Renowned throughout the world as a fly fishing mecca, the lodge has offered guided fishing for the last 30 years.

How to Get There: Connect to Belize City from Miami or Houston. Upon arrival in Belize City, your passport or picture identification and notarized birth certificate will be checked, a brief immigration form filled out, and $15 U.S. paid. **Special note: Some non-U.S. visitors need visas and credit cards and travelers checks are NOT accepted for the $15 airport departure tax.**

Once you have cleared customs, a Turneffe Island Lodge representative handles your bags, shepherds you through the airport, and conducts you to the island.

Money: While the peso is the local currency, most places in Belize accept travelers checks and credit cards. Bring along small amounts of cash for tips and sundries.

Language: English, Spanish, and Creole are spoken.

Climate: The trade winds continuously cool Belize's tropical climate, with daytime temperatures ranging from 80 to 90 degrees Fahrenheit year-round. Water temperatures range from 79 to 84 degrees F. Since a wind shift may signal the occasional insect assault, bring repellent.

131

Arrow Crab by Lois Hatcher

Diving: To dive Turneffe Atoll is to experience pristine, blue water, wilderness reef diving at its best. The endless variety of sealife on the reef includes rays, turtles, dolphin, sharks, and exotic fish. Most dives are a five minute boat ride from the island and consist of wall drift dives ranging from 60 to 90 feet deep. Nearly all between-dive breaks are spent back at the lodge.

There are three dives every day, two in the morning and one in the mid-afternoon. Once your gear has been set up for the first time, you won't need to handle it again. It will be assembled and waiting on the boat for you each morning. At the end of the day your gear will be washed and stored for the next day's dives.

Equipment: Bring your own regulator, mask, and fins, and check with the lodge on any other dive gear you might need. Service your equipment before your trip, as hard-to-find parts can pose problems. Check before your arrival on what the water temperatures will be during your stay. In the cooler months, a light neoprene or a Polartec suit is ideal. During the warm season, a Lycra suit works fine.

Don't forget to bring your C-card and dive log. A re-compression chamber is located at the Belize City airport.

THESE ARE SOME OF OUR FAVORITE DIVE SITES:
ELBOW
Huge pinnacles and valleys of white sand are dotted with patches of coral, sponges, and sea fans. Grouper, snapper, Atlantic spadefish and jack inhabit this reef. You will see eagle rays and jewfish, as well as occasional sharks. This magnificent dive is the premier attraction of the reef and features plenty of big, impressive fish.
BLACK BEAUTY
Found at a depth of 80 feet and **named for a huge black coral** growth that was cut and removed, this spectacular ledge is covered with black bush and other varieties of coral.
GAIL'S POINT
Great second dive at about 75 feet. This is a wall drift dive, and the place to spot numerous turtles and rays, along with some nurse sharks.
THE BLUE HOLE
This is a very different dive meant for the experienced diver only. This is a hole in the sea floor. You descend to 130 feet to explore a cavern filled with stalactites. The bottom time is approximately six minutes. Certainly a dive to be remembered.
HALF MOON WALL
Beautiful 80-feet-deep wall dive. This is a 360 degree dive, filled with abundant sea

SCUBA AND SNORKELING QUESTIONNAIRE

NAME: **Turneffe Island Lodge**
ADDRESS: **P.O. Box 480 Belize City**
Belize, C.A.
CONTACT: **Warwick & Barbara Lowe**
TITLE: **Managers**
TELEPHONE: **5012 12011**   FAX   same

CAPITOL: **Belmopax**   GOVERNMENT: **Parliament**
POPULATION: **30,000**   LANGUAGE: **English**
CURRENCY: **$1 US = $2 BZ**   ELECTRICITY: **110V**
AIRLINES: **Tala, AA, CO**   DEPARTURE TAX? **Y**
NEED VISA/PASSPORT   **Yes**   PROOF OF CITIZENSHIP?   **Yes**

YOUR FACILITY IS CLASSIFIED AS: SCUBA CENTER   RESORT **Both plus fly fishing**
BUSINESS HOURS: **0600 - 2200**
CERTIFYING AGENCIES: **PDIC, PADI**
LOG BOOK REQUIRED?   **No**
EQUIPMENT: SALES **Y**   RENTALS **Y**   AIR FILLS **Y**
PRIMARY LINE OF EQUIPMENT?   **Sherwood**
PHOTOGRAPHIC EQUIPMENT: NO   SALES   RENTALS   LAB

CHARTER/DIVE BOAT AVAILABLE?   **Yes**   DIVER CAPACITY **10**
COAST GUARD APPROVED?   **Yes**   CAPTAIN LICENSED? **Yes**
SHIP TO SHORE?   **Yes**   LORAN? **No**   RADAR? **No**
DIVE MASTER/INSTRUCTOR ABOARD? **Yes**   **Both**

DIVING AND SNORKELING: **Salt**
TYPE OF DIVING/SNORKELING IN AREA: WALL **Y** BEACH WRECK REEF CAVE ICE
DIVING/SNORKELING IN YOUR AREA IS BEST SUITED FOR: BEGINNER **Y** INTERMEDIATE **Y** ADVANCED **Y**
BEST TIME OF YEAR FOR DIVING/SNORKELING:
TEMPERATURE: NOV-APRIL: **80F**   MAY-OCT.   **84F**
VISIBILITY: DIVING: **100+ Ft.**   SNORKELING **30+ Ft.**

PACKAGES AVAILABLE: + FISH   DIVE **Y**   DIVE STAY   SNORKEL **Y**   SNORKEL STAY
ACCOMMODATIONS NEARBY: HOTEL **Y**   MOTEL   HOME RENTALS
ACCOMMODATION RATES: EXPENSIVE   MODERATE **Y**   INEXPENSIVE
RESTAURANTS NEARBY: EXPENSIVE   MODERATE **Y**   INEXPENSIVE
YOUR AREA IS: REMOTE **Y**   QUIET WITH ACTIVITIES   LIVELY
LOCAL ACTIVITY/NIGHTLIFE: **Island is 30 minutes from mainland**
CAR NEEDED TO EXPLORE AREA: **No**
DUTY FREE SHOPPING: **No**

COAST GUARD: BELIZE MARITIME
CALLSIGNS: **Channel 16**   AUTHORITY: **Sub-Aquatic safety**
TELEPHONE: **026-2852**   TELEPHONE: **02-35312**
                                  LOCATION: **San Pedro**

life and breathtaking coral formations. This dive is generally done as a second dive after the blue hole

Space does not permit adequate descriptions of the Turneffe Atoll's many spectacular dives. Find out for yourself!

"They do it right at Turneffe Island Lodge." We felt comfortable during our stay, and part of a family. This was a true vacation in paradise! We can hardly wait to return.

Belize Tourist Board
421 7th Avenue Ste 701
New York, NY 10017

COSTA RICA

Cocos Island

Lois Hatcher

Cocos Island is located about 280 miles off the coast of Costa Rica. Its history dates back to the 1500's, when it was used as a stopover for seamen, mostly pirates. There are tales that pirates left millions, possibly billions, of dollars worth of treasure on the island. Little of it has ever been found, though many people have invested a lot of time and money trying to recover it.

Palm trees pigs and goats were transplanted on the island over time. There is an abundance of fresh water; I've never seen so many waterfalls that seem to appear from nowhere. Cocos averages 26 feet of rain per year, however there is little or no effect on the visibility from run off. We never got to see the top of the 14 square mile island, as it was continually enshrouded in clouds. We had unusually dry weather for September, even though it rained every day. All the divemasters were in agreement that **the best time of year to visit is during the rainy season from May through October.**

To me the real treasure lies underwater. Many kinds of exotic fish were viewed on every dive, including the King Angelfish and Barberfish that set up cleaning stations for the Hammerheads to swim through.

Cocos Island is the most exciting place that I have ever dived. It was truly amazing! From the minute my eyes broke the surface on my first descent until climbing out of the water on my last memorable dive, I could look down and see sharks, sharks and more sharks.

The abundance of large marine animals made up for the lack of flora on the walls and bottom, which consists of dark volcanic rock. At night the beautiful tubastrea coral would feed, transforming the bleak landscape into a riot of orange and yellow and most of the larger more interesting creatures were hiding (feeding?) in deeper water.

The crossing from Puntarenas to Cocos is not always calm; ours took almost forty hours and was rough! We were told that it is usually rougher going than returning, which ended up being true. However, on the way there about two thirds of the passengers suffered from some form of seasickness, and some could barely leave their bunks during the forty hour ordeal. We were told that our crossing was unusual, and that it was not always that rough, but it can happen! **Passengers that are prone to seasickness, and even those that aren't, should take some form of medication to prevent seasickness before they get on the boat.**

Okeanos, originally built as a research vessel is 120 feet long and has a crew of eight. In the eleven years it has been running they have maintained a spotless safety record. The boat is equipped with marine radio and phone so it can maintain contact with shore. All the safety equipment that is needed is on board.

The dive and meal schedules were on time with no one feeling rushed. E6 processing was done daily, so one could keep track of their progress and make sure photo equipment was working. A group video is shot during the week and available with added music at the end of the trip. No stock footage is used; they don't need to.

The crew was extremely helpful and willing to do anything to make it a better trip. Some of the more hefty divers had problems hoisting themselves out of the water and on to the Zodiacs. The crew was there to help haul them up and I'm sure there were a few sore backs at the end of the trip.

The night before we left Cocos, a celebration was held with a top-deck barbecue that included T-bone steaks, baked potatoes, corn-on-the-cob, and the best chips and salsa I've ever tasted. There was a preponderance of food. The chef had a thing for Jell-O as this seemed to be the main ingredient in his deserts. Fresh fish was served several times which made me wonder where they were getting it. I think they actually bought some of it from a fishing boat that was anchored at the island.

Soft drinks, wine and beer were free. Wine was offered at all the evening meals. Most people did not imbibe as the divemasters were continually reminding us about the ways to avoid decompression sickness, excessive drinking of alcohol being one of them.

The water temperature stayed around 76. There were thermoclines that made it quite cool at times. Some people dived the entire week in a Polartec. I wore a 5-mm wetsuit adding a hood later. **If you are prone to get cold, I would definitely take extra protection.**

Hammerheads were everywhere! I got within about 15 feet. They were quite unpredictable. Sometimes they were deep, over the one hundred and twenty-foot maximum that was set for us. At other times they were shallow, the schools stretching up to just below the surface. At all times they were awesome!

Dives were scheduled at 8:00 a.m., 11:00 a.m. and 3:00 p.m., and a night dive. The first dive that we did was the backside of **Manuelita Island.** We rolled over the side of the chase boat and descended to a gradually sloping volcanic base that merged with a sandy bottom at around fifty feet. This was also the site that most night dives were done on as it is protected from the current.

School of Hammerheads by Lois Hatcher

We only glimpsed Hammerheads in the distance, but they were there. **Whitetips were so numerous that I soon started to think of them as "Reef Fish," which is what the divemasters called them.** I also encountered one of the biggest Sea Turtles I've ever seen. Once again exotic fish were everywhere and included several kinds of Puffers, Trumpet and Angelfish.

Manuelita appeared to be one of the favorite dives of the crew. The backside, which we dived several times, dropped off in steps to depths well out of our range. It was here that we had the most Hammerhead action. There were several cleaning stations manned by the Angel and Butterfly cleaners and at these stations we had numerous close encounters with single Hammerheads. There was also a pair of bright orange Frogfish that had set up residence at about ninety feet. Eagle rays were commonly seen in pairs and they were the biggest I've ever seen.

The most exciting dive we did was at a location named **Submerged Rock,** which is a submerged rock on the Pacific side of Cocos. We were escorted to the site by a pod of friendly dolphins that continued to do swim-bys for the duration of the dive. There is a gorgeous archway at around 60-70 feet that was packed full of so many different kinds of Jacks, Snappers and other fish that we almost missed it. As we continued on the dive, we encountered the usual array of Whitetips and Marble Rays. Some people were lucky enough to see a Manta Ray cruise by and I had several good close encounters with Hammerheads.

Towards the end of the dive we came across a large school of Jacks that formed an endless spiral to the surface. They were broken up by the dolphins swimming through them and then by the appearance of a couple of curious silky sharks.

No trip would be complete without a dive to Dirty Rock. We did several. Once again it was a dive site full of life. with the usual sharks and large schools of Jacks.

Other sites we dived were **Dos Amigos, Viking Rock, Isla Pajara** and **Ulloa Island.** All were good, but depended on the currents as to how much action was taking place.

It seemed impossible to have a bad dive at Cocos and I never heard anyone complain about any of the dives other than they had been looking the wrong way when the Hammerheads swam by. **You can't begin to imagine the thrill of descending through schools of jacks that are so thick they block out the sun, or seeing a twelve foot Manta Ray cruise by.** We saw Hammerheads on every dive, though they were quite shy and kept their distance. On a couple of occasions we saw massive schools that stretched as far as the eye could see. On the very last dive I managed to get amongst a school that had over three hundred Hammerheads!

The whitetip sharks were present in large numbers on every dive, as were the marble rays, which swam with no concern within inches of you, sometimes brushing you with their wings.

You have to go here!
For more information on booking an *Okeanos* cruise:
Contact Aqua Expeditions at
E-MAIL info@aquax.com

Honduras
Roatan
Bay Islands

Charlene Taylor

When asked to write of my experience diving Roatan in the Bay Islands, which lie 40 miles off Honduras, I could not decide which dive resort to recommend. I've been to "Cocoview" and "Anthony's Key Resort". It would be comparing apples to oranges. If you like the "local friendly tavern" type of atmosphere then "Cocoview" is for you. If you like a more romantic and exotic hotel setting, then try "Anthony's Key Resort". If you just want to dive, try either! After all you will be diving in the second largest barrier reef in the world. "Cocoview" is on one side of the island of Roatan; "Anthony's Key": is on the other. Both are quality dive destinations.

Lying 40 miles off the coast of Honduras, you land via American Airlines, on a narrow airstrip sandwiched between rocky bluffs and the clear Caribbean. Close your eyes and imagine any tropical isle with white sandy beaches, gentle breezes and bats in the palm trees. Then douse yourself with "Skin-so-Soft" to keep away the "no-see-ums" from making you black polka-dotted underwater from head to toe. The sunsets and rises are as breathtaking as you can imagine. The people are cordial, if not overly friendly, and speak English. But most importantly, the sea around it is clear, warm and full of beauty.

"Cocoview"has excellent beach diving and snorkeling. It truthfully advertises a wreck (*The Prince Albert*), and a 100 foot wall right out its back door. You can reach them both in a few minutes of diving. Between the *Prince Albert* and shore is an area populated by garden eels. **On one night dive I saw and octopus, a beautiful stripped**

lobster, sea cucumbers, a six-legged orange starfish, crimson sponges and many color-ful drowsy fish.

From "Cocoview" we also visited the famous "Mary's Place". A 100-foot "struc-tured" divemaster-led dive; **"Mary's Place is magnificent"**. Tunnels filled with thousands of silversides were an enchanted world when the diver ahead of you disappears momen-tarily amidst them. Even at 100 feet they shimmered with light and flashes as they moved as one to let us pass. Beautiful banded shrimp also caught my eye.

"What a party" by Ron Stretter

One interesting thing about "Cocoview" was the orientation dive we had to do. The divemaster made us buddy breathe, clear our masks and show him our buoyancy control. They checked dive logs. In ten years, one diveboat captain in Alabama on the Gulf of Mexico and one in the Florida Keys asked me for my dive log and no one has checked my skills before or since.

"Anthony's Key" boasts a DC-3 in its Channel dive site just off its pier. On a night dive here, we saw a twelve-inch long spiny lobster, completely out and away from any hidyhole. I was able to measure the lobster by my dive light. He looked like something out of a science fiction movie. There was a large grouper in the cockpit of the DC-3 who looked out at us through the window. On the wing of the plane was the biggest featherduster tubeworm I'd ever seen. Another dive site that impressed me was **"Herbie's Fantasy"** The divemaster fed huge groupers for our entertainment. One had a remora attached. This 40-foot dive had "canyons" with occasional roofs an twists and turns which revealed sea fans with flamingo tongues, small moray eels and lobsters. **"Overheat Reef"**a finger-reef formation, had a large friendly school of yel-lowtails that swam with us and actually let us touch them. I saw some incredibly bright blue banded shrimp that fascinated me. I'd only seen red banded ones before. Two jolly juvenile drums also showed themselves and some squid appeared briefly. At "Anthony's Key" there is an experience I'd recommend to anyone. They have a "swim with dol-phins" program. We spent about twenty minutes, **feeding and snorkeling** with these beautiful creatures. The trainers are very protective of their charges and no tanks or camera equipment is allowed. The animals themselves dictate how long they will allow you to play with them. Their swiftness and accurate swimming over and around you without causing a ripple seemed almost uncanny. And their intelligent gazes almost gave me the spooks. I could swear they were laughing at our feeble swimming abilities!

For the non-diver, there's a botanical garden just down the road and a guide will take you through the jungle to the top of a hill with a gorgeous view of the resort and a large portion of Roatan. However, beware of the guide asking you to smell some of the crushed leaves of plants. Most of them are genuine herbs and spices you will rec-ognize, but a favorite joke on tourists is to crush one species they call the "lipstick" plant. Yes, you guessed it. It gets a bright red juice all over your hands and face if you're not careful! (It washes off easily though.)

Rating these two destinations for diving is easy. They're both A-1. "Cocoview" is better than "Anthony's Key" for snorkeling. Shopping or nightlife is not so great at

Wreck of The Prince Albert by Louise Seddon

either, although "Anthony's Key" had a nice bar and some organized activities. **Food was better at "Cocoview" but both were good.** It's quieter and cozier at "Cocoview" but "Anthony's Key" is bigger and more social. Take your choice, the hard part is getting there. The plane schedules are subject to delays and you can't land on Roatan in bad weather. We spent an interesting night in San Pedro Sula, inland on Honduras, on one of the trips. It was a kick. All in all, I'd go again in a minute!

Honduras Embassy 202 966 7702

Editors note: Snorkeling from a canoe has become a popular new pastime-Sea Blades at the West End offers beginner lessons.

CHINA

Hong Kong
"Dive The Dragon"

Don Lanman

From the Great Wall of China in the North the mighty Kun Lun Shan mountain range of central Asia snakes south to the coast like a giant serpent. Where the great mountains submerge into the South China Sea there's a magical place that Chinese spiritual teachers, "Fung Shui Masters", say the dragon lives. This place is Hong Kong.

The area surrounding Hong Kong is known as Kowloon or "Nine Dragons" after the eight hills that surround it to the north. Local legend holds that a Chinese emperor arrived in search of the Nine Dragons, throwing himself into the sea when he counted only eight, never understanding that he represented the ninth.

With a strong desire to dive the Dragon, I arrived in Hong Kong at the peak of the Typhoon season (June to August). Before leaving, however, I tried to uncover information on diving facilities, requirements, conditions, and the environment.

This research turned out to be a great journey in itself. Local dive shop owners simply laughed, asking why would I dive in that cesspool. So much for the "no sea too rough" mentality.

Of equal help, *Skin Diver Magazine*, PADI and NAUI could provide no information to assist me in preparing for diving in the South China Sea. Finally I contacted Aqua

Expeditions and learned that information was sparse for this dive location. In fact, the only dive operation they had on file was **Bunn's Divers Institute Ltd.**

Bunn's is the <u>only</u> official dive operation in Hong Kong. Formed in 1958 to produce diving equipment, Bunn's is a full service dive operation with divers certification training, equipment sales/service, dive trips and a wide variety of water sports activities including: water skiing, wind surfing and snorkeling.

The dive operation is licensed for several organizations including PADI, NAUI, British Sub-Aqua Club (BSAC) and the Confederation Mondiale Activities SubAquatiques (CMAS). Bunn's offers a full range of classes from beginner to dive master with a sincere focus on safety through "Equipment, Knowledge and Technique".

There are two key drawbacks to Bunn's; they schedule dive trips on the weekends only and preference is given to local club members. This fact severely limits the diving opportunities and requires at least two weeks-advanced reservations.

In addition, they have only two dive boats; the newest being an 80-ft. custom boat named *Diver's Pro*. While it's comfortable, air conditioned and fully equipped, there is only room for 20 divers, again limiting access to divers.

The dive masters and instructors seemed competent and attentive to safety. However, there is a language issue to consider, so I found it important to listen very carefully to each dive briefing.

While many divers do not associate Hong Kong with scuba diving, given the high level of pollution in the harbors, the destination is growing in popularity. **Outside the harbor areas, the eastern waters have remained relatively clear and support a wide range of marine life.**

The typical visibility is only about 30 feet and sea temperature ranges between thirteen and twenty-eight degrees Celsius. This wide variety of temperature creates an environment for many temperate and tropical marine species to exist. **There are no true coral reefs, however there are over 50 species of coral growth on wrecks and other solid objects.**

"I see you" by Lois Hatcher

The sea is void of any large fish due to unrestricted fishing in the area. However, there is a nice variety of other sea creatures including; crabs, sea slugs, miniature octopus, small damselfish, and pink and white fan worms. If you are lucky you may see small reef sharks and sea bass.

In an attempt to protect the environment, the WorldWide Fund for Nature Hong Kong, and other government departments, have set aside the first marine protected area in the Hoi Ha Wan Bay located at the mouth of the Tolo Harbor. The plan is to build a marine studies center at the bay for students, visitors and divers.

From Ping Chau in the North to Po Toi in the South, there are over 235 islands in the region, most of them uninhabited. This provides the adventurous diver with an unlimited source of dive locations including great spots like Tap Mun, Breaker Reef, Fung Head, Long Ke and Pak Chau.

For the snorkeler there are some great spots at Repulse Bay, Clear Water Bay and Stanley Bay. Stanley, once an old pirate city, still resembles a sleepy fishing village like

SCUBA AND SNORKELING FACILITIES QUESTIONNAIRE

NAME: **BUNNS DIVERS INSTITUTE, LTD.**
ADDRESS: **Kwong Sang Hong Building, Shops E & G**
188 Wanchi Road, Wanchi, Hong Kong
CONTACT : **Anthony C.F. Ho, Simon K.K. Yu**
TITLE: **Manager and Centre Manager**
TELEPHONE: **852-893-7899** FAX: **852-834-0039** TELEX: **81003 BUNNS HK**

CAPITAL: **Hong Kong**
POPULATION: **6 Million**
CURRENCY: **Hong Kong Dollar**
AIRLINES: **UA, Cathay, Singapore**
VISA/PASSPORT: **Yes**

GOVERNMENT: **English Crown Colony**
LANGUAGE: **English & Chinese -Canton**
ELECTRICITY: **220 V, 3 Pin British type**
DEPARTURE TAX: **$20 US**
PROOF OF CITIZENSHIP:

YOUR FACILITY IS QUALIFIED AS: **SCUBA CENTER**
BUSINESS HOURS: **10 am - 6 pm daily, diving on Weekends only - advance booking**
CERTIFYING AGENCIES: **PADI, NAUI, BSAC, CMAS**
LOG BOOK REQUIRED: **NO**
EQUIPMENT: **SALES AND RENTALS**
PRIMARY LINE OF EQUIPMENT: **Complete Pro Shop, custom wet suit**

CHARTER/DIVE BOAT AVAILABLE: **YES** DIVER CAPACITY: **20**
COAST GUARD APPROVED: **YES** CAPTAIN LICENSE? **YES**
SHIP TO SHORE: **YES** LORAN : **YES** RADAR: **YES**

DIVING & SNORKELING: **SALT**
TYPE OF DIVING/SNORKELING IN AREA: **WALL**
DIVING/SNORKELING IN YOUR AREA IS BEST SUITED FOR: **INTERMEDIATE**
BEST TIME OF YEAR FOR DIVING/SNORKELING: **September to November**
TEMPERATURE: NOV-APRIL **60 - 75 F** MAY-OCT: **75 - 90 F**
VISIBILITY: DIVING **35 FT** SNORKELING: **20 FT**

PACKAGES AVAILABLE: **DIVE, SNORKEL**
ACCOMMODATIONS NEARBY: **HOTEL**
ACCOMMODATIONS RATES: **EXPENSIVE, MODERATE, INEXPENSIVE**
RESTAURANTS NEARBY: **EXPENSIVE, MODERATE, INEXPENSIVE**
YOUR AREA IS: **LIVELY**
LOCAL ACTIVITY/NIGHTLIFE: **UNLIMITED**
CAR NEEDED TO EXPLORE AREA: **NO**
DUTY FREE SHOPPING: **YES**

LOCAL EMERGENCY SERVICES: NEAREST HYPERBARIC TREATMENT FACILITY:
COASTGUARD **On file with Dive Shop** AUTHORITY: **Hong Kong Royal Navy**

LOCAL DIVING DOCTOR:
NAME: **Any local hospital. On file with Dive Shop**
LOCATION:
TELEPHONE:

you might find in Mexico. It has interesting sights, shopping, Old English Pubs and plenty of history.

As a tourist destination, Hong Kong has much to offer -sensational shopping, fabulous food, great nightlife, diverse sightseeing and a remarkable cultural heritage. In addition to being a dive destination Hong Kong is a fascinating fabric of local culture, state-of-the-art shopping complexes, bobbing sampans, English tradition, modern world influence and the history of an Eastern civilization that dates back thousands of years. **So, if you're looking for a unique dive location, plus, then...Dive the Dragon.**

ACCOMODATIONS

REGENT HOTEL (FIVE STAR)
  No. 18 Salisbury Road
  Tsimshatsui, Kowloon
  Tel: 852-2721-1211
  Fax: 852-2739-4546
  Email: No
GREAT STANFORD HARBOUR VIEW (FOUR STAR)
  70 Mody Road
  Tsimshatsui, Kowloon
  Tel: 852-2721-5161
  Fax: 852-2732-2233
  Email: gshv@netvigator.com
KOWLOON HOTEL (THREE STAR)
  19-21 Nathan Road
  Tsimshatsui, Kowloon
  Tel: 852-2369-8698
  Fax: 852-2739-9811
  Email: khh@peninsula.com

BISHOP LEI INTERNATIONAL HOUSE (BUDGET)
  No 4, Robinson Road
  Mid-level, Hong Kong
  Tel: 852-2868-0828
  Fax: 852-2869-9829
  Email: resvtion@bishopleihtl.com.hk
SALISBURY HOUSE (YMCA) (BUDGET)
  41 Salisbury Road
  Tsimshatsui, Kowloon
  Tel: 852-2369-2211
  Fax: 852-2739-9315
  Email: info@ymcahk.org.hk

CYPRUS

Cherry Dobbins

Cydive, Ltd. Offers dive trips for qualified divers (one star or above) twice daily at 9:00 and 14:00 hours. They return to the center between dives to allow for those who prefer to make only a single dive each day.

Safari trips are also available, which take you through some beautiful remote parts of the island, normally inaccessible, and include two dives with barbecue or buffet. Safaris are only available April to October.

Besides the "safari," they can also organize day trips by Land Rover or boat when numbers and conditions are suitable. Divers family and friends are welcome when space is available. Night dives with a beach barbecue and full-day boat trips are also possible.

It is a recognized BSAC and PADI five star school, and as such, runs courses for all levels and in specialist subjects, such as Photography. For those without underwater cameras, both movie and still equipment are for hire.

Cydive has a large stock of quality equipment for the use of visiting divers. For shore dives they use a long-wheel base Land Rover, and for boat dives, a 10-meter wooden dive boat with radio, echo sounder, boarding platform and shade from the sun for those who prefer it. Non-diving relatives and friends are always welcome on dives when there is space in the Land Rover and for a small fee on the boat.

Other watersports are available in **Paphos**, including windsurfing and water skiing.

In the true tradition of Cyprus, a warm and friendly atmosphere prevails and Cydive is fortunate to have Dougie and Gill next door serving breakfast, snacks and drinks in the **Divers Den**. Evening entertainment may include a slide show, barbecue or visit to a local tavern for a meze.

DIVE SITES
THE WRECK OF THE *ACHILLEAS*
A Greek vessel, which mysteriously sank in 11m of water in 1975, it is in three main sections and good condition. There are still some portholes. The bronze propeller is still attached and the bow section may be entered. The winch and large grab are also of interest.

BIG STEPS
This site is 20 minutes by boat from the harbor, and drops down to 25 meters in a series of small drop-offs. Lots of small holes to examine and plenty of marine life.

THE SHOALS
This site is an isolated rocky area about 3 kilometers from the shore. **The rocks come just to the surface and in ancient times a large number of ships were wrecked there. The rocks are littered with amphorae, mostly broken, and in some places concreted together in the shape of the hold of the ship from which they came.** There are many other remains such as stone anchors but none of the artifacts can be removed. The site takes 20 minutes to reach by boat. Depths are between 2 to 10 meters.

THE VALLEY
This site takes less than 15 minutes to reach by boat. The site is an underwater "valley" of about 100m length and about 60m deep. The deepest end of the valley is 26m. There is much encrusting marine life under the overhanging walls of the valley and there are a few small caves.

WRECK OF THE *Vera K*
This wreck is near some small islands called Moulia Rocks . It takes 25 minutes to reach the site by boat. The *Vera K* went aground in 1972. It was blown up as a hazard to shipping in 1974. The vessel is a large Lebanese freighter of about 200m length. The wreck is in four main sections and is completely submerged. It lies in a "crater" in the

Blue Star Fish by Victor Organ

seabed that is 8m deep. Just beside the wreck is a large rock archway where a family of groupers live, the largest of which (1.5m) is known to local divers as Uncle George. Close to the archways there is a system of fairly narrow tunnels suitable for experienced divers.

VALLEY OF CAVES

A large valley with many small caves and 100m away a large crater contains large boulders and more caves. Maximum depth is 15m.

N.E. REEF

N.E. Reef is a popular site not far from the valley. Rocky bottom, lots of small holes and interesting marine life. Maximum depth is 18m.

100 FOOT DIVE

The 100-Foot Dive is an interesting dive to depths of between 26m and 34m. The clear water means the boat is visible from the bottom. Lots of small caves and drop-offs.

BREAM BAY

A favorite dive site. Sand and rock bottom with many crevices, valleys and tunnels in 26m of clear water and lots of marine life. The beautiful red and purple algae and coral encrust many of the holes so taking a torch is a good idea. Maximum depth is 30m.

THE SLOPE

The Slope has a rocky bottom area with small holes and interesting marine life. **The remains of a Roman anchor (lead cross bar) may also be seen here.** The area slopes down from 16 to 26m fairly quickly.

THE COLUMN

The pieces of amphorae to be seen at this site suggest a Rhodian wreck (similar to the Kyrenia wreck). It was carrying building materials, and the column with fitting holes is still clearly discernable.

THE ROMAN RUBBISH PIT

The Roman Rubbish Pit is an area with great many shards of amphorae and pieces of artifacts. Archaeologists believe this to be "Anchorage Gash"—broken items junked by sailors.

WALRUS FLATS

No walrus have ever been spotted here, but it is still a very attractive site. It has a sandy bottom with rocky outcrops, valleys and small caves.

GROUPER HOLES

A popular site that is only 15 minutes by boat from harbor. Depth is 16 to 23m. An area with gullies and small holes inhabited by grouper. Also a good area to see pina clams and fan worms.

DEEP SLOPE

Only 10 minutes by boat to this site, then down the shot line to 40m and a calcified coral bed on a fairly steep slope.

ANCHOR REEF

The Anchor Reef is an interesting dive in depths between 9 and 20m. It has a rocky bottom with small gullies. The site is so called because of a large Danforth anchor and a very large Admiralty pattern anchor only 200m apart.

THE FOLLOWING SITES ARE ACCESSIBLE BY SHORE

CORALLIA POINT

A variety of caverns, craters, archways and tunnels make this a good dive for scenery and interesting marine life, especially fan and peacock worms in the shallower caverns. Also to be seen is the lovely red and purple coral and algae that encrusts most of the caves around Paphos.

MORAY COVE

Half a mile past Corallia Point, this small white cliffed bay is a popular site. It has attractive underwater scenery of small drop-offs down to 20m. On the far side of the bay a stepped crater was once thought to be a submerged amphitheater.

WOLF BAY

Past Moray Cove, the next small bay gives yet another marvelous dive for scenery and marine life.

THE OLD HARBOR WALL

Opposite the center is a submerged line of rocks where one can find the remains of the original Roman harbor wall and numerous small fish, sponges and octopus. Also to be seen are amphorae remains and the spare propeller from the *Achilleas*. Maximum depth is 7m. This is an excellent site for a first or night dive.

OCTOPUS POINT

A popular and well-protected dive site with very easy access. It has an interesting rocky bottom with small holes and crevices, leading to 14m. You can also see some broken amphorae.

SAINT GEORGE

From the beautiful small fishing harbor of Ayio Yeorgos is this shore dive in depths down to 14m, with a large crater, cavern, archway, and plenty of amphorae.

LIGHTHOUSE WRECK

Only 5 minutes from Cydive, this is an ideal snorkel or first dive in 6m. The *Ektimon* was a 5,000-ton Greek freighter that ran aground in 1971. It is very broken up but the two propellers are still here.

PISTOL BAY

This is normally a shore dive, and is about a 20-minute drive from Paphos. It is near the island of Ayios Yeorgos. Maximum depth is about 12m. The main feature of this dive is a system of tunnels over 100m long. To fully explore the caves a torch is required. **The caves are not suitable for novice divers.**

MANIJIN ISLAND

This dive can be made from the shore, in which case it is a 10-minute snorkel to reach the island. To reach the site will take 30 minutes by land or 90 minutes by boat. For this reason, we usually go by boat if we go for a day trip and will make a second dive elsewhere that same day. Most divers consider this as one of the best dives. The island is small enough to swim around during a dive. There are drop-offs, caves, a large archway, and a lot of marine life. Maximum depth is 22m close to the island.

THE MAZE

As the name suggests, the site is a maze of channels, tunnels and archways in 12m of water. An "out of the way" site, but well worth a visit.

AREAS OF INTEREST

A short drive from Kato Paphos gives access to many beautiful quiet beaches and coves. On the more popular beaches windsurfing and water skiing are for hire and lessons are available. Alternatively, one may use the watersports facilities at **Kato Paphos Harbor.**

UNESCO has recently placed Paphos on the "World Heritage" list. There are many sites of antiquity, including the famous Mosaics, Tombs of the Kings and a lovely amphitheater.

The **old harbor of Paphos**, sentried by a small fort from Crusader times, is a popular attraction. Here are a number of taverns and bars where you may sit and watch the local fishing boats.

Nor should one miss a day in the **Troodos Mountains** with the cool, pine clad slopes, streams, waterfalls, monasteries and Byzantine Churches.

Cyprus has many local handicrafts including lefkara lace, pottery, filigree, silverware and basketwork. These may all be purchased from the shops in Kato Paphos or one can visit the villages and see the crafting in progress. **Mesoiya**, only a few miles from Paphos is famous for its basketwork and the village of **Yeroskipos** makes **Turkish Delight.**

SCUBA AND SNORKELING FACILITIES QUESTIONNAIRE

NAME   **Cydive**
ADDRESS   **1 Poseidon Ave.**
                Kato Paphos, Cyprus
CONTACT   **Cherry Dobbins**
TITLE   **Ms.**
TELEPHONE ****357-6-234271**   FAX ****357-6-235307**   TELEX
CAPITOL: **Nicosia**   GOVERNMENT: **Republic of Cyprus**
POPULATION: **200,000 +/-**   LANGUAGE: **Greek**
CURRENCY: **Cyprus Pount**   ELECTRICITY: **240v**
AIRLINES: DEPARTURE TAX?
NEED VISA/PASSPORT?   YES **x**   NO   PROOF OF CITIZENSHIP?   YES **x**   NO

YOUR FACILITY IS CLASSIFIED AS: SCUBA CENTER **x**   RESORT
BUSINESS HOURS: **9 a.m. - 5 p.m.**
CERTIFYING AGENCIES: **PADI**
LOG BOOK REQUIRED?   YES **x**   NO
EQUIPMENT: SALES **x**   RENTALS **x**   AIR FILLS **x**
PRIMARY LINE OF EQUIPMENT: **Seaquest, U.S.D., Spiro, Suunto**
PHOTOGRAPHIC EQUIPMENT: SALES   RENTALS   LAB

CHARTER/DIVE BOAT AVAILABLE?   YES **x**   NO   DIVER CAPACITY **40**
COAST GUARD APPROVED?   YES **x**   NO   CAPTAIN LICENSED? YES X   NO
SHIP TO SHORE?   YES **x**   NO   LORAN? YES NO **x**   RADAR?   YES NO **x**
DIVE MASTER/INSTRUCTOR ABOARD? YES **x**   NO BOTH
DIVING & SNORKELING: SALT **x**   FRESH
TYPE OF DIVING/SNORKELING IN AREA: WALL **x**   BEACH **x**   WRECK **x**   REEF **x**   CAVE **x**   ICE
DIVING/SNORKELING IN YOUR AREA IS BEST SUITED FOR: BEGINNER **x** INTERMEDIATE **x** ADVANCED **x**
BEST TIME OF YEAR FOR DIVING/SNORKELING: **Sept/Oct**
TEMPERATURE: NOV-APRIL   **16C**   MAY-OCT: **26C**
VISIBILITY: DIVING: **80-100FT** SNORKELING: **80-100FT**

PACKAGES AVAILABLE: DIVE **x**   DIVE STAY   SNORKEL   SNORKEL-STAY
ACCOMMODATIONS NEARBY: HOTEL **x**   MOTEL   HOME   RENTALS **x**
ACCOMMODATION RATES: EXPENSIVE **x**   MODERATE **x**   INEXPENSIVE **x**
RESTAURANTS NEARBY: EXPENSIVE **x**   MODERATE **x**   INEXPENSIVE **x**
YOUR AREA IS: REMOTE   QUIET WITH ACTIVITIES **x**   LIVELY
LOCAL ACTIVITY/NIGHTLIFE: **Dining, dancing, disco, bars**
CAR NEEDED TO EXPLORE AREA? YES **x**   NO
DUTY FREE SHOPPING?   YES   NO **x**

LOCAL EMERGENCY SERVICES   NEAREST HYPERBARIC TREATMENT FACILITY
COASTGUARD **Paphos Harbour Marine Police**   AUTHORITY: **Akrotiri RAF Base**
TELEPHONE: **242911**   LOCATION: **Akrotiri**
CALLSIGNS: TELEPHONE:

LOCAL DIVING DOCTOR:
NAME: **Dr. Chris Theophanides**
LOCATION: **Rochester Medical Centre, Paphos**
TELEPHONE: **06-233966**

Paphos has a very low crime rate and is safe for everyone to walk at all hours of the day and night.

Cydive organizes slide shows at the center with a barbecue afterwards and meze nights at local restaurants. A meze is a Cypriot meal of about twenty different dishes.

There are numerous bars and restaurants in Kato Paphos and many restaurants have displays of local dancing on certain nights each week. A visit to some of the village taverns is a must for very good food and local color.

There are three discotheques and a number of **"Bouzouki" nightclub**s. At the latter you will find live music and singers.

GREECE

Corfu
"An Island of Contrasts"
Wendy Canning Church

The wooden isle Corfu (Keri Keri), named Corcyra in ancient times, sits peacefully and stately alone in the north Ionian Sea. The island stretches in front of the coast of Epirus and Albania. A narrow strait separated it from the mainland some millennia ago.

Founded in 734 BC by the Corinthians, Corfu fell under Roman control in 229 BC, but regained independence in the 6th century. In 1402, the Venetians paid the King of Naples 30,000 gold ducats for the right to rule and inhabit Corfu. Homer sang Corfu's praises and Shakespeare selected it as a background for his Tempest. It is also the place that Ulysses chose to make a last stop before his long journey home to Ithaca after a 20-year absence.

Corfu is an island of contrasts, the modern and the ancient; they dwell in concert, side by side, offering those rare opportunities to feed the mind and the soul. Corfu is a kaleidoscope of bright, clear color.

The climate is Mediterranean attracting year-round guests, providing modern accommodations and amenities for any pocketbook.

We urge travelers to rent a car or scooter and set out to explore all of Corfu. Begin your journey along the shores where sun-filled skies meet gin clear waters. Pause and delight, or join in the activities of bathers, boatmen, or fishermen on your way. Climb into the hills and with every turn notice the valleys dressed in lush green vegetation. The oak, pine, cypress and olive trees lovingly share their space with fruit trees and flowering cactus.

Noble, stately villas amaze you, as they are perched precariously on the hillside to catch the gentle winds and view the sparkling sea beyond.

At the many points in your journey there will be clearings. Stop and take in the mesmerizing views. At times the entire coast will stretch before you. You will soon become aware of shrines built at a curve in the road. The shrines have either colored or white facades. Most are simple, but some are expensive and ornate. The shrines are memorials. The white, memorials to those who had died in traffic accidents, the other colors are for those who survived. The victims' families tend these shrines.

As you approach the villages, learn to use caution driving through the narrow cobblestone streets fit for only one car. Beware of the natives on donkeys loaded with wares going to or coming from market. Learn to exercise caution and always think there is something very big coming around the next corner. Many times you will be correct. It is the Mercedes buses that really get your attention.

Corfu by Wendy Canning Church

The order and cleanliness of each small sun-washed house adds to an air of quiet and order and a feeling that all is well with these people. Every town has at least one church. The interiors are beautifully appointed with frescos and icons.

On your return home perhaps the sun will be setting. Stop at a tavern and take a glass of local wine. As you slowly sip it perhaps you will feel as we did, that we began to understand the pace and continuity of these lovely people and the serenity evidenced in their lives.

CORFU TOWN

Our first day's destination was to Corfu Town. We made our way along the shore and into the capital of Corfu, the only urban center on the island. Of Corfu's 92,000 inhabitants, 29,000 live in Corfu town.

We approached the **Spinanada,** or Esplanade. This is the Town Green, the largest square in all of Greece and some say it's most beautiful. On one side of the square are shops and restaurants. To the left are the stately Venetian homes, a reminder of the long centuries of occupation.

The **Civic Center**, which is on the Spinanada, is a lovely example of Venetian architecture. Built in 1663 as a club for Venetian nobility it was later a theater and in 1902 became the Town Hall. The Corfu branch of the Greek National Tourist Association is now housed there.

A little further along the shore route is the **Heraion Acropolis**, the Venetian fortress separated from the town by a moat. Of all its foreign occupiers, the Venetians are the most beloved and respected.

The many architectural influences are apparent. The Neapolitan Cantounia houses, which are French in design, sit side by side with English Georgian style houses. Farther along are Byzantine Churches, which are an architects delight.

Many of the smaller shops are located down narrow back alleyways that are paved with blocks of stone (Kantounia). No cars are allowed in these alleyways, making touring easier. The quality of merchandise ranges from expensive furs and leathers to cheap souvenir shops. The gold jewelry, much of it fashioned after museum pieces, is exquisite! If you are a shopper, Corfu is your town. If you are not a shopper, browse anyway. Look at the local wares, for they tell a great deal about the people and their culture.

GASTOURI

Nine kilometers from the city we came upon Gastouri, a town of Old World charms. It is here that many of the aristocratic families of Greece built their summer homes. The Empress Elizabeth of Austria was so taken by its beauty that she built her summer palace here. She named it the **Archillion Palace** in honor of the mythical figure Achilles. At the palace she sought refuge from the indifference of her husband and the intrigues of the Hapsburg Court. In recent years past the palace has served as a museum.

The neoclassical Palace and gardens have a commanding view of the Northern Coast. The interior of the palace has decorative inlayed ceilings; the furnishings are tasteful and simple. A stroll in the garden will introduce you to Gods and Goddesses fashioned of pure white marble. The gardens are ablaze in color. In the rear courtyard are two statues of Achilles. The first is the wounded Achilles with an arrow in his foot, looking brave and noble. The second Achilles stands 11' 6" high in full military dress ready for battle. The statue overlooks the sea and entire valley beyond.

Traveling through what seemed to be miles of olive groves, we noticed something curious. Tucked in one branch of every olive tree was a roll of black mesh. We were told that many olive trees are too tall for the farmer to pick the olives, so when the olives ripen the mesh is unrolled and placed under the trees. The trees are then shaken and the olives gathered in the mesh.

Adjacent to the Archillion Palace is the **Buena Vista Restaurant**. Here we dined on fresh fish, vegetables, fruit and one of the best bottles of wine we had ever savored. **The food was perfect**, and our table overlooked the sea. The view was sensational. The full moon, the candlelight, and the lights of Corfu Town in the distance illuminated the coastline.

AGIOS GORDIS

Each day we would wind our way to Agios Gordis, a distance of 16 kilometers, or one half hour, from Corfu Town. We always took a different route, allowing extra time to discover and photograph the sun-splashed seaside villages or the historic old towns tucked away in the luxuriant valleys between the mountains.

The true photographic rewards were the people. Many would look, hesitate, then smile at us, but most scrutinized us carefully and then continued on about their daily chores in the same fashion as their ancestors did centuries before. The women are very shy, and it is difficult to get close for a photograph. One woman, perhaps for vanity or posterity, stopped for us, removed her shawl and said: "Please."

Our first glimpse of Agios Gordis was from high in the hills. Tall, noble, cypress trees and flowering cactus parted before us as if on schedule. The glistening sea seemingly stretching to infinity dazzled our eyes. What seemed a tiny dot bobbing up and down near the shore, was our boat. The small houses fit snugly into the hills that run down to the sea.

The beach, long, sandy, beautiful and one of the most swimmable on Corfu, is where the action takes place day and night. Here you will find restaurants, discos, hotels and pensions. A myriad of activities is offered beachside, such as water-skiing, para sailing, pedal boats and canoes. Sunbeds and parasols are also for hire.

The **Calypso Diving Center**, and its adjacent restaurant and pension, are also located on the beach. The center carries a full line of Mares equipment that is up to date, well serviced and available for hire or purchase.

Editor's Note: Since our last visit to Corfu, Calypso has become a PADI resort, which is still offering CMAS, BSAC and ANIS course certification.

THE SCUBA DIVING AND SNORKELING

Mr. and Mrs. Dukakis have run the Calypso restaurant and pension for 36 years. The restaurant specializes in Italian cuisine, but Greek favorites are also offered. The food is simple, fresh and delicious. Their son, Andreas, runs the **Calypso Diving Center**.

Most of these waters have been over fished, but Andreas knows where they hide, so fresh fish is always available.

For those on a budget, the Diving Center offers an inexpensive dive/stay package. Andreas also offers two bedroom apartments with kitchenettes for families or a small group. The apartments are simple, but charming. However, a new block of apartments has recently opened which offer upgraded accommodations. Those who want quieter surroundings should opt for a hotel further from town.

The Center plans a variety of excursions which include trips to quaint villages like **Sinarades**, which produces some of the islands best wine, a boat trip to **Paxi**, museums, nights out at local discos, and restaurants such as the **Tripa**.

The Center caters to divers of all levels of experience and separates them accordingly. Divers dive in small groups. Strong winds can blow in making for rough seas. Divers should use caution and common sense before booking a dive!

The guides are experienced and knowledgeable. An anchor line is dropped along with a safety line at the bow. The buddy system is adhered to. Divers diving with the Center are covered by insurance, which covers evacuation to the decompression facility in Italy. To date they have never had to use it!

Do not even think about bringing home an artifact that you are lucky enough to find underwater! It is illegal! The Greeks are passionate about their national treasures, both discovered and undiscovered. Treasure hunters abound worldwide and the Greek government is adamant that none of their artifacts yet uncovered beneath its waters leave the country! This is the main reason why scuba diving is not encouraged throughout Greece and why so few permits are given to individuals or scuba centers.

You can imagine our enthusiasm therefore, when we learned that the Calypso Diving Center had obtained a permit to dive the entire western coast of Corfu and that we would be able to explore, and film its beauty.

FOUR METER REEF AT PALEOKA STRITSA

Our gear was loaded in the boat and the small group boarded. Our group was a mix of divers, snorkelers and non-divers. The dive plan was given, we buddied up, and dropped into some of **the clearest water I have ever seen.**

We descended down the anchor line to 40 feet and swam toward the reef. To my amazement the reef's topography resembled a Roman amphitheater. The coral was formed in a semi-circular shape with ledges running from 40 feet almost to the surface.

Andreas introduced me to the undersea photographic opportunities. The Dive Center schedules special scenic photography outings.

A moray eel caught our eye as it peered out from inside a crevice in the ledge. It made its way toward us, mouth open, looking as if we might be lunch. The first time I saw a moray, I was quite apprehensive. Then I learned that the moray eel breathes through its mouth, thus it is always open, not just when it's hungry!

Swimming further along the reef, we caught sight of two 30 to 40 pound grouper at about 60 feet. We dropped down and swam along with them. They soon became bored with us and took off.

Our bottom time up, we ascended. The wind had come up and the currents had become strong, so we opted for a slow scenic tour back.

Andreas pulled the boat close to shore and maneuvered it into the mouth of a large cave. **Here lie the remains of a British ship dive bombed by a Messerschmidt during World War II.** The ship is still intact and you can see many objects aboard.

ERMONES BEACH

The winds and the sea were up, so a decision was made to use the inflatable. After the gear and the divers were abroad, we headed off into choppy seas. We anchored off two huge rocks. The dive plan was to descend the anchor line, drop 50 feet, swim towards the rock, pass through a huge arch and return to the boat. We were warned not to go on the north side for the currents would carry us out to sea. There would be many crevices to investigate, so we took our dive lights.

SCUBA AND SNORKELING QUESTIONNAIRE

NAME: **Calypso Diving Corfu**
ADDRESS: **Marasli 24**
Corfu, Greece 49100
CONTACT: **Sam McLeod**
TITLE: **Liason and Instruction**
TELEPHONE: **661-53101** FAX **661-53369** TELEX
CAPITOL: **Corfu** GOVERNMENT:
POPULATION: **110,000** LANGUAGE:
CURRENCY: **Drachma** ELECTRICITY: **220**
AIRLINES: **Olympic** DEPARTURE TAX?
NEED VISA/PASSPORT YES **x** NO
PROOF OF CITIZENSHIP? YES NO **x**

YOUR FACILITY IS CLASSIFIED AS: SCUBA CENTER **x** RESORT **x**
BUSINESS HOURS: **08:00 - 21:00**
CERTIFYING AGENCIES: **96 - PADI (PIRA)**
LOG BOOK REQUIRED? YES NO **Dive card essential**
EQUIPMENT: SALES **x** RENTALS **x** AIR FILLS **x**
PRIMARY LINE OF EQUIPMENT? **Mares**
PHOTOGRAPHIC EQUIPMENT: SALES RENTALS **x** LAB **x**

CHARTER/DIVE BOAT AVAILABLE? YES **x** NO DIVER CAPACITY **30**
COAST GUARD APPROVED? YES **x** NO CAPTAIN LICENSED? YES **x** NO
SHIP TO SHORE? YES **x** NO LORAN? YES **x** NO RADAR? YES NO
DIVE MASTER/INSTRUCTOR ABOARD? YES **x** NO BOTH **x**
DIVING AND SNORKELING: SALT **x** FRESH
TYPE OF DIVING/SNORKELING IN AREA: WALL **x** BEACH **x** WRECK **x** REEF CAVE **x** ICE
DIVING/SNORKELING IN YOUR AREA IS BEST SUITED FOR: BEGINNER **x** INTERMEDIATE **x** ADVANCED **x**
BEST TIME OF YEAR FOR DIVING/SNORKELING: **May - November**
TEMPERATURE: NOV-APRIL: **15 - 17C** MAY-OCT. **17 - 28C**
VISIBILITY: DIVING: **30 - 90Ft.** SNORKELING **30 - 90Ft.**

PACKAGES AVAILABLE: DIVE DIVE STAY **x** SNORKEL SNORKEL STAY **x**
ACCOMMODATIONS NEARBY: HOTEL **x** MOTEL **x** HOME RENTALS **x**
ACCOMMODATION RATES: EXPENSIVE MODERATE INEXPENSIVE **x**
RESTAURANTS NEARBY: EXPENSIVE MODERATE INEXPENSIVE **x**
YOUR AREA IS: REMOTE QUIET WITH ACTIVITIES **x** LIVELY
LOCAL ACTIVITY/NIGHTLIFE: **2 disco/clubs, 4 restaurants with music and dancing**
CAR NEEDED TO EXPLORE AREA: YES **x** NO
DUTY FREE SHOPPING: YES NO **x (only at airport-ferry port)**

LOCAL EMERGENCY SERVICES: NEAREST HYPERBARIC TREATMENT FACILITY:
COAST GUARD: **Corfu Port Police** AUTHORITY: **Greek Naval/Private**
TELEPHONE: **Corfu Port** LOCATION: **Athens 2.5 hrs. by helicopter**

LOCAL DIVING DOCTOR:
NAME: **Spiro Cardacaris**
LOCATION: **Corfu Hospital, 16 km. distance**

With our lights we were able to see both families of shrimp and an upside-down crayfish.

We had two shark fanciers along with us that day, who had inquired about the possibility of seeing sharks in these waters. In July 1990 sharks were first seen in Corfu waters. They ranged in size from 7 to 20 feet. The "yellow pollution" prevailed in the Italian waters and the sharks swam down the channel. No sharks were seen on this dive, but to my delight we saw the Antheas, the world's smallest grouper.

Homeward bound, our guide had a delightful surprise. We pulled up to a small islet out of the wind. The waters were calm and the most beautiful shade of clear emerald green one will ever see. We noticed well-worn stone steps reaching up the side of the cliff. We disembarked and climbed to the top where we found a small church, simply but lovingly fashioned, bleached white by salt air, sun and rain.

Upon entering, we were awestruck to find beautiful icons, intricate hand-painted frescos and a silver chalice. Each year on August 15th, worshippers make the short journey and climb the steps to this tiny chapel to celebrate the Feast Day of the Virgin Mary. We toured the grounds and although it was mid-October, the yellow cactus and prickly pear were in full bloom.

In less than three hours we had discovered two unique and wondrous places, one above, and one beneath the sea.

Does the diving compare to the world's virgin spots such as the Red Sea, Roatan, Palau or Australia? The answer is yes and no. There is certainly not an abundance of fish life, but there is the beauty of the drop-offs and the caves, the wrecks, the clarity of the water, the reef formations, and the interesting family of fish that is endemic to these waters that more than compensates.

THE TRIPA

Run for generations by the same family, the Tripa is famous throughout Greece. The food and wine come from their own farms and vineyards.

On first approach, the Tripa seems a simple tavern. Inside you will find a small dining room with walls filled from floor to ceiling with every wine and liquor bottle imaginable. Many of these are hundreds of years old. In the rear there is a large garden for dining in good weather.

The upstairs of a small house across the street caters to large groups. They have live music and I expect this is where the plates are broken a la Zorba.

There is a fixed menu. It begins with mezes followed by grilled, herbed lamb, small potatoes braised in cheese and very long pasta dressed with a light red sauce. Both white and red table wines from the Tripa vineyards are served throughout dinner. Dessert is fresh fruits, rum and raisin cake, a white cake and the most heavenly yogurt topped with honey from their own beehives.

The Tripa is a must for travelers to Corfu!

Greek National Tourist Organization
645 Fifth Avenue
New York, NY 10022
Tel 212 421 9777

Crete

Orville S. Carman

PUBLIC SNORKELING SITES

Anywhere on the coast, the snorkeling is nice. The water is cool, but you do not need a wet suit. These waters have been picked over for years. I have seen some small fish, cuttlefish, octopus, and shells.

Kalathas Beach has a restaurant that is open only in the summer with three bar/water stands. This is the main beach that the U.S. Navy personnel use. It is also where I found a W.W.II gun shell.

Tavros Beach has one restaurant and one bar/water stand. It also has a marina and is the other beach that the American Navy uses.

The coastline between these two beaches is filled with caves, most of which do not go very far. **You can snorkel in these, but without a light you cannot go in very far**.

ACTIVITIES

Both beaches are topless. They also have a volleyball area. Kalathas has water-skiing, jet skiing, windsurfing, and a better restaurant. It is also closer to Hania, which is the main city. There you can find bars, restaurants, cafes and museums. Hotels also abound in Hania. The average price of a room is $30.00/night.

Mykonos

Chris Politopoulos

Mykonos artifacts by Wendy Canning Church

Visit the famous island of Mykonos, queen of Cyclades, and explore the fantastic underwater world with Lucky Scuba Divers and let them surprise you with their hospitality.

You will find **Lucky Scuba Divers in Ornos Beach** and a few meters from the beach you will see the 17-meter boat, *Agios Andreas*. All the international dive certifications can be used. The scuba gear Lucky Scuba Divers offers is Scubapro, US Divers, Dacor, and Sherwood.

The dive sites for both diving and snorkeling are **Dragon Island, Paradise Reef, Lazaros Islands, Green Islands, and Paraga Reef**. All of these sites are about 5-30 minutes away from the diving center. These sites have a combination of walls, reefs, wrecks, caves, and offer a variety of fishlife.

The most interesting site of all is the archaeological site of Mykonos, which is under the surface of the sea. There you can enjoy what has been left by our ancestors and their great civilization amphorae, house walls left of old cities, etc. They have all been there for thousands of years. The visibility is 80 feet for diving and 65 feet for snorkeling. The temperature is about 70 degrees F.

152

SCUBA AND SNORKELING FACILITIES QUESTIONNAIRE

NAME **Politopoulos, Chris**
ADDRESS **Summer-Oznos beach (Mykonos) GR.84600**
Winter-Aztemidos 3 Acylon GR25100
CONTACT **Chris Politopoulos**
TITLE **Diving Instructor**
TELEPHONE **094-322716 (Mobile Phone)**   FAX **(0030)-691-21331**
CAPITOL: **Athens**   GOVERNMENT: **Presidential Democracy**
POPULATION: **1,500,000**   LANGUAGE: **Greek, Eng.,German, French, Ital**
CURRENCY: **Greek Drachma**   ELECTRICITY: **220v**
AIRLINES: **Olympic Airlines**   DEPARTURE TAX? **Yes**
VISA/PASSPORT? **Yes**   PROOF OF CITIZENSHIP? **Yes**

YOUR FACILITY IS QUALIFIED AS: **Scuba Center, Resort**
BUISINESS HOURS: **10:00-18:00**
CERTIFYING AGENCIES: **NUR, ITAS, TSCO, TUI**
LOG BOOK REQUIRED? **Yes**
EQUIPMENT: **Rentals, Airfills**
PHOTOGRAPHIC EQUIPMENT: **Rentals, Lab**

CHARTER/DIVE BOAT AVAILABLE? **Yes**   DIVER CAPACITY **45**
COAST GUARD APPROVED? **Yes**   CAPTAIN LICENSE? **Yes**
SHIP TO SHORE? LORAN   RADAR?
DIVE MASTER/INSTRUCTOR ABOARD? **Yes**

DIVING & SNORKELING: **Salt**
TYPE OF DIVING/SNORKELING IN AREA? **Wall, Beach, Wreck, Reef, Cave**
DIVING/SNORKELING IN YOUR AREA IS BEST SUITED FOR: **Beginner, Intermediate & Advanced**
BEST TIME OF YEAR FOR DIVING/SNORKELING:
TEMPERATURE: NOV-APRIL **50 F** MAY-OCT: **70 F**
VISIBILITY: DIVING **80 FT** SNORKELING: **65 FT**

PACKAGES AVAILABLE: **Dive, Divestay, Snorkel, Snorkelstay**
ACCOMMODATIONS NEARBY: **Hotel, Motel, Home Rentals**
ACCOMMODATIONS RATES: **Moderate, Inexpensive**
RESTAURANTS NEARBY: **Moderate, Inexpensive**
YOUR AREA IS: **Quiet With Activities, Lively**
CAR NEEDED TO EXPLORE AREA? **No**
DUTY FREE SHOPPING? **No**

LOCAL EMERGENCY SERVICES: NEAREST HYPERBARIC TREATMENT FACILITY:
COASTGUARD **Uykonos Island, Greece**   AUTHORITY: **Marine Hospital**
TELEPHONE: **0030-289-22218**   LOCATION: **Piracus**
CALLSIGNS: **VHF Channel 12-16 "Marine"**   TELEPHONE: **0030-1-4654611**

LOCAL DIVING DOCTOR:
NAME: **Houtomitzus, Thzasyboulos**
LOCATION: **Mykonos (Greece)**
TELEPHONE: **(0094-338292) 24211**

All levels from beginner to advanced are suited for the site. The location's scuba and snorkeling facilities are so good that nobody has ever left disappointed.

DINING & ACCOMMODATIONS

For accommodations there are rooms for rent, houses, villas and apartments.

There is great dining in our restaurants with a variety of Greek and other kinds of food. Excellent seafood, traditional Greek hospitality and exciting nightlife.

For more information and dive/stay packages contact: Chris Politopoulos, Lucky Scuba Divers, (Summer) Ornos Beach, Mykonos 84600, Greece. Tel: 0030-289-22813 Fax: 0030-289-23764. (Winter) Artemidos 3, Aegion 25100, Greece. Tel: 0030-691-21849 Fax: 0030-691-2133.

THE INDIAN OCEAN

The Comoros Islands
Wendy Canning Church

For those who are not content with landscape alone, but also love history, for those who always keep an eye on the sea, for those who are able to distinguish one island from another, for those who dream of a holiday with all their senses fully awakened, the archipelago of the Comoros, some hundreds of kilometers west of Madagascar, holds the promise of love at first sight

The Federal Islamic Republic of The Comores, situated in the Indian Ocean, northwest of Madagascar, comprises the islands of Grande Comore, Moheli, and Anjouan, while the fourth island of the archipelago, Mayotte, has chosen to stay under French rule. An area of 1900 km and a population of 420,000, its capital is Moroni. The archipelago is situated in the Mozambique Channel, between the northwest coast of Madagascar and the African mainland. The islands are all of volcanic origin.

Our air carrier was Air Mauritius (1 800 537 1182) U.S. address 560 Sylvan Ave., Englewood Cliffs, New Jersey Tel 201 871 6983. They can arrange package tours.

The islands offer the tourist: striking natural beauty, palm fringed beaches, wonderful corals and game fish. Fascinating too, are the perfumes, spice crops and coconut groves. **The Comores are the home for the Coelacanth, the 350-year-old fish believed until recently to be extinct.**

After immigrations of African, Malagasy and others to the islands, they became a French colony in the 19th Century. In a referendum in 1974, the majority voted in favor of independence.

The cool season is between May and October, the hot season is between November and April with tropical downpours. Sea breezes and high humidity are consistent.

The people are of mixed African and Arab decent. The official languages are French and Arabic. The majority of people speak Comorian – a mixture of Arabic and Swahili. Few people can speak English. Swahili is also used commercially.

A visa is required, but this can be obtained upon arrival from Tourism Services Comores.

The Comores is an Islamic Republic, a country with many customs and traditions, which are to be respected and adhered to by visitors. Drinking of alcohol in public places is forbidden (although Hotels and Restaurants are fully licensed). No photographing of Comorian women before asking their permission. Female visitors should be dressed with decorum. If visiting a Mosque, please have a Comorian accompany you.

The food is a mixture of French and Comorian cuisine. Seafood is in good supply as are tropical fruits such as bananas, mangoes, coconut, jackfruit, and breadfruit. The economy is almost entirely agricultural, the soil being very fertile. **The islands are**

Starfish found only in Comores by Claudia Stuerzenbecher

among the most important producers of perfume and spice crops in the world. The Comores supply 70% of the natural base requirements (Ylang Ylang) of the French perfume industry. They rely on this plus vanilla, cloves, copra, nutmeg, pepper and sisal. The majority of the population lives from fishing and agriculture. Industrialization is at a minimum and tourism is only starting to develop.

Malaria is prevalent in the Comores. Precautions must be taken and insect repellent is useful. Electronic destroyer and a supply of vapor mats are recommended. Remember to bring any basic medication that you may need with you.

THE SCUBA DIVING AND SNORKELING

The NAUI Dream Resort Dive Club is located at the Galawa Beach Hotel and Casino. **Island Ventures** dive/snorkel school, boathouse and office are situated at the northeastern end of the main beach. It is a leisurely stroll beneath the palms.

The climate is tropical and watersports are scheduled throughout the year. The rainy season is from mid-November to mid-March. The multilingual instructors will take care of your every need. Priding themselves on having **a professional approach to diving and snorkeling,** they cover over twenty sites, including their own 2500-ton wreck. The center has a 38-foot Prout catamaran equipped for sailaways. The catamaran has three cabins en suite including a full service bar.

Day Cruises: The **Sundowner** is a two hour cruise with full bar.

There is also a five-hour cruise to **Castle Rock** where you can snorkel the time away and soak up the sun. A lunch of cold cuts, salad and a full bar are included.

Moheli is your opportunity to see one of the other islands in the group. Sail away on the catamaran and visit the mystical isle of Moheli, **snorkel or scuba dive** in its' once great volcano among a myriad of tropical fish, turtles and giant coral fans. At night you might hear sounds of pirates as they ground their ships on Moheli's beaches. Blackbeard's lair, it was. This a minimum four day trip

Anjouan, once named Joanna, was the main watering hole for the British ships sailing to the east, stopping at **Mayotte** with its barrier reef, **calm waters, and magnificent scuba diving and snorkeling.** This is a five-day trip.

Mayotte is a minimum six-day sail and **a great scuba diving and snorkeling adventure.**

The three questions I am most often asked about my diving experiences are: "Have you ever seen a shark? "How deep have you dived?" and "What is your favorite destination?

My answer to the first is "Yes", to number two is "Deep Enough", and to number three "The Comores". I have to rank them as one of the most perfect dive destinations in the world. I would return in a heartbeat and maybe never leave.

The following were a sampling of the sites I dived:

Masiwa is a drift dive named after the village it sits off. We spent forty minutes drifting along in the shallows and were amazed by the exceptional colors and variety of the marine life. **There were geometric moray eels, dragon wars, decorated sea horses, and chocolate corms.** Beneath us was a wonderful bed of lush kelp that we cruised over very closely so we would not miss the smallest creature.

The *Misawa* is the wreck of the ship that belonged to Bob Denard who has led an untold number of attempted coups on Grand Comore. It was sunk intentionally in 1991 after the government asked him to vacate the island. The staff at Island Ventures have cleaned her up and put pulleys inside the hull so that you can penetrate her as you pull yourself along. Her bones have attracted multicolored marine life and fish abound in and around her. Small round faced batfish, leaf fish, clown triggerfish, moray eels, shark and rays live in her.

The Captain has to position the boat directly over the site of **Banc Vailleur or Sea Mount.** It is a two and one half-hour ride from the hotel. The swift currents and the depth of 96 feet require a negative live boat entry. You will see all varieties of fish both pelagic and diminutive. Shark, spotted rays, giant clams, clown triggerfish, bi-colored parrotfish, schools of blue stripped snapper, and blackside hawkfish. **This site is for experienced divers.**

Hahaya Wall is another wonderful spot. "See it all-dive the wall". Divers descend 60 feet to the shallows. The wall resembles an artist's palette encrusted with rainbow hard and soft corals. The fish life was plentiful and varied. Sea cucumber walked along the sandy bottom on blackfeet, white spotted boxfish, bright green and lemon moray eels, six-stripe soapfish, blue spotted puffers, and a small turtle. This was just a sample of what we saw.

The night dive on the *Mosque* should not be missed, nor the two different dives at **Castle Rock** or any other dives on their list.

The water is iced vodka clear. The reefs are rife with marine and fish life, some of which I had never seen. Each dive is challenging whether a novice or an advanced diver. Combine this with a staff that treats you like a VIP and every guest is spoiled.

"We make your dreams come true" is the motto of Island Adventures. They certainly do.

"The Coelacanth"

Claudia Stuerzenbecker

Editors note: Claudia Stuerzenbecker was kind enough to write of her experience with the coelacanth and give us beautiful photographs.

On a sleepy sunny morning, March 3, 1995, on the Corian Island off Grande Comore we were sitting at the breakfast table when a telephone call brought life to our group. **A fisherman had caught a Coelacanth, the first found since 1938. Explorers had continued to try to find the secret of this fish and sent expeditions to the Comoros Islands. Finding and studying the Coelacanth is difficult, for it lives in a depth of 200 to 700 meters and it is very seldom that a fisherman can catch one.**

One hour after the phone call, our group of eight divers was on the way. After 40 minutes, we reached our destination. Galawas (fishing boats) were already in the water. The whole village was on the beach and the children welcomed us in the water. It was indeed a bustling marketplace atmosphere. We were very excited and couldn't wait to see "our" Coelacanth.

Was he still alive, could he escape, how big would he be?

We saw a Galawa breaking away from the others. A dark object was being pulled behind it. The fisherman asked us to follow him. We maneuvered our boat around the galawas and followed the single boat offshore.

On command, we all jumped overboard and as the air bubbles around us disappeared, we saw him just a meter away from us, and about 1.70 meters and 70 kg heavy.

The Coelacanth was still hanging on the fishermen's hook. We were excited and shocked at the same time. **This steely-blue majestic fish was so helpless on that hook, and at the same time it was something none of us had seen before. He was still alive, but very weak (for a fish that lives so deep, it is terrible to stay in the shallow water for such a long time). It's habitat in depths extending 200 feet and below amongst a haleanic layer. Here it's colonization serves as camouflage from predators.**

We took a couple of photos and our boss started negotiating with the fisherman to buy the Coelacanth. After a while, they made a deal and the Coelacanth was ours. We wanted to give him back his freedom.

Taking him off the hook, we brought him back into deeper water. The deeper we went, the more life came back into him. The backfin went up, his breast fins started moving, and as we released him at 42 m (where our limits for sport diving stopped us from going any further) it looked like we had brought him through. But it turned out he was too weak, and after a while he gave up and floated back to the surface where we couldn't help him anymore - he died

We took him into our boat and brought him back to our dive base. A few weeks later, Robin Stubs, one of the restaurateurs of J.L.B. Smith came to dissect our Coelacanth. It turned out "he" was a female. Everybody can see our "Ivy", as we called her now, at the **Island Ventures** dive base on Grande Comore, where she will always remind us of the treasures the sea can offer us.

Editor's note

To study the Coelacanth gene, marine biologists need more information on its relationship to other species from that era. This will enlighten them as to the evolution between sea and land - living vertebrates.

ACCOMMODATIONS

Thirty minutes from the airport, The Galawa Beach Hotel and Casino is situated at Mitsamiouli along one of the islands loveliest beaches, which is ringed by a coral reef. It stands in the shade of coconut trees, vast yet intimate since the setting always has the place of honor. Everything opens onto one of the most splendid beaches of Grand Comore, the largest of the four islands. It is a member of the Sun International Hotel Group. Personalized service provides for your every comfort under the keen eye of Christian Antoine, General Manager.

Coelacanth by Claudia Sturzenbenbecker

157

From aquatic sports to the exotic aromas at the sumptuous buffets, from parties in full swing to dreamy siestas, from energetic tennis tournaments to moments of calm, there is nothing to equal the Comoros. So enjoy it. Enjoy its Arab heritage. Today, allied with African customs, it is an astonishing marriage in which ancestral mosques and spice markets live together in an unusual harmony.

All 182 attractive rooms have private baths and showers. Superior rooms have separate shower and suites have separate shower and bidet. All standard rooms can accommodate two children on single foldout couches - Superior rooms have double pullout couches. All rooms are decorated with floral fabrics and wicker furniture, air-conditioning, telephone, music,and a lounge area facing the sea.

There are two dining areas seating 200 guests and a Bistro overlooking the sea. Regular theme evenings include delicious fresh Comorian, Sultan, Tropical, Pirate, Gatsby, and Seafood cuisine. These take place around the pool, or on the beach. They also have live bands and dancing every night. Slide presentations on the Comoros and its culture, films on Coelacanth and underwater expeditions are shown regularly.

The Casino Bar is open every night. It has three Roulette tables and three Blackjack tables and 40 slot machines. Guests may use credit cards to purchase chips.

The Hotel Public Relations Department organizes a daily entertainment program with fun activities like basket weaving, chess tournaments, Galawa races and cross-country hikes. A game room offers board, indoor games, Olympic games and body painting.

The mini club organizes daily entertainment for children up to 12 years. A baby-sitting service is available.

The hotel also offers tennis (two floodlit courts), volleyball, table tennis, soccer, darts, water gymnastics, aerobics - all free to hotel guests. Free aquatic sports include boating, canoeing, paddle skiing, sailing, snorkeling, windsurfing, and water-skiing. There is a charge for scuba diving, deep-sea fishing, para sailing, cruises, and the glass-bottom boat.

A boutique, hairdressing salon, baby-sitting, medical room, laundry, car-hire and excursions, beauty salon and massage can also be found on the premises.

Editors note: Request Room 2243

Le Galawa Beach
Hotel and Casino
BP 1027 Moroni, Grande Comore
Republique Federale Islamique des Comoros
Telephone: (269) 738119
Facsimile: (269) 738251

THE MALOUDFA BEACH BUNGALOWS

For those on a budget the Maloudfa is just a five-minute walk from the Galawa. The Maloudfa was the only Sun International Hotel before the Galawa was built.

Private wooden bungalows have A/C, fan, private baths and terraces that overlook a beautiful beach club with a sapphire sea beyond. Coconut trees shade all bungalows. A staff member will happily climb one and pick you a fresh coconut. He will cut off the top and present it to you with the broadest of grins.

Meals can be taken at the Galawa for a few extra francs.

Scuba diving and snorkeling can be arranged at Island Ventures.

Editors note: Request Bungalow #1002-right on the beach, or #1014 which has a lovely garden for privacy.

The Maloudfa Beach Bungalows
B.P. 1027 Moroni Grande Comore
Republique Federale Islamique des Comoros

AREAS OF INTEREST

Thanks to the excursions organized by the hotel, you can enjoy the **Karthala** volcano and its spectacular panoramic view. For another change of scenery, enjoy **Moron**i, the capital, and **its Medina, the old Arab quarter. Be sure to see the century-old baobabs, the mysterious salty lake, and the beaches endlessly encircling the island.** Below is a description of the various tours Tourism Services Comoros offers through the hotel. **TSC is a partner of White Sand Tours on Mauritius and is exceptional for quality guides and services.**

Visit the **Yang Distillery** (which produces basic element essences for luxury perfumes) in **Mitsamiouli**, the second largest town before continuing to **Moroni**, the Capital. Visit a Sultan's Palace ruins at **Itsandra village**.

In Moroni, the guides will take you to the Historical and Literary Museum and at Badjanani - the Great Friday Mosque and Port area. You will then proceed to Iconi, a fishing village that became famous for the Coelacanth fish.

Make-up for market by Wendy Canning Church

Continue along the South coast, stopping at Singani to view the top of the Karthala Volcano where the last lava flow erupted in 1977. On the way you will see a wide variety of spice plants.

Stop at Chindini Beach for swimming, sunbathing and picnic lunch. After lunch, proceed to **Chomoni** where the black solidified lava flows contrast with the powder white sandy beaches. At **M'samdou village**, you will see a four century old Baobab tree (now devastated with time, weather and termites) which encloses a glorious history in its trunk.

Chaine du Dragon at **Ivoini** is an impressive natural display of lava rocks. Your last stop is at **Lac Sal**, an extinct crater reputed to heal skin diseases.

SHOPPING IN MORONI

Travel along the West Coast to **Moroni**, the Capital and main trade center. Visit the typical and traditional colorful market with its spicy flavor and quality souvenirs from Madagascar and the Comoros.

Walk in the **Medina**, the old quarter of Maroni before contemplating the old **Great Friday Mosque** where the call to prayer is heard five times a day. The Mosque was built in 1427 and the Minaret completed in 1912.

NATURE WALK/THREE CRATERS

This tour takes you to three interesting sites with different characteristics, each one offering a breathtaking panoramic view, each one as attractive as another.

The **Lamnavaliya Crater,** 100 meters in depth offers a bird's eye view of the Northern Coastline and beautiful scenery.

Climb up the **Chaine du Dragon**, a fascinating phenomenon of natural volcanic rock that erupted some 600 years ago. From the top, you can contemplate the scenic mountain ranges in front and the clear crystal blue lagoon behind.

You will have a very clear view of **Turtle Island**. Walk around the rim of the **Lac Sal**. Enjoy a cool refreshing drink whilst viewing the sun sinking behind the mountain range.

LA GRILLE RAIN FOREST

Drive through the town of **Mitsamiouli** where the *Chiraziens Princes* landed in the 12th century and established Sultanates.

The tour will take you to **Maweni village** at 1000 meters altitude amidst dense tropical vegetation. Enjoy a nature walk in the **Tropical Rain Forest** and a deep valley covered with different species of indigenous trees and wild orchids. This tour is conducted in bush taxis and comfortable walking shoes are recommended.

FULL DAY CHOMONI/MARONI

This is a half circle tour of the island. The day starts with a visit to the **Lac Sal**. On the way, you will have a good view of the **Chaine du Dragon** at a distance. At **M'Beni village**, the guide will take you to a spice and vanilla boutique where a wide variety of essence of spices and other medicinal plants can be seen and purchased. At **M'tsamdou,** you will see an old Baobab tree.

Stop at **Chomoni Beach** for swimming and sunbathing. Then proceed over the mountain at the slope of the **Karthala Volcano** to Ntsoudjini where you will see different spice plants.

Lunch at a typical Comorian restaurant in **Moroni**. After lunch proceed to **Iconi village** famous for its **Coelacanth fish**. Visit an old **Sultan Palace** and admire the high cliffs, which hide a sad story linked with pirates' invasion.

Visit the **National Museum** in Moroni and discover the history of the islands with its Pirates, Sultans, ancient African and Persian cultures and other general information on aquatic treasures. Stop at **Itsandra village** and visit Historic Monuments and Ramparts. Continue along the West Coast and view the lava flow at **Hahaya**. The last stop is at a **Ylang Ylang distillery** at Mitsamiouli.

KARTHALA TROPICAL RAIN FOREST

Drive to **M'vouni village** at the foot of the **Karthala Volcano**. Walk up the slope to 1500 meters altitude. You will walk through different plantations of guavas, bananas, spices and wild orchids.

This is a 5 to 6-hour walking expedition for people in good physical condition. A picnic lunch is scheduled half way.

KARTHALA EXPEDITION

Spend one night at the top of the **Karthala Volcano**. You depart early from the hotel and drive to M'vouni Village at the foot of the Karthala. Walk up 2361 meters to the top and enjoy light snacks on the way. Visit the top and the fascinating crater with its green sulphurous lake, whilst the guides and porters set up the camping tents.

By sunset, a lighted bonfire will warm you up and a freshly grilled barbeque will help to restore some energy. Camping tents, sleeping bags, food and drinks are provided. This tour is for VERY energetic and for physically active people.

For more details and prices visit the Tourism Services Comoros Desk in the foyer of the Galawa Hotel or contact:

Tourism Services Comoros
Veerapen Govindan
Itsandra Hotel,
P.O. Box 1226
Moroni
Federal Islamic Republic of the Comoros
Telephone (269) 73.30.44
Telefax 269) 73.30.54

SCUBA AND SNORKELING FACILITIES QUESTIONNAIRE

NAME **Island Ventures**
ADDRESS **La galawa Beach Hotel**
Grande Comores
CONTACT **Tony Kay**
TELEPHONE **09269 - 738119**   FAX   **09269 - 738251**
CAPITOL: **Moroni**   GOVERNMENT:
POPULATION: LANGUAGE:
CURRENCY: **Comorian/French Franc**   ELECTRICITY: **220v**
AIRLINES: **Air France**   DEPARTURE TAX?
VISA/PASSPORT? **No**   PROOF OF CITIZENSHIP?

YOUR FACILITY IS QUALIFIED AS: **Scuba Center, Resort**
BUISINESS HOURS: **7:30am - 5:30pm**
CERTIFYING AGENCIES: **PADI, NAVI, CMAS**
LOG BOOK REQUIRED? **No (Certification is)**
EQUIPMENT: **Sales, Airfills**
PRIMARY LINE OF EQUIPMENT: **Sherwood, Buddy**
PHOTOGRAPHIC EQUIPMENT: **Rentals**

CHARTER/DIVE BOAT AVAILABLE? **Yes**   DIVER CAPACITY **10**
COAST GUARD APPROVED?   CAPTAIN LICENSE? **Yes**
SHIP TO SHORE? **Yes**   LORAN ? **Yes**   RADAR **Yes**
DIVE MASTER/INSTRUCTOR ABOARD? **Yes**

DIVING & SNORKELING: **Salt**
TYPE OF DIVING/SNORKELING IN AREA? **Wall, Beach, Wreck, Reef**
DIVING/SNORKELING IN YOUR AREA IS BEST SUITED FOR: **Beginner, Intermediate & Advanced**
BEST TIME OF YEAR FOR DIVING/SNORKELING: **Nov - Apr**
TEMPERATURE: NOV-APRIL **28 C**   MAY-OCT: **25 C**
VISIBILITY: DIVING **30 M**   SNORKELING: **40 M**

PACKAGES AVAILABLE: **Dive, Divestay**
ACCOMMODATIONS NEARBY: **Hotel**
ACCOMMODATIONS RATES: **Moderate**
RESTAURANTS NEARBY: **Moderate**
YOUR AREA IS: **Quiet with activities**
LOCAL ACTIVITY/NIGHTLIFE: **Disco, Casino .**
CAR NEEDED TO EXPLORE AREA? **Yes**
DUTY FREE SHOPPING? **No**

LOCAL EMERGENCY SERVICES: NEAREST HYPERBARIC TREATMENT FACILITY:
COASTGUARD **VH7**   AUTHORITY: **Richards Bay RSA**
TELEPHONE: **Moroni Port Control**   LOCATION: **3 Hours with Medical**
CALLSIGNS: **Channel 7**   **Procedure Evacuation**
TELEPHONE:

LOCAL DIVING DOCTOR:
NAME: **Dr. Rachid**
LOCATION: **Clinic at La Galawa Beach**
TELEPHONE: **Moroni Hospital**

The Maldives

"The Nearest Place to Paradise"

Andy Cobb

I have two passions other than my family, the ocean and the sharks. The reason I was lured to the Maldives was for the shark diving.

The Maldives is an amazing archipelago consisting of 1190 islands. The various atolls have their attendant islands and the main economy of the Maldives is based on tourism, hence the 79 tourist resorts.

Our aircraft landed on the Airport Island. The airport takes up the whole island. We then had two options to reach our final destination; an island situated on the most northern end of the Archipelago called Kuredu. The first option was by ferry, which would take 5 hours, and as my wife and I are not good travelers, we took the option of going by seaplane.

The month of May was the beginning of the monsoons and the big cumulus nimbus clouds hovered over us in their ominous and dominating splendor. Once in the plane I seem to suddenly remember stories about "Biggles" the intrepid airman. The storm was fierce with its heavy rain as the pilot negotiated around the clouds.

Morning Dive, Maldives by Alan Marquardt

The landing on rough water certainly had me holding onto the seat. After the second wave bounce, the pilot put the nose of the aircraft up and changing the pitch of the propellers provided enough retro action to allow the aircraft to land like a duck or goose.

The rain prevented the normal welcoming reception by the staff, and by the time we got to our rooms we were drenched, and I bought a sarong from the shop as our luggage was 4 hours behind us on the ferry and I had nothing else to wear.

The Moldavians are gentle people and devout Muslims; we enjoyed the freedom from peddling, pimping, violence and theft. It was an incredible experience, and to mingle with a society of people who have learned to cohabitate was very peaceful. Our guide took us to all the back streets, and we were told we would not see policemen, as they are not needed. Typical Asian trading was the order of the day. The more you bought the bigger the discount.

In the bars or wherever alcohol is served, the employees are Sri Lankan, as the Moldavians being strict Muslims are not allowed to handle alcohol.

All accommodations are sea facing-some without air-conditioning-but all it takes is 10 steps from the front door and you are swimming. Swimming is also entertaining as fish that no doubt have had snacks from previous visitors soon surround you. **For non scuba divers, there are snorkeling safaris and windsurfing rentals and lessons**. The swimming around the island is ideal for a family holiday, as it is safe and warm at any time of day.

It was a joy to be at a resort that did not support any form of unsustainable fishing, i.e. reef or spearfishing, and that wherever we dived we were not perceived as predators by the marine creatures. They did not flee, but portrayed normal animal behavior patterns in our presence.

The Moldavian tuna fishermen are dolphin friendly and catch off Kuredu island 50 tons of dog toothed tuna a day all on hand line. All of the tuna is processed at the fish factory on an adjacent island and on the same atoll as Kuredu.

The only discordant note was that the shops in Male were filled with shark jaws, as the Moldavian fishermen have tapped into the lucrative and unsustainable shark fin industry.

On the water taxi to Male Island, I met a fellow Kenyan called Mohammed Ali of African origin. Mohammed is well known in the Maldives, as he has lived there for 10 years and plays soccer for their national team. Mohammed and I caused a stir as we conversed in Swahili for 10 to 15 minutes. We were soon like long lost brothers. The South Africans in our group were amazed at our sudden bond since we looked so totally different. Integration in Kenya was never a problem. Mohammed started off as a stowaway and when found was thrown overboard with a drum as a flotation device. Mohammed held on to the drum for 5 days and was rescued by some Moldavian fishermen and has stayed there ever since.

Yes, the Maldives is a place for some superb diving and an excellent holiday. It is a pleasure to have these gentle and disciplined people as your hosts.

THE DIVING

The infrastructure of Kuredu is well equipped to cater to every need for large diving groups. Kuredu operates a large supply ship and three transfer ferries. In season they can cater for 500 divers a day, however, as there are so many dive sites there are never two boats at one site and the planning and coordination of the boats and diving was well done.

The dive resort is well run and there is a set of rules, which at times takes patience to accept. The resort will organize all sorts of evening activities. What I found was that everyone came in a group and stuck with a group for meals, dives and competition activities and that there were not many groups cross socializing, which to me was a pity.

Everyone arriving to dive is required to dive on the house reef. Each diver is checked to see if they can mask clear, buddy breathe and have buoyancy control before they are allowed to continue with a dive program. This home reef is an ideal area for shore entries and snorkeling. This check off dive is an excellent practice for safety and the sustainability of the reefs.

Pretty Shoals, Maldives by Alan Marquardt

163

SCUBA AND SNORKELING QUESTIONNAIRE

NAME   **La Pirogue Diving School**
ADDRESS   **La Pirogue Hotel - Wolmar - Flic-en-Flac**
              Mauritius
CONTACT   **Thierry De Chazal**
TITLE   **Instructor - Owner**
TELEPHONE **H538441**   FAX   **H538449**
CAPITOL: **Port - Louis**   GOVERNMENT: **Democracy**
POPULATION: **1,200,000**   LANGUAGE: **French, English**
CURRENCY: **MRU Rupee**   ELECTRICITY: **220v**
AIRLINES: **Air Mauritius**   DEPARTURE TAX? **RS 100**
VISA/PASSPORT?   **Yes**   PROOF OF CITIZENSHIP? **Yes**

YOUR FACILITY IS QUALIFIED AS: **Resort**
BUISINESS HOURS: **8.30am.**
CERTIFYING AGENCIES: **PADI - CMAS**
LOG BOOK REQUIRED?   **Yes**
EQUIPMENT: **Rentals, Airfills**
PRIMARY LINE OF EQUIPMENT: **Spiro, US Divers, ScubaPro**
PHOTOGRAPHIC EQUIPMENT: **Rentals**

CHARTER/DIVE BOAT AVAILABLE?   **Yes**   DIVER CAPACITY   **12**
COAST GUARD APPROVED?   **Yes**   CAPTAIN LICENSE? **Yes**
SHIP TO SHORE?   **Yes**   RADAR   **No**
DIVE MASTER/INSTRUCTOR ABOARD? **Yes**
DIVING & SNORKELING: **Salt**
TYPE OF DIVING/SNORKELING IN AREA?   **Wreck, Reef**
DIVING/SNORKELING IN YOUR AREA IS BEST SUITED FOR: **Beginner, Intermediate & Advanced**
BEST TIME OF YEAR FOR DIVING/SNORKELING: OCT - APR
TEMPERATURE: NOV-APRIL   **27-28 C**   MAY-OCT: **20-25 C**
VISIBILITY: DIVING **60 F**   SNORKELING: **60 F**

PACKAGES AVAILABLE: **Dive**
ACCOMMODATIONS NEARBY: **Hotel**
ACCOMMODATIONS RATES: **Moderate**
RESTAURANTS NEARBY: **Inexpensive**
YOUR AREA IS: **Quiet With Activities**
LOCAL ACTIVITY/NIGHTLIFE: .   **Bar, Restaurant, Disco, Casino**
CAR NEEDED TO EXPLORE AREA?   **Yes**
DUTY FREE SHOPPING?   **Yes**

FACILITY Flic en Flac:
COASTGUARD   AUTHORITY: **Special Mobile Force**
TELEPHONE: LOCATION: **Vacoas**
CALLSIGNS: TELEPHONE: **686-1011**

LOCAL DIVING DOCTOR:
NAME: **Serge Maurice**
LOCATION: **Georgetown QBournes**
TELEPHONE: **454-8053**

The dive sites are varied. The Maldavian government has a law that no dive can exceed 100 feet and no dive profile longer than 60 minutes. The temperature of the sea is warm enough to use a Lycra suit and enjoy a full dive profile without getting chilled.

The shark diving was an anti-climax as all I saw was a couple of small white tip and gray reef shark. The gray reef shark is not as territorial as those observed in other oceans. The bio diversity on the reef dives, wall dives, wreck dives and night dives makes the diving memorable and been modified for scuba divers. The space is quite palatial for a S.A. diver. The water conditions gentle. Each dive site is accessed by typical Maldavian style fishing craft that have been modified for scuba divers.

Pro Divers run the Maldives operation at "Kuredu Island Resort", on Kuredu Island of the Republic of the Maldives. Tel: +960 23 0343. Email prodiver@netlink.net.mv

Mauritius

Wendy Canning Church

Mauritius lies 500 miles east of Madagascar in the Indian Ocean. With Its 1,865 square kilometers (160 of which are coastline, almost all of which are surrounded by coral reefs), the visitors to this wonderful paradise will never, and I mean never, be bored.

Although known to the early traders, the first visitors from Europe were the Portuguese, who landed in 1510. They used the island as a victualer on the way to Goa and Malacca, but did not settle there. The Dutch, who arrived in 1598 named the island Mauritius after Prince Maurice of Nassau, made the first attempt at colonization. They introduced sugar, Malagasy slaves and a herd of Javanese deer, but were heedlessly destructive and were responsible for the disappearance of the magnificent ebony forests and the extinction of the Dodo. They eventually abandoned their settlements in 1710.

The French occupied the island, which they re-named Isle de France, between 1715 and 1810 and many place's names are reminders of this period. Mahe de Labourdonnais, who took over as governor in 1735, rebuilt Port Louis, the Capital, and opened the first sugar mill. In 1810, the British conquered the island and renamed it Mauritius. The abolition of slavery in 1835 led to the importation of Chinese and Indian indentured laborers, who were followed by traders of their own nationalities.

Mauritius gained independence on March 12, 1968 and since then has been an independent sovereign nation within the British Commonwealth. Under the Constitution, which is based on the British Westminster model, political power is vested in the Prime Minister and Cabinet. Elections are held every five years in the democratic tradition.

ACCOMMODATIONS

We stayed at **La Pirogue,** one of the fine resorts on the island owned and run by the Sun International group. Sun resorts has always offered quality to the tourist.

Under the very watchful eye of Managing Director Andrew Slome, it is one of the most successful hotels in the country. La Pirogue takes its' name from the local fishing boats–strong, yet elegant crafts with a single mast that still sail across the lazy lagoons. Hence, the roof of the three story main building looks like a pirogue sail billowing in the wind. It is incidentally a world acknowledged design to withstand the cyclones that occasionally roll across Mauritius.

Under a large domed, overhanging roof you will find the Terrace restaurant stretching languidly alongside the hotel's swimming pool. Breakfast, lunch and dinner are served here. The cuisine is a mixture of Indian, French, Chinese and authentic Creole. Luncheon is also served at the beach bar and at the adjacent Paul and Virginie restaurant. The cuisine at each spot is excellent and the service is warm and friendly and highly professional. **Andrew sets the standards of a five-star hotel for La Pirogue and its staff.**

On other floors you will find comprehensive conference facilities, a spacious bar and the casino and slots area. The hotel has two boutiques, a gift shop, a hairdresser, and a masseuse on the premises. A doctor is also on call at any time and the hotel has a dispensary with a nurse and a comprehensive range of pharmaceuticals.

The accommodations are a comfortable blend of air-conditioned luxury and a seaside cottage. Take your choice of twin-bedded rooms, twin-bedded suites or inter connecting rooms. **Each bungalow resembles an upturned pirogue basking on the beach. The highly peaked roofs are heavily thatched – to exclude both heat and noise – while the interiors, each with an informal lounge area, contain everything you need:** private bath, piped-in music, telephone, individually controlled air conditioning, electric razor plug (110/220v) and a secluded patio. The wonderful service helps to make this cottage your own private hideaway, yours to enjoy with prompt and efficient bar service, scrumptious continental breakfasts and gentle trade winds breathing through cascades of bougainvillea.

White cucumber, "very rare", by Karl Heinz Berger

Share your mornings with an inquisitive Mynah bird, your sun soaked days with groves of sighing Casuarina trees and your evenings with the delicate fragrance of exotic flowers that bloom in lush profusion.

La Pirogue is a perfect spot for the single diver, diving couple, family, or group of divers, as well as non-divers. Not only is there good diving nearby, but there are plenty of other activities at the hotel to keep everyone happy.

Parents of young children will be delighted to note that La Pirogue also has resident Children's Hostesses, experienced in the ways of junior guests. A complete program to entertain children has been organized and each child over the age of three years can become a member of the Young Pirates Club and will be given a T-shirt and a membership card. They can enjoy supervised swimming in the pool or in safe, shallow lagoon waters, as well as an endless variety of games and pastimes. Arrangements can be made for a babysitter, and children's meals are served between 18:00 and 19:00.

Please see our "Honeymoon and Anniversary Section" for more information on the newly renovated Le Touessrok and Paradise Meridian Cove Resorts.

THE SCUBA DIVING AND SNORKELING

The waters off La Pirogue hold some of the best diving and snorkeling spots in the area. Corals, rock caves, submarine cliffs and, of course, the abundance of fish guarantee excitement with every dive.

Scuba divers and snorkelers will be delighted with the scuba center at La Pirogue and its' personnel. The resort is up-to-date, fully equipped with tanks, compressor equipment, and a lecture room. **The director, Thierry De Chazal, a native, has been head of the diving operation for more than 15 years.** The sites are only minutes away from the hotel, which is a plus. Between diving, you sit at the charming beach restaurant at the water's edge and have an expresso or cappuccino with Thierry, and other divers while you fill out your log books, identifying all the new fish and beautiful corals you have just discovered.

Aquarium: This is a shallow dive to a maximum of 45 feet, aptly named because of the abundance of fish of many varieties which are quite accustomed to terrestrial visitors. A moray named Kong is the star attraction.

L'Eveille: Here the depth is 83 feet. The rock formation and drop off allows divers the opportunity to view gardens of sea anemones, black coral, schools of yellow and brown clownfish, snowflake and grey moray eels, goldsaddle goatfish, schools of green chromis, and sergeant major, spotted eagle rays and lionfish.

Cathedral: One of the most interesting underwater rock formations comprising two drop-offs leading to a cave. The waters abound with crayfish, kingfish, lionfish, and schools of soldier fish. A torch is recommended to explore the surrounding small crevices. The depth here reaches 28m and you have a bottom time of about 30 minutes.

Canon: At 66 feet, this 19th century wreck is buried partially in the sand. **An old cannon can be seen and copper nails can be found in the sand, making for exciting exploration.** There are lots of rays, shark, barracuda, lionfish, and a variety of reef fish that call this site home.

Couline Bambou: At a maximum depth of 90 feet, this dive takes you through a series of tunnels and caves. A torch is needed to see all the sea life and black coral. **This is an excellent site for close-up photography.**

Rempart-Suisse: One of the longest reefs in Mauritius found at an average depth of 75 feet. Here you will find copious fish and marine life, especially the balloon fish.

Night Dives: The Aquarium, because of its abundance of fish, is the ideal spot for a night dive. Depart from the hotel at sunset and return two hours later in time for dinner. Aptly named, you will see every kind of reef fish and perhaps spot turtles, giant wrasse, or even the big nose unicorn fish.

Seven Colored Sands by Wendy Canning Church

The dive center receives high praise for its professionalism, adherence to safety standards, and for making each dive an interesting and adventurous one. Many warm thanks to Thierry and his staff for a fantastic week!

DEEP-SEA FISHING

The resort is fast gaining a reputation as the world's premier center for big-game fishing. The coveted Sun International Marlin World Cup is presented annually at La Pirogue. Deep-sea fishing trips can be arranged by contacting the Fishing Office at the beach, and fully equipped boats take day cruises out into the blue depths where fishermen will find marlin (the black and blue striped varieties), tuna, barracuda, bonito, kingfish, wahoo, sailfish and shark. The best time for fishing in

Mauritian waters is October to March. Jackfish and barracuda, however, are caught close to the reefs between June and September.

TRIMARAN CRUISE

For those who wish the pleasure of a cruise without fishing, the hotel's private trimaran takes guests on a never-to-be-forgotten trip up the reef on the West Coast. The trimaran excursion departs from Black River, only 15 minutes away, and includes a luncheon of smoked salmon and champagne. **Snorkeling equipment is provided to explore Aladdin's Cave of neon-colored fish and coral.**

TAKING IN THE SCENERY

It is tempting to never leave the grounds, but Mauritius has a variety of sights to investigate and the entire island should be seen. **White Sand Tours has a desk in the lobby at La Pirogue** and can arrange for a private car or tour bus to take you to Port Louis and open air markets filled with sensual aromas of spices, hand sculptures, native crafts, or to the spectacular Pamplemousse Gardens, the Aquarium, or one of the many beautiful beaches. **We always arrange to have their driver pick us up at the airport and give us private tours throughout our stays. The drivers are trained guides.**

Be sure to visit the **Green Island Rum Factory** and bring some home to friends even if you do not drink! It's more of a sipping rum, similar to brandy and just as delicious!

Not to be missed is a day on the **Isle Aux Cerfs**. Take a ten minute boat ride and you will be able to soak up the sun on one of the most beautiful beaches in Mauritius. There are two luncheon restaurants on the island; one specializes in seafood and the other in Mauritius cuisine. There is also a bar, which serves tropical cocktails, drinks and snacks. A wide range of water sports is available at the boathouse. **It is a great spot for snorkelers.**

GETTING THERE

We flew Air Mauritius from Paris to Mauritius. They have many worldwide gateways outside of the U.S. and can arrange a package tour to fit any budget.

Air Mauritius
Telephone: 1-800-537-1172
Facsimile: 1-203-871-6983
La Pirogue Hotel and Casino
Wolmar, Flic en Flac
Mauritius.
Telephone: 203-453 8441/2/3
Telex: 4255 IW. Fax: 203-453-8449
IBL Tourism Division
White Sand Tours
P.O. Box 738
M1 Motorway
Port Louis, WS
Mauritius
Telephone: 1-203-208-8524

Reunion

"An Unusual French Experience"

Al J. Venter

There is an island in the Indian Ocean that is neither independent nor yet a colony in the strict sense of the word. Administered directly from Paris, in the same way as Tahiti, Martinique, Guadeloupe and other members of the former French Empire they are still members of metropolitan France. It offers some really exciting diving.

The Francophonic Ile de Reunion "is" France. In spite of often violent protests by a very vocal and radical minority, the Elysee Palace clearly has no intention of changing the state of things, either now or in the future.

There are sometimes as many as three or four Air France Boeing 747's parked on the apron at the airport at any time. This is all "domestic" traffic.

These aircraft bring in anything from yesterday's Paris newspapers, chilled Norman beef, fresh supplies of "pate de foie" and a small army of French civil servants who keep the administration and the mechanics of the island comfortable and in trim.

The Reunionnais public transport system is almost the most efficient in the entire Indian Ocean basin west of Australia. Modern double-lane highways have been built round the entire circumference of the island.

French domestic television is relayed by satellite live from Marseilles, Paris and Lyons and the schools follow the same curriculum as French schools. The lessons for each day are centrally determined on a nationwide basis.

Municipalities, hospitals, security, sewage, ports, the city hall, recreation, rubbish disposal and evening activities are exactly as the visitor would find them in a French provincial capital "chez nous".

Much of the infrastructure on La Reunion is distinctly advantageous to the enthusiast who proposes to use the island as a base for serious diving.

Although it is situated in an isolated corner of the Indian Ocean, Reunion is half an hours' flight from Mauritius, which itself has direct links with the Far East, Europe, Africa and Australia. That makes it two interesting destinations for the price of one.

Since the climate is not as balmy as that of Mauritius, it has a rather different undersea marine life, topography, terrain, and ecology. The ocean floor is of lava, and much of it is of fairly recent volcanic origin. In places it is "visually" almost like diving off the Cape Peninsula in South Africa, though the water is not nearly as cold.

Reunion is less tropical than Mauritius. There are more and larger fish (including sharks) which have presented serious problems to non-divers in the past few years; there have been several attacks on swimmers and sailboarders. There are also more wrecks, and the diving is generally deeper.

Reunion has some excellent small hotels and restaurants. You can also find accommodation at family-run pensions or "gites".

There are about two dozen diving operations in Reunion, run with professional French competence. Safety controls are rigorously maintained.

There are also a dozen doctors trained in diving medicine emergency facilities with helicopters. All these provide a remarkable experience in an area that a few years ago offered only the bare essentials.

While on Reunion Island I have tended towards the two western towns of St. Gilles, my favorite, and St. Pierre, a little farther to the south. Much of the area around St. Gilles is sheltered by coral reef several hundred meters out, and the beach is good, with a shallow sanded lagoon. Many of the beaches on the rest of Reunion are of black coral sand, but the diving is none the worse for that. The sea life is rich and varied.

St. Gilles nearing the 21st century is a "Cote d'Azur" in the Indian Ocean. Ten years ago it was a sleepy little backwater. Now it is a swinging modern holiday center where you can pay a lot of money for two cokes or coffees and croissants for breakfast in an unpretentious coffee bar.

THE DIVING

Any diving of consequence is centered in the area of the harbor, where eight clubs operate at a very competent level. There are five clubs in **St. Denis** and two more in **St. Paul.**

All the clubs have very good boats and equipment, and the dive masters are all French-qualified and sticklers for procedure. Your won't get a dive if you cannot produce a recognized certificate. Nor will you get your bottles filled.

The dive masters check out all newcomers, even if they claim to be related to the Cousteaus.

Probably the most enterprising of the diving groups at St. Gilles is the Groupe Exploration Ocean, known as GEO. Thierry Donatien acquired the place not long ago and he offers perhaps the most reasonable service for overseas visitors. He has made the point that anyone from the English-speaking world would be well looked after, though he needs a little help with his broken English.

Thierry has an arrangement with a local small hotel. There is a kitchen for self-catering. They suggest that anyone who proposes to come to the island should write and arrange a package deal. **Telephone Reunion 245603 or write to GEO, Enceinte Pouruaire, 97434, Saint Gilles-les-Baines, La Reunion.**

It matters little whether the diver has his own gear; the charge is standard. GEO has a seven-meter Zodiac rubber duck, among others, 28 tanks and a Bauer 28 compressor.

Diving is a very well established sport. The thousand or so members of clubs and diving centers welcome visitors but again, it does not help if you cannot communicate in French. Very few islanders speak any English.

Diving takes place all year round on Reunion. There is a cyclone season between January and April, but unlike Mauritius, you need to be unlucky to have your activities curtailed by the weather. If you cannot dive one side of the island, you can always try the other.

Even during cloudy weather, the visibility underwater is excellent largely because the level of pollution is low.

Thierry Donatien lists 17 dive locations within easy reach of St. Gilles. According to Thierry only very experienced divers are allowed to participate in deep diving, and then with adequate back up in the event of problems. **Strong currents are a feature of this rugged coastline.**

There have been several diving accidents off Reunion in spite of precautions; some of these have resulted in loss of life. As a consequence, all deep dives off Reunion are carried out with a 15 liter tank coupled to four octopus rigs strung on a line five or six meters below the surface.

These people also like to keep an oxygen bottle and rig onboard and are great believers in drinking large quantities of fruit juice and a little salt immediately on returning to the boat after a dive. **Many French divers will also take an aspirin tablet for better blood flow. If there are any "silent bubbles", it has been shown that the aspirin will reduce the possibility of clotting.**

TROISE GROTTES

This is an area offshore from St. Gilles-les-Baines at a depth ranging from about 20 to 24 meters. The reef is made up of strips of granite between 30 and 40 meters in length with connecting caves crisscrossing the reefs and interspersed here and there by connecting caves and passages. Very complicated, but interesting! This dive is not recommended for anyone whose size may cause him or her to get stuck in a tunnel.

The gorgonians on Troise Grottes are spectacular. Plenty of emperor and angelfish as well as a wide variety of butterflyfish.

BOUCAN CANNOT

This reef is situated about 200 meters offshore from the village of Boucan and lies at depths ranging from about 10 and 20 meters. It is made up largely of cooled lava rock, again interspersed with cavities and caves. Because the reef acts as a break for incoming waves, there is sediment in the water and visibility is not what it is elsewhere along the coast, but still an interesting dive. There is usually a current running, so divers tend to drift along the reef. There are a great number of smaller reef fish, clownfish and lionfish.

PIERRE AUX MEROUS

At depths of about 30 meters there is a small reef about 15 meters in height, riddled with tunnels and caves and home to several large rock cod that are tame enough to be touched. During one dive, one of the grouper was trying, from behind, to get my head into his mouth in a moment of tomfoolery. Who says that fish don't have a sense of humor?

BARQUE *ST. PAUL*

This barge measures 20 meters by 10 meters, is a meter and a half high and sits in 26 meters of water. It was sunk as an artificial reef five years ago and is alive with a huge variety of marine life including hard and soft corals and stonefish.

A 30-meter length of chain is attached to the wreck and this allows for some excellent macro-photography. One will see plenty of lionfish, honeycomb electric rays, skate, game fish and the occasional moray. The barge is a marvelous experience and is not to be missed.

Clearly, diving in La Reunion is an unusual and very "different" experience. Diving in these French waters is not the kind of "resort" experience that one finds offered by Mauritius hotels, largely because dive operations on La Reunion are run as independent businesses and are dependent - not so much on novice holiday makers - as local residents, the majority of whom are CMAS qualified. **To the French, NAUI and PADI qualifications are American and therefore inferior to European standards.**

Thierry Donatien and his associates play a prominent role in maintaining adequate standards and offering the kind of services that you would have difficulty equaling elsewhere in the Indian Ocean.

SEYCHELLES

"Still a Coveted Destination"

Al J. Venter

Weave a pattern of orchidaceous tropical hues with an azure sea and dotted islands and you have happiness. Add to that the resplendent colors of a flaming sunset on the Indian Ocean and you enter a new realm. This is the Seychelles; you will find a cordial welcome here. Unquestionably, the diving is excellent in the tradition of the Red Sea or the Maldives.

Tucked away in a remote part of the vast Indian Ocean, 1,110 km from the northern tip of Madagascar and 1,600 km from the East African mainland, this variegated group of 92 islands was a legend for much of the twentieth century. Until the airport was completed on Mahe in 1971, the only way to reach Victoria, the capital, was by boat either from India or from Mombassa on the Kenya coast. Only the most determined travelers took the trouble, for so much time was needed for the passage that few people could spare it in those days. Now, all that has changed. The island paradise is only hours away from anywhere in the world.

The lore of centuries is embedded in the history of the Seychelles. The islands are believed to have been discovered by the Portuguese navigator Mascarenhas in 1505, nearly a century and a half before the first Dutch settled at the Cape of Good Hope. At that time there was no sign of human life on any of the clusters. Captain Sharpleigh of the British East India Company arrived off Mahe in 1609.

The present indigenous are the descendants of early French settlers and slaves who came from the then French Island of Mauritius. A number of freed African slaves were landed on the island from time to time by British man-of-war. Most of the islanders still speak French, or a Creole patois of French, which is also spoken on some of the other Indian Ocean islands. Although British traditions go deep, most of the inhabitants are still Roman Catholics.

The islands were also the haunts of European privateers that scoured the Indian Ocean in search of prizes centuries ago. One was the notorious French pirate Olivier de Lasseur, who captured a Portuguese treasure ship in 1721. He paid for his crimes by being hanged ten years later, but not before he managed to dispose of his treasure believed to be still

Flower Garden by Victor Organ

buried somewhere on Mahe. It included gold and jeweled religious ornaments belonging to the Archbishop of Goa. There are still people searching for the treasure.

Relics of other wrecks are on display in Victoria. At the end of the old Long Pier stands a small, well-ordered museum that has a number of artifacts recovered from the sea, including an old bronze cannon recovered from a wreck off the outer island.

Above and below the water, the Seychelles islands are rich in fauna and marine life. So far, about 800 species of fish have been identified on the continental shelf. About 85 percent of these species are wide-ranging forms that are found in whole tropical areas from Africa to the western and mid-Pacific.

Many of the islands in the group are renowned for their bird life. On the island of La Digue, for example, a special reserve has been created to protect the magnificent Paradise Flycatcher.

Because of the steady flow of tourists, the government recognizes the prime need to protect the natural beauty and resources of the islands. Spearfishing has therefore been totally prohibited within the entire area. No guns for that purpose may be brought in and these measures have had their reward.

Almost 80 percent of the population of the Seychelles live on Mahe. The rest are clustered on the nearby islands of La Digue, Praslin (pronounced Prahlin), the Farquhars and others. **A small community lives on the Amirante islands, a beautiful group about 240-km southwest of the main island. There the diving is some of the best in the world, with the visibility often as much as 50 meters horizontally and vertically.**

Little more than 27 km long and between five and eight kilometers across, **Mahe Island is a tapestry of sandy beaches and palm-fringed coves almost unequaled anywhere else.** Granite peaks are interspersed with luxuriant forests.

Victoria is the busy capital of the islands. The shops stock a fair array of goods, many of them duty free. Town life provides cinemas, nightclubs, a public house and a hotchpotch of cultures that represent both East and West; Chinese, French, Malaysian, Indians, Creoles, Africans and British mix easily and affrably. There are several car hire firms that provide daylong safaris into the interior.

It is possible to take a late afternoon dip on **Beau Vallon Beach** and afterwards, drink in hand, to contemplate the beauty of an Indian Ocean sunset in an atmosphere and climate that demand little formality.

Praslin is the second largest island in the archipelago, where life goes on with a rhythm of its own. Unlike Mahe, there isn't a real "town" life as such. The simplicity charms most people who visit the place, for there are not enough vehicles to cope with

172

the steady stream of visitors who come to **visit the famous Vallee de Mai, which General Gordon believed was the site of the Garden of Eden.**

He may have been right, for the sheer unspoiled beauty and towering trees, many hundreds of years old would seem to confirm the myth of paradise lost. Huge green fronds hem the visitor in a green temple of silence and, if you are lucky, you may hear the call of the black parrot. Few visitors have seen the bird, but if you do, it is said you have been blessed with longevity.

The valley is the only place in the world where the coco de mer grows naturally. For centuries the fruit of this tall plant was reputed to have aphrodisiac qualities, particularly in the East.

Some visitors who stay for a while spend their time at the **Cote d'Or Fishermen's Lodge** over looking the tiny island of St. Pierre. The diving there is good and the fish are abundant.

THE SCUBA DIVING & SNORKELING

The best months for diving are April-May and October-November when the seas are the calmest, visibility can be over 30 meters on offshore sites, and the water can reach 29 degrees Centigrade.

Most dive facilities are situated at the beachside hotels. The Association of Professional Divers, Seychelles (APDS), sets strict standards of operation for its members and requires that all activities should be supervised by qualified staff. The Seychelles Tourist Board recommends dive operations that are members of the APDS.

There are many sites around the main island of Mahe that are easily accessible to divers and snorkelers.

ST. ANNE MARINE NATIONAL PARK

This park is based around the islands east of Victoria. All the travel agencies run trips out to the park from the Marine Charter Association. Since a narrow channel directly outside the main commercial port reaches it, the park does suffer from silting, and much of the coral is in poor condition.

Snorkelers should head for reef patches to the north of Cerf Island and the fringing reef to the north and east of Moyenne Island. Here corals still flourish, and the shallow water species of fish can be observed at close range.

Divers should make for Beacon Island, its granite outcrops form-interesting archways frequented by many fish.

NORTH-WEST BAY

From **L'Ilot Island to Sunset Beach Hotel** the coast is made up of rugged granite which provides many crevices for fish to hide in and **it is a good snorkeling area.** L'Ilot is an interesting spot for diving, with lush soft coral formations in some places. There are other submerged granite outcrops off Petit Blanche Bay and Sunset Hotel.

A fringing reef extends from the **Sunset Hotel to Beau Vallon Beach,** and it is typical of this type of formation. The shallow inner reef of hard dead coral is covered by seaweed with only a few isolated coral colonies but many long-spined sea urchins. **Snorkelers should concentrate on the reef front, and be careful to avoid areas of wave action that might drive them on to the coral.** The top three or four meters of the front consists mainly of staghorn coral which shelters many timid fish; below that there is a zone of large coral heads interlaced with beds of leather corals. Larger fish and an occasional hawksbill turtle are seen in this slightly deeper zone.

Beau Vallon Beach itself is just sand. However, the local diving centers run trips out to the patchwork reef that extends across the bay from **Sunset Hotel to Danzilles,** which is very exposed during the northwest monsoon. The inner reef is mainly covered with soft leather corals; it then slopes away to the reef front, which starts at a depth of about ten meters. The diving in this area is rewarding; there is a wide variety of coral species and some giant coral "bommies" that give shelter to a wealth of fish.

There are diving centers at several of the main hotels that arrange daily boat dives round the bay. **Glass-bottomed boats are also available for trips round the bay and into the neighboring marine park.** For the more adventurous there are also various boats to be hired for longer expeditions.

BAIE TERNAY AND PORT LAUNEY SPECIAL MARINE RESERVE

The fringing reef at Baie Ternay is one of the best areas of live coral round the island. A shallow lagoon up to 800 meters wide separates it from the shore. **Many surge channels cut the shallow inner reef and it is a favorite spot for snorkelers and glass-bottomed boats, with a wide range of fish life.**

The reef deepens to its edge, which starts at about 12 meters and extends to the rocky point of Cap Ternay right across the bay except for a hundred-meter gap by the opposite shore. **This is an area of large hard coral "bommies"** interspersed with a multitude of smaller coral heads of different species; areas of dead coral are quickly overgrown by the subtly shaded mats of Alcyonarian soft leather corals. The deeper parts of the reef are home to a number of larger reef fish and are often visited by species from the deeper waters, especially rays.

Port Launay has narrow fringing reefs off the rocks at either end of the beach. They consist mainly of smaller coral heads and leather coral mats, but there are, however, some large coral "bommies" off the southern point.

SOUTHERN END

The southern end of the island has some idyllic coves and beaches, however, they are exposed to big surf and strong currents, and **it is wise to seek local advice before snorkeling or diving. Petite Police Bay is well worth a visit, as is the reef next to Barbarons** Hotel.

ANSE ROYALE

On the eastern coast the northern end of Anse Royale has some good coral formations and fish life, while the outer reef at Anse aux Pins is too far from shore for most snorkelers. Both of these reefs are exposed to large waves during the southeastern monsoons.

TROIS BANCS

An amazing, almost sheer granite outcrop off the West Coast of Mahe rises from the seabed at 23 meters to five meters from the surface. It is a natural focus for fish of all kinds, and the larger pelagic fish, predators and large shoals of eagle rays frequent it. Because of its exposed position, visit this site only on very calm days.

THE WRECK OF THE *ENNERDALE*

The *Ennerdale* was a Royal Fleet auxiliary tanker, which struck an uncharted rock about 12 km off the northeastern point of Mahe in 1970. The Royal Navy, who considered her to be a hazard to shipping, sank her and she now lies in 15 fathoms of water. She is in three sections, her bow still more or less intact, a tangled middle section and her stern. The stern section is dived most often, and the aft deck gear is easily accessible. The bridge has been blown off the deck and lies upside down on the sand next to the stern. Fish life is abundant round the wreck, which has given shelter to many large moray eels and some big groupers. **Care must be taken because of the many-sharp steel edges round the wreck.**

BRISARRE ROCKS

Also off the northeast of Mahe, these granite **outcrops provide an amazing fish watching spectacle to both divers and snorkelers; snorkelers should attempt this site only if it is calm, as waves surge powerfully round the area.** Giant Napoleon wrasse live here, also large bump-head parrotfish, snappers, groupers. Sweetlips and dense shoals of fusiliers; some large morays have also made their homes in the granite crevices and whitetip sharks can often be found in the larger caves.

SILHOUETTE

Silhouette, a beautiful granite island with towering palm-clad mountains, also has some good diving. While there is little coral, the granite rock outcrops are home to many large fish. Although the island is large, **there is little boat traffic, so that pelagics are seen regularly in the shallow waters round the coast.**

LA DIGUE AND NEIGHBORING ISLANDS

The West Coast of La Digue is bordered by a well-developed fringing reef, with the exception of the harbor area at La Passe, which has been dredged to improve facilities for boats. **Although the reef top is shallow enough for snorkeling, the coral here is in poor condition because of silting.**

North of La Passe, the fringing reef off Anse Severe is in better condition with colorful live coral colonies along the reef front. On the northern end there is a shallow zone of staghorn coral down to about five meters below which is an area of larger boulder corals that extends to the sand seabed at 12 meters.

AVE MARIA ROCKS

This granite outcrop is a spectacular diving site with extensive coral formations covering the rock walls; it is visited regularly by the diving centers from both Praslin and La Digue. It tends to be exposed to currents, but there is almost always an area of calm sea. **Large offshore fish often visits these waters,** and shoals of eagle rays are not uncommon.

COCOS ISLAND AND ALBATROSS ROCKS

A thicket of coconut palms crowns this pretty granite island and it has always been popular with tourists. **It is one of the best shallow water sites in the Seychelles, with an amazing profusion of fish life.** The coral formations are mainly dead staghorn although there are several flourishing banks of live staghorn. The encrustation of algae on both granite and dead coral is the main reason for the huge shoals of powder blue and convict surgeonfish. **Access to this island has been restricted because of littering by visitors, so ask the hotels or tour operators what the present position is.**

FRIGATE ISLAND AND CHIMNEY ROCKS

Chimney Rocks is another spectacular diving spot when the visibility is good; again the granite rocks bear good branching coral formations. Being further away from the main boat passages, the area tends to harbor an abundance of large fish and predators. Back fish are frequent visitors, and the various species of shark, large Napoleon wrasse, bump-head parrotfish and groupers are all found round these rocks.

Frigate Island itself presents similar opportunities for fish watching round the rocks to the right of the landing area. **The fringing reef itself is unfortunately often too rough to dive or snorkel near.**

DIVING FACILITIES

Most facilities are situated at the beachside hotels. The Association of Professional Divers, Seychelles (APDS), sets strict standards of operation for its members and requires that all activities should be supervised by qualified staff. The Seychelles Tourist Board recommends dive operations, which are members of the APDS.

Editors note: Seychelles Underwater Center has a shop on Mahe and liveaboards that go to the Inner and the Southern Islands.

Tel/Fax: (00 248) 344 223
mailto: Divesey@seychelles.net
www.diveseychelles.com.sc

INDONESIA

Bali
Jochen Kem

Samur, Kuta and Nusa Dua are the famous lodging areas and each area has its own scuba center. Most visitors to Bali stay in these areas, using them as a base, diving and snorkeling there, and then taking day trips to more remote areas, getting to know Bali both above and under the water.

Lion Fish by Victor Organ

You drive on the left side and must have an international driver's license. Make sure to check your vehicle for damages before hand and show any small scratches to the renter to guarantee a disturb-free return! Benzene (gasoline) is very inexpensive, the roads are very nice and the countryside beautiful, with wonderful scenery of rice fields and palm trees.

PALAU MENJANGAN
Pulau Menjangan is located on the northwest coast of Bali. It is a four-hour drive from the hotel area.

Here you will find the most marvelous wall reef with a drop to 140 feet. The reef is protected and you must obtain a license at the small security station. A boat brings you to the island, taking about twenty minutes The boat is great carrying ten people including diving equipment. You must bring your equipment from your hotel, 2 tanks for a 2-tank dive, spare O-rings and your lunch.

Make sure you have underwater photography equipment - the 80 ft. visibility will reveal a fantastic assortment of marine life including: clams, pearl mussels, sea anemones, umbrella anemones, lobster, sea shells, flyer snails, all kinds of coral fish, large jacks and if you are lucky, the monstrous 40 foot shark wall - outstanding!

Stop on the road on your return and drink a coffee Bali - one of the real strong ones!

When diving this beautiful Menjangan wall reef be certain that you don't break anything or carry anything away. The reef is protected and I want to go back and enjoy the reef just like my last dive.

SINGARADJA

Forty minutes after Padangbay in the direction of Singaradja on the East Coast road to Bali (opposite Lombog) offshore, only 20 minutes from the stony beach, can be found the wreck of the *S.S. Liberty.*

The *S.S. Liberty* was a U.S. Navy transport, torpedoed by the Japanese in World War II. She lies on her right side in depths of 8 to 40 feet making this of interest to both the snorkeler and scuba diver.

The engine room and other parts are filled with sand and volcanic ash from the 1962 mountain eruption. This beautiful site unveils a myriad of marine life. Your offering of bananas or bread brings you to a center of thousands of colorful fish.

The wreck is two hours by car from the major hotel resorts.

Twenty minutes after Padangbay is another dive called the **Killershell Place**. The dive at 40 feet must be entered through a barricade of heavy waves.

One more destination is behind the Padangbay Harbor. **You can visit a cave with depths of 40 feet and see up to twenty sharks sleeping on the ground.**

BENOA

In Benoa there is a passage to the open sea to the right of Turtle Bay and to the left of Nusa Dua passing into the harbor of Benoa. This passage is fantastic for drift diving and has depths of 80 feet. There are large lobster colonies, a few big sharks, pilot fish and many small coral fish.

NUSA PENIDA ISLAND

South of Sanur is the large island of Nusa Penida comprised of channels with depths of 150 feet. You must travel by boat for 3 hours. Most of the boats are deep-sea fishing boats so you will have a chance to catch marlin, dolphin, jack and tuna. These may be cooked and served free in the fishermen's restaurant at the Hyatt Hotel. A full day's charter includes lunch and equipment. **Nusa Penida has heavy current and therefore you should dive with not only your buddy, but also a guide that knows these waters.**

SANUR

South of Bali is Sanur one of the richest hotel areas and also my former workplace.

A wall reef fronts Sanur. On the island side of the reef it is 6 feet deep. **Perfect for snorkeling or diving** and over the wall on the seaside the depth is 30 feet. There is a break in the center, which makes a passage for the wooden outriggers; the local boats called Sakung.

The reef is fully alive with marine life. All kinds of coral fish, watersnakes, lobster, young barracuda, schools of octopus, large ball fish, small sharks, seasnails, prawns, fire fish, stone fish and moranes can be found.

The current is strong! Make sure you wear a wetsuit or heavy T-shirt and gloves as the water is not deep and a collision with coral is possible.

A second site is perfect for the snorkeler or diver, as at its deepest it is 10 feet. You can leisurely visit the home of beautiful sunfish or stingrays, yellow and black angelfish, the gracious looking trumpet fish and more, more, more.

Snorkelers and divers beware and don't forget the reef passage on the right side from land to sea is very dangerous! Please stay at the left side only!

NUSA DUA

Nusa Dua is the new established tourist area. Like Sanur it is fronted by a wall reef that is mostly dead, but still has some marine life.

The depths outside the reef are 60 feet. **The Scuba Centre is next to the Nusa Dua Beach Hotel.**

Make sure your equipment is in good shape because there is no decompression chamber in Bali.

When you go to Bali, give my regards to this island of the Gods!

SCUBA AND SNORKELING FACILITIES QUESTIONNAIRE

NAME   **Bali Marine Sports**
ADDRESS   **Jl. By Pass Ngura Rai, Blanjong - Sanur**
                Denpasar 80228 Bali, Indonesia
CONTACT   **I Made Wirawan**
TITLE   **Managing Director**
TELEPHONE   **+62 361 289308, 287872**   FAX   **+62 361 287872**
CAPITOL: **Denpasar**   GOVERNMENT: **Indonesia**
POPULATION: **2,000,000**   LANGUAGE: **Indonesian**
CURRENCY: **Any Currency**   ELECTRICITY: **220v**
AIRLINES: **Garuda Indonesia, etc.**   DEPARTURE TAX? **Rp. 15.000,-**
VISA/PASSPORT? **Yes**   PROOF OF CITIZENSHIP?   **Yes**

YOUR FACILITY IS QUALIFIED AS: **Scuba Center**
BUISINESS HOURS: **6:30am - 11:00pm**
CERTIFYING AGENCIES: **PADI**
LOG BOOK REQUIRED?   **Yes**
EQUIPMENT: **Sales, Rentals, Airfills**
PRIMARY LINE OF EQUIPMENT: **US Diver, ScubaPro, Seaquest**

CHARTER/DIVE BOAT AVAILABLE?   **Yes**   DIVER CAPACITY **15**
COAST GUARD APPROVED?   **Yes**   CAPTAIN LICENSE? **Yes**
SHIP TO SHORE?   RADIO **x**   RADAR **No**
DIVE MASTER/INSTRUCTOR ABOARD? BOTH

DIVING & SNORKELING: SALT
TYPE OF DIVING/SNORKELING IN AREA?   **Wall, Beach, Wreck, Reef**
DIVING/SNORKELING IN YOUR AREA IS BEST SUITED FOR: **Beginner, Intermediate & Advanced**
BEST TIME OF YEAR FOR DIVING/SNORKELING: **All Year**
TEMPERATURE: NOV-APRIL **80 F**   MAY-OCT: **80 F**
VISIBILITY: DIVING   **70 FT**   SNORKELING: **80 FT**
PACKAGES AVAILABLE: **Dive, Divestay, Snorkel, Snorkelstay**
ACCOMMODATIONS NEARBY: **Hotel, Home Rentals**
ACCOMMODATIONS RATES: **Expensive, Moderate, Inexpensive**
RESTAURANTS NEARBY: **Expensive, Moderate, Inexpensive**
YOUR AREA IS: **Lively**
LOCAL ACTIVITY/NIGHTLIFE: **Bar, Disco, etc.**
CAR NEEDED TO EXPLORE AREA?   **Yes**
DUTY FREE SHOPPING?   **Yes**

LOCAL EMERGENCY SERVICES: NEAREST HYPERBARIC TREATMENT:
COASTGUARD **Kuta Beach, Bali**   AUTHORITY: **Indonesian Naval Hospital**
TELEPHONE: **+62 361 51999**   LOCATION: **JL. Gadung No. 1 Surabaya**
CALLSIGNS: **YC9ZRV**   TELEPHONE:

LOCAL DIVING DOCTOR:
NAME: **Not available in Bali, only in Surabaya (East Jawa)**
LOCATION: **Indonesian Naval Hospital in Surabaya (East Jawa)**
TELEPHONE: **+62 31 816053**

BIAK

Tropical Princess Live-Aboard

Glenn Mullin

I have been diving twice on the *Tropical Princess* and have been equally impressed on both trips. American, Japanese and Taiwanese divers book expeditions and are interesting and fun to dive with. The diving expeditions are never the same as the Dive Master and Captain adjusts the sites to the conditions and guest consensus. There are more dive sites within range of the *Tropical Princess* than can be visited in ten expeditions.

There are three notable dive sites: **Mapia, Asia,** and **Ayu.** The diversity of fish and coral species is amazing and the submarine terrain is made up of a seaward reef front with sand terraces, vertical walls and drop-offs. The reefs are decorated with Gorgonians and black corals. Nearly all dive sites will interest deep or shallow divers. Night dives are spectacular with giant Spanish dancers and many lobsters.

Over 250 different common species, including pelagics, gobies and wrasse, damselfish, groupers, blennies, cardinalfish, moray eels, butterflyfish, surgeonfish, pipefish, parrotfish, scorpionfish, jacks, snapper, snake eels, emperors, wormfish, dartfish, triggerfish frequent these waters. **Read up on the fish to be seen in Micronesian Reef Fish (Meyers).**

The safety of the boat and crew is outstanding. The Zodiac crew is excellent at spotting surfacing divers. Post dive return to boat is very quick.

The meals are excellent, with fresh vegetables and a wide assortment of meat and fish. Snacks are always available. The cabins and public areas of the ship are well thought out and very spacious. Bring a couple of favorite compact discs or choose a video from the ship's large movie library.

An expedition on the *Tropical Princess* may visit a small (100 person) fishing village on one of the remote islands or visit W.W.II Japanese caves when back in port in Biak.

Do not be dismayed by the long flight to Indonesia. **Biak is rare in that one can fly to such a remote area of the world without first transiting through a city or another country first.**

Two's Company by Lynn Funhouser

Booking Information
Aqua Expeditions
(617) 723-7134

MANADO
CELEBES

Lucky Herlambang

Calling all nature lovers, especially divers and other sea lovers. If you have been yearning for an exciting and unusual destination for your next holiday, your first choice should be Manado, a beautiful city on the north tip of Sulawesi, the orchid shaped island with the ancient name Celebes. It is the south of the Philippines and split in two by the equator.

Manado, an accessible travel destination, offers many unique and unmatched sea and land attractions, especially the fascinating dive sites and endless variety of dive programs, shallow and deep dives on the colorful flat reefs or dramatic drop-offs, drift or current dives, wreck dives and night dives. All of these should keep even the most experienced diver busy for at least ten days.

Pink Skunk Anemone Fish by Lynn Funhouser

THE DIVING

Just 30 minutes from the marine park, is the **Nusantara Diving Center** or N.D.C., your inexpensive joyful home base for exploration, in the seaside village of Molas.

Nusantara Diving Center is owned, operated and dedicated to divers. It was the founder of diving activities in Manado. Established in 1975, **this organization received the Kalpataru Award in 1985. This is the highest honor for pioneering works in environmental conservation. Kalpataru means "tree of life".**

N.D.C. only organizes small group tours in their typical outrigger dive boats. This assures you a completely hassle free, cheerful vacation with uncrowded exploration to remote dive sites. Daily two-dive programs depart at 9 a.m. and return at 4 p.m.

This dive center offers you a homey atmosphere with 20 rooms in local type seaside cottages that are fan-cooled with western-styled private baths and hot water. Superb home cooked meals of Indonesian, Chinese, European and regional specialties. Don't plan to lose weight. Also for your pleasure: mini-bar, disco, bamboo music band, billiards, aquarium, volleyball court, motor bike rental and game fishing.

It will be a delight to get to know and dive with these young competent Indonesian divers. They are qualified and look after your every need. At night they entertain you with a singsong, guitars, Manadonese bamboo music, marimba or dancing.

In this tropical paradise, N.D.C. will help you explore the world's most unspoiled marine wilderness area. These marine parks are fully protected from spearfishing, coral, or fish collecting:

- **Bunaken - Manado Tua Marine Preserve** of 75.265 hectares, off the north coast of Minahasa peninsula, in Celebes Sea, including the 5 islands of Bunaken, Manado Tua Old Manado, Siladen, Montehege and Nain.
- **Lembeh Island and Pulau Dua Island** (sister island), off the south coast of Minahasa peninsula, in Molucca Sea.

A white sand beach with breathtaking beauty of colorful shallow coral reefs and magnificent deeper coral gardens surrounds each island. The water is usually calm and visibility often exceeds 30 meters (100 feet). The water temperature remains about 30 degrees centigrade (84 degrees Fahrenheit) all year round. **The excellent diving can be found anytime of the year, only disturbed by the occasional monsoon west wind. Then the diving will be on the opposite coast.**

Coral reef formation begins with a flat reef to about five meters (15 feet) deep, then slopes down forming underwater valleys, or drop-offs, vertically down to hundreds of meters. **This forms fantastic "underwater great walls", cut with many narrow vertical clefts, large caves and hanging masses of corals.**

On these unique coral reefs a tremendous collection of marine life thrives, red and orange encrusting sponges, Christmas tree worms, basket and tube sponges, soft and hard corals of all colors, sea anemone stocked with clown fish, red-blue-pink and brown starfish, bright colored crinoids, giant tunicates, sea-whips, nudibranch, Spanish dancer, transparent and red stripped coral shrimps, lobsters, mollusks, thousands of ornamental coral fish and large pelagics, often seen giant Napoleon wrasse, angelfish, cattlefish, turtles, blue ribbon eels, moray eels, stingray and eagle ray, harmless sea snakes, sharks, barracuda, tuna, snapper and dolphin.

Nightlife begins after the sunsets. Take your underwater torch to observe sleeping fish, mating shells and invertebrates, the swinging lantern fish and colorful feeding corals.

Completing the diving experience are the exciting W.W.II wrecks in 25 meters (80 feet) of water. These are encrusted with marine life such as color sponges, soft and hard corals, deepwater gorgonias and serve as a home for large schools of fish including lion-fish, stonefish, the upside-down shrimpfish, batfish, trumpetfish, jacks and mother of pearls. **Shallow water snorkeling and observation through a glass bottom boat provides an excellent experience as well as diving.**

AREAS OF INTEREST

Awaiting you on the surface is the fascinating land of the Minahasa region. Here you will meet the delightful light skinned Minahasan people with their quick smiles and keen interest in visitors. **In this region you have many optional activities:** Climbing volcanoes to see the smoking caldron and colorful Crater Lake exploring the rain forest to observe species unique to Sulawesi such as: the tarsius, at 15 cm it is the smallest car-nivorous monkey in the world; the maleo, a small pigeon with 10cm eggs; the tailless black monkey; the marsupial kukus; babirusa (pig-deer); anoa the dwarf buffalo; horn-bill birds and hundreds of other bird and butterfly species.

Tour by car to enjoy the mountain scenery, beautiful lakes, sulfuric hot springs, clove, nutmeg, and coconut plantations, vanilla and tropical vegetable farms, cinnamon trees on the road side and all sorts of tropical flowers and fruits. **Especially interesting are the Waruga, stone burial containers dating from the pre-Christian animist days of megalithic age.**

The city of Manado is fully stocked with your needs for medicines, film and film pro-cessing, bookstores and markets of every kind. You can buy souvenirs, clothes and spices. There are inexpensive quick service tailors who will make suits, shirts or dresses from Indonesian batik, silk sarongs or kerawang (pulled thread embroidery). **You can also play golf, tennis or enjoy an expert oriental massage or accupressure.**

SCUBA AND SNORKELING FACILITIES QUESTIONNAIRE

NAME: **Nusantara Diving Centre**
ADDRESS: **Molas Beach Dusun III**
P.O. Box 1015 Manado Indonesia
CONTACT : **Lucky/Katiman Herlambang**
TELEPHONE: **0431 63988 & 60638**   FAX: **0431 60368 & 54668**

CAPITOL: **Manado**   GOVERNMENT: **North Sulawesi Province**
POPULATION: **350,000**   LANGUAGE: **Indonesia & English**
CURRENCY: **Rupiah**   ELECTRICITY: **220 volt**
AIRLINES: **Silk Air, Garuda, Bouraq**   DEPARTURE TAX: **Yes**
VISA/PASSPORT: **Yes**   PROOF OF CITIZENSHIP: **Yes**

YOUR FACILITY IS QUALIFIED AS: **Scuba Center, Resort**
BUISINESS HOURS: **07:00 - 22:00**
CERTIFYING AGENCIES: **SSI & PADI**
LOG BOOK REQUIRED: **Yes**
EQUIPMENT: **Rentals, Airfills**
PRIMARY LINE OF EQUIPMENT: **Scuba Pro.**
PHOTOGRAPHIC EQUIPMENT: **Rentals, Lab**

CHARTER/DIVE BOAT AVAILABLE: **Yes**   DIVER CAPACITY: **10 divers/boat**
COAST GUARD APPROVED: **No**   CAPTAIN LICENSE: **Yes**
SHIP TO SHORE: **Yes**   LORAN: RADAR : **Yes**
DIVE MASTER/INSTRUCTOR ABOARD: **Yes**

DIVING & SNORKELING: **Salt**
TYPE OF DIVING/SNORKELING IN AREA: **Wall, Beach, Wreck, Reef, Cave**
DIVING/SNORKELING IN YOUR AREA IS BEST SUITED FOR: **Beginner, Intermediate, Advanced**
BEST TIME OF YEAR FOR DIVING/SNORKELING: **Year round**
TEMPERATURE: NOV-APRIL   MAY-OCT:
VISIBILITY: DIVING **99 ft**   SNORKELING: **99 ft**

PACKAGES AVAILABLE: **Dive, Dive Stay, Snorkel, Snorkel Stay**
ACCOMMODATIONS NEARBY: **Hotel**
ACCOMMODATIONS RATES: **Moderate, Inexpensive**
RESTAURANTS NEARBY: **Moderate, Inexpensive**
YOUR AREA IS: **Remote, Quiet with Activities**
LOCAL ACTIVITY/NIGHTLIFE: **Disco**
CAR NEEDED TO EXPLORE AREA: **Yes**
DUTY FREE SHOPPING: **No**

LOCAL EMERGENCY SERVICES: NEAREST HYPERBARIC TREATMENT FACILITY:
COASTGUARD: **Harbour Master**   AUTHORITY: **Manado Hospital**
TELEPHONE: **0431 - 51875**   LOCATION: **Manado City**
CALLSIGNS: TELEPHONE: **0431 - 53191**

LOCAL DIVING DOCTOR:
NAME: **Dr. Bambang Suharianto**
LOCATION: **Manado City**
TELEPHONE: **0431 - 60334, 51583, 66751**

IRELAND

Simon Nelson

The rugged coastline of County Cork at the southwestern corner of the Republic of Ireland offers some of the best cold water diving that is available anywhere in the world. Off its most southwesterly point lies the famous Fastnet Rock - the last piece of Ireland seen by those emigrants that have left for America in the last century. The adjoining coastline is deeply indented with long bays and towering headlands and a scattering of quiet towns and villages.

Being at the very edge of Europe and in the path of the Gulf Stream, the area has clear unpolluted water and an abundance of marine life. The area is remote and under-developed and facilities for the diver are few and far between. However, for the intrepid diving group that is looking for more than an easy trip to a popular reef which has been dived by thousands, here there is spectacular diving in an area that has yet to be explored.

The village of **Schull**, just nine miles from **Fastnet Rock**, has become popular in recent years with those on holiday and has a good range of accommodations. Schull also has the only dive shop in the area. It is possible to rent tanks and weights, but you must bring all the rest of your gear with you, or rent it in Dublin. You must also bring your own diving buddy, as you are unlikely to find any lone divers to match up with. Similarly, any boat diving is by way of boat charter. There are no scheduled boat trips to join up with.

Fastnet Rock by Simon Nelson

So much for the difficulties! Here is a sampling of the myriad of possible dive sites:

FASTNET ROCK

This famous rock lies 3 miles southwest of **Cape Clear Island** and is 9 miles from Schull. A magnificent lighthouse that seems to grow from the very rock itself tops it. It is at the tip of an underwater reef that is about one mile long and 200 yards wide. The reef rapidly plunges down to 50 meters on all sides. **It is an area of tricky currents and an experienced local skipper is a must for safe diving.** The visibility underwater is always good and in settled weather you can easily see the boat from 30 meters down. The reef is split into a maze of gullies whose rock faces are carpeted with jewel anemones of every possible color. Huge shoals of Pollack and Mackerel abound and can all but block out the light as they swim overhead. This is an advanced dive and you need to keep your wits about you, but on a good day it is a world-beater.

THE NESTORIAN

Lying close under the cliffs of Cape Clear Island lie the remains of this **400-ft ship**. The *Nestorian* ran aground early in 1917 and sank in 20 meters of water. Being exposed to the full force of the Atlantic storms for 75 years means there is little structure left in tact. **However, its cargo of large steel ingots and empty shell casings lie scattered amongst the plates of this once proud vessel.** Being close up under a westerly facing cliff means this site is inaccessible if there is any swell rolling in from the open Atlantic. When conditions are calm however, it makes a splendid scenic setting to an interesting wreck dive with good visibility and extensive marine growth on the pinnacles and rock faces.

TOOR PIER

The coastline of this area is dotted with small isolated landing points, built in the last century to promote fishing in the bays. **These now offer the diver some excellent sites for shore diving.** They are easy to find - given a good map and a bit of local advice. The best of them all is **Toor Pier** which is a lonely spot near the end of **Dunmanus Bay** about 12 miles from Schull. **As with shore diving in the area, it is vital to check that you can cope with the somewhat limited facilities for entering and leaving the water. Slippery and broken concrete steps can be difficult with the water surging around you with the swell.**

This site offers excellent diving starting at 10 meters and running down into deep gullies at 25 meters with their tops in 15 meters. **Visibility is usually excellent and the marine life extensive.** Swimming the other way brings you to a large arch that runs right through the rock and is the home to several inquisitive seals. With a maximum depth of 10 meters and rocks reaching almost to the surface, this is an excellent area for advanced snorkelers as well.

LOUGH HYNE MARINE RESERVE

One of the first marine reserves to be set up in Europe, this one-mile square lough is connected to the open sea by a narrow set of rapids and reaches depths of 50 meters in places. However, the area of main interest is in 15 meters close to the entrance of the rapids. **An exciting experience is to snorkel through the short stretch of rapids where the tide runs at about 10 knots - it is then easy to climb out and return by foot.**

THE DINGLE DOLPHIN

This world-renowned wild dolphin has lived close to the town of **Dingle** for the last 7 years and has sought out human company. It is easy to snorkel out to his "playground" at slack water and the experience of meeting a 10 foot wild dolphin who just wants to come and play is very exciting. Dingle is about a three-hour drive north of Schull through stunning scenery and the trip can easily be made in a day.

In describing these sites I have tried to portray the beauty and remoteness of the area without glossing over the potential problems that can confront the diver who is used to easier conditions. However, once you start diving here, the effort is well worth your while.

GENERAL INFORMATION

During the summertime the water temperature is 15 C and a 6-mm wetsuit is the minimum needed for diving in comfort.

It is illegal to pick up any shellfish or to use a spear gun while using SCUBA.

A permit is required to dive in the Marine Nature Reserve at Lough Hyne. It can be obtained for free by writing to: Conservation Section, Wildlife Service, OPW, Leeson Lane, Dublin 2. **All wrecks over 100 years old are protected and a permit is required to dive them.** There is no legal requirement to hold a diving certificate to dive or rent gear. However, you should be competent in dealing with diving in a thick wetsuit, sudden low visibility and rough surface conditions.

The national federation coordinating diving in Ireland is the Irish Underwater Council, Haigh Terrace, Dun Laoghaire, Co. Dublin.

The local dive shop is **Schull Watersports Centre**, The Pier, Schull. Telephone 028-28554 or 28351. They can also help arrange accommodations.

In case of emergencies the local doctor is trained in diving medicine and the nearest recompression chamber is only one and a half-hours away.

Non diving activities include: golf, sailing, pony trekking, spectacular walks and enjoying the relaxed Irish way of life!

DIVERS FACT SHEET FOR WEST CORK DIVING RELATED ACCIDENTS
(BENDS/EMBOLISM)

- Contact the local diving doctor, Dr. Larry O'Connor, Schull. Tel 028-28311 for conformation of symptoms and arrangements for chamber recompression.
- If symptoms occur while offshore contact VALENTIA RADIO on Ch.16 and ask for phone link to the doctor. In case of potential helicopter requirement for an evacuation to the chamber and there is a delay in contacting the doctor, ask to be put through to Marine Rescue Coordinator at Shannon Airport to arrange transport. Head to shore, but do not leave the boat unless requested to do so. (Helicopter officially only for rescue at sea).
- If you are unable to contact the doctor, call the chamber direct to ascertain that it is available, before setting off.
- Directions to Haulboeline (1 3/4 hrs from Schull). Head for Cork via Bandon. After Innishannon turn right at sign for airport and ferry. Follow signs to Ferry and Ringaskiddy. In the docks area, pass the ferry terminal and cross the bridges into the Irish Steel complex. Finally, turn left into the naval base.
- Directions to Galway General Hospital (4 1/2 hrs from Schull). Head for Galway via Cork and Limerick. Heading into Galway keep straight on at all roundabouts until you cross the river. Straight across the next lights then left at the next roundabout. Right at the T-junction and right again at the next crossroad. Hospital is on your left. Head for 'Fever Dept'.

Note: Oxygen Kit and large capacity cylinder belonging to WCSAC is available in an emergency from Catherine Arundel, Arundel's Bar, Schull.

EMERGENCY TELEPHONE NUMBERS

Doctor	028-28311
Marine Rescue Coordinator, Shannon	061-61969/61219
Recompression Chambers	
Duty Officer, Naval Base, Haulbowline, Cork	021-811246
Dept. of Anaesthesia, Galway General Hospital	091-24222
Local Hospital	027-50133
Regional Hospital, Cork	021-546400
Valentia Radio	0667-6109
Baltimore Life-boat Station	028-20119

USEFUL TELEPHONE NUMBERS

Schull Watersports Centre	028-28554(w)
	028-28351(h)
Met Office (weather forecast)	021-965974/964600
	or 1199
Harbour Master (Schull)	028-28136
Garda Station (Schull)	028-28111
Mizen Head Lighthouse	028-35115

IRISH TOURISH BOARD
345 PARK AVENUE,17TH FLOOR
NEW YORK, NY 10154
TEL 212 418 0800

South West Ireland

County Cork

Paul James

In September, our group of twelve divers from England set sail on the *Swansea* to board the Cork Ferry for the overnight crossing to County Cork, Ireland. Our intention was to dive the South Western most tip of Ireland, where the Atlantic Ocean batters the coast for most of the year. Our research showed there to be hundreds of wrecks on the seabed around that part of the coastline.

We arrived at Cork at 7am the following morning laden with diving equipment and bottles of Irish Whiskey. Richard Jackson, the owner of **Sea Trek Dive Centre**, was waiting with transport to take us to our final destination, **Union Hall**, a small fishing village consisting of about forty houses and five very friendly pubs.

Our accommodations for the next six days were basic, but very comfortable. The standard of accommodation in Ireland is excellent and the size of your pocket decides whether its hotel accommodation, or like us, bed and breakfast for the week. I can't recommend Richard's breakfast enough, we had to tell him to stop bringing us food. They were massive and made up of mostly traditional Irish fare.

WRECK DIVING

We told our boat skipper, Nick, we wanted to dive the wrecks in the area. Nick is a very serious wreck diver's skipper, he has previously taken divers out to the *Lucitania*, which is a one hundred plus meter dive only to be undertaken on mixed gas by the most advanced enthusiast.

Our first dive was to be on the *Mignonette*, a British sloop that sank in 1917. Full of anticipation, we arrived at the harbor to see our dive boat. It was a fast offshore 105 with twin 375 hp diesel engines. The trips out to the wrecks don't take long at 30-35 knots. **The Mignonette was an excellent dive at 35 meters,** there were plenty of things to look at, soft corals, sponges and a myriad of fish and crustaceans. **It is illegal in Southern Ireland to take crustaceans whilst scuba diving.**

We dived seven wrecks that week. *The Crescent City* (the silver dollar wreck) sank in 1871. She was carrying a cargo of general goods and four chests of newly minted Mexican silver dollars. One of our party found two of them; they were absolutely beautiful.

The next wreck was *The Kowloon Bridge*, a massive tanker that sank in 1987 while carrying 165,000 tons of iron ore. **She is reputedly the largest wreck in the world.**

The Asian, built in 1898 and sank in 1924 on Stag Rocks, which rise out of the Atlantic like a set of shark's teeth.

A submarine, the U260, sank in 1945 in 43 meters of water is a small craft. We managed to fin from the propellers to the nose and back to the conning tower and surface with minimal decompression.

The Alondra, a British steamer that sank in 1916 was the penultimate dive. She was 298 ft long and weighed 2,248 tons.

Towards the end of the week the sea was extremely calm. **Nick took us out to Cape Clear, which is near the famous Fastnet Lighthouse; to dive a wreck called** The *Nestorian*. She sank in 1917 while carrying a very expensive cargo of stainless steel bars; they are still there. The bars are approximately 10ft long and 2ft or 1ft thick.

All the wrecks that we dived were excellent dives. The visibility varied from 5 meters up to 20 meters and Richard assured us that **there are hundreds more in the area yet to be dived,** and added that we had missed some fantastic scenic diving.

Our evening entertainment was provided by the five pubs where the food was unbelievably good. I put on 8 pounds in the six days we were there. The people of southern Ireland were wonderful; you would be hard pressed to find a more friendly and hospitable place.

Cork has an airport and a ferry port, so it is very accessible. **Personally, I can't wait to go back again, the diving is great and the welcome is warm, I highly recommend it.**

All divers facilities are available. We dived with Richard Jackson of Dive Trek, Blind Harbour House, Reen, Union Hall, County Cork. Tel/Fax 028 33092 Int: +35328 33092. U.K. Contact out of season Tel: 01429 837573

MARSHALL ISLANDS

Bikini Atoll

Mike Innis

U.S.S. Saratoga by Michael Innis

Getting there is not half the fun. From the States, you go to Honolulu. After a night in Honolulu, you catch a weekly flight at 8:30 a. m. to the island of Majuro. You spend the night in Majuro, then catch an 8:00 a.m. flight to Enue, which is part of the Bikini Atoll. From Enue you take a 50-minute boat ride to Bikini proper; then a 5-minute truck ride to your quarters. 15 time zones and one International Date Line later, I was glad to settle in.

However, the travel is worth it! I can now say that I am one of less than fifty people who have first dived these wrecks since they were driven to the bottom more than 50 years ago.

After years of testing and months and months of negotiation, **these historic shipwrecks are finally open to advanced recreational divers.** The negotiations took place between the Bikinian government and scores of eager dive packagers from all over the world. The testing was done, and is still being done, by the DOE, to ensure that the levels of radiation are low enough to permit safe diving in the lagoon. **The results of the tests show that you are exposed to more radiation in Los Angeles today than you are in Bikini.**

Marshalls Dive Adventures were awarded the exclusive rights to the dive operation.

My first dive with them was the wreck of the *U.S.S. Saratoga*. I put a puff of air into my BC and hover, 5 feet off the flight deck, 100 feet down in Bikini Lagoon. The visibility is 80 feet. I look to my right across the expanse of the flight deck and it smears into blue haze; looking left, it's the same thing: no end in sight. I don't bother looking fore and aft, since she's 880 feet long. During WW II, **the Japanese claimed they sunk "SARA" on 7 different occasions. The reality is that our own hands in a nuclear holocaust called Operation Crossroads in 1946, sank her.**

Deeper into the wreck at the hanger deck level, I see 500 pound bombs, racks of rockets,

U.S.S. Pilotfish by Michael Innis

187

stacks of torpedoes. A couple of fighter planes, Thunderbolts, sit broken in the silt; and behind them, an Avenger, like the one George Bush flew, appears out of the murk.

My next dive was on the *Nagato*. From the bridge of this massive battleship, Admiral Yamamoto launched the aerial attack on Pearl Harbor.

Then on to the *U.S.S. Pilotfish*, which was in Tokyo Bay at the surrender ceremonies.

The *U.S.S. Carlisle*, the destroyer that searched for weeks for Emelia Earhart, was our next dive site.

...And on it went, through six incredible days of diving.

MEXICO

Akumal
Bill Hull

Tulum Ruins by Wendy Canning Church

From the international airport at Cancun the drive to Akumal is about 65 miles.

Aqua Expeditions arranged for a rental house, a pleasant casa about a mile to the north of the dive shop. Several more topes and a tended gate soon accustom everyone to a more leisurely pace, and ensure an atmosphere of peace and quiet for watching the water, sky, birds, lizards and insects.

Our casa was right on the Yal-Ku, a relatively shallow lagoon with a protecting reef at its mouth. We could swim right from our front steps or walk a short distance to the head of the bay to begin explorations of its upper regions.

The Yal-Ku has been described as a natural aquarium and coral garden.

Why are there so many fish? Are they attracted by the flow of fresh water from the head of the bay? Has someone been feeding them? On our first swim from the front steps we encountered French grunts, three-spotted damselfish, small Spanish hogfish, a spotted ray with a stubby tail and a golden spotted eel. On a later excursion we startled a small sea turtle. In the lagoon itself, the layering of fresh and salt water sometimes produces a "halocline" that blurs the scenery.

The more we discovered the more interesting it became. We found a group of large, midnight blue parrotfish. What were they eating? I thought their diet was largely coral and there isn't a great abundance in the Yal-Ku. I watched carefully- but all I saw was some nibbling on vegetation growing on rocks. In addition to schools of sergeant majors there were quite a few larger fish such as gray snappers and Bermuda chub. On one dive we saw many Atlantic needlefish, some solitary others in schools. There were trumpetfish, brittle stars, very large sea urchins: such a variety of creatures to see that it is hard to remember, or identify all that was encountered. One is apt to see more fish when swimming very slowly or drifting.

On our first swim in the upper Yal-Ku I was preparing to slip into the water from a convenient rocky shelf — mask, snorkel, fins, wet suit and weight belt all adjusted — when there was a sudden impact on my dangling calf — no blood drawn, but it was startling. When I checked it out from below I discovered a line of small and fiercely territorial damsel fish. Their impact is all out of proportion to their size. Exclamations from others, preparing to swim by cooling their legs off as I had done suggested that generations of damsel fish from this short stretch of shore had been practicing full speed head-on collisions on relaxed calf muscles.

We chose Akumal for a family vacation because we wanted easy access to the water and favorable conditions for introducing two grown daughters to SCUBA diving.

My wife and I had received our certification two years ago, but had not had an opportunity to practice our skills. Most of all we wanted an opportunity for extended observation of underwater life. I have had a long term fascination with diving and was particularly interested that other members of our family have an opportunity to experience the richness and complexity of SCUBA diving in a safe and supportive setting.

Diving has always had a compelling fascination for me, perhaps because it is a strong challenge to one's senses to operate in such a different environment. I was very excited to find that it was possible to float at any depth by adjusting the amount of air in my lungs or buoyancy compensator. The ability to go up and down so easily in three dimensions is fascinating in itself. Gliding down the side of reefs, controlling buoyancy by the amount of air in one's lungs gives a sense of effortless flying in worlds of incredible diversity and beauty.

The resort refresher course was very well handled.

The shore session packed a great deal of information into a short time and then we waded into the water with small tanks to check out the equipment, practice clearing the regulator and masks, breathing from our buddy's octopus, etc. We hadn't understood that

Akumal Casa

189

SCUBA AND SNORKELING FACILITIES QUESTIONNAIRE PRIVATE

NAME **THE ORIGNAL AKUMAL DIVE SHOP**
ADDRESS **POSTAL #1**
AKUMAL, Q. ROO, MEXICO
CONTACT **DON BREWER**
TITLE **OWNER**
TELEPHONE **011 52 987 59032**   FAX **987 59033**

CAPITOL: **CHETUMAL**   GOVERNMENT: **MEXICO**
POPULATION: LANGUAGE: **SPANISH / ENGLISH**
CURRENCY: **PESOS**   ELECTRICITY: **YES**
AIRLINES: DEPARTURE TAX? **YES**
VISA/PASSPORT? **YES**   PROOF OF CITIZENSHIP? **YES**

YOUR FACILITY IS QUALIFIED AS: **SCUBA CENTER**
BUISINESS HOURS: **8:00 AM TO 5:00 PM**
CERTIFYING AGENCIES: **PADI NSS CDS TDI 5 STAR MIXED GAS AND REBREATHER**
LOG BOOK REQUIRED? **NO BUT MUST HAVE PROOF OF CERTIFICATION**
EQUIPMENT: **SALES RENTALS AND AIR FILLS**
PRIMARY LINE OF EQUIPMENT: **SHERWOOD**
PHOTOGRAPHIC EQUIPMENT: **SALES**

CHARTER/DIVE BOAT AVAILABLE? **YES**   DIVER CAPACITY **EIGHT**
COAST GUARD APPROVED? **YES**   CAPTAINS LICENSED? **YES**
SHIP TO SHORE? **YES**   LORAN ? **NO**   RADAR **NO**
DIVE MASTER/INSTRUCTOR ABOARD? **YES**

DIVING & SNORKELING:
TYPE OF DIVING/SNORKELING IN AREA?   **SALT AND FRESH WATER**
DIVING/SNORKELING IN YOUR AREA IS BEST SUITED FOR: **ALL LEVELS INCLUDING REEF AND CAVE**

BEST TIME OF YEAR FOR DIVING/SNORKELING:
TEMPERATURE: NOV-APRIL   **79F**   MAY-OCT: **84F**
VISIBILITY: DIVING **80 TO 100 FT**   SNORKELING: **50 FT**

PACKAGES AVAILABLE: **DIVE AND DIVE/STAY**
ACCOMMODATIONS NEARBY: **HOTELS CONDOS AND HOME RENTALS**
ACCOMMODATIONS RATES: **MODERATE**
RESTAURANTS NEARBY: **MODERATE**
YOUR AREA IS: **QUIET WITH ACTIVITIES**
LOCAL ACTIVITY/NIGHTLIFE: **NEARBY MAYAN RUINS**
CAR NEEDED TO EXPLORE AREA? **YES**
DUTY FREE SHOPPING?

LOCAL EMERGENCY SERVICES: **MEDICAL CLINIC 5 KMS**
NEAREST HYPERBARIC TREATMENT FACILITY: **PLAYA DEL CARMEN 25 KMS**

LOCAL DIVING DOCTOR:
NAME: **EDUARDO RODRIGUEZ**
LOCATION: **PLAYA DEL CARMEN**
TELEPHONE: **987 31365**

this was to be followed by a boat dive the same morning, but we were soon wading out to a dive boat. This time carrying full-sized tanks.

The trip through the reef entrance seemed very rough, but it was a short trip to the "Escuela" or school site where there was a mooring. The pitching was less in deeper water, but still a bit intimidating for beginners who found themselves being asked to roll over backwards under these conditions. **La Escuela is a fine location for a beginning dive.** I wish we had been able to return there. The sand bottom with coral canyons to swim through at a depth of 25 feet and the abundance of marine life was marvelously exciting.

The best dive was off Akumal Point a mile or more to the south and well offshore. The water was much clearer and the bottom visible at 70'.

With such good visibility we could get a good overhead view of the reef configuration on our slow descent. The bottom was sandy with coral forming vertical walls and canyons. It was similar to the Escuela site, but on a much larger scale. I had the sense that I was viewing something quite ancient. How many years had this reef been here in a similar form, I wondered?

Tulum and Coba make wonderful cultural excursions for non-dive days, and a nearby biosphere reserve.

For more information on diving centers and cassa rentals contact; Aqua Expeditions, 92 Mt. Vernon Street, Boston, MA 02108; Fax: (617) 227-8145

Editors note: Our writer Ray Elman took the casa in 1998 and agrees. He raves about the spot for a family vacation and cannot wait to return. He dived the Cenotes for the first time and felt very comfortable with the "Buttoned Up" scuba center.

BAJA
LOS CABOS

Wendy Canning Church

The area known as "The Capes" is comprised of the towns of San Jose del Cabo and Cabo San Lucas.

Along the eighteen miles of highway that separate the two towns are spectacular views of sixteen beaches with the cobalt blue Sea of Cortez on one side and the Pacific Ocean on the other. Mountain ranges and the golden yellow desert sprinkled with three hundred-year-old flowering cacti act as a backdrop. To further whet the visitor's appetite there are five well maintained championship golf courses along the way.

Los Cabos is less than two hours from Los Angeles on daily direct and connecting flights from most major cities. It is located on the tip of the beautiful Baja peninsula. U.S. and Canadian citizens need proof of citizenship. All others need a valid passport to enter Mexico. Although the distance between the two towns is short, the ambience of each is worlds apart.

Cabo San Lucas [the slender one] with a population of twenty-one thousand, extends eastward of the Baja peninsula's southern tip. **It is a bustling tourist area, hotels, condominiums, guest houses, restaurants, nightclubs, watersports, including some of the best scuba diving and fishing in the world combined with 365 days of sunshine make this a tourist Mecca.**

San Jose del Cabo on the northern end of the corridor is seductively quiet, a small town, few restaurants, and no nightclubs.

Spanish explorers discovered Los Cabos in 1533 and the first mission was founded in 1730. By 1767, all of the Indians had died of European diseases or in skirmishes with the Spanish. Los Cabos remained a native fishing community until Budd Parr built the beautiful Hacienda Beach Resort.

In Cabo San Lucas we chose the Hotel Hacienda Beach Resort that has been awarded the prestigious *Gran Turismo* rating, achieved by only a few elite hotels in

Cabo San Lucas Villa

Mexico. It offers its guests an uncompromising blend of beauty, luxury, comfort, service and relaxation with miles of wide, uninterrupted beach embracing the gentle curve of the dramatic, calm and protected Cabo San Lucas Bay.

Located on its own peninsula, protected by the Sierra De Laguna Mountains, it juts into the calm bay. The Hacienda has the only safe swimming beach in the area.

Accommodations range from garden patio rooms to deluxe two bedroom townhouses. All have air conditioning, telephones, television, and mini bars. Townhouses come with complete kitchens, perfect for families.

The spacious and immaculate rooms, studios, suites, beach cabana rooms, and town-houses with patios or balconies and panoramic ocean views were designed for privacy and comfort. Exotic bougainvillea and tropical landscaping provide an impressive and peaceful ambiance. The cuisine is delicious and beautifully presented. The visitor will sample the freshest of foods prepared in Mexican and International style in the romantic dining room overlooking the Sea of Cortez. A superb wine list is available.

Do everything under the sun or nothing at all...

Tennis, marlin fishing, windsurfing, scuba diving, whale watching, snorkeling, sailing, dove hunting, duck hunting, water skiing, sun swept beaches, horseback riding, glass bottom boats, coastal cruises, paddle tennis, beach volleyball, trap shooting, surf/shore fishing, putting green, fresh water pool, fantastic 11-piece Mariachi band, complete and modern dive shop, all sports equipment available, private beaches and secluded coves, safe anchorage for private yachts. Three beautiful indoor and outdoor bars, poolside lunches served on request, box lunches available for excursions. Car rental and taxi service. Unique shopping plaza and courtyard.

The Hotel Hacienda Beach Resort stands alone, like an exclusive club amid lush tropical gardens and "Old World" fountains on a private estate. Under the keen eye of owner and manager Mark Parr this is a first rate resort. This is definitely our first choice for the perfect hideaway in Cabo San Lucas.

FOR RESERVATIONS:
Hotel Hacienda Beach Resort
Cabo San Lucas
Baja, Mexico
Tel: 011 52 114 30664

"Lands End" by Wendy Canning Church

Hotel Service Corporation
6523 Wilshire Boulevard
Los Angeles, CA 90048
Tel: 1 800 733 2226
Fax: 213 655 3243A

OTHER ACCOMMODATIONS
Los Cabos –Mexico's Best Kept Secret offers Lovely condominiums and villas on empty white sand beaches that stretch for miles. Ocean or golf course views.
Contact:Aqua Expeditions Tel: (617) 723-7134

Three km northeast of Cabo San Lucas off Mexico 1, the **Vagabundos del Mar RV Park** [Tel 3-02-90; 707 374 5511 in the U.S.] Has full hookups. Additional guests are extra. Discounts are available for members of the Vagabundos del Mar travel club.

Facilities include flush toilets, showers, a pool, and laundry.

LOCAL TRANSPORT
Taxi service from Los Cabos International Airport to Cabo San Lucas is available. In Cabo itself, you can easily get around on foot, bicycle, or scooter.

Auto Rental: VW sedans or vans are easily rented at Los Cabos International Airport.

THE SCUBA DIVING AND SNORKELING
Cabo San Lucas has unique underwater terrain. The sand in the Bay of Cortez travels in circles building huge canyons or monoliths at lands end. These create sand waterfalls descending to depths of 100 feet marking the end of the landmass in the bay. Ones next stop is Antarctica. These open sea conditions provide prolific sea life in all varieties and size.

Diving off Cabo San Lucas is quite different than the diving off San Jose del Cabo. Here the waters are calm, although at some sites you will find swift currents. These sites are for advanced divers only.

We dived with **Cabo Aquadeportes**, conveniently located at the Hotel Hacienda Beach Resort. **Owned and operated by John and Molly Fox for the past fifteen years.** Their center upholds the highest safety standards. **The multilingual staff guides divers and snorkelers to the perfect pristine underwater kingdom in the bay.**

Dive boats leave at 8:00 am, 10:00 am and 1:30 p.m. Night dives are available by reservations. They offer divesites to suit every level of experience. **Snorkelers are welcomed aboard.**

PELICAN ROCK
This is a mellow dive suited for all levels. **At 45 feet divers and snorkelers have time to view Cortez damselfish, leather bass, schools of Mexican goatfish, China rockfish, painted greenling, wolf eel, turbot, and yellow eye rockfish.** Hundreds of fish swam above and below us as the sand fell like waterfalls. Beautifully shaped slopes in a panorama of color made a sensational backdrop for the tunnels and alleyways waiting to be investigated. **A must dive!**

SAND FALLS
This is a deep dive at 90 feet, giving the diver only 20 minutes to sight Pacific angel shark and swell shark, bat rays, stingrays, banded guitarfish [half ray half shark] and

eagle rays. The Pacific manta are magnificent creatures and cruise at 20 feet below the surface where you will meet them on ascent or descent.

ROOKERY

Here you will dive with the Sea Lions and their pups. At times the currents are quite strong. It is best to just go with them. The divers will also encounter huge beautiful green moray eels sometimes as many as four or five in one crevice. The parrot and puffer fish were the largest I have seen anywhere.

THE POINT

Not for the faint of heart, this dive has very swift currents but the reward is the sighting of the pelagics. From December to March it is home to whale sharks. **Words of caution, follow the dive plan to the letter, the next landmass is Antarctica and you will be there without a passport!**

SNORKELING

The best snorkeling is in the northeast on your way to San Jose del Cabo where you can view colorful reef cornetfish, king angelfish, guinea fowl puffer, tube blenny, giant seahorse and rough jaw frogfish.

Sea Lion, Cabo San Lucas, Mexico by Lynn Faukhouser

DINING

DaGiorio's in Cabo overlooking the arch is a glorious place for a cocktail at sunset.

The Peacock serves the freshest of seafood, prime meats [steak and lamb] prepared by a German chef. Alfresco dining, weather permitting, is delightful.

Alfonso's is a tiny romantic restaurant with white table linen.

Mia Casa serves wonderful Mexican food indoor and alfresco. There are splendid murals on the walls and a shop with Mexican artworks and furniture.

Al's Burger is popular with residents and serves both burgers and American breakfast.

The Trailer Park serves the best seafood at the best prices.

ACTIVITIES
CABO SAN LUCAS

There are few historical sites to visit.

The Old Lighthouse at Mar Bermejo [Red Sea].

SCUBA AND SNORKELING FACILITIES QUESTIONNAIRE

NAME   Cabo Acuadepoutes S.A de C.V.
ADDRESS   Apdo, Postal 136
            Cabo San Lucas, Baja California Sur, Mexico
CONTACT   Joe and Molly Fox
TITLE   Owners
TELEPHONE   (011)-52-114-30117   FAX (011)-52-114-30117   TELEX

CAPITOL: **Mexico City**   GOVERNMENT: **Mexico**
POPULATION: LANGUAGE: **Spanish/English**
CURRENCY: **Peso, U.S. $**   ELECTRICITY: **110-120v AC 60 cycle**
AIRLINES: **Alaska, Aero Mexico, Mexicana**   DEPARTURE TAX? **Yes**
NEED VISA/PASSPORT?   YES x   NO   PROOF OF CITIZENSHIP?   YES x   NO

YOUR FACILITY IS CLASSIFIED AS: SCUBA CENTER   RESORT x
BUSINESS HOURS: **8:00 a.m. - 4:00 p.m.**
CERTIFYING AGENCIES: **PADI (5-star), NAUI (Pro Eclty), SSI**
LOG BOOK REQUIRED?   YES   NO x
EQUIPMENT: SALES x   RENTALS x   AIR FILLS x
PRIMARY LINE OF EQUIPMENT: DACOR
PHOTOGRAPHIC EQUIPMENT: SALES   RENTALS   LAB

CHARTER/DIVE BOAT AVAILABLE?   YES x   NO   DIVER CAPACITY   **60**
COAST GUARD APPROVED?   YES   NO   CAPTAIN LICENSED? YES x   NO
SHIP TO SHORE?   YES x   NO   LORAN? YES NO   RADAR?   YES   NO **n/a**
DIVE MASTER/INSTRUCTOR ABOARD? YES x   NO BOTH x
DIVING & SNORKELING: SALT x   FRESH
TYPE OF DIVING/SNORKELING IN AREA: WALL x BEACH x WRECK x REEF x CAVE x ICE
DIVING/SNORKELING IN YOUR AREA IS BEST SUITED FOR: BEGINNER x INTERMEDIATE x ADVANCED x
BEST TIME OF YEAR FOR DIVING/SNORKELING:
TEMPERATURE: NOV-APRIL   **65+F**   MAY-OCT: **80+F**
VISIBILITY: DIVING: **60FT**   SNORKELING: **60FT**

PACKAGES AVAILABLE: DIVE x   DIVE STAY x   SNORKEL x   SNORKEL-STAY x
ACCOMMODATIONS NEARBY: HOTEL x   MOTEL x   HOME RENTALS x
ACCOMMODATION RATES: EXPENSIVE x   MODERATE x   INEXPENSIVE x
RESTAURANTS NEARBY: EXPENSIVE x   MODERATE x   INEXPENSIVE x
YOUR AREA IS: REMOTE x   QUIET WITH ACTIVITIES x   LIVELY x
LOCAL ACTIVITY/NIGHTLIFE:
CAR NEEDED TO EXPLORE AREA?   YES   NO
DUTY FREE SHOPPING?   YES x   NO

LOCAL EMERGENCY SERVICES   NEAREST HYPERBARIC TREATMENT FACILITY
COASTGUARD   **N/A**   AUTHORITY: **Sub-Aquatic Safety Services**
TELEPHONE: LOCATION: **Plaza Las Glavias Hotel, Cabo**
CALLSIGNS: **Ch. 16 VHF**   **San Lucas**
                                          TELEPHONE: **Plaza Marinatt E-16,**
                                                        Tel/Fax (114) 33666

LOCAL DIVING DOCTOR:
NAME: **Dr. Alfonso Navar**
LOCATION: **Cabo San Lucas**
TELEPHONE: **(114) 31218**

SCUBA AND SNORKELING FACILITIES QUESTIONNAIRE

NAME **Dive Pamilla**
ADDRESS **P.O. Box 37**
Cabo San Lucas, B.C.S. Mexico
CONTACT **Ignatius Ayuso Arderius**
TITLE **General Manager**
TELEPHONE **(114) 3 29 86**   FAX **(114) 3 15 21**   TELEX

CAPITOL: **La Pas BCS, Mexico**   GOVERNMENT: **Democratic Republic**
POPULATION: **30,000**   LANGUAGE: **Spanish**
CURRENCY: **Peso**   ELECTRICITY: **110 Volt**
AIRLINES: **Alaska, Mexicana, Aero California**   DEPARTURE TAX? **$10.00 U.S.**
NEED VISA/PASSPORT?   YES   NO **x**   PROOF OF CITIZENSHIP? YES **x**   NO

YOUR FACILITY IS CLASSIFIED AS: SCUBA CENTER **x**   RESORT
BUSINESS HOURS: **9:00 -17:00 hours**
CERTIFYING AGENCIES: **PADI**
LOG BOOK REQUIRED?   YES **x**   NO
EQUIPMENT: SALES **x**   RENTALS **x**   AIR FILLS **x**
PRIMARY LINE OF EQUIPMENT: SEA QUEST
PHOTOGRAPHIC EQUIPMENT: SALES   RENTALS   **LAB Only films & disposable U/W cameras**

CHARTER/DIVE BOAT AVAILABLE?   YES **x**   NO   DIVER CAPACITY **8 people**
COAST GUARD APPROVED?   YES **x**   NO   CAPTAIN LICENSED? YES **x**   NO
SHIP TO SHORE?   YES **x**   NO   LORAN? YES   NO **x**   RADAR?   YES   NO **x**
DIVE MASTER/INSTRUCTOR ABOARD? YES **x**   NO BOTH
DIVING & SNORKELING: SALT **x**   FRESH
TYPE OF DIVING/SNORKELING IN AREA: WALL **x**   BEACH **x**   WRECK **x**   REEF **x**   CAVE   ICE
DIVING/SNORKELING IN YOUR AREA IS BEST SUITED FOR: BEGINNER **x** INTERMEDIATE **x** ADVANCED **x**
BEST TIME OF YEAR FOR DIVING/SNORKELING: **October/February**
TEMPERATURE: NOV-APRIL   **84-69F**   MAY-OCT: **65-84F**
VISIBILITY: DIVING: **60FT**   SNORKELING: **60FT**

PACKAGES AVAILABLE: DIVE **x**   DIVE STAY **x**   SNORKEL   SNORKEL-STAY
ACCOMMODATIONS NEARBY: HOTEL **x**   MOTEL   HOME RENTALS
ACCOMMODATION RATES: EXPENSIVE **x**   MODERATE   INEXPENSIVE
RESTAURANTS NEARBY: EXPENSIVE **x**   MODERATE **x**   INEXPENSIVE
YOUR AREA IS: REMOTE   QUIET WITH ACTIVITIES **x** LIVELY
LOCAL ACTIVITY/NIGHTLIFE: **Golf courses, fishing, tennis course, bars and discos**
CAR NEEDED TO EXPLORE AREA?   YES **x**   NO
DUTY FREE SHOPPING?   YES **x**   NO

LOCAL EMERGENCY SERVICES   NEAREST HYPERBARIC TREATMENT FACILITY
COASTGUARD **C.G. VHF #16**   AUTHORITY: **Dr. Alfonso Najar**
TELEPHONE: **2 03 16**   LOCATION: **Cabo San Lucas B.C.S**
CALLSIGNS: TELEPHONE: **3 36 66 Radio VHF Channel #16**

LOCAL DIVING DOCTOR:
NAME: **Alfonso Najar**
LOCATION: **Recompression Chamber**
TELEPHONE: **(114) 3 36 66**

Cabo Pulmo, Puerto Chileno and Punta Palmilla offer a variety of watersports
The San Lucas Marina. Cabo San Lucas has the finest fishing waters in the world. One will find great fishing and boating.
The Los Cabos Shopping Mall has decorative objects and native clothing.
Do not leave without at least one piece of the magnificent silver jewelry the workmanship and quality is excellent and embarrassingly inexpensive.
Curious Cong has shops in both towns. You are expected to bargain!

SAN JOSE DEL CABO
Boulevards Mijares and Zaragonza are the two main streets intersecting at Plaza Mijres. The local fiesta is held here every Saturday night. In this area you will find many small boutiques and restaurants.

DINING
Damina offers patio dining under lush bougainvillea's trees. The wonderful cuisine is complimented by the music of strolling guitarists.
Another romantic spot is **Pietro's,** an Italian restaurant serving great pasta.
The bargain on dining is Ricardo's, housed in a simple white washed building serving luncheons fresh from the sea.
Café Europa, a cozy bistro serves Mexican coffee, omelets, and fresh pastries made on the premises.

Cancun

Jeffrey Ray Noordhoek

Being a lover of the outdoors I have always been curious about the mystical underwater world of scuba diving and anxious to learn how to dive. Therefore, when I was planning my trip to Cancun, Mexico I solicited advice from Aqua Expeditions as to where to get certified while I was on vacation.
I was staying at Club Med which only offers a "Club Certification", only accepted at other Club Med and I had heard rumors of overloaded dive boats diving reefs. These horror stories obviously made me a bit leery of "Club" diving and I wanted to receive a full certification that I would be able to use all over the world not just at Club Med. Wendy Canning Church of Aqua Expeditions highly recommended **Scuba Cancun.**
The day I arrived at Club Med I took a taxi to Scuba Cancun to schedule my classes and open water dives. I met with my instructor everyday for the next 5 days. It was a rigorous schedule for one week, but well worth it.
I was assigned a personal instructor, Juan Carlos Marin. He is everything anyone would want in an instructor and in a friend. He is a professional diver with over 15 years of diving experience 7 of which were spent in the Gulf of Mexico working on offshore oil wells. He has only one motive for being an instructor - to introduce those in search of adventure to the incredible beauty and magic of the underwater realm.
One of Juan Carlos' greatest attributes is his uncanny ability to simulate underwater sounds, sights and human reaction. The demonstrations were humorous, yet they completely prepared me for what I was about to experience. He made me feel comfortable with my equipment and my skills, making any traces of apprehension disappear. We practiced my underwater skills again and again until we both felt that I was completely prepared for the open water dives.
The actual open water dives were beyond imagination. It is almost impossible to describe the sensations and sights that I experienced during my first "adventures" underwater.
On my very first dive I saw sea turtles, six foot barracuda, lobsters, and so many fish that I am still attempting to learn all their names. On another, I had the opportunity to play with an eel and swim amongst enormous schools of jacks.

SCUBA AND SNORKELING FACILITIES QUESTIONNAIRE

NAME   **Scuba Cancun (5 star PADI Dive Center)**
ADDRESS   **P.O. Box 517**
                Cancun, Q. Roo 77500 Mexico
CONTACT   **Edith and Luis Hurtado**
TITLE   **Owners**
TELEPHONE   **98831011 898842336**   FAX **98 842336**

CAPITOL: **Mexico City**	GOVERNMENT: **Democratic**	
POPULATION: **50,000**	LANGUAGE: **Spanish**	
CURRENCY: **Peso**	ELECTRICITY: **110-60**	
AIRLINES: **Various**	DEPARTURE TAX? **$12**	
VISA/PASSPORT? **Yes**	PROOF OF CITIZENSHIP? **Yes**	

YOUR FACILITY IS QUALIFIED AS: **Scuba Center**
BUISINESS HOURS: **8am - 6pm**
CERTIFYING AGENCIES: **PADI**
LOG BOOK REQUIRED?   **Yes**
EQUIPMENT: **Sales, Rentals, Airfills**
PRIMARY LINE OF EQUIPMENT: **Sherwood**
PHOTOGRAPHIC EQUIPMENT: **Rentals**

CHARTER/DIVE BOAT AVAILABLE?   **Yes**   DIVER CAPACITY **14 - 55 Pax**
COAST GUARD APPROVED?   **Yes**   CAPTAIN LICENSE? **Yes**
SHIP TO SHORE   **Yes**   LORAN   RADAR
DIVE MASTER/INSTRUCTOR ABOARD   **Yes**

DIVING & SNORKELING: **Salt**
TYPE OF DIVING/SNORKELING IN AREA?   **Reef**
DIVING/SNORKELING IN YOUR AREA IS BEST SUITED FOR: **Beginner, Intermediate & Advanced**
BEST TIME OF YEAR FOR DIVING/SNORKELING: **Apr - Oct**
TEMPERATURE: NOV-APRIL   **80 F**   MAY-OCT: **80 F**
VISIBILITY: DIVING   **80 FT**   SNORKELING: **80+ FT**

PACKAGES AVAILABLE: **Dive, Snorkel**
ACCOMMODATIONS NEARBY: **Hotel**
ACCOMMODATIONS RATES: **Expensive, Moderate**
RESTAURANTS NEARBY: **Expensive, Moerate**
YOUR AREA IS: **Lively**
LOCAL ACTIVITY/NIGHTLIFE: **Lots.**
CAR NEEDED TO EXPLORE AREA?   **No**
DUTY FREE SHOPPING?   **Yes**

COASTGUARD   **Isla Mujeres**   AUTHORITY: **I. Mujeres**
TELEPHONE: **2 00 34**   LOCATION: **Naval Clinic**
CALLSIGNS: **VHF Marine CH 16**   TELEPHONE: **Ch 16**

LOCAL DIVING DOCTOR:
NAME: **Jorge Garcia**
LOCATION: **Cancun**
TELEPHONE: **84 65 23**

The waters of Cancun are an ice blue, yet warm and abound with plant and fish life. The current is strong and so most of the dives are drift dives where the boat follows your bubbles and picks you up when you surface after your dive.

I was impressed with the other staff members at Scuba Cancun. For my last two dives we went out with 6 other divers and we had 2 dive masters aboard. We were given a full description of the site and the dive plan. We were told how we would proceed, what order we would get into the water, how deep we would be going, what we could expect to see, the current conditions and changes along the way, and how long we would stay down. The dive itself was equally as organized and professional.

On a scale of 1 to 10, I would give my overall certification experience a 12. Edith Hurtado and her husband Luis and their entire staff are a delight. The shop also has the only hyperbaric chamber in Cancun, another plus! Luis was in charge of search and recovery for divers for 25 yrs!!!

Scuba Cancun is located downtown and is on the hotel route so you can reach it by bus from any of the hotels, a much better deal than the taxis. You can leave your equipment at the shop if you are diving for an extended period, so you only need to cart yourself back and forth.

I will undoubtedly return to Scuba Cancun for more pleasure diving - and maybe even an Advanced Certification! I highly recommended it to all!

Cozumel

Jane and Richard Goulston

Cozumel is the largest island in Mexico, ten miles off the Yucatan peninsula, nine miles wide and twenty miles long. It is a Spanish speaking island, albeit English is spoken as well. A valid passport or a birth certificate with a picture is needed for entry.

We decided after our previous visit to Cozumel to return to this island of such extreme beauty and one of the great diving destinations. We were curious to see if Cozumel had changed in the last five years. Cozumel had changed, but in a way that only added to our pleasant experience. We chose to go diving between Christmas and New Year. We were able to get lodging at one of the better hotels on the island. The next six days were spent exploring and enjoying Cozumel's reefs. **Drift diving at its best!**

DIVING

We enjoyed diving Chancanab Reef, Yocab Reef, the Santa Rosa Wall, Palancar Caves, and Colombia Gardens. The reefs are still in good shape given the amount of traffic they see. This is due to the constant cautioning by the local divemasters regarding touching or damaging the reef. There were times the reefs were pretty crowded. It was not unusual to be on a reef with 4-6 other boats. In fact it was pretty easy to get mixed up with a group from a different boat, and in fact this happened to some on our boat. The dives were generally on the order of a 70-90 ft first dive, and a 40-50 ft second dive with about an hour sit time. Make sure you have knowledgeable professionals to set up your dive package, and help you with your dive plan. We were generally back at the hotel for lunch at 1:00 p.m.

The food was delicious. It was possible to get a freshly prepared meal that was close to home cooking. We never worried about getting sick from the food, although **we did always order bottled water.**

Cozumel has grown. It's become a very busy place. We saw as many as 7 cruise ships in the harbor at one time. But you know this is a good sign. Cozumel is safe, the food is good, the shopping varied, (yes there are a few bargains, but you have to know what you're buying), and the diving and the island are great. Transportation is by taxi unless you rent a car. (Make sure you get one that's completely functional.) **We'd go back again in a heartbeat, maybe not at Christmas, but I'd definitely be up for another "re-visit".**

Clownfish in Anemones by Lynn Faukhouser

Dive Paradise can arrange dive/stay packages to fit any pocketbook. The following are dive sites offered in their brochure:

Editor's note: The currents in Cozumel can be extremely strong. Therefore it is important to choose a reputable facility and stay with your buddy and guide.

USE THIS KEY TO HELP DETERMINE MINIMUM DIVE SKILL NEEDED TO SAFELY ENJOY OUR MOST POPULAR DIVE PARADISE SITES:

N=Novice   I=Intermediate   A=Advanced   E=Expert

1-VILLA BLANCA WALL   I
Sloping wall with huge sponges and gorgonians, big schools of jacks and angelfish. (50-100')

2-PARADISE REEF   N
Abundant marine life. Often shaded by multitudes of snorkeler's overhead. Popular night dive (Max 45')

3-CHANCANAB REEF   N
Abundant marine life. Popular night dive. (Max 55')

4-BALONES OF CHANCANAB   N
Series of balloon-shaped coral heads. Colorful abundant marine life lobsters and crab. (60-70')

5-SAN FRANCISCO REEF   I
Shallowest wall dive. Abundant marine life. Exciting, not-to-be-missed dive. (Best 35-50')

6-SANTA MARIA REEF   I
Beautiful diving with large schools of angelfish. (40-60')

7-YUCAB REEF   N
Dense reef full of abundant color and marine life including grouper, eels lobster and crab. (Max 60')

8-PUNTA TUNICH   I
Discover friendly grouper, lobster, crabs and eels while drifting along a vibrant, colorful reef. (Best 40-60')

9-TORMENTOS REEF   I
Colorful coral heads teeming with marine life including eels and angelfish. (40-70')

10- PASO DE CEDRAL   I
Spectacular dive with abundant marine life in a dense, colorful setting. (Max 60')

11-SANTA ROSA REEF   I

Impressive sponges colorful overhangs. Divemaster can show you great, safe tunnels. (Min 50')

12-VIRGIN WALL   A

Lush, pristine reef that lives up to its name. Dived only with small groups due to strong current. (40-130')

13-LA FRANCESA REEF   N

Good site for first time ocean divers. Wide spectrum of colorful marine life. (Max 75') Dives 14-19 comprise the famous ìPalancar Reef.î

14-PALANCAR GARDENS   N

Beautiful dive with lots of color. Many nice caverns. (Best 40-70')

15-LITTLE CAVES   N

Labyrinth of colorful canyons, deep ravines and narrow crevices. (Best 50-70')

16-BIG HORSESHOE   N

Giant coral heads come within 20' of surface. (Max 100')

17-SHALLOW PALANCAR   N

Lots of color and marine life. Narrow, winding tunnels for experienced divers only. (Best 20-40')

18-BROKEN REEF OR LITTLE HORSESHOE   N

Majestic coral ridges rise up over impressive canyons and caverns. (Best 60-80')

19-PALANCAR CAVES   N

Beautiful canyons, tunnels and caves alive with abundant marine life. (Best 60-90')

20-DEEP PALANCAR   A

Pristine, rarely dived site. Spectacular at 100-120' with variable current. Always stunning. (Min 90')

21-CEDRAL WALL   I

Fairly flat but brimming with color and life. Cover a lot of reef in the normally strong current. (50-90')

22-COLUMBIA REEF   I

Coral pinnacles tower over an impressive drop off. Frequently see big marine life. (Best 60-80')

23-SHALLOW COLUMBIA   N

Never ending sea garden teeming with color and marine life. Shallow depth means a long dive. (15-35')

24-CHUN CHA KAB   A

If you're lucky enough to find it, expect a virgin fairyland. Most difficult site to locate. (90-120')

25-BARRACUDA & SAN JUAN REEFS   E

Virgin reefs due to extreme currents that can quickly carry divers to sea. Not worth the risk. (Min 70')

26-MARACAIBO REEF   A

Too deep for enjoyment at 140-160 feet. Lush, huge coral heads highlights shallower diving in from the wall at Maraicaibo/Lighthouse Reef (60-90'). (Min 100')

27-PUNTA SUR   A

Incredible topography and huge caverns. Home of the widely acclaimed "Devil's Throat." (Min 90')

MEXICAN GOVERNMENT TOURIST OFFICE
405 PARK AVENUE, STE 1401
NEW YORK, NY 10022

SCUBA AND SNORKELING FACILITIES QUESTIONNAIRE

NAME	**Dive Paradise**
	601 Melgar
	Cozumel, Mexico
CONTACT	**Renee Applegateana**
TITLE	**Owner Operator**
TELEPHONE	**011-52-987** FAX **21061/24316**

CAPITOL:	**Mexico City**	GOVERNMENT:	**Democracy**
POPULATION:	**45,000-60,000**	LANGUAGE:	**Spanish**
CURRENCY:	**Peso**	ELECTRICITY:	**110v**
AIRLINES:	**Continental, Mexican**	DEPARTURE TAX?	**$12**
NEED VISA/PASSPORT? **Yes**		PROOF OF CITIZENSHIP? **Yes**	

YOUR FACILITY IS QUALIFIED AS:	**Scuba Center**
BUISINESS HOURS:	**8am - 9pm**
CERTIFYING AGENCIES:	**PADI, SSI, NAUI, CMAI, IDEA**
LOG BOOK REQUIRED?	**Preferred**
EQUIPMENT:	**Sales, Rentals, Airfills**
PRIMARY LINE OF EQUIPMENT:	**Sherwood, Mares**
PHOTOGRAPHIC EQUIPMENT:	**Sales, Rentals**

CHARTER/DIVE BOAT AVAILABLE?	**Yes**	DIVER CAPACITY	**6-24**
COAST GUARD APPROVED?	**Yes**	CAPTAIN LICENSED?	**Yes**
SHIP TO SHORE? **Yes**	RADAR **No**		
DIVE MASTER/INSTRUCTOR ABOARD?	**Yes**		

DIVING & SNORKELING: **Salt**
TYPE OF DIVING/SNORKELING IN AREA   **Wall, Beach, Reef, Cave**
DIVING/SNORKELING IN YOUR AREA IS BEST SUITED FOR: **Beginner, Intermediate & Advanced**
BEST TIME OF YEAR FOR DIVING/SNORKELING:

TEMPERATURE:	**NOV-APRIL**	MAY-OCT:
VISIBILITY:	DIVING	SNORKELING:

PACKAGES AVAILABLE:	**Dive, Divestay**
ACCOMMODATIONS NEARBY:	**Hotel, Home Rentals**
ACCOMMODATIONS RATES:	**Expensive, Moderate, Inexpensive**
RESTAURANTS NEARBY:	**Expensive, Moderate, Inexpensive**
YOUR AREA IS:	**Lively**
LOCAL ACTIVITY/NIGHTLIFE: .	**Discos, Museum**
CAR NEEDED TO EXPLORE AREA?	**No**
DUTY FREE SHOPPING?	**No**

COASTGUARD **X**	AUTHORITY:	**Port Captain**
TELEPHONE: **n/a**	LOCATION:	**North of Town**
CALLSIGNS: **12(channel)**	TELEPHONE: **20169**	

LOCAL DIVING DOCTOR:
NAME: **Gustavo and Ambriz - S.S.S.**
LOCATION: **Local SSS Chamber or Central de Sacud Hospital**
TELEPHONE: **22387, or Channel 21**

MICRONESIA

The Republic of Palau
Sun Dancer II
Lynn Funkhouser

Divers have known Palau as an underwater paradise for many years, even being called "one of the Seven Underwater Wonders of the World." Also known locally as Belau, it is the westernmost island group of the Caroline archipelago. Only 14,000 people inhabit the 340 islands that stretch from 400 miles north of the equator and for 400 miles north towards Japan. It is located midway between the Philippines and Guam.

The islands of Palau are incredibly picturesque! Emerald green, mushroom shaped islands are sprinkled on turquoise blue waters, usually with an assortment of puffy white clouds on the horizon for added visual pleasure. Continental/Air Micronesia serves Palau from the USA through Guam and the Philippines. **Consider spending a day or two in Guam or Palau before the dive trip to recover from jetlag and allow any of your luggage that missed your flight to catch up.**

Upon arrival, we were met and transported by bus to the beautiful **Palau Pacific Resort** where we all shared a room for changing clothes and had use of the swimming pool and other resort facilities until 4:00PM when it was time to board the *Sun Dancer II*. At the end of the cruise, one night is included at the PPR in the price of the trip. There are wonderful hiking and running trails around the resort providing the opportunity to see the beautiful local flora and fauna. **Snorkeling is good in front of the resort.**

Palau is rich in legends, fables and folklore. In early times plain legends were carved and painted on Bais, which are the men's meeting houses. **Now the legends are carved on wooden storyboards, the most popular souvenir from Palau.** Storyboards can be purchased at the PPR boutique or check out the local jail where inmates carve some very nice ones at good prices.

The best thing to happen for divers visiting Palau is Peter Hughes' *Sun Dancer II*. She is 138' long with a beam of 26'. There are 10 beautifully appointed staterooms that can accommodate 20 passengers. The Owner's Suite features two twin beds, which can be made into a king size bed and an entertainment center with TV and VCR. There are two Master Staterooms with queen bed, TV, and VCR. The other seven Deluxe Staterooms feature two twin beds or one king bed. All cabins are independently air-conditioned and all have volume controls for the cabin audio system.

Sun Dancer II **has all the comforts of a luxury hotel!** Large picture windows are especially appreciated so the awesome beauty of the islands is visible from your room. Large fluffy terry bathrobes are provided for each guest. **The private bathrooms are fabulous! (Finally a bathroom that we women can appreciate!)** There are flush toilets, wash basins, showers with plenty of hot water (the desalinator makes 3200 gallons per day), mirrored vanity cabinets with hinges that pull out to let you check even the back of your hair, great lighting, hair dryers, and fresh towels daily. Ample storage space is provided with a large closet and built-in drawers under the beds. The attention to detail is remarkable. Hand towels have embroidered anemonefish on them, and shell soaps, liquid hand soap, and shampoos are provided. Local storyboards and beautiful marine art decorate the cabins and passageways throughout the ship. Chocolates on the pillows at night and the fin shaped "do not disturb" signs with a request to be awakened with coffee, tea, or hot chocolate are wonderful touches.

The ship's food is excellent consisting of American and Island style meals. "Palauan Night" is a special treat. Breakfasts and lunches are served buffet style. Dinners are full service complete with elegant table settings, fresh flowers, cocktails, wine, and after dinner drinks for the non-night divers. (All drinks are included in the package.) We often viewed videos during dinner on the large screen TV. Snacks are outstanding.

Palau's diving is legendary and one of the most legendary dive sites is Blue Corner. It certainly lives up to its reputation as a high intensity dive! True, unfortunately, the top of the reef shows a lot of diver damage, but the blue water action is adrenaline producing. There were moments when I had sharks above me, below me, and beside me. Awesome! **Big Al, the giant Napoleon wrasse, hangs out here and greets all divers.** There are large schools of jacks, barracudas, and snappers swirling around. Large tuna zip by regularly. If the current takes you over the top of the reef there are plenty of butterflyfish, angle fish, a beautiful red anemone with anemonefish and other reef critters to check out. The group on board when I was on *Sun Dancer II* opted to dive Blue Corner (a.k.a. Holy S— Dive!) five times. Dive it early, before all the small day boats arrive. 11 sharks were coming toward us as we left one morning.

Jellyfish by Lynn Funkhouser

The *Sun Dancer* boutique sells or rents special reef hooks which allow you to attach yourself to a dead part of the reef with the hook so that you can hold your place in the currents. It works very well. On one dive the current was so strong that I could not hand hold my strobe up to shoot photos I even hooked it to a dead coral head. **Shark and fish action was spectacular and I shall always remember it.** Without a hook I would have been swept across the reef. "Current surfing" is awesome and sure beats tearing up the reef!

Blue Holes start in 10' and open into a large cavern. The shafts of light coming through the holes were fabulous. I exited around 100' and saw two threadfin pompano. The light on them took my breath away. (If you swim down the wall you can reach Blue Corner from this dive.)

Aulong Channel is a very special site. It is the breeding grounds for many groupers so it is closed to divers and fishermen around the first of March each year. (What a great idea to protect the groupers!) We dropped in over a sandy bottom. Soon I was enveloped by a school of barracuda. Then a school of surgeons intermixed with them. Two large jacks charged through the schools with a grey reef shark under the schools also charging through to feed. Afterwards I allowed the gentle current to carry me through the channel past the most magnificent stand of leaf coral I have ever been privileged to see. Hundreds of groupers were hanging out everywhere. **There were also numerous sharks. I laughed at a Titan triggerfish charging a shark. (Divers should be warned of these instead of sharks!)** The dive ended in a beautiful coral garden with lots of tabletop corals.

At **Giant Clam Garden**, there are dozens of these magnificent animals in just 10' to 30' where snorkelers as well as divers can enjoy them. Some of the giant clams are arranged in rows and others in fields. **It is a spectacular site, especially if you realize how rare it is to see even one large giant calm alive.** Unfortunately this species is becoming rare throughout the Indo-Pacific due to over-harvesting and illegal poaching. **Giant Clams are listed in Threatened Species under CITES, the Convention on International Trade in Endangered Species.** Palau's Micronesian Mariculture Demonstration Center

(MMDC) produces millions of baby clams and can be visited if you spend any time in Korror, capital of Palau.

Another advantage of the *Sun Dancer II* is that it can take you to more distant (less dived!) sites like Peleliu, Kayangel, and Angaur. Pelelie Wall is spectacular, decorated with yellow soft corals everywhere, which give you wonderful photographic backgrounds. A 300-lb. grouper left a cave as we approached. Sharks, large anemones with anemonefish, eels, parrotfish, wrasse, angels, butterflyfish, crinoids, etc. here in abundance. The safety stop was a real test of discipline: 10 large tuna (one almost as large as me) kept circling, maintaining eye contact, and luring me deeper. Didn't know if they were curious or if I was being sized up as part of the food chain. Great dive!

Don't miss snorkeling in the legendary Jellyfish Lake, located in the interior of Eil Malk Island. It is one of the most fascinating lakes in the world. Every morning, the estimated 1.6 million peach-colored Mastigias jellyfish migrate to the sunny side of the lake. In the afternoon they pulsate back across the lake. This beautiful non-stinging jellyfish is known to exist only in this lake. One other species of non-stinging jellyfish, three species of fish, and one species of anemone are the only other known species to inhabit Jellyfish Lake. After a short hike up to it, you arrive at a fantastic stand of mangroves and a little channel to the lake. It is a wonderful experience.

I must confess that I was last on the *Sun Dancer* I in 1995. The boat, the tender boats, and most of the crew have changed since then. With Peter's attention to detail, however, the operation has to be even better now and I have no problem recommending it.

The new *Sun Dancer II* has a crew of 10. Chief divemaster Frank Ladner, who is still there, gave the most informative and entertaining briefings, complete with multi-colored drawings and plastic animals that might be seen at the site–the best I've ever seen. Frank and the rest of the crew worked very hard to make the trip outstanding. I'm sure that the new crew is excellent also.

There are currently 2 new safe boats, one 32', the other 28' with 400 h.p. jet engines used as tenders. Buoyant foam incorporated in the boats makes them unsinkable. When I was there, after some frustration, I finally reorganized divers into two boat groups–the "easy breathers" and the "less-easy breathers" so that our dives could last a little longer and not have divers waiting in the rain or sun. Luckily for me a Japanese man usually surfaced after the others so I surfaced when he did. (I can't deal with short dives. The best stuff is always found at the end of a dive, especially if you only dive an area once.)

Water temperatures range from 80' to 84' throughout the year. Since you may be doing four or five dives a day and will be in a safe boat for most of those dives, consider taking a wetsuit or at least a diveskin for thermal (and sun) protection. Palau can have strong currents, which are caused, by the tides, that can be over eight feet, and the filling up and emptying of the huge lagoon. A lot of water rushes through the channels and cuts at least four times a day. Strong downdrafts and updrafts can also occur on the reefs. Remember, it is these currents which attract all the big fish and nourish all the beautiful corals! *Sun Dancer's* divemasters are wonderful, providing assistance to those who need it or want it and leaving others alone. It is, in your best interest to dive in the vicinity of the group so that you are not swept out to sea alone.

Safety is of the utmost importance on the *Sun Dancer*. Everyone is required to carry a safety sausage and have a Dive Alert whistle attached to his or her BCD. They are provided free of charge for the trip if you do not have them. (However, quantities may be limited and diving will not be permitted without both.) Cyalume light sticks are required for night dives. You may bring your own or purchase them on board.

When you get back to the *Sun Dancer*, a hot towel right out of the dryer and a snack await you. A plastic barrel is provided for a camera rinse and two showers to rinse off divers. A large two-tier table provides safe space for all the photographic equipment on board. E-6 processing, camera and video rental, and photo and video instruction are available. A light table and slide projector is provided in the lounge/library. A CD player

SCUBA AND SNORKELING QUESTIONNAIRE

NAME: **Peter Hughes Diving, Inc./Sun Dancer II**
ADDRESS: **1390 S. Dixie Highway #1109**
Coral Gables, FL 33146
CONTACT: **Patricia Rose**
TITLE: **Manager**
TELEPHONE: **305-669-9391**   FAX **305-669-9475**   EMAIL   **dancer@peterhughes.com**

CAPITOL: **Koror**
POPULATION:
CURRENCY: **US Dollars**
AIRLINES: **Cont./Air Micronesia**
NEED VISA/PASSPORT   YES   NO **x**

GOVERNMENT: **Republic of Palau**
LANGUAGE: **English**
ELECTRICITY: **110 volt**
DEPARTURE TAX? **$12.00**
PROOF OF CITIZENSHIP?   YES **x**   NO

YOUR FACILITY IS CLASSIFIED AS: SCUBA CENTER   RESORT   LIVEABOARD
BUSINESS HOURS: **24 hours**
CERTIFYING AGENCIES: **PADI/ NAUI/TDI**
LOG BOOK REQUIRED?   YES   NO **Preferred/recommended**
EQUIPMENT: SALES   RENTALS **x**   AIR FILLS **x**
PRIMARY LINE OF EQUIPMENT?   **Nikonos**
PHOTOGRAPHIC EQUIPMENT: SALES   RENTALS **x**   LAB **x**

CHARTER/DIVE BOAT AVAILABLE?   YES **x**   NO   DIVER CAPACITY **20**
COAST GUARD APPROVED?   YES   NO **x** CAPTAIN LICENSED?   YES **x**   NO
SHIP TO SHORE?   YES **x**   NO   LORAN? YES **x** NO   RADAR? YES **x** NO
DIVE MASTER/INSTRUCTOR ABOARD? YES **x**   NO   BOTH **x**

DIVING AND SNORKELING: SALT **x**   FRESH
TYPE OF DIVING/SNORKELING IN AREA: WALL **x**   BEACH   WRECK **x**   REEF **x**   CAVE   ICE
DIVING/SNORKELING IN YOUR AREA IS BEST SUITED FOR: BEGINNER   INTERMEDIATE **x** ADVANCED
BEST TIME OF YEAR FOR DIVING/SNORKELING:
TEMPERATURE: NOV-APRIL: **80 - 84F**   MAY-OCT.   **80 - 84F**
VISIBILITY: DIVING: **80 - 200Ft.** SNORKELING **80 - 200Ft.**

PACKAGES AVAILABLE: DIVE   DIVE STAY   SNORKEL   SNORKEL STAY
ACCOMMODATIONS NEARBY: HOTEL **x**   MOTEL   HOME RENTALS
ACCOMMODATION RATES: EXPENSIVE **x**   MODERATE   INEXPENSIVE
RESTAURANTS NEARBY: EXPENSIVE **x**   MODERATE   INEXPENSIVE
YOUR AREA IS: REMOTE **x**   QUIET WITH ACTIVITIES   LIVELY
LOCAL ACTIVITY/NIGHTLIFE:
CAR NEEDED TO EXPLORE AREA: YES   NO **x**
DUTY FREE SHOPPING: YES **some**   NO

LOCAL EMERGENCY SERVICES:
COAST GUARD:
TELEPHONE:
CALLSIGNS: **V3TD5**

NEAREST HYPERBARIC TREATMENT FACILITY:
AUTHORITY:
LOCATION: **Koror**
TELEPHONE:

provides background music. Openwater, specialties, advanced, and nitrox diving instruction is also available.

Visibility on the outer reefs of Palau is usually 100' to 200'. In the lagoon where the wrecks are located, visibility is around 60'. The best time of the year for diving is November through March. Rainy season is April through September. Rough seas are most likely from mid-June through October. However, the worlds weather pattern seems to be abnormal so weather is getting harder to predict. Luck and Murphy always prevail.

Few countries in the world can offer such beautiful scenery above and underwater as the Islands of Palau and *Sun Dancer II* will allow you to see it in luxury.

POHNPEI

Donna Marchetti

My decision to go to Pohnpei was instantaneous and gut-deep, and oddly enough, it had nothing to do with diving. I was flipping through a book on Oceanic art one day, past elongated, strangely modernistic figures and elaborately carved war clubs, when I came to a photograph of magnificent stone ruins. Nan Madol, the caption told me, was built from the 13th through 17th centuries. The complex is made up of ninety-two man-made islands crowned with structures made of log-shaped basalt stones that were mysteriously hauled to the site by a method archeologists have yet to figure out. The image stared back at me from the page, enigmatic and beckoning, and I knew this was a place I had to see.

Nan Madol may be the island's biggest claim to fame, but it's not the most pervasive. Once you visit Pohnpei, the mention of the word instantly conjures up another—water. Rain pelts out of the sky at the rate of 400 inches per year. When the downpour pauses, the landscape drips. When the sun comes out, everything steams. Water gushes down mountain rivers and cascades over waterfalls, past ferns and bromeliads glistening with raindrops that never dry. At its shores, the wetness takes the form of saltwater—a seventy-square-acre lagoon, with the deep blue of open ocean just beyond. There simply is no avoiding water of one kind or another on Pohnpei. If you stand still long enough, you'll feel as though you're beginning to sprout.

Despite all the dampness, or maybe even because of it, **Pohnpei is a spectacular place.** Unlike the flat coral atolls of the Marshall Islands to the east, Pohnpei rises from the ocean like a giant green hulk, its mountains looming from mist-covered heights. Vegetation is lush, flowers are abundant, birds are ever present and the surrounding reefs teem with life.

Located just above the Equator and about midway between Honolulu and Manila, Pohnpei consists of one main island and eight outlying atolls, with a total landmass of 127 square miles. Pohnpei is the capital of the Federated States of Micronesia, which also includes Kosrae, Yap and Chuuk (Truk). The Pohnpeian population of approximately 35,000 is almost entirely Micronesian, although the people who inhabit the farthest atoll, Kapingamarangi, are Polynesian. In the early part of this century, drought drove many Kapingamarangans from their atoll to the main island of Pohnpei. Their descendants live today just outside the capital city of Kolonia in Porakiet, a village known as one of the best places in Micronesia to buy high quality handicrafts.

Like the rest of Micronesia, Pohnpei has borne the influence—and sometimes the exploitation—of many foreign cultures. Spain, Germany, Japan and the U.S. have each claimed dominion over the island throughout the centuries following the arrival of the first Europeans in 1595.

Japan took over in 1914, and embarked on full-scale colonization. By World War II, Japanese outnumbered Pohnpeians three to one. After the war, Pohnpei became part of the Trust Territory of the Pacific Islands under the jurisdiction of the United Nations, which mandated control to the United States. In 1979, Pohnpei united with Kosrae, Yap and Chuuk (Truk) to form the Federated States of Micronesia. Self-government for the FSM came in 1986 when the Compact of Free Association with the United States went into effect, permitting the U.S. military access to the islands in return for hefty amounts of financial aid.

THE DIVING & SNORKELING

I spent a week diving with the Village, and though that isn't enough to declare myself an expert, it is enough to say that Pohnpei is an undiscovered underwater paradise. Hurry up and get there, before everyone else does. When I visited, there were never more than two divers on the boat, and only once did we even see another dive boat.

Our first dive was at **Manta Road,** a sandy-bottomed channel where rays come to feed during the tide changes. The current was quite strong, nearly impossible to swim against, so my guide and I hung onto a rock and waited. We didn't have to wait long. I looked up to see a six-foot manta hovering just over our heads, majestic in both its size and grace. I had to resist the urge to reach out and touch it. After a minute or so, it drifted back gently, carried with the current until it was out of sight.

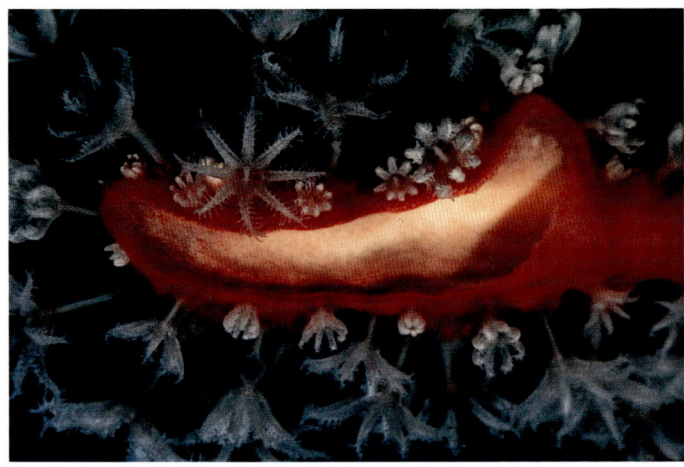

Soft Corals by Lynn Faukhouser

We dived the next day at **Paliker Pass** on the island's northwest coast, just outside the barrier reef. As I was floating along with a gentle current, admiring the 100-foot-plus visibility, **I glanced to my right and was amazed to see a school of about thirty reef sharks. Several large blacktips swam by in the distance. Above me, fifty or so great barracudas appeared, and seconds later, hundreds of skipjacks glided across the current directly in front of me.** Everywhere I looked, there was something to rivet my gaze. It reminded me—forgive the blasphemy—of Palau's legendary Blue Corner.

Blue Reef drop-off, to the northeast, is a vertical wall of incredible beauty, covered with soft corals in shades of pink, purple, peach and orange. Giant sea fans, anemones with clownfish, cobalt blue sea stars and a variety of small reef fish are among the attractions on this dive. When I was there, the visibility was relatively poor by Pacific standards—about 30-40 feet. After the dive, my guide Robert confirmed what I was beginning to realize—that the **visibility at all dive sites around the main island varies a great deal according to tides, currents and other factors.** A site with 100-foot visibility one-day may offer only 30 the next. Likewise, on any given day visibility at sites within a half-hour's boat ride of each other may vary considerably.

This, however, is not the case at **Ant Atoll,** about an hour-and-a-half away by boat.

Ant is the tropical island of fantasies—jungle-covered, ringed with sugar-white beaches and a pristine reef, uninhabited except for a few wild pigs. The water here is consistently clear, and the reef teems with life. In addition to the usual array of vibrant-hued reef fish we saw eagle rays, whitetip and blacktip reef sharks, eels and Napoleon wrasse.

Like all other dives I did on Pohnpei, the dives at Ant were done as drift dives even though the current was very slight. Swimming along the reef then turning around to swim back to the boat could have done nearly all dives, but drifting allowed us to see more. All dives ended with a safety stop on a shallow section of reef, offering another opportunity to explore the abundant underwater life.

Diving on Pohnpei is as relaxed as the breezes that stir the palms. There is no rushing to get the boat back to pick up another load of divers. There is no rush to get into the water, and for that matter, no rush to get out, unless safety dictates it. Lunches are long, languorous affairs that often include a nap. Surface intervals stretch to two hours at times, particularly when the extended lunch is followed by a forty-minute ride to the next dive site. In short, don't be in a hurry when you dive on Pohnpei. Expect to spend the entire day and don't have aspirations of afternoon sightseeing. Relax and enjoy it— scenery doesn't get much better than this.

The Village's dive boats are large, fast, Boston whaler-type boats that meet the local conditions well, but are not decked out as dive boats. Some may find it difficult to don equipment while sitting on the floor of the boat and then move to the side for a back roll entry. I found that the key to dealing with these small inconveniences was simply to move slowly and carefully.

The dive guides at the Village are experienced and quite capable, but though they are certified advanced or rescue divers they are not divemasters or instructors. For this reason, although the diving on Pohnpei is not considered difficult, visiting divers should be experienced and sure of their underwater skills. There is no rental scuba equipment available at the Village, so be sure to bring your own. They will supply weights and tanks. Rental snorkel gear is available.

There is ample opportunity for snorkelers on Pohnpei. Aside from snorkeling off the beach from the Village, there are several small islands accessible by boat that offer good visibility and interesting sights. We stopped at Long Island one day on our way to see the ruins at Nan Madol. The current tends to be strong here, so caution is advised. We saw abundant reef fish, including butterflyfish, wars, Moorish idols, angelfish and chromis.

Lenger Island, which served as our lunch stop during several days of diving, is even more interesting. Though the island is uninhabited now, it once served as the base for a World War II seaplane landing strip. The ruins of the strip are still there, extending a couple of hundred feet into the water. The somewhat turbid water attracts different species of fish than are found in clearer waters.

ACCOMMODATIONS

If your vision of the ideal dive vacation is not complete without a five-star luxury resort with nightlife galore, you'll probably want to skip Pohnpei and head straight for Guam, where you're likely to drop a couple of hundred dollars a night. That said, you can be quite comfortable on Pohnpei, and you won't spend a fortune doing it.

There are several small hotels in the capital of Kolonia, though it's not a particularly attractive town. The Joy Hotel (PO Box 484, Kolonia, Pohnpei, FM 96941; phone 691-320-2447, fax 691-320-2478,) has a restaurant and ten rooms with phones, A/C and refrigerator. The hotel also rents scuba gear and can arrange diving tours.

Yvonne's Hotel (PO Box 688, Kolonia, Pohnpei, FM 96941; phone 691-320-5130) has six rooms with phones, A/C refrigerator and TV.

The choice of most divers, and the place with the most beautiful setting, is the Village, about five miles outside Kolonia (PO Box 339, Pohnpei, FM 96941; phone 691-320-

2797, fax 691-320-3797). Owned and run by Americans Patti and Bob Arthur, the Village has developed a steady clientele over the past twenty-one years. Accommodations are twenty-one thatch-roofed bungalows in a jungle setting high on a hillside overlooking the water. Each spacious bungalow has two waterbeds, 24-hour electricity, ceiling fan and full bath with plenty of hot water. The atmosphere is casual, and the staff is friendly and helpful. **A path down the hillside leads to a small private beach that is a good entry point for snorkelers.** The Village also offers land tours and guided dive tours. Every morning the hotel van goes into Kolonia; guests can ride into town for free and catch a taxi back if they want to explore the town.

DINING

The **Tattooed Irishman,** the Village's restaurant and bar, **has excellent food at reasonable prices.** The island-style open-air building has a dramatic view of the lagoon and surrounding islands. You can get American or Japanese breakfasts; as can be expected on a lush tropical island, the fresh fruit is delicious. Lunches are served at the restaurant, or if you're going on a tour for the day, the staff will pack a lunch for you. **Be sure to try bento (boxed lunch Japanese-style)** — steamed rice, fresh tuna steak, cucumbers and sausage wrapped up in a banana leaf.

Dinner is served daily, and you can be sure you won't walk away hungry. Meals include salad, rolls, soup, entree, rice or potatoes and vegetables. The fresh seafood is excellent.

A good value if you're eating lunch in town is the **Joy Restaurant,** down the street from the Joy Hotel (the hotel also has a restaurant; this can be confusing). An enormous, made-from-scratch Japanese lunch will set you back only $4 or $5. The restaurant also has a gift shop. If you don't have time to go to the workshops where local crafts are made, this is the best place for one-stop souvenir shopping. Joy Restaurant is open for lunches only Monday through Friday and dinner only on Sundays. It is closed on Saturdays.

AREAS OF INTEREST

Don't limit your exploration of Pohnpei to the underwater realm. It's an easy island to get to know, and you'll find the people friendly and helpful. What appears to be shyness may be some degree of discomfort with English, which nearly everyone speaks, but which is not the first language for most.

If you are a woman, you may want to take note that, traditionally, Pohnpeian women keep their thighs covered. Especially when touring remote areas, respect for this custom will make everyone more comfortable. Likewise, bikinis are frowned upon, and bathing suits of any kind are appropriate only on the dive boat or in the water.

Many visitors rent a vehicle to explore the road (most of it unpaved) that circles the perimeter of the island. If you have a choice, a pick-up is preferable to a car; in either case, be sure there's a spare tire. Car rentals are available in Kolonia, at the airport and through many hotels.

The capital city of Kolonia is worth exploring. The staff at the tourist office, on the main drag close to the post office, is very helpful. Highlights in the town include the remains of a wall built by the Spanish in 1887 and the old Catholic mission, of which only the bell tower remains, the rest having been dismantled during the war to supply building materials for the Japanese military.

Down by the water next to the public market you'll find **Island Traders,** producers of export-quality pepper that is known among gourmands around the world. It's possible to tour the small facility, and you can buy pepper there cheaper than you may find it elsewhere on the island.

Just outside of Kolonia is **Porakiet,** the village of the Kapingamarangans. Handicraft shops are operated out of private homes, so it seems a bit bewildering when you first try to figure out which places have goods for sale without appearing to stare. Don't worry, they'll find you. Be sure to take plenty of small bills. (The U.S. dollar is the currency of

Pohnpei.) Some of the most striking handicrafts offered by the villagers are sharks and other marine animals carved from local wood. You can buy a dolphin small enough to fit in your pocket or a three-foot hammerhead—it just depends on what you're willing to haul onto the plane. You'll also find small figures carved from a local nut, necklaces made of shells, and woven mats of various types.

Opportunities for hikers abound on Pohnpei. Those who are interested in hiking can pick up an excellent guide there, Pohnpei: An Ecotourist's Delight, for $2. Trails can be slippery and many cross private property, so a guide is advised. Most hotels, including the Village, can arrange for guides. The tourist office in Kolonia can also make arrangements.

A visit to Pohnpei is not complete without a tour of the ruins at Nan Madol, off the southeast coast of the main island. Although it is possible to reach the ruins by wading through the ocean at low tide, it is far more enjoyable and informative to visit the area by boat with a guide. Ruins of this caliber are found nowhere else in Micronesia.

The most impressive and best preserved of the ninety-two manmade islands is Nan Douwas, the main fortress. The basalt walls made of huge stone "logs" rise twenty-five feet above the surrounding channels. The eerie quiet that surrounds the site today seems fitting for a place that was once the refuge and holy place of the great chiefs of Pohnpei. A tour of Nan Madol is often paired with a visit to Kepirohi Waterfall, a magnificent cascade that tumbles seventy feet over black basalt rocks to form a pool ideal for swimming.

Beach lovers won't find what they're looking for on Pohnpei proper, since mangrove swamps surround the island. The mangroves have their own beauty, though, which divers are often treated to when dive boats take short cuts through them during high tide. **The Village also rents sea kayaks, which are ideal for touring the swamps.**

There are several cultural centers that offer an experience of traditional Pohnpeian life, including food, weaving, handicrafts and *sakau* making. Sakau, made from the roots of the pepper plant, is a mild narcotic that plays a central role in the Pohnpeian culture. It is used in a variety of ceremonies and as a social drink. Look out! It leaves your mind clear but your legs like jelly.

For anyone who wants a comprehensive guide to Pohnpei, I recommend Pohnpei, An Island Argosy by local author Gene Ashby. It is available at many hotels or by writing to Rainy Day Press, 1147 E. 26th Ave., Eugene, Oregon 97403.

For more information contact:
Office of Tourism and Parks
PO Box 66
Kolonia, Pohnpei FSM 96941.

SCUBA AND SNORKELING FACILITIES QUESTIONNAIRE PRIVATE

NAME: **THE VILLAGE**
ADDRESS: **BOX 339; POHNPEI, FM 96941**
CONTACT: **PATTI ARTHUR**
TITLE: **MANAGER**
TELEPHONE: **+699 320-2797** FAX: **+699 320-3797**

CAPITOL: **POHNPEI** GOVERNMENT: **FEDERATED STATES OF MICRONESIA**
POPULATION: **35,000** LANGUAGE: **ENGLISH/POHNPEIAN**
CURRENCY: **US $** ELECTRICITY: **110V 60 CYC - 24 HRS**
AIRLINES: **CONTINENTAL, MICRONESIA** DEPARTURE TAX? **$5.00**
NEED VISA/PASSPORT? **YES** PROOF OF CITIZENSHIP? **YES**

YOUR FACILITY IS CLASSIFIED AS: **RESORT**
BUSINESS HOURS: **7AM - 24:00PM**
CERTIFYING AGENCIES: **NONE**
LOG BOOK REQUIRED? **NO, C-CARD IS**
EQUIPMENT: **RENTALS, AIR FILLS**
PHOTOGRAPHIC EQUIPMENT: **SALES RENTALS LAB**

CHARTER/DIVE BOAT AVAILABLE? **YES** DIVER CAPACITY: **6-8 DIVERS**
COAST GUARD APPROVED? CAPTAIN LICENSED? **NO**
SHIP TO SHORE? NO LORAN? **NO** RADAR? **NO**
DIVE MASTER/INSTRUCTOR ABOARD? **NO**

DIVING & SNORKELING: **SALT**
TYPE OF DIVING/SNORKELING IN AREA: **WALL, REEF**
DIVING/SNORKELING IN YOUR AREA IS BEST SUITED FOR: **BEGINNER, INTERMEDIATE, ADVANCED**
BEST TIME OF YEAR FOR DIVING/SNORKELING: **YEAR ROUND**

PACKAGES AVAILABLE: **DIVE STAY**
ACCOMMODATIONS NEARBY: **HOTEL**
ACCOMMODATION RATES: **MODERATE**
RESTAURANTS NEARBY: **MODERATE**
YOUR AREA IS: **QUIET WITH ACTIVITIES**
CAR NEEDED TO EXPLORE AREA? **TAXIS AND TOURS AVAILABLE**
DUTY FREE SHOPPING? **NO**

LOCAL EMERGENCY SERVICES NEAREST HYPERBARIC TREATMENT FACILITY
COASTGUARD AUTHORITY: **GUAM**

LOCAL DIVING DOCTOR:
NAME: **DR. AMINIS DAVID**
LOCATION: **POHNPEI HOSPITAL**
TELEPHONE: **+691 320-2212-14; 320-2226**

ROTA

Commonwealth of the Northern Mariana Islands

Donna Marchetti

I first went to Rota with expectations that seemed impossibly optimistic: I pictured deserted white beaches fringed by coconut palms, an ice-blue ocean, blazing sunsets that fade to indigo, grass huts surrounded with fragrant plumeria—sort of a Pacific reverie. I was right about everything but the grass huts -not bad not for the realization of a fantasy. Rota drew me back a second time and will no doubt beckon again.

Just forty miles north of Guam, the 33-square-mile island of Rota seems half a world away from the glitzy high-rise hotels and American fast food of its neighbor. Songsong, Rota's main village, is a sleepy, quiet place near the water—a block of small restaurants, family-run groceries, a couple of modest hotels, an ice cream shop or two. Nearby, Mt. Taipingot rises from a peninsula like a multi-tiered confection, thus its nickname of Wedding Cake Mountain. Away from the one paved road that runs from the village to the airport, Rota is a patchwork of jungle vegetation, grass savannah and taro fields. Only about 1,500 people inhabit the island—everyone seems to know everyone else, and visitors are no exception after they've spent a week on the island. Getting to Rota is easy. There are daily flights from Guam.

Rota's history parallels that of most Micronesian islands—early discovery and domination by the Spanish, brief ownership by Germany around the beginning of the 20th century, followed by Japanese take-over and exploitation that lasted until the island fell to the Americans at the end of World War II. Today, Rota and the better-known islands of Saipan and Tinian make up the Commonwealth of the Northern Mariana Islands, an arrangement that provides for local governing of internal affairs, but offers U.S. protection and recognizes the sovereignty of the U.S. Constitution. The residents of Rota are U.S. citizens.

The indigenous people of the island are Chamorros, as are the people of Guam and the other islands of the Marianas group. No one knows exactly how they got there, but the oldest archeological remains on the islands date from 2000 BC. While the Chamorro language is widely spoken, English is the official language of the Northern Mariana Islands.

THE DIVING & SNORKELING
Diving on Rota is a treat. There is only one dive shop—**Dive Rota**, located in Songsong. Owners Mark and Lynne Michael cater to small groups of experienced divers. Some dives are done in the protected waters of Sosanjaya Bay near the village, while others are done in the swift currents and considerably choppier conditions outside the bay. **The depth of most dives (typically 80-110 feet), the strong currents and the challenging surface conditions make Rota a dive destination unsuitable for novice divers.**

Certification cards are required, and logbooks are recommended. The staff of

Male Trunkfish by Lynn Faukhouser

Dive Rota screens divers carefully before taking them to advanced sites (and most of them are advanced), so if you're new to diving, get more experience under your belt before heading for Rota. Water temperatures are warm year-round and 100-foot visibility or better are the norm.

The biggest underwater attraction is the 393-foot *Shoun Maru*, a Japanese cargo ship that was downed by an American pilot in 1944. It sits in 110 feet of water, breathtakingly visible from the surface of Sosanjaya Bay. **While the mid-section, which took the torpedo blast, is a twisted reminder of a violent demise, much of the rest of the ship is intact.** On board are trucks, bicycles, a bathtub and two steam engines. Nudibranchs and crinoids can be found over the ship's surfaces, while a colony of garden eels lives nearby.

Outside the bay, at **Harnom Point** and forty feet below the surface, is the entrance to **Senhanom Cave. Along the walls there are red lace corals, cowries, and lobsters, their eyes glowing in the beams of dive lights.** Occasionally you can spot a scallop, with its weird glowing iridescence that makes it look like a miniature flying saucer. Lionfish are often found here, and the place literally swarms with glassy sweepers. A little way into the cave, the passage opens into a large room where sunlight streams from an opening overhead. If you are there at the right time of day, and position yourself in the right place, the sunlight appears as an azure waterfall frozen in time.

A drift dive along **Harnom Point** is also a favorite. **The waters of the Pacific Ocean and the Philippine Sea come together here, swirling around each other like the bubbles of divers doing their safety stops.** This is Mark Michael's favorite site, he told me. "You never know what you'll find there," he said. "I've seen sailfish, mantas, groupers, wahoo and mahi-mahi." Reef sharks are not an unusual sight.

Pona Point, on the other side of Sosanjaya Bay, offers a wild ride if ever there was one. This is a drift dive of sometimes alarming velocity that takes divers along a wall, whisking past crinoids and sea fans, while large pelagics are often visible in the deep water opposite.

Other dive sites include **Sailigai Tunnel,** a lava tube that begins at seventy feet and exits at forty; and **Cable Run,** ruins from the Japanese phosphate industry that flourished during the war.

Snorkelers will also find Rota interesting. Dive Rota will take snorkelers to sites within the bay, or they can go to nearby **Teteto Beach,** where the reef lies just offshore. Snorkeling at Teteto, however, should be timed for high tide since the coral is close to the surface.

For more information contact Dive Rota at P.O. Box 941, Rota, MP 96951; phone 670-532-3377; fax 670-532-3022.

ACCOMMODATIONS

Hotels on Rota range from modest to luxurious, with a few oddities thrown in. The best bargain for divers may be the **Coral Garden Hotel** (P.O. Box 597, Rota, MP 96951, phone 670-532-3201, fax 670-532-3204), located just outside Songsong, about a quarter-mile from the island's only dive shop. The hotel is new, comfortable, and reasonable.

At the opposite end of the spectrum is the new **Rota Resort** (P.O. Box 938, Rota, MP 96951, phone 670-532-1155, fax 670-532-1156), located high on a hillside overlooking the ocean at the northern end of the island, about ten miles from Songsong. If you stay here you will probably want to rent a car (available at the airport) since the resort is quite isolated. **There is a golf course, pool and restaurant.** All accommodations are suites, either two-bedroom or four-bedroom. The suites are beautifully decorated, but could have been transplanted straight out of an American suburb—there is no Pacific theme here. The restaurant is quite good. An interesting alternative is the **Coconut Village Hotel** (P.O. Box 855, Rota, MP 96951, and phone 670-532-3448, fax 670-532-3449), built on an old coconut plantation close to the water at the north end of the island. The hotel consists of eight duplexes built in a Pacific style, overlooking the water. There is a restaurant and pool. It has seen better days, but the Coconut Village is very quiet and is in a beautiful location. A rental car will be desirable since it also is isolated.

Many hotels on Rota do not accept credit cards, so check when making a reservation. **For more information contact the Marianas Visitors Bureau, Box 861, Saipan, MP 96950; phone 670-234-8325.**

DINING

When hunger strikes; don't expect a gourmet feast on Rota. You'll find decent, but not extraordinary, food. **Valentine's,** in Singsong, offers consistently good, reasonably priced fare, mostly Filipino- Rota-style.

The **Root Resort** is good, but more costly, but the sunsets are worth it.

It's possible that the best meal you'll have on Root will be at **Jack's Raman House,** located, logically, in Jack's house. During the day you could walk by and not notice it, but at night, Jack opens up his back room and serves the best ramen and cold beer on the island.

AREAS OF INTEREST

Non-diving hours can be spent exploring the island, and for such a small place, there's quite a lot to see. **There are remnants of the Japanese occupation—cannons peaking out of hillsides and a cave that were used as a hospital during the war.**

There is also a small **zoo,** a **bird sanctuary,** and a mysterious **stone quarry** used by the Chamorros centuries ago, where you can see the large latte stones used for construction that were hewn out of solid rock by some unknown means.

For a magnificent view of the island, drive up **Mount Sabana,** past the **Peace Memorial,** to a vantage point that looks out over **Songsong, Sosanjaya Bay** and **Wedding Cake Mountain.** On a clear day **Guam** is visible in the distance.

If you're looking for nightlife and excitement, don't go to Rota. But if you want a little piece of serene pacific paradise sweetened with first-class diving, this may be just the place.

Truk (or Chuuk) Lagoon

SS Thorfinn

Lynn Funkhouser

I had not been diving in Truk Lagoon since 1978. My first experience was shaped by unfriendly people, only two dives per day, (often with only a short surface interval after a deep dive), absolutely no night dives, no choice of dive sites and horrible food. The frosting "off the cake" was staying 3 extra days for the purpose of diving the *Shinkoku Maru,* and then never being allowed to go there. I can still remember the dive guide sitting on the wing of an aircraft and throwing pieces of coral at a blue faced angel I was trying to photograph. Twenty years later, it would be interesting to see how the wrecks had changed, but I wasn't particularly excited to go back.

The *S.S. Thorfinn* has changed all that! Captain Lance Higgs understands what a diver wants. Five dives a day are offered, including the deep wrecks and night dives. Diving depth limitations are 200 plus (on a non-deco basis). All dives are done safely with nice long safety stops; extra tanks tied off, and guide to assist the divers. You can see up to 30 wrecks in a week of diving on the *Thorfinn!*

Even more exciting, there are four 24-foot twin engine dive tenders so there are no more than 6 divers per boat and on each wreck. We had a *"Thorfinn* appreciation dive" when another operator tied onto the *Fujikawa Maru* and dropped 14 divers in with us. (The *Thorfinn* tender boats tie up to buoys. The other operator ties directly onto the wrecks *Thorfinn* operates 365 days a year and offers 7 days of diving in a 7-day package! **Many liveaboard operators only offer 5 1/2 days of diving in a 7-day** package.) Tenders can take divers to the sites even when the *Thorfinn* is anchored at the Truk Continental Hotel during weekend guest changeovers or fueling at a commercial pier.

The *S.S. Thorfinn* **is 170 feet in length with a wide 30-foot beam, which makes her one of the largest liveaboards in the world. She recently had a $1.5 million renovation.** She has 11 fully air-conditioned staterooms, which accommodate up to 22 guests in spacious comfort. Eight of the staterooms feature very comfortable queen size beds and an additional berth for extra camera gear or a possible third guest. These staterooms also have a private shower, head, and wash basin. Each room has a TV and VCR. The size of the *Thorfinn* gives her rock solid stability and her Antarctic designs and background make her one of the safest diveboats in operation.

There is a spacious main salon which features plenty of comfortable couches, a full bar, large salt aquarium, great windows for viewing the beautiful scenery, and state of the art entertainment center with big screen TV, VHS and 8mm VCRs, Dolby surround sound stereo, and a good video library. Every morning laminated pages detailing the wrecks that will be dived that day are on the tables to be studied.

The private dining room has also been redecorated and food on the *Thorfinn* is excellent. The cook awakens at 3:30 AM to begin making homemade breakfast rolls for the early risers. We were served wonderful meals including prime rib, duck a l'orange, fresh tuna, lamb chops, lobster, BBQ ribs, homemade pastas, breads and incredible desserts. Wine is offered at the evening meals unless you are going on the night dive.

A custom designed ocean hot tub with seating for 8 on the back deck is really wonderful after a night dive or any dive, for that matter. There is a nice sun deck with chaise lounges and a shaded area for relaxing.

The *Thorfinn* **has 21 crewmembers to serve a maximum of 22 guests, which is one of the highest ratios of crew to guests in the world. The dive guides are excellent.** Since there is so much to see and time is limited at deeper depths, they guide you to the best parts of the wrecks to see the most important things most efficiently. Gear is stowed and/or put on board the dive tenders for you. There are fresh water rinse buckets for cameras, camera maintenance tables, battery charging (110 and 220 voltage) stations, daily E-6 film processing, and light tables for photographers.

To say the least, **I found Turk to be a much better experience now than 20 years ago.** Sure, some of the wrecks have deteriorated a bit, but the corals are even more fabulous. **Amazingly, you can still see newspapers, gas masks, skulls, bones, saki bottles, lanterns airplanes, trucks, china dishes, etc. on the Japanese wrecks.** The *Thorfinn* enables you to safely experience more of the wrecks and do it comfortably. The Chuukees are much friendlier, waving and talking to visitors now. They have realized that their economy

Wreck of The Nippon by Lynn Funkhouser

SCUBA AND SNORKELING QUESTIONNAIRE

NAME: **Seaward Holidays Micronesia Inc.**
ADDRESS: **P.O. Box 1086, Chuuk, FSM, 96942**

CONTACT: **SS Thorfinn - L. Higgs**
TITLE: **Captain/Director**
TELEPHONE: **691-330-3040**   FAX **691-330-4253**   SHIP   **91-330-4302**
CAPITAL: **Chuuk, SM**   GOVERNMENT: **Elected**
POPULATION: **60,000**   LANGUAGE: **English / Chuukese**
CURRENCY: **USA dollar**   ELECTRICITY: **110 Volt 60 cycle**
AIRLINES: **Cont., Micronesia**   DEPARTURE TAX? **$10 US**
NEED VISA/PASSPORT YES   NO **X**   PROOF OF CITIZENSHIP? YES **X**   NO

YOUR FACILITY IS CLASSIFIED AS: **Dive live aboard ship**
BUSINESS HOURS: **24 hours 365 day a year**
CERTIFYING AGENCIES: **PADI, NAUI**
LOGBOOK REQUIRED? YES **X**   NO
EQUIPMENT: SALES   RENTALS **X**   AIR FILLS
PRIMARY LINE OF EQUIPMENT? **All dive accessories including Video**
PHOTOGRAPHIC EQUIPMENT: SALES   RENTALS   LAB

CHARTER/DIVE BOAT AVAILABLE? YES **X**   NO   DIVER CAPACITY **22**
COAST GUARD APPROVED? YES **X**   NO   CAPTAIN LICENSED? YES **X**   NO
SHIP TO SHORE? YES **X**   NO   LORAN? YES **X**   NO
RADAR? YES **X**   NO
DIVE MASTER/INSTRUCTOR ABOARD? YES **X**   NO   **Both**

DIVING AND SNORKELING: SALT **X**   FRESH
TYPE OF DIVING/SNORKELING IN AREA: WALL **X**   BEACH   WRECK **X**   REEF   CAVE   ICE
DIVING/SNORKELING IN YOUR AREA IS BEST SUITED FOR: BEGINNER **X** INTERMEDIATE **X** ADVANCED **X**
BEST TIME OF YEAR FOR DIVING/SNORKELING: **All year**
TEMPERATURE: NOV-APRIL: **82-85F**   MAY-OCT. **83-85F**
VISIBILITY: DIVING: **50-120Ft.**   SNORKELING **50-120Ft.**

PACKAGES AVAILABLE: DIVE **X**   DIVE STAY **X**   SNORKEL   SNORKEL STAY
ACCOMMODATIONS NEARBY: HOTEL   MOTEL   HOME RENTALS
ACCOMMODATION RATES: EXPENSIVE   MODERATE **X**   INEXPENSIVE
RESTAURANTS NEARBY: EXPENSIVE   MODERATE   INEXPENSIVE
YOUR AREA IS: REMOTE **X**   QUIET WITH ACTIVITIES   LIVELY

LOCAL ACTIVITY/NIGHTLIFE: **Limited**
CAR NEEDED TO EXPLORE AREA: YES   NO **X**
DUTY FREE SHOPPING: YES   NO **X**

LOCAL EMERGENCY SERVICES: NEAREST HYPERBARIC TREATMENT FACILITY:
COAST GUARD: AUTHORITY: **US Navy**
TELEPHONE: LOCATION: **Guam**
CALLSIGNS: TELEPHONE:

LOCAL DIVING DOCTOR:
NAME: **Dr. Herlib Nowell**
LOCATION: **Chuuk General Hospital**
TELEPHONE: **691-330-2210**

depends on tourist dollars. One word of caution, the governor of Chuuk disappeared with the funds to operate the island, so it is a struggle to provide such basic services as electricity, water and operating the airport. For that reason, you should consider trip insurance and keep in contact with the *Thorfinn*, which could arrange to pick divers up elsewhere if there is a problem.

If you prefer to dive reefs instead of wrecks and would enjoy the luxury of the *Thorfinn* you might want to try one of the 2 week trips being offered. The *Thorfinn* is offering four Pan Micronesian "Voyage of Discovery" trips to very remote islands. Trip #1 includes Truk Eastbound via East Fayu, Murilo Atoll, Minto Reef, Oroulk Atoll, Pakin Atoll, Ant Atoll, Madolenihm Harbor to Pohnpei. Trip #2 includes Pohnpei via Ujelang Atoll, Enewetak Atoll, Bikini Atoll, Wotho Atoll, to Kwajalein Atoll. Trip #3 is the reverse of trip #2 and Trip #4 is the reverse of trip #1.

Two great books to own if you want to study the wrecks in depth are: *Hailstorm Over Truk Lagoon* by Klaus Lindermann and *26 Principal Shipwrecks of Truk Lagoon* by Capt. Lance Higgs of *S.S. Thorfinn*.

The *Thorfinn* makes Truk the wreck diver's paradise it should be!!!!

Yap

Mike Innis

If you've ever wanted to dive with BIG manta rays, Yap is a "must do" destination. During a recent five-day stay, we saw mantas on every dive. Up close and personal. Within arm's length. These beautiful creatures, with 12-foot wingspans and weighing up to 1500 pounds, performed aquatic ballets for an appreciative, awe-struck audience of divers. At times only one ray was visible; and then, out of the blue haze, another one would materialize. Then another. Sometimes six of them glided by, circling, hovering, as cleaner wrasse picked parasites from their skins and darted in and out of their mouths and gill rakes to complete their grooming duties.

On several dives, curious whitetip and blacktip sharks cruised by to see what we were doing, and during the five days of diving we spotted turtles, moray eels, barracuda, lionfish, clownfish flashing in and out of carpet anemones, and clouds of jacks. The reefs appeared healthy, with the entire food chain represented in impressive numbers. Forests of staghorn coral, acres of lettuce coral, and brain coral heads as large as a Volkswagen bombarded your senses.

This is pristine diving, untrammeled by the thundering herds of divers that are literally beating the life out of some of the more popular, accessible dive destinations of the world. Certified divers with just a small amount of experience can comfortably dive here, but practice your buoyancy control so that you stay off the coral! The islanders are justifiably proud and protective of their natural resource.

While there were no snorkelers in our group, it is definitely a place that the snorkeler would enjoy.

The manta experiences took place in a couple of the channels leading in from the fringing reef. We would moor the boat at the edge of these channels, in 8-10 feet of water, and then slide down to 50-60 feet to look for rays. While decompressing under the boat, there was enough activity going on in and amongst the coral formations to keep even the most jaded snorkeler happy awaiting our return. We visited one site, Sunrise, out beyond the reef, which would also offer more of the same. The visibility in the channels varied from 50-100 feet, depending on the tide; out on the reef, true 120-foot visibility was the norm. The water was a constant 86 degrees.

A Swiss ex-pat, Freddy, manages the PADI 5-star dive operation, and it runs like a watch. The boats leave promptly at the published departure time, the crews are courteous, knowledgeable and proficient, and safety is the watchword. Freddy keeps a large, well-maintained inventory of rental gear available for use by the guests. It was a pleasure diving with Yap Divers.

Steven Fish, the local photography pro who runs Manta Visions, is another of Yap Divers' excellent human assets. Steve, a professional land based photographer for years, took up U/W photography and videography with a vengeance over 10 years ago. He freely shares his enormous knowledge of how to effectively capture images on film, and was always there to answer any questions we had. He has produced truly top quality "stock" videotape of Yap and the diving around Yap, and will, upon request, customize the stock tape with clips of you and your party.

Manta Ray by Michael B. Innis

ACCOMMODATIONS & DINING
I stayed at the **Manta Ray Bay Hotel**. The rooms are spacious, clean and air-conditioned. Every day housekeeping placed a small arrangement of gorgeous tropical flowers on the bed pillow. Prettier than the usual chocolate mint, and much better for you.

I also took all my meals at the Hotel, based on the recommendations of previous visitors to the island. The wiseness of this decision was reinforced by a few guests I talked to who had ventured out to eat "native". They were disappointed with the quality of the food and service, and all expressed some concern about the cleanliness of the eateries. Meals at the hotels are fixed price. Beverages are additional. The quality and variety of the food was quite good.

AREAS OF INTEREST
If you are dived or snorkeled out, and want to spend some time out of the water, the Hotel can arrange several different tours for you:
- a 1/2 day land tour
- transfers to and from a local beach, including lunch and a drink
- a boat tour of the mangrove areas and O'Keefe Island
- a "cultural" tour, Sundays only, with a visit to a local village
- a guided stone path walk from the hotel at no charge
- Yap Anglers will make arrangements to take you fishing, and will develop a price for you depending upon the type of fishing you wish to do.

As you can tell, there's something for everyone who visits Yap. Make your arrangements directly with Mr. Bill Acker at the Manta Ray Bay Hotel.

SCUBA AND SNORKELING FACILITIES QUESTIONNAIRE

NAME: **Manta Ray Bay Hotel**
ADDRESS: **PO Box MR**
YAP FSM 96943
CONTACT: **Bill Acker**
TITLE: **General Manager**
TELEPHONE: **011 691 350 2300**   FAX: **011 691 350 4567**
CAPITOL: **COLONIA**   GOVERNMENT: **Federated States of Micronesia**
POPULATION: **8000**   LANGUAGE: **English**
CURRENCY: **VS $**   ELECTRICITY: **110V 60 HZ**
AIRLINES: **Continental Micronnesia**   DEPARTURE TAX? **No**
VISA/PASSPORT? **Yes**   PROOF OF CITIZENSHIP? **Yes**

YOUR FACILITY IS QUALIFIED AS: **Resort**
BUISINESS HOURS: **24 Hours**
CERTIFYING AGENCIES: **PADI**
LOG BOOK REQUIRED? **No**
EQUIPMENT: **Sales, Rentals, Air Fills**
PRIMARY LINE OF EQUIPMENT: **Scuba Pro**
PHOTOGRAPHIC EQUIPMENT: **Rentals, Lab**

CHARTER/DIVE BOAT AVAILABLE? **Yes**   DIVER CAPACITY: **5 Boats 8-20 passangers**
COAST GUARD APPROVED? **No**   CAPTAIN LICENSE? **No**
SHIP TO SHORE? **Yes**   LORAN ? **No**   RADAR? **No**
DIVE MASTER/INSTRUCTOR ABOARD? **Yes, Both**

DIVING & SNORKELING: **Salt**
TYPE OF DIVING/SNORKELING IN AREA? **Wall, Reef**
DIVING/SNORKELING IN YOUR AREA IS BEST SUITED FOR: **Beginner, Intermediate, Advanced**
BEST TIME OF YEAR FOR DIVING/SNORKELING:
TEMPERATURE: NOV-APRIL   **79 F**   MAY-OCT: **82 F**
VISIBILITY: DIVING   **30-150 FT**   SNORKELING: **30-150 FT**

PACKAGES AVAILABLE: **Dive, Dive-Stay**
ACCOMMODATIONS NEARBY:
ACCOMMODATIONS RATES: **Expensive**
RESTAURANTS NEARBY: **Expensive**
YOUR AREA IS: **Remote**
LOCAL ACTIVITY/NIGHTLIFE: **Cultural Tours**
CAR NEEDED TO EXPLORE AREA? **No**
DUTY FREE SHOPPING? **Yes**

LOCAL EMERGENCY SERVICES   NEAREST HYPERBARIC TREATMENT FACILITY
COASTGUARD   AUTHORITY:
TELEPHONE: LOCATION: **Palav**
CALLSIGNS: TELEPHONE:

LOCAL DIVING DOCTOR:
NAME:
LOCATION:
TELEPHONE:

NEW ZEALAND

Picton

Paul Snowman

If you take a globe of the world and rotate it so that New Zealand is in the center you will see more than land. "Our" half of the world is 90% ocean, with nearly half of the remaining 9% made up of the continent of Antarctica.

New Zealand is at the center of the water hemisphere. This makes us the most maritime nation on earth. It has a long coastline (approx. 15,000km or 9500 miles). Our coast is varied and includes fiords, sounds, vast bays, harbors, beaches and cliffs. We have everything except coral reefs and icebergs. Almost all of New Zealand is accessible by car or boat with the sea never more than 120km (75 miles) away. New Zealand's human population of a little over 3,000,000 is small when distributed over a land area approximately equivalent to Japan or the British Isles.

The waters of New Zealand lie between the 33rd and 47th parallels which includes the subantarctic to the subtropical, the shallow continental shelf to the abysmal depths. Because our country lies in the "Roaring Forties" (westerly winds circumnavigating the earth at 40 degrees to the South) the west coast is rugged and almost incessantly pounded by ocean waves and high winds. Our proximity to Antarctica affects our water temperature which ranges from winter lows of 10 degrees centigrade (50 degrees Fahrenheit) to summer highs of 32 degrees centigrade (72 degrees Fahrenheit), depending on your location. Obviously, the further south you

Anash Rock by Paul Snowman

go, generally, the colder it gets. **January and February are our warmest months** (25.C - 30.C) **with July the coldest** (-5.c - 12.C)

Picton lies at the base of the Marlborough Sounds, at the very top of the South Island. Picton is a quiet town of 4,000 people and because of its role as a "Getaway to the South" it prides itself on its tourist-oriented outlook.

THE DIVING

Diving from Picton centers on the **Marlborough Sounds**, 1,400km (900 miles) of coastline containing a unique drowned valley system. The vast collection of bays, islands and subtidal reefs create numerous habitats supporting a great variety of New Zealand's endemic marine species. Water temperatures range from 14 degrees centigrade (57 F.) to 20 degrees centigrade (68 F.) with the warmest water and more settled weather usually being experienced from January to April. Year round diving is possible although 7-mm wetsuits are the norm regardless of the seasons. Water clarity is not comparable to the tropics, ranging from 2m (6ft) in bad weather to 20m (65ft) in good.

Novice divers will find excellent safe scenic diving within the Sounds at sites such as

221

Cooper's Point, Motuara Island or the wreck of the *Koi*. These sites are also suitable for snorkelers, diving shallow rocky reefs covered in kelp and supporting large varieties of marine life.

The more ambitious experienced diver is catered for at sites such as **Cape Koamaru, Cape Jackson, Brother's Island** and the more distant **D'Urville Island**. These sites are generally kelp covered; rocky reefs with some tidal currents experienced resulting in exhilarating diving. Fish life is prolific with both conservationists and hunter being satisfied.

The Sounds sports numerous wrecks from small launches to 100 year old sailing ships and coastal steamers to our most recent, the 20,000 ton Russian liner *Mikhail Lermontov* which struck rocks and sank in the outer Sounds in February 1986. This

Nudibranch (Sea Slug) by Paul Snowman

wreck is immense and needs many dives to gain a perspective of its size. The ship lies on its side in 36m (120ft) with 13m (45ft) at its shallowest point. However, due to the regular poor visibility and the numerous "enticing" windows and doors accessing the wreck, this is not a dive for the beginner and like all wreck dives, requires proper planning with local knowledge preferable.

No scheduled dive operation runs to the *Lermontov* but trips for groups of 4 or more can be arranged but can cost up to $120/day per person.

Several other, much older, shipwrecks lie in the outer Sounds many with opportunities for photography, relic hunting or just observing the resident fish population.

Excellent snorkeling opportunities exist in Tory Channel for spearfishing; Paua (Abalone), pronounced "Par-wah", hunters; photographers; or those just content to observe.

Because the Marlborough Sounds are largely sheltered from the effects of ocean waves and winds, there is always a dive site available for all levels of diving ability. Dive charters are available at the Picton town wharf. Self-drive charter vessels ranging from 5.0m runabouts to 12.0m launches and sailboats are available for independent divers while skippered charters are available for groups of four to sixteen divers. Because the best dive sites are 35km (21 miles) from Picton, it is advisable to set a full day (or more) aside to do justice to the area.

The best diving value would have to be as a guest of the Picton Underwater Club which runs monthly dive trips into the Sounds. Most trips are held on the 2nd or 3rd Sunday of the month, so timing your arrival in Picton for this event would ensure your participation.

The club (30 members) has good local knowledge and use members private boats. The boats used by the club are fast runabouts, so dive sites are accessed within 30 minutes of Picton compared to 2-3 hours taken for charter launches.

Contact with club members can be made through the dive store in Picton.

ACCOMMODATIONS
There are numerous restaurants, hotels, motels, hostels and retail outlets geared to accommodate the tourist, with all budgets catered for.

SCUBA AND SNORKELING QUESTIONNAIRE

NAME: **Diver's World - Picton**
ADDRESS: **London Quay, Picton**
New Zealand
CONTACT: **Bill Lines**
TITLE : **Manager**
TELEPHONE: **03-5737323**   FAX: **03-5737323**
CAPITOL: **Picton**   GOVERNMENT: **New Zealand**
POPULATION: **4,000**   LANGUAGE: **English**
CURRENCY: **NZ Dollar**   ELECTRICITY: **230v ac**
AIRLINES: **Air NZ, United, Continental**   DEPARTURE TAX? **$20 NZ Dollars**
VISA/PASSPORT? **Yes**   PROOF OF CITIZENSHIP? **Yes**

YOUR FACILITY IS QUALIFIED AS: **Scuba Center**
BUISINESS HOURS: **0830-1730**
CERTIFYING AGENCIES: **PADI, SSI**
LOG BOOK REQUIRED? **No**
EQUIPMENT: **Sales, Rentals, Air Fills**
PRIMARY LINE OF EQUIPMENT: **Sherwood**
PHOTOGRAPHIC EQUIPMENT: **Lab**

CHARTER/DIVE BOAT AVAILABLE? **Yes**   DIVER CAPACITY:
COAST GUARD APPROVED?   **Yes**   CAPTAIN LICENSE?
SHIP TO SHORE?   **Yes**   LORAN ? **No**   RADAR? **Yes**
DIVE MASTER/INSTRUCTOR ABOARD? **Yes, Both**

DIVING & SNORKELING: SALT
TYPE OF DIVING/SNORKELING IN AREA?   **Wall, Beach, Wreck**
DIVING/SNORKELING IN YOUR AREA IS BEST SUITED FOR: **Beginner, Intermediate, Advanced**
BEST TIME OF YEAR FOR DIVING/SNORKELING: **Summer, Autumn**
TEMPERATURE: NOV-APRIL   **70 F**   MAY-OCT: **60 F**
VISIBILITY: DIVING   **15-65 ft**   SNORKELING: **15-65 ft**

PACKAGES AVAILABLE: **Dive, Snorkel**
ACCOMMODATIONS NEARBY: **Hotel, Hostels**
ACCOMMODATIONS RATES: **Expensive, Moderate, Inexpensive**
RESTAURANTS NEARBY: **Expensive, Moderate, Inexpensive**
YOUR AREA IS: **Quiet with Activities**
LOCAL ACTIVITY/NIGHTLIFE: **4-wheel drive tours, wine trails, harbour cruises, hotels,**
restaurants, nightclubs
CAR NEEDED TO EXPLORE AREA? **Yes**
DUTY FREE SHOPPING? **No**

COASTGUARD: **Picton Police**   AUTHORITY: **Canterbury Area Health Board**
TELEPHONE: **03-5736439**   LOCATION: **Princess Margaret Hospital,**
Christchurch

LOCAL DIVING DOCTOR:
NAME: **Dr. John C. Welch**
LOCATION: **Picton**
TELEPHONE: **03-5737901**

Accommodation ranges from backpacker hostels to top class hotels/motels. There are no diving resorts in Picton, but a number of resorts in the Sounds cater to dive groups.

Picton is the South Island terminal for an inter-island ferry service and this as well as the scheduled bus; train and plane transport is regular and convenient. Picton also sports a large fleet of rental vehicles with all the major companies represented.

Pre-bookings for accommodation and all modes of travel can be made through the **Picton Information Center, The Station, P.O. Box 332, Picton, New Zealand.** Phone (03) 5738838 within New Zealand. Diver's World - Picton is the sole dive retail center in Picton and boasts a full range of both hire and retail equipment. The store has full testing and filling facilities and undertakes recognized Scuba training (PADI & SSI) by qualified instructors. Dive charters are also arranged with groups of 4-16 divers. Trips do not normally include a dive master, but can if required.

THE PHILIPPINES

Introduction

Lynn Funkhouser

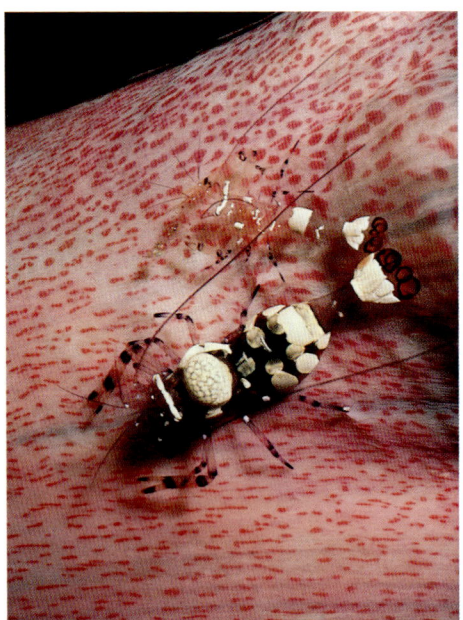

Dive 7000 by Lynn Funkhouser

More than 7,000 islands comprise the Republic of the Philippines and these islands are surrounded by some of the world's most exquisite coral reefs. This region is noted for having the greatest U/W species diversification in the world. The reefs, a living work of art built by more than 400 species of corals, cover approximately 27,340 square miles. Conservative estimates count more than 2,000 species of fish supported by the massive reef systems and at least 5,000 species of shells. Many more species are yet to be discovered.

The country lies from 5°N to 21°N latitude and has a coastline that stretches approximately 10,850 statue miles. **It lies on the western edge of the Pacific Ocean and the eastern edge of the South China Sea.** Other seas, including the Sulu Sea, Celebes Sea, Bohol Sea, Visayan Sea, Sibuyan Sea, and the Philippine Sea surround the islands and contribute to the diversity. Each area has its own unique species and/or distribution of species.

The Philippines are also diverse in their human culture. Malayo-Polynesian, Spanish, Chinese, Indian, and American influences can all be seen in varying degrees. The national language of the country is Philipino or Tagalog, but there are at least 75 other languages and dialects scattered among the numerous islands and tribal groups. English, the second official language, is widely spoken.

Few countries in the world can offer as many colorful and contrasting attractions as the Philippine Islands with everything from the most fabulous underwater scenery to vibrant festivals and fiestas; from beautiful secluded sandy beaches to pulsating

nightlife, from somber war memorials to modern malls and unique handicraft shops. However, its greatest asset is its exceptionally friendly and hospitable people. I first visited the islands in 1976 and have spent approximately 2 months every year since diving there because of the exquisite reefs, the myriad and diverse critters, and wonderful people. This is one country that divers want to return to many times, often to dive the same destination and then to sample different ones.

PHILIPPINES, BATANGAS PROVINCE, LUZON, ANILAO, DIVE 7000

Dive 7000 is a dive resort run by divers. It may not be as posh as many of the resorts featured in this book, but in my 30 years of diving, it is still my favorite place in the world for critters. **This area of Batangas Province, near the village of Anilao, is a "little hotbed of evolution". It is so rich in marine life that scientists have discovered more than 300 species of nudibranchs new to science in the last few years.** Other species of critters are just as well represented. You will see octopus, cuttlefish, nudibranchs, lionfish, schools of catfish, ghost pipefish, harlequin shrimp, etc. in 3 feet of water. You can enjoy diving with 10 species of anemonefish residing in anemones the size of wagon wheels, numerous species of lionfish, Spanish dancers, sea goblins, crinoids in every color, many species of shells, fish, corals, and invertebrates in less than 20' of water. There are plenty of deeper dives also–just follow the sloping walls down to 120 ft. if you prefer. There is so much to see in shallow water that you can get plenty of bottom time. **Night diving is SPECTACULAR! This area is great for snorkelers.**

Dive 7000 got its name from the 7000 islands of the Philippines. Owner, Dr. Tim Sevilla, was going to construct a resort on each of the 7000 islands, but the diving was so good in Batangas that he never got around to building the other 6,999. He picked the site on the point because it was naturally air-conditioned by the breezes and made sure nobody had ever gotten malaria in the area. There are very few bugs and definitely no no-see-ums.

Dive 7000 is approximately 50 miles south of Manila, but due to slow traffic it takes two and half hours by private car or van. You may want to stop along the way for fascinating photo opportunities and can even **take a side trip to Lake Taal and the volcano within the lake.** For a treat, sample the fresh hot buko (young coconut) pie sold at roadside pie stands.

Once you arrive at this rustic Philippine style resort your stress will magically disappear. There are 7 newly renovated rooms constructed of native materials to add to the 5 existing rooms, all with private bathrooms. Accommodations are for a maximum of 24 divers.

Dr. Sevilla and his wife, Luz, are wonderful hosts. You will never have to hassle with your dive gear. **Experience the wonderful hospitality of the Filipino people who will take care of all your needs, including assembling your dive gear, carrying it to the bancas (outrigger boats) or shore, rinsing it after dives, putting it away, and more – all with a smile.**

Three excellent family-style meals, and usually an afternoon snack, are served each day. Food is abundant, consisting of the most wonderful tropical fruits, fresh seafood, vegetables, with native and international dishes served buffet style. There is even a Japanese hibachi for special dinners. Lunches are usually cooked and served on a variety of beautiful beaches.

Dive 7000 has fantastic diving right off the shore. Cathedral, one of three marine sanctuaries in Batangas, is just a short swim from shore. It started out as two rather barren rocks at 40' to 50' to the tops of them dropping to 90' at the bases with only a few pieces of black coral growing on them. Dr. Sevilla and several other divers started to transplant hard and soft corals, (tying some of them into place with ropes) sponges, shells and other animals, etc. from various areas, creating a remarkable reef teeming with an extremely colorful profusion of life. The reef then attracted many species of butterflyfish, angelfish, frogfish, leaffish, groupers, jacks, parrotfish, wrasse, pufferfish, triggerfish, trumpetfish up to 4' in length, etc. **General, now Philippine President, Fidel V. Ramos, an avid diver, donated the cross, which was blessed by Pope John Paul II,**

SCUBA AND SNORKELING QUESTIONNAIRE

NAME: **Dive 7000 Resort Located in Batangas Province, Anilao village**
ADDRESS: **P.O. Box 7545 ADC-MIA**
Pasay City, Metro Manila, Philippines
CONTACT: **Dr. Tim Sevilla**
TITLE: **General Manager**
TELEPHONE: **632-741-2130** FAX **632-741-2130** CELL PH. **632-0912-340-6300**
CAPITAL: **Manila** GOVERNMENT: **Democratic**
POPULATION: **10 million (Manila)** LANGUAGE: **Philipino & English**
CURRENCY: **Philippine peso** ELECTRICITY: **220 volt**
AIRLINES: **PAL, United, NW** DEPARTURE TAX? **500 pesos ($20 US)**
NEED VISA/PASSPORT V IF STAY OVER 21 DAYS YES **X** NO PROOF OF CITIZENSHIP? YES NO **X**

YOUR FACILITY IS CLASSIFIED AS: SCUBA CENTER RESORT **X**
BUSINESS HOURS: **24 hrs.**
CERTIFYING AGENCIES:
LOGBOOK REQUIRED? YES **X** AND NO **X**
EQUIPMENT: SALES RENTALS **X** AIR FILLS **X**
PRIMARY LINE OF EQUIPMENT?
PHOTOGRAPHIC EQUIPMENT: SALES RENTALS LAB

CHARTER/DIVE BOAT AVAILABLE? YES **X** DIVER CAPACITY **5 passengers max. per boat**
COAST GUARD APPROVED? YES **X** NO CAPTAIN LICENSED? YES NO
SHIP TO SHORE? YES NO X LORAN? YES NO X RADAR? YES NO X
DIVE MASTER/INSTRUCTOR ABOARD? YES X NO BOTH **X**

DIVING AND SNORKELING: SALT **X** FRESH
TYPE OF DIVING/SNORKELING IN AREA: WALL **X** BEACH **X** WRECK **X** REEF **X** CAVE **X** ICE
DIVING/SNORKELING IN YOUR AREA IS BEST SUITED FOR: BEGINNER **X** INTERMEDIATE **X** ADVANCED **X**
BEST TIME OF YEAR FOR DIVING/SNORKELING: **December through May**
TEMPERATURE: NOV-APRIL: **80F** MAY-OCT. **82F**
VISIBILITY: DIVING: **60Ft.** SNORKELING **60Ft.**
PACKAGES AVAILABLE: DIVE X DIVE STAY **X** SNORKEL **X** SNORKEL STAY
ACCOMMODATIONS NEARBY: HOTEL MOTEL HOME RENTALS
ACCOMMODATION RATES: EXPENSIVE MODERATE **X** INEXPENSIVE
RESTAURANTS NEARBY: EXPENSIVE MODERATE INEXPENSIVE
YOUR AREA IS: REMOTE **X** QUIET WITH ACTIVITIES X LIVELY
LOCAL ACTIVITY/NIGHTLIFE:
CAR NEEDED TO EXPLORE AREA: YES NO **X**
DUTY FREE SHOPPING: YES NO **X**

LOCAL EMERGENCY SERVICES: NEAREST HYPERBARIC TREATMENT FACILITY:
COAST GUARD: AUTHORITY: **Manila Philippine Commission**
TELEPHONE: LOCATION: **on Sports, SCUBA Diving**
CALLSIGNS: **(PCSSD), Dept. Of Tourism**
T. M. Dalaw St., Rizal Park
Manila
TELEPHONE:

LOCAL DIVING DOCTOR:
NAME: **Ramon Suter, MD**
LOCATION: **Makait Medical Center**
Manila
TELEPHONE: **632-58-58-57 / 50-37-35**

and had it placed between the two rocks. Dr. Tim, as he is often called, can frequently be seen picking up corals that have been carelessly kicked by divers and placing them back. He does his "gardening" underwater.

The key to it all is the amount of plankton in the water, which feeds the incredible number of invertebrates, and anthias (fish) which feed all the larger fish that make this such a rich area. **Visibility is usually around 60 feet. Water temperature is 80 degrees F.** A wetsuit is suggested because **your dives can last 2 hours or more** if you choose to hang out in the shallow depth so you can get cold and there are many creatures that sting, some of them are plankton.

Other good dive sites include the two other marine sanctuaries of Twin Rocks and Arthur's Rock, Carboy's Rock, Laying Rock (Ship's Rock), Cabana Cove, Coral Garden, Bethlehem, Red Palm, Maillot Point, Beatrice Rock, Abjure, Septic Wall, Sombrero Island, and Devil's Point. If you are into deep dives, Mapping features an interesting cave at 150'. These sites are reached by bancas with no more than five divers in each. If you plan it well, the different bancas can go to various sites so there will only be a few divers at each location. You can meet for lunch and scatter again.

If you love critters, you will marvel at the incredible diversity of marine life in Batangas. **Dive 7000 is my favorite place.**

Northern Palawan

Club Paradise

Lynn Funkhouser

Club Paradise is perfectly named. It encompasses the whole island of Dimakya, owned by Juergen Warnke, a German international textile entrepreneur. Getting there is an adventure in itself. It is reached by daily flights on Air Ads, Aerolift and Pacific Air. The 70-minute flight from Manila to Busuanga, viewing some of the most picturesque islands scattered over intense blue seas, passes quickly. A smiling Club Paradise employee meets the flight and collects you and your luggage for the half-hour jeepney ride. Next you arrive at a small harbor where a wooden plank bridge with handrails stretches for approximately a quarter mile spanning a magnificent mangrove swamp. Luckily your luggage is carried for you! A large banca (outrigger boat) with soft drinks and sandwiches awaits you at the end of the bridge and transports you past magnificent panoramas on the final 45-minute leg of your journey to Club Paradise.

The island is beautiful and its essence and ecology have been preserved. 40 private cottages built of nipa, bamboo, and rattan feature king size beds, large marble bathrooms, intercom phones (for room service), and spacious terraces. Large tropical trees provide privacy and visual delight. Half the cottages are large enough to accommodate families. **Did you know that many resorts have to import sand for their beaches? At Club Paradise the local white sand is accumulating rapidly** – probably thanks to a resident school of 40 large bumphead parrots processing all that coral.

Special treats are the small Calamian deer, which can be encountered grazing behind the cottages in the evenings. There is a marked hiking trail on the hilly side of the island to view even more flora and fauna and it provides great views of the island and surrounding islands. Some of the trees are identified and cashew nut trees can be seen. A small swamp was left in the middle of the island and if you are patient you can observe four foot long monitor lizards.

A spacious lounge offers comfortable couches, a video viewing room, a friendly bar, pool tables, large library, plenty of games and karaoke facilities. **In addition to diving and snorkeling,** tennis, windsurfing, sailing, fishing, hiking, swimming in the large pool or lagoon, sunset cruises, other island tours, and special events are offered.

The Clubhouse has a large terraced restaurant with a view of the ocean and the sky. The chef is from Germany and the food is excellent, abundant and varied. Native fruits, seafood and specialties are served in addition to international cuisine. It is served buffet style, with friendly staff to attend to your beverages and special requests. Even though the resort is German owned, Filipino personnel manage it, so **it retains the marvelous hospitality that makes the Philippines so special.**

Diving off the white sand beach, in front of the lounge, is amazing. Upon entering you can encounter schools of fish, small blacktip sharks, a school of 40 bumphead parrots up to 4 feet long, large giant clams, several species of anemonefish, an assortment of tame reef fish, many species of corals, and invertebrates. **In 10 feet of water there is a white sandy area which is called the classroom, perfect for teaching SCUBA.** At the far end of the reef is an extensive garden of delicate staghorn corals with a wonderful school of goatfish, other schools of fish, large crocodile fish, etc. **A small wooden ship was sunk as a wrecksite nearby, providing a hiding place for an assortment of great angelfish, groupers, and other reef fish.**

Walking off the beach in front of the dining room brings you to a site called Dugong Park, a bed of turtle grass where you can occasionally see the very rare dugong and often watch sea turtles feeding. Guards are posted to inform the dive guides when a dugong (a relative of the manatee) arrives and guests are escorted out for a very special experience. In addition, a large school of jacks in 10 feet of water, lots of helmet shells, and saddleback anemonefish are all right there.

Club Paradise by Lynn Funkhouser

On September 24, 1944 Admiral Halsey ordered a bombardment of the "camouflaged small moving islands" around the Coron and Calamian Islands. That day American forces sank 24 Japanese freighters and warships. One of those wrecks, located near Dimalanta Island, about 40 minutes away by banca, is the ***Kyokuzan Maru***, an excellent wreck dive. She is approximately 170 meters long, resting upright, and mostly intact with anemones with anemonefish, great cock's comb oysters, red encrusting sponges, schools of jacks and fusiliers, a large grouper in one of the holds and a myriad of reef fish decorate the wreck.

The island next to Club Paradise is Calauit, a wildlife sanctuary that was established in 1976. You can take a safari to see Philippine animals, which are native to Palawan, such as Calamian deer, mouse deer, bearcats, and Palawan porcupines. It also has exotic African animals such as zebras, giraffes, impalas, antelopes, tobies, and elans roaming freely on the island creating wonderful photo opportunities. Rangers have devoted their

SCUBA AND SNORKELING QUESTIONNAIRE

NAME: **Club Paradise**
ADDRESS: **Bldg. #4, Celery Rd., FTI Complex**
Taguag, Metro Manila
CONTACT: **Liza Moralis**
TITLE: **Manager**
TELEPHONE: **632-816-6871**   FAX   **632-818-2894 & 818-8474**   TELEX

CAPITAL: **Manila**   GOVERNMENT: **Phils. Style Democracy**
POPULATION: LANGUAGE: **English/Tagalog**
CURRENCY: **Peso**   ELECTRICITY: **220**
AIRLINES: **Air ADS, Aeronet**   DEPARTURE TAX? **500 pesos ($20 US)**
NEED VISA/PASSPORT   YES **X** NO   PROOF OF CITIZENSHIP?   YES   NO **X**

YOUR FACILITY IS CLASSIFIED AS: SCUBA CENTER   RESORT **X**
BUSINESS HOURS:
CERTIFYING AGENCIES: **PADI, NAUI, PDIC**
LOGBOOK REQUIRED?   YES **X**   NO
EQUIPMENT::   SALES   RENTALS **X**   AIR FILLS **X**
PRIMARY LINE OF EQUIPMENT?   **US Divers, Sea Quest, Scubapro**
PHOTOGRAPHIC EQUIPMENT: SALES   RENTALS   LAB **soon**

CHARTER/DIVE BOAT AVAILABLE?   YES **X**   NO   DIVER CAPACITY 8 PAS. DAY BOAT
COAST GUARD APPROVED?   YES **X**   NO   CAPTAIN LICENSED?   YES   NO
SHIP TO SHORE?   YES   NO   LORAN?   YES   NO   RADAR?   YES   NO
DIVE MASTER/INSTRUCTOR ABOARD? YES **X**   NO   BOTH

DIVING AND SNORKELING: SALT **X**   FRESH
TYPE OF DIVING/SNORKELING IN AREA: WALL **X**   BEACH **X**   WRECK **X**   REEF **X** CAVE   ICE
DIVING/SNORKELING IN YOUR AREA IS BEST SUITED FOR: BEGINNER **X** INTERMEDIATE **X** ADVANCED **X**
BEST TIME OF YEAR FOR DIVING/SNORKELING: **Nov. - May Good all year**
TEMPERATURE: NOV-MAY: **28-31C**   MAY-OCT.   **29-31C**
VISIBILITY: DIVING: **60-100Ft.**   SNORKELING   **60-100Ft.**
PACKAGES AVAILABLE: DIVE **X**   DIVE STAY   SNORKEL   SNORKEL STAY
ACCOMMODATIONS NEARBY: HOTEL   MOTEL   HOME RENTALS
ACCOMMODATION RATES: EXPENSIVE   MODERATE **X**   INEXPENSIVE
RESTAURANTS NEARBY: NONE   EXPENSIVE   MODERATE   INEXPENSIVE
YOUR AREA IS: REMOTE **X**   QUIET WITH ACTIVITIES   LIVELY
LOCAL ACTIVITY/NIGHTLIFE: **video, disco, pool, bar, billiards, darts, board games, special events**
CAR NEEDED TO EXPLORE AREA: YES   NO **X**
DUTY FREE SHOPPING: YES   NO **X**

LOCAL EMERGENCY SERVICES: NEAREST HYPERBARIC TREATMENT FACILITY:
COAST GUARD: **Manila**   AUTHORITY: **V. Lona Medical Center,**
TELEPHONE: **Coron PNP**
CALLSIGNS: LOCATION: **SOS Oil Rig, Offshore**
                                           TELEPHONE: **Via Radio**

LOCAL DIVING DOCTOR:
Resident doctor on resort 24 hours

lives to protecting the animals. A 1933 Toyota truck will transport you around the island when it is running.

The brochure says "Club Paradise fulfills the greatest recipe for happiness: doing what you want – when you want – how you want it!" I would add that they do it beautifully.

Northwestern Palawan

Miniloc, Pangulasian, and Lagen Islands
El Nido Resorts

Lynn Funkhouser

El Nido Resorts are surrounded by some of the most picturesque islands on this planet. Lofty limestone cliffs, marble mountains, hidden lagoons, secluded beaches, and tropical treasures will delight your eyes and lift your spirits the moment you board a banca at the airport to take you to one of the resorts.

El Nido is a municipality on the northwestern tip of Palawan. 12 out of 18 of its barangays have been declared a protected area called the El Nido Marine Reserve. The vision of Ten Knots Development Corporation, owner and operator of the El Nido Resorts, has been to develop it into a world class tourist destination with emphasis on involving members of the community, staff, and resort guests in the conservation and protection of the area's natural resources. Among many things, they have been instrumental in protecting hatchling turtles and raising them until they are large enough to have a better chance in the wild.

El Nido, meaning "the nest", is home to the swifts which build the nests that are the main ingredient in the popular Chinese bird's nest soup. Nest gatherers scale the limestone cliffs, barefoot and without benefit of safety lines, from December to May in search of the nests. The resorts are reached by flights on Soriano Aviation. Only 15 kilos or 33 lbs. is allowed as free baggage.

Miniloc Island, the first El Nido resort, is located in a spectacular cove. Recently renovated, it has 31 native-style cottages: Water cottages built on stilts over the lagoon, garden cottages surrounded by beautiful tropical foliage, and Cliff cottages nestled in the hillside. All of these cottages now have private bathrooms. In addition, there are five seaview rooms, also built over the water, which are connected by a long veranda, which

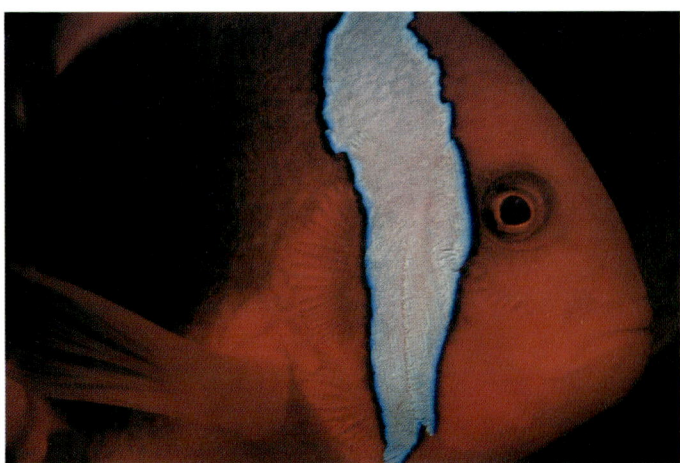

Tomato Anemone Fish by Lynn Funkhouser

provides a spectacular view of the entire cove. Shower and toilet facilities for these rooms are located at the end of the veranda. All cottages have air-conditioning, mini bars, and refrigerators. **Miniloc is known as the "Island of the Gods".**

Pangulasian Island, about 15 minutes away from Miniloc by banca, is built on a spectacular long stretch of white sand beach lined with rows of palm trees. It has 30 native style cottages with private marble bathrooms, air-conditioning, refrigerators, and mini-bars. Each cottage has a breathtaking view from its private veranda. **Pangulasian is known as the "Island of the Sun".**

The third resort, Lagen Island, opened its doors in January 1998. It is located about 10 minutes away from Pangulasian Island by banca and has 51 luxuriously appointed cottages.

All three resorts have complete diving and marine sport facilities. **You can also enjoy snorkeling,** wind surfing, kayaking, hobie cat sailing, and exploring countless hidden beaches, secret lagoons, and isolated coves. You can even pick your own private island, and be put on your private beach with food, beverages, blankets, your favorite dive buddy, and your fantasies, and claim it yours for the day! You can arrange to be "rescued" at a pre-determined time.

Food at these resorts is excellent and the variety is special. You will experience all the wonderful Filipino dishes, Japanese specialties, and international cuisine. **One of the highlights of a week at these resorts is the sunset beach dinner served on a perfect beach to watch the sun set, complete with dining room furniture from the resort and flaming torches. A bar and several tables laden with incredible food from lechon (a whole roast pig) to lobster, fresh fish, chicken, salads, fresh fruits, and fabulous desserts are set under the sparkling stars with musicians playing in the background.** Traditional dances performed by the very talented staff in costumes (and a few brave guests at the end) make it a memorable evening.

The best news from El Nido is that they are finally offering night dives at all resorts! There are more than two dives per day! Either a third dive or a night dive is now being offered at an additional rate. Two dives are included in the regular package. The night dives are beach dives. **The Aquarium,** off the pier at Manioc resort, has been a fish feeding station for years and has attracted so many fish to that area it has to be spectacular at night. During the day, large groupers, schools of jacks, angels, butterflyfish, wrasse, triggerfish, parrotfish, etc. pose for your camera while waiting for their daily handout. Maroon anemonefish can be found right off the pier.

Diving is excellent year-around, but the best time to go is from March to June. The rugged terrain above water extends underwater. There are many areas with large boulders, deep crevices, caves, and tunnels swarming and silversides in 10' to 70' of water. **Black Coral Forest** teems with numerous volitan lionfish suspended above the black coral in 100'. **Twin Rocks** offers a large number of blue-spotted stingrays in approximately 50' of water. Another area features a colony of ribbon eels. Some species of fish that you see in the El Nido area such as copperband butterflyfish, annularis angels, etc. are not found in many of the other areas. Invertebrates are well represented, including many species of nudibranches, octopus, squid, crabs, shrimp, lobster, shells, etc. **One of my all time favorite dives was across from Miniloc in hundreds of large pink jellyfish. Drifting in inner space felt outer space.**

These idyllic islands and spectacular seascapes will fill your senses and renew your spirit.

SCUBA AND SNORKELING QUESTIONNAIRE

NAME: **Pangulasian Island Resort**
ADDRESS: **El Nido, Northern Palawan,**
Philippines
CONTACT: **Mr. John A. Tanjangco**
TITLE: **Sales and Marketing Manager**
TELEPHONE: **632-894-5644**   FAX: **632-810-3620**   E-MAIL   **elnido@mailstation.net**
CAPITAL: **Manila**   GOVERNMENT: **Democratic**
POPULATION: **70 million**   LANGUAGE: **English/Tagalog**
CURRENCY: **Philippine Peso**   ELECTRICITY: **110V/220V**
AIRLINES: **PAL**   DEPARTURE TAX? **500 pesos ($20 US)**
NEED VISA/PASSPORT   YES **X**   NO   PROOF OF CITIZENSHIP?   YES   NO **X**

YOUR FACILITY IS CLASSIFIED AS: RESORT: **PADI Accredited Resort**
BUSINESS HOURS: **24 hours**
CERTIFYING AGENCIES: **PADI and NAUI**
LOGBOOK REQUIRED? YES NO
EQUIPMENT: SALES RENTALS **X** AIR FILLS **X**
PRIMARY LINE OF EQUIPMENT? SCUBA PRO AND US DIVERS
PHOTOGRAPHIC EQUIPMENT: SALES **X** RENTALS LAB

CHARTER/DIVE BOAT AVAILABLE? YES NO **X** DIVER CAPACITY
COAST GUARD APPROVED? YES NO CAPTAIN LICENSED? YES NO
SHIP TO SHORE? YES NO LORAN? YES NO RADAR? YES NO
DIVE MASTER/INSTRUCTOR ABOARD? YES NO **Both**

DIVING AND SNORKELING: SALT **X** FRESH
TYPE OF DIVING/SNORKELING IN AREA: WALL **X** BEACH **X** WRECK REEF **X** CAVE **X** ICE
DIVING/SNORKELING IN YOUR AREA IS BEST SUITED FOR: BEGINNER **X** INTERMEDIATE X ADVANCED
BEST TIME OF YEAR FOR DIVING/SNORKELING: **March - May**
TEMPERATURE: APRIL-NOV: **26 - 29C** DEC.-MARCH **24 - 26C**
VISIBILITY: DIVING: **10-30m** SNORKELING **3-10m**

PACKAGES AVAILABLE: DIVE X DIVE STAY **X** SNORKEL SNORKEL STAY **X**
ACCOMMODATIONS NEARBY: HOTEL MOTEL HOME RENTALS **X**
ACCOMMODATION RATES: EXPENSIVE MODERATE **X** INEXPENSIVE
RESTAURANTS NEARBY: EXPENSIVE MODERATE INEXPENSIVE X
YOUR AREA IS: REMOTE **X** QUIET WITH ACTIVITIES LIVELY
LOCAL ACTIVITY/NIGHTLIFE:
CAR NEEDED TO EXPLORE AREA: YES NO **X**
DUTY FREE SHOPPING: YES NO **X**

LOCAL EMERGENCY SERVICES: NEAREST HYPERBARIC TREATMENT FACILITY:
COAST GUARD: AUTHORITY: **Phil Commission on Sports**
TELEPHONE: LOCATION: **Manila**
CALLSIGNS:

RESORT GUESTS COVERED BY:
NAME: **the S.O.S. Program**
LOCATION: **Manila**
TELEPHONE: **632-503-735/585-587**

Tunicate by Lynn Funkhouser

Palawan

Captain Victor Organ

Palawan is the fastest growing area for tourism in the 7,000-island archipelago of the Republic of the Philippines. These lush tropical islands have mountains blanketed with rainforest filled with exotic hard woods like Nara, unspoiled sand beaches, low population density, and both a sea life and coral reefs seldom matched anywhere. Little is know about the area, so the Philippine Government, under the leadership of President Ramos and Palawan Governor Socrates, has targeted the Palawan region for tourist development.

The dive guide of the Philippines available from the Department of Tourism will reveal the importance of Palawan as a diving destination. This is especially true of the islands in northern Palawan in the Calamian Group. Busuanga and Cullion are the largest in this group with hundreds of smaller islands, or keys, just off shore. It is here that the South China Sea, Indian Ocean and the Celebes Sea rendezvous bringing with them nutrient-rich water. Little wonder there is a Mecca of sea life, including fish, shells, crabs, and over eight hundred species of corals. There is even a very distinct squid season in February.

The dry season starts in late November and stretches into June when the monsoon season, known locally as the Habagat, arrives. Water temperature averages a warm eighty degrees, but is cooler in the winter, so wet suits are recommended.

Fishing has traditionally been the life stay of the indigenous people of Busuanga. Their way of life and hand to mouth existence went undisturbed for thousands of years until World War II when maganese mining in Busuanga began to flourish. Sheltered deep anchorage in the channel between Busuanga and Cullion islands was an advantage the Japanese invaders could not ignore, so early in the war the Busuanga port of Coron fell into Japanese hands.

When historians reminisce about naval wars in the Pacific, names like Midway, Truk Lagoon and the Battle of Leyte come to mind. There was however a major route of the Japanese fleet in the Calamian Islands. Admiral "Bull" Halsey advancing on the uncharted

Calamian Islands needed reconnaissance to chart a safe passage. On September 24, 1944 planes were dispatched to take aerial photographs near the Japanese occupied town of Coron. The photographs revealed 24 floating islands that actually turned out to be heavily camouflaged cargo ships and their gunboat escorts. They were anchored in Sangat Bay conserving their fuel for the larger class battleships.

Admiral Halsey ordered immediate bombardment of the area. Torpedo planes were dispatched. All 24 ships were sunk or beached with the loss of only one U. S. Navy aircraft. **To date 15 wrecks have been found of which eight are divable by sport divers. The other nine have yet to be located.** Two gunboats that were beached, either because they were sinking, or because things were too hot in the area, **offer the snorkeler and the photographer an unusual opportunity of seeing a wreck in clear water with good light.**

WRECK DIVING

The freighter called the **North Wreck** rests on its starboard side in 50 to 100 feet of water. Another freighter locally called *Hector's Wreck* after the fisherman that guided earlier divers to its location, sits upright in 110 feet and the refrigeration ship, *Irako*, lying at 150 feet, is one of the deeper wrecks to be explored in Sangat Bay.

Two of the ships that were not sunk at anchorage and were able to get under way were the flying tender *Akitsushima* and the tanker *Tae-Ie Maru* or *Concepion Wreck*. The *Akitsushima* is a favorite deep dive because the vessel lies on her port side at eighty to 120 feet and the antiaircraft guns on her deck are intact.

The *Concepion Wreck* is known for soft and black corals and a large abundance of aquatic fish life. Upright in the middle of the channel, *Concepion Wreck* has the strongest tidal currents and the best visibility of all the wrecks in the area. Couple that with its close proximity to the beach resorts that are exclusively located in northern Palawan, and it is easily understood why it is probably the most popular wreck in the Philippines.

DIVE-STAY ACCOMMODATIONS

The oldest dive operation in the area is **Concepion Divers,** (owned and operated by Andy Pownall), located on the bay in Concepion. Nipa cottages and simple, but scrumptious home-style meals are available at reasonable rates. Concepion is the main jumping off place for traveling to the beach resorts on the outer island with names like **Treasure Island and Calumbayan Island.**

For the more discriminating, **Las Hamacas Resort,** located on a peninsula north of Salvation, is for you. **Daniel and Belen Prejger offer cozy cottages and the finest of European and Filipino cuisine to be found in all of Palawan.**

The newest resort in the area is **Kaniki Point Resort** with over a half mile of the best sand beach on Busuanga. Designed, built and operated with eco-divers in mind, by Gulfstream Enterprises Corporation, an American-Filipino consortium. **The reef offers great swimming, snorkeling and shallow depth for open water training, night diving and photography. There are two hundred thousand square meters of hills covered in exotic fruit trees** such as Carabao Mango, Star Apples, Calamansi Lime and over two hundred coconut trees. The coastline is shaded by dap dap, ficus and three varieties of banana trees. Vegetables are grown next to one of the few fresh water springs found on these islands. It is very possible that the fruit and vegetables served for dinner were still on the tree at lunch!

Kaniki Point Resort occupies the center third of Kaniki Island separated from Busuanga by mangroves and a narrow channel navigable by small craft only. Kaniki Island lies just ten minutes west of Concepion by boat and is within twenty minutes of the wrecks to the south. Excellent reef diving offshore is just one hour out by banca. **The gentle lapping of waves on a sand beach, sun setting over China Sea keys, fresh coconut milk seasoned with calamansi lime and a liberal dash of Tanduay rum in hand after an exhilarating days diving, this is the medicine of the mind, body and soul.**

234

GETTING THERE

To get to Busuanga at one time meant an overnight cruise on a coastal passenger freighter, a treat still available to the economy conscious back packer or those seeking adventure. Construction of a domestic airstrip and a native terminal opened the island to air travel. **Three domestic lines have regular scheduled flights, of these Air Ads and Pacific Air are the most dependable.** The national carrier Philippine Airlines (PAL) has resumed flights now that the renovation is completed. The flight from Manila, the capital, is one hour.

Both Air Ads and Aero Lift offer private charters to a landing strip along the China Sea near the barangay of Old Busuanga at reasonable rates. Once on the island you travel by Jeepney, a locally manufactured vehicle that closely resembles the American World War II jeep extended into a bus. This adds local flavor to the journey. The cost of hiring Jeepney service to Coron, the port town in the south, and to Salvation to the north, varies and bargaining is expected.

Some travelers visit Coron, stay over night at the Bayside Inn, and then take a two-hour banca (long narrow boat with two outriggers powered by small inboard engines) ride to the wrecks and resorts further north.

Rare Flamboyant Cuttlefish by Lynn Funkhouser

Reefs of Tubbataha

M/Y Tristar

Lynn Funkhouser

The Reefs of Tubbataha are the Philippines largest coral reef atoll and its only national marine park. The name Tubbataha means a long reef exposed at low tide. In 1994 the World Conservation Union declared Tubbataha Reef a World Heritage Site, the first in the Philippines. This area is noted for its great visibility–up to 200 ft., incredible walls, fabulous soft corals, large fish, large schools of fish, mantas, eagle rays, turtles, sharks, whale sharks, etc. and beautiful perfect coral gardens.

When traveling from the US, it is best to allow at least a day in Manila for getting over jetlag, sightseeing and/or shopping. This also allows a day for your luggage to arrive if it didn't get on your flight.

To get to Tubbataha take Philippine Airlines (PAL) from the new Manila Domestic Airport to Puerto Princesa, Palawan, which is an 80-minute flight. **Tip: If you travel with** a lot of scuba and camera gear you can get an extra 30 kilos (66 lbs.) weight allowance for all PAL domestic flights by applying to PAL for their Flying Sportsman Diver card. Cost is $15. Most international flights allow 2 bags of up to 70 lbs. each, plus 1 carry-on bag per passenger. PAL domestic flights allow 2 bags of up to 40 lbs. each, plus 1 carry-on bag. The Flying Sportsman card will save you overweight charges on all PAL domestic flights.

In Puerto Princesa, the *Tristar* crew meets your flight and starts taking care of you. They even claim your baggage. They deliver you to the *Tristar* and bring your luggage to your room later. A "Welcome Aboard" drink is served at the bar on the sun deck.

Depending on the PAL schedule, you may have several hours to explore the unique markets and sights in Puerto Princesa before the *Tristar* departs on the 100 nautical mile trip to Tubbataha. **The mayor of Puerto Princesa is very progressive and it is the cleanest city in the Philippines.** Litter is conspicuous by its absence. If you are interested in conversation, stop by the International Marinelife Alliance, Philippines, office and check out the CDT (Cyanide Detection Test) lab and other ecology programs. If you have forgotten to pack something or want to buy you can stop at the local supermarket and get most anything. Often a dive is offered at TableTop Reef before departing for Tubbataha.

The M/Y *Tristar* is a 110-ft., fully air-conditioned, motor yacht/liveaboard diveboat. She has a 20.5' beam which makes her feel even larger. She has 6 twin-berth and 2 six-berth fully carpeted cabins, which can accommodate up to 24 guests. (The trip will be more comfortable if only 3 guests occupy the six-berth rooms for a total of 18 divers.) She has 4 common showers and 4 common heads. The main dining salon can seat everyone comfortably. Meals are served buffet style and the food is excellent. On the upper deck, the *Tristar* features a comfortable lounge with TV, VCR, and stereo. This is a great place to relax, work on cameras, and/or view the latest dives on videos. The upper deck also has a large, covered gear-up area with hangers for your wetsuits and bins for your equipment, a bar for soft drinks, juices, water, alcoholic beverages and a spacious sundeck.

The greatest part about diving on the *Tristar* is the level of service! She has a well-trained, efficient, and friendly crew consisting of the Captain and crew of at least 19, plus several dive masters. Your tanks will be set up and waiting for you (unless you prefer to rig them yourself) and then placed in the chase boats. There are 2 chase boats and they almost never have more than 6 divers in them. Often there are fewer. **You can sign up for your dives on a clipboard on the hour or half-hour so it gives you much more flexibility and fewer divers at the same site.** On the dive, there is usually 1 divemaster to every 2 to 4 divers. If you want to be left alone, you will be. If you want someone to hold your hand and point out everything, they will do it. Buddy teams are always free to dive their own computer profiles.

Another great part of diving with the *Tristar* is you never have to swim back to the boat after your dive–the chase boats will come get you (no guilt delivered) usually within a few minutes of surfacing. There are numerous drift dives with unpredictable currents, which is where and why you will see so many big fish. Enjoy the ride! Sometimes the current will take you one way on the reef, reverse, and take you back to where you started. (Try it at a different depth, if you want to see something different on the way back.) **When the divemasters talk about the El Presidente current at Basterra, pay attention.** The divemasters can keep you out of most currents if you don't like them. **Bring a safety sausage.** *Tristar* may not be a new luxury yacht, but she makes up for everything with her diving service! If you are there to get the most out of your dives, you will love her.

The diving season for Tubbataha is only March through May because of possible high winds and bad weather at other times. This has helped to protect it from too many divers and fisherman. North Tubbataha, also called Bird Island, has nesting brown boobies, masked boobies, noddy terns, and various other birds. South Tubbataha has a lighthouse and many birds. There is finally a ranger station between the islands staffed by military personnel. It would be better to have rangers as staff and a better boat with bigger motor to patrol the area, but at least it is a start.

Other islands you may visit on your trip are Jesse Beasley, Basterra, and possibly Arena and Bancoran. All are superb and I include them as part of the Tubbataha experience, even though they are not in the marine park and are not protected. Hopefully, at least Jesse Beasley and Basterra will be added to the list soon.

In 1996 there was evidence of earthquake activity at South Tubbataha and Basterra. It gets reported as blast fishing, but if it was, the fisherman blew themselves, their boat, and the fish to pieces. After all, the Philippines is in the huge Pacific Rim ("Ring of Fire") which contributes to making it so interesting and diverse. **There are many fascinating deep crevices and caves in the reefs, probably from ancient earthquake or volcanic activity,** so these crevices are just a couple of new news, which will be interesting to watch and see how they develop. **There is some blast fishing and anchor damage in the area, but there are plenty of magnificent reefs to see. I have seen *Tristar* owners Geggy and David Choy do a heroic job of protecting the area.** They board fishing boats to inform the fisherman that they are in a sanctuary and see that they are not doing anything illegal. They have ordered fisherman to leave and seized nets and lines and turned them in to the coastguard in Puerto Princesa. David even removes fishing lines and cables littering the reefs.

Tubbataha has the high intensity diving that makes it world class. These reefs are a haven to a diversity of marine life equal to or greater than any comparable area in the world. There are dives where schools of jacks mix with schools of barracudas which mix with schools of unicornfish, which mix with fusiliers, and sometimes whitetip sharks circling underneath. Most dives have plenty of whitetip sharks with occasional leopard sharks, nurse sharks, and grey reef sharks, oceanic whitetips and sometimes hammerheads. **North Tubbataha has an area, which usually has about 50 shovelnose sharks sleeping in the white sand.** There are walls festooned with banner butterfly fish, schools of Moorish idols, many species of butterfly fish, angel fish, wrasse, anthias, parrots, surgeons, squirrelfish, purple queens, triggerfish, sweetlips, anemonefish, lionfish, groupers, snappers, an occasional tuna or several, etc.–all adding their colors and antics to the reefs. **Many of the reefs start in 10′ of water or less and drop much deeper than divers can go, so after a dive you can do your safety stops in perfect coral gardens instead of just blue water.**

Dusk is an especially exciting time, thousands of fish come sweeping into the reefs to find safe places to spend the night. Many mating critters make their appearance and you can see two species of flashlight fish, parrotfish sleeping in cocoons, eels hunting, lobster and shrimp, many species of shells, nudibranchs, corals feeding, huge basketstars, squid, cuttlefish, octopus, and all those fish that you couldn't approach during the day, sleeping. It's also a good time to notice all that great macro life that you were too busy to observe during the day when the blue water critters were occupying your attention.

A tip: due to PAL's schedule you will probably need to spend at least one night in Manila before departing on your international flight home unless it leaves late. There are good tours, wonderful restaurants, and great shopping to enjoy.

Tubbataha has it all and holds a special place in many hearts. Numerous divers return to it multiple times. (I have returned there every year since 1978.) Even people who have never seen it are very committed to its preservation. It must be protected!

SCUBA AND SNORKELING QUESTIONNAIRE

NAME: **M/Y Tristar, Tristar Sea Ventures Corp.**
ADDRESS: **2038 Kalamansi St.**
Das MariÒas Village, Makati, Metro Manila, Philippines
CONTACT: **David Choy**
TITLE: **Owner**
TELEPHONE: **632-816-7340**   FAX   **632-810-9180**   TELEX

CAPITAL: **Manila**
POPULATION: **10 million**
CURRENCY: **Peso**
AIRLINES: **PAL**
NEED VISA/PASSPORT √ IF STAY OVER 21 DAYS   YES   NO

GOVERNMENT: **Democratic**
LANGUAGE: **Philipino and English**
ELECTRICITY: **220 volts**
DEPARTURE TAX? **500 peso ($20 US)**
PROOF OF CITIZENSHIP? YES   NO

YOUR FACILITY IS CLASSIFIED AS: **Live aboard dive boat**
BUSINESS HOURS: **NA**
CERTIFYING AGENCIES:
LOGBOOK REQUIRED?   YES **X**   AND   NO **X**
EQUIPMENT: SALES   RENTALS   AIR FILLS **X**
PRIMARY LINE OF EQUIPMENT?
PHOTOGRAPHIC EQUIPMENT: SALES   RENTALS   LAB

CHARTER/DIVE BOAT AVAILABLE?   YES **X**   DIVER CAPACITY 18-24
COAST GUARD APPROVED?   YES **X**   NO   CAPTAIN LICENSED?   YES **X** NO
SHIP TO SHORE?   YES **X**   NO   LORAN?   YES **X** NO   RADAR?   YES **X**   NO
DIVE MASTER/INSTRUCTOR ABOARD? YES **X**   NO   BOTH **X**

DIVING AND SNORKELING: SALT **X**   FRESH
TYPE OF DIVING/SNORKELING IN AREA: WALL **X**   BEACH   WRECK **X** REEF **X**   CAVE   ICE
DIVING/SNORKELING IN YOUR AREA IS BEST SUITED FOR: BEGINNER   INTERMEDIATE **X**   ADVANCED **X**
BEST TIME OF YEAR FOR DIVING/SNORKELING: **Tubbataha March through May**
TEMPERATURE: NOV-APRIL: **80-86F**   MAY-OCT.
VISIBILITY: DIVING: **60-200Ft.** SNORKELING   **60-200Ft.**

PACKAGES AVAILABLE: DIVE   DIVE STAY **X**   SNORKEL   SNORKEL STAY
ACCOMMODATIONS NEARBY: HOTEL   MOTEL   HOME RENTALS
ACCOMMODATION RATES: EXPENSIVE   MODERATE   INEXPENSIVE
RESTAURANTS NEARBY: EXPENSIVE   MODERATE   INEXPENSIVE
YOUR AREA IS: REMOTE **X**   QUIET WITH ACTIVITIES   LIVELY
LOCAL ACTIVITY/NIGHTLIFE:
CAR NEEDED TO EXPLORE AREA: YES   NO **X**
DUTY FREE SHOPPING: YES   NO **X**

LOCAL EMERGENCY SERVICES:
COAST GUARD:
TELEPHONE:
CALLSIGNS:

NEAREST HYPERBARIC TREATMENT FACILITY:
AUTHORITY: **PCSSD-Philippine Commision**
LOCATION: **on Sports, SCUBA Diving,**
Dept. of Tourism, T.M. Kalaw St.
TELEPHONE: **Rizal Park, Manila 632-58-58-57 / 50-37-35**
M/Y Tristar operates this schedule:
March through May - Tubbataha
June through Oct. - Ceby and Bohol
Oct. through. Feb - Busuanga

RED SEA

EGYPT
Hurghada
Captain Victor Organ

When one conjures up visions of Egypt, the first thing that comes to mind is Cleopatra and the Pyramids, cruising down the Nile or digging for ancient artifacts in Luxor. Everyone knows there is a sea on the Eastern Shore. Moses parted it when he made his "Great Escape". Few people realize however, that Egypt has over twelve hundred miles of sand and limestone coast along the Red Sea.

In the last ten years, diving tourists have started to show interest in the Red Sea area. The Sinai Peninsula has blossomed into a world class resort area with hotels and dive shops to cater to this growing need. The diving is excellent, but the atmosphere is sterile. All the ultra modern hotels create a squeaky clean ambiance in the middle of a desolate desert. The Sinai is a stark contrast to the congested streets, noise and various smells for which Cairo is famous. Tourists travel to exotic places to experience the culture of the lands they visit by air, land and sea...but in comfort of course. To that end, **Hurghada is the obvious choice for divers. It blends the old with the new and offers world class diving as well.**

Pink Eel by Victor Organ

Hurghada is an old port town with a population of about thirty thousand. Protected by several large uninhabited off shore deserted islands, the bay is shallow with scattered reefs and coral heads. The old section of town is similar to Cairo minus the crowds and traffic. Fishing continues to be an important industry, however tourism is the main source of income today. This is evident by the many souvenir shops along the narrow streets. Prices are lower for like items found in Cairo, but beware as the quality is not as good and you must bargain in earnest to get an exceptional deal.

ACCOMMODATIONS

Along the desert shore, many hotels and townhouses are either opening or under construction. The finest of these is the newly opened **Hurghada Marriott Beach Resort**. The resort is situated on the water, has two hundred and fifty rooms and twenty-five suites, all of which have a spectacular view of the bay. For recreation and leisure, the Marriott Beach Resort offers a clean sandy beach for sunbathing and swimming. Need a cool refreshing drink while lounging in the sun? *Mafi Mushkila! (No problem)*. You can order from the Poolside Bar or take a refreshing swim out to the Island Garden equipped with an open-air bar. There is a wood bridge for those who would prefer to walk across to enjoy the unobstructed view of the Marina or Bay. The Island Bar is the perfect venue to end the day while watching a flaming sunset over the resort.

Diving and other water sports such as windsurfing, parasailing, fishing, water skiing, and sailing are the main attractions at Hurghada.

Indoor facilities include a fully equipped health club with massage, whirlpool and sauna. Sports activities include tennis and air-conditioned squash courts.

For your dining pleasure, the Shorouk Restaurant serves traditional favorites in a relaxed setting and the Tuscany Restaurant offers delightful Italian cuisine. The Lobby Bar is located in the garden courtyard surrounded by water and fountains. The appropriately named Aquarius Entertainment Lounge overlooks the pool, and the bay. The Poolside Bar features light fare.

THE SCUBA DIVING

The Barracuda Dive Shop is located at the pier and offers daily excursions to the outer reefs for diving, snorkeling and swimming. The boats leave the pier at nine and return between four and five o'clock. These very functional craft are locally made and quite spacious. Duly licensed Egyptian skippers captain them.

After an hour cruise we anchored at our first dive site named **Abu Ramada south** that is next to a reef that skirts a sand and limestone island. The reef is similar to those off the Saudi Arabia coast. Uli Neukater, our German instructor/guide, briefed us about the seabed below, we made buddy checks, donned gear and entered the water by giant stride off the dive platform.

The first thing any diver from the Arabian Peninsula will notice is the water temperature. **Good wetsuits and hoods are desirable.** We recommend renting these and all your dive gear from the Barracuda Dive Shop. The rates are reasonable and the equipment is state of the art and well maintained. We proceeded to tour the reef while hunting things to photograph. The visibility along the reef was excellent and we found all the familiar creatures and corals associated with the Red Sea.

Unlike Jeddah where we are accustomed to diving, **the fish swam around us in schools begging to be photographed.** Like many of the resort areas around the world, the practice of feeding fish is commonplace.

Shab Abu Ramada, was our second dive site. We swam around the end of the reef and were greeted by Humphead Wrasse, Sweetlips in schools of hundreds and some very playful Butterfly Fish. Goatfish hovered above the corals and moved only for the occasional diver who passed through their midst. Blue Spotted Rays rested under Table Coral oblivious to the light show I was putting on with my underwater strobe.

The lazy days that followed were much the same, short boat trips, gin clear visibility, and close encounters of the fishy kind. Laurenz Geihsler, the Austrian/American manager of Barracuda Divers, looked after our diving needs while spinning plenty of yarns about his experiences living in the Maldives. He was an instructor guide there for seven years before he transferred his operation to Hughada. Over the years he has done over 4,000 dives. The dive shop offers scuba instruction at all levels and can certify either CMAS or RSTC (PADI etc.)

AREAS OF INTEREST

We did manage to get out and see the town. Almost every hotel or resort had some kind of entertainment to offer. We met some Egyptian friends that insisted we see **the latest rage -belly dancers from Russia.** They were very good of course and even added a little pop and ballet to their routines.

Sindbad Submarine beckoned from the bay and I wondered what it would be like to experience the underwater world dry. A *Mark III* is a third generation passenger submarine specially designed for the tourist market. It can carry forty-six passengers comfortably and a crew of two. The passenger compartment is fully air conditioned with comfortable seats and a separate television monitor for each view port.

Egypt Air has daily flights from the Kingdom of Saudi Arabia to Cairo with late afternoon connecting flights to Hurghada. Starting in June there will be direct Jeddah-Hurghada flights on Wednesdays.

We decided to return to Cairo by a privately rented van. The cost was about one hundred twenty dollars all-inclusive and it was a very comfortable journey along the sea to Port Said. Porpoise performed a short demonstration of their acrobatic skills then swam off into the emerald waters.

Just before we reached **Port Said** we turned west to transverse the desert plain to **Cairo**. There was evidence of mining both old and new. We stopped at a roadside stand and bought honey. I wish that we had purchased a gallon, as it is the closest I have had to orange blossom honey since I left Florida twenty-five years ago.

Any trip to Egypt is incomplete without visiting the **Nile** and the **Pyramids**. To experience the romantic flavor, for which the Nile is famous, a cruise is required. The pyramids are every bit as auspicious as history has painted them. Unfortunately we did not have time to see the light show. I understand it gives the already impressive pyramids a majestic aurora.

Hurghada Marriott Beach Resort has developed dive packages and can combine a fantastic dive holiday with other Egyptian tours, guaranteed to please the most discriminating traveler. For more information on all the fun just contact:

Hurghada Marriott Beach Resort
P.O. Box 38 Hurghada,
Red Sea, Egypt
Tel. 2065-443950
Fax 2065 443970
EGYPTIAN EMBASSY
2310 DECATUR PLACE N.W.
WASHINGTON, D.C. 20008
TEL 202 232 5400

Jordan

Aqaba

"The Jewel of the Red Sea"

Gill Balchin, Rod Abbotson, Elja E. Vries

Geographically, **Aqaba is bounded on the west by Israel and to the south by Saudi Arabia, with the coastline of the Sinai Peninsula in sight.**

Jordan is a politically stable country, however in the past it frequently suffered from the "backlash" of events in neighboring countries. As a consequence, many travelers have been cautious about visiting the country, although those that did were always more than pleasantly surprised at the genuine friendliness and open hospitality of the local people. Since the historic signing of the Peace Treaty between Israel and Jordan, travelers now feel more at ease to venture here.

Jordan is a land waiting to be discovered. You will be enthralled by the marine life, enchanted by the people, fascinated by the history and heritage and captivated by the spectacular scenery.

DIVE SITES

Whether you are an experienced diver, or dive only a few times a year when on holiday, Aqaba has something to offer, **from shallow fringing reefs abundant with marine life and numerous examples of hard and soft corals, to drop-offs and wrecks.**

The diving and snorkeling sites start 8kms south of Aqaba town, extending to the border with Saudi Arabia, offering a diveable coastline of around 10 kms, with 20 different and varied sites. Aqaba has not suffered the onslaughts of mass tourism and has a unique advantage over other Red Sea destinations with unspoiled reefs. The only crowds are the myriads of small reef fish! **Seastar Watersports** is a PADI Dive Center, (S2500), a BSAC Dive School (R87) and affiliated to CMAS. There are three instructors, Rod Abbotson (British), Elja De Vries (Dutch), and Nabeel Aqbarawi (Jordanian), between them speaking 7 languages. All levels of diving are catered to and courses are offered to give as much flexibility as possible to fit in with the clients' requirements and program; afterall, "it's your holiday".

Aqaba is an area of mainly fringing reef, hence dive sites are easily accessed from the shore, just "one step into the water" and the reefs are right there. Even the wreck is only 100m offshore.

First Bay, which is also the location of Seastar's new dive center, provides an excellent Home Reef, with two main entry points each giving a different aspect of the reef. Among the most curious species found at this site is the frogfish.

Black Rock is excellent for both divers and snorkelers and is used regularly as our "orientation" dive, with an easy entrance from the shore. It is also popular as a site for frequent turtle sightings.

The *Cedar Pride* is a Lebanese freighter deliberately sunk 10 years ago to provide a dive site. She lies on her port side across two reefs, so at 27m you can actually swim under her. She supports a large variety of soft corals, as well as being part of the territorial range of many larger fish. The reef, which leads out to the wreck, is also well worth a dive on its own and Napoleon wrasse are frequent visitors.

Gorgon 1 and 2 are excellent afternoon dives, being in shallow water (14m). Gorgon 1 consists of 3 pinnacles covered with lionfish, a resident Arabian angel and on the way, a cabbage coral the size of a house!

There are several dives located at the Saudi border that offer excellent reef outcrops at shallow depths and are ideal for inexperienced divers and snorkelers, plus for the more advanced, the drop-off starts 30m offshore and falls away beyond 50m with some small caverns at 30m.

Blue Spotted Ray by Victor Organ

The **Japanese Gardens** is an excellent shallow dive at 14m with little paths wandering through small pinnacles resembling a garden of Bonsai trees, hence the name.

There are many other sites, but we have found that these are the most popular.

ACCOMMODATIONS

Accommodations in Aqaba range from 4-star standard to small "local" hotels. **The Alcazar Hotel** is a 3-star hotel offering a European standard of accommodation, services and amenities including the largest swimming pool in Aqaba, 25m x 10m, which with a deep end of 4m, makes it ideal for diver training. Other facilities include 2 bars, of which the "Dolphin Club" is particularly popular with divers, and two restaurants, "The Khayam", which serves European and Arabic cuisine, and "The Teppanyaki", where a Mongolian barbecue is available. The Alcazar Hotel is unique in Aqaba with its Arabic architectural style, private balconies, 2 inner courtyards and traditional Arabic interior, with local artifacts, antiques, carpets and wall hangings.

Dining out in Aqaba is also a pleasure. In addition to the restaurants at other hotels, there are many delightful local restaurants serving "Mezze"—a selection of local salads and hors d'oeuvres followed by local fish or lightly spiced grilled meats and chicken.

AREAS OF INTEREST

Jordan also offers more than "just another diving holiday". It is a land steeped in history and tradition, with numerous archaeological and biblical sites, plus regions of spectacular scenery.

From Aqaba one may easily visit fabled **Petra**, the "Rose Red City," carved out of the sandstone mountains, or journey to the awesome desert scenery of **Wadi Rum**. North of Petra are the magnificent crusader castles of **Kerak** and **Shobauk**. Like ancient Rome, the capital, **Amman**, was built on 7 hills and has many fine archaeological remains including the **Roman Amphitheater** and **Citadel**.

Less than one hour's drive away is **Jerash**, the Greco-Roman City of the Decapolis.

North of Jerash you can continue on to the **Roman baths at Umm Quais** or the black basalt remains of **Umm el Jamal**, a once prosperous and thriving center on the caravan route.

Northeast of Amman are the **desert castles of the Umayyad period**, which includes **Azraq, the headquarters of Lawrence of Arabia**, where today there is a wildlife sanctuary.

JORDANIAN EMBASSY
3504 INTERNATIONAL DR. NW
WASHINGTON, D.C. 20008
TEL 202 966 2664

Saudi Arabia
Jeddah

"Pride of the Red Sea"

Captain Victor Organ

Jeddah, pride of the Red Sea, has been long been known as the "Islamic Port" to the Moslems making the pilgrimage to Mecca. Shallow reefs guard the port and entry by ship to this day is at best tricky. This accounts for the forty-three known shipwrecks within a ten-mile radius of the Port of Jeddah. The reef structure and aquatic life around Jeddah is much the same as the popular Sinai at the northern end of the Red Sea, but the water temperature is on average five to eight degrees warmer. The water temperature in the summer months is a warm 85 degrees. In winter it drops to 72 to 75 degrees, depending on the location and depth.

Black Flat Worm by Victor Organ

The Red Sea is known for fantastic visibility, which can be as much as two hundred feet on a good day. The average visibility is one hundred feet. The basic reasons for this is that there is little fresh water drainage, as the land on the African and Arabian shores are primary deserts. With the exception of Jeddah and Yambu on the eastern coast, and Port Said in Egypt and Port Sudan in Sudan on the western coast, there are only small fishing villages sparsely scattered along the shore, thus pollution by man is minimal. The shifting of the African continent to the west has left much deeper water than that of the Mediterranean Sea to the north.

When planning a dive there are basically two ways to get into the water, either by walking in along the shore or by chartering a boat to dive the coral reefs a few miles offshore.

SHORE DIVING

The shore diving is absolutely unparalleled. This is a bold statement, but indisputable as the Saudi Arabia coast stretches for some seven hundred miles. A walk in over hard flat coral will average about fifty to one hundred and fifty meters. Most of the coastal reefs plummet to depths of twenty to sixty meters with some walls dropping even further. A four-lane highway along the sea locally called **"The Corniech"** stretches south of Jeddah for more than forty miles. Not a single building or residence can be seen on either side except for the three stone Coast Guard stations that guard the shore.

THE MECCA

The first dive site south of the city is one of the longer walks, but well worth the hike. *The Port Authority scuttled the Mecca wreck, a cargo ship about three hundred and forty feet long, in 1978.* Stern ashore, she rests on her port side in fifty feet at the stern and the bow lays in eighty feet of water straight out to sea.

A recent inspection and survey executed by a PDIC sanctioned wreck diving class of the Red Sea Dive Club has verified reports that the hull has split in two about two hundred and thirty feet aft of the bow. It is now possible to swim through one of the cargo holds, the cargo floor, and out the bottom as the split is nearly three feet in width.

Apart from typical hundred feet plus visibility, the *Mecca* wreck is known for the abundance of fish that make the wreck their home. For years divers have made the trek to photograph and video the sweet lips, red snapper and other pelagic fish, like the jacks and tuna, which visit from the depths in hope of catching the schools of baitfish off guard.

WILLI'S POINT

Further south just past the second Coast Guard station is **Willi's Point,** the areas most frequently dived site. Willi's Point, named after PDIC instructor trainer Captain William Victor Organ, has been a favorite dive training site for many of Jeddahs instructors.

The walk in is short. There are two distinctive white sand-training sites at depths of thirty and fifty feet. The fifty feet training area has concrete cannons, treasure chests and other underwater toys for training purposes.

MARS REEF

There is a three hundred foot long reef outside of the fifty foot training site that rises to twenty feet and then drops straight down to one hundred and thirty feet with three coral heads known as *Mars Reef* a little further out. **For deep divers *Mars Reef* is a must.**

There is sheet coral on the top of the coral heads. Down the sides are black coral, all the clams, shrimp, crags and other creatures. Olive green branches sway gently in the current.

The best way to enjoy the dive is to plan a step dive by snorkeling out fifty meters, descending to **Mars Reef** and then return by ascending the outside reef, across the fifty foot training area and finishing off with a safety stop at ten feet on the reef at the shores edge.

AL SHUAIBA

Seventy miles south of Jeddah is the ancient Islamic port of **Al Shuaiba**. Now a small fishing village and also the site of the desalination plant that supplies fresh water to Mecca. Like Willi's Point, the walk to the dive site is short, especially north of the Coast Guard station. North of the villas the water is shallow with many coral heads scattered across the bottom. Typical coral heads in the Red Sea rise majestically from the bottom like the Pillars of Hercules with heights exceeding twenty feet. Typically they are covered with an abundance of soft corals, gregorian sea fans, pipe organ sponges and sheets of fire coral.

Soldierfish are found guarding the table top coral and bright red coral grouper glide in and out of the many crevices. Nearly every head has a resident moray eel, many of which grow to more than five feet in length. Glistening fusilier fish dart above and the brightly colored blue spotted rays excavate the sugar sand below in search of food. This frenzy of feeding and the kaleidoscope of colors in pristine water is beyond imagination and can only be believed if seen.

BOAT DIVING

Boat diving excursions begin from the **Abhor Creek** seven miles north of Jeddah. Sharm Abhor is not actually a creek but is a deep-water inlet that is four miles long and averages three hundred yards in width and eighty feet in depth. **Night diving, especially for macro photographers, is excellent.**

There are several marinas from which to rent a dive charter boat such as **Andalus Marina**, the **Red Sea Marina**, and Jeddahs newest dive training facility and marina, the **Saudi Under Water Dive Village,** located on the north side of the creek.

In addition to the marina the **Saudi Under Water Dive Village** has a thirty four-foot dive boat named *My Fal 2* that will accommodate 12 divers comfortably. They also have a dedicated scuba instruction pool, dive shop, and 41 two-bedroom bungalows complete with kitchen and living room. Each apartment is accessible by car and there is a separate pool for swimmers and sunbathers by the clubhouse and restaurant.

After you have selected your charter and cleared the Coast Guard formalities at the mouth of the creek, a virtually unlimited array of dive locations and varied dive experiences await. **There are over a thousand coral reefs and coral heads in the two hundred square miles of the Eliza Shoals.** So many in fact, all the navigation charts exclude the area for safe navigation to larger ships. There are thirteen known vessels resting comfortably on the bottom that did not follow this advice much to the delight of local divers.

Aside from wrecks and coral formations, there are deep-water canyons, sea mounds protruding from fifteen hundred fathoms and great drift diving through channels formed by the coral reefs. **There are some drawbacks to visiting and diving such exotic places. You will not find mixed gasses like nitrox, nor is it easy to get a visa to visit.** Most divers are expatriates employed in various places around the kingdom. **Tourist visas are not available except to Moslems wanting to do the pilgrimage. There is a possibility of getting a business visa if a company or Saudi citizen will sponsor you. Saudi Under Water Dive Village is the best source of information on visas.**

SCUBA AND SNORKELING FACILITIES QUESTIONNAIRE

NAME   **Saudi Underwater Dive Village**
ADDRESS   **P.O. Box 50817 Jeddah, K.S.A. 21533**

CONTACT   **Eric Mason**
TITLE   **Site Manager**
TELEPHONE   **966-2-681-3134**   FAX   **966-2-681-3134**   TELEX

CAPITAL   **Riyadh**   GOVERNMENT: **Kingdom**
POPULATION: **4 million**   LANGUAGE: **Aribic/English**
CURRENCY: **Riyal**   ELECTRICITY:
AIRLINES: **Saudia**   DEPARTURE TAX?
VISA/PASSPORT? **Yes**   PROOF OF CITIZENSHIP?

DIVING & SNORKELING:
TYPE OF DIVING/SNORKELING IN AREA?   **Wrecks(18), Beach**

SOUTH AMERICA

Brazil
"Beyond Carnival"
Wendy Canning Church

The Portuguese Navigator Pedro Alvares Cabral discovered Brazil in 1500. Brazil remained a colony for 300 years until the Portuguese King arrived in 1808 and set up court in Rio de Janeiro. John Pedro I ruled as Emperor but was forced to resign. His son, Pedro II, ruled until 1821 and in 1822 declared independence from Portugal and declared Brazil an empire.

After his death in 1831, his son Peter, only 5 years old, became ruler. He declared himself Emperor in 1841 when only 14 years old. He could speak 8 languages and proved to be a very progressive leader, bringing positive changes to the country. In 1872 he invited Alexander Graham Bell to install the beginnings of a telephone system. He reigned as Emperor from 1841-1889 and died at age 63.

Peter II became Emperor, and proclaimed Brazil a Federal Republic in 1889. The landed gentry were not happy with this as it came hand in hand with the abolishment of slavery. The New Republic came to an end in 1930. The country and its people were soon to be as they are now, living in a democratic state.

Brazil, meaning wood, is the world's fifth largest country. Every country in South America, except for Ecuador and Chile, borders it. Most of its population of 127 million

Dolphins by Danielle Currlin

residents are under twenty-four and descend from European, African, Asian, and Native American backgrounds. The Portuguese language sets Brazil apart from its neighbors in South America.

Brazil has some 8,000 kilometers or 5,000 miles of beaches making it one of the best locations in the world for water sports. Couple this with warm temperatures throughout the year and you have an unbeatable combination for fun and sun!

There is severe poverty and conversely, great wealth in Brazil. The middle class is struggling. As a result, there is crime as in any large city. One should not travel with expensive jewelry or flaunt a camera in crowded areas.

On the plus side, **Brazil is one of the most beautiful countries you will ever visit.**

With its size, almost that of the United States, you have a range of topography: lush high mountain ranges, plains covered in colorful fragrant orange groves, cattle ranches, and the verdant jungles. **The sea and its islands, with untold treasure from sunken wrecks, offer the scuba diver and snorkeler a world that is almost virgin.**

"Carnival", celebrated each February, an occasion similar to Mardi Gras in New Orleans, has always been the most played up attraction in Brazil. As much local color, excitement, and fun this celebration brings to both native and visitor, we feel that there lies another side to Brazil that world travelers should know about.

You will be astounded by the variety of fruits and vegetables, the high caliber of cuisine and the immense portions that you are served.

And the people? Well, all I can say as a world traveler, you'd have to go a long way to find a friendlier, more helpful group. Everywhere I went I was presented with a gift, whether it was a small flower or a piece of native art. The 9 million Rio natives, or "cariocas," love life and like to play night and day.

GETTING THERE

We left Boston on a very cold November evening, connecting out of J.F.K. International Airport in New York, and landed in Rio de Janeiro early the next morning in spring.

RIO DE JANEIRO: THE RIVER OF JANUARY

On January 1, 1502, Captain Gaspar de Limos and his Portuguese fleet landed in Guanabara Bay and called it Rio de Janeiro or River of January. Salvador, in northern Brazil, was the first capital until gold was discovered inland. Rio was the nearest seaport to transport the gold to Portugal so it became the capital and remained so until 1960 when it was moved to Brasilia. Rio is divided into two areas, Zona Sue and Zona Norte. These lie to the north and south, with the business district in the center.

One will marvel at the beautiful neoclassic style mixed with the modern architecture dispersed throughout these districts. The neighborhoods, or "barrios," where you will find the population especially concentrated are Ipanema and Copacabana. They are where most tourists stay in the many hotels lining the beach. A quieter barrio is Leblon. It is quite beautiful and the one I prefer.

We planned to spend three days in Rio for a little R&R and some sightseeing. The **Hotel Inter-Continental** (U. S. TEL l 800-327-0200, Rio FAX 011-55-21-322-5500) was our choice of hotels. We wanted to be far away from the hustle and bustle of Copacabana and Ipanema, yet near enough to take advantage of the hotel's free shuttle to visit and yes, be part of the action...and action there surely is! **Under the watchful eye of Director of Marketing and Sales, Paulo Senise, this hotel-resort is run with the utmost of professionalism.** The entire staff has been expertly trained and is truly warm and helpful.

You really never need to leave the compound for everything is provided for the traveler whether their mission is pleasure or business. The rooms and suites are large and tastefully decorated many with views of the beach that stretches for miles.

At sunset, the lights of Rio come on and it's Christmas all over again as they twinkle and light up the night and the beat goes on to the Latin rhythms until the wee hours of morning.

The hotel has three swimming pools set in exuberant tropical gardens, a small pool on the upper deck for more privacy, or swim in the pool with waterfalls, or savor a cool drink at the swim-up bar. There are three tennis courts with a multi-lingual pro shop and cabana bar adjacent to a spectacular eighteen-hole golf course. Surf fans can catch waves on the beach, while hang-gliding, squash and ice-skating are all available just a few minutes from the hotel.

All beaches are public, and this is taken advantage of both during the week and on weekends. **My advice would be to sightsee on the weekends, especially Sunday, or book a dive or a boat cruise because it is really body to body at the beach.**

To watch the parade go by is better than any movie. **No matter what age, the girls from Ipanema, and for that matter Copacabana, love the thong bikini, jokingly referred to as**

"dental floss". They say the bikinis are so small they can be wrapped up in the price tag.

We loved the fruit bars, or "suco," where for very little money you can purchase freshly squeezed mango, papaya, passion fruit, or watermelon juice. Vendors also pass with coconuts. They cut off the top and you drink the fresh milk. Afterwards, you use the top to scrape out the meat. This is not only delicious, but also apparently good for you and any stomach ailment. The local beer, Brahma, is not bad either!

OTHER AREAS OF INTEREST

Little shops are filled with local handmade crafts. The more fashionable sell precious stones in beautiful settings, leather goods, and gold. These are good buys, and if budget allows, take advantage of them. Bargain!!

The **Opera House** is a copy of the one in Paris, only smaller, in jewel-like colonial style. The Brazilian Navy now uses the original Customs House; its architecture is Moorish style.

The **Maracana,** or soccer stadium, is the largest in the world, holding 200,000 fans. It was constructed in 1950 for the World Cup match between Brazil and Uruguay. In the final game, Uruguay won. It is common knowledge that the Brazilians are passionate about soccer, so you can imagine the riot that followed this game. There is a saying in Brazil that when you see a man playing dominoes, you know he is a senior citizen, because he has given up soccer.

Don't miss the museums: **Museu Nacional de Belas Artes, Museu de Arte Moderna, Museu da Republica, Museu Historico Nacional, Museu do Indio** and **Jardim Botanico.**

Most of us are familiar with two other sites in Rio. The first in the southern end is **Sugar Loaf Mountain** (1,300 feet high) which is reached by cable car. Here you can get a spectacular view of the city. The second is situated inland on **Hunchback Mountain**, a 2,400 foot peak where an enormous statue of Christ stands with arms outstretched. This statue can be viewed from almost any point in Rio. When you see it you wonder if the Brazilians are correct when they state, "God is a Brazilian".

DIVING

We dived with **Aqua Life** run by Joselio Da Silva, a former Brazilian Navy Seal. He runs a good, safe operation, following all safety regulations.

The boat we used was quite small, but he assured us if there is a larger group he could secure a larger boat. There is a boat person on the boat at *all* times. My only critique would be that this small boat has no canopy. The last day was spent entirely in the sun and the Brazilian sun can be brutal! So when you book him, ask for a boat with a canopy. Our dives were off **Ilha Grande**.

Our first dive was a wall of about 60 feet. As we descended to a sandy bottom, we made our way to the wall. The entire bottom was covered with black and purple sea urchins. There was a tremendous variety of fish, starfish, Moorish idol, sergeant majors, yellow goatfish, four-eye butterfly fish, porkfish and a large Nassau grouper.

This was a good first dive and you could tell that Joselio had picked a mellow one so he could size up our experience. I always respect that with a guide.

The wind really was kicking up, so we decided to call it a day and head for the little island of Ilha Grande. Since it was Thursday, the island was very quiet and we had a good chance for a complete tour. Victor, our guide for the entire trip, took us into a little Pousada and introduced us to the owner. We decided to come back over the weekend and spend a night there.

The next day we dove off **Abraao Island,** a very small island off Ilha Grande. Rolling over, we descended to 30 feet and swam to the reef. It was covered with red and orange sponge, sea stars, and sea urchins. There must have been a thousand sand dollars on the sandy bottom between the reef and the boulders.

Grooved brain coral, elliptical star coral and smooth star coral were also abundant. There were crabs and spiny lobster and tiny jellyfish. Although this was a shallow dive, it was interesting for there was a current and that carried us in and out of the boulders and through openings in the reef.

On Friday, we headed out for Ilha Grande late in the day. We had dinner at one of those small little seaside restaurants and just watched the world go by. I can highly recommend the **Aqua Viva Pousada on Ilha Grande.** It is not just clean and neat, it is a little gem. Carlos and his wife are charming proprietors of this resting-place. You really shouldn't pass up seeing the island even if just for the day. There is ferry service from Portogalo. Address Aqua Viva Pousada, Ilha Grande, Brazil.

On Saturday morning we dove **Enseads Das Pamas.** This was a rock wall dive with sandy bottom. As we descended, a small ray darted past us. As we went deeper, we came upon a moray eel hidden amongst the rocks in the wall. It was quite long and came out to investigate us, winding in and out of his rock. Ocean triggerfish, small mouth grunt and porkfish swam along with us.

AREAS OF INTEREST

We made a day trip to the 18th century colonial town of **Paraty**, three hours from Rio by car. **In the 18th and 19th century this beautiful, historic town was one of Brazil's most important ports. It was from here that gold and sugar were shipped back to Portugal.**

Rich landowners, merchants and shipping magnates, along with those who controlled the mines (they received 1/4 of the price of gold, Portugal retained the other 3/4) built beautiful houses both in and around Paraty. It is a charming town which reached its height in 1750. As gold ran out, so did Paraty's power. When the Empire came into being in 1822, Paraty became all but forgotten.

It was left to decay until UNESCO stepped in and declared it a national monument and began refurbishment. No renovation can be made unless UNESCO grants permission. No cars are allowed in most parts of the city; therefore, one can walk about and marvel at its architecture.

As you travel throughout the historic cities of Brazil, you will notice that the shutters of the buildings are painted in various colors. The royal family or palaces of the Emperor were white with pink shutters. Blue was attributed to the second degree of royalty, the Barons. One could become a Baron by virtue of wealth as well as birth. The "Coffee Barons" appeared from 1830-1850. The Emperor bestowed these titles.

The old families of Rio would utilize white with green shutters. Throughout Paraty we could distinguish the owners' position in society by the colors of the shutters.

Today, the town has almost been completely restored and Paraty has become an antique and arts center. If you are lucky enough to find a piece of furniture made from Jacarava, grab it, for this wood is 600 years old and quite novel in its appearance.

There are boutiques to roam through, open-air markets selling native crafts and wonderful little restaurants. We wandered down to the port and had fish, salad and dessert which was simple yet delicious and made with fresh ingredients. Served with a smile, it cost very little.

Paraty is not to be missed if you are in the area and even worth a trip from Rio. There are many Pousadas where one can overnight.

We made our way out of Paraty and arrived at **Fazenda Murycana** about twenty minutes out of town. Today it is home to a zoo, restaurant and a distillery, where the Caipirinha Sugar Cane Rum is made.

Angelita Murycana, second wife of the owner, now runs all three. She is both delightful and interesting and gave us a private tour and a tasting of the many varieties of liquor. It seems her husband purchased the land for a cattle farm, but soon it became the first farm in the region to produce sugar cane. Twenty years ago, they began to travel worldwide and collected exotic animals, beginning their zoo.

The restaurant on the premises, serves food produced on the farm. All meat is cooked on a wood stove and is fantastic! Drink the Murycana over ice with lime. This is the typical Brazilian drink.

Her husband, rumored to be a violent man, never drove an automobile, although they owned several. Each day he would ride into town on his horse, dressed like a cowboy complete with pistols at his side. One year ago, whilst just inside the farm, three shots were fired, and he was killed. To this day, no one knows why!

As you ride through the countryside, take note of the beautiful old colonial farmhouses, two stories in height. On the first floor the stock was kept and the second floor was the residence. The right side of the house was the commercial side where the farmers conducted business. The middle of the house served as the social center, and on the left side, parents hid their daughters until marriage so they would go to their marriage bed pure not only of heart but body. Behind the house there was a winter garden. Slaves were kept in small buildings away from the main house.

The aristocracy planted four Imperial Palms in front of their homes. In front of houses were large rock walls where coffee would be placed and dried. From the 17th to the 19th century, rich landowners thrived and were very much part of the power structure.

CABO FRIO

We set out for Cabo Frio in early afternoon, a two hour drive from Rio. We left Rio and within 15 minutes were in the countryside where all one could see for miles were orange groves. **Which is no surprise since Brazil is the second largest exporter of oranges in the world.**

Just outside of Cabo Frio, the **sea salt mines** came into view. This is also the place that each year, September to December, you can stop along the roadside and buy shrimp and crab. They come in such quantities that they cost very little.

Cabo Frio is still the most important fishing port in Brazil and has the best octopus fishing on the coast, catching 50-150 octopus a day. **It has the richest fish life in Brazil because the current of the Falklands passes through and the plankton comes up, creating a food chain.**

We stayed in Arraial do Cabo, a moderately large seaside village. Quiet in off-season, it really swings from December 15th until March.

The delightful **Thalassa Pousada** is run by Giselle and Bernard Rubiere, an elegant and lovely ex-patriot Frenchwoman and her husband. Patrick, their son, handles the scuba and snorkeling end of the operation.

Beds are dressed in ironed linens. Baths are furnished with French soaps. There is a central room where groups can gather, games to occupy children, and a TV set. Flowers grow profusely from the center atrium that runs through the Pousada.

Breakfast is included. It will be the typical Brazilian fare of juice, fresh fruit, rolls, bread, ham, cheese, and, of course, wonderful Brazilian coffee. Madame will surprise you each morning with one of her homemade goodies i.e. tomato preserves.

DIVING

The rich marine life of Arraial do Cabo is due to the phenomenon of the flora of the cold, deep waters (around 350 meters/1140 ft.) which, despite their richness in nutrients, are not productive as they are out of sunlight's reach. With the resurgence of the deep waters, the phytoplankton, the most basic level of marine life, receive solar energy, and then are consumed by plankton, which in turn feed the other species on up the food chain. The result of this process is rich and varied waters that make it possible to see both whales and sunfish in the same dive.

The diving conditions on the leeward side of Cape Island are excellent with the bay reaching a maximum depth of 65 feet, visibility from 10 to 65 feet, and a sandy bottom, which meets the coast with burrows and small coral banks. There you can dive among the ruins of the English vessel, *Wizard*, shipwrecked in 1821, which is a real treat. Among the marine life to be found here are lobster, sea turtles, starfish, rays and moray eel.

On the windward side of the island, the conditions are quite different: huge walls between 100-150 ft., and cold waters of 13 degrees Celsius, producing the resurgence phenomenon, and visibility of between 10-100 ft. The bottom is sandy with pebbles near the deep walls. There is a **big cave** with a submarine entrance and an exit to a **chimney** about 260-ft. inland.

We loaded our gear on the little "putt putt" and were off on a sunny morning. A **small cove** about an hour from shore was chosen as our first dive. Since it was out of season, there were only two divers on the boat, Jezzeco, my buddy (who, by the way, holds the world record for free diving 320 ft.) and myself.

We rolled over and descended to 45 feet to inspect a beautiful long wall. I couldn't believe the diversity of fish. Each time we found another variety we thought that would be our last great find of the dive, but then another fish appeared. All in all, we came upon a conger (sea snake), spotted flounders, two sea horse, pufferfish, French angelfish, bluewing sea robin, black-ear wrasse, spotted scorpion fish, porkfish, squirrelfish, Atlantic spadefish, rockbeauty crevalle jack, snowy grouper, scarlet lady and moan jellyfish. The entire sea floor was covered with vegetation that resembled a field of lettuce.

The *Thetis* was a British frigate serving Spain. It sank in 1830 while returning to port. Quite foggy the Captain mistook a cave for the opening to the Harbor. She now lies off this cove in open sea 25 feet to 69 feet. The visibility was not more than five feet.

If you dive this area any time of year, you will need a thick wet suit, hood and gloves. The weather and water temperature can change by the hour! Calm seas can become treacherous ones in a matter of minutes. This is not an area for the faint of heart!

The British ship, *Fuentas Das Mulheres,* sunk in 1906 in 66 feet of water. She was transporting French prostitutes from Rio. Half the women drowned, and so the area is now called "The Cove of Women"

The *Wizard,* located off Saco Do Leste, was a British Steamer sunk in 1821. She lies in 90 feet of water in open sea.

The *Imbetiba,* off Praia Grande, was caught in the fog in 1888, got stuck in the sand and the waves broke her to pieces. **She's only 50 to 100 feet from the beach so she makes a good snorkel.** There is a rich population of fish on her. **Here these waters are *always* cold, and so you *must* come prepared. Cabo Frio means cold coast, so travel with correct gear.** One day it can be warm with wonderful visibility, but on a moment's notice, it can change. **If you are willing to brave the cold waters, it is a location you MUST dive!**

For those who wish to come in a group and want to rent a villa, there is a beautiful 5 bedroom, 5 bath villa that sits high in the hills, overlooking the ocean. It has its own pool and there are steps to the beach. Maid service is provided. This villa assures the ultimate privacy. For villa information in the U.S. fax Aqua Expeditions. (617) 227-8145

RECIFE: THE VENICE OF BRAZIL

Recife is the fifth largest city in Brazil (incorporating nine towns). Its population of 2.8 million comprises Portuguese, Indians, French, Dutch and Africans. The first settlers were the native Indians. The Portuguese brought slaves from Africa in 1526 to fight the Indians and to tend the sugar cane crops. Recife became a commercial port during colonial times, exporting sugar cane, tobacco, and cotton.

Thirty years ago, developers discovered the city, and since then it has become one of the favorite resorts for both Brazilians and world travelers. **It is known as the "Venice of Brazil," because of its many bridges and rivers which criss-cross the area and eventually run into the sea.**

We stayed at the Petribu Sheraton Hotel whose five stars are well deserved. It is fifteen minutes from the airport and offers the traveler a quiet oasis from the busy downtown area. Opening in November 1991, its owners were determined to create an ambiance of local color. Therefore, its architecture, furnishings, paintings, ceramics, and carpet are fashioned by Brazilian artisans. The flowers throughout lend a touch of grace. The hotel faces the Atlantic Ocean. The public rooms are large and airy with intimate areas for meetings whether social or business. Guestrooms are large and comfortable, with marble baths, cable TV, direct dial phone, mini bar, safety deposit box, and 24-hour room service. There is a *hotline* so that if a guest has a problem or questions, they will be attended to immediately. Fax and telex are available. (Sheraton Hotels in the U. S. 1-800-325-5335, fax Recife 011-55-81-468-1118.)

The **Quebra** is the tastefully decorated dining room, serving local food always arranged beautifully in buffet style or a la carte. On Fridays and Saturdays, the **Ocean Reef Club** and lounge, which is located on the top floor of the hotel is open. This is a special place to dine and take in the commanding views of Recife. Be there for the sunset!

There is a sauna, masseuse, hairdresser, and boutique on the premises. A doctor is on call at all times. Babysitting can be arranged. Golf, tennis, and scuba diving are nearby.

There are two pools, one for children, one for adults, and a pool bar and restaurant. The beach that stretches for miles down the coast is a wonderful one to walk and catch all the local color. There is a hotel guard at the gate to the beach. Please do not take any valuables or cameras with you. Just don your swimsuit that's all you need!

There are apartment buildings and private homes along the beach, and since all beaches are public, local vendors set up their booths or carry their wares up and down selling hats, suntan lotion, ice cream, etc.

The *Jangadas*, replicas of the age old fishing raft, sit on the beach waiting to take you for a ride. Originally for fishing, they are made of wood, very flat, and truly seaworthy.

AREAS OF INTEREST

Sunday is family day, and everyone goes to the beach. This is where you will observe the real Brazilian family at play. This is a good day to take in the local attractions!

There are many tourist sites and one that surely should not be missed is the **Museu Do Doman Do Nordeste**, the Museum of Northeastern Man. Gilberto Freyre, a sociologist, is responsible for its creation. The museum, although not large, depicts the history of Recife from its first inhabitant to modern times.

The Governor's Palace is also quite beautiful and there is a very good modern art museum.

Outside of Recife, the little town of **Olinda** is where the artists live. Here you will find beautiful museums, monasteries, and convents. The architecture spans many centuries and styles. Olinda was the liveliest of all the towns surrounding Recife.

If you want to skip carnival in Rio, remember there is one held in Recife, that starts a week earlier. This is so they can practice for Rio, but rumor has it that it is because the natives of Recife want a week's more of "anything goes".

DIVING

We dove with **Brasmar**, a company that was highly recommended to us. From my first encounter with Joel, the owner, and a tour of his facility, I could understand why. Brasmar is a full service scuba center with diving trips and certification. Joel has a good boat, well maintained, with a permanent canopy to shade you from the sun, deck topside for sun worshippers, and more than ample room for tanks, gear and divers.

Joel does not believe in taking the students from the pool to the open ocean to do open water check outs. He has built a cylindrical tank (the only other one we know of is in San Paolo), of concrete that is 120 feet high. Students are trained in the pool, then checked out in the tank and then taken to the open ocean for final checkouts. It is such a terrific idea! How many times have you seen divers panic on their open water checkouts?

Recife means reef, and reefs abound but are not charted. Therefore most of the diving is wreck diving located out at sea. Our first dive was on *The Pirapama*, a steamboat carrying cargo, which collided with another ship, the *Vapor de Bahia*, in 1889. Her frame is still intact, including a giant paddle wheel. Our trip from the dock was about 1 and 1/2 hours. No one on board spoke English, but somehow we had a running conversation and a great many laughs.

The dive was at 72 feet, which gave us enough time to inspect the entire wreck and the abundance of sea life, which has grown on her, and play in and around her frame.

On descending, we spotted a large turtle swimming around the wreck. Further on, yellow jack, blue tang, Portuguese man of war, squirrelfish, fairy basslet, rock beauty and plume worms. A long, whip-like tail hidden in the sand gave evidence to a large ray that darted off. The corals, both hard and soft, growing on the wreck were in various brilliant colors, purple, pink and orange.

Bottom time up, we ascended, and took time for a safety stop.

Because the seas were high and the visibility became less clear, we chose to do the second dive in the same spot. Our reward was the spotting of five rays, one right after the other. They stayed quite close this time which is unusual for rays in open water.

Recife is the perfect place for the diver who loves to explore the graveyards of the sea.

NATAL

Founded in 1599, Natal is in the most eastern part of Brazil. The entire archipelago is 26 square km. During the Ice Age it was part of Africa. Its topography is really quite interesting. Miles and miles of beach, not good for scuba diving, but a favorite of surfers with it's awesome waves. Its hillside resembles a desert.

During World War II, Natal was the site of the largest U.S. Air Force Base outside the United States. It was built from scratch in 1941 with the help of the Brazilians, 440 buildings included lodgings, supply, hospitals, and aircraft maintenance. The base employed 6,000 Brazilians and housed up to 15,000 troops. No one knows the exact number. By 1943, it was handling outgoing aircraft every three minutes. It could accommodate 1,000 people in transit overnight. In addition, it was a base of operations for submarine surveillance, ferrying aircraft and crews to Europe, and the support system for the North African invasion.

Hitler, in two major speeches, singled out Natal for destruction. As a result there were untold blackouts. On August 26, 1942, Brazil declared war on Germany and from that time on Brazil has been a U.S. ally. Brazilians served with the 5th Army in Italy as General Mark Clark's "Brazilian Expeditionary Force".

You could fly from Washington to Natal in 21 hours. USO shows used this route and President Roosevelt came through twice. The United States gave the base free of charge to the Brazilian government in 1945. They use it as their international airport and a training school for air force pilots.

My plan was to overnight at the **Genipabu Hotel** in Natal, before flying on to Fernando De Noronha which is about a 1-1/2 hour flight from Recife, on the northeastern shore of Brazil. The hotel's complimentary bus transfers you to and from the airport. Perched high in the hills, its setting and architecture gives you an immediate sense of a less hurried world. The 24 double rooms are quite large with balconies overlooking the valley below with all color of vegetation, and the desert-like hillside that runs to the sea. They are furnished in a way that reminds one of the Orient, simple, yet beautiful: TV, mini bar, and no phone or air-conditioners, just a ceiling fan.

After lunch, Victor suggested a buggy ride on the dunes. I thought this a splendid idea that should teach me never to say yes until I have inquired just what a new adventure entails. **It takes a *very* experienced driver for this sport because of the strong wind from the sea and the desert sands shift constantly from area to area. It is similar to a roller coaster ride, only I'm not sure which makes my heart beat faster.**

Along the way we encountered a father and his son who give donkey tours of the dunes. I shall never forget the father's face, so weathered, so gentle, and the boy, so young but a little man. It can be a hard life in Brazil.

For more information contact:

Genipabu Hotel
Caixa Postal 2640
Natal – RN – Brazil
Tel: (084) 225-2063
Fax: (084) 231-4602

FERNANDO DE NORONHA

The next afternoon our small plane took off for the hour trip to Fernando De Noronha, about 360 km from the Natal coast. As our plane flew over, we viewed the steep pinnacle rocks, in varying shapes and sizes rising from the sea, beautiful deserted beaches and century old buildings in a state of disrepair. It was as if time had stood still in this naturalist's paradise.

Americo Vespucci, sailing from Portugal, discovered this vast archipelago two hundred miles off the coast of Natal, comprising six main islands and fourteen rocky outcroppings.

The government allows only a certain number of visitors per day, and this is strictly enforced. When you land you must fill out a form with length of stay, Pousada, passport number and pay a fee or tax that goes towards preserving these islands.

There are few places to stay at this writing. Most are very rustic and do not have hot water. If you can do without fancy amenities, you will partake of some of the finest diving anywhere.

Here we dived with Patrick Muller. He and his wife Ana, own the Genipabu Hotel in Natal. Patrick had come to Fernando De Noronha to secure a license for a scuba diving operation, (not an easy feat, since the government in 1988 declared most of this island a National Park) and they are very cautious about any new development or enterprise, especially by non-Brazilians.

Patrick's two boats, the *Atlantis I* (32 feet long) and the *Atlantis II,* (35 feet long) have two 155 horsepower engines, head, permanent canopy, flybridge, bow for sunning, and enough room to comfortably hold 8 divers and their gear.

We motored out of the small cove, heading towards our destination about forty-five minutes away. This gave me a good opportunity to see the island close up. What a beauty it must have been in her day when the wood exporting business gave it riches and prominence.

As we passed the "Bay of Dolphins", a group of them came out and followed the boat. They are such gentle and friendly creatures; I marvel at how they move through the water at great speed and wonderful grace.

Finally reaching our dive site, **Iuias,** in front of Cape Caracas, we entered the water by giant stride for a drift dive. We swam amongst many huge rocks and through caves and tunnels. The variety and size of fish was unbelievable. Catching sight of a 12 foot nurse shark, we watched it as it slept, then awakened by the Nikonos, dart away. There were turtles, barracuda, French angelfish, schools of squirrelfish, parrotfish, African pompano, blackjack, quelly jack, Atlantic spadefish, a large horse-eye jack, a green triggerfish with the brightest yellow tail I have ever seen, spiny lobster, dog snapper, banded butterfly fish, yellow pea chub, silver porgy, tiny shrimp, and black margate. The barracuda that met us on our descent followed us the entire dive. **I can say this was one of the best dives I've ever made.**

Patrick told me that in good weather the visibility is 200 feet. Descending, we swam into the grotto at **Sapata Cave** and investigated hiding places for fish. We spotted another large nurse shark, a school of barracuda, spotlight parrotfish, blue tang, butterfly fish, coney, and black margate. We caught sight of a jewfish that weighed at least 150 pounds and followed it for the rest of our dive.

On my next trip to Brazil I will head here and just dive, dive, dive. I can put up with simple accommodations for the world class virgin diving. Patrick is both an able and safety concious fellow who has created a full service scuba center with dive/stay packages. He is probably one of the most charming and accommodating fellows you will ever meet!

BACK TO RIO

We flew back to Rio the next day and I confess I vegged out after this whirlwind trip. Because I enjoyed the Sheraton in Recife so much, I decided to book the 5-star **Sharaton Rio Hotel and Towers.** The hotel offers enough luxury and privacy to please any sybarite. It is also the only hotel located directly on the beach in Rio with sea view, and recreational

SCUBA AND SNORKELING FACILITIES QUESTIONNAIRE

NAME **Atlantis Divers**
ADDRESS **Caixa Postal, 20 - CEP 53990-000**
CONTACT **Patrick Muller**
TITLE **Owner**
TELEPHONE **(0055) 81 619.1371**   FAX **(0055) 84 231.4602**   TELEX

CAPITOL: **Fernando De Noronha/PE**
POPULATION: **2,000**
CURRENCY: **Real**
AIRLINES: **Varig/Nordeste**
NEED VISA/PASSPORT?   YES **x**   NO

GOVERNMENT: **Brazil**
LANGUAGE: **Portuguese**
ELECTRICITY: **220v**
DEPARTURE TAX?
PROOF OF CITIZENSHIP?   YES **x**   NO

YOUR FACILITY IS CLASSIFIED AS: SCUBA CENTER **x**   RESORT
BUSINESS HOURS: **8 a.m. - 10 p.m.**
CERTIFYING AGENCIES: **PDIC Professional Diving Instructors Corp.**
LOG BOOK REQUIRED?   YES   NO **x**
EQUIPMENT: SALES **x**   RENTALS **x**   AIR FILLS **x**
PRIMARY LINE OF EQUIPMENT: **Sherwood, US Divers, Mares**
PHOTOGRAPHIC EQUIPMENT: SALES   RENTALS   LAB

CHARTER/DIVE BOAT AVAILABLE?   YES **x**   NO   DIVER CAPACITY **16**
COAST GUARD APPROVED?   YES **x**   NO   CAPTAIN LICENSED?   YES **x**   NO
SHIP TO SHORE?   YES **x**   NO   LORAN?   YES   NO **x**   RADAR?   YES   NO **x**
DIVE MASTER/INSTRUCTOR ABOARD?   YES **x**   NO   BOTH **x**

DIVING & SNORKELING: SALT **x**   FRESH
TYPE OF DIVING/SNORKELING IN AREA: WALL **x**   BEACH **x**   WRECK **x**   REEF **x**   CAVE **x**   ICE
DIVING/SNORKELING IN YOUR AREA IS BEST SUITED FOR: BEGINNER **x**   INTERMEDIATE **x**   ADVANCED **x**
BEST TIME OF YEAR FOR DIVING/SNORKELING:
TEMPERATURE: NOV-APRIL   **28C**   MAY-OCT: **28C**
VISIBILITY: DIVING: **Up to 200FT**   SNORKELING: **Up to 200FT**

PACKAGES AVAILABLE: DIVE **x**   DIVE STAY **x**   SNORKEL **x**   SNORKEL-STAY **x**
ACCOMMODATIONS NEARBY: HOTEL **x**   MOTEL   HOME RENTALS
ACCOMMODATION RATES: EXPENSIVE **x**   MODERATE **x**   INEXPENSIVE
RESTAURANTS NEARBY: EXPENSIVE   MODERATE **x**   INEXPENSIVE
YOUR AREA IS: REMOTE   QUIET WITH ACTIVITIES **x**   LIVELY
CAR NEEDED TO EXPLORE AREA?   YES   NO **x**
DUTY FREE SHOPPING?   YES   NO **x**

LOCAL EMERGENCY SERVICES
Natal - Navy Base (180 NM)
COASTGUARD   **Recife**
TELEPHONE: **(0055) 81 224.2269**

NEAREST HYPERBARIC TREATMENT FACILITY
AUTHORITY: **Administrator**
LOCATION: **Fernando De Noronha**
TELEPHONE: **(0055) 81 1305**

LOCAL DIVING DOCTOR:
NAME: **Natal - Navy Base**
TELEPHONE: **(0055) 84.216.3413**

SCUBA AND SNORKELING FACILITIES QUESTIONNAIRE

NAME   Joselio Sebastiao Da Silva
ADDRESS   Aqualife Conceieao De Jacarei - Mangarafibs
TITLE   2 stars Instructor – Navy
CONTACT   Fjevitour/Rio - y Setembro 92/1706
TELEPHONE   507-2211   FAX 224-6319   TELEX

CAPITOL: Rio/Brasilia/Brazil   GOVERNMENT: Democratic
POPULATION: 145 million   LANGUAGE: Portuguese
CURRENCY: Crueeiros Reais   ELECTRICITY: 110v
AIRLINES: Varig   DEPARTURE TAX: $16 U.S.
NEED VISA/PASSPORT?   YES x   NO   PROOF OF CITIZENSHIP? YES   NO

YOUR FACILITY IS CLASSIFIED AS: SCUBA CENTER x   RESORT
BUSINESS HOURS: 9 a.m. - 6 p.m.
CERTIFYING AGENCIES: International
LOG BOOK REQUIRED?   YES x   NO
EQUIPMENT: SALES   RENTALS   AIR FILLS
PRIMARY LINE OF EQUIPMENT: Luxfer Aluminum/3000 PSI USI Divers
PHOTOGRAPHIC EQUIPMENT: SALES   RENTALS   LAB
CHARTER/DIVE BOAT AVAILABLE?   YES x   NO   DIVER CAPACITY 3
COAST GUARD APPROVED?   YES x   NO   CAPTAIN LICENSED?   YES x   NO
SHIP TO SHORE?   YES   NO x   LORAN? YES   NO x   RADAR?   YES   NO
DIVE MASTER/INSTRUCTOR ABOARD? YES x   NO   BOTH x

DIVING & SNORKELING: SALT x   FRESH
TYPE OF DIVING/SNORKELING IN AREA: WALL x BEACH x WRECK x REEF x CAVE x ICE
DIVING/SNORKELING IN YOUR AREA IS BEST SUITED FOR: BEGINNER x INTERMEDIATE x ADVANCED x
BEST TIME OF YEAR FOR DIVING/SNORKELING: Summer
TEMPERATURE: NOV-APRIL   21C   MAY-OCT: 17C
VISIBILITY: DIVING: 30FT   SNORKELING: 36FT

PACKAGES AVAILABLE: DIVE x   DIVE STAY x   SNORKEL x   SNORKEL-STAY x
ACCOMMODATIONS NEARBY: HOTEL x   MOTEL   HOME RENTALS x
ACCOMMODATION RATES: EXPENSIVE x   MODERATE x   INEXPENSIVE x
RESTAURANTS NEARBY: EXPENSIVE x   MODERATE x   INEXPENSIVE x
YOUR AREA IS: REMOTE x   QUIET WITH ACTIVITIES x   LIVELY
LOCAL ACTIVITY/NIGHTLIFE: WEEKENDS
CAR NEEDED TO EXPLORE AREA? YES x   NO
DUTY FREE SHOPPING?   YES   NO x

LOCAL EMERGENCY SERVICES   NEAREST HYPERBARIC TREATMENT FACILITY
COASTGUARD   Yes   AUTHORITY: Marine/Navy Capitania
TELEPHONE: Yes   LOCATION: Angra Dos Reis

LOCAL DIVING DOCTOR:
NAME:
LOCATION: Angra Dos Reis
TELEPHONE:

SCUBA AND SNORKELING FACILITIES QUESTIONNAIRE

NAME   **Patrick Rubiere**
ADDRESS   **Rua Bernardo Lenz, 114 Pousada Thalassa**

CONTACT   **Figuiton — Pousada Thalassa**
TITLE   **Tour Angene Pousada (Hotel)**
TELEPHONE **502-2211 0246-222285**   FAX **2246319**   TELEX **021-21408 EEFP - BR**
CAPITAL: **Rio**   GOVERNMENT: **Democracy**
POPULATION: **14 million**   LANGUAGE: **Portuguese**
CURRENCY: **Crueeiros Reais**   ELECTRICITY: **100v**
AIRLINES: **Varig**   DEPARTURE TAX? **$17 U.S.**
NEED VISA/PASSPORT? YES **x** NO   PROOF OF CITIZENSHIP? YES **x** NO

YOUR FACILITY IS CLASSIFIED AS: SCUBA CENTER **x**   RESORT **x**
BUSINESS HOURS: **9 a.m. - 6 p.m.**
CERTIFYING AGENCIES: **Figuitoun**
LOG BOOK REQUIRED?   YES **x**   NO
EQUIPMENT: SALES **x** RENTALS **x**   AIR FILLS **x**
PRIMARY LINE OF EQUIPMENT: **Boat 26 ft - 12 bottles Beauchrat - Regulators/B.C.**
PHOTOGRAPHIC EQUIPMENT: SALES   RENTALS   LAB

CHARTER/DIVE BOAT AVAILABLE?   YES **x**   NO   DIVER CAPACITY **8-30**
COAST GUARD APPROVED?   YES **x**   NO   CAPTAIN LICENSED? YES **x**   NO
SHIP TO SHORE? YES NO **x**   LORAN? YES NO **x**   RADAR? YES NO
DIVE MASTER/INSTRUCTOR ABOARD? YES **x** NO   BOTH **x**
DIVING & SNORKELING: SALT **x**   FRESH
TYPE OF DIVING/SNORKELING IN AREA: WALL **x** BEACH **x** WRECK **x** REEF **x** CAVE **x** ICE
DIVING/SNORKELING IN YOUR AREA IS BEST SUITED FOR: BEGINNER INTERMEDIATE ADVANCED
BEST TIME OF YEAR FOR DIVING/SNORKELING: **Summer**
TEMPERATURE: NOV-APRIL **14-25F**   MAY-OCT: **14-25F**
VISIBILITY: DIVING: **60 FT**   SNORKELING: **60FT**

PACKAGES AVAILABLE: DIVE **X**   DIVE STAY **x**   SNORKEL **x**   SNORKEL-STAY **x**
ACCOMMODATIONS NEARBY: HOTEL **x**   MOTEL POUSADA **x**   HOME RENTALS **x**
ACCOMMODATION RATES: EXPENSIVE **x** MODERATE **x** INEXPENSIVE **x**
RESTAURANTS NEARBY: EXPENSIVE **x** MODERATE **x** INEXPENSIVE **x**
YOUR AREA IS: REMOTE   QUIET WITH ACTIVITIES **x** LIVELY

LOCAL ACTIVITY/NIGHTLIFE: **Bars with live music**
CAR NEEDED TO EXPLORE AREA?   YES **x**   NO
DUTY FREE SHOPPING?   YES   NO **x**
LOCAL EMERGENCY SERVICES   NEAREST HYPERBARIC TREATMENT FACILITY
COASTGUARD   AUTHORITY: **Capitania - Navy**
TELEPHONE: LOCATION: **Arraial Do Cabo/Cabo Frio**
CALLSIGNS: TELEPHONE: **0246-432840**

LOCAL DIVING DOCTOR:
NAME: **Angelo Lima**
LOCATION: **Arraial Do Cabo**
TELEPHONE: **0246-222218**

facilities. **The tennis courts are ranked among the 10 most beautiful in the world by Tennis Magazine.**

BRAZILIAN EMBASSY
3006 MASSACHUSETTS AVENUE N.W.
WASHINGTON, D.C. 20008
TEL 202 745 2828

Colombia

Renee Burt

It is extremely difficult to answer the question as to what my favorite dive spot is in Colombia. Here are a few of my favorite places:

The islands of San Andres and Providencia are the Hawaii of Colombia, it is a favorite place for honeymooners and vacationers from surrounding countries.

The natives speak Spanish, English and Papiamento. The islands are located 480 km north of Colombia on the Caribbean Sea.

Another good diving location is Santa Marta, a big Colombian tourist spot and home of the legendary "Lost City" of the Sierra Nevada Mountains. Santa Marta is the capital of the Magdalena department of Colombia (population 300,000), the third largest Caribbean port, and is 96 km east of Barranquilla at the mouth of the Manzanares River. Santa Marta lies on a deep bay with high shelving cliffs. The climate ranges from hot, to hot and pleasant in February and March.

I found a nice diving school called **Pro-Buzos de Colombia.** The instructor, Alvaro Riascos, took us on two excursions either out of the goodness of his heart, or because he liked American women. We ended up paying a nominal fee for air and transportation and had an unforgettable diving experience. Be sure to visit the little fishing village of **Taganga.** The natives build their own boats and fish the way they did over 100 years ago.

Bahia Solano is a nice place to dive. It is where I took my first open water diving lessons. The waters range from 20-25 Centigrade with visibility of 10-15 kms.

Capurgana is located in the Gulf of Uraba, and is very close to Panama. **The Calypso Hotel is a first-class luxury hotel** with air conditioning, satellite television, a swimming pool, playground, tennis and basketball courts. They also have excursions to **the beaches of Panama and the San Blas islands**. I have never been diving there, but if you have your own equipment, there is a place that will fill your tanks and take you via speedboat to the nice diving areas.

Bahia Solano and Capurgana are not your typical tourist locations, so some degree of Spanish is necessary as no one speaks English.

Cartegena is a very popular vacation spot, especially for Canadians, and most natives speak English. It is also one of the most interesting cities in South America. It is steeped in history. In the 1600's Cartagena was one of the storage points for merchandise sent from Spain and for treasure collected from the Americas to be sent back to Spain. A series of forts protecting the approaches from the sea and the walls that were built around the city made it impregnable.

Of more interest to the diver are the **Rosario islands,** about 45 minutes away from the city by speedboat. All of the major hotels have daily excursions to the islands. We made reservations to stay at **La Isla Pirata** for two nights, which included a nice cabana and food. **Be sure to get tanks filled in the city beforehand as there are no diving facilities on the islands.**

COLUMBIAN EMBASSY
2118 LEROY PL.
WASHINGTON, D.C. 20008
TEL 202 387 8338

Columbia

Cali

Karen Rodriguez

Mr. James Baker put Cali and our road to Buenaventura on the map. I can't say that makes me very happy, but I suppose it forces me to put our dive expeditions on the high adventure list.

You can fly from Miami to Cali direct on Avianca or American Airlines in three and half-hours. I will pick you up at the airport and baby-sit you for your entire stay. Cali is three hours from the Pacific Coast where we keep the *Asturias* (our banana boat).

Now I know Mr. James Baker was an important person and should know what he was talking about but...I have not had any trouble in twenty-five years either in Cali or driving the road to Buenaventura at any hour of the day or night.

GORGONA NATIONAL PARK

There are two places that divers go, one is Gorgona National Park, a ten hour crossing to this park, which is the mating ground for the humpback whale from July through November. A beautiful, lush jungle island with white beaches and coconut trees. It was once a prison island, but now only receives park visitors.

Spearfishing is not allowed. You may fish with a line, and you are only allowed to take photographs and memories home with you. You will see the big stuff here, but not much in the way of coral. At different times of the year we have devil mantas, hammerheads, whale sharks, huge snappers, amberjacks, tuna, and barracuda. I have always seen white tips. We can see everything in less than 100 feet, but the visibility can be anything from thirty to eighty feet. Most of the time the temperature is around 78 degrees Fahrenheit, but I recommend a light wetsuit for protection. I take open water students to Gorgona for certification. Advanced divers enjoy some of the advanced dive spots.

I'm a mother hen...and since our chamber is a good nine hours away, I keep an eye on all divers. We dive in small groups with an instructor or dive master guiding the way.

MALPELO ISLAND

My other high-high adventure trip on our "Regressor Banana Boat" is to Malpelo Island, which is a thirty five-hour trip. It is well worth the wait. A stark rock, 400 meters high, with lots of smaller rocks scattered around. There are tunnels, sheer walls, and more fish life than most people see in a lifetime. Unfortunately the Colombian government can't protect this outpost from fishing trawlers. I fear the schooling of hammerheads is in danger. We do spearfish there but only by free-lung, and we only take what we can eat. Other divers are discovering this treasure and if we are going to continue to go there we must protect it!

This is an eight-day trip for experienced divers only. I would expect any diver to use all standard required equipment and come with an internationally recognized certificate and logbook. There are no special fees for sport diving in Colombia. At the Gorgona National Park there is no spearfishing or taking by hand of aquatic life. In other areas there is no enforcement of any kind.

VENEZEULA

Wendy Canning Church

In 1498, on his third voyage, Columbus discovered Venezuela. But like so many of his findings, he never laid down a permanent settlement. Amerigo Vespucci followed in 1499 and mapped much of the area. One of his favorite spots was Lake Maricaibo which Indian tribes had settled. They lived in houses built on stilts, and traded along

SCUBA AND SNORKELING FACILITIES QUESTIONNAIRE

NAME **Karen Rodriguez**
ADDRESS **Apartado Aereo 6963, Cali, Colombia**

TELEPHONE **515008**   FAX **688452**   TELEX

CAPITOL: **Bogata**   GOVERNMENT: **Democratic**
POPULATION: **30 million (approx)**   LANGUAGE: **Spanish**
CURRENCY: **Peso**   ELECTRICITY: **110v**
AIRLINES: **American/Avianca**   DEPARTURE TAX?
NEED VISA/PASSPORT?   YES **x**   NO   PROOF OF CITIZENSHIP?   YES **x**   NO

YOUR FACILITY IS CLASSIFIED AS: SCUBA CENTER   RESORT
BUSINESS HOURS:
CERTIFYING AGENCIES: **PADI, NAUI, FEDCAS**
LOG BOOK REQUIRED?   YES **x**   NO
EQUIPMENT: SALES **x**   RENTALS **x**   AIR FILLS **x**
PRIMARY LINE OF EQUIPMENT: VARIETY
PHOTOGRAPHIC EQUIPMENT: SALES   RENTALS **x**   LAB

CHARTER/DIVE BOAT AVAILABLE?   YES **x**   NO   DIVER CAPACITY **18**
COAST GUARD APPROVED?   YES **x**   NO   CAPTAIN LICENSED?   YES **x**   NO
SHIP TO SHORE?   YES **x**   NO   LORAN?   GPS **x**   NO   RADAR?   YES **x**   NO
DIVE MASTER/INSTRUCTOR ABOARD? YES **x**   NO   BOTH

DIVING & SNORKELING: SALT **x**   FRESH
TYPE OF DIVING/SNORKELING IN AREA: WALL **x**   BEACH   WRECK   REEF   CAVE   ICE
DIVING/SNORKELING IN YOUR AREA IS BEST SUITED FOR: BEGINNER **x** INTERMEDIATE **x** ADVANCED **x**
BEST TIME OF YEAR FOR DIVING/SNORKELING: **All year**
TEMPERATURE: NOV-APRIL   **78-80F**   MAY-OCT: **78-80F**
VISIBILITY: DIVING: **40 FT**   SNORKELING: **40FT**

PACKAGES AVAILABLE: DIVE **x**   DIVE STAY **x**   SNORKEL **x**   SNORKEL-STAY **x**
ACCOMMODATIONS NEARBY: HOTEL **x**   MOTEL   HOME   RENTALS
ACCOMMODATION RATES: EXPENSIVE   MODERATE **x**   INEXPENSIVE **x**
RESTAURANTS NEARBY: EXPENSIVE   MODERATE **x**   INEXPENSIVE **x**
YOUR AREA IS: REMOTE **x**   QUIET WITH ACTIVITIES   LIVELY
LOCAL ACTIVITY/NIGHTLIFE:
CAR NEEDED TO EXPLORE AREA?   YES   NO **x**
DUTY FREE SHOPPING?   YES   NO **x**

LOCAL EMERGENCY SERVICES   NEAREST HYPERBARIC TREATMENT FACILITY
COASTGUARD **Naval Base, Bahia Malaga**   AUTHORITY: **Naval Base**
TELEPHONE: **34114-34120**   LOCATION: **Bahia Malaga, Pacific Coast,**
                            Colombia

LOCAL DIVING DOCTOR:
NAME: **Carlos Botero**
LOCATION: **Buenavetura, Colombia**
TELEPHONE: **34865**

SCUBA AND SNORKELING FACILITIES QUESTIONNAIRE

NAME **Aquarium Dive Shop**
ADDRESS **P.O. Box 1692**
San Andres, Isla-Colombia-Sur America
CONTACT **Pablo E. Montoya A.**
TITLE **PADI Open Water Scuba Instructor - CMAS 3 Star Instructor**
TELEPHONE **6649 - Home: 6378** FAX **40126 Hansa CO** TELEX

CAPITOL: GOVERNMENT:
POPULATION: LANGUAGE:
CURRENCY: ELECTRICITY:
AIRLINES: DEPARTURE TAX?
NEED VISA/PASSPORT? YES **x** NO PROOF OF CITIZENSHIP? YES NO

YOUR FACILITY IS CLASSIFIED AS: SCUBA CENTER **x** RESORT **x**
BUSINESS HOURS: **All the time, Summer & Winter**
CERTIFYING AGENCIES: **PADI, CMAS, FEDECAS**
LOG BOOK REQUIRED? YES NO
EQUIPMENT: SALES **x** RENTALS **x** AIR FILLS **x**
PRIMARY LINE OF EQUIPMENT: SALES AND RENTALS
PHOTOGRAPHIC EQUIPMENT: SALES RENTALS LAB

CHARTER/DIVE BOAT AVAILABLE? YES **x** NO DIVER CAPACITY **20**
COAST GUARD APPROVED? YES **x** NO CAPTAIN LICENSED? YES **x** NO
SHIP TO SHORE? YES **x** NO LORAN? YES **x** NO RADAR? YES **x** NO
DIVE MASTER/INSTRUCTOR ABOARD? YES **x** NO BOTH

DIVING & SNORKELING: SALT **x** FRESH
TYPE OF DIVING/SNORKELING IN AREA: WALL **x** BEACH **x** WRECK **x** REEF CAVE **x** ICE
DIVING/SNORKELING IN YOUR AREA IS BEST SUITED FOR: BEGINNER **x** INTERMEDIATE **x** ADVANCED **x**
BEST TIME OF YEAR FOR DIVING/SNORKELING: **All year**
TEMPERATURE: NOV-APRIL F MAY-OCT: F
VISIBILITY: DIVING: FT SNORKELING: FT

PACKAGES AVAILABLE: DIVE **x** DIVE STAY SNORKEL **x** SNORKEL STAY
ACCOMMODATIONS NEARBY: HOTEL **x** APARTMENT **x** HOME RENTALS
ACCOMMODATION RATES: EXPENSIVE MODERATE INEXPENSIVE
RESTAURANTS NEARBY: EXPENSIVE MODERATE INEXPENSIVE
YOUR AREA IS: REMOTE QUIET WITH ACTIVITIES **x** LIVELY
LOCAL ACTIVITY/NIGHTLIFE:
CAR NEEDED TO EXPLORE AREA? YES NO
DUTY FREE SHOPPING? YES NO

LOCAL EMERGENCY SERVICES NEAREST HYPERBARIC TREATMENT FACILITY
COASTGUARD AUTHORITY: **Juan Martin Velasquez - Fabio Acevedo**
TELEPHONE: LOCATION: **Hospital Santander - San Andres Isla**
CALLSIGNS: TELEPHONE:

LOCAL DIVING DOCTOR:
NAME: **Juan Martin Velasquez**
LOCATION: **Hospital Santander, San Andres, Isla**
TELEPHONE: **3596**

the waters in dugout canoes. This reminded him of Venice; thus he named the country Venezuela, meaning "Little Venice".

Spain, with its lust for gold, had a strong foothold for 300 years. Simon Bolivar, then and now a hero, was an aristocrat born only 57 miles from Caracas. He overthrew the tyrants, and Little Venice became a democracy.

Today, Venezuela remains a democracy of over 20 million people, the preponderance of which are under 40.

Situated in the Caribbean with 1,800 miles of coastline and seventy-five islands, it is bordered by Guyana, Colombia, and Brazil. **Its 352,150 square miles are comprised of some of the most diverse and beautiful topography one will find anywhere. Stretches of jade green mountain ranges run throughout. The wild, verdant Amazon, bubbling rivers, deserted islands, huge waterfalls, solitary beaches in colors of perfect gemstones are yours to discover. Its waters are crystalline clear, virgin and the government protects most as reserves.**

It is a country of dichotomies like so much of South America. There are the old great fortunes from gold and the new from oil, and there are the favelas of the city that one always wants to turn their eyes away from.

Caracas, the capitol, is the most populous city, with four million people living in a cosmopolitan area with many historic sites.

I was amazed to learn that a large percentage of the population is of Italian decent and that one can find 5-star Italian cuisine at little cafes throughout Caracas.

Do be at the airport at least two hours ahead of time and re-confirm 24 hours before departure when leaving Caracas. There is a great deal of paperwork. You pay taxes at a counter other than the check in. There are at least two securities checks before boarding the aircraft.

You do need a Visa, and don't lose it or you'll spend two days going through a lot of red tape at your Embassy.

VENEZUELAN PERMANENT MISSION TO THE UNITED NATIONS
7 EAST 51ST STREET
NEW YORK,NY 10022
TEL 212 826 1660

Venezuela

Live-Aboard in Los Roques

Donna Marchetti

Picture Caribbean diving at its best and you're likely to think of Cozumel, Bonaire or the Caymans. But the relatively unknown Venezuelan archipelago of Los Roques offers some of the most pristine diving in this part of the world. Located about a hundred miles north of Caracas, this group of more than 300 islands and its surrounding water make up the largest and oldest marine sanctuary in the Caribbean.

Most of the islands within Los Roques National Park are uninhabited and accessible only by boat. The handful of islands with permanent residents have traditionally supported fishing villages, though this is changing rapidly as more tourists are discovering these unexpected pieces of paradise. **The island most favored by visitors, Gran Roque, has a small landing strip and a number of small, informal hotels called *posadas*.**

Ironically, these islands called Los Roques—"The Rocks"—are primarily sand spits, many of which disappear with high tide. Only the island of Gran Roque is actually rock, formed by the shifting of tectonic plates millions of years ago. The others, says park director Miguel Matanay, were formed by centuries of wind and wave action, creating sedimentary layers of dead coral that have resulted in the fine, powdery, chalk-white beaches found there today.

I had come here to spend a week diving Los Roques from the *Antares III*, an 85-foot live-aboard based in Gran Roque. The prospect of a day of complete relaxation drew me to Gran Roque a day before I was to board the *Antares*. The relatively short flight from Miami got me into Caracas by 2:00 p.m., where I was met by a representative from the *Antares*, who made sure I made my connection to the commuter flight. By 5:00 I was standing in the sand with my luggage at the edge of Gran Roque's airstrip. It was a short walk from there to my posada, perched at the water's edge.

Gran Roque is one of those places we tend to fantasize about when life gets overly demanding. There simply isn't much to do but relax and take in the charm of the scene. There are no streets, just sand. Rows of houses arranged in neat lines are painted in pastel shades, their doors and windows shuttered against the hot sun. Kids play on the dock, taking turns jumping into the water. Brightly colored wooden fishing boats rest at the water's edge, waiting for tomorrow's work. The sea is an impossible aqua, reflected on the white wings of the terns that hover overhead.

Like the other islands in the archipelago, Gran Roque depends on shipments from the mainland to keep it supplied with essentials. All food and other goods must be brought in. Although there is a desalinization plant, it is apparently unable to keep up with the demand, since fresh water is also brought to the island. Aware of these considerations, I had no expectations for a dinner beyond the ordinary, but I was proved wrong. Perhaps it was watching the sun set over the water while sitting at a table under the darkening sky, my feet luxuriating in sand still warm from the afternoon heat, that made the food taste especially good.

I headed out the next morning for an all-day catamaran excursion to Sarqu, an island to the west, where snorkeling and walking the long, sandy shore were the perfect preparation for a week's exploration of these beautiful islands.

DIVING WITH ANTARES III

I boarded the *Antares III* that evening and enjoyed the first of many delicious meals, prepared in part by Dominique, who admitted by week's end that he had once been in the restaurant business in Paris. For Captain Dominique Delmas, the *Antares* is home, and a source of great pride. There are six guest staterooms, each with private bath including cold-water shower. A large communal area serves as dining room and entertainment center, with TV, VCR, stereo and a well-stocked library of books in several languages. An upper deck offers a quiet place for sunbathing or reading. The completely refurbished boat is filled with rich natural wood and decorated with original art. The English-speaking crew, which includes Dominique's son and brother-in-law, are quick to make guests feel welcome.

We spent the first day of diving—a Sunday—anchored in the harbor at Gran Roque, using a tender to go to the dive sites. Leaving the island, explained Dominique, is always delayed until Monday as a courtesy to those who can't get to Gran Roque until Sunday. We did, in fact, pick up another passenger that evening—Miguel Matanay from the national park, who would dive with us while checking the health of the reefs.

PIEDRA DE LA GUASA

In many ways, that first day offered the most remarkable dive of the week. After a ten-minute ride to the site, called **Piedra de la Guasa** (Jewfish Rock), we dropped over the side and descended. Visibility was cloudy but cleared somewhat at about 30 feet, when we reached the top of a coral-covered pinnacle that begins on the ocean floor at 130 feet. We continued our descent to about 75 feet, then began working our way slowly around the pinnacle and up.

We were surrounded by swarms of schooling fish—jacks, snappers, creole wrasse, thousands of boga, bonnetmouth and rainbow runners. Ceros came curiously close to us, while a large queen triggerfish, filefish and a jumbo-sized hogfish swam by. There

Antares III by Donna Marchetti

were midnight parrotfish so large it seemed you could saddle them up and ride off into the sunset.

The top of the pinnacle was teeming with smaller life—blennies, juvenile angelfish, small damsels and tiny juvenile spotted drums. A group of eight large squid hovered just out of camera range, flashing their iridescent colors. An inquisitive moray eel swam boldly out of his crevice and right into the lens of the video camera one diver was carrying. We went back for a second dive and were once again amazed at the diversity and plenitude of life.

I was surprised that the water was downright chilly by Caribbean standards, about 77 F—and this was July. My suspicions were confirmed when I learned that the cooler water comes with the currents up the South American coast from the Atlantic Ocean off Brazil. There is little seasonal fluctuation in water temperature, which along with high levels of oxygen and the usually clear water results in healthy coral.

"You can find coral at depths of 90 feet here," Miguel told me, "because the sunlight penetrates that far. The coral is healthy because we've been monitoring these waters for 25 years." His claim was verified throughout the week, when despite the visibility it was obvious that the reefs of Los Roques are untouched, pristine and lush.

PUNTA SALINAS

We moved early the next morning to the southern barrier reef, arriving at our new dive site, **Punta Salinas**, at about 9:30. The area had seen human presence long before Europeans set foot here, Dominique told me. Fishermen used to come from the mainland for the conch, turtles and fish, which they would salt for preservation. The conch shells they used to collect fresh water are still there, concentrated into huge mounds.

We spent two days diving at Punta Salinas, beginning with a drift dive along a wall with caverns at about 80 feet and again at about 60 feet. The current was quite strong— the strongest we encountered all week—meaning that if you weren't in the right lane on the freeway, so to speak, you missed the exit, and before you knew it thc cavern was behind you—which is exactly what happened to me. I was consoled at the safety stop, however, when thousands of tiny fry made the sea sparkle with aquatic glitter.

Punta Salinas abounds with gorgonians, some very tall, waving like an underwater forest, their brown shades punctuated by the occasional soft lavender of rope sponges. There are huge formations of sheet coral, flower coral and brain coral as well as sea fans and sea whips, bringing a new backdrop with every turn of a corner. Stingrays and eagle rays are common, as are spotted moray eels and barracuda. The reef fish are the best of Caribbean technicolor—damsels, chromis, wrasse, filefish, butterflyfish, snappers, porkfish, coneys and parrotfish.

It's worth noting that other than the strong current on our first dive at Punta Salinas,

there were no other factors that would make Los Roques inappropriate for novice or intermediate divers. Surface conditions were calm, currents generally slight, and the depths shallow. Though one dive bottomed out at 90 feet, most were in the 60-80 range.

BOCA DE COTE

We moved to **Boca de Cote**, almost directly south of Gran Roque. We could even see the jagged rocky hill that sprouts an old lighthouse. But if we pulled anchor and headed directly toward it, said Dominique, we'd be in trouble. The island that seemed so near could only be approached by going around the outside of the archipelago, so shallow is the water of the inner lagoon.

At Boca de Cote we were awed by more gorgeous gorgonians, some of the tallest I had ever seen, along with purple stovepipe sponges and living room-sized brain coral. Despite the unusual soupy visibility, I was able to spot the tiniest of spotted drums and a minuscule juvenile filefish concealed in the waving fronds of a gorgonian. There were surprise encounters with a large nurse shark resting in the sand and a turtle making its way toward the surface. On one dive we were greeted upon descent by the sight of eight spotted eagle rays swimming gracefully into the distance.

ESTACIÓN SUR

We departed Boca de Cote two days later, stopping **at Estación Sur to dive and to go ashore to visit the marine research station there, where turtles are hatched and later released into the sea.** By afternoon we were back on Gran Roque and exercised our "sea legs" by going ashore to climb the hill to the lighthouse. We were rewarded by a magnificent view of the turquoise and deep blue sea stretching as far as the eye could see.

I left the *Antares* just after dawn the next morning, reluctant to say good-bye to newly made friends, but looking forward to three days of land tours on the mainland.

AREAS OF INTEREST

While the Venezuelan landscape is both varied and beautiful, no part of it may be more mysterious than the **Gran Sabana**, where jungle-covered tepuis rise from the grassy plains. These tepuis, "mountains" in the Pemón Indian language, have been the source of much speculation since Europeans first discovered them in the late 1800s. **The plateau-topped mountains support species that have been cut off from the rest of the world for millions of years and therefore exist nowhere else on earth.**

The most popular tourist destination in the Gran Sabana is **Canaima National Park**, deep within Bolivar State. (Movie buffs may like to know that the opening sequence of *Anaconda* was filmed here, and that Steven Spielberg wanted to film *Jurassic Park* at

Angel Falls by Donna Marchetti

Canaima, but park officials declined.) **The highest waterfall in the world, Angel Falls, is located within the park.** At 16 times the height of Niagara Falls it makes an impressive sight. The most common way to view it is from the air.

The park is located on a wide, peaceful section of the Rio Carrao known as the **Laguna Canaima,** which offers a magnificent view of **Saltos Hacha,** a series of seven waterfalls. The water is reddish-brown, colored by natural tannins, while the sandy shore has a pink hue. An excursion by dugout canoe, followed by a short hike, will take you to **Salto El Sapo.** It is possible to walk behind this thundering waterfall, emerging at the other side for a spectacular view of rushing water.

But the most memorable of my land experiences was at **Arekuna,** a camp in a remote area of Bolivar. Built on a grassy hill at the jungle's edge, Arekuna can be reached only by plane. There are ten cement-floored, grass-roofed huts, each with two units that include beds, a desk, a hammock and bath. Owned by the large tourism company, LTA, Arekuna is powered completely by solar energy, and uses water distilled from the nearby Rio Caroni. Food and supplies must be flown in.

The most striking thing about Arekuna is the absolute quiet, the absence of any sounds of civilization. It is almost disconcerting at first, accustomed as we are to a certain level of noise. A group of us took an afternoon hike that began with a boat ride on the Caroni, passing a gold mining camp and a Pemón village. Our trek ended at a roaring waterfall, and I couldn't help but feel privileged to be one of the relatively few to see this sight. A hike the next morning took me through the jungle, verdant and dripping from a torrential cloudburst the night before.

Although mosquitoes are not a concern around Los Roques, they are a problem in many other parts of Venezuela, including the areas around Canaima and Arekuna. They can transmit malaria and dengue fever, so prophylactic medication and/or strong insect repellent is recommended for visits to these areas.

GETTING THERE

Getting to Venezuela from the United States is easier than getting to many Caribbean islands. **American Airlines** and Continental both **fly to Caracas,** as well as several Venezuelan airlines. Flights from Caracas to Los Roques run several times daily and can be arranged when booking a dive charter or land tour. Visitors are not required to have visas unless they are going for business, but tourist cards are issued by the airlines.

Exchange money at the airport if you want to play it safe; few places cash travelers checks and fewer accept credit cards. Don't expect to find many English-speaking people except in major tourist areas or on a tour. For a better experience, brush up on a bit of Spanish.

There's no bad time to visit the country, **diving is best during the summer rainy season because the water tends to be calmer.** (Though "rainy" sounds unpleasant, the showers come and go quickly; it's rare to encounter more than a brief downpour.) Unlike many Caribbean destinations, hurricanes are not a concern, as Venezuela is not in the hurricane track. Summer is also a better time to visit Canaima National Park and Angel Falls, since the increased rainfall makes for more spectacular waterfalls.

For information on dive charters or land tours contact Dominique Delmas on the *Antares* at 011 58-14-16-40-07 (phone and fax).

Venezuela

Puerto La Cruz

Wendy Canning Church

One half-hour flight to Barcelona, or a four-hour drive from Caracas, gets you to Puerto La Cruz, also known as "The Gateway to the East".

Just ten short years ago this area resembled Los Roques, a remote fishing village on the map overlooked by tourists. Today, the traveler will find a humming city replete with five-star hotels, beautiful waterfront villas, condos, and marinas in whose berths lie fabulous yachts. There is also the American infusion of McDonalds and Burger King. Whether their introduction was due to the Americans working the oil fields or demand from the locals is anyone's guess.

You will be a bit dazzled by the area's facelift and its obvious building boom geared to the rich and famous. If you spend a little time, you will find the old city, built in colonial times, with small cafes serving delicious cuisine and little shops selling charming handicrafts.

Once out on its waters, the true beauty of the area becomes apparent. Many small islands lie offshore that are surrounded by waters protected by the government. They were designated a Marine Park five years ago. The government judiciously patrols the Park.

Scuba divers can take nothing dead or alive from the waters. There is no spearfishing. Fish can only be taken on a line. Limits are set for the fishermen and there are times of the year when allocated species may be caught.

New housing cannot be built upon the islands in the Park. Call it poetic justice if you will, but a group of wealthy people built expensive houses without permission. The government tore them down, allowing only the small, modest houses of the fishermen whose livelihood has been culled from these waters for centuries to remain.

You can sail for miles and never see another boat. Every island has a reef. Some islands have more than two! Most of the islands are deserted. The reefs are virgin, the waters pristine. Couple this with a year round temperature of 80 degrees and you have a perfect destination for lovers of watersports.

THE DIVING

We dived with **Lolo's,** a first class operation situated about one-half hour from our hotel, *The Golden Rainbow*, Maremares Resort and Spa. Some days we would be picked up by Eddy Revelant, our dive master and we would leave from the scuba center. Other days, he and the captain would bring the boat around and we would leave from the marina at the hotel.

Lolo's has three boats, all in good condition, comfortable, with enough room for divers and equipment and canopy for shade from the intense sun.

The scuba center is up to date. The equipment provided is in good shape and well serviced. They carry wet suits, which you will need. **Don't laugh, but a hood and gloves are also necessary.** Even though it was April, the waters were quite cold!

THE SCUBA DIVING AND SNORKELING

THE BUBBLE OFF EAST LAS CARACAS ISLAND
This is a wall dive suited for all levels. We rolled over and descended to a maximum depth of 100 feet. As we descended we saw bubbles rising to the top. Eddy stopped along the way and showed me different areas where hot water was coming out of the rocks. The bubbles are caused by natural gas coming out from under the bottom of the wall at 100 feet.

As we ascended, there was a field of beautiful corals and reef fish, parrotfish, angelfish, grunt, squirrelfish, deep-water grouper, small snapper, sergeant major, and a pair of spotted drum. The abundance of healthy corals was astounding, star, brain, knobby brain, and large flower corals with brilliant red and green coloring.

LAS PENAS OFF SANTA FE GULF
A reef dive suited for all levels depending on the time of year and current. This applies to every dive in Venezuela. If there is heavy current, drift dives are done.

The pinnacle reaches almost to the surface. The dive plan is to begin at the last pinnacle in shallow water and make your way to the West Side, which is comprised of a sandy slope. The hard and soft corals were beautiful. The entire dive site was covered with anemones, which resembled bouquets of flowers. Small shrimp were hidden amongst the rocks along with arrow crabs and a large variety of reef fish. We spotted two moray eel, stonefish, and sea cucumbers littered the sand.

This dive used to be called Anemone Garden and one can understand why. We swam through fields of them our entire dive.

THE CATHEDRAL OFF BARRACUDA ISLAND

This is a reef dive suited for every level and a good site for a night dive. We dropped down to forty-five feet and swam along the reef toward the northwest to a cave in the wall. The cave is full of passages filled with sea life and beautiful colored sponges. It has two openings at the top.

Ascending, I heard a voice. Eddy said, "Hi." Obviously, we had hit an air pocket. These happenings underwater are what gets we divers hooked!

We came out of the cave and descended to 60 feet. There were parrotfish, angelfish, a snake eel, a green moray eel, and something strange, which I first thought might be an octopus, but rather it was fire worms eating eggs of other fish.

LA BALLENA

La Ballena is off Borracho Island. We approached the reef by going under a large ledge of rocks. It resembled an amphitheater. Its slope, made up of hard corals, went downward. There were schools of red snapper, two huge blue parrotfish; schools of butterfly fish swam along with us.

TIQUITIQUE

Tiquitique is a reef dive that is shaped like a mountain so you can dive both sides, the deepest point being 120 feet. Here we spotted the big fish, manta rays, nurse shark, grouper and big red snapper.

Lolo's has innumerable dive sites but on our last day the first dive's visibility was poor. We decided to go further inland and find better visibility. This was a new site. It was a wonderful dive. I liked this very much about the operation. Their flexibility was always keyed not only to the safety of the diver, but their enjoyment of the site. Lolo's is first rate and I thank them all for a wonderful underwater stay in Puerto La Cruz.

ACCOMMODATIONS

The **Golden Rainbow, Maremares Resort and Spa,** is situated only 20 minutes from the airport and minutes from town. It is definitely <u>the</u> place to stay in Puerto La Cruz. A five-star hotel by Venezuela's standards, it is the most complete resort you will find in the area.

Guests are lodged in attractive rooms with private baths and balconies in three-story pink pastel buildings. I don't think anyone could possibly get bored with the myriad of activities offered. The food is delicious.

The world class spa is a joy. Lifestyles of the Rich and Famous filmed it for one of its TV episodes. Interestingly enough, by the world's standards and prices, the Golden Rainbow is very affordable.

Golden Rainbow Maremares Resort and Spa
Puerto la Crue
Tel 011-58-081-1011
Fax 011-58-081-814449

AREAS OF INTEREST

Diving in Venezuela is an all day affair. You start off early in the morning, motor to your first site, complete the dive, then set out for an island to picnic. In early afternoon, a second dive is done and you are back on shore between three and four. Those not wanting to go each day can opt for every other and just relax or sightsee.

Old Town is well worth a visit being very picturesque. Walk to Boulevard El Paseo Colon. When oil was discovered, the big American companies ran the refinery until the Venezuelan government bought them out. Here you will see the American influence. It is an interesting contrast, restaurants, hotels, and craft shops situated on the sea. You will not find any big shopping malls yet; little souvenir shops abound.

SCUBA AND SNORKELING FACILITIES QUESTIONNAIRE

NAME   **Lolo's Diving Center**
ADDRESS   **Sector Punta De Meta Guantamarina Guanta Edo, Anzoategui**

CONTACT   **Pedro Rodriguez/Eddy Revelant**
TITLE   **President/Marketing Director**
TELEPHONE   **081-683052 014-801543 014-205073**   FAX **081-682885**   TELEX

CAPITOL: **Barcelona**   GOVERNMENT:
POPULATION: **1,000**   LANGUAGE: **Spanish, Little English**
CURRENCY: **Bolivar**   ELECTRICITY: **110v, 60 cy**
AIRLINES: **Charter Flight Aeroejecutivo/Aereotuv**   DEPARTURE TAX? **National Park Fee**
NEED VISA/PASSPORT?   YES **x**   NO   PROOF OF CITIZENSHIP? YES **x**   NO

YOUR FACILITY IS CLASSIFIED AS: SCUBA CENTER   RESORT **x**
BUSINESS HOURS: **7:30 a.m. -7:00 p.m.**
CERTIFYING AGENCIES: **PADI**
LOG BOOK REQUIRED?   YES   NO **x** **Certification is required**
EQUIPMENT: SALES **x**   RENTALS **x**   AIR FILLS **x**
PRIMARY LINE OF EQUIPMENT: **Seaquest - Technisub**
PHOTOGRAPHIC EQUIPMENT: SALES   RENTALS **x**   LAB NONE

CHARTER/DIVE BOAT AVAILABLE?   YES **x**   NO   **DIVER CAPACITY 10 people w/each D.M.**
COAST GUARD APPROVED?   YES **x**   NO   CAPTAIN LICENSED? YES **x**   NO
SHIP TO SHORE?   YES NO   LORAN? YES **x**   NO   RADAR?   YES **x**   NO
DIVE MASTER/INSTRUCTOR ABOARD? YES **x**   NO BOTH **x**

DIVING & SNORKELING: SALT **x**   FRESH
TYPE OF DIVING/SNORKELING IN AREA: WALL **x** BEACH   WRECK **x**   REEF **x**   CAVE **x**   ICE
DIVING/SNORKELING IN YOUR AREA IS BEST SUITED FOR: BEGINNER **x** INTERMEDIATE **x** ADVANCED **x**
BEST TIME OF YEAR FOR DIVING/SNORKELING: **May - October**
TEMPERATURE: NOV-APRIL   **80F**   MAY-OCT: **80F**
VISIBILITY: DIVING: **40-80 FT** SNORKELING: **80FT**

PACKAGES AVAILABLE: DIVE **x**   DIVE STAY **x**   SNORKEL   SNORKEL-STAY
ACCOMMODATIONS NEARBY: HOTEL   MOTEL   HOME RENTALS **x**
ACCOMMODATION RATES: EXPENSIVE **x** MODERATE **x**   INEXPENSIVE **x**
RESTAURANTS NEARBY: NONE **x**   EXPENSIVE   MODERATE   INEXPENSIVE **w/package**
YOUR AREA IS: REMOTE **x**   QUIET WITH ACTIVITIES   LIVELY
LOCAL ACTIVITY/NIGHTLIFE: **During high season there are parties in the plaza**
CAR NEEDED TO EXPLORE AREA?   YES   NO **x**
DUTY FREE SHOPPING?   YES   NO **x**

LOCAL EMERGENCY SERVICES   NEAREST HYPERBARIC TREATMENT FACILITY
COASTGUARD **(Has emergency helicopter)**   AUTHORITY: **Centro Clinico Hiperbarico**
TELEPHONE: **VHF Channel 16**   LOCATION: **La Guaira**
CALLSIGNS: **Guardacosta Los Roques**   TELEPHONE: **35.29.33/242.84.77/242.93.25**

LOCAL DIVING DOCTOR:
NAME: **Adolfo Gonzalez Poarrio**
LOCATION: **Centro Clinico Hiperbarico, La Guaira**
TELEPHONE: **35.29.33/242.84.77/242.93.25**

270

If avid shoppers need their "fix", **Margarita Island** makes a good day trip.

When we inquired of knowledgeable dive operations in Venezuela and about good diving areas, Margarita Island was sold to us more as a duty-free port than a dive destination. A ferry service runs each day from the end of Boulevard El Paseo Colon. It is a four-hour trip.

Or you can take a plane and visit **Angel Falls**, named for American aviator, Jimmy Angel. In 1937 on a quest for gold, his plane crashed on top of "Auyan-Zepuy" or Tabletop Mountain. The party survived and when they emerged from the forest they came upon this waterfall, the highest in the world.

A TASTE OF THAILAND

Forward
Wendy Canning Church

Known as Siam before 1949, Thailand is located in south east Asia and is shaped like an elephant's head. Thailand shares borders with Burma, Cambodia and Vietnam. On her west side is the Andaman Sea and on her east, the South China Sea.

Approximately the size of France, geographically speaking, Thailand is divided into six major regions: the mountainous north where elephants work forests and winter temperatures are sufficiently cool to permit cultivation of temperate fruits such as strawberries and peaches; the sprawling northeast plateau, largely bordered by the Mekong River, where the world's oldest Bronze Age civilization flourished some 5,600 years ago; the central plain, one of the world's most fertile rice and fruit-growing areas; the eastern coastal plain where fine sandy beaches support the growth of summer resorts; western mountains and valleys suitable for the development of hydro-electric power; and the peninsula south where arresting scenic beauty complements economically vital tin mining, rubber cultivation and fishing.

Thailand has three seasons, summer March-May, rainy June-September and cool October to January.

Thailand is a constitutional monarchy. Since 1932, Thai kings, including the present monarch, H.M. King Bhumibol Adulyadej (Rama IX), have exercised their legislative powers through a national assembly, their executive powers through a cabinet headed by a Prime Minister, and their judicial powers through the courts.

The population is 58 million, only 15% are over 50. 90% are practicing Buddhists.

Equidistant between China and India, Thailand has served as a crossroads in southeast Asia. This country is made up of a diversity of ethnic backgrounds: Thais, Mon, Khmer, Laotian, Chinese, Malay, Persian, and Indian. These people are both light and dark skinned. Most are petite. Eighty-five percent of the population is literate.

Thai is the predominate language. Roadsigns are in both Thai and English. Major hotels have English speaking staff.

Lodgings range from five-star hotels to bungalows, guesthouses, houseboats, hostels and beachside huts.

Bangkok is Thailand's major gateway. Most visitors arrive through Bangkok's Don Muang International Airport, which is connected by daily flights to Europe, North America, Asia and Australia .

A passport is needed to enter. Check with your consulate or tourist authority on visa requirements. Domestic air, rail and road transport in Thailand is surprisingly inexpensive. Your travel clinic can advise you about necessary shots or medicines needed to travel throughout Thailand. Travelers leaving the country must arrive at the airport two hours before their flight. Security check is long and elaborate.

Please see the Honeymoon and Anniversary Section for the Oriental Bangkok and The Sukhotai Hotel

Bangkok

"City of Angels"

Wendy Canning. Church

I arrived in the City of Angels at 2 a.m. after a 26-hour flight. During the drive to my hotel, a flurry of activity and a cacophony of voices shocked me even in my semi-comatose state. Men and women wearing masks (because of the pollution) were building the new subway. Discos, massage parlors, nightclubs and hostess bars were blasting noise. All offered a thousand delights to their clients. I could not help but think which one of these delights a tourist might not ask for but return home with.

"What are all these people doing up at this time of night?" I inquired of the driver.

"Bangkok is a city that never sleeps. The tourists are here for fun and delight and we are here to please."

Was this the city I had traveled thousands of miles to visit and learn of her culture and people? What I had seen was an assault on my senses.

A visitor to Bangkok will find it difficult to imagine that 1500 years ago this sprawling metropolis was covered with rice paddies fed by ocean waters. Over time monsoons and swift currents pushed the waters further and further into the Gulf of Thailand. Houses were built on stilts and Bangkok was destined to take her place as one of the most economically viable cities in Asia.

The Chao Phya River runs through the city and canals connect many districts. During the monsoon season the river overflows, hence Bangkok is also known as the "Venice of Thailand". Bangkok has no central financial, diplomatic or shopping district. It takes time to get to know this exotic and faraway place.

Bangkok, the capital of Thailand since 1782 spans 6,261 square miles and is home to eight million people. It is also home to towering office buildings, shopping malls, condominiums and horrendous traffic jams. Bangkok also has the dubious distinction of being the hottest city in the world.

Away from the hotel and down side streets and alleyways I discovered the real Thailand. Sidewalk stalls are set up so close together that they almost spill their wares into one another. They teemed with exotic fresh fruit, vegetables and flowers in a rainbow of hues that was a feast for the eye. The orchids were breathtaking in a kaleidoscope of color. Motorcyclists and tuks (3 wheeled taxis) came perilously close to shoppers while monks in saffron robes strode amid this chaos with slow graceful strides.

Jellyfish, "The Mornings Catch" by Wendy Canning Church

When I asked if I could photograph the vendors they were quite amenable. **Travelers will learn in Thailand that there is no such word in their vocabulary as no. Their motto is "Don't worry, be happy."**

272

I was very hot and I was tempted to buy a freshly squeezed drink at the juice bar, but had been warned ahead of time: **buy nothing to eat from street vendors, and drink only bottled water.**

Returning to **The Oriental**, I found a haven from the flurry of activity outside. As always, I was greeted with a smile and bow from each of the doormen and those at the front desk. (**Please see Honeymoon and Anniversary Section for more information on The Oriental Hotel.**)

From my room I looked out at the Chao Phraya River abuzz with activity. River taxis, tour boats, and commercial vessels were ferrying passengers and wares. I began to understand the way a visitor must approach both Thailand and its people. One must look beyond the ribbons of concrete for they only seem to dwarf the ancient temples. Never allow the noise of traffic to drown out the sounds of the sweet greetings of the people. Bangkok is a city of extremes, yet a City of Angels, for she's a rowdy city with gentle people.

AREAS OF INTEREST

Bangkok's major tourism attractions include:
- Wat Phra Kaeo (Emerald Buddha Chapel) and Grand Palace complex
- Wat Arun (Temple of Dawn); Wat Pho (Temple of the Reclining Buddha)
- Wat Saket (Golden Mount); Wat Benchambophit (Marble Temple)
- Wiman Mek Palace, favorite residence of King Chulalongkorn (1868-1910) and the world's largest golden teak building
- The Royal Barges
- The Pasteur Institute's Snake Farm, where poisonous snakes are fed daily, and venom is milked from cobras and kraits to make invaluable serum
- Jim Thompson's House Museum, which contains a superb collection of Asian objets d'art
- Suan Pakkad Palace's lacquer pavilion, which is decorated with medieval gold leaf murals
- The world's largest Crocodile Farm
- The Ancient City, a 200-acre open air museum
- Entertainment and recreational complexes, such as Siam Water Park, Safari World, King Rama IX Park and Dusit Zoo
- Unrivaled shopping opportunities for some of the world's most admired handicrafts. The Best Buys are silk and gems
- Exceptionally fine dining featuring some of the world's favorite cuisine
- A liberated, almost legendary, nightlife.

Phuket

"The Pearl of the South"

Wendy Canning Church

Phuket is the largest island in Thailand, approximately the size of Singapore and shaped like an irregular pearl, hence referred to as "The Pearl of the South". Just a one-hour flight from Bangkok, she is also linked by a causeway at its northernmost tip so is accessible by car. Formerly Phuket's wealth came from rubber, tin and pineapple. While these still produce revenue, tourism has become the main livelihood. Make no mistake Phuket has been found.

During the dry season, November to April (also the best time for scuba diving) planes land one after the other at the new international airport.

A visitor will find accommodations in all price ranges, simple or luxurious, quiet and with a Thai ambiance.

The visitor must travel beyond Phuket Town and Patong Beach with her high-rises, condos, discos and bars which stay open to the wee hours to find her wonders.

Here Phuket's natural attractions unravel: solitary silver beaches, sheltered coves and anchorage's, lush forest clad mountains, sheer cliffs dropping into the crystalline waters and a virgin Eco-system underwater that bedazzles the eye.

Phuket is a center for charter boats, and you can hire a yacht, with or without crew, for as long as you like, while fully equipped deep-sea fishing boats generally offer charters for one to five days.

To fill days away from the beach, visits can be enjoyed to the Marine Biological Research Center, the Butterfly Garden and Aquarium, the Talang National Museum, the Crocodile World and Sea Aquarium, the Naga Pearl Working Farm and the Thai Village where daily cultural shows give a splendid insight into the traditional ways of southern Thailand. Take in a Thai boxing match.

Sea-canoeing is another thrilling option, exploring island caves during one - to seven - day voyages entering a hidden world as unspoiled as anywhere on earth.

These caves were discovered by chance by a gentleman from Hawaii fishing off them. Only at high tide can one notice the openings. They are so low that a canoe barely can enter them. Even then one must lie down. Once inside, the eye delights in a wondrous world of tall limestone cliffs rising above azure waters, covered in a profusion of vegetation. Wildlife abounds birds, monkeys and even bats. After exploring each of the three caves lunch is served aboard the boat. It is a typical Thai meal, resplendent in color, taste, and freshness. A swim at a nearby beach follows and then you head home which takes 1 and 1/2 hours. It's a perfect outing for the entire family. Reservations through Sea Canoe, P.O. Box 276, Phuket, Thailand, 83000. Tel/Fax (076) 212172, (076) 212252.

Phuket and its off islands, and the Similian Islands 50 miles northwest, are where you will find the best scuba diving and snorkeling in Thailand.

Canoe Trip by Wendy Canning Church

The Andaman Sea reefs encompass 1,200 square miles. These have been declared a Marine National Park to insure they remain as pristine and virgin 100 years from now as today. This means no anchoring and no collecting of shells or marine life.

My itinerary took me to **The Laguna Beach Resort** where by day I dived the off islands, took the canoe trip and toured Phuket. I then booked the Andaman Explorer liveaboard for 6 days and 5 nights, diving and snorkeling the Similian islands.

LAGUNA BEACH CLUB

A short 30 minute drive from Phuket International Airport, **Laguna Beach Club's (LBC)** atmosphere of beauty and tranquility seem worlds away from much of this commercial, busy island.

Located at Bangtao Bay on 20 acres of prime land nestled between the lagoon and the Andaman Sea, it features a four-acre water park incorporating waterfalls, water slide, Jacuzzi swimming pools and scuba pool. All this is surrounded by hand sculptured walls and is reminiscent of ancient Thai artwork. The entire low-rise resort is built to reflect typical Thai architecture.

Throughout the resort one will find beautiful antique Thai carvings, sculpture and textiles. As one walks to the dining area or different activities you find yourself pausing to reflect on the artifacts which in a true sense envelope the guest in the ambiance of the culture of Thailand both past and present.

Guestrooms face the sea stretching as far as the eye can see or the sapphire blue lagoon. All rooms feature open-air balconies and private sitting areas. Every room comes with two oversized double beds, mini bar and fridge, color TV with free videos and international cable channels, in room safe, air conditioning and a ceiling fan. The bathroom has a luxurious huge sunken tub plus a complete selection of toiletries including a hairdryer.

Clubmates from all over the world coordinate sports, instructions, activities and nightly entertainment all in an environment of pure fun and Thai hospitality. In the LBC tradition of the all-inclusive all 30 on-site sports and activities are at no cost (except scuba diving which is extra). These consist of 3 outdoor tennis courts, 1 indoor tennis court, auto-tennis practice area, volleyball, golf practice range, 2 squash courts, archery range, bicycles, game room with billiards, table tennis, darts and board games, fitness center, badminton, four acre water park with waterslide, lap pool, Jacuzzi, scuba pool, plunge pool, water volleyball, water basketball, water polo, and sea sports facilities which include kayaking, sailing, **snorkeling***, windsurfing, and scuba diving.

*There is excellent snorkeling off a little island not far from the beach. A longtail boat can be hired to take you there.

The "Kid's Club" is a real plus for parents who wish to take time to enjoy their favorite adult activities. Children from the age of 4-12 are supervised in any or all of three sessions daily, which last from 9 a.m. to 9 p.m. Younger children may attend if supervised by an adult.

Treat yourself to a typical Thai massage. Excellent Thai and Continental cuisine rounds out the LBC Experience. A meal plan is available. There is a clinic in-house and a doctor on call. Complete conference facilities make this an excellent choice for business meetings and a post holiday stay.

The Resort is under the direction of experienced and very imaginative General Manager, John Green, and his proficient staff who go about their tasks with sincere warmth and an ever-ready smile. In tandem they work to offer guests of any age a wonderful holiday with an authentic Thai flavor while including all modern amenities.

Laguna Beach Club
Bangtao Beach, Cherngtalay Thalang,
Phuket, 83110, Thailand
Tel (66) 076-324-352 Fax (66) 076-324-353

SCUBA DIVING AND SNORKELING

Scuba Diving is the island's most popular and best developed sport. The Andaman Sea boasts some of the world's finest dive spots, deep and shallow, presenting scuba enthusiasts with the full gamut of underwater scenes — coral walls, a web of caves, tunnels and swim-throughs, wrecks and more.

The Andaman Sea Triangle encompasses some 1200 square miles comprising Phuket's off islands, the Similian group, Surin and the Burma Banks.

FANTASEA DIVERS DAYDIVES

Fantasea Divers operates two liveaboards and two-day boats. Divers making day trips will be picked up at their hotel and dive any one of the off islands of Phuket.

The *Reef Runner* and *Panamphon* spend the week taking divers to varied and interesting locations. Divers of all experience levels can dive these sites except for Raja Noi, geared to the more experienced. A professional divemaster leads each dive or a buddy team may go off on their own.

SHARKPOINT
Depth: 10-27 meters Viz: Fair to excellent.
Boat Trip: 1 H 15 min.
This large reef with colorful soft corals and a great variety of fish is everyone's favorite. Home of the leopard sharks! This trip also visits Ko Doc Mai and Anemone Reef.

PI-PI ISLANDS
Depth: 6-24 meters. Viz: Poor to excellent
Boat Trip: 2 Hrs.
PI-PI's world famous cliffs continue straight down underwater offering wall and cavern diving as well as shallow coral gardens.

RAJAH ISLANDS
Depth: 10-35 meters. Viz: Good to gin-clear.
Boat Trip: 1H 30 min.
Rajah's clear waters offer deep rock formations and sloping coral reefs. Your best chance to see bigger fish.

Fantasea is professional in every detail. Their comfortable boats have a permanent canopy, the aft deck has lots of room for divers and equipment, fresh water shower, rinse tank for cameras, a head, galley (from which are created delicious hot lunches with a Thai accent) and an upper deck for sunning. Cold drinks are available all day and beer after the diving is over. Towels were handed to us between dives.

The entire staff was capable from the divemaster (helpful, informative about the sea and its creatures that abound in it) to the captain, second mate (who sets up all your equipment, helps you put it on, takes it off and breaks it down) to the chef who somehow presents starving divers with a delicious different lunch each day and fresh fruit between dives.

The first day we set off from Chalong Harbor for Sharkpoint. On the way we were given a tour of the vessel, C-cards were checked and safety instructions explained. Each diver was given an "orange sausage". This is folded up and kept in the pocket of your B.C. If needed it can be inflated to signal the captain and crew of a diver's whereabouts in the water. Most of the dives are drift dives so this is an important piece of equipment. We commend Fantasea for utilizing it. A little over one hour later we reached our destination. Lucy, our diveguide briefed us on the site and minutes later a giant stride led us into the underwater topography.

The deadronephthia soft corals in pinks and purple which covered an enormous area of rock, were a feast to the eye along with large fans and sponges that are prevalent. There were schools of lionfish, four species of moray eels,

Liveaboard M/V Fantasea by Wendy Canning Church

barracuda, snappers, emperors, and squid, along with banded sea snakes, cuttlefish, and nudibranch. Here I sighted the first leopard sharks I ever encountered. They lay on the bottom sleeping; their bodies appeared bedecked in spotted pale grey velvet.

After lunch our second dive was at Koh Doc Mai. We dived the shallow western side which was wondrous, so virgin and full of flaring color and sea life. **Suddenly we spotted a whale shark, another first for me. Swimming along with this immense creature (the world's largest fish) that moved through the water with such grace and stature was inexplicable.** One has to experience an encounter with these creatures to understand the thrill and delight we all felt.

KOH BIDA

The following day we were off to the Pi-Pi Islands east of Phuket on the *Reef Runner*. They consist of two main islands — Pi-Pi Don and Pi-Pi Lay and a handful of smaller ones. Pi-Pi Don is the only island that is inhabited and can be reached by a longtail boat or the ferry.

After a two and a half-hour ride we came upon them, rising vertically from the sea surrounded by white sand beaches A shower of marine life flows between the many caverns, swim throughs and walls.

We suited up and were in the transparent waters in minutes. You can go around the pinnacle jutting out of the sea in either direction. One side goes straight down to 26 meters and the other side gradually slopes to a shallow depth of between 6 and 15 meters.

This is a perfect spot for snorkeling. Many longtail boats, the most common form of water transport, had brought groups of two and three to enjoy the day snorkeling and lunching at a nearby beach. There was too much to see in one dive. The profusion of hard and soft corals was a palette of every conceivable color. The walls and reef were a repository of sponges, gorgonias and sea fans in every hue. We spotted a leopard shark (zebra are the juveniles). In the juvenile stage the zebra is striped, not spotted. There were six lionfish. It is very unusual to see these in groups. All types of reef fish called this home: Moorish idols, clownfish, chromis, reef pufferfish, squid and greenfish.

Just about the time we were to reboard, another diver spotted two whale sharks under the boat. Bottom time was up so we could not remain to seek them out. During lunch we discussed if we should move to the next site or stay here and try to find the whale sharks. The decision was unanimous. We would dive this site again.

Descending we sighted the two whale sharks and accompanied them as they swam along with the remoras (the fish that are hitch hikers). The remoras attach themselves to bigger fish so that they can catch the scraps the bigger fish feed on and also a faster ride to any food available.

Leopard Shark by Mark Strickland

Whale Shark with diver by Mark Strickland

We dived Racha Noi off Ray Ban on the southern tip the third day. The site is tricky to find. The captain must use radar. Once found divers must enter the water quickly because of the current, hence this is a live boat negative dive making a fast descent while at the same time swimming away from the vessel. The boat's engines are not shut off. This is rather tricky; **thus a dive which is geared for experienced divers.**

Racha Noi is a sunken rock formation beginning at 12 meters down to 50 meters. The huge brown boulders slope down to a deep sandy area. There is an enormous area of deadronephthai, soft corals, and gardens of sea fans. There is an excellent chance of spotting the pelagics: mantas, whale sharks, eagle rays, marbeled stingrays, leopard sharks, gray reef sharks, schools of barracuda, surgeonfish, fusiliers, and big red snapper.

M/V *Fantasea Divers* two live-aboards are quite different. The M/V, a motor vessel, carries 16 passengers. *Fantasea* cruises the Similian Islands, Richelieu Rock, and the Burma Banks for 6 days and 7 nights. She is air-conditioned. Each cabin is carpeted and has its own porthole, stereo and multi-system TV/VCR, library, gear locker, sundeck, and freshwater showers. There is a water maker onboard. You have nonstop hot water.

There is a camera person's dream come true with a large table for cameras on the dive deck, fresh water rinsing tanks, processing lab, and camera rentals.

The *Andaman Explorer*, a sailboat, carries 9 passengers and 4 in crew. She was the first liveaboard in these waters, beginning her trips in 1983. The antithesis of *M/V Fantasea*, there is no hot water and no air conditioning and only one head onboard. The vessel only cruises the Similian Islands.

I booked the *Explorer* because the *Fantasea* was full. To my surprise, I never missed hot showers or the air conditioner. Many slept on deck. I never found the need to. The nights were cool and I had a small fan in my room. Most cabins are small but since one spends the day in the water or topside, this is a moot point. We had 5 days and 6 nights aboard this charming sailing ship.

Actually it was very soothing not having the noise of engines. The only harsh sounds aboard were the compressors when they filled the tanks. We had the option to go to a nearby beach, snorkel or dive. The cook was first rate. **The food was delicious. The divemaster, Bobby, excellent. The first mate who set up our gear, put it on, broke it down and ran the beach bus and picked divers up after ascending from drift dives (most dives were drift dives) was always helpful and on target.** All were as professional as they come.

We covered 9 islands in 5 days.

One could make as many dives as they wished as long as they had a buddy and stayed within the dive tables or the computers. (Computer rentals were free the first day). A safety stop was required (15 feet for 3 minutes after each dive). Every diver was given a safety sausage. Each dive was guided but you could go off on your own as long as you had a buddy.

There were two featured guided dives a day at 9 a.m. and 2 p.m. Night dives began at 7:30. There is no diving after 9 p.m. Most dives were done from the boat, a handful from a dinghy.

The Similian Islands are 50 nautical miles northwest of Phuket and encompass 10 miles. All have been declared a Marine National Park. **Nothing is to be taken from the waters and there is no dropping of anchors.**

On its east side one finds gently sloping coral reef while on the west side there are boulders one atop each other creating caves, tunnels and archways.

Our first dive was at **Beacon Beach.** It was a very easy relaxed dive. There was a sloping coral reef that bristled with fish life: Moorish idols, a big trumpetfish, a family of checkerboard wrasse, six bar wrasse, powderblue surgeon, coral grouper, sharpnose pufferfish, stonefish, schools of yellow fusillier and yellowtail jacks. We began the dive up current and swam back with the current.

Christmas Point is a wonderful site. There are archways and tunnels, which we swam through. The valleys in-between were incrusted with hard and soft corals. As one ascended there was always something to observe — schools of oriental silvertips, undulating moray eels, lionfish, dusky batfish, clown triggerfish, crescent angelfish, big eye emperor and starry pufferfish. The black coral was abundant and healthy. No wonder the site is also known as Coral Gardens.

Elephants Head was another outstanding site. This was done as a live boat dive because of the currents. There were large swim throughs and huge jumbled boulders alight with wondrous color. The gorgonias and nudibranch were plentiful. A big shovelnose ray joined us on this dive.

Fantasea Reef, named after our dive center, was a typical multi-level dive. This is a large reef so we dived it twice. We swam through a large cavern coming upon a sandy area. We turned left and ascended to a valley called the Bronx. There were shovelnose rays, fire goby, blackwedged butterfly fish, peacock grouper, a spider crab, giant clams, blue triggerfish, starry pufferfish, feather star, Christmas tree worms and feather duster worms. On both dives the currents brought both the reef fish and pelagics to this spot simultaneously. A whale shark was spotted.

Cuttlefish mating by Mark Strickland

SCUBA AND SNORKELING FACILITIES QUESTIONNAIRE PRIVATE

NAME **Fantasea Divers Co. Ltd**
ADDRESS **P.O. Box 20, Patong Beach**
        Phuket 83150, Thailand
CONTACT **Maarten Brusseters/Jeroen Deknatel**
TITLE **Director of Marketing/ Director of Operations**
TELEPHONE **66 76 340088, 295511**   FAX **66 76 340309**   TELEX

CAPITOL: **Bangkok**   GOVERNMENT: **Constitutional Monarchy**
POPULATION: **8 million**   LANGUAGE: **Thai**
CURRENCY: **Baht**   ELECTRICITY: **220v/50Hz**
AIRLINES: **All major ones**   DEPARTURE TAX? **Baht 200**
NEED VISA/PASSPORT?   YES **x**   NO   PROOF OF CITIZENSHIP?   YES   NO **x**

YOUR FACILITY IS CLASSIFIED AS: SCUBA CENTER **x**   RESORT
BUSINESS HOURS: **07:30 - 21:30**
CERTIFYING AGENCIES: **PADI**
LOG BOOK REQUIRED?   YES **x**   NO
EQUIPMENT: SALES   RENTALS X ON TOURS ONLY   AIR FILLS
PRIMARY LINE OF EQUIPMENT: **US Divers, Seaquest, Cressi**
PHOTOGRAPHIC EQUIPMENT: SALES   RENTALS   LAB

CHARTER/DIVE BOAT AVAILABLE?   YES **x**   NO   DIVER CAPACITY **20**
COAST GUARD APPROVED?   YES **x**   NO   CAPTAIN LICENSED? YES **x**   NO
SHIP TO SHORE?   YES **x**   NO   LORAN? YES   NO **x**   RADAR?   YES   NO **x**
DIVE MASTER/INSTRUCTOR ABOARD? YES **x**   NO BOTH **x**

DIVING & SNORKELING: SALT **x**   FRESH
TYPE OF DIVING/SNORKELING IN AREA: WALL   BEACH   WRECK   REEF **x**   CAVE   ICE
DIVING/SNORKELING IN YOUR AREA IS BEST SUITED FOR: BEGINNER **x** INTERMEDIATE **x** ADVANCED **x**
BEST TIME OF YEAR FOR DIVING/SNORKELING:
TEMPERATURE: NOV-APRIL   **80-90F**   MAY-OCT: **80-90F**
VISIBILITY: DIVING: **30-80FT** SNORKELING: **70-80 FT**

PACKAGES AVAILABLE: DIVE **x**   DIVE STAY   SNORKEL   SNORKEL-STAY
ACCOMMODATIONS NEARBY: HOTEL **x**   MOTEL   HOME RENTALS
ACCOMMODATION RATES: EXPENSIVE **x**   MODERATE **x**   INEXPENSIVE **x**
RESTAURANTS NEARBY: EXPENSIVE **x**   MODERATE **x**   INEXPENSIVE **x**
YOUR AREA IS: REMOTE   QUIET WITH ACTIVITIES   LIVELY **x**
LOCAL ACTIVITY/NIGHTLIFE: **Open air markets, herbal saunas, Thai massage, night life, Thai**
                             kickboxing, karaoke bars
CAR NEEDED TO EXPLORE AREA? YES **x**   NO
DUTY FREE SHOPPING?   YES   NO **x Airport Only**

LOCAL EMERGENCY SERVICES   NEAREST HYPERBARIC TREATMENT FACILITY
COASTGUARD   **N/A**   AUTHORITY: **Royal Navy Hospital, Bangkok**
TELEPHONE: LOCATION
CALLSIGNS: TELEPHONE: **(2) 460-1105**

LOCAL DIVING DOCTOR: **Royal Navy Hospital, Thonburi**
NAME: **N/A**   **Recompression Dept., Hyperbaric Medicine**
LOCATION: **Somdeth/Phra, Pin, Kloa**
TELEPHONE:

One word of caution. We dived during the week of the full moon. The currents were very strong. Try to book at other times. Always dive with the guide if you are uncomfortable diving under these sea conditions!

Starting in July 1995 *M/V FANTASEA* began cruising to Western Sumatra until October when she resumes her normal Similian Islands/Burma Banks schedule.

FANTASEA DIVERS CO. LTD.
P.O. BOX 20, PATONG BEACH
PHUKET 83150, THAILAND
TEL: 66 76 340 088, 66 76 295 511
FAX: 66 76 340 309

Before returning home I spent three more days in Bangkok at the **Sukhothai Hotel. Please see the Honeymoon and Anniversary Section**

Many thanks to the Thailand Tourist Authority in New York City, especially Kim Vacher-Ta, for assisting us with extensive information on the country.

TURKEY

"A Tapestry"
Wendy Canning Church

Turkey is a beautiful country with a landmass of 780,000 square kilometers that is populated by some 60 million inhabitants. One might compare its six centuries of continuous but diverse culture to an antique tapestry. A bit threadbare yet finely woven by the influence of the Hittites, Frigians, Urartuans, Lydians, Ionians, Persians, Macedonians, Romans, Byzantines, Selijuks, and Ottomans into a work of art that touches every sense of ones being.

If you are fortunate enough to visit their remarkable country, your mind will be stretched by Turkish history and your eye delighted by its natural beauty and architectural heritage. Quite subtly a sense of a higher power will be awakened by the essence of spirituality that embraces the panoramic views of pine forests sloping to the seas and olive groves stretching as far as the eye can see. Indented coastlines and hidden inlets in a panoply of color where one hears families laugh while playing, swimming, or fishing, the grandeur of century old monuments, mosques, synagogues, and churches that call for pause. Her ancient cities, some in ruins, set the mind to roaming with their history and mythology.

The official language is Turkish, but it seems most of the population speaks fluent or passable English.

Tourism is a main source of revenue. I have yet to find friendlier people. From Istanbul down the coast to Kas there is a very low crime rate. **However one avoids travel to the southeastern part of the country.**

I was amazed at the freshness and variety of fruits and vegetables. A perfect meal begins with raki (a drink similar to anisette) mixed with water, which is referred to as "lions milk". This is taken with meze (an assortment of hot and cold hors d'oeuvres prepared with meats, fish, fowl, vegetables and rice) followed by the entree. The cuisine is similar to French or Chinese. Breakfast was a bit difficult to become accustomed to. The typical fare is olives, tomatoes, cucumbers, feta cheese, bread, hardboiled eggs and Turkish coffee!

The famous Turkish baths (public bathhouses or hamman) date back to medieval times. There are separate facilities for men and women. My first experience was at the Cirogen Palace Hotel and was wonderful! You enter a room and lay on a large heated

Children with Gypsy Wagon by Wendy Canning Church

stone. When you have perspired the required amount of time, the attendant takes something similar to a loofa and rubs your entire body. Intermittently the attendant throws cool water over you. This is followed by a shampoo. If you really want the complete treatment, **ask for the Sultans Delight! You will not be sorry.**

Turkey is a country with many natural resources: coal, iron, copper and bauxite. Tourists will find good buys on carpets, copper, silver, onyx jewelry, embroidery, suede and leather as well as native handicrafts.

How will you ever be the same after you have visited the shrine of the Virgin Mary which was her home where Christ, before he died, asked St. Paul to take her.? Or after you have climbed to the top of the summit where the enormous Temple of Artemis, the Golden Goddess, once stood (numbered amongst one of the seven wonders of the ancient world) or walked the marble streets in Etes? Or taken a moonlight swim in the Dardanelles as the phosphorescent waters danced about you, or tied a piece of cloth to the wishing tree at the Temple of Athena, Goddess of Love, or dived the world's oldest known intact Bronze Age shipwreck?

Embrace Turkey and its people and they will embrace you. They will lovingly share their tapestry of treasures with you. If you will let yourself, somehow in some magical spiritual way, you will become woven into and become a part of it.

The Turkish Department of Tourism (821 U.N. Plaza, New York, New York, 10017, Telephone 212-687-2194, Fax 212-599-7568) sent me reams of information.

I suggest you begin your visit in Istanbul once called Constantinople. At one time, Constantinople and Rome were the two greatest capitals of the Western World. Today, Istanbul is the commercial center of the Turkish Republic. Since 1910, there has been a constant migration from rural to urban. Towering office buildings, new five star hotels and couture boutiques live in harmony with small wooden structures once houses in the 18th century, are now small hotels.

The Grand Bazaar covers 5 acres. Under its roof are 4,000 small shops. Here it is a sin not to bargain. It is approached from a street filled with shops catering to lovers of haute couture. There are small, intimate native restaurants nested near those of 4 and 5 star caliber.

Commuters take ferries to and from work. Many of these go from the Asian to the

European side across the Bosphorus. In Istanbul Europe meets Asia either by ferry or the Galata bridge.

DAY ONE

Awakened early, we set out for the old city, visiting the **Hippodrome**. In Byzantine times, this was the center of cultural events and the chariot races. Columns and statues surrounded the edifice. Today, only three of these remain. **The obelisk of Theodosius, the bronze serpentine column and the column of Constantine.**

Next we visited the **Museum of Turkish and Islamic Art**, originally built as a private residence by Ibrahim Pasa. The museum houses some of the oldest carpets in Turkey: a collection of textiles, ceramics, metalwork, miniatures and calligraphy. Take notice of the architecture -the beautiful high ceilings for ventilation, enormous fireplaces for heating and cooking and the exquisite woodwork .

The Blue Mosque is famous for its delicate blue ceramic tiles. Next we visited Saint Sophia: church turned mosque turned museum takes one's breath away with the size of its interior and its magnificent dome.

Next we visited the spectacular **Topkapi Palace**. Built on one of the seven hills of Istanbul, this huge complex commands views of the Sea of Marmata, the Bosphorus and the Golden Horn. It was the seat of government for the Ottoman Empire for many centuries.

DAY TWO

The following morning started with a visit to the aromatic **Spice Bazaar,** where the smells of cinnamon, cloves and thyme rise from hundreds of colorful muslin bags at every storefront. We boarded our ferryboat for a relaxing cruise along the shores of the **Bosphorus**, the natural gateway that divides Asia and Europe. As you sit back and enjoy Turkish coffee or well-brewed tea from traditional small cups, summer palaces and palatial homes pass by .

The **Aya Sofa Pension** near Sultan Ahmet Square offers comfortable rooms in 19th Century mansions.

DAY THREE

On our third day we began our trip to **Canakkale**. It's best to have a car with air-conditioning. There is only a two-lane highway with a speed limit of 140 kilometers per hour (around 85 M.P.H.). Take your time.

About one half hour out of Istanbul the pace begins to slow and another Turkey shows its face. We passed well-tended farms with many varieties of fruits and vegetables, miles of sunflowers grown for the seeds, and small ranches with cattle, goats and donkeys.

The countryside opened up as we climbed into the mountains with breathtaking views of the sea and descended through acres and acres of olive groves. In the countryside they still lead a life of century old customs. You see very few women and the cafes are filled with men.

We began our scenic drive down to **Gallipoli**, the site of many WWI battles.We crossed the second strategic waterway, the **Dardanelles** and proceeded to **Troy** which has nine cities superimposed one upon another. Troy VI pertains to the famous Trojan War where the legendary heroes Agamemnon, Achilles, Ulysses and Nestor were on the Greek side and Priam, Hector and Paris on the Trojan side.

We checked into our **Hotel Tusan** in Canakkale which turned out to be a good choice -simple, comfortable, on the sea, with excellent cuisine.

DAY FOUR

On our journey to **Izmir**, we stopped by the hauntingly beautiful **Pergamon**. Among the impressive structures of this city, dating from 399 BC, we saw the **Altar of Zeus, Temple of Dionysus** and the **200,000 volume library** which was surpassed only by that found in Alexandria at the time. The **Asclepieum of Pergamon** was a famous health center where methods of treatment included blood transfusions, music therapy and meditation.

Leaving Pergamon , we settled at our hotel, the Hilton, in Izmir. It has all the modern amenities. The casinos for gambling where all attendants are dressed as cowboys and cowgirls, free drinks, cigarettes and American music.

DAY FIVE

We proceeded to the old section of Izmir called **Kadife Kale** which was built by Alexander the Great. Heading further south, we arrived at the ancient city of **Ephesus** and visited the **Basilica of St. John,** who came here to write his Gospel.

Southwest of the Basilica stands the **Isa Bey Mosque** and further in the same direction is the **Temple of Artemis,** one of the seven wonders. Ephesus was undoubtedly one of the most important cultural centers of the ancient world. **Impressive structures include the Library of Celsius, Temple of Hadrian, and the Theatre of Odeon.**

We also visited the Museum of Seljuk. **Close by is the House of the Virgin Mary where she is believed to have spent her last years.** On August 18, 1961, Pope John XXII proclaimed the House of the Virgin Mary at Ephesus to be sacred. You can take a phial of Holy Water from the Sacred Spring.

DAY SIX

We journeyed to **Priene,** which is a fine example of a city whose history dates back to the 10th century BC. **Highlights include the Temple of Athena Polias, the Ecclesiasterium and the Agora.**

We next visited **Miletus,** where the philosopher, **Thales,** was born. He coined the phrase "Know Thyself". We inspected the **Delphinion, Baths of Faustina** and the **Council Chamber.** Our last visit was to Didyma, which served as a religious sanctuary to the god Apollo. The oracular inscriptions date as far back as 600 BC. Among the highlights are the **Temple of Apollo** and the **Stadium.**

DAY SEVEN

We proceeded down the coast to the **Bodrum Peninsula,** where the Mediterranean meets the Aegean.

We drove through the steep mountain ranges and at intervals caught glimpses of the sea. On the outskirts of **Halinarnassu** (Bodrum)as it was called in the 4th century BC (the birthplace of Heredotus, where the tomb of King Mausolus was built and considered one of the seven wonders of the ancient world), we began to get a feeling for the town.

White washed sun bleached houses dot the lush green hillside where orange and tangerine orchids are grown. Boats in the harbor appear as miniature models bobbing up and down. On the other slope we caught a glimpse of new high rise apartment houses and villas. These were a sign to us that our little secret was not so secret. Bodrum has been found and has started to develop into a major tourist center.

Motif Dive Center was the facility I chose to dive with. They offer a dive stay package in a comfortable, simple hotel right on Gumbet Bay. I stayed at **The Antique Theatre Hotel** which was highly recommended to me.

The hotel is perched high on a hill with a panoramic view of Bodrum. Rooms are approached by sun washed stucco steps with bougainvillea running along the sides. My room was comfortable and large with adequate bath and air conditioning. The windows were shuttered against the mid-day sun. The view from my window was postcard perfect. I could take in all from my private little terrace, the guest rooms on separate levels, the turquoise pool, other beautiful small villas fitting snugly in the lush and colorful ledges and the calm bay with all matter of vessels from fishing boats to luxury yachts.

The remains of the 15th century medieval castle of St. Peter built by the Knights of Rhodes is now the Museum of Underwater Archeology. My feeling was more of being a guest in a large villa than that of a hotel. This view was mine for a week and each morning at sunrise I never missed opening my shutters so as not to miss its awakening.

The service and the food at the hotel are at the same time subdued and elegant. It is of five star quality. One can be assured of a comfortable stay in this wonderful little gem of understated elegance.

For more information contact: Antique Theatre Hotel, Kibris Sehitleri Caddesi, 243, Bodrum 48400, Turkey, Phone: 90-252-316-6053 or Fax: 90-252-316-0825.

THE SCUBA DIVING & SNORKELING

After unpacking I met with Catherine Woods, a delightful Canadian from **Motif Divers**, who became a good friend. She checked my certification card, logbook and medical form and told me about the center and our schedule for the next days.

Divers in Turkey are covered by insurance, which is rolled into the price of their dive. **No one is allowed to dive or get their tank filled without presenting a recognized certification card and logbook. They cannot dive without a guide.**

There is a recompression chamber in Bodrum. One of our guides who worked on the *Viking* during the week works at the chamber on weekends.

The *Viking* leaves in the morning for a day at sea and all divers and snorkelers are picked up and delivered to their respective hotels free of charge. The *Viking* is a 55-foot

Motif Dive Boat by Wendy Canning Church

replica of the traditional ancient ships. A woody built in 1986 and in mind's eye, more of a yacht than a dive boat. Simply, she is beautiful, comfortable and roomy, adequate for a day's outing or long charter.

These Bodrum built Gullets are exact replicas of the ancient ships except for the modern amenities of galley and head. They are built locally at one of three yards, which have been in existence for centuries. The ships have pointed bows, broad beams and rounded stern, making them especially comfortable. During the Gulf War when tourism was off they sold for $8,500.

The *Viking* leaves her berth at 10 A.M. and returns at 4:30. On the way, all certification cards, log books, and medical forms are checked. The site chosen to dive or snorkel depends on sea conditions. There are numerous sites on the *Viking's* roster.

After reaching the site, the vessel is moored, the dive plan given and divers and snorkelers from all corners of the globe suit up. The ratio of divers to guide is 4 to 1. There is a lead guide and a follow up guide.

One of the great features of the yacht is the ladder Zeki, who is part owner, designed. It is stationary, so a diver can enter the boat fully equipped (sans fins of course).

BLACK ISLAND

We moored that day off (Karaada) Black Island, which is about thirty minutes from Gumbet Bay. There were small swells but the visibility was 75 feet. Even though it was August and the temperature was 100 degrees Fahrenheit, and the water was 85 degrees

Fahrenheit, there were cold rushes of current at spots throughout the dive. This occurred on every dive. **At first I laughed when I saw the crew put on heavy wet suits, gloves and hoods. Believe me, after a day or two I didn't think it hilarious. I knew they were right!**

We entered the water and slowly descended to the reef. Leveling off at 60 feet, we began to investigate the territory. There was a giant grouper who is king of the reef. Different species of wrasse swam by. There were many caves and tunnels to investigate. Seals used to live in them, but the great number of divers drove them away.

Ascending slowly, we moved toward and made our way along the wall. I marveled at the beautiful sea fans. I had never seen these before. They are tube-like and these had the most beautiful bright pink flowers. When you touched the flower, it receded back inside.

On the bottom, we both spotted pieces of amphora. At closer range we could see the inscription on the inside. It looked as if these were all parts of larger vessels. What a wonder to see and feel an object of art and beauty thousands of years old.

There were sea urchins, octopus, moray eels and starfish. The wall was a blaze of orange coral in different hues. Bottom time up, we ascended, made a safety stop and reboarded.

Equipment is stowed aft so that divers and snorkelers have plenty of room. They can be shaded in the salon or go topside for sun.

GUNEY UCU

After lunch the swells increased, so we pulled anchor and sailed for a small, secluded cove. The cove was spectacular. Giant boulders rose from the sea to lush green hillsides, which surround a lovely little beach with a small cove at either end. Good for exploring before our second dive.

Guney Ucu, our second site, was on the opposite side of Black Island. Average visibility was 80 feet. We dropped down to a grassy area and swimming further on came to a sandy bottom and the reef, resplendent in all colors of sponges and hard and soft coral. We made our way to the wall, which was covered in peacock weed.

Small tunnels and caves turned out to be hiding places for huge sea urchins. Small multicolored reef fish, wrasse and bleeny swam by. A bright green moray eel pushed out, seemed bored, and tucked its head back in. On this dive we came across beautiful bright orange sea fans and a small ray darted by.

LITTLE REEF

The second day we sailed to **Little Reef** right off the Bay of Gumbet. This is a deep dive at 90 feet maximum. The interesting feature of the dive was the topography. The reef had a wall all around it like a ledge. The Aussies call it a Bombie.

The water was quite cold at this depth. We did see large groupers, crayfish, played with an octopus at the end of the dive and then slowly ascended.

GORECIK ISLAND

The current and swells picked up, so we pulled anchor and headed for **Gorecik Island. These waters were calm and crystal clear, good for both divers and snorkelers.**

This is the site of many wrecks. Greek galleons and Turkish merchant ships would come around the corner from the other side of the island not knowing about the treacherous reef—their ships would be broken like match sticks.

One can also see the signs of lava which flowed into the sea. The topography was certainly of great interest. Huge boulders surrounded volcanic rock. There were huge black sponges, hollow in the middle with broken shells and pebbles inside. We spotted many pieces of amphora, surely the last remnants of these unfortunate ships meeting their end on the reefs.

This is a good site for beginners and snorkelers and a good place for a night dive. The seas are calm which makes for stable anchorage.

KAGAKGI KOUV

On our third day our routine changed. It was Monday. It seems every Monday in the summer a group of Scandinavians books resort courses. We took two boats as we had 25 people for the resort course and three scuba divers.

We returned to Black Island and dove at Kagakgi Kouv. Because we had so many resort course divers and because Zeki had assessed our level of diving , he suggested the certified divers go off on our own.

There were slight swells but no current and we were moored in a very shallow protected cove. The three of us decided to swim out to a further depth and descend to 80 feet to check out the wall. Despite the slight swells, once under water we had good visibility.

There were few fish but the topography once again was quite interesting. We descended to a sandy bottom laden with orange starfish and swam along coming to a nice wall with hundreds of little ledges. To our surprise, the more we looked, the more little critters we found hiding in them, i.e., lots of shrimp. Sea fans covered the walls and they were in varying shades of pink and orange. A baby octopus came out to play.

To Zeki and his crew, I must give heartfelt congratulations. They spent at least 15 to 30 minutes with each person. There was not one soul who returned not turned on to diving. Motif Centers is a credit to the dive industry!

After lunch, the three of us set off again. This time we investigated the other side of the inlet. To our surprise we found the same kind of wall and ledges with again an assortment of critters. We took lots of time just looking and showing each other what we had found. As we swam along we saw a stonefish, scorpion fish and another eel.

Motif's motto is "Our Promise Safety Enjoyment Service". All of this is true of them. If I may, I would like to add one, "New Friendships".

Sharing a day's journey with people of another culture, living in other parts of the world and speaking another language and being able to not just communicate in a basic way but to understand and share a common philosophy. It makes you realize things are different, people aren't.

YACHT DIVE CHARTERS

For a dive charter you may have a guide. A captain, cook and seaman aboard can be arranged. A compressor and tanks are supplied along with weight belts. You supply your own equipment. You can bring your food or send a list and they will purchase it and bill you. The usual charters are one week and go from Bodrum to Dates, Gokova Bay, stopping at bays along the way and spots when there is nightlife and one can dine off the boat. For more information, contact:E-mail info@aquax.com

DAY ELEVEN

We left Bodrum and continued down the Southwest coast towards the small town of **Kas** (pronounced Kash). It seemed the deeper we drove into the countryside, the more modern architecture faded away.

Houses constructed in the same centuries old fashion were visible throughout our journey. Donkeys were used by many to transport themselves and goods from village to village. The fields were tilled and plowed using cattle. The preponderance of women were still dressed in black from head to toe, only their eyes were visible.

The countryside is exceedingly lovely with forested hillsides harboring remote villages awash in the colors of nature. All this interspersed by ancient ruins.

We arrived in the small town of Kas known in ancient times as Antiphillos, meaning "across from Phellos". Along this ancient route, the large Lycian settlements were connected after the Republic was founded in 400 BC. Antiphillos was renamed Kas, meaning the arch of the eyebrow, because of its position to the Assas mountains reaching out beyond the town in the shape of an arch.

The remains of the Lycian culture can today be seen in the form of ruins in sarcophagi, rock tombs, cisterns, ancient inscriptions and an open-air theatre.

The **Aqua Park Hotel** had been highly recommended to us and again we chose wisely! Set out of town, high in the hills leading down to the sea, the Aqua Park is a wonderful complex of accommodations. Here you can indulge in the sun and serenity and be only 5 km away from all the activities of town. The hotel runs a complimentary shuttle bus to Kas.

The positioning of the Hotel is such that it lies on a sloping area and one can partake of breathtaking views of not only the Mediterranean, but other Turkish and Greek islands, which lie just off the shore.

I chose one of the 31 apartment rooms, which are large and spacious, fully air-conditioned, with well equipped kitchen, terrace with sea view, satellite TV and direct dial telephone.

I must confess if one were not a scuba diver they would probably spend most of their vacation at the hotel (with side trips into town) for the Aqua Park Hotel is a complete resort. It has a 400 sq. foot swimming pool, children's pool, waterfall, pool bar, barbeque beach bar, disco, mini market, fitness room, billiards, game room, table tennis, and a 103m waterslide.

Although I only had breakfast there, I found the food to be excellent. Every morning there was a bountiful buffet with a delicious variety of foods. The service was excellent and executed with warmth and charm.

Apartments have daily maid service. There are also 39 standard rooms bringing the hotel units to 70 which is a very manageable number.

The manager, Abdullah Bayrak, is seen throughout the hotel, making sure that all is in tiptop shape for his guests.

It was lovely to see so many families vacationing there from all over the world. They seemed to delight in the sea and the activities catering to every age. **Aqua Park would be my choice on a return visit! For more information contact: Aqua Park Hotels, Andifi Mah - Bahce No. 30/A, Kas – Antalya, Turkey, Phone: (9-3226) 1908-1909, Fax: (9-3226) 1906-1905.**

THE DIVING AND SNORKELING

I dove with Barrakuda Club. The owner, Augur Ergo, is a CMAS, two star instructor. Their dive boats go out at 9:30, 12, 3 and 4:30. Each trip offers a one-tank dive.

We met at 9:30 at the dock in Kas the next morning aboard one of the two boats, the *Barrakuda,* which Augur and his wife, Gabrielle, operate. The craft is well suited for diving. She is 16 meters long, 5 wide with a 210 horsepower engine. She can carry a maximum of 25 divers at a good clip to the more than 15 dive and snorkeling sites offered along the coast or near one of the islands lying offshore. She has ample space in the stern for both equipment and divers who are shaded by a permanent overhead. There is a sunroof atop.

All levels of divers are welcomed on each trip and of course snorkelers. A diver must present an internationally recognized certification card, log book and fill out a medical form. If one's malady would prevent them from diving, they must have a doctor's report (not more than 2 years old) that says they are in condition to dive.

Safety is an important factor with this outfit. Everyone goes through a check out. A diver is asked to ascend to 8 meters remove mask , clear it, take the regulator out of their mouth and practice buddy breathing. If you pass muster, you will be buddied up and can dive with the group.

Unbeknownst to you, while on your first dive you are also being evaluated so that if you prove to be an experienced diver on the second day you will be buddied up with another diver of your experience and you both can dive without the group.

I commend them for their high safety standards. We all should remember that when these kinds of safety regulations are practiced, they are practiced not only for our good but for others as well. The vessel is coast guard approved, has a radio, loran, and carries a backboard, first aid kits, oxygen supply and a blood pressure monitor aboard.

FLYING FISH II

Our dive and snorkel site that morning was the Flying Fish II, about 1/2 hour from the marina. Augur gave the dive plan. It was a reef dive with a nice wall further out.

We headed toward the reef, and then descended to a maximum of 30 meters (90 ft.). The seas were calm with average visibility of 90 feet. As Augur and I descended, we noticed a slight current. It carried us over to the reef where we investigated blue snails (without shells), lobsters and two moray eels.

The current carried us along to the wall, which was really beautiful, bedecked in all colors of anemones. A special highlight of the dive was broken amphora, which we both lovingly picked up. To our elation, its parts fit together perfectly. We placed them back very gingerly! As we returned to the boat, a school of larger grouper swam by leading our way.

Aboard, delicious hot apple tea (a favorite drink in Turkey) was ready for us. This was welcomed, for, the waters can be cold in Turkey even in August.

All their equipment is in good condition and they take great pride in their operation. A dive/stay package can be also arranged. I would book an apartment at the Aqua Park, take advantage of their shuttle to Kas, and dive with Barrakuda. The town is bustling both day and night and it's great to have the serenity of Aqua Park to return to.

AREAS OF INTEREST IN KAS

Do take some time and investigate the little town. If you plan to cook, there is an open-air market once a week with all kinds of food available. They also sell local handicrafts and practical goods. It's similar to a flea market. I marveled at the beautiful jewelry more valued for its workmanship than gems. The cost was embarrassingly little. If you leave Turkey without buying a carpet, you will forever regret it.

There are also little grocery shops, small bakeries and little "delis". There are innumerable restaurants serving delicious cuisine.

Many thanks to the Director of Tourism, Ferhat Moilcan for his help and that of his staff. The office in the middle of Kas is small, but they offer a wealth of information both written and oral.

Temple of Apollo, Wishing Tree, by Wendy Canning Church

About an hour and a half away in Entail is one of the most incredible restaurants I have ever been to. The Cigar Restaurant has a natural spring flowing into a great round basin in the middle of their outdoor dining room. Small tables with candlelight glowing were placed around it, and diners were eating the most fantastic smelling foods from vessels that had little fires under them.

Waiters would fetch fresh water for their tables from the spring surrounded by giant trees and beautiful vegetation. The musical sound from the springs and the beauty of

SCUBA AND SNORKELING FACILITIES QUESTIONNAIRE

NAME   **Zeki Arslan - Motif Diving Center**
ADDRESS   **Neyzen Tevfik Cad. no: 80**
              Bodrum, Turkey
CONTACT   **Zeki Arslan**
TITLE   **Owner**
TELEPHONE   **614-62997**   Home; Work: **614-66252**   FAX **614-63522**

CAPITAL: **Ankara**   GOVERNMENT: **Democratic**
POPULATION: **70 million**   LANGUAGE: **Turkish**
CURRENCY: **Turkish Lira**   ELECTRICITY: **220v**
AIRLINES: **Delta**   DEPARTURE TAX?
NEED VISA/PASSPORT?   YES **x**   NO   PROOF OF CITIZENSHIP?   YES **x**   NO

YOUR FACILITY IS CLASSIFIED AS: SCUBA CENTER **x**   RESORT
BUSINESS HOURS: **10:00 a.m. - 5:00 p.m.**
CERTIFYING AGENCIES: **PADI, CMAS**
LOG BOOK REQUIRED?   YES **x**   NO
EQUIPMENT: SALES   RENTALS **x**   AIR FILLS **x**
PRIMARY LINE OF EQUIPMENT: **Scubapro, Cressi-sub, Spiral**
PHOTOGRAPHIC EQUIPMENT: SALES   RENTALS   LAB

CHARTER/DIVE BOAT AVAILABLE?   YES **x**   NO   DIVER CAPACITY   **25**
COAST GUARD APPROVED?   YES **x**   NO   CAPTAIN LICENSED?   YES **x**   NO
SHIP TO SHORE? YES **x**   NO   LORAN   YES   NO   RADAR?   YES   NO
DIVE MASTER/INSTRUCTOR ABOARD?   YES **x**   NO   BOTH **x**

DIVING & SNORKELING: SALT **x**   FRESH
TYPE OF DIVING/SNORKELING IN AREA: WALL **x**   BEACH   WRECK   REEF **x**   CAVE **x**   ICE
DIVING/SNORKELING IN YOUR AREA IS BEST SUITED FOR: BEGINNER   INTERMEDIATE   ADVANCED
BEST TIME OF YEAR FOR DIVING/SNORKELING: **May - October**
TEMPERATURE: **NOV-APRIL:**   **80 F**   **MAY-OCT:**   **100 F**
VISIBILITY: **DIVING:**   **100 FT**   **SNORKELING: 50 FT**

PACKAGES AVAILABLE: DIVE   DIVE STAY **x**   SNORKEL   SNORKEL-STAY
ACCOMMODATIONS NEARBY: HOTEL **x**   MOTEL   HOME RENTALS
ACCOMMODATION RATES: EXPENSIVE **x**   MODERATE **x**   INEXPENSIVE
RESTAURANTS NEARBY: EXPENSIVE **x**   MODERATE **x**   INEXPENSIVE **x**
YOUR AREA IS: REMOTE   QUIET WITH ACTIVITIES   LIVELY **x**
LOCAL ACTIVITY/NIGHTLIFE: **Wide variety**
CAR NEEDED TO EXPLORE AREA?   YES **x**   NO
DUTY FREE SHOPPING?   YES **x**   NO

LOCAL EMERGENCY SERVICES   NEAREST HYPERBARIC TREATMENT FACILITY
COASTGUARD: AUTHORITY: **Ali Erkal**
TELEPHONE: **VHF**   LOCATION: **Bodrum**
CALLSIGNS: **Channel 16**   TELEPHONE: **614-61143/62491 F: 614-62492**

LOCAL DIVING DOCTOR:
NAME: **Sezgin Gokmen**
LOCATION: **Bodrum**
TELEPHONE: **614-62385**

the scene is something I shall never forget. For more information contact: Cigar Restaurant, Mustafa Kay, Ulupinar-Kemer-Antalya, Tel: 9-(3135) 7208 Fax: 7209.

Perhaps now you have some idea why I left Turkey with the feeling it had been one of my best trips. I also had the pleasure of staying at The Ciragan Palace in Istanbul, for more information please see the Honeymoon and Anniversary Section.

UNITED KINGDOM

Dover England
The Largest Cast-Bronze Weapon Arm Treasure Site in Europe
"300 Years Old and it is Underwater"

In 1976, members of the Dover BSAC (British Sub Aqua Club) were diving about a mile off-shore east of Dover Harbour at a depth of 10 meters (30 ft), when they came across what appeared to be a number of implements and tools lying scattered on the seabed. Unsure of what exactly they had stumbled across, the divers gathered a couple of samples and marked the site. With a mixture of curiosity and excitement, they promptly presented the items to the local museum for answers. Perhaps they had stumbled across a long lost bounty.

The museum curator, after much deliberation, tentatively identified the items as weaponry and possibly 3000-year-old cast-bronze -a rare and unusual find. He was clearly excited and following his recommendation, it was decided that further consultation was required from the experts. The artifacts were transported, under a heavy insurance policy, to the British Maritime Museum in Greenwich, London. Chief Diving Officer, Dr. Martin Dean of the Underwater Archeological Division, quickly confirmed the authenticity of the find as very old cast-bronze weaponry.

The find generated further excitement and interest among the professional ranks, resulting in two major decisions. First, the site was designated a protected underwater archeological site of great historical value (permission was required by anyone to dive the site further). Second, a major exploratory expedition, to be conducted by professional underwater archeological divers of the Maritime Museum, was to be launched.

THE EXPLORATION AND SALVAGE OF 3000 YEAR OLD CAST-BRONZE ARTIFACTS

As members of the Dover BSAC, we were permitted to volunteer to assist in the project since we discovered the site, and extra divers were required. The first expedition was planned for the month of August in 1980.

A 10,000 square meter area was to be explored. A grid system was laid on the seabed divided into 50 square meter squares. Two-meter wide corridors searched each square. The project had two main objectives: to assess the viability of the site for further exploration according to the number and range of artifacts discovered, and to produce a "topographical map" outlining the perimeters of the site.

Was there any evidence of wreckage and from where could the artifacts have originated? These were the questions for which answers were sought. Mapping was to be conducted by hand drawn visual inspection, and the search of artifacts was to be assisted by use of underwater metal detectors. As a young lad at the time, I felt very lucky and privileged to be able to participate in such an adventurous expedition. I can still recall the combination of nervousness, excitement and trepidation when I entered the water for the first time in search of treasure.

The search for artifacts was hampered by the discovery of large quantities of shrapnel debris and various forms of ammunition, both products of the Second World War, where Dover featured as a major strategic port. At its most dangerous extreme we even came across a live, unexploded bomb of considerable size. The British Royal Navy later dealt with it. Also a large number of musket and cannonballs were regularly cropping up. Each of these items, even in its smallest form, resulted in a positive contact on the metal detectors and much time was consumed digging up war debris.

Every time a genuine find was made, however, its position and location were precisely recorded and the find was tagged, photographed and then brought to the surface. Items such as knife blades, dirks, handles and hilts, axe heads, and even crude broken pins and sewing needles were discovered in quantity. Over 50 individual artifacts were recovered. An impressive amount already equaling in quantity to other large cast-bronze weaponry finds. It was very unusual to find so many items on one site.

The success of the initial exploration was tremendous, resulting in a full five-year expedition plan, where the British Maritime Museum Divers would conduct one month to six weeks of exploration and salvage every year.

Speculation began as to how the artifacts came to Dover and what the reason was behind their final resting place being the ocean floor. 3000 years ago, the British did not possess the technology to produce cast-bronze. Tracking the origin of the artifacts was narrowed down to a couple of locations in Europe. France and Italy, I believe. But had the weaponry been stored as a stockpile hidden along the famous White Cliffs of Dover and the cliffs since receded, or had there been an ancient vessel wrecked in a storm and sunk in the murky depths? No evidence of any wreckage whatsoever had been discovered in the first year of our exploration, and it appeared as if no attempt at salvage had previously been made, at any time, due to the nature in which the artifacts were haphazardly around the sea floor.

I had the good fortune to participate in 3 of the 5 expeditions and witnessed the recovery of over 400 individual items. **Words cannot describe the sense of awe and amazement one experiences upon discovering an artifact buried several feet in the sand that hasn't been touched or seen by another human for 3000 years** - it is a thrill and a rush. Sometimes you would find one item, other times a hoard of 5 or 6 buried together. I lucked out on one occasion when I discovered 11 knife blades, one stacked on top of the other, in only a foot of sand. It was as though they were put there only yesterday. **The largest hoard discovered was 17 different items, the single largest hoard ever made anywhere, worldwide!**

The weather could often make conditions quite demanding at times, but even in the poorest conditions, with near zero visibility, making a discovery made it worth while.

All of the artifacts recovered required a lengthy chemical treatment, cleaning and restoration process. After several years, a major permanent archeological exhibit was established in the British Maritime Museum, where the objects can be viewed. The mystery of how the artifacts ended up where they did was solved by studying the positions of all the finds. A map outlining all of the discoveries was produced.

As far as the theory of the cliffs receding, it was decided after further study that it would not have been possible for the cliffs to have receded so far back in such a short time. The site is not excavated and it is still marked as an area of historical value. **Only members of the Dover Sub Aqua Club are permitted to dive and take people diving on the site.**

Only the White Cliffs of Dover lay witness to the weapons final demise and continue to preside over one of the true hidden and lesser-known underwater wonders of the world. Every now and then, the site still yields a very old, rare and valuable artifact of genuine historical importance. Additionally, since **Dover was a port of major strategic value during the war, there are many other underwater treasures to explore - Submarines, U-boats, freighters, destroyers, Merchant Marine and Coast Guard vessels, and even the odd Spitfire and German war plane.** The ocean floor is simply littered with ammunition from pitched battles at sea, both on and above the water. **The most discerning of divers will find many underwater wonders.** Happy diving.

As for the historical importance of the discovery, the find may have helped contribute in understanding the trade route of ancient mariners who sailed the oceans, and how different natures and cultures had developed relationships and liaisons previously unknown or unexplained. A full account of the sites discovery and contribution into mapping out history can be rediscovered at the British Maritime Museum in Greenwich, London, where one of the most important and largest records of world maritime history is recorded.

BRITISH TOURIST OFFICE
551 FIFTH AVENUE ,SUITE 1501
NEW YORK , NY 10017
TEL 212 986 2266

SCOTLAND

Stephen John Dye

Diving in Scotland can be cold and hazardous and the ill-prepared diver could quickly find him/herself in trouble. Water temperature changes from winter to summer are in the range of 5C to 15C, give or take a few degrees. Subsequently air temperatures can range from below freezing in winter to 60C - 70C in summer.

Winter diving presents the stiffest challenge and I would strongly recommend the following equipment: Dry suit with direct feed, thick neoprene gloves, a good hood, stabilizer/ABLJ with emergency air supply, S.M.B. (surface marker buoy to mark position of divers), compass, depth gauge, watch, and torch.

In summer many divers prefer a wet suit or semi-dry suit, although I much prefer to wear my dry suit with less undergarments. I would also recommend wearing a hood all year round although gloves may not be necessary.

The sea state can change quickly from calm to rough so getting a weather forecast before setting out is essential.

Divers should always indicate their position by attaching S.M.B. lines to themselves, which lets the dive boat not only know the divers' position but also be able to warn other approaching boats. The dive boat should have a radio on board (VHF is sufficient) and the Coast Guard should be informed of any diving which will take place and the location. H.M.S. Coast Guard should be contacted by VHF radio on channel 16 or by dialing 999 in an emergency.

THE WEST COAST

The visibility depends on the time of year and the sea state. **The best visibility is found on the west coast** and can be anything up to 30m, the visibility on the east coast tends to be about half that.

On the east the diver finds himself in the North Sea which can be cold and treacherous and lies on the continental shelf. The west faces onto the Atlantic Ocean and is affected by the warmer water of the North Atlantic Drift.

OBAN

Oban, which is situated on the west coast of Scotland, is a dive site I have been visiting for the past five years. It as the diving 'Mecca' of Scotland, everything is here: dive sites to suit all levels of diver, equipment hire, boat hire, plus plenty of accommodation and public houses to provide comforts.

On several of our expeditions there we have stayed at the Oban Divers campsite. The accommodations we chose could be best described as a bunkhouse, bunk beds three high with a cooker, heater and sink. Showers are next door in the washroom (be pre-

The Summer Isles by Stephen John Dye

pared to queue). It sounds basic, but for only a few pounds per night it is good value and is an ideal 'divers residence'. No need to worry about getting carpets dirty, or messing up a nice kitchen while preparing the 'catch' for dinner.

S.S. BREDA

A popular dive in Oban is on the wreck of the **SS Breda**. This is a wreck of a British convoy vessel, which was bombed in World War II and is very well preserved.

It lies upright and pretty much intact on the seabed, which is at the 30m mark, although a diver on the deck would be nearer the 20m mark, which would suit the experienced diver.

On one particular visit to the **S.S. Breda** we decided to launch our RIB from a beach close by (the wreck is not far offshore), in search of the wreck which we found using transits. Upon fixing our position we dropped a short line on which we would descend and ascend for safety. On reaching the seabed we saw we were close to the stern. Swimming along the deck level the fish life was excellent, shoals of cod and pollock taking of the food the wreck provides. Sitting perfectly intact on the deck about midship is a 4-ton lorry, although the tires are a bit flat. On returning across the sandy seabed to the shoreline I came across a cuttlefish, which when startled by my approach, changed color instantly and shot off at an angle, brilliant to see. Unfortunately, as we had touched 30m our no-stop time was twenty minutes and our dive was over all too soon, but still very rewarding.

MAIDEN ISLAND

Another excellent dive close by Oban is a drift dive round Maiden Island, which is a relatively small rock island inhabited only by seabirds and seals.

The particular dive provides me with my favorite underwater pursuit, diving for scallops. It presents a challenge, a purpose for the dive, and the reward of the highly prized shellfish, which is delicious. Again this would suit the more experienced diver and is reached by boat, although is only a very short distance offshore.

Jimmy (my buddy) and I rolled over the side of the inflatable and descended down the sloping rocky face. On making bottom, we swam a short distance away from the rock face and onto the sandy bottom, which is the home of the scallop. Each armed with a net bag; we set off in pursuit, which we soon found to be successful by indented half-moon crescents in the sand, which gave their position away.

While drifting along we also encountered a large edible crab which unfortunately only had one claw and so we let it be. Further on we drifted past an anglerfish, the first one I

294

had seen underwater and was great to see. As the deepest we reached was 18m we had plenty no stop time and we surfaced after forty minutes with a haul of about twenty largish scallops between us.

Oban also provides plenty of good dives for the novice with good visibility and interesting marine life.

GAVANNACK

One particular site is at Gavannack Beach where divers can enter the water from the beach and swim through the kelp forests full of life and rocky coastline in depths around the 9m mark.

The coastline on the west is very different to the east; it is generally very broken and rugged with many islands dotted along its coast (many of these islands cater to the diver and offer excellent diving sites).

There are also many beautiful beaches with fantastic scenery along its shore. Hill walking, scenic coach tours, sailing and windsurfing are all pursuits available to the holiday visitor.

ACCOMMODATIONS

Accommodations range from expensive hotels to bed and breakfasts to campsites for pitching tents. Hotel prices tend to range from fifty pounds up, bed and breakfasts from fifteen to twenty pounds and campsites from a few pounds per night. Prices and availability obviously depend on the season, summer being the busiest (May-August) although Easter (April) and Christmas and New Years are very popular times for people to get away.

THE EAST COAST

The East Coast of Scotland provides good dive sites, many which are rarely, if ever, dived. Unfortunately the east has not been developed for the scuba diver. There are, however, boat skippers who will charter their boats to divers, and regularly do so. Equipment hire is not available, (although in the future this may not be the case) but air is available from certain sources (dive shops and commercial outlets). For this reason the east would suit divers who have the necessary equipment.

The water along the east coast is the North Sea, which is known for its cold and hostile waters.

Lying on the Continental Shelf the depth increases very gradually from the shore (9 meters is about as deep as the diver would expect to find going from the shore). Tides can be quite strong and shore dives should be planned to coincide with the incoming tides around hightide/slack water for safety. Further offshore, however, greater depths are available to the diver (the North Sea is several hundred meters deep).

Before diving it is always a good idea to contact the local Coast Guard station for a weather report and to inform them of your intentions.

Charter a boat to **May Island/Bass Rock**. No equipment is for sale or hire. Be sure a knowledgeable skipper/ex-diver knows the dive sites and is experienced with divers accompanies you. Both these sites are only for experienced divers.

Dive sites that I have first hand knowledge and experience of are: Crail (a shore dive which suits novices, but still a very interesting dive), Bass Rock and May Isle, both of which lie offshore and would suit the experienced diver.

MAY ISLE AND BASS ROCK

May Isle lies about 6 miles out from the Firth of Forth and Bass Rock lies to the south of the island. Both are uninhabited and offer wonderful sanctuaries to both seabirds and seals. Visitors landing must keep to pathways and respect birds nesting and not get too close. The islands are very impressive sites from a small boat and stand very high with rocky faces. **Many boats offer charter trips for either people wishing to visit the islands and study the wildlife or for divers.** My investigation has shown that although many boats are available I have not come across any skippers who hire equipment, but are experienced in taking divers and have a good knowledge of the sites.

Scattered around the rocky islands are the remains of many wrecks but, as is the case on most of the east, they are very broken and scattered.

Close into the island are caves, drop-offs and rocky reefs leading to sandy bottoms. Depths range to roughly 70m (210 ft). **Seals and other forms of marine life can be studied at close quarters and are great attractions.**

Summer would be the ideal time to visit these sites as the seas are warmer, air temperatures higher, and sea conditions calmer. The winter can be very cold and rough seas make venturing out very dangerous.

CRAIL

The date was February 2nd, the air temperature was slightly above freezing and we had recorded the sea temperature at 3.6 degrees centigrade. We had just arrived at Crail on the Fife coast for our first dive of the year. We planned to take advantage of the calm seas resulting from two weeks of windless westerly weather. The visibility was good; light green and dark patches indicating the varying bottom conditions.

Suited up we made our way to the water's edge and fitted our fins, masks, regulators in place and submerged heads into the icy water. The first couple of minutes are the worst, then numbness takes over and comfort is felt, the hard part of the dive over.

Swimming out on an easterly compass bearing for approximately twenty minutes, a compass is a very useful tool here for navigation. No need to surface for direction, also poor surface conditions may exist. On our way out we encountered little fish life as they move further offshore in winter, which is in total contrast to summer when wrasse, lobsters, edible crabs, codling, flatfish, starfish and sea urchins are just a few of the species which may be encountered, although plenty of starfish and sea urchins and a sea lemon over areas of kelp forests, sandy bottom and rock outcrops were viewed. After swimming far enough out (the cold helped us decide!) we turned around 180 degrees and swam westwards back in.

On surfacing, inflating our jackets; spat out the regulators and remarked to each other how good the visibility was with numb mouths. At this point Stuart realized his fingers were too numb to remove his fins for the walk ashore, even though he was wearing neoprene gloves (another essential). Luckily my gloves had proved more effective and I was able to help him (for a small fee!).

Once out of our dry suits we brought ourselves back to life with a hot cup of coffee, which Stuart had brought along (yet another essential piece of equipment). Looking back, the challenge of winter

Crail by Stephen John Dye

diving in Scotland was well worth the effort of all the preparation, planning and the cold water.

Apart from diving there are plenty of other attractions for the visitor along this part of the coast. There are rages of magnificent beaches to walk along. One beach I particularly like is Tentsmuir. This beach is home to a large gray seal colony, which are not too shy. **Further north to Tentsmuir is Dundee and to the south is St. Andrews, the world famous home to golf, historic ruins, beautiful beaches and golf courses.** There is also very good accommodation and restaurants in and around St. Andrews.

NORTH WEST SCOTLAND- THE SUMMER ISLES

Winter Diving by Stephen John Dye

The Summer Isles of Northwest Scotland are particularly beautiful. This is a very remote, largely uninhabited and an unspoiled part of the world. It is diveable year-round because of the shelter offered by the isles. The water gets a bit cool in the winter (5 degrees C). It is not commercialized with only one-charter boat offering dive charters.

The remote Summer Isles are beautiful and unspoiled both above and below the water in Scotland. **This part of the country is excellent for wrecks.**

In April, I decided to expand my diving horizons and visited the Summer Isles, which lie about 25 miles from Ullapool at the end of a single-track road.

The road leading to the Summer Isles takes you through a very beautiful part of Scotland. There are mountains galore on either side of the road as well as hill lochs (be prepared to drive slowly as it may be necessary to chase sheep away). As you wind your way slowly around the road you are eventually met by a spectacular view of the Summer Isles. The largest is Tannera More which is not far from shore.

The islands name conjures up pictures of sunkissed days (which can be true in summer), but in April it was very different. We kitted up for the first dive in the shelter of a small island in falling snow. Heavy-duty diving equipment is needed here- drysuits, gloves and hoods.

The wreck of the **M.V. Heron** was sitting in about 10 meters of water below, and glancing over the side I could see the bottom with its patches of white sand between the rocks. The dive provided plenty of marine life to study and the water was very clear.

I returned to dive the Summer Isles again in August with the specific intention of wreck diving. The contrast between the two visits could not have been greater (from snow and freezing temperatures to sun and shorts). It was a different place altogether.

Our first dive was on the wreck of the *Fairweather*, a ship approximately 150 feet in length and more or less intact. She sits on the seabed around 30 meters. The mast of the ship is still intact and encrusted with anemones with fish curling around it- a wonderful sight.

The next day we decided to dive a wreck that had just been located. The name of the wreck was not known. The problem was that she was lying on the seabed at 40 meters, which would not give us much bottom time, but we were very keen so we went ahead with it. Upon arrival at the wreck, it was noticeable that not much sea life was present due to the depth. The wreck was very much intact. We saw that the mast had been broken and was lying at a right angle to the wreck. **We followed it out and downwards and noticed something on the sand. It was the ships bell still attached to its ornate hanger and bearing the name of the ship –** *Innisjurra and the date 1913.*

The history of the wreck has been difficult to research. An older local man remembers the sinking of a coastal barge during World War II that was carrying German prisoners over to help build a harbour pier. Mystery solved?

Atlantic Diving Service is the only dive charter that I know of around the Summer Isles. They have a very good skipper/diver who is friendly and honest. As with most

SCUBA AND SNORKELING FACILITIES QUESTIONNAIRE

NAME   **Oban Divers, Ltd.**
ADDRESS   **Cologin Homes, Lerags by Oban**
           Argyll, Scotland, UK
CONTACT   **Henry Woodman**
TELEPHONE **0631-64501**   FAX   TELEX

CAPITOL: GOVERNMENT:
POPULATION: LANGUAGE:
CURRENCY: ELECTRICITY:
AIRLINES: DEPARTURE TAX?
NEED VISA/PASSPORT?   YES   NO   PROOF OF CITIZENSHIP?   YES   NO

YOUR FACILITY IS CLASSIFIED AS: SCUBA CENTER x   RESORT
BUSINESS HOURS: **Varies**
CERTIFYING AGENCIES: **BSAC**
LOG BOOK REQUIRED?   YES x   NO
EQUIPMENT: SALES x   RENTALS x   AIR FILLS x
PRIMARY LINE OF EQUIPMENT: SCUBA
PHOTOGRAPHIC EQUIPMENT: SALES   RENTALS   LAB

CHARTER/DIVE BOAT AVAILABLE?   YES x   NO   DIVER CAPACITY
COAST GUARD APPROVED?   YES x   NO   CAPTAIN LICENSED? YES x   NO
SHIP TO SHORE?   YES   NO x LORAN? YES NO x   RADAR?   YES   NO x
DIVE MASTER/INSTRUCTOR ABOARD? YES x   NO   BOTH

DIVING & SNORKELING: SALT x   FRESH
TYPE OF DIVING/SNORKELING IN AREA: WALL x   BEACH x   WRECK x   REEF   CAVE   ICE
DIVING/SNORKELING IN YOUR AREA IS BEST SUITED FOR: BEGINNER x INTERMEDIATE x ADVANCED x
BEST TIME OF YEAR FOR DIVING/SNORKELING: **Summer**
TEMPERATURE: NOV-APRIL   **30-50F**   MAY-OCT: **50-60F**
VISIBILITY: DIVING: **100FT**   SNORKELING: FT

PACKAGES AVAILABLE: DIVE x   DIVE STAY x   SNORKEL   SNORKEL-STAY
ACCOMMODATIONS NEARBY: HOTEL x   MOTEL x B&B'S x   HOME RENTALS x
ACCOMMODATION RATES: EXPENSIVE x MODERATE x   INEXPENSIVE x
RESTAURANTS NEARBY: EXPENSIVE x MODERATE x   INEXPENSIVE
YOUR AREA IS: REMOTE x   QUIET WITH ACTIVITIES   LIVELY
LOCAL ACTIVITY/NIGHTLIFE: **Oban - Bars, restaurants, nice walks, scenic and hillwalking**
CAR NEEDED TO EXPLORE AREA? YES x   NO
DUTY FREE SHOPPING?   YES   NO

LOCAL EMERGENCY SERVICES   NEAREST HYPERBARIC TREATMENT FACILITY
COASTGUARD   AUTHORITY: **Fasclane Naval Base**
TELEPHONE: EMERGENCY **Dial 999**   LOCATION:
CALLSIGNS: **Channel 16 on VHF radio** TELEPHONE:

LOCAL DIVING DOCTOR:
NAME:
LOCATION:
TELEPHONE:

SCUBA AND SNORKELING FACILITIES QUESTIONNAIRE PRIVATE

ADDRESS   **30 Dreelside**
            Anstruther, Fife, Scotland, UK
CONTACT   **Jim Raeper**
TELEPHONE   **0333-310103**   FAX   TELEX

CAPITOL: **Edinburgh**	GOVERNMENT: **U.K.**	
POPULATION: **I Million**	LANGUAGE:	
CURRENCY: **Sterling**	ELECTRICITY: **Yes**	
AIRLINES:	DEPARTURE TAX?	
NEED VISA/PASSPORT? YES **x** NO	PROOF OF CITIZENSHIP? YES **x** NO	

YOUR FACILITY IS CLASSIFIED AS: SCUBA CENTER   RESORT
BUSINESS HOURS:
CERTIFYING AGENCIES:
LOG BOOK REQUIRED?   YES   NO **x**
EQUIPMENT: SALES   RENTALS   AIR FILLS
PRIMARY LINE OF EQUIPMENT:
PHOTOGRAPHIC EQUIPMENT: SALES   RENTALS   LAB

CHARTER/DIVE BOAT AVAILABLE?   YES **x**   NO   DIVER CAPACITY
COAST GUARD APPROVED?   YES **x**   NO   CAPTAIN LICENSED?   YES **x**   NO
SHIP TO SHORE?   YES   NO **x**   LORAN?   YES   NO **x**   RADAR?   YES   NO **x**
DIVE MASTER/INSTRUCTOR ABOARD? YES **x**   NO   BOTH

DIVING & SNORKELING: SALT **x**   FRESH
TYPE OF DIVING/SNORKELING IN AREA: WALL **x**   BEACH **x**   WRECK **x**   REEF   CAVE **x**   ICE
DIVING/SNORKELING IN YOUR AREA IS BEST SUITED FOR: BEGINNER INTERMEDIATE **x** ADVANCED **x**
BEST TIME OF YEAR FOR DIVING/SNORKELING: **May - October (Summer)**

TEMPERATURE:	NOV-APRIL	**40-50F**	MAY-OCT:	**60F**
VISIBILITY:	DIVING:	**50FT**	SNORKELING:	**FT**

PACKAGES AVAILABLE: DIVE   DIVE STAY   SNORKEL   SNORKEL-STAY
ACCOMMODATIONS NEARBY: HOTEL **x**   MOTEL **x**   HOME RENTALS
ACCOMMODATION RATES: EXPENSIVE   MODERATE **x**   INEXPENSIVE
RESTAURANTS NEARBY: EXPENSIVE   MODERATE **x**   INEXPENSIVE
YOUR AREA IS: REMOTE   QUIET WITH ACTIVITIES **x**   LIVELY
LOCAL ACTIVITY/NIGHTLIFE: **St. Andrews/Edinburgh are fairly close**
CAR NEEDED TO EXPLORE AREA? YES **x**   NO
DUTY FREE SHOPPING?   YES   NO **x**

LOCAL EMERGENCY SERVICES   NEAREST HYPERBARIC TREATMENT FACILITY
COASTGUARD **Forth Coastguard,**   AUTHORITY: **Rosyth Naval Base**
            Fifeness & Crail   LOCATION: **Rosyth (Firth of Forth)**
TELEPHONE: **0333-5066/Emergency Dial 999**   TELEPHONE:
CALLSIGNS: **Channel 16 on VHF radio**

LOCAL DIVING DOCTOR:
NAME:
LOCATION:
TELEPHONE:
˜WPCV°˜2XB
(J˜R

SCUBA AND SNORKELING FACILITIES QUESTIONNAIRE

NAME: **ATLANTIC DIVING SERVICES**
ADDRESS: **Summer Isles, Achilitibue**
Ullapool, Ross-Shire, Scotland IV26 2YN
CONTACT: **Andy Holbrow**
TELEPHONE: **01854 622261**

CAPITAL: **Edinburgh**
POPULATION: **5 million**
CURRENCY: **Sterling**
AIRLINES:
VISA/PASSPORT: **yes**

GOVERNMENT: **Conservative**
LANGUAGE: **English, Gaelic**
ELECTRICITY: **yes**
DEPARTURE TAX: **no**
PROOF OF CITIZENSHIP:

YOUR FACILITY IS QUALIFIED AS: **Scuba Center**
BUISINESS HOURS: **7 days a week**
CERTIFYING AGENCIES:
LOG BOOK REQUIRED: **yes**
EQUIPMENT: **air fills**
PRIMARY LINE OF EQUIPMENT: **dry suit, scuba**

CHARTER/DIVE BOAT AVAILABLE: **yes** DIVER CAPACITY: **12**
COAST GUARD APPROVED: **yes** CAPTAIN LICENSE: **yes**
SHIP TO SHORE: **yes** LORAN: RADAR: **yes**
DIVE MASTER/INSTRUCTOR ABOARD: **both**

DIVING & SNORKELING: **salt**
TYPE OF DIVING/SNORKELING IN AREA: **wall, beach, wreck, reef**
DIVING/SNORKELING IN YOUR AREA IS BEST SUITED FOR: **inter/advanced**
BEST TIME OF YEAR FOR DIVING/SNORKELING: **April - October**
TEMPERATURE: NOV-APRIL **45 F** MAY-OCT: **60 F**
VISIBILITY: DIVING SNORKELING:

PACKAGES AVAILABLE: **Dive**
ACCOMMODATIONS NEARBY: **Hotel, Home Rentals**
ACCOMMODATIONS RATES: **Moderate**
RESTAURANTS NEARBY: **Moderate**
YOUR AREA IS: **Remote**
LOCAL ACTIVITY/NIGHTLIFE: **2 Public Houses, Ullapool 25 miles away**
CAR NEEDED TO EXPLORE AREA: **Yes**
DUTY FREE SHOPPING: **No**

LOCAL EMERGENCY SERVICES
COASTGUARD
TELEPHONE: **999**
CALLSIGNS: **VHF CHANNEL 16**

NEAREST HYPERBARIC TREATMENT FACILITY
AUTHORITY:
LOCATION:
TELEPHONE:

LOCAL DIVING DOCTOR:
NAME:
TELEPHONE:

Scottish charters, there are no frills – solid boats whose appearance reflects the environment they are exposed to. Atlantic Diving Service is not a diving school, but will suit experienced divers with their own equipment. **To anyone wishing to dive the West of Scotland, I would thoroughly recommend this location and this charter.**

This is also a popular part of the world for walkers and climbers, and you can catch a ferry from Ullapool to Stoneway (Western Isle).

Editors Note:
Would you enjoy a stay in a converted lighthouse? For travelers to Scotland, treat yourself to a stay at The Coursewall Lighthouse Hotel, near Straenraer. For reservations call – 01776-853220 Yes, it is a converted lighthouse. One of its six bedrooms has a private patio. Guests can warm themselves while dining before a blazing log fire in the oak beamed restaurant.

UNITED STATES

California
La Jolla
Richard H. Cassens

Diving can be done year-round, but the best visibility will be found October through December. Depth ranges from 30 to 65 feet. During peak season, visibility ranges to 40 feet. The rest of the year, it averages around 20 feet. Temperature ranges from the high 40s to 60 degrees with an average of 55 degrees during peak season.

Spearfishing is allowed, but a state license is required. Check dive store for local regulations.

Restricted Diving Areas: The La Jolla Ecological Reserve. (Look - but don't touch) No person should disturb or take any plant, bird, mammal, fish, mollusk, crustacean, reptile, or any other form of marine life, plant life, geological formation or archeological artifacts.

BEACH DIVING SITES
HOSPITAL POINT
Beach/surf experience is a must for this area. Check with the lifeguards for information and conditions. Hospital Point is located off the 300 block of Coast Blvd., La Jolla, San Diego. It is also known locally as Whale View Point. Hospital Point is located between Wipeout Beach to the north and Horseshoe Reef to the south.

The Hospital Point Reef is made up of sand channels, giant kelp forest and parallel reef structure that extends to a depth of approximately 55 feet. The extensive reef and kelp forest offers the diver a large lobster population, abalone and all forms of kelp life. The reef structure offers the photographer excellent photo opportunities. Whale View Point is a very beautiful dive site. It's well worth the time devoted to learning the area by talking to local divers and the San Diego lifeguard personnel. The more the divers know about the area, the more enjoyable the dive will be. **At Hospital Point Reef, care must be taken in getting into and out of the water. Because of the constant surf and slippery moss covered rocks, the divers must be ever alert to conditions of the area.**
CASA COVE
Casa Cove, also known as the "Children's Pool", depending on conditions of the day, is grand diving for the beginning diver all the way to the most advanced. Always check

with the lifeguard on duty for conditions and tips on diving the area. The entry into the ocean is easy because of the rip current, but knowledge of the area is a must for returning to the beach. **The lifeguards or local divers will be happy to give you a detailed description of proper technique to exit. It's not hard, but the proper method must be utilized.**

The Children's Pool offers a variety of vertical reef walls, the giant kelp forest of Southern California and great varieties of kelp life. The **Children's Pool also offers beautiful photo opportunities both in and out of the water. Casa Cove is perhaps one of the most popular dive sites in the La Jolla area for both new and "old divers" alike. Because of the variety of reef structure, kelp forest and marine life, it offers the chance to covort with local sea lions, poke at the resident lobster or be thrilled by the sight of a moray eel. The Casa is a varied and diverse diving area.**

N.O.S. SEA TOWER

Selecting a dive site along the California coast can be difficult—there's just so much to choose from. One favorite site off the coast of Southern California is the N.O.S. Sea Tower. **The tower rests off Mission Beach in San Diego in an area known as Wreck Alley.**

Coral Gems by Lynn Funkhouser

Local divers say the sea tower, formerly used as an observation tower, can be compared to an oilrig dive. The tower went down in January 1988 and rests in 60-65 feet of water on the sandy bottom about one half mile offshore.

The rig, approximately 150 feet long, attracts an abundance of marine life to the area, including calico bass, sand bass and blacksmith. Soft corals, starfish and a multitude of sponges have taken up residence, and an occasional white anemone can be seen.

Giant stars and nudibranchs also abound. Spearfishing is allowed, but divers need to be aware of local regulations and seasons.

Divers say the tower, lying on its side, looks like a big jungle gym covered with corals and growth. The top can be reached at 30 feet, the bottom at 65 feet.

This boat dive is for intermediate to advanced divers. Several local charter boats run out of Mission Bay. It is only a 10-minute boat ride from the dock.

It is possible to dive this area year-round, but the best time is during the fall months of October, November and December when visibility is best. During this time visibility ranges to 40 feet; the rest of the year it averages 20 feet.

SNORKELING
The following locations are recommended for the beginners:
- Scrips Pier, No. La Jolla
- La Jolla Shores
- Marine Room, So. La Jolla
- La Jolla Cove
- Casa Cove

The following locations are recommended for the experienced skin and scuba divers:
- Devil's Slides
- La Jolla Cove
- Goldfish Point
- Shell Beach
- Casa Cove
- Hospital Point (Whale View Point)
- Horseshoe Reef
- Big Rock Reef

SAN DIEGO FULL SERVICE DIVE SHOPS
- Diving Locker, 1020 Grand Ave., 92109   619-222-1120
- Diving Locker, 8650 Miramar Rd., 92126   619-271-5231
- Diving Locker, 405 N.Hwy 101, Solona Beach 92075   619-775-6822
- San Diego Divers Supply 7522 La Jolla Blvd. 92037   619-459-2691
- Sports Chalet, 3695 Midway Sr., 92101   619-636-9191
- Buhrow Into Diving, 1536 Sweetwater Rd. #D, National City, 92050   619-477-5946
- Water Education Training (WET), 2525 Morena Blvd., 92110   619-275-1822
- Ocean Enterprises, 7710 Balboa Ave., 92111   619-565-6054
- Ocean Enterprises, 191 N. El Camino Real   619-942-3661

AREAS OF INTEREST
For the non-diver and/or for after diving, the San Diego area offers plenty of activities, including visiting Sea World, shopping, sightseeing at local historical sites and sporting events.

ACCOMMODATIONS
If you are planning to travel to San Diego to dive or visit, the following list is offered to help you in making arrangements before you arrive.
- Bahia Resort 998 W. Mission Bay Dr. (619) 488-0551
- Budget 1-800-225-9610
- Best Western 2901 Nimitz Blvd.1-800-528-1234
- E-Z-8 (619) 223-9500
- Capri Beach 1-800-542-2774
- Image Inn on Mission Bay 1-800-282-8111
- La Jolla Inn, Pacific Beach 1-800-367-6467
- Travel Lodge 1-800-869-0562
- Days Inn 3350 Rosencrans St.1-800-828-8111
- Comfort Inn 1-800-622-2102
- Grosvenor Inn & Super B 3145 Sports Arena Blvd. In CA: 1-800-222-2929 Outside CA: 1-800-232-1212
- Western Inn 1-800-439-6888
- Hyatt Islandia Hotel, 1441 Quivira Rd.1-800-233-1234
- Days Inn 1-800-325-2525
- Ramada Inn, Hotel Circle 1-800-228-2828
- Quality Inn 1-800-228-5151

Southern California

Kurt Turner

The visitor to Los Angeles will find a wide variety of diving adventures awaiting their pleasure. From the kelp beds of Leo Carrillo State Park to the urchin-encrusted reefs of Laguna Beach, the conditions qualify as world class. As is so often the case however, you must know how to get around and where to go. If not, you will come away with the attitude that a lot of good water is going to waste.

Upon arrival at Los Angeles National Airport (LAX), the first problem you face is contending with Southern California geography. If you expect public transportation to fill your needs, you will be setting yourself up for frustration and disappointment. **There is only one way to cope. Get a car.** The Yellow Pages list a wide variety of rental agencies. A phone call to one of them from the airport lobby will have you on the freeway in 30 minutes.

Sea Lions by Wendy Canning Church

Where do you stay? Since **Pacific Coast Highway follows the coastline**, I would recommend you stay on this route. This will keep you located near the water, and **this route is home to many good restaurants**. Since you are contemplating dive activity, I recommend renting a motel room. The large hotels do not deal well with wet dive gear in their lobbies. Stay with a national chain such as Holiday Inn, Motel 6, or Best Western. **Be sure to ask for a ground floor room. Carrying equipment up several flights of stairs will not improve your disposition.**

BEACH DIVING

For scuba diving purposes, divide the beaches of Los Angeles and Orange Counties into two groups. West facing beaches offer good conditions when seas are from the south. South facing beaches are better when the seas are from the west. This places the surf action at an angle to the beach offering easier entry and exit. Don't worry about the seas from the north. Do to the shape of the coast, waves never come from the north. Occasionally there is a hot wind called the Santa Anna that blows from the deserts lying to the east. During these Santa Anna conditions, diving is near perfect. The ocean blows flat and an upwelling begins.

The shape of the coastline gives each beach its unique character. At the north end the coast follows an east-west direction. This gradually curves to the south as it passes Malibu and Santa Monica resulting in a north-south coastline to Palos Verdes. There it wraps around the cliffs again going east west through Long Beach. The Long Beach area does not offer diving because the beautiful beach lies within the Federal Breakwater. It is illegal to dive on the harbor side of the breakwater. Some divers do dive the ocean side; however, this would be quite foolhardy for the visitor. The caves formed by the large boulders could be very dangerous. After Long Beach, the coast again curves to the south through Laguna Beach. This is a popular west facing diving area. Here the reefs come to within a few feet of the shoreline and offer spectacular underwater conditions.

MALIBU

Initially, consider the south-facing beaches. The first of these is in the Malibu area. Go north on the Pacific Coast Highway. After you pass through Malibu and before you get to the Ventura County line, you will see signs for **Leo Carillo State Beach**. This is a large area offering many entry and exit points. Check in with the lifeguards and seek their advice about the local area.

After entering the water, you notice several large kelp beds on the reefs that run parallel to the shore and out 25 to 50 yards. The depths here are shallow (20 to 35 feet) inside the kelp beds. You should be able to spend all day making 3 or 4 dives without falling off the tables. **Don't go on the outside of the kelp beds as there is a sharp drop off and the rip currents can be unpredictable.**

PALOS VERDE PENINSULA

The second south-facing beach is **White Point** near the eastern end of the Palos Verde Peninsula. The trip begins on the Pacific Coast Highway. From there turn south on Western Avenue to the coast in San Pedro. Turn right on Paseo Del Mar then again to the right at the entrance to Royal Palms Beach. At the bottom of the hill bend to the left and go as far as you can. You'll see the ruins of a hotel foundation in the water. These ruins are seaward of the rocky beach entry area.

The diving here is shallow. I have been out 1/2 mile and still only found 45 feet of water. If you swim out 1/8 to 1/4 mile, you will have no more than 35 feet. This is a unique area. **Several underwater hot springs spew forth-mineral water.** You will visually notice them first as a patch of black sand. Position yourself over the patch and you will feel the hot water. Very noticeable in the area are strings of fungus that look like egg whites. They are harmless, but quite interesting, as they live on the sulfur from the hot springs. Purple sea urchins cover most of the rocks. There are also some large octopus. Plan on spending the whole day here and making 3 or 4 dives.

LOS ANGELES COUNTY

In Los Angeles County there are only two west-facing beaches worth mentioning. They can both be done in a single day. The first is Veterans Park in Redondo Beach. Start again from Pacific Coast Highway and turn westbound on Torrence Boulevard. This street will dead-end at Veterans Park. The parking lot is on the south side and access to the beach is by concrete steps. The bottom drops off quickly. You'll be in 40 feet of water within 75 yards of the beach. It then drops off quickly into the Redondo Canyon. You'll probably see many sheep crabs and a few rays. There are many fish here and some get to be quite large. Pay special attention to the sandy bottom and you'll spot some good size halibut. Plan on making only one dive here. It will be a deep dive, but stay above 90 feet so you'll have time left on the tables at the next site.

Our second west facing location is **Malaga Cove,** a few miles to the south. Go back to Torrence Boulevard and then turn south on Pacific Coast Highway. Turn south bound on Palos Verdes. Drive West. As you pass Malaga Cove Plaza, turn right on Via Corta, which becomes Via Almar. Turn right on Via Arroyo and as you pass the Malaga Cove school you will be on Paseo Del Mar. You'll see a large parking area with a gazebo on one end. From that vantagepoint you can see the area quite clearly. To the north is a sandy beach that stretches all the way to Ventura. To the south are the rocks and cliffs of the Palos Verde Peninsula. Suit up in the parking lot and follow the steep path down to the shoreline. This transition point from a flat sandy beach to rocky cliffs is an interesting dive site. Here is a combination of rocks, reefs, and sand. The added kelp bed provides cover for a variety of aquatic lives. On the sandy side you'll probably see some angel sharks near the rocks. In the rocks you'll find lobsters, abalone, and rockfish. The kelp bed will be home to schooling fish.

These dives will be shallow, 20 to 30 feet. Plan on doing as many as the tables will safely allow.

ORANGE COUNTY

The remaining west facing beaches are at **Laguna Beach** located in Orange County. Go south on Pacific Coast Highway and as you enter Laguna Beach look for Fairview Street or Wave Street. A right turn on either one will put you on Cliff Drive, which runs parallel to the ocean. Many well-marked sites are available along this street. They are all easily accessible. Although quite similar, each spot has an individual flavor. Sometimes it is difficult to find parking in this area. **On weekends it is not uncommon to see a dozen classes**. It is for good reason that instructors select these sites. Usually the surf is only 2 or 3 feet, so the wave action is negligible. Visibility is between 15 and 30 feet, and there is plenty of beautiful reefscape to enjoy.

The bottom terrain includes both rocks and sand with all the attendant creatures. There are numerous gorgonias, nudibranchs, and anemones adorning the rocks. Also in abundance are the ever-popular Garibaldi, constantly begging the diver to break open a sea urchin which they readily devour.

I would like to offer a word of caution on the taking of game to eat. **You will see many legal fish, scallops, lobster, and abalone, but my advice is not to take any.** Enjoy them visually. Those that come behind you will be grateful. Furthermore, eating these critters is not a safe practice. **The Santa Monica Bay is a dumping area for sewage effluent and over flow.** For decades, the waters of Palos Verde were a chemical dumping ground. Most notably, DDT and heavy metals lie in the silt leeching their way into the food chain.

A portion of Orange County is a game refuge, but even if legal I wouldn't want to eat anything caught there. The storm runoff carries all manner of pollution into the ocean. The filter feeders absorb this chemical stew and the food chain becomes polluted. If you wish to eat fresh seafood, go to one of the fine restaurants in the area. They offer a menu of government inspected items that are safe to eat.

BOAT DIVING

The most important step to insure a successful dive boat trip in Southern California is planning the schedule. This is because you need reservations for anything to do with a boat. They fill up fast. Your primary tool for making a reservation is the publication entitled **"Dive Boat Calendar and Travel Guide"**. It lists the charters by destination, and provides a telephone number to call for your reservation.

Most of the charters in the Los Angeles area operate out of 22nd Street Landing in San Pedro. This is an excellent facility, recently remodeled and offering plenty of convenient parking. It is easy to find and offers special access to off load passengers and gear. Most of the boats allow you to board the night before. They provide a bunk complete with blanket and pillow. I strongly recommend that you take advantage of this service. Doing so removes all the anxiety of trying to find your way to the dock during the morning commuter rush. You'll wake up to hot coffee after a pleasant sleep, and be able to enjoy the harbor dawn without a care. When you call to make your reservations, get good directions to the dock, and tell them you wish to sleep onboard.

Boat diving destinations usually are the Channel Islands with the most common being the "near side" of Catalina Island. This is an excellent choice. There are a wide variety of dive sites for the captain to chose from. Depths can range from 20 feet to over 100 feet, so use caution in forming your dive plan.

If you are lucky enough to catch a boat going to the "back side" of Catalina Island, you are in for a real treat. Farnsworth Banks is an advanced site that never fails to deliver

some exciting activity. The banks consist of two peaks rising from the ocean floor. One comes to within 60 feet of the surface and the other to 90 feet. The actual depth depends upon the daily sea conditions. These peaks fall off very sharply, straight down in some places. As a result there is the need to monitor depth and bottom time carefully. The peaks exhibit a wide variety of sea life. One worth noting is the purple coral. Also, it is not uncommon to see several species of sharks and rays.

Local dive shops are a valuable resource for gaining insight into the current diving scene. They can offer invaluable advice about the conditions at the beach. **It is not unusual for dive conditions to change on a weekly basis.** A good shop operator can tell you what is hot on any particular day. The shops book boat charters, and offers specialty courses that may interest your party. In addition, most of them sell copies of "Dive Boat Clanedar and Travel Guide".

While at the shop, inquire about any additional equipment that you may need to buy or rent. **In addition to the basics, you will definitely need a wet suit.** The minimum is 1/4 inch if cold doesn't bother you. For myself, I use a 3/8-inch complete with hood and gloves. Remember to adjust your weight. Many of the shops have a training pool on their premises. Ask if you can try out the wet suit and get yourself neutrally buoyant. If you are neutrally buoyant in fresh water, add 2.5% of your fully suited weight to your belt. That should be just right for the ocean.

As you contemplate diving in the varied beach areas, you must realize that it is of the utmost importance that you have the necessary training. This will add to your enjoyment of the area, and it will enhance your safety. In this regard, you must be comfortable in traversing the surf line. A very frightening scene is that of inexperienced and untrained divers caught in moderate surf. The wave action will toss them about, out of control and in a state of panic. They will lose equipment and possibly suffer serious injury. Such a disaster is avoidable with a course of instruction in surf diving. **To receive the finest instruction, contact the Underwater Instruction Association. The Los Angeles County Department of Parks and Recreation, Underwater Unit, Carson, CA, will provide a roster.** Telephone a couple of members and be specific with your request. Tell them that you wish to learn how to deal with sandy beach and rocky beach surf. A day of instruction will enable you to enjoy some excellent beach diving in safety and comfort. Most of these instructors are also available for guide service.

Don't overlook the fun of linking up with a local dive club. There are at least two dozen in the area that are very active with monthly boat trips and many beach activities. The mid-week meetings are open to the public. Potential buddies will swamp you with offers of diving trips, once the members learn you are a visitor. A partial listing of clubs in available in the "Dive Boat Calendar". Take the time to contact one or more of them. You are sure to add some lasting friendships to your diving adventures.

There are many other sites available. For the visitors, however, these few offer the best access and reasonable assurance of good beach diving conditions. Now that I have whetted your appetite for blowing bubbles, make plans to visit some of the finest sites for world class diving. Even if you spend a full two weeks exploring the area, you will only see a small portion of what is available. I guarantee that you will want to return. **As you become more familiar with the area, you will discover that it offers an endless variety of conditions. Enjoy them and bring your friends!**

Florida

Crystal Springs

Tom Boyd

Crystal River is situated on the West Coast of Florida about an hour north of Tampa. I've been a witness to its development and it isn't the sleepy little town it used to be years ago. There is a power plant, plenty of homes and too many boats. Each dive at Crystal River becomes ever more meaningful to me as I'll never be sure if it is to be my last encounter with the manatees.

The Florida Manatee is probably one of the gentlest creatures in the marine environment. I feel privileged to have been able to dive with them, especially since their survival is doubtful. **I've taken numerous newcomers to encounter a manatee and after snorkeling and diving with them, everyone seems to be wearing a grin and walking on water.** That's why I dive. I don't believe I'll ever become bored with the feelings of awe when I see something new or am able to make a connection with a marine animal.

Every year between November and March the manatee head into the warm springs of Florida. **Crystal River is one of the main area that manatees come and the only place I know that you can snorkel/dive with them.** Snorkeling is the preferred way to encounter a manatee, as they don't seem to like the noise and bubbles created by scuba gear.

King's Spring is the main spring and is about 30 feet deep. The river itself isn't very deep and around the spring it can be only 8 to 10 feet (plenty of room to enjoy a meeting with a manatee). Be aware there are strict laws governing harassing a manatee, classified as an endangered species. They also have restricted sanctuary areas where no one is allowed so the manatee has a place to get away when it wants to be left alone. If you are lucky enough to have a manatee approach you and initiate contact, enjoy the opportunity to touch it's almost leather -like hide (although authorities prefer you don't). Don't think about grabbing onto or chasing the manatee as there are stiff fines and any decent diver would understand this action could force the manatee into colder waters of the river, which is harmful to their health. **A word to the wise for divers and snorkelers, due to the large number of boats in the manatee sanctuary areas, stay within the area of your dive flag.**

Although visibility on the river isn't always crystal, you'll know when you are about to have a manatee encounter, they are about 10 feet long and can weigh up to 3,000 pounds.

A month ago, I was shooting some footage of a manatee calf and was having a great time. He seemed to love having his picture taken and I thoroughly enjoyed his company. Wherever I went, he kept right along side. I felt honored to have such a unique friend or dive buddy. As we came near the main spring, my new friend drifted quite close until a group of inconsiderate divers began to chase him. I knew I had connected with this manatee because as I was shooting this sequence of events, he turned to look at me and decided to beeline to my side keeping distance between him and his undesired pursuers (I will always cherish that footage). Needless to say, the divers weren't happy with the calf's adopted bodyguard, but my friend obviously felt safe and the feelings I have are virtually undesirable.

The following quote I discovered while working on the manatee documentary and which I feel could possibly summarize why I dive other than my love of shark encounters; sightings of beautiful tropical fish; the

"Murry," Manatee by Joseph R. Tatusky

whales and the manatees; and the hope that my manatee buddy will be around for a very long time:

"For in the end we will conserve only what we love. We will love only what we understand. We will understand only what we are taught."

Baba Dioum: Senegalese Naturalist

CRYSTAL RIVER ACCOMODATIONS AND DIVE CENTERS

Port Paradise Hotel, P.O. Box 516, Crystal River, FL 32629, (904) 795-3111
Port Paradise Manatee Dive Center, P.O. Box 214, Crystal River, FL 32629, (904) 563-2810
Bay Point Dive Center, 300 NW Hwy 19, Crystal River, FL 32629, (904) 563-1040
Crystal Lodge Dive Center, P.O. Box 456, U.S. 19 & 98 North, Crystal River, FL 32629, (904) 795-3171, (904) 795-6798 (dive shop)
Plantation Inn & Golf Resort, (800) 632-6262 (Eastern U.S.), (904) 795-4211, (904) 795-5797 (dive shop)

The Florida Keys

America's Caribbean Island Chain

Bill Roe

Home to Indians, then Spaniards, wreckers, cutthroats, and thieves from all nations, the Florida Keys have endured a rich history that predates the landing at Plymouth Rock. Even today is doesn't hurt to have a little pirate in your soul if you live there.

The waters surrounding these islands hold the last great natural coral reef system in this country, the bones of ships and their cargo, some dating back nearly 400 years and an abundance of maritime history. That is where SCUBA diving comes in, and there is plenty of it, as diverse as the island chain itself. In almost 120 miles, the Keys offer different lifestyles in different places, and great diving wherever you go. There are five different areas of the Keys. Each has it's own flavor and uniqueness, both above and below the water. Those areas are, Key Largo, Tavernier/Islamorada , Marathon, the Lower Keys, and of course Key West. These magical isles are linked by the Overseas Highway, also known as U.S.1. It is "Main Street" in the Keys.

A pioneering developer and railroad owner, Henry Flagler built a railway down the east coast of Florida. As he went, he would build magnificent hotels for the tourists who rode his trains. His dream was to terminate in the southern most city in Florida, the seaport town of Key West. The majority of the Overseas Highway is laid on the old railroad bed of Flagler's railway which was washed away in the 1929 hurricane. The original "Seven Mile Bridge" below Marathon was built to carry rail cars before it carried autos.

Most travelers fly into Ft. Lauderdale or Miami and drive down from there although both Marathon and Key West have airports with commercial links. Drive south on Florida's Turnpike until it ends in Florida City, you will come to the Overseas Highway and progress down the "Eighteen Mile Stretch." Eighteen miles of two lane road that has claimed the life and limb of many an impatient driver. This is the ideal time to get into "Keys Time", a relaxed, unhurried state of mind that slows the pace of life to an island beat

Dozens of Osprey nests are perched atop power poles and road signs. In the late winter and early spring, you see young sea hawks testing their wings at nests edge.

As you near the end of the "stretch" water appears on both sides as you ride the ribbon of asphalt. Key Largo is dead ahead, just past Lake Surprise. Lake Surprise is actually a narrow strip of land that is the first piece of the roadway to flood in a hurricane, (surprise!).

Key Largo is the largest of all the islands in the chain. It boasts John Pennekamp Underwater State Park (305 451 1621) and the Key Largo National Marine Sanctuary under the direction of the National Oceanographic and Atmospheric Administration.

"Close encounter with a dolphin" by Ron Streeter

Captain Corkys Divers World offers snorkeling charters and live aboard excursions, (MM 99.5,P.O. Box 1663, Key Largo, FL 33037, 305 451 3200).

Some of the most legendary diving in the country is done around Key Largo. It seems to be the unwritten law in diving, that you HAVE to dive **"The Statue" in Pennekanmp Park.**

French Reef is punctuated with small caves and swim throughs that are often home to clouds of glassy sweepers and other small fish.

Molasses, The Elbow, Carysfort, are all beautiful dive and snorkelers sites served by any and all of the operators.

Lodging in Key Largo is varied, from rustic campgrounds, the ubiquitous Mom and Pop roadside motel, to the absolute lap of luxury. For sheer comfort, at a modest price, the **Best Western Suites of Key Largo** (MM 100, 201 Ocean Drive, Key Largo, FL 33037. 800 462 6079) is my favorite. Upstairs there is a master bedroom with phone, T.V. and private bath, downstairs, a sofa that opens to a queen size bed, separate bath, a full size kitchen, another T.V. and phone. All have a commanding view of the dive boat fleet that runs out to Pennekamp twice daily.

You can also get a glimpse of the original "African Queen" of the classic Bogart/Hepburn movie, ferrying passengers about from her base at the Holiday Inn.

Across the canal is **Marina Del Mar,** (MM 100, P.O. Box 1050, Key Largo, FL, 33037, 305 451 4107) another fine hotel, loaded with nighttime fun. The view from their rooftop sundeck shows Key Largo in all her splendor unlike any other vantage point on the island. Housed in Marina Del Mar is **Ocean Divers, and Hyperbarics International,** (MM 100, 522 Caribbean Drive, Key Largo, FL 33037. 305 451 1113) where veteran dive instructor and diving pioneer Dick Rutkowski teaches "nitrox"diving.

Nitrox is rapidly coming to the forefront in sport diving discussion today, and is a useful skill to have if you want to take full advantage of diving the ***Bibb*** or the ***Duane,*** **twin Coast Guard Cutters,** sunk as artificial reefs several years ago. In over 100' of water, just outside Park boundaries, these ships are huge, and nitrox diving can maximize safe bottom time for viewing these awesome wrecks.

You can scuba or snorkel with **Dolphins Plus,**(147 Corrine Place, Key Largo,33037, 305 451 1993) advance reservations are required. This little known attraction does have a waiting list at times.

Restaurants are not in short supply, the bill of fare is wide, but throughout the Keys, seafood is clearly the mainstay. **Senior Frioles',** (MM 103.9, 305 451 1592) offers great Mexican food and a great sunset view.

For a neat yet out of the way waterfront dining experience, try **The Fish House**

(MM 102.4, 305 451 4665), a little south of Key Largo proper. As you leave the main business district, heading toward Tavernier, notice the beautiful three-story mural on your left that welcomes you to the Keys.

Tavernier and Islamorada have more of a small town feel than the comparative hustle and bustle of Key Largo. Even the dive operators have a more laid back style.

Without the hype of Pennekanmp, they are less pressured, and you will find most of the boats carry either 6 or 12 passengers max. For dive operators, **Rainbow Reef Dive Center** (MM 85,Oceanside, Islamorada, FL. 33036 305 664 4600) or **Conch Republic Divers** (90311 Ocean Highway, Tavernier, FL 33070, 305 852 1655) will charm you and treat you to personalized service you won't forget.

Ken and Pat Kock have one of the more charming operations in the area. Rainbow Reef Dive Center is tucked away in the rustic **Pirates Cove Hotel and Marina** on Windley Key. The will show you true Southern Hospitality. When you dive with these people, you know they want you to have a good time.

Or stay with Brad Neat at his **Island Bay Resort** (MM 92.5, Bayside, Tavernier, FL 33070, 305 852 4087). Clean tastefully decorated apartments, on the Gulfside with Brad's dive boat, the *Do Wa Diddy*, docked right there. Brad has a compressor on site and runs complete dive charters. One of the most experienced and respected operators in Islamorada, he has been known to occasionally gift his guests with a complimentary bottle of wine. They can enjoy it at sunset with their feet propped on a circa 1733 cannon at waters edge. Brad recovered the cannon in the 70's, let him tell you about it.

If you like to blend some hard partying in with your dive vacation, you should probably check in at the **Holiday Isle Resorts and Marina** (MM 84, 84001 US Highway 1, Islamorda, FL. 305 664 2321). Accommodations range from royal to economy. The Holiday Isle now is compromised of several hotel properties all linked by shuttle service when not within walking distance.

This is a self contained resort. Holiday Isle Dive Shop offers snorkeling trips as well as scuba (305 664 4145) , a huge fishing fleet, boat rentals, jet ski rentals, several of the areas best eateries, all the shopping you could do plus...the legendary Tiki Bar, where the classic Keys Rumrunner was born and still reigns as king. One of the hottest night spots in the Keys , many do not make it any further south on their vacation. Those that do will find wonderful dining at the Whale Harbor, the seafood buffet at the **Cart Grill** (the locals call it the "Oral Thrill"), is another "must" for seafood lovers. **The Green Turtle Inn is fabulous.** Closed on Monday when... "the turtle rests"(MM 81.5, 305 664 9031 –Stone crabs and Key Lime pie a must). **Rip's Island Ribs'N Chicken** features entrees prepared on thick granite slabs that are heated to 600 degrees and brought to your table. (305 664 5300) **The Old Lighthouse** has a wonderful seafood buffet (MM 83.5, 305 664 4959)

For diversion, you can spend an afternoon at Theater of the Sea. A long time attraction, it puts you close to the many ocean inhabitants and is an ideal way to introduce non divers of all ages to the wonders we experience. You will probably learn a few things yourself.

Diving is different here than it is on Key Largo. It is a place where you can see if your depth gauge works below 35 feet. Where your dive can be as rewarding if you carry a camera bag, a bug bag, (in season, with a license) or a pole spear (license required also).

If you rent a boat go snorkeling around Alligator Light, and visit the historical Indian Key Park. You will learn about the early days of Florida when people lived by "wrecking", and this tiny island was the first Dade County seat, why the Indians wanted the white man out, what they did to achieve this, and what little the Government could do to stop it. It all makes a fascinating story.

There is allegedly a state run boat to ferry tourists out to the island, I have yet to see one running. Before we go down to Marathon, a few last fond memories, sitting on the deck of the *Lady Cyana III* (MM 85.9, Islamorda, FL 305 664 8717), coming back from two great dives and just smiling...bringing my own boat down on a trailer and staying at the Drop Anchor Motel.

You can get on "Keys Time" very quickly in Islamorada.

MARATHON ... THE HEART OF THE KEYS

Almost exactly halfway between Miami and Key West, the community of Marathon was born in 1904. Now, ninety year later, **the area is losing its status as one of the Keys best kept secrets for divers.** The word has gotten out.

Home to Indians as far back as 2000 B.C., the reefs off Marathon saw many a Spanish Galleon and British Merchant vessel alike break their backs and die on the coral in storms and in darkness. **There are wrecks still being discovered today, laden with booty and history.** The rich fisheries on both the Atlantic and Gulf sides of the islands attracted only a handful of hardy settlers by the early 1900's.

Marathon gained its name during pioneer Henry Flagler's headlong rush to build a railroad through to Key West. Flagler built a major construction camp on the island of Key Vaca as midway depot to house men and materials to complete the project. Because of the frenzied push for completion, a worker was heard to say, "Building this railroad has become a regular Marathon!" That was enough to give the camp a name. The name stuck.

Today the railroad is gone. U.S. 1, the Overseas Highway, has replaced the rails and beams with a ribbon of asphalt that runs down the spine of the Keys and leads divers to a host of Middle Keys diving delights. The Marathon area begins with Duck Key, Mile Marker 61 and wanders down to the Seven Mile Bridge at M.M. 45. Along this expanse the coastline offers divers dozens of reef sites and *The Thunderbolt*, a deep wreck that is quickly becoming as much of a "must" for traveling divers as the "Statue" in Pennekanmp Park.

More of a "must" is Sombrero Reef, a labyrinth of coral caves and arches, home of Marathon's first mooring buoy project. Tying off to one of these buoys saves the reef from anchor damage, while putting divers on some of the prettiest "bottom" in all the Keys.

There are a number of operators in the area, most do not run any further south than Sombrero Reef for they don't need to. **Hawk's Cay Resort and Marina** (MM 61, Duck Key, Marathon FL 33050 305-743 7000) offers snorkeling trips from 30 to 40 feet. Marathon is even blessed with a Gulfside body of water that is deep enough and diverse enough in plant and fish life to make for an exciting dive.

Marathon is still a fishing community. The marinas and dockside moorings are littered with long liners and shrimpers. Aged and with their nets drying in the sun, they stand as a testimony to the generations of fishermen who have sought a living from the sea, and who remain here today. Many times throughout the year sponge divers are seen plying their trade on the Gulfside. The sight is a tribute to the ability of nature to rejuvenate herself, and a reminder of our oceans struggle to supply mankind with it's needs, at the same time.

The important thing to remember is, in Marathon, the Gulfside can still provide diving thrills when the Atlantic can't. In the shallows of the "inside", you are more or less in the nursery of the ocean. It is here that you can witness another strata of the food chain, much less visible in the open sea. Even if the weather is perfect for open water diving, you might elect to check with an operator and take one of these more ecologically oriented underwater tours. Days when it is a total "blowout" are almost nonexistent.

From the 25'-30' tall coral formations at the **Pillars** off of Duck Key, to the fantasy of arches and "swim throughs" that Sombrero Reef touts, Marathon diving has it's own unique and diverse menu.

Rule of thumb says the depths average 40'-60' on the reefs, but at places like **Coffins Patch,** the depth can be 10 feet or less. Ideal for snorkelers, bottom time like you can't believe for scuba divers.

For deeper wreck thrills, the *Thunderbolt* offers the challenge. Sunk a few years as an artificial reef, she lies in 110 feet with appropriate growth to make photographers giggle in their regulators with glee.

Other sites include the **Fish Market, East Washerwoman, Delta Shoals, the Delta Shoal Wreck,** the wreck of the *Ignacio, and the Ivory Wreck.*

312

For some reason divers either stop much further up in the Keys, or drive past in search of other things. Marathon is a well kept secret by many divers. The lack of fear in the marine life when approached proves this.

Aside from Marathon being a fishing community, many commercial tropical fish collectors are based here alongside the shrimpers and long liners. Some offer special "collecting" charters, and while it may be fun to learn the habits of these animals and the thrill of actually catching them, shipping them home can be a costly, logistical headache, equal to having a "trophy" fish mounted and shipped home.

Accommodations in the Marathon area can satisfy any budget and taste. Most operations are the "Mom and Pop" variety; clean rooms and friendly attention highlight them, many have boat ramps and dockage available to guests. There are nationally advertised chain hotels, (**Holiday Inn** MM 54, 800 224 5653, **Howard Johnson Resort** MM 54 800 654 2000) and some truly first class "Resorts" that will pamper you silly. Some give package rates for divers.

Hawk's Cay located on Duck Key, is one of the most elegant resorts in the Caribbean let alone the Keys (MM 61, Duck Key, FL 33050, 800 432 2242) . Designed in a 50's island style, if you like chocolates on your pillow at night, and never lift a finger service, stay here. Of the few, Triple-A listed, five star restaurants in the lower Keys, two are on the premises of Hawk's Cay, as is **Marathon Underseas Adventures**, the dive shop. They have been honored for their work with the Handicapped Scuba Association (HSA) and have certified more student instructors than nearly any operation in Florida.

The Diving Site (MM 53.5, Marathon FL 33050, 305 289 1021) offers both reef and Gulfside ecology-oriented tours as well as great, friendly diving.

Good things to say for **Tilden's Pro Dive**(MM 49.5, Marathon FL 33050 800 223 4563) Bill and Heidi at **Abyss Pro Dive Center**(MM 54 , Marathon FL 33050, 800 457 0134) and **CJ's Dive Center** (MM 48.5, Marathon, FL 33050, 305 289 9433) as well.

If you are not eating dinner at the **Sombrero, or Hawk's Cay**, try the **Anglers Lounge** at MM 48 or **Kelsey's** at MM 48 is a sure favorite. **The Hurricane Raw Bar and Restaurant** at MM 49.5 has a great menu, reasonably priced. Try an evening dinner cruise with **Latigo Charters** at MM 47.5. **Porky's Too** has well priced take-out.

As for nightlife, the larger hotels have clubs, there are a number of restaurants and nightspots that offer live entertainment and dancing. Margaritas and moonlight dancing on the water to an island backbeat. If you don't feel like diving, try a seaplane ride or a flying lesson. Marathon has a large airport serviced by commercial air carrier connecting links. **You can fly to your dive destination!**

If you have the chance, stop in at the Dolphin Research Center on Grassy Key. There are some very dedicated people doing amazing things to learn from, save, and protect those wonderful mammals.

Your donation for admission will give you access to some rare and insightful information on these cetaceans. You will walk away feeling a little 'different', and you will have helped support this ongoing program. The Marathon area is rich in diving delights, and steeped in maritime history.

THE LOWER KEYS-LOOE KEY

At the end of the Seven Mile Bridge is Bahia Honda. One of the Nations 10 most beautiful beaches can be found here.

A Mecca for campers who either fish or dive and bring their own boat, you can literally just walk around the premises and feel refreshed and relaxed. The skeleton of Flagler's old bridge/trestle stands to one side of the "new" Overseas Highway, a historic reminder of days past. If you can stop for a picnic at Bahia Honda, from here down to Big Coppitt Key, the lodging is "Mom and Pop" style with the exception of the Sugar Loaf Lodge and Looe Key Reef Resort.

The main attraction for diving and snorkelering in this area is the Looe Key Marine Sanctuary.

Director Bily Causey's high-profile style of management has put this place on the map. Each July, the Sanctuary holds it's Underwater Music Festival, another unique Keys event. The local radio station provides programming that Park Rangers relay to divers in the Park via hydrophones. Gliding among the coral heads to a slow island beat as the fearless groupers and myriad tropical fish swim past is a treat. (Sorry I can't say the same about the insurance commercial I heard, the fish didn't seems to be too impressed either.)

Looe Key was named after the wreck of **H.M. Looe** a frigate lost around the turn of the century.

Big Pine Key is one of the largest and most interesting islands in the Keys, although you would not guess so by your passage along the Overseas Highway. The island is much wider that what you experience on U.S. 1, and most of it is a refuge for the rare (and endangered) Key Deer. These deer are so tiny, a full grown male would not necessarily come up to the height of your car fender. They wander across the road at all times of the day and because of their size are in constant danger of being hit by unobservant drivers. (The 45 mph/35 mph night speed limits are strictly enforced).

The Key Deer National Refuge is on Big Pine Key, and a few miles of country road driving can put you in another place on earth and time. A primeval landscape of scrub pine and palmetto, the Refuge has a visitor station and supplies maps to spots where you might see one of these tiny creatures sneaking a drink of fresh water, or crossing a path. If you have the time stop in to see nature before it is all gone.

On Big Pine, **Underseas, Inc.** at MM 30.5(305 872 2700) is your connection. Marianne Rockett, the owner operates one of the Keys oldest and best stocked dive shops. Underseas can run you out to the reef any day and many nights.

Onward to Key West, if you stop at Looe Key Reef Resort on Ramrod Key , you can have it all, spacious clean rooms, the dive boat out your back door, a restaurant and pool side Tiki bar at your front door, where do you need to go?

If you don't need the Tiki Bar and all it's attendant fun, look up **Parmer's Place Resort Motel** (MM 28.5, 305 872 2157) on Little Torch Key, its a little hard to find, but absolutely Key's quaint and a spotlessly clean establishment.

On Little Torch Key dive with **Scuba Concepts** on Pirates Road (305 872 9766).

Compared to other areas of the Keys, the Lower Keys are probably the slowest paced, "closest to nature" part of the island chain. You come to the Lower Keys to truly get away from it all.

Heading down, deeper into the Keys, the throaty, roaring whine of military jets overhead from Boca Chica Naval Air Station, heralds your approach to **Key West. A diving treat, and the ultimate party town.**

Reefs, wrecks and even a wall highlight the diving around the Key West area.

No where else in the world can you be so totally immersed in such a divergent atmosphere, steeped in the lore of the sea, rum runners, smugglers of all kinds, as well as heroes both military and artistic. Rogues of all descriptions have haunted the narrow streets of Key West.

After dive entertainment can begin with a walk at sunset on Mallory Square, as a man balances a bicycle on his chin while bagpipe music fills the air. Or watching the sunset from a sailboat, champagne in hand. Maybe a walk through a museum stuffed with the treasure of long dead kings or the quaint gingerbread homes passing by as you view them from a motor tour. "People that say, there's not much good diving in this area haven't had a good look around these parts" says Tim Taylor of **Looker Diving Center** (305 294 2249)

There are plenty of great spots around the Key West area. **Sand Key** is probably one of the more familiar reefs and **Western Dry Rocks** is also recorded in a lot of logbooks. Their spur and groove formation give many a diver a thrilling view of spotted eagle rays (the most I have seen at one time).

There is a wall on another portion of Western Dry Rocks that trails from 35-40 feet down to 110. It is a small area but one worth seeing if you are a wall diver.

"One nice thing about our island is that it doesn't have a "Gulfside" said Mimi Dye of **Lost Reef Adventures** (800 633 6833). We've got diving all around us. When the wind is strong on one side, we just dive the calmer, better visibility of the other side".

Dive sites for all tastes are available. From shallow brightly colored snorkeling reefs that are perfect for resort course and checkout divers to deep wrecks and even treasure hunting on the bones of sunken galleons.

The named sites in Key West include: Rocky Key, Nine Foot Stake, Western Sambo, Little Sambo and Pelican Shoals. Boats sailing out of Key West are as varied as the sites they dive. From the muted thunder of powered charter boats, to the silent whisper of sails pushing you out to the Marquesas and Dry Tortugas in search of underwater excitement and pleasure. You can even put on a trench coat and pretend you're an underwater spy riding the "James Bond Boat", the *Sea Eagle*.

Or you can sail away on intimate liveaboards and trace the path of treasure hunters and rogues in the Marquesas or the Dry Tortugas.

If your diving tastes lean toward the deeper, technical side of the sport, stop in at **Captain Billy's Key West Diver,** on Stock Island (305 294 7177) just before coming into Key West. Captain Billy Deans in one of the most experienced in this highly specialized area, he has visited the *Andria Doria,* and even dove the *Monitor*.

When it comes to lodging, food and nightlife, Key West has it, hands down. At the **Ocean Key House Suite Resort and Marina (800 328 9815**) at the end of Mallory Square, you can luxuriate in a two bedroom suite with a Jacuzzi in your master bath with balconies that overlook both the square and the sea.

The sunset view from the rooftop bar at **La Concha**, (430 Duval Street) will take your breath away.

Key West is also rife with quaint little B&B's, nestled in refurbished, but authentic "Conch" houses, many over 150 years old. A real taste of the Old Town, but inconvenient at best lugging wet dive gear up and down the stairs and halls. If you want to stay at a B&B, best rent the major share of your gear.

If you prefer staying a little farther from the madding crowd, the other side of the island, away from Mallory Square, offers ocean view hotels and motels with the beach across the street.

There is also some liveaboard boats that run weekend trips out to Fort Jefferson in the Dry Tortugas. You can dive this unspoiled wonderland with *The Yankee Freedom* or the *MV Spree*. They both offer a great trip, excellent diving and a tour of historic Ft. Jefferson. If you want to see the Fort, "home" to Dr. Samuel Mudd after Lincoln's assassination without taking the time for the diving and the cruise you can fly out to the Fort via a number of seaplane charter operators.

If you really like to walk on the wild side, try to be here in October when Fantasy Fest is going on. It's Key West's answer to Mardi Gras, a wilder time, you won't soon find.

Don't forget, this is also "Margaritaville", and if you don't like Jimmy Buffett songs, wafting from bars everywhere, you'll have trouble adjusting.

Home to Hemingway, and a host of famous writers, both living and dead, Key West is also an artists colony, many recognizable names and faces float around the town.

You might even catch a glimpse of Mel Fisher, the world famous treasure hunter, using a small gold bar for a swizzle stick. Hit **Sloppy Joe's,**at the corner of Duval and Greene Streets, **The Hog's Breath Saloon,**400 Front Street, **The Turtle Kraals** at the Gulf end of Margaret Street and **The Half Shell Raw Bar** in Lands End Village. See at least one sunset at Mallory Square.

Check out the art, both in the galleries, and with street vendors.

Take one sunset, champagne sailboat cruise.

Try not to buy a T-shirt in every shop that sells them.

Thanks for letting me share my Keys with you.

Florida

West Palm Beach
"Dive The Golden Palm"

Don Lanman

It was about 10 a.m. when I entered the crowded shop. I was seeking the treasure map I knew had to be hidden among the scores of books, trinkets and dive equipment that littered the little shop The bright sunlight reflected off the water and streamed through the windows, casting an eerie glow on everything in the shop, including a group of browsing patrons who resembled a school of barracuda. But I was looking for a specific map, a guide that would lead me to the location of scores of sunken galleons and their cache of silver coins, gold and pieces of Eight. I had to move quickly for fear the "Cudas" would get there first.

From the corner of my eye, I could see the hint of a rainbow reflecting off a shelf of books and I knew it marked the spot. Not wanting to alert the others, I moved slowly toward the location to secure the book containing the map, as quietly as possible, and slipped away unnoticed.

Just then, the tall slightly built young man with a deep tan, long tangled yellow hair and a pirate's earring moved swiftly toward me, and in a soft voice said, "May I help you Sir?"

In an instant, my daydream adventure had evaporated, so I replied that the warm summer day was perfect for diving and all I needed was a new mesh bag to collect shells and other interesting artifacts from the ocean floor, thank-you very much.

The shop was filled with interesting friendly people, the type you usually find at a dive location, but this scene was unusual since this was a pro shop -for divers.

In fact, this pro shop was part of a dive company called **The Scuba Club**, a country club setting designed specifically for divers and located in one of the most beautiful settings in the world -West Palm Beach!

Florida is renowned for its diving; however, the focus is usually on the Keys. Interestingly, some of the best diving these emerald green waters have to offer is just north from Miami at Vero Beach.

Easy to reach, low cost, and with no foreign exchange or difficult third world travel, Palm Beach offers everything a diver could want and more -warm Gulf Stream waters that average 78 to 84 degrees Fahrenheit, to diving with visibility that frequently reaches 100 feet or more.

The Gulf waters of the Palm Beaches are teaming with all the types of sea life that you generally expect to find in more exotic locations like Grand Cayman or Truk.

Almost every dive produces encounters with a variety of creatures, including; turtles, lobsters, barracudas, sharks, moray eels, stripers, groupers, amberjacks, rays and an amazing variety of sea fans, and soft and hard corals.

To make this location even more exciting, it has one of the largest artificial reef systems in the world. If your passion is wreck diving, you'll have hundreds to choose from by diving this part of the Gold Coast.

The Scuba Club itself is a 25-year-old diving country club that was formerly known as the Norene Rouse Scuba Club. They have a pro shop, dive boats, swimming pool, deep tank, hot showers, steam room, photo lab and picnic area. Best of all, the diving is only 30 minutes from the dock.

The key to this country club is fun and safety. They offer NAUI, PADI and YMCA courses. All visitors are welcome, the rates are very reasonable, and memberships are available but not required. If you are a first time guest, be prepared to show your C-Card, log book and demonstrate your basic proficiency. There is a hyperbaric chamber in Miami.

The dive sights are numerous and exciting including: the **Breakers, Ron's Reef, North**

SCUBA AND SNORKELING FACILITIES QUESTIONNAIRE

NAME **The Scuba Club Inc.**
ADDRESS **4708 North Dixie Highway**
West Palm Beach, FL 33407
CONTACT **Mr. J.D. Duff**
TITLE **Manager**
TELEPHONE **407-844-2466**   FAX 407-844-8256

CAPITAL: **Tallahassee**   GOVERNMENT: **Democratic**
POPULATION: LANGUAGE: **English**
CURRENCY: **US dollar**   ELECTRICITY **120v**
AIRLINES: **All major U.S. carriers**   DEPARTURE TAX?
NEED VISA/PASSPORT?   YES   NO **x**   PROOF OF CITIZENSHIP?   YES   NO **x**

YOUR FACILITY IS CLASSIFIED AS: SCUBA CENTER **x**   RESORT **x**
BUSINESS HOURS: **Tuesday-Sunday 8:00 am to 5:00 pm**
CERTIFYING AGENCIES: **PADI, NAUI, SSI**
LOG BOOK REQUIRED?   YES **x**   NO
EQUIPMENT: SALES **x**   RENTALS **x**   AIR FILLS **x**
PRIMARY LINE OF EQUIPMENT: **US Divers**
PHOTOGRAPHIC EQUIPMENT: SALES **x**   RENTALS **x**   LAB **x**

CHARTER/DIVE BOAT AVAILABLE?   YES **x**   NO   DIVER CAPACITY **25**
COAST GUARD APPROVED?   YES **x**   NO   CAPTAIN LICENSED?   YES **x**   NO
SHIP TO SHORE? YES **x**   NO   LORAN   YES **x** NO   RADAR?   YES **x**   NO
DIVE MASTER/INSTRUCTOR ABOARD?   YES   NO   BOTH **x**

DIVING & SNORKELING: SALT **x**   FRESH
TYPE OF DIVING/SNORKELING IN AREA: WALL **x**   BEACH   WRECK **x**   REEF   CAVE **x**   ICE
DIVING/SNORKELING IN YOUR AREA IS BEST SUITED FOR: BEGINNER **x**   INTERMEDIATE **x**   ADVANCED **x**
BEST TIME OF YEAR FOR DIVING/SNORKELING: **Year round**
TEMPERATURE: NOV-APRIL: **70-80F**   MAY-OCT: **75-85F**
VISIBILITY: DIVING: **100+FT**   SNORKELING: **50FT**

PACKAGES AVAILABLE: DIVE **x**   DIVE STAY **x**   SNORKEL   SNORKEL-STAY
ACCOMMODATIONS NEARBY: HOTEL **x**   MOTEL **x**   HOME RENTALS **x**
ACCOMMODATION RATES: EXPENSIVE **x**   MODERATE **x**   INEXPENSIVE **x**
RESTAURANTS NEARBY: EXPENSIVE **x**   MODERATE **x**   INEXPENSIVE **x**
YOUR AREA IS: REMOTE   QUIET WITH ACTIVITIES **x**   LIVELY **x**
LOCAL ACTIVITY/NIGHTLIFE: **All available**
CAR NEEDED TO EXPLORE AREA?   YES **x**   NO
DUTY FREE SHOPPING?   YES **x**   NO

LOCAL EMERGENCY SERVICES   NEAREST HYPERBARIC TREATMENT FACILITY
COASTGUARD: AUTHORITY:
TELEPHONE: LOCATION:
CALLSIGNS: TELEPHONE:

LOCAL DIVING DOCTOR:
NAME:
LOCATION:
TELEPHONE:

Hook, **Jupiter High Ledge**, wrecks of the *Esso Bonaire*, *Mizpah*, PC-1170, *Amaryllis* and a **Rolls Royce** automobile (honestly).

Of all the sites, however, my favorites are the *Mizpah* and *Amaryllis*. The *Mizpah* is a Greek luxury liner. She is intact and very easy to penetrate. Since she has been down for over 25 years, there is a wonderful collection of sea life from great barracuda to turtles and groupers.

The *Amaryllis* is a beautiful wreck of a 400-foot freighter. There's not much left except for the ribs, but drifting over her grave gives one the feeling of being in a surrealistic painting.

Beyond the wrecks, reefs, walls, warm clear water and sea life, you always have the chance of drifting over a 300 year old Galleon. If diving adventure has a name, it must be West Palm Beach, the Golden Palm of the Caribbean.

Two Angels by Alan Marquardt

The Hawaiian Islands

Forward

Wendy Canning Church

Hawaii, our 50th state, comprised of 132 islands, is situated some 2,000 miles from the American Continent and 2,000 miles away from any other major island making them the most isolated archipelago in the world.

The island chain is less than 6,500 square miles. Its topography is made up of vast mountain ranges, sloping green valleys leading to coastal flatlands, and beyond to coral reefs.

Only in the last few decades has the science of archaeology been utilized to ascertain its people's origins, which are thought to be Asian.

It is believed, through the use of carbon dating, that the first settlers came from the Marquesas Islands in the 8th century.

The Polynesians dated events by generations and reigns of Chiefs, thus an exact chronology is difficult to confirm. Settlements were in small groups, their governments were tribal with the Chief as ruler. They worshipped many Gods and the priests brought the Gods' messages to its people. Their diet consisted of fish and poi (a paste made from cooked and processed taro root); a variety of fruits and meat was also available.

The main occupations were agriculture and fishing. By the time white settlers arrived in the late 18th century, 300,000 people populated the largest islands in the chain which were Hawaii, the biggest island, Maui, Molokai, Lanai, Kahoolawi, Oahu, Kauai and Niihan.

British Captain James Cook on his third mission to find a sea passage from the Pacific to the Atlantic across the north of the American continent came upon Oahu on January 18, 1778.

Oahu meaning "The Gathering Place" is 40 miles long and 26 miles at its widest point, an area of 595 square miles.

In its earliest days Oahu was known to sailors worldwide as the crossroads to the Pacific because it had the only safe protected harbor on its southeastern shore. Today Oahu is noted for its tourism. It also houses major military bases, four sugar plantations, three pineapple companies and maintains a large service industry to accommodate the tourists and year round population.

On his fourth mission Captain Cook landed with his two ships **H.M.S. Discovery** and **H.M.S. Resolution** in Keolakekua Bay on January 17, 1770 and Hawaii or the "Big Island" was discovered.

Editor's note: Rainy season begins in November and ends in March.
HAWAII VISITORS AND CONVENTION BUREAU
P.O. BOX 8527
HONOLULU, HI 96830
TEL: 800-GO-HAWAII

Oahu

"The Gathering Place"

THE DIVING AND SNORKELING

"Bubbling Enterprises" is owned and operated by Jack and Adele Papas. They provide a full range of water activities. Offering both NAUI and PADI, openwater through instructor level courses; night and twilight dives, spear fishing and lobster hunting.

Jack has a wonderful sense of humor and amazed us with his wealth of information. For example, the state fish is the Humuhumu-nukunukua Pua'a. There is a legend that if you look closely at this fish, you will eventually see the blue stripe, which represents the ocean, and the red along the side represents a volcanic lava floor.

Try the excitement of a jet-ski trip, the beauty of viewing Oahu from a para sail soaring along the coast, or the heart-stopping thrill of an open jet boat ride. Whatever your favorite water activity - they can help to make it safe and fun. Twenty plus years of showing the beauty of Hawaii's ocean to visiting friends make this the place to call in planning your Hawaiian Ocean Adventure.

Bubbling Enterprises can arrange dive-stay vacations on Oahu for every budget.

DIVE SITES

Haleiwa Trench - This is a wall dive with depth and visibility of up to 100 feet. It has an abundant coral formation - finger coral, mushroom coral, crisp coral, razor coral and a thriving colony of green sea turtles, an endangered species, some of which weigh up to 400 pounds. Most divers see 7 to 14 of these rare and graceful creatures with an occasional manta ray. The shallow coral area (up to 40 feet) is perfect for beginners while the deeper wall dive is tops for experienced divers.

Pupukea (or Sharks Cove) - on the beautiful north shore is a protected marine reserve with mazes of lava tubes and caverns. **The bay with tremendous schools of fish and curious and friendly octopus is for the beginner diver while the lava tube system in a once-in-a-lifetime experience for the experienced diver.**

Lanai Lookout - This spectacular dive site on the rugged east coast is definitely for experienced divers only. A current dive with arches, caves, 80 food depth and an average visibility of over 100 feet, is a don't miss area for every experienced diver.

Magic Island - This area is also known as Rainbow Reef due to the unparalleled number of colorful reef fish that congregate there: turtles, spotted eagle rays. Magic Island is also world renowned for the rare varieties of nudibranch. Suitable for both beginners and experienced divers with a maximum depth of 40 feet and an average visibility of 70. Perfect for underwater photos.

Kahe Point - On the quiet west shore of Oahu, Kahe Point offers 100-foot visibility and large schools of fish attracted by the warm water exhaust from the Electric Plant. Suitable for both beginner and certified divers with an average depth of 30 feet.

BEST SNORKELING AREAS

Alii Beach - in Haleiwa, has a profusion of coral varieties with a depth of 3 to 20 feet.

Sharks Cove – is a marine sanctuary with a depth of 5 to 25 feet; clear, calm waters with a tremendous variety of fish.

Hanauma Bay – is world renowned for the shallow fringing reef, this nature reserve offers everything from beginner to advanced snorkeling.

Keehi Lagoon – is shallow, calm and protected; feed the fish by hand and perfect for underwater photos.

BEACHES AND PARKS

Ala Moana - This beach is a favorite of the Kama'ainas (locals). Excellent swimming and sunning can be found here. Good beach for kids. Facilities and parking are available. Ala Moana is a 10-minute drive from the pier.

Waikiki - The most famous and popular beach in the islands, is actually a series of beaches stretching from Duke Kahanamoku Lagoon to Kaimana Beach at the foot of Diamond Head. Waikiki offers swimming, sunning, and people watching. The water is excellent for beginning surfers. Catamaran and outrigger rides are available. Sand is fine and groomed daily. Facilities and parking are available.

Haunauma Bay – offers **Oahu's best snorkeling**. Beautifully situated in a now submerged volcanic crater. Good swimming, snorkeling, and sunning. Gets crowded - go early. Facilities, snackstand and parking are available.

Makapu'u Beach - Below Makapu'u Lighthouse and across from Sealife Park. Very scenic. Good sunning and swimming. Bodysurfing good but waves can be very dangerous. Facilities and parking are available. Makapu'u is a 50 minute ride from the pier.

Kailua Beach Park - beautiful powdery white sand beach. Conditions are very good for swimming and sunning. Facilities and parking are available. Kailua is a picturesque 40-minute drive from the pier.

Kahana Beach Park - A beautiful and tranquil bay. Good swimming and sunning. Facilities and parking are available. Kahana is a 60-minute drive from the pier.

Sunset Beach – **has ideal snorkeling**, swimming and sunning are found along this popular North Shore beach during the calm summer months. In winter, this beach provides excellent surfing (for the experienced only). Facilities and parking are available. Sunset Beach is a 60-minute drive from the pier.

POINTS OF INTEREST

Aloha Tower - Honolulu's familiar landmark is open to visitors and offers an excellent view of the harbor area.

Aquarium - On Kalakaua Avenue across from Kapiolani Park at Waikiki, the aquarium contains a world-famous collection of beautifully colored tropical fish.

Beaches - Beautiful beaches, wherever you go, for swimming, surfing, fishing or a picnic.

Bishop Museum and Planetarium - At 1525 Bernice Street, the museum houses the world's foremost collection of Hawaiiana and Polynesian antiquities.

Blow Hole - Near Koko Head, playful Mother Nature forces the mighty sea through a tiny hole in a lava ledge and blows miniature geysers high into the air.

Byodo-in Temple - Japan's 900 year-old architectural treasure is duplicated in exact detail at the Valley of the Temples Memorial Park, beneath the majestic cliffs of the Koolau mountains. The beautiful Oriental Garden setting also has a carp pool, massive 9 foot Buddha statue and a teahouse.

Castle Park - Hawaii's first theme park, this family entertainment center is adjacent to Aloha Stadium.

Chinatown - Unlike the Chinatowns in other American cities, this section of downtown Honolulu is an exciting blend of shops, restaurants and markets displaying not only Chinese goods but wares and foods typical of the countries of origin of Hawaii's early day immigrants.

Diamond Head - This world-renowned landmark bounds Waikiki Beach on the south. An extinct volcano, it is said to have once been the home of Pele, the fire Goddess.

East West Center - A center for cultural and academic interchange between the peoples of Asia and the United States. Established by the US Congress in 1960, the center has since become a public, non-profit educational corporation with offices and facilities adjacent to the University of Hawaii campus.

Foster Botanic Garden - Remarkable botanic displays including photogenic orchid section in a 20 acre setting in downtown Honolulu.

Hanauma Bay - A delightful sea cove in Koko Head Park, its rugged grandeur was created by volcanic action 10,000 years ago when Pele made her last attempt to find a home on Oahu, as legend tells. A favorite spot for swimming, picnicking and snorkeling.

"Peek A Boo"

Hawaii Maritime Center - Includes Aloha Tower plus the square-rigged sails of Clyde and the Hokule, a Polynesian sailing canoe.

Honolulu Academy of Art - A registered national and state historic place, renowned for an extensive collection of Asian and Western art and the beauty of its grounds and buildings.

Honolulu International Airport - Nine miles west of Waikiki, the Honolulu Airport is the hub of the Pacific for Trans-Pacific Airlines as well as several inter- island airlines.

Iolani Palace - Only throne room under the American flag, where Hawaii's last two monarchs lived and ruled. Completed in 1882, the building has been entirely renovated, displaying a magnificent interior.

Kamehameha Schools - Established by a member of Hawaii's royal family for boys and girls of Hawaiian ancestry.

Kaneana Cave - Near Makua just before the end of Farrington Highway, Kaneana, the Sharkman Deity, is supposed to have made his home in this cave which is volcanic and coral in formation.

Kawaiahao Church - Dedicated in 1842, the "Westminster Abbey" of Hawaii offers Sunday services in Hawaiian and English.

Kewalo Basin - Sampans and other fishing boats moor in this small boat harbor which is also the departure point for Pearl Harbor cruises.

Mission Houses - The oldest existing buildings, erected by the first missionary contingent to Honolulu, are in the civic center area as are many other historic sites.

Mormon Temple - Built in beautiful Laie in 1920, it is the first Mormon Temple to be constructed outside of Salt Lake City.

National Memorial Cemetery of the Pacific - Puowaina, literally translated "Hill of Sacrifice" is the final resting-place of thousands of World War II, Korean and Vietnam War veterans. Open seven days a week, it overlooks the vast expanse of Pearl Harbor, Honolulu and Waikiki.

Nuuanu Pali - Oahu's scenic masterpiece, at the head of Nuuanu Valley, is where Kamehameha the Great defeated the Oahuans in a bloody battle in 1795. Forcing thousands of warriors over the precipice, to meet death on the jagged rocks below he added Oahu to this realm.

Old Sugar Mill - Near Kaaawa are the stone ruins of the first sugar mill on Oahu erected in 1864.

Paradise Park - Situated in Manoa Valley, the park is an extensive tropical exhibit set amidst ethnic gardens depicting Hawaii's golden people. Hundreds of tropical birds inhabit the park which features an entertaining demonstration of trained birds. Stroll along trails through bamboo forests, jungle growth, mountain streams and waterfalls.

Pearl Harbor - the USS Arizona Memorial, above the sunken battleship, is a tribute to American fighting men killed during the attack on December 7, 1941. The USS Bowfin, a restored World War II submarine, is on exhibit next to the Arizona Memorial ground facility.

Polynesian Cultural Center at Laie - Located on the north shore of Oahu, the center is made up of native villagers representative of those in Fiji, Tonga, New Zealand, Tahiti, Samoa, Marquesas and Hawaii.

Queen Emma Summer Place - A charming home, located in Nuuana Valley, this former summer palace has been restored to its original appearance and houses a fine collection of Hawaiiana.

Rabbit Island - Near Waimanalo, this is one of the many interesting islets that border Oahu. It looks like the head of a rabbit and was once overrun with them.

Royal Mausoleum - Resting-place of Hawaii's former rulers, with well informed guide-custodians.

Sea Life Park - Located at Makapuu Point, Sea Life Park features an outstanding display of Hawaii's exotic marine life in a truly beautiful oceanside setting. The 30,000-gallon Hawaiian Reef Tank is one of America's finest aquariums, housing 2,000 island specimens: shark, rays, moray eels, turtles and exotic reef fish. Giant whales, dolphins, sea lions, penguins and a variety of sea birds can also be enjoyed.

Waimea Bay - Between Haleiwa and Kakuku, the beach is fine for picnicking but the bay is dangerous for swimming when surf is 6 feet or more.

Waimea Falls Park - This narrow canyon extending into the Koolau Mountains was once a heavily populated Hawaiian village. Today, the 1,800-acre site between Haleiwa and Kahuku, is a dwelling for nature's lovely, unspoiled environment of tropical plantlife, birds, hiking trails and a truly beautiful waterfall.

ACCOMMODATIONS
THE KAHALA MANDARIN ORIENTAL

In an ere of new, glitzy mega-resorts, the Kahala Mandarin Oriental (before a $75 million dollar renovation) retains the grace and elegance of another era while at the same time sacrificing nothing to maintain a high standard of service. Its location lends to the complete aura of serenity for it is situated in Oahu's exclusive Waialai Kahalai residential neighborhood. One has the Koolau Kahalai mountain range as a backdrop, with frontage on the waters of Manaulua Bay and the Pacific Ocean.

We stayed at the **Lagoon Terrace Wing**. Our accommodations were spacious with views of the lagoon where bottlenose dolphin romp and the pool and sea beyond. It was decorated in light pastels with a comfortable sitting area, cable television, large bath and dressing area, mini-bar and a wonderful terrace to take breakfast, read or sun.

Each table in the open-air dining room has a view of the sea.

SCUBA AND SNORKELING FACILITIES QUESTIONNAIRE

NAME   **Bubbling Enterprises**
ADDRESS   **c/o Kahala Hilton**
                5000 Kahala Avenue, Honolulu, Hawaii 96816
CONTACT   **Mr. Jack Pappas**
TITLE   **Owner**
TELEPHONE   **808-735-8979**   FAX **808-737-2478 c/o Kahala Hilton**

CAPITAL: **Honolulu**   GOVERNMENT: **USA**
POPULATION: **100,000**   LANGUAGE: **English**
CURRENCY: **US $**   ELECTRICITY: **Yes**
AIRLINES: **All major carriers**   DEPARTURE TAX? **$3.00**
NEED VISA/PASSPORT?   YES   NO **x**   PROOF OF CITIZENSHIP?   YES   NO **x Not for US**
citizens

YOUR FACILITY IS CLASSIFIED AS: SCUBA CENTER   RESORT **x**
BUSINESS HOURS: **0800 - 1700**
CERTIFYING AGENCIES: **PADI, NAUI**
LOG BOOK REQUIRED?   YES   NO **x**
EQUIPMENT: SALES **x**   RENTALS **x**   AIR FILLS **x**
PRIMARY LINE OF EQUIPMENT: **Scuba PRC**
PHOTOGRAPHIC EQUIPMENT: SALES   RENTALS **x**   LAB

CHARTER/DIVE BOAT AVAILABLE?   YES **x**   NO   DIVER CAPACITY **14**
COAST GUARD APPROVED?   YES **x**   NO   CAPTAIN LICENSED? YES **x**   NO
SHIP TO SHORE? YES **x**   NO LORAN YES **x** NO   RADAR? YES **x**   NO
DIVE MASTER/INSTRUCTOR ABOARD?   YES **x**   NO   BOTH **x**

DIVING & SNORKELING: SALT **x**   FRESH
TYPE OF DIVING/SNORKELING IN AREA: WALL **x**   BEACH **x**   WRECK **x**   REEF   CAVE **x**   ICE
DIVING/SNORKELING IN YOUR AREA IS BEST SUITED FOR: BEGINNER **x** INTERMEDIATE **x** ADVANCED **x**
BEST TIME OF YEAR FOR DIVING/SNORKELING: **April - November**
TEMPERATURE: **NOV-APRIL:**   75-85 F   **MAY-OCT:**   80-90 F
VISIBILITY: **DIVING:**   50 FT   **SNORKELING:**   50 FT

PACKAGES AVAILABLE: DIVE **x**   DIVE STAY   SNORKEL **x**   SNORKEL-STAY
 ACCOMMODATIONS NEARBY: HOTEL **x**   MOTEL   HOME RENTALS
ACCOMMODATION RATES: EXPENSIVE **x**   MODERATE **x**   INEXPENSIVE **x**

RESTAURANTS NEARBY: EXPENSIVE **x**   MODERATE **x**   INEXPENSIVE **x**
YOUR AREA IS: REMOTE   QUIET WITH ACTIVITIES   LIVELY **x**
LOCAL ACTIVITY/NIGHTLIFE: **Everything and anything**
CAR NEEDED TO EXPLORE AREA?   YES **x**   NO
DUTY FREE SHOPPING?   YES **x**   NO

LOCAL EMERGENCY SERVICES   NEAREST HYPERBARIC TREATMENT FACILITY
COASTGUARD: **Pier 4 Honolulu**   AUTHORITY: **USCG - Art Arnold, MD, Dive Medicine**
TELEPHONE: **808-541-2064**   LOCATION: **Honolulu, Hawaii 42 Ahui Street**
CALLSIGNS: **KQ21 531**   TELEPHONE: **808-523-9155**
LOCAL DIVING DOCTOR:
NAME: **J. Wood Ferren**
LOCATION: **K-K Medical Centre**
TELEPHONE:

If you are a shopper, the many boutiques will entice you with their tasteful wares. Do you play chess or backgammon? Perhaps shuffleboard is your hobby. Do you wish to snorkel, windsurf or scuba dive? All this is available on the premises.

The Maunalua Bay Club is minutes away by complimentary shuttle. This Oceanside tennis and fitness club is for the use of members and guests of the hotel.

Don't leave the children behind. Despite its sophistication, the hotel has hosted many of the same families year after year. **Kamp Kahala is run for ages 6-12.** Junior hosts and hostesses supervise it each day. Except for transportation and admission fees, the children's program is free. Babysitting services are also available.

The discriminating executive will find the Kahala a perfect, quiet retreat while at the same time conducting business in an international atmosphere.

When booking, request the rooms overlooking the lagoon. They are more expensive, but are worth every penny. We will return for Vol. III for an update. Our question is how will they have improved on perfection!!

For more information contact

Kahala Mandarin Oriental
5000 Kahala Avenue
Honolulu, HI 96816-5498
Telephone: 808-739-8888
Fax: 808-739-8800

Campers and hikers write or call:

Hawaii Geographic Society
P. O. Box 1698
Honolulu, HI 96806-1698
Tel: 808 538 3952

Hawaii

The "Big Island"

Touring the "Big Island" is a real adventure. Hawaii's vast size is nearly that of Connecticut and it has a wide variety of climates and attractions. All about the island you will discover traces of the ancient Hawaiian civilization and view relics from Monarchy days. You go from sandy beaches to lava wastelands, from rocky deserts to sweet mountain meadows, from peaceful bays to volcanic craters.

Kona, on Hawaii's leeward side is the gateway to the Big Island. Visitors may also arrive at Hilo or Kamuela. Hilo curves gracefully around a bay. Surrounded by fields of orchids and anthurium, it is the floral center of the islands.

On the nearby coastal plains you'll wander through immense orchards of macadamia nut trees and lush groves of succulent papaya.

From Hilo you can drive 30 minutes to Hawaii National Park and gigantic Kilauea Crater. Kilauea is the legendary home of Madame Pele, Hawaiian goddess of fire. Sulfurous steam billows from deep fissures to scorch the earth. Charcoal trees attest to past volcanic furies, ancient lava flows mark the island's growth. You can stand on the rim of Helemanumau Firepit in the Kilauea Caldera and with luck watch Pele at play as lava foundations spring up from the firepit floor. **You can even walk through a long lava tube, created by a molten stream centuries ago. The outside cooled first while the inner stream flowed on, leaving an eerie cave.**

After exploring these awesome wonders of nature primeval, **swing south along the coast to the famous beaches of black sand** then around to Hawaii's leeward side and the Kona coast. It was down these sandy stretches that defeated warriors once raced for their lives toward the Pu'uhonua O Honaunau (Place of Refuge), now a National Historic Park.

The calm ocean is perfect for swimming and boating, but the big lure of Kona is deep-sea fishing for the mighty Pacific Blue Marlin. The colorful Kailua-Kona fleet awaits you. Each summer the world's best sportfishermen converge on Kailua for the Hawaiian International Billfish Tournament.

Challenging golf is played on several public courses scattered around the island. The distinctive Kona coffee bean, sought by connoisseurs, grows on the lower slopes of the mountains. Kona coffee is the only coffee produced commercially in the United States. In this balmy county you'll likely meet your first Hawaiian cowboy down on holiday from Parker Ranch.

The State's finest hunting is found on the slopes of Mauna Kea and Hualalai which teem with pheasant, chukkar partridge, wild boar, goat and sheep. Almost any sort of vacation you want is for the asking on the "Big Island".

POINTS OF INTEREST

Akaka Falls - North of Hilo, plunges over 420 feet in a sheer drop over volcanic cliff.

Black Sand Beaches - of Kaimu and Punaluu, made up of pulverized lava, are on the southeastern shoreline.

Captain Cook Monument - at Kealakekua Bay, is a tribute to the British navigator and discoverer of the Hawaiian Islands who was killed on the shoreline in 1779.

American missionaries who first landed on this coast in 1820 erected the first Christian Church at Kailua-Kona.

Hawaii Volcanoes National Park - One of the top scenic attractions in the Aloha State, has an array of unique volcanic formations, forests of giant tree ferns, steaming craters and a volcanological museum, which has free color movies daily.

Hulihee Palace - In the village of Kailua-Kona, was once the summer home of Hawaiian royalty and now houses a rare collection of Hawaiiana.

Kamehameha Statue - in Kohala, was lost at sea during shipment to Hawaii and later recovered after a replica had been made and erected in Honolulu.

Kamuela Museum - in Kamuela/Waimea, with royal Hawaiian treasures from Iolani Palace, ancient Hawaiian artifacts and art objects from around the world.

Lapakahi State Historical Park - north of Kawaihae, was once an ancient Hawaiian fishing village.

Laupahoehoe - which literally translated means "leaf of lava" is one of the Hamakua Coast's many scenic and historic spots.

Lava Flows - are marked by warrior signs, which designate flows, which have surged down the mountains of Mauna Loa and Kilauea since prehistoric times.

Lyman Mission House and Museum - in the city of Hilo, contains a collection of historic Hawaiian relics.

Orchids and Anthuriums are grown in profusion on Hilo and surrounding areas for export to far parts of the world.

Painted Church at Honaunau St. Benedict's is the oldest Catholic Church on the island constructed in 1875. The church has brilliantly hued murals depicting biblical scenes on the interior walls. A priest painted the murals in the Star of the Sea Catholic Church at Kalapana over a half century ago.

Parker Ranch - in the Waimea-Kamuela district at the foot of Mauna Kea, is the second largest cattle ranch under the American flag.

Pololu Valley - in Kohala, was once the locale of a number of ancient Hawaiian heiaus (temples).

Pu'uhonua O Honaunau (Place of Refuge) A National Historical Park, is said to have been built at the Honaunau location in the 12th century to provide political and religious asylum.

Puukohola Heiau - near Kawaihae, was built by Karnehameha the Great and is now a national historical site.

Rainbow Falls - one of the Big Island's loveliest waterfalls, is located in Hilo.

Waha'ula Heiau - at the foot of the Chain of Craters Road is maintained by the National Park Service as part of Volcanoes National Park. Walking tours available.

Waipio Valley - north of the town of Honokaa, was once the home to the kings of Hawaii.

White Sand Beaches - at Hapuna State Beach Park, Anehoomalu Beach, and Magic Sands Beach, Kailua, all on the western side of the island.

HAWAII - KONA

White Sands - Also known as "Disappearing Sands" because surf often washes away the sand. This beach offers great body surfing when the sand is "in". Facilities available. Parking limited. White Sands is a 10-minute drive from the pier.

Kahalu'u - A popular coarse sand beach offers **good swimming, sunning and snorkeling**. Facilities and parking available. Kahalu'u is a 15 minute drive from the pier.

Pu'uhonua O Honaunau - Vestiges of old Hawaii, life size tikis, grass shacks and an ancient outrigger canoe can be experienced at the famous Place of Refuge located in this state park. **The area is also good for snorkeling** and scuba diving. Facilities and parking available. Pu'uhonua is a 45 minute drive from the pier.

Hapuna - One half mile of Hawaii's most beautiful beaches, this popular park **offers great snorkeling**, scuba and swimming with some caution. Sunning good. Facilities and parking available. Hapuna is a 40-minute drive from the pier.

HAWAII - HILO

James Kealoha - Small white sand beach. Rest rooms, freshwater and picnic tables. Parking available. James Kealoha is a 10-minute drive from the pier.

Onekahakaha - Small white sand beach with tidal pool. Restrooms, fresh water and picnic tables. Parking available. Onekahakaha is a 10-minute drive from the pier.

Leleiwi Beach Park - crowds of inshore tropical fish.

Hawaii

The Big Island by Sea

The Kona Aggressor II

We arrived after a thirty-minute flight; one of the crew from the *Kona Aggressor II* greeted us with a wonderful smile, hug and a lei. The lei is a customary welcome in these islands, yet each time I am greeted this way I am touched This handiwork of beauty, so delicate, emitting a sweet, subtle fragrance embodies the essence of the Hawaiian Islands.

The yacht lay before us, painted red, white and blue in Honokolau Harbor. **She is a comfortable yacht and perfectly outfitted for the scuba diver.**

The following morning we awoke to the sound of engines. No need for an alarm clock on this boat. At seven o'clock the Captain starts the engines and heads off to a new destination.

Our cruise took us along the western shore of the Hawaii and Kona coasts. There we found waters filled with multi-colored fish of all varieties and sizes and bays and villages steeped in Hawaiian history. We cruised not more than a mile from shore and were able to video and photograph the mountain ranges, jagged hills and green valleys interspersed with lava flow.

Eighty-five miles long, the Kona coast is warm during the day and cooled by the evening tradewinds. It is those same tradewinds shifting suddenly that can drive a sailor in search of a safe harbor. This was to be our luck for the next two days.

The Captain told us that one of the reasons that there are so few private charters in these waters is due to a dearth of moorings. He and the crew have put down thirty such moorings along the coast. They chart their location and let others use them.

Our destination for the next two days was Keolakekua Bay. On our way we watched in awe as whales breached off our bow. We even saw a pair breach, which is quite unusual. The whales are in these waters this time of year where they come to mate and calve.

One can do repetitive dives as long as they adhere to the Navy tables. Diving must be in buddy teams.

Each diver has a locker and behind each locker are two tanks. There is an area for drying wet suits, large camera station with rental equipment, battery chargers and space for personal equipment. An E-6 processing lab is onboard and a rinse tank is provided for cameras.

The large dive platform has two ladders. Entry is giant stride. A blackboard is provided and a map of the area of the dive site is sketched out along with the names of fish, plant life and coral you might see. A bar is thrown over the side for ascents with a regulator for out of air situations.

Kona Agressor II courtesy of Kona Agressor

The meals are buffet style, simple but the food is fresh and well prepared. Soft drinks, wine, beer and liquor are included in the price of charter.

KEOLAKEKUA BAY

The bay was calm, beautiful and steeped in history. Captain James Cook landed here on January 17, 1779 during festival time. His welcome was a warm one. He set out on February 4, 1779 but returned because of storm damage to his ship. Returning to the bay for repairs, he laid anchor. During the night a boat from his Flagship **H.M.S. Resolution** was stolen. This was unthinkable to Captain Cook and he went ashore to take Chief Kalanipuu as hostage. A fight broke out and Cook fired on the natives. Captain Cook was struck down, bludgeoned to death and his flesh was eaten. A lovely stark white obelisk stands at water's edge, a memorial to this courageous man, Captain, chart maker, a leader of men, an explorer's explorer.

THE AQUARIUM

There are one hundred and seventy-six species of fish endemic to these waters.

The Aquarium is aptly named for it is here that the scuba diver or snorkeler will find a myriad of reef fish. Depths range from relatively shallow down to 110 feet.

We dropped down to fifty feet making our way along the wall. We were armed with peas, a favorite of the nenui, gray in color, so you much watch closely for them. Dozens of pink tail durgeons sashayed by followed by pennant fish, yellow tang, barred fire fish, snowflake, yellow margin zebra, Hawaiian squirrelfish and saddle wrasse.

The sun was high and shone brightly through the water making a flash for cameras unnecessary. Schools of butterhead parrotfish, forceps fish, butterfish and yellow tang came out for the shoot and what actors they were! At one point I just remained still and watched the parade go by!

HAMMERHEAD POINT

Just outside of the bay is Hammerhead Point. It is here that one can make a date with Barney the turtle at exactly 8:45 each morning. Make sure you bring Barney breakfast, he expects it.

The yacht pulled in close to the site where the visibility was 100 feet. We descended to 40 feet. Our guide was armed with a goodie bag. Barney didn't keep us waiting. Much to the consternation of his buddies, Barney had center stage. Definitely the lead in this shoot! He frolicked and ate, swam around us, left us, turned around and came back.

MILOLII

This tiny village of Milolii is the oldest continuous settlement on Hawaii where natives earn their living from the sea. Although fishermen now use outboard motors on their canoes, they still haul their boats up the rocky shores by hand. The fish are salted and dried in the sun.

We went ashore to photograph its stone walls covered in night blooming Cereus, a charming yellow church, small straw huts and canoes. There is nothing to buy, only a tiny grocery store, but it was good to be on land for a while and to walk an interesting stretch of black lava shoreline.

TABASTREA TUNNEL

Our first dive off Milolii was Tabastrea Tunnel. On this dive you are likely to find turtles, mantas, octopus, and eagle rays. Be sure to bring your light and perhaps you will see the white tip shark which inhabits one of the three caves. They were not present on that dive. We were especially delighted by the beautiful cup coral and the nudibranchs.

THE LIGHTHOUSE

We found that the site was of interest not so much for the fish life but for the topography. The archways were magnificent. There were peaks and valleys and one felt as if they were discovering a mountain range beneath the water with the sun glistening down the slopes.

KAULUOA POINT

It was time to begin our journey home. We stopped along the way and dived Kauluoa Point. Here we found a three-room cave. As if one of the Gods knew our cruise was coming to an end they sent out ghost shrimp, pin cushions, sea stars, lionfish, conger eels, leaf fish, cowlies and Hawaiian slipper. Unfortunately Cozy, the conger eel, was somewhere else that day.

ROB'S REEF

In Skull Cave on Rob's Reef there were nudibranchs, blennies, gobys, and other divers came upon yellow margin, moray eels, conger eels, fatworms, but no whale sharks or manta rays which are usually present.

Dome Cave was our next site. For photographers this is known as "Nudibranch Haven." Sailfish, tangs, eels, cowries also were spotted along with all types of reef fish. There is a complex of caves filled with fascinating topography.

This was the last dive of the trip. The charter runs from Saturday to Saturday. I have never seen a crew work harder or longer hours. The schedule allows for a 2 p.m. arrival where guests can either leave the boat and continue their stay ashore or can take the launch into town for shopping and dinner ashore with leave taking place very early the next morning.

We bid farewell to the crew, exchanged addresses and hopes that we would meet again on the high seas.

Mohalo to the crew of the Kona Aggressor.

Note: Due to seasonal and unexpected seas, we suggest inexperienced divers check weather conditions when booking.

Reservations
Agressor Fleet, Ltd.

328

P.O. Drawer K
Morgan City, LA 70381
Tel : 800 348 2628

Hawaii

"Hawaii by Land"

Kona Village Resort

Wendy Canning Church

Our car pulled off the Queen Kaakumanu Highway and after following a long road we approached the gatehouse, giving our name the guard waved us on. This procedure is a preamble of the attention to detail the Kona Village Resort gives to each guest's privacy and comfort.

Proceeding down the long road the resort's beauty unfolded before us. 82 acres of lush greenery was interspersed with century old lava flow and lovely examples of Polynesian architecture. In the distance the sea sparkled in various shades of blue and emerald green.

The Kona Village Obana (family) numbers two hundred and thirty. **Fred Duerr, General Manager for twenty-six years, is referred to by some of the guests as "Father".** You will meet Fred at the managers' cocktail party on Tuesday night.

There are 125 individual hales(thatched huts), the largest group in Hawaii. They are dispersed over the eighty-two private acres situated either on the lagoon, in the gardens or by the sea. Surrounded by tens of thousands of acres of undeveloped land, the complex sits at the foot of Mount Hualalai and runs to the water's edge.

According to ancient legend, the fire goddess Pele, unleashed her anger in 1801 on Mount Hualalai. The mountain erupted and its fiery entrails were strung over the small, thriving fishing village. Miraculously, one small area around Kahuwai Bay and fifteen acres of petroglyphs were spared. In 1965, one hundred and fifty years later, Johonno Jackson built his paradise on this very spot.

In those days there were only forty hales. Guests and supplies arrived by boat or plane since there was no road and each arrival was an event. Guests and staff would turn out not only to greet the new arrivals, but also to check out the shipments of supplies.

We arrived at our hale, the Na Hale, one of 65 renovated in 1996, it's architecture is representative of one of the lighter styles of ancient Polynesian culture. It sat on stilts, the embodiment of the South Pacific. Hale Moana and Hale Samoa were refurbished in 1997.

Entering our hale, we found our new home to be sun splashed and spacious. The decor was in shades of pastel. There was a king size bed and an alcove, which doubled as a dressing room and another sleeping area. A small refrigerator was stocked with mineral water and juices, a coffee maker with built-in coffee grinder and local Kona coffee beans was a nice touch for early risers.

After unpacking I stepped out on the balcony, listening to the sounds of silence. When man works in harmony with nature he creates a beautiful canvas.

What you will not find in your room are televisions, radios, phones, or air conditioning. This is in keeping with the aura of tranquillity that envelops you during your stay.

We set off for luncheon, which is served in the oceanside Hale Moana. Luncheon is buffet style, not only pleasing to the eye, but replete with a wide variety of selections to satisfy any palate. Breakfast is also served at the Hale Moana.

At dinner time guests have the option of dining at the Hale Moana or the Hale Samoa where gourmet dining is available every night except Wednesday and Friday.

On Wednesday evenings a Pariolo (cowboy) steak fry is served at the Hale Ho'okipa

329

Hospitality House set on the beautiful lagoon and gardens. On Fridays, guests enjoy a luau and Polynesian show in the same spot.

The Kona Resort's daily rate is all inclusive, three meals (FAP) plus more activities. If adults are not content to swim in one of the two pools or in the bay, and sunning or reading is not their choice, then there are myriad of other activities offered. They are included in the daily rate: unlimited use of Sunfish, sailboats, snorkeling gear, outrigger canoes, tennis courts, Scuba is extra.

Throughout the week, lessons in lei making and snorkeling are scheduled for the guests. There is also a tennis clinic. Scuba diving, catamaran sailing and tennis lessons are optional Golf can be arranged at a nearby 18 hole course.

Willie Ward is in charge of the scuba diving. One can become certified, take advanced courses, have a video made or book a dive. Willie says he separates divers on dive tours according to their level of experience. From what we've seen in these waters a dive/stay at the Kona Village Resort would delight any diver! The Kona is also a superb choice for the scuba diver traveling with a non-diver or snorkeler for it provides many optional interesting activities.

Although its atmosphere is a sophisticated one, this resort if very family oriented. There is **a daily children's program supervised** by junior hosts and hostesses. A children's pool was built in 1987. We think a very nice option is the early children's dinner hour at 5:30 p.m. This gives parents the opportunity to dine leisurely at a later hour. Children's movies are shown after dinner. **It is no wonder that families return year after year.**

The business traveler is also warmly received. What a perfect spot for a pre or post conference visit, or a meeting in an ambiance of taste.

We returned to our room to rest before dinner, placing our pineapple outside our door, which means: "Do Not Disturb."

The following day we arranged for a car and toured the island. There is a great deal to see. A complimentary van transports guests to the airport five and a half miles away to pick up your car. A van will return you to the hotel in the afternoon. Remember to request a picnic the night before.

Only a short drive away is the petroglyph field, Pu'abonua O Honacnau, or "The Place of Refuge." It was here that ancient Hawaiians would come to be given a second lease on life. You will find ancient carvings of dogs, turtles, fish and stick figures in the rocks telling stories of earlier times.

All that's needed when arranging for the Kona Village Resort's 'Island Wedding' package is the bride and groom - the resort provides everything else.

As I sat on my balcony the bright, orange-red sun slipped away and night fell. The breezes carried the subtle fragrances of Hawaii.

The Kona Village Resort is at the same time elegant yet informal; offering a choice of activities in a leisurely atmosphere. Its setting reflects ancient times, yet offers twentieth century amenities. Its aura is one of serenity, simplicity and good taste reminding one of a time when life was sweeter and gentility was more a rule than an exception.

Editors Note: Kona Village has celebrated the completion of a beautiful new fitness and massage center. You'll be pleased with the assortment of aerobic machines, indoor/outdoor massage rooms, saunas and juice bar. The facility is adjacent to the tennis courts, and will eventually offer yoga and t'ai chi classes as part of their wellness program. Fred has thought carefully about creating the perfect place for healing at Kona Village. **We plan to cover the Spa in Volume III.**

Kona Village Resort
P.O. Box 1299
Kailua - Kona - Hawaii 96745
1-800-432-5450 (from US)
1-800-432-5450 (from Hawaii)

Kauai

The Garden Isle

Linda Bail

What you really come to Kauai to see is the marine life. Twenty-nine percent of the fish are endemic to the Hawaiian Islands. Which means you aren't going to see one third of its fish anywhere else.

South Shore diving means turtles. Big Hawaiian green sea turtles reaching 300 pounds. These large graceful reptiles socialize with their young giving us families of multiple generations to visit underwater. Through long term tagging, studies have shown that there are only 750 adult female green turtles. In 1978, all turtles in Hawaii became protected under the Endangered Species Act. This Act has allowed the population to replenish themselves again, but turtles grow slowly, not reaching sexual maturity until 25 years.

THE SCUBA DIVING AND SNORKELING
BUBBLES BELOW
There are dozens of dive sites where divers can swim with the turtles and learn to distinguish between the males and the females. Experience the turtles, the lava tubes, the thick black coral garden and the friendly fish of the south side.

TURTLE BLUFFS
The depth range is 45 feet to 90 feet. Many female turtles live in this area, a great place to see shark, eagle rays, eels and octopus. Some rare fish sightings can occur here. Often we drift from the Bluffs to Fishbowl.

FISHBOWL
Depth range from 45 feet to 80 feet. Schools of blue stripe snappers and other species fill the bowl to the brim so divers are immersed in swimming fish. There is also a resident white tip reef shark.

THE GENERAL STORE
Depth ranges from 55 feet to 90 feet. This is a site of a 19th century shipwreck. Huge anchors encrusted with coral are amongst the rubble, which was once a large metal hull. There are also three lava tubes here, full of life, many fish, turtles and black coral.

BRENNECKE'S LEDGE
The top is 50 feet with a beautiful lava overhang down to 90 feet. We dive it at 80 feet. Large black coral trees hang down from the ceiling interspersed with mauve cup coral. Long nose hawk fish and sponge crabs live as neighbors. Several resident sharks and turtles live here.

PYRAMI MAGIC
Lava fingers are complimented with many, many reef fish. Excellent variety of species of fish as well as coral. We dive this sight as an 80-foot dive. The magic here is with the pyramid butterflies. There are hundreds of them packed in formation.

DEEP PINNACLE
The top is 90 feet, the bottom a remotely visited 200 feet. This pinnacle becomes a market for activity, with pelagics frequently cruising by. There is a great covering of red sponge, which makes photography colorful.

SHERATON CAVERNS
User friendly at it's best! This is a series of lava tubes, which produce beautiful images. Visit the lobster rookery, which is also a turtle burial site. The top is 35 feet; the bottom is just 65 feet. Many tame, friendly eels, large schools of taape and quite a few turtles. **If you've always wanted a picture of a lionfish, this is your chance.**

SUPER BOWL SUNDAY
A shallower dive with much variety of life. It is a sloping dive to 50 feet. A good place for turtles, eels, octopus and the white checked surgeonfish.

Hanalei Sea Tours by Craig Wall

SCULPTURED REEF

The lava has been sculptured giving relief from 20 feet to 50 feet. An excellent site for octopus and schooling fish.

FAST LANES AND BEACH HOUSE ARCH

Do these separately or in combo at 90 feet, the top is 60 feet. Friendly eels, turtles, and occasional sharks visit these areas.

THE ICEBOX

Lava fingers with encrusting corals, 50 feet to 90 feet. Excellent fish life. This is a good location for macro photography.

OASIS REEF

A great second dive. The top is 2 feet; the bottom is 35 feet. Pennantfish (Heniochus) school here along with lots of other critters. Truly a mecca for reef fish as this pinnacle juts up in the middle of vast sandflats.

TORTUGAS

A very pretty place to visit with a large resident population of horned helmet shells. Appropriately named for large turtles that live here. Depth is 50 feet.

AREAS OF INTEREST

The colorful town of Lihue, Kauai's commercial center, is the starting point for your tour of either half of the Garden Isle. If you are off to the north shore, first stop will be the Wailua River for a fascinating, three-mile ride on one of the river launches. At the very end passengers disembark to explore the hauntingly beautiful Fern Grotto. **Your north shore trip will be liberally sprinkled with a host of perfect beaches, sugar and pineapple fields and a variety of unusual churches. But the highlight will be the incredible beauty of Hanalei Valley and Hanalei Bay.** Their magic will linger in your memory for decades to come. Pat Hanalei and Haena Point are the unmatched spectacle of the Na Pali Coast. Helicopter services offers flights into this lost world of breathtaking beauty. Boat trips are also available along this spectacular coastline.

Kauai's South Shore is equally as lovely. You'll travel high up into Kokee State Park to view Waimea Canyon - The Grand Canyon of the Pacific. **While there, you'll also visit**

Kalalau Lookout for a view of an awe-inspiring Na Pali Coast valley whose emerald cliffs plunge 4,000 feet to the crashing surf below. Enroute down from the park you will catch a glimpse of the privately owned island of Niihau. Stops at the Menehune Ditch, Spouting Horn, Hanapepe Valley, Captain Cook's Landing, Poipu Beach, Menehune Fish Pond, and Nawiliwili Harbor are other highlights of your memorable south shore adventure.

AREAS OF INTEREST

Botanic Gardens - Abounding in natural vegetation, Kauai also has four botanic gardens, which are open to the public for small fees. The Smith's Tropical Paradise at Wailua, Olu Pua Gardens at Kalaheo, Kiahuna Plantation Gardens in Poipu, and National Tropical Botanical Garden in Lawai, offer an unusual assortment of flowers, shrubs, cacti and other magnificent species of plant life.

Captain Cook's Landing, Waimea Bay - The first place in which the intrepid British explorer set foot in Hawaii in January, 1778. This bay was for many years a favorite provisioning point with pacific traders and whalers.

Fern Grotto - This hauntingly beautiful cave, luxuriantly festooned with growing ferns, is reached from the Wailua Marina.

Grove Farm Homestead - Founded in 1864 by George Wilcox, the homestead is now a museum complex that includes the old family plantation home, washhouse, teahouse, guest cottage and other amenities. The homestead is typical of the old Hawaiian plantation experience and tradition. It is just south of Lihue.

Hanalei Valley - Another name for Hanalei is Hanohano, meaning "glorious." You will want to stop at the vantagepoint near the marker to gaze at this sweeping scene of majestic tranquillity.

Hanapepe Valley - Note the red cliffs and the handsome color accent they give the valley's myriad shades of green·and blue.

Kalalau Lookout - Once peacocks preened their plumage in this tropic Eden and families cultivated terraces of taro. No one lives here now, nothing remains but one of the most beautiful views on earth.

Kamokila Hawaiian Village - Above the great bend of the Wailua River, where war canoes of the King of Kauai, Kaumualii, once assembled, lie the ruins of an old Hawaiian village.

Kauai Museum - The museum in Lihue presents a factual history of the Garden Isle, using artifacts and photographs. Other historical and art exhibits are also displayed.

Ke'e Beach Park - A fine beach at the end of the road where the trail begins to the Na Pali Cliffs.

Kilauea Lighthouse & Kilauea Point National Wildlife Refuge - A refuge for nesting seabirds. The isolated promontory where the lighthouse sits is open to visitors.

Kokee State Park - Adjacent to Waimea Canyon this park has picnic grounds, cabins and a wide variety of outdoor activities including hunting, trout fishing and hiking. The NASA Kokee Tracking Station is located nearby.

Lamahai Beach - Chosen for Nurses' Beach in "South Pacific", this lovely spot is undoubtedly the most photographed beach on Kauai.

Menehune Ditch - Only small portions remain of what was once a great watercourse of aqueduct. Archeologists say it was built before Hawaiians came, possibly by the Menehune.

Menehune Fish Pond, Niumala - Remarkable stone walls are said to have been built in one night by the Menehune. The fishpond they enclose is still in use.

Ols Russian Fort (Fort Elizabeth) - Hoping to seize Kauai for his Czar, an employee of the Russian Fur Company of Alaska built this fort near the mouth of the Waimea River in 1817. Rocky ruins are all that remain of his efforts and dream.

Opaekaa Falls - The Wailua River makes a dramatic plunge over a high cliff. Opaekaa means, "rolling shrimp" and dates from days when swarms of shrimp were seen rolling in turbulent waters at the base of the falls.

Poipu Beach - Exceptionally fine bathing beach.

Royal Birthstones, Wailua - Women of Hawaiian nobility always tried to reach these sacred stones in time to give birth to insure the royal status of their children.

Sleeping Giant - The outline of a mountain ridge shows a striking resemblance to a reclining giant.

Smith's Tropical Paradise - this 23 acre site has gardens, lagoons, exotic birds and a narrated trainride which meanders through a rain forest, a Polynesian village, a Japanese island, a Filipino village and other interesting areas. Kauai's ethnic heritage is reflected nightly in a 75-minute musical production in the Lagoon Theater.

Spouting Horn - When the tide is running high, waves pressured through lava tubes are forced through a hole in coastal rocks to burst noisily into spectacular fountains of a salt spray and foam.

Wailua Falls - Nicknamed Fantasy Island Waterfalls.

Waimea Canyon - This is more than a view; it's an experience! You'll treasure in memory its grandeur and jewel-tone colors, and its awesome depth and breadth.

Waioli Mission House - Visitors are welcome to look through this quaint home, built in 1834 and restored by descendants of the first missionaries.

Wet and Dry Caves of Haena - These eerie caverns, one dry, the other two filled with limpid green water, are where chiefs are said to have gathered in ancient times.

KAUAI

Kalapaki: This beautiful and popular white sand beach is predominantly calm and inviting. Good for swimming and sunning. Facilities available. A 10-minute walk from the pier.

POIPU

A series of beautiful and popular white sand beaches along the southern coast of the island. Excellent swimming and snorkeling are found here as well as good boogie-boarding and surfing. Facilities and parking available. A 25-minute drive from the pier.

Anahola Beach Park - "Bali Hai" in the movie *South Pacific*. Scenic beach. **Good snorkeling, safe swimming at south end.** Facilities and parking available. A 40-minute drive from the pier.

Lumahai Beach - Probably Kauai's most photographed beach. Also seen in South Pacific. Good for walking and sunning. Not safe for swimming. Short hike from road. No facilities. A 45-minute drive from the pier.

Haena Beach Park - Long stretch of beach across the road from the wet and dry caves, **Good for strolling, sunning, snorkeling and hunting for puka shells.** Sand is course. Facilities, picnic tables and snack stand. Parking. Haena is a 60-minute drive from the pier.

Bubbles Below can arrange a dive/stay package.

Maui & Lanai

Allen H. Glaberson

Maui has a well-deserved reputation as a great place to take a diving vacation. In addition to having the best overall weather in the Hawaiian Islands it also has a tremendous variety of activities and natural beauties to see when you are not diving. Whatever accommodations you pick, the best advice is to rent a car at the airport. Maui has NO public transportation.

Lahaina has historical sights from the time of the whalers and was the original capital of the Hawaiian Islands during the monarchy. There are a number of buildings of historical interest; forts, prisons and the oldest lighthouse in the Pacific. In addition,

SCUBA AND SNORKELING FACILITIES QUESTIONNAIRE

NAME   **Bubbles Below Scuba Charters**
ADDRESS   **6251 Hauaala Road**
             Kapaa, Kauai, Hawai 96746
CONTACT   **Ken or Linda Bail**
TITLE   **Owner/Operators**
TELEPHONE   **808-822-3483 (DIVE)**   FAX

CAPITAL:	**Honolulu**	GOVERNMENT:	**USA**
POPULATION:	**50,000**	LANGUAGE:	**English**
CURRENCY:	**US $**	ELECTRICITY:	**110v**
AIRLINES:	**United Airlines**	DEPARTURE TAX?	**No**
NEED VISA/PASSPORT?	YES NO **x**	PROOF OF CITIZENSHIP?	YES NO **x**

YOUR FACILITY IS CLASSIFIED AS: SCUBA CENTER   RESORT
BUSINESS HOURS: **7 a.m. - 7 p.m. 7 days a week**
CERTIFYING AGENCIES: **PADI, NAUI**
LOG BOOK REQUIRED?   YES   NO **x**
EQUIPMENT: SALES **x**   RENTALS **x (Boat customers only)**   AIR FILLS
PRIMARY LINE OF EQUIPMENT: **Scubapro/Sherwood**
PHOTOGRAPHIC EQUIPMENT: SALES   RENTALS **x (Boat customers only)**   LAB

CHARTER/DIVE BOAT AVAILABLE?   YES **x**   NO   DIVER CAPACITY   **6 per trip**
COAST GUARD APPROVED?   YES **x**   NO   CAPTAIN LICENSED? YES **x**   NO
SHIP TO SHORE?   YES **x** NO GPS YES **x** NO   RADAR? YES   NO **x**
DIVE MASTER/INSTRUCTOR ABOARD?   YES **x**   NO   BOTH **x**

DIVING & SNORKELING: SALT **x**   FRESH
TYPE OF DIVING/SNORKELING IN AREA: WALL **x**   BEACH   WRECK   REEF **x**   CAVE   ICE
DIVING/SNORKELING IN YOUR AREA IS BEST SUITED FOR: BEGINNER **x** INTERMEDIATE **x** ADVANCED **x**
BEST TIME OF YEAR FOR DIVING/SNORKELING: **Year round**
TEMPERATURE: **NOV-APRIL:**   **73 F**   **MAY-OCT:**   **76 F**
VISIBILITY: **DIVING:**   **70 FT**   **SNORKELING: 30   FT**

PACKAGES AVAILABLE: DIVE **x**   DIVE STAY   SNORKEL   SNORKEL-STAY
ACCOMMODATIONS NEARBY: HOTEL **x**   MOTEL   HOME RENTALS **x**
ACCOMMODATION RATES: EXPENSIVE **x**   MODERATE **x**   INEXPENSIVE **x**
RESTAURANTS NEARBY: EXPENSIVE   MODERATE **x**   INEXPENSIVE **x**
YOUR AREA IS: REMOTE   QUIET WITH ACTIVITIES **x**   LIVELY
LOCAL ACTIVITY/NIGHTLIFE: **Limited: Mostly at local hotels**
CAR NEEDED TO EXPLORE AREA?   YES **x**   NO
DUTY FREE SHOPPING?   YES **x**   NO

LOCAL EMERGENCY SERVICES   NEAREST HYPERBARIC TREATMENT FACILITY
COASTGUARD: **246-0390**   AUTHORITY: **Hyperbaric Treatment Center-Honolulu**
TELEPHONE: **911**   LOCATION: **Kauai Veterans Memorial Hospital, Waimea**
CALLSIGNS: **HA 333CP**   TELEPHONE: **338-6431**

LOCAL DIVING DOCTOR:
NAME: **Dr. Robert Overlock**
LOCATION: **Kauai Veterans Memorial Hospital**
TELEPHONE: **338-9431**

Lahaina is full of shops, restaurants and art galleries. At night it offers a wide range of live music and entertainment.

In addition to hiking and scuba there are 18 golf courses on the island as well as numerous tennis courts, submarine rides and horseback riding.

THE SCUBA DIVING AND SNORKELING

Maui offers lots of diving opportunities at all levels of experience. The best known location is **Molokini Crater,** a cindercone situated in mid channel between Maui and the island of Kahoolawe. Nearly three miles off the Maui shore; Molokini rises from depths of 250' to 350' to form a half-moon islet with sheer cliffs going up nearly 200' above the ocean floor. **Inside the crater is the largest hard coral concentration in the state of Hawaii.** The rock ridges and coral reefs form a bowl inside with several coral ridges separated by sand channels that slope down to depths of 130 feet or more. Much of the inside is less than 40 feet deep and filled with fish. **Molokini is a major snorkeling location as well as a diving one.** Hanauma Bay on Oahu is a similar formation to Molokini as it is a fish and bird preserve and no one is allowed on the islet or to take anything, including shells. **Sea life is abundant and fairly familiar with the diver.** There are a number of semi-tame moray eels; a good population of docile white tip reef shark and often manta rays are seen when the plankton counts are high.

Visibility at Molokini is usually 100+ feet and 150 to 200 feet days are common. Water temperature varies from a low of 72 degrees F in mid winter to 80 degrees F by mid summer and stays warm through the end of October.

On the outside flanks of Molokini erosion has cut the walls away to near vertical drops with many ledges and overhangs dropping off to 300+ feet on the sides and 250+ feet on the back (south) wall. Again, visibility is so good that is often possible for divers to be at 80 or 90 feet and look down and see the bottom. **These 'outside' dives are all done as drift dives and as there is effectively no bottom. They are considered a more advanced dive. Often, when on these dives in the winter (whale season which is usually December through early April), divers are able to hear and even sometimes see humpback whales.** The humpbacks, especially the yearlings, seem to like the crater and can often be seen circuiting it during the day.

On the *No Ka Oi IV*, they usually split the dive sites doing the first dive at Molokini then moving on to another site to give the divers a change of topography. They leave at seven in the morning with the intention of getting out to Molokai ahead of the rest of the fleet, so divers are returning from their dives when the majority of the other boats divers are just getting in the water (and in each others way).

The *No Ka Oi IV* is a 37-ft Toli Craft with a twin diesel. She is a seaworthy and roomy boat with a large main cabin to get out of the sun, or the spray and a lot of deck space for lying out and sunning between dives. Fresh water shower and toilet add to the comfort. They serve a continental breakfast and fruit and veggie trays for snacking. Most people want to try Buzz's or the Fish Co. for lunch and they are back in plenty of time for them to do so.

As they only take a maximum of 12 divers (average load is usually around 8), there is plenty of space for everyone to spread out and be comfortable. With any more than 6 divers they put on an additional dive leader so the groups stay small and manageable and each diver gets the right amount of personal attention.

While certainly a must see, Molokai is by no means the only good diving location on Maui. In fact most of the resident divers like other locations even better. **All along the south west or Wailea/Makena shore are numerous excellent diving locations. Two favorite dives are Red Hill (or Up Olai in Hawaiian) and Five Caves.** While both are possible to be done as shore dives they entail such long swims (500+ yards) that they are better from a boat and are usually one of the second dives after a dive at Molokini.

Red Hill is a cindercone similar to Molokini.Instead of being in the middle of the channel it forms a peninsula and is one of the major features on the south west coast of Maui. The dive is a shallow one seldom deeper than 45 feet and usually less than 25 feet. Because of this, **it is a good spot for snorkelers to follow along with the divers.** It is a tremendously rich site in sea life, with several turtle nests, good coral and reef fish population.

The dive is done along the north face of the Hill where a number of pinnacles and ledges make interesting topography. As the hill juts out into the Alalakeiki channel between Maui and Molokini there are often moderate to brisk currents that move the diver along. A shallower dive is usually done as a drift and the boat picks the snorkelers and divers up off the end of the point. This eliminates a long, tiring swim back.

At the end of the point is a large cavern with several chimneys. **The cavern is big enough to put the boat in and is full of residents ranging from a 6 foot white tip reef shark and several good sized eels down to a healthy lobster community and a number of frog fish.** The current usually does a good job of keeping the water clear and visibility is often in the 50 feet+ range, sometimes getting up to 80feet+.

Five Caves (or Nahuna Point) is also on the Wailea/Makena coast about a fifteen-minute sail away from Red Hill. This is a shallow dive with a maximum depth of 45 feet, most of it in the 30 foot range. **This dive is an excellent place for snorkelers.** Shore access is better than at Red Hill and the swim out to the site is only about 250 yards and can be done from a beach on the south side of the peninsula.

The site is comprised of two parallel fingers of lava sticking out due west from the shore about 50 yards apart. These fingers are actually lava tubes, the tops of which start just below the surface (the north finger has a wash rock which breaks surface at low tide) and then run out and down ending about 100 yards offshore in about 40 feet of water. They make a dramatic mini wall effect rising abruptly out of the surrounding sand bottom.

Between the two fingers are a number of pinnacles, which provide anchorage for lots of staghorn coral trees and nesting sites for about a dozen green sea turtles. **Being air breathers the turtles have to come up every 20 to 40 minutes and as such are a prime attraction for snorkelers.**

The fingers themselves are covered with coral and support large populations of reef fish and eels. Erosion has caused parts of the tubes to collapse making archways and grottos that inexperienced divers can swim through. On the ceiling of a triple archway on the south finger there is a small black coral bush in only 30 feet of water. **This is a rare opportunity for a novice diver to be able to see a coral which usually is only found in water over 100 ft deep.**

The north finger has a large cavern right under the wash rock and breaks in the overhead let in a church lighting effect on sunny days. In a small gallery off to one side of the main entrance, a good sized (6 to 7 foot) white tip usually can be found dozing in the daytime.

Five Caves is a great dive for experienced and novice divers alike. The experienced diver will enjoy the caverns and archways, as well as the abundant sea life. The novice will feel comfortable with the modest depths and the well defined ledges of the dive makes navigation easy. Just following the fingers into shallow water will bring the diver back to shore and as we usually anchor at the end of one finger or the other finding the boat is also easy.

Snorkelers will like the site as well. It is shallow enough that they can follow the divers around, or go explore the reefs on the lava tubes by themselves. Being inshore the visibility is usually in the 40 to 60 foot range. Freshwater runoff can make for some "cool spots" but water temperature is usually in the same 72 to 80 degree F range.

LANAI

While most diving is done off the coast of Maui (and there are literally dozens of spots around the island), and there are special trips to the island of Lanai for groups of 6 or more divers. The Lanai trip is an all day event. The island is 25 miles or a two and a half-hour run from Maalaea. While our normal 2-tank morning run leaves at 7 a.m. and returns by noon, the Lanai trip leaves at 7 a.m., but doesn't return until 3 p.m.

Lanai does offer some spectacular diving. The two favorite sites are the 1st Cathedral

"Eye to Eye" by Lynn Funkhouser

and **Sweetheart Rock.** The Cathedral is a huge volcanic structure reaching up from 60 feet of water, capped by a wash rock that is clear even at high tide. Below are a major cavern, 100 feet long, and 40 to 50 feet high and 30 feet wide with several side galleries branching off. It is usually entered through a 10-foot high opening on the west side, which quickly opens to the main cavern.

At the other end is a thin wall of rock, which formed in such a way as to suggest a stained glass window. Right below these "windows" are rocks which look just like an altar. Off to either side are tubes and galleries that also provide light and exits. **The whole effect is pretty dramatic and weddings have been conducted there (the Captain of the *No Ka Oi IV* is also a minister) for REALLY committed dive couples.**

Sweetheart Rock is close to the Cathedral and offers more outstanding underwater topography. There is an area of shallow valleys and walls created by volcanic activity with some interesting archways and cul-de-sacs.

It has a very healthy lobster population and the area is frequented by a large (100+) pod of spinner dolphins.

If the group has a mix of divers and snorkelers this is fine. Snorkelers are welcome on the *No Ka Oi IV*. While PADI allows a ratio of 1 instructor to 6 intros on the boat, they never have more than 1 to 4.

Remember, "Maui No Ka Oi" -Maui is the best; and for the perfect mix for vacation and diving, I have to agree.

ACCOMMODATIONS

Accommodations on Maui range range from campgrounds close to Maalaea Harbor (windy but close to the dive boats) to condominiums spread all along the west (leeward/sunny) coast of the island, to full service hotels and top luxury resorts: **Stouffers Wailea Beach, Grand Wailea (formerly Grand Hyatt) and the Kea Lani.**

Unless money is literally no object, the rental condominiums offer a good value for the money. With kitchens included they can help keep the high cost of dining out down. In Kihei, **Nani Kai Hale** offers a great rate with a good central location (73 North Kihei Rd, Kihei Hi, 96753 808-879-9120).

A bit further down in Kihei (but still only 15 minutes from Maalaea Harbor) is **Kihei Garden Estates.** They have excellent accommodations: pool, Jacuzzi, lovely interior garden court and an unbeatable proximity to the post office, banks, two supermarkets, and a brand new shopping center. It is still quiet and affordable, especially for a week or longer stays. (1822 Uluniu St. Kihei HI, 96753, phone: 808-879-6123).

On the west side (Lahaina & Kaanapali), **Embassy Suites** and the **Marriott** offer excellent resort accommodations. While these Kaanapali resorts have been somewhat superseded by the newer resorts on the south side (Kihei/Wailea) and are a bit far away from activities on the rest of the island, they still offer a good vacation experience.

DINING

There are a few great restaurants. **The Waterfront** in Maalaea Harbor is excellent for dinner with a great view of the Harbor and Molokini Island.

At Maalaea is **Buzz's Wharf**, which is perfect for a Mahi Mahi burger and a beer after the morning dives, or if you have a craving for Tahitian Prawns or Teriyaki Steak and fries for dinner and want to watch the sunset redden the clouds on Haleakala.

For those who want something simpler, or want to bring home some fresh fish to cook at their own condo, the **Fresh Island Fish Co.** in Maalaea (across from the Coast Guard Station) sells a good selection of fish caught by the local fishermen.

The **Ocean Activities** sunset dinner cruises on the Wailea Kai combines a hearty dinner, drinks and a sunset off west Maui.

On the way to Hana and the weather shore is **Cafe Paradiso** in Paia (about 30 minutes from Kihei, 45 from Lahina), on the Hana highway. They offer excellent northern Italian cuisine at a reasonable price.

Towards Haleakala, in Haliie Maile is the **Haliie Maile General Store**. They serve Nouvelle cuisine, and are expensive, but worth it.

If you are going up to see the top of Haleakala (usually referred to as 'the Crate') be sure to stop at the **Kula Lodge** for a late breakfast or early lunch. Great coffee, Eggs Benedict and other more local dishes with a stunning view of the isthmus and the west Maui Mountains.

In Lahaina one of the best dinner experiences is the Ocean Activities cruise from 5 p.m. to 7 p.m., open bar and some of the best food I have ever had on the Island. Sailing in the calm of the 'Lahaina Triangle' as the sun sets behind Lanai, lighting up the west Maui Mountains dramatically, with a live band playing mellow Hawaiian and popular music is a very romantic experience.

AREAS OF INTEREST

Baldwin Home now serves as a museum. This is an excellent example of early island missionary homes.

The Banyan Tree was planted in 1873. This magnificent tree is said to be the largest Banyan tree in Hawaii

Hale Hoikeike: Historical Society Museum in old Bailey Mission Home built in 1841. Interesting display of early missionary items and Hawaiian artifacts.

Hale Paahao is an old jail that was built for drunken and disorderly members of the whaling crews that roared through Lanaina in the mid-1800s. The whole Lanaina area, royal capital of the islands until 1845, is filled with sites and scenes of great interest to students of Hawaiian history.

Hale Pa'I: here you will see the quaint old press on which Hawaii's first newspaper was printed in 1834.

Haleakala National Park is where according to Polynesian legend, the demigod, Maui captured the sun and held it captive to give his people more daylight hours, and it is here that you will stand to capture an unforgettable scenic memory. From the crater's topmost rim to its floor is a drop of 3000 feet. The floor measures 25 square miles, a fascinating area of richly colored cinder cones. Haleakala's last eruption was more than 200 years ago. A public observatory stands on the rim of the volcano's crater. The outer wall of the volcano, cut by ravines and gullies, slopes down to the shore of the island.

Halekii Heiau are ancient temples of worship, sacrifice and refuge, ordered destroyed by King Kamehameha II in 1819, it is now being partially restored.

Iao Valley is an enchantingly tranquil park. This was the site of a bloody battle in 1790 when Kamehameha conquered Maui in the famed battle of Kepaniwai.

Kaahumanu Church is the oldest Congressional Hawaiian church in central Maui; the original section was built in 1837.

Kaanapali is one of the top resort areas, situated along three miles of golden sand beach with a misty mountain backdrop. Lors of recreational facilities - golf, tennis, riding, and swimming - and a unique whaling museum/shopping center.

Kaiwaloa Heiau: There are eerie legends about spirits that walk from this Heiau at night, and about daring humans that followed them and were never seen again.

Kanaha Bird Sanctuary: Each winter, migrating birds from the northwest make this park their island home.

Kaumahina Park is located halfway between Kahului and Hana. It is the perfect place to pause and picnic.

Lahaina was the first capital of the islands and the historic heart of Maui, this colorful town is steeped in the memories of whaling days, missionaries, ancient Hawaiian rulers and the plantation workers of various ethnic origin who migrated to the island.

Lahainaluna School is the oldest school west of the Rocky Mountains, established in 1831. A stone building which still stands on the modern school grounds, replaced its first building of poles and grass.

Maui Tropical Plantation is Hawaii's agricultural showplace located in Waikapu Valley. Working plantation with acres of tropical fruits, sugarcane, coffee and macadamia nuts.

Maui Zoological & Botanic Gardens offers an entertaining and educational view of animals and plants from many parts of the world. It is situated on a three-acre site in Wailuku, across from the Maui War Memorial Stadium.

Ohe's Stream (Seven Pools) is truly a photographer's paradise. It is said that in these crystal pools, the mother of Maui, the demigod, used to wash and bleach her tapa-cloth.

Puaa Kaa Park is a gem of a park whose name means "the place of the rolling pigs"- dating from days gone by when plump wild pigs were said to have rolled down the slick steep grassy hills in this area.

Tedeschi Winery is Hawaii's only winery. Taste its light pineapple wine, a forerunner to the production of grape wine from vineyards on the slopes of Haleakala.

Waianapanapa Caves: Strong swimmers and scuba divers by diving into a pool and swimming underwater can reach a big inner cave. It is a legendary trysting place for lovers of old.

Wailea Lookout offers a choice view of the entire Keanae Peninsula and its spectacularly lovely coastline.

Whaler's Village Museum has hundreds of antiquities recalling the boisterous, rowdy years of the great whaler's house in a picturesque atmosphere of yesteryear.

For more information contact the **Maui Visitors Bureau.**

1727 Wili Pa Loop
Wailuku, HI 96793
Phone: (808) 244-3530

SCUBA AND SNORKELING FACILITIES QUESTIONNAIRE

NAME **Ocean Activities Center**
ADDRESS **1847 So. Kihei Road #203**
Kihei, Maui 96753
CONTACT **Captain Allen Glaberson**
TITLE **Senior Captain, No Ka Oi IV**
TELEPHONE **808-879-4781** FAX **808-879-7427**

CAPITAL: **Honolulu** GOVERNMENT: State of Hawaii
POPULATION: **90,000 (Maui)** LANGUAGE: English
CURRENCY: **US $** ELECTRICITY 110v
AIRLINES: **United, Delta, American** DEPARTURE TAX? No
NEED VISA/PASSPORT? YES NO **x** PROOF OF CITIZENSHIP? YES NO **x**

YOUR FACILITY IS CLASSIFIED AS: SCUBA CENTER RESORT
BUSINESS HOURS: **0600 -2100**
CERTIFYING AGENCIES: **PADI**
LOG BOOK REQUIRED? YES NO **x**
EQUIPMENT: SALES RENTALS AIR FILLS
PRIMARY LINE OF EQUIPMENT: **Scubapro**
PHOTOGRAPHIC EQUIPMENT: SALES RENTALS LAB

CHARTER/DIVE BOAT AVAILABLE? YES **x** NO DIVER CAPACITY **12 per trip**
COAST GUARD APPROVED? YES **x** NO CAPTAIN LICENSED? YES **x** NO
SHIP TO SHORE? YES **x** NO LORAN YES NO **x** RADAR? YES NO **x**
DIVE MASTER/INSTRUCTOR ABOARD? YES NO BOTH **x**

DIVING & SNORKELING: SALT **x** FRESH
TYPE OF DIVING/SNORKELING IN AREA: WALL **x** BEACH **x** WRECK REEF **x** CAVE **x** ICE
DIVING/SNORKELING IN YOUR AREA IS BEST SUITED FOR: BEGINNER INTERMEDIATE **x** ADVANCED
BEST TIME OF YEAR FOR DIVING/SNORKELING:
TEMPERATURE: NOV-APRIL: **75 F** MAY-OCT **80 F**
VISIBILITY: DIVING: **100 FT** SNORKELING: **50 FT**

PACKAGES AVAILABLE: DIVE DIVE STAY **x** SNORKEL SNORKEL-STAY **x**
ACCOMMODATIONS NEARBY: HOTEL **x** MOTEL HOME RENTALS **x**
ACCOMMODATION RATES: EXPENSIVE **x** MODERATE **x** INEXPENSIVE
RESTAURANTS NEARBY: EXPENSIVE MODERATE **x** INEXPENSIVE
YOUR AREA IS: REMOTE QUIET WITH ACTIVITIES **x** LIVELY
LOCAL ACTIVITY/NIGHTLIFE:
CAR NEEDED TO EXPLORE AREA? YES **x** NO
DUTY FREE SHOPPING? YES NO **x**

LOCAL EMERGENCY SERVICES NEAREST HYPERBARIC TREATMENT FACILITY

COASTGUARD: **Maalea Station** AUTHORITY: **University of Hawaii**
TELEPHONE: **244-5256** LOCATION: **Honolulu Kewalo Basin**
CALLSIGNS: **WTM 3510** TELEPHONE: **1-523-9155**

LOCAL DIVING DOCTOR:
NAME: **Dr. Norm Estin**
LOCATION: **Napili Tower, Suite 100, 200 Nohea Kai Dr. Lahina**
TELEPHONE **667-7676**

"Angels in Love" statue at The Ocean Club, Nassau, Bahamas
by Wendy Canning Church

Two's Company by Alan Marquardt

HONEYMOON AND ANNIVERSARY SECTION

Barbados
The Coral Reef Club
"An Intimate Atmosphere with a Carefree Spirit"

Wendy Canning Church

The Coral Reef Club is a member of Small Luxury Hotels of the World and the Elegant Resorts of Barbados, who describe Coral Reef as having "an atmosphere, whilst intimate, will appeal to those of a carefree spirit". It is as close to the perfect holiday home as you will ever find. It is 18 miles from the airport on Barbados' famed west coast. This little jewel sits on 12 acres with its comely talcum powder beach that is opposite the resort's namesake reef, a short swim from shore.

For nearly forty years, the O'Hara family has owned and managed the club. They provide warm hospitality and impeccable service for guests residing in the 69 rooms, cottages and junior suites, named after native plants. All are set amidst beautiful gardens, which are tended from dawn to dusk overlooking the topaz blue sea by sixteen gardeners and groundskeepers. There are numerous delightful places for guests to relax and enjoy cool tropical drinks or traditional English tea.

Air-conditioned accomodations are spacious with large baths and either a terrace or large covered patio, ceiling fans, refrigerators, telephones, lovely rattan furniture, a stocked bookcase and mini-bar, hair dryer and a toaster. Television is available.

The reception desk where guest requests are speedily and warmly granted is located in the main house along with the spacious lounge and restaurants. All open onto a

Coral Reef Club by Wendy Canning Church

beachfront terrace where one dines in perfect ambiance al fresco. The food and service are impeccable.

An extensive breakfast room service menu is put on your door each evening and served on your private patio the next morning. During high season (generally December 15 to April 15), a buffet luncheon is served in the restaurant. An a la carte luncheon is taken at the terraces of the Reef Bar during the summer season. Please note that swimsuits are not allowed in the restaurant or lounge. Dinner is served from 7:30 to 9:30 pm. The requested dress is casually elegant - with black tie, or jacket and tie, requested for Christmas night and New Years Eve.

There is entertainment nightly during the winter, and three to four evenings per week during summer. Each Monday guests are invited to the managers cocktail party followed by a Bajan buffet.

On Thursdays they serve a barbecue buffet with floor show that includes limbo, and a steel band. The Sandpiper, Sandy Lane, and **Coblers Cove** are on the west coast and exchange dining privileges with Coral Reef.

The beach offers colorful and vaired snorkeling on a coral reef just below the surface directly opposite the Clubhouse. It is marked by buoys to the right of the beach, which is excellent for swimming. The whole area is an underwater park. Scuba diving is available through **High Tide Watersports**. There is a free pick up and drop off service for scuba divers and snorkelers. (Please see chapter on Barbados).

Tennis courts are immediately across the road from the sister hotel – the **Sandpiper Inn**. Courts are lighted for night play. Complimentary snorkeling, sunfish, laser and hobie cat sailing is also available at the watersports shop. Water-skiing is available at a special hotel rate.

Golf can be arranged at the new Robert Trent Jones designed course at the Royal Westmoreland, just one mile away.

Horseback riding through the sugar cane fields in the country or on the beach can also be arranged. If a private sail is in mind, take a cruise on their 32 foot Catamaran.

The Beauty Spot offers cosmetic and beauty therapy - message, ozone bath, etc., and is located in the Coral Arms building near the hotel entrance.

Nanny and baby-sitting can also be arranged; and children's meals are available on request.

Intimate with a carefree spirit aptly describe "The Coral Reef Club." The Coral Reef Club offers Honeymoon and Golf packages.

For reservations contact:

Ralph Locke
P.O. Box 492977
Los Angeles, CA 90049-8477
1-800-223-1108

BERMUDA

SOMERSET

CAMBRIDGE BEACHES

Wendy Canning Church

Cambridge Beaches is ranked in the top 10 resorts in the world, and is often described as the best of Bermuda. A $10 million dollar face-lift was completed in 1995. Under the direction of experienced Managing Director, the Honorable Michael J. Winfield, the project sacrificed none of its Old World ambiance and standard of excellence, yet brought 21st century amenities to the resort.

Situated on the western tip of the island in Somerset Parish, one half-hour from the airport, this idyllic cottage colony sits on a 25-acre peninsula surrounded by five palm-fringed beaches with numerous hidden coves. The private and public areas are tucked away among meticulously kept, lush vegetation giving the environs a sense of calm and serenity.

All accommodations have private terraces and superb views of the bay or the Atlantic and are tastefully decorated with English antiques and comfortable furniture covered in floral chintz. Many cottages have fireplaces. The large baths have Jacuzzis, fluffy bathrobes and baskets of amenities. **One would think they were a guest in an English country manor house.**

Be sure to inquire about the Heart and Soul Honeymoon Holiday. Request, Sunrise or Sunset: these charming cottages can accommodate 2 guests.

Windswept (a house for a larger group) is a wonderful property. It sits atop a hill over-looking the Atlantic with a private cove on one side and the harbor on the other. Sur-rounded by old stone walls, guests can enter separate quarters by private paths.

The charming 275-year-old Club House includes the registration area and a lounge where afternoon tea is served. Here one finds the Port O'Call and resident bars, the newly refurbished formal, indoor Tamarisk Room, and the outdoor Mangrove Bay Terrace for candlelight dining. **Five star chef, Jean Claude Garzia, and his staff create award winning gourmet cuisine.** Lunch is served at the Beach Cafe, poolside, or a picnic basket may be individually prepared. There is exchange dining with four other Bermuda Collection properties: Lantana, Pompano Beach, The Reefs, and Stonington. A romantic dinner can be served in your cottage.

There is nightly entertainment (in season) with special evening cruises, concerts and dancing. For those of you who are not content to laze, suntan, or read, you can take the new hotel ferry to Hamilton for shopping and sightseeing or **go for a sail on the private yacht to historic St. George's for snorkeling and a picnic. A sunset sail and after-dinner moonlight cruise are also offered.**

Swim in the natural ocean pool and lunch on the pool terrace, play croquet, try your hand on the putting green or a set of tennis on one of the 3 courts (one lit for night play). A full-service marina with power and sail boats, windsurfing and snorkeling equipment, as well as canoes and kayaks offer other options for fun. A full-service diving center, **Fantasea Divers,** is located in nearby Warwick.

Rent a moped or cycle to tour the island. A visit to a popular Bermuda historical site, the **Royal Navy Dockyard,** and shopping center nearby is a must!

Cambridge Beaches' membership at every Bermuda golf course means easy access for guests. **The Port Royal Golf Course** is five minutes away by taxi.

THE SPA

Many guests travel from all over the world for the purpose of de-stressing at the professionally run New European Health and Beauty Spa. **The new unisex spa is Bermuda pink with talcum white walks and an ambiance as soothing as the therapies and treatments of its expertly trained European technicians.**

I took advantage off all the luxurious Guniot of Paris beauty treatments time would allow. One can be pampered from head to toe, and pampered I was. My program included therapeutic massage, aromatherapy, super cathiodermic facial, paraffin body treatment deluxe, manicure and pedicure with paraffin mask. If I had had more time, I would have chosen the complete menu.

Cambridge Beaches, Bermuda
Courtesy of Cambridge Beaches

Many guests stay for a Spa Week and utilize the beauty salon, universal gym exercise facility, personalized and group fitness programs, fitness and nutrition consultations, and of course, sauna, steam and whirlpool. For serious spa enthusiasts, Cambridge Beaches internationally acclaimed gourmet cuisine will include special Spa menus. The staff is pleased to suggest a personalized program for you to follow at home.

I shall remember my sunwashed, pink cotton candy cottage with vanilla ice cream roof. It overlooked the winsome harbor, the oldest drawbridge on the island and blue Atlantic beyond. Each morning I awoke to find a small boat of muted coloration anchored there cradled in, the gently lapping waters. It was aptly named " Satisfaction", a synonym for my visit to Cambridge Beaches.

For information or reservations, or to request a video, write:
Cambridge Beaches
30 King's Point, Somerset MA02 Bermuda
Phone: 800 468 7300 (USA); 800 463 5990 (CDN)
Fax: 441 234 3352

THE SCUBA DIVING & SNORKELING

I give Fantasea Divers top marks for safety standards, selection of sights and a terrific crew. They are a PADI 5 star dive center offering wreck and reef diving mornings and afternoons 7 days a week. Every member of the staff is internationally and locally licensed through the Bermuda Dive Association.

There are 2 service technicians at Fantasea for those last minute repairs or tune-ups of equipment. They have a well-stocked retail shop for most of your diving needs as well as shirts, hats, snacks and postcards. Their comfortable boat, *Bottom Time*, with head, rinse tank, permanent canopy and a bridge for sunning, has ample room for divers and their equipment.

Many people have touted the dive season to run between March and November. **Graham Allen, manager of Fantasea** is now tailoring packages for cold water wreck diving in off-season. At that time of year the water is crystal clear because of its temperature. There is no plankton. Besides servicing Cambridge Beaches, they happily accommodate guests at other hotels and can arrange packages to suit any pocketbook.

Fantasea offers daily snorkeling trips to many of the reef and wreck sites. They also offer snorkel/sail trips on their 55ft-luxury catamaran, which takes two trips a day, 7 days a week. The catamaran *Aristocat* is also available for group and private charters.

SOME OF THEIR MOST POPULAR WRECK SITES INCLUDE:

Wreck	Depth	Experience Level
Constellation	30 ft	all
Lartington	25-35 ft	all
Madiana	25-35 ft	all
Caraquet	30 ft	all
North Caroliner	25-45 ft	all
Darlington	15-30 ft	all
Minnie Breslauer	45-65 ft	intermediate-advanced
Hermes	75 ft	intermediate-advanced
Mari Celeste	55 ft	intermediate
King	65 ft	intermediate
*Critobal Colon**	30-70 ft	intermediate-advanced
*Pelinaion**	35-70 ft	intermediate-advanced
*Zovetta**	20-70 ft	intermediate-advanced
*Iristo**	50 ft	intermediate

*For group or private charters only

THIS IS JUST A SMALL SELECTION OF MANY REEF DIVES:

Reef	Depth	Experience Level
South West Breakers	35 ft	all
Inbetweenies	35 ft	all
Hole in the Wall	30-45 ft	all
Shell Hole	30 ft	all
Eastern Blue Cut	25-50 ft	all
Parrots Landing	30-50 ft	all
Truk Hole	45 ft	all
Dudley Hill	45 ft	all

Bonaire

Harbour Village Beach Resort

Wendy Canning Church

There is nothing on Bonaire that can lay claim to her position as the undisputed Queen of resorts on Bonaire. Guests arriving by the Harbor Village Beach Resort's private Turbo Prop Airlink from Curacao, or by sea on their sleek yachts, will find a comely, serene, private playground under the able guidance of Managing Director Carol Upper.

Harbour Village Beach Resort is situated on the leeward side of Bonaire, a short ten-minute ride from the airport. It is a perfect jewel shining forth on its own four-acre peninsula within the hundred-acre development of Harbour Village

Narrow flower scented pathways in a kaleidoscope of color lead the way to 72 spacious air-conditioned guestrooms, including one and two bedroom suites. (**Be sure to request room 223**). Accommodations are sprinkled across a quarter mile chalk white

Harbour Village, Bonaire Courtesy of Harbour Village

beach, shaded by leafy coconut palms and flaming orange trees. Others overlook court-yards ablaze in tropical foliage spilling over sun splashed walls falling to patios below.

Tastefully decorated, the air-conditioned rooms are complimented by rattan fur-nishings and white tile floors dressed with native straw rugs. A full wet-bar, cable TV, hairdryers, terrycloth robes and personal amenity packages are welcomed additions.

The entire complex is reminiscent of the tranquil atmosphere and relaxed hospitality of the Mediterranean with the panache of destinations like Bonifacio, Sardina or Provence. Its architecture is of an open-air design awash in a rainbow palette of ripe can-taloupe, watermelon green, and rich lemon yellow.

The guest is tempted never to leave the grounds, but is inveigled by activities offered both on and off property. Sun worshipers can read and relax on the beach or at the sparkling pool. You can windsurf, charter a boat at the marina for deep-sea fishing, or shop at the boutiques (offering everything from designer clothing to newspapers). Other options include renting a bicycle, going hiking or on a picnic, **snorkeling, or diving on the nearby island of Klein Bonaire.**

The hotel can also arrange for you to play tennis on one of the four-lighted tennis courts at the Tennis Center. The Center offers private lessons from Peter Buswash, a trained professional. For those of you thinking "pamper me", you can indulge in an afternoon, or even a week, of unadulterated pampering at **the New European Spa.**

All these activities will surely permit you to partake of the delicious and beautifully presented cuisine. Take breakfast on the seclusion of your terrace, luncheon at Captain Wook's situated at the Marina or dinner at the open-air tri-level Kasal Coral restaurant. **Not to be missed is the Friday night seafood buffet with local band.**

Romantics can opt to order a candlelight dinner served on their patio, choosing from the chef's daily menu. You sip the perfect glass of wine suggested to compliment each course as the sun hands over its reigns to the moon, which illuminates your own special private parcel of paradise.

I chose to divide my time between scuba, the spa, and touring. It was the perfect pre-scription for a stressed out executive. I returned home refreshed in body, mind and soul.

THE SPA

Located in a quiet area of the grounds, **the spa is an oasis of tranquillity and beauty.** The tri-level facility was built to include a variety of activities, from yoga classes to outdoor massage. There is a state-of-the-art fitness center and outdoor Roman-style freshwater pool and whirlpool along with a myriad of treatments (massage, facials and body treatments). **A full service beauty salon is located across the tiled corridor.** The complete fitness program encompasses hiking, biking, exercise classes, Tai Chi and yoga classes.

You can choose a week's spa program or individual treatment. Upon arrival, each guest is given a pass to use the saunas, whirlpool, and upstairs solarium and fitness equipment.

Begin the day with either an indoor or outdoor fitness class. Indoor classes offer aerobics, water, body contouring, and yoga. Outdoor classes include Tai Chi Trail, Walk This Way, and 1000 Step Trek. Walks include a guide, and are a great way to become acquainted with the Bonaire countryside and get fit.

Personal Trainers will provide either a custom-tailored workout or motivational session in weight training, nutrition, cardiovascular conditioning, meditation, and stress management.

Therapeutic massages at the Spa are designed to relax and eliminate stress through release of tension in tight muscles, improved circulation and enriched overall well-being. The spa also offers a thirty-minute "mini-stress buster", an ultra customized massage and Shiatsu. This may be given in or outdoors or by request in one's own room.

Your complexion is enhanced with skin care services specifically designed to cleanse, hydrate and nourish. An assortment of cleansing and replenishing body treatments are designed to leave you feeling refreshed and reborn, i.e. a Phytomer Back Treatment or the Bonarian Salt Exfoliate, a body polish, algae full body mud, after sun relief mask, and cellulite relief mask.

DIVER'S SPA PACKAGE

For divers who want to relax the mind and body after a day of diving, a special program includes a massage, a body exfoliation to clean and refresh your body, and the calming effects of a Tai Chi class.

The least one should choose is the above plus the ultra customized facial, manicure with hand paraffin, pedicure with herbal footbath and hair and scalp treatment.

I should like to say, "donki", to each member of the staff at Harbour Village Beach Resort. I took away fine memories and new friends.

Harbour Village Beach Resort
P.O. Box 312
Kralendijk, Bonaire,
Netherlands Antilles
Tel. 5997-7500 Fax 5997-7507
Toll free in US and Canada (800) 424-0004

THE SCUBA DIVING & SNORKELING

Under the keen eye of Ms. Marion Wilson, Great Adventures receives the highest grade one could give for it's all round attention to safety standards and level of service.

Their boat, a 30-foot island hopper is roomy and comfortable with canopy, hot water shower and rinse tank for cameras. Cold drinks are served between dives. Equipment is set up, broken down and rinsed off. The center provides secure personal lockers for equipment storage.

The first day on the boat I was introduced to a new safety measure that I wish every dive boat would emulate. Role call was taken and we signed the roster as the boat made its way to the dive site. After our first dive, role was taken again, we signed off once more and each diver was asked for his/her time underwater and PSI remaining.

The following are two of my favorite sites among the 85 marked and protected dive sights available:

RED SLAVE

This dive site is 30 minutes from the resort and is aptly named, for it sits off shore directly in front of the old slave quarters bedecked with red roofs near the salt pans. At 80 feet, large tiger groupers and yellow jack swam along with us. Halfway into the dive, we moved to shallower water. Here the divemaster taught us how to look for sea horse. All in all, we counted six of them in varying sizes and colors (navy, red and yellow).

THE HELMA HOOKER

Situated on the south side of Bonaire, the 1,000-ton wreck is 300 feet long. Her topside starts at 60 feet and goes to down to 120. A former drug boat, she was confiscated and sunk by the Bonaire Navy in 1984. There are three buoy lines attached to her, thus the dive is suited for the intermediate to advanced diver. Her bones are dressed in beautiful bright yellow tube coral and flaming orange sponge coral. The first time I dived her, a large school of enormous chubb swam in and out of her at a depth of 90 feet. They appeared very territorial and quite frankly fairly ominous.

Each day after our first dive, we lowered anchor off one of Klein Bonaire's 24 marked dive and snorkeling sites. On these shallower dives, we glided leisurely over the abundant, healthy hard and soft corals spotting a variety (in all shapes and sizes) of the 200 species of fish found in these waters... turtles, rays, schools of yellow tail snapper, and trumpetfish in every color. Pairs of Queen and French angelfish and the enchanting micro were always present. **Each dive on Bonaire brought new discovery and delights to the eye.**

British Virgin Islands

Virgin Gorda

North Sound

Biras Creek

Wendy Canning Church

Biras Creek is a flawless resort in a formidable setting. It is cradled in lush velvet green hills, surrounded by three bodies of water, the North Sound an enormous protected lagoon, the thunderous Atlantic and the blue Caribbean.

Burt Honmer, a 14-year vacationer at Biras, bought the property in 1995 and after a multi million-dollar renovation it reopened in 1996. **Its 140-acre peninsula can readily be counted as one of the world's top resorts.**

Reservations should be made well in advance. Future reservations are made by a phone call to Ralph Locke's booking agency that will assure that guests will be able to return to their favorite cottages.

Biras Creek is accessible via the North Sound Ferry, not far from Beef Island Airport on Tortola, or by the resort's private launch.

The property accommodates guests in 21 deluxe suites scattered along Benchers Bay on the Atlantic side and nine other hidden among sea grape and tamarisk plantings.

Cottage configuration assures guests the ultimate in serenity and privacy. All have A/C, ceiling fans, and large pastel hued decorated comfortable sitting rooms with mini bars and coffee makers. The bedroom compliments the sitting area in design and has a separate tiled bath with alfresco shower. Fresh flowers, English toiletries and mini bar are replenished daily.

Your private terrace allows for sunning, reading and viewing the beautiful sunrises and sunsets.

We reached many of our destinations on the two bicycles allotted each cottage. There are no cars on the island.

The heartbeat of the property is the stone "Castle" which sits high on the hill and is reached by tiled staircases. It houses the reception area, office, the terrace bar and the open air restaurant.

At dinner gourmet international cuisine is served at tables lit by flickering candles. There is a superb wine list to select from. Surrounding hills and valleys as well the nearby islands provide a serene backdrop.

Our path home was lit by moonlight and we were lulled to slumber by the lapping waves.

After dinner, big screen TV, a game of snooker, or a good book can be found at the Arawak Pavillion.

It was tempting for us never to leave the property outside of scuba diving and our private picnic excursions to isolated islands on one of their many Boston Whalers.

But we decided to partake of other activities offered: the trip to Anegada with lobster lunch, and the morning trip to the Baths, which is one of the most beautiful sites in the BVI's. We tried our hand at water-skiing, glass bottom boat rides, deep-sea fishing and a guided tour of the surrounding islands by speedboat.

We dove with Kilbrides Sunchaser Scuba Center located at the Bitter End Yacht Club. Their boat picked us up at the dock in the morning and afternoon. Other mornings we would take a picnic and a Boston Whaler and be off to a nearby island to swim and snorkel.

Biras Creek by Jamie Holmes

Another day, Alvin Harrigan, head gardener, gave us a guided tour of his gardens. A hike on one of the well-marked trails proved a delight. The estate's hills are filled with the essence of wild nutmeg, tamarisk, frangiapani, white cedar and a multitude of Turks Head cactus. The stunning views as you reached the top of a hill are magical.

At any time of year bird watchers will marvel at the variety of species.

Swim in the freshwater pool, which appears to flow directly into the sea or at Deep Bay's protected beach where luncheon is served three times a week under thatched huts for shade. Go off island on their 44-foot yacht on an overnight sailaway. Sample the Hobbie cats, sunfish, laser, windsurfers or kayaks. The choice is yours.

Whatever you do visit Biras Creek. Dollar for dollar it's one of the best buys we have come across for a luxury resort. 140 pristine acres of perfection, privacy and protection (no rain days). Request Cottage 5B.

Under the watchful eye and highly professional General Manager, Jamie Holmes and his staff Biras Creek Resort is a flawless resort in a formidable setting.

Reservations: inquire about wedding and special packages
North American and UK
Ralph Locke Islands
P.O. Box 492477
Los Angeles, CA 90049
USA
Tel: 1-800-223-1108
Fax: 1-310-440-4220
Toll-free from the UK
Tel: 0-800-894-057

British Virgin Islands

Virgin Gorda,
North Sound
Bitter End Yacht Club
Understated and Unexcelled

Wendy Canning Church

At the last point of land on Virgin Gorda where sailors could turn back to find tranquility from the often-turbulent Atlantic waters sits an idyllic retreat. Understated and unexcelled, the Bitter End Yacht Club can unabashedly lay claim to be amongst the world's top resorts.

Twenty-five years ago its owners sailed into this comely harbor and never left. Instead, they started a small resort for sailors where good grog, good food and good friends were available in an unfettered and unpretentious ambiance. Today, little has changed at the resort except for its size and the innumerable activities offered; most centered on the water. One might liken "Bitter End" to an upscale camp for grown-ups with all the toys and bells and whistles usually younger campers get to indulge in.

The resort is accessible only by the North Sound Ferry or by yacht. Accommodations spill from high up in the hibiscus-covered hills to the palm fringed vodka water below. Yachts of all sizes bob at anchor at the dock. Guests move about the property at a lively pace yet there is a quiet hum here, active yet serene.

ACCOMMODATIONS

All accommodations are West Indian style architecture. They are dispersed throughout the large property so a feeling of privacy prevails. The charming beachfront villas take advantage of the offshore breezes with no A/C but ceiling fans. All have a mini fridge. A private terrace completes your hideaway only steps from the beach.

Hillside cottages are nestled between a kalleidoscope of foilage filled with hummingbirds and covered with lush green vegetation. The views are spectacular. The tradewinds supply the A/C.

The Commodores Club is the newest addition to the resort. Essentially, it is a resort within a resort. The suites are situated away from other accommodations and activity centers. Reached by jitneys, the bungalows have panoramic ocean views and sit high in the hillsides which are ablaze with lush plantings .

Large and tastefully decorated, the 20 A/C suites have nice mini kitchens, the choice of king or queen size bed, telephone, radio, VCR and roomy terrace. Splurge and book one of these special romantic retreats. Each terrace gives an unforgettable view of the surrounding islands, yachts coming and going, sunfish skimming the water, and the private pool and beach below. All of this with the sound of silence.

The Commodores Club has its own private dining room where you will enjoy five star cuisine with five star views. A complete vintage wine list is available. The bar is fun place to trade tales of the day's adventures. The Quarterdeck Club is a private club for boat owners cruising in the area. Yachtsmen from all over the world dock here and take advantage of electrical hookups, private on-dock facilities and the other services available.

This is the home of the Freedom 30 fleet.

Marina Rooms are located near the Quarterdeck Club. The live-aboard Freedom 30s and the Marina Rooms, at the heart of the waterfront action, make a perfect land-and-sea combination package.

View from Commodores Club Villa; Bitter End Yacht Club by Wendy Canning Church

DINING

The cuisine at the waterfront pavilion restaurant or the Steak and Seafood grill offer food and service of high quality. Each restaurant has a different atmosphere.

There is also a small pub/deli/grocery store for casual fare.

SCUBA DIVING AND SNORKELING

With a year round semi-tropical climate, virgin waters, unlimited visibility, and 300 uncharted shipwrecks, Virgin Gorda makes an ideal vacation spot for the scuba diver and snorkeler.

The resort is headquarters for Kilbrides Underwater Safari dive operation. We took advantage of their morning and afternoon excursions both here and at Biras Creek which is situated nearby; reached by footpath or a short boat ride.

Instructors only need apply to work here. Mike, the manager sets high standards for the staff and in turn they set the highest safety standards for the guests whether snorkeler or diver. They do this with a serious albeit gentle manner. Once the rules are set down, the dive plan laid out, the fun begins. I found that each guide loves the sea, respected it and saw that each diver/snorkeler left bedazzled by what they encountered underwater. We were not only more informed but quite mellow after each dive.

Diving at Kilbrides is geared to all levels. Dive sites are chosen by weather conditions so there is not a fixed schedule.

The boat is a 40-foot Sunchaser, with plenty of room for divers/snorkelers and their equipment. A sun deck is at the bow and entry is by giant stride with two good ladders for re-entry. Refreshments are served between dives. There is a maximum of six divers to one guide

Mountain point is situated off Virgin Gorda at its northern most point. Formed by three large rocks with narrow cuts to swim through. The large drop off leads to sharply edged walls with a sandy bottom as backdrop making this a dramatic dive. Hard and soft corals were healthy, varied in a cacophony of color. Reef fish were plentiful and our reward was a ray darting from his sleep on the sandy bottom, a nice size turtle and a nurse shark. At 60 to 70 feet we got a good 40 minutes bottom time to eye the lobster, crabs, moray eels and barracuda.

The Wreck of the *Bertha* is located at Ingnass Bay off Cooper Island sunk intentionally as an artificial reef, we were lucky to dive here in 1997. She could be completely penetrated which will most likely not be possible in the near future. The *Bertha* is an old cargo ship 210 feet long that landed perfectly upright in 80 feet of water. Growth is beginning on her bones. I dived her three times and saw up to six rays on each dive, corals, nurse sharks, and a queen angelfish. A large remora catching a ride on a filefish was sighted signaling that this will become a first class dive site.

Big Grotto and Little Grotto off Mountain Point are shallow dives, but there is a long swim between grottos. At 30 feet you get lots of bottom time. There are huge boulders, gullies and swim throughs with plentiful reef fish. At the second grotto you ascend to the top and before you is a large open cave, a delight.... A must dive.

ACTIVITIES

One would have to stay for a month in order to take advantage of all the activities offered. **If you are a sailor, past or present or have an interest in learning to sail, The Bitter End is a top choice.** The **Nick Trotter Sailing School** teaches beginner to advanced courses from navigation to racing techniques.

Thirty Boston Whalers are ready for guests to take for a sojourn to nearby islands. **Necker, Prickly Pear, Statia and Cactus Reef are wonderful snorkeling and picnic spots.**

The 50-foot *Prince of Whales* **waits to whisk you off to Anegada for a lobster lunch and snorkeling. Another day sail is to the famous Baths.**

The *Paranda*, the resorts 48-foot catamaran makes day and sunset cruises.

The fleet of Freedom 30's is at the disposal of sailors who wish to bareboat or have instruction.

Try your hand at windsurfing and take a lesson at the resorts Mistral School.

Unlimited sailing is offered for qualified skippers on Lasers and Rhodes 19's.

It is exhilarating to return from vacation having tried your hand at a new experience. This is one of the greatest assets of Bitter End. You are learning a new talent from highly skilled professionals who take their job seriously. They aren't dropouts to Sun City.

Potters Taxi will give you an Island Tour - Gorda Peak National Park, Spanish Town and the Copper Mine.

Bitter End, book it for yourself or the entire family. Your visit will be one of the more memorable ones. Vacation, honeymoon or anniversary, **The Bitter End Yacht Club Hotel and Resort is understated and unexcelled.**

Bitter End Yacht Club
Virgin Gorda, BVI, Box 46
809-494-2746
FAX: 809-494-4756

Bitter End Yacht Club International, Inc.
875 North Michigan Avenue
Chicago, Illinois 60611
1-800-872-2392
FAX: 312-944-2860

Cayman Islands

Little Cayman

Pirates Point

Wendy Canning Church

The smallest of the three islands, this coral atoll lies seventy miles northeast of Grand Cayman. Little Cayman is cigar shaped and is surrounded by a diamond bright sea.

We landed at Edward Bodden International Airport that consisted of a grassy airstrip and a small shack to handle cargo and passengers. Disembarking, I heard a loud voice say, "Wendy, I'm over here. Come say 'Hi' while they sort out the luggage."

Interior of Cottage, Pirates Point, Little Cayman courtesy of Pirates Point

I greeted Gladys Howard, owner and my hostess for the next three days at Pirates Point Resort. Gladys' personality, professionalism and warmth are as big as the State of Texas from which she hails—Tyler, Texas to be exact.

Guests are accommodated in octagonal shaped cottages. The interiors have high ceilings, and are furnished in rattan with tasteful tropical decor. Half of the rooms are seaside, with a ceiling fan and air conditioning, but no telephone or TV.

The bathrooms have showers with wonderful soap, fluffy towels and all the hot water you would want. Believe me, this is a real luxury on such a remote island (they have a reverse osmosis plant).

Don't even think about roughing it at Pirates Point. Before she became a hotelier, Gladys was a celebrated caterer in Texas and studied under the likes of Julia Child and James Beard. Luncheon is casually elegant served with linen and silver, al fresco, under the shade of a perfusion of sea grape trees. Dinner is served with all the amenities of a five-star restaurant. Linen, fine crystal and candlelight dress the tables.

As I bade goodnight to Gladys, I asked about dive time. She said very casually, "Oh, about ten o'clock. Our guests are here on vacation to rest. No sense in rushing anyone."

"My style of management makes Pirates Point more of a second home for my guests than a resort. **My guests set their own schedules for diving and fishing, and the kitchen never closes.** I have traveled and dived all over the world and I have incorporated into this small resort all the things that I have liked the best. Here I have the opportunity to get to know my guests and to cook for them creatively, which I enjoy. I feel **Pirates Point provides a unique experience that our guests will never forget.**" I could not have said it better.

SCUBA DIVING

The next morning we all loaded our gear in the truck and were off to board the *Newton*. She's a 42-foot boat with a permanent canopy for shade, room for sunning and a head. There is cold juice, fresh fruit, and fluffy towels on board. There are always two instructors on board. The *Newton* has a VHS radio, oxygen mask and carries a backboard for injuries. A giant stride is made from a platform and a ladder is used for re-entry. You are asked not to feed the fish. Gloves are not allowed.

MIXING BOWL

Twenty minutes from shore, this site is situated between **Jackson Reef** and **Bloody Bay Wall**. It's an interesting dive since the sand holes at Jackson Wall at 90-95 feet change as you make your way over to the top of Bloody Bay Wall, being back on the line at 700 PSI at 15 feet for a 5 minute safety stop.

As you descend, you are at the top of the wall at 18 to 20 feet and then drop down where there are many holes and crevices. You go through the wall at 100 feet, gradually ascending. Turtles, schools of yellow jack, tiger grouper, queen angelfish, schools of snapper, banded butterfly fish, spotted drum, grouper, jewfish, black durgeon, ocean trigger, file fish and trumpet fish were spotted.

The topography was incredible. The most impressive sight was a sponge, the color of celedon china.

GREAT WEST WALL, BLOODY BAY

Our next dive off the **Great West Wall, Bloody Bay**, was an incredible dive for the wall is sheer. You descend to 18 feet and then it's like going over the side of a building. Keeping to the right at 50 feet, we swam along spotting a pea green moray eel. Making our way further along, we saw lobster, a yellow and an orange sea horse, hog fish, grouper, black durgeon with wrasse cleaning them, and a huge rainbow parrotfish. Leafy lettuce sea slugs covered almost the entire area. We had a tremendous amount of light even at that depth which made for outstanding visibility.

Unfortunately, I only had time to make these two dives at Little Cayman because of my flight schedule. But I agree with the gentleman and his wife that I met in the Bahamas. He asked, "Have you dived Little Cayman?" I said, "No." He retorted, **"Get there before it's found!"**

AREAS OF INTEREST

Gladys took me on an hour tour of the island, educating me as to the history, topography, scuba diving and gossip. The island is only 9 miles long and 1 mile wide and is home to a mere 50 permanent residents.

As we drove along the road (all roads are now paved and 30 feet wide), other vehicles would appear and each driver pulled over to greet the other. "We're having a good old fashioned barbecue tonight, ribs and chicken. Do you and the family want to join?" "Sounds great, Gladys. Expect us there at seven."

Little Cayman has its pirate legends. On **Spot Bay Road** that cuts across the island the pirates could walk through on foot and have an exit and entrance to the sea on either side.

We passed papaya trees growing along the road and Gladys remarked how they make great meat tenderizers. We stopped to smell the Star of Bethlehem flowers. The fragrance is similar to lime. We picked and tasted the seeds from the Nase berries. They are round and look like big seeds and taste like a cross between an apple and a pear. Further along, we picked cockspur seeds from the cockspur vine. These are used to play the game of Waurie that dates back to the time of the pirates and now is played on a special board.

Gladys is Chairman of the National Trust for the island and knows the scientific names of the birds and plants both indigenous and those brought to the island. She is adamant about preserving the wildlife and I wouldn't want to be the one to tread on her philosophy.

We rode past a 15-acre tarpon pond, a small shopping center (the only one on the island), **The Iguana**, a souvenir shop, and the state-of-the-art dump. The only problem with the dump is they can't find anyone who wants to be the trash man—any takers?

Bird watchers! You'll see the most beautiful bird life in the woodlands and wetlands, mangrove cuckoos, bananaquits, woodpeckers, and the colorful and rare purple gallinule. The island has the largest sanctuary for red footed boobies and the magnificent frigate in the Western Hemisphere.

Take a rowboat from Little Cayman to **Owen Island**, just 200 yards away. The untouched island is only 11 acres with a white sandy beach and a blue lagoon—the most beautiful place to picnic and spend a peaceful day.

Enjoy a game of Waurie, a strategy game reputedly enjoyed by Hemingway and Blackbeard. Slaves brought the game to the West Indies from Africa.

When I think of Little Cayman, I remember a beautiful, remote spot where God's handiwork is mostly untouched. An island where one is reminded, when diving, of a paperweight. You turn it upside down, then upright and the entire underwater scene is of a perfect undersea garden where nature's beauty has been left intact, surrounded and filtered by the radiant soft light of the sun. I remember a lady that I would not hesitate to call aunt or Mom who was at all times gracious, and warm to all the guests; someone you really would like to see again.

Little Cayman and Pirates Point are the perfect complement and to be shared with that special someone. The island really is a small model of perfection. The bright red flamboyant trees touching the Northfolk pine intermingled with all varieties of fauna, the wild iguana, the egrets and boobies, the tarpon pond, all surrounded by a sea with **some of the best bone fishing, scuba diving, and snorkeling to be found anywhere.**

Guadeloupe

Le Hamak

Panache With Understated Sophistication

Wendy Canning Church

Under the direction of Jean Francois Rozen, Owner and General Manager, Le Hamak embodies the panache and elegant as the gentleman himself. This hideaway sits serenely on its own private lagoon facing the tradewinds.

Until 1966 the eastern part of Grand Terre, 34 km from Raizet Airport at Pointe-a-Pitre airport, was an area of great sugar cane plantations. Slowly four and five-star resorts began to replace them and by 1977 the once sleepy village of St. Francois became a haven to the finest resorts in Guadeloupe.

Le Hamak's guests will find a lively area with many attractions, which include an 18 hole Robert Trent Jones golf course, airport for light planes, 140 berth marina, water sports and tennis facilities, small boutiques, a supermarket, cafes, discos, nightspots, and casinos.

Its 52 bungalows are woven amongst five acres of tropical gardens who's flowing hibiscus and oleander perfumes intermingle with the fresh sea air. **When booking, ask for bungalow 29D at the far end with its own little beach — a family of 4 would enjoy adjoining 29D and 29F.**

One's accommodation is large with soft, peach-colored rattan furnishings covered in pastel floral fabrics. There is a writing desk and a separate sitting area, and an abundance of closet space. All are air-conditioned, have direct dial telephone, mini fridge stocked with any array of liquor or wine that you request, cafe expresso machine, and TV if desired.

Le Hamak by Wendy Canning Church

The bathrooms are a good size, replete with hairdryer and French toiletries. To my delight, there is a terrace with a shower surrounded by a wall for privacy and one's own little garden. Here you cannot only shower, but read, relax and sunbathe au natural. It is also a perfect spot for small children to entertain themselves.

Et bien sur, on your patio facing the crystal waters one has a hammock. Each one is individually designed; some with lace borders others with French chintz or madras. These inviting patios inveigle the guests to breakfast here or while away the afternoon napping, have an evening cocktail while watching the sunset, or take an expresso and brandy after dinner. Beachfront bungalows have their own little private beach.

The cuisine is excellent, a mixture of European and Creole, the wine list superb, served beachside or in the main dining room. A mood music bar doubles as the restaurant in summer.

A boutique is replete with everything from chic clothing to sundries.

Play toys include a soft water spa jacuzzi and windsurfers. Private charters to Petit Terre and rental car can be arranged.

To keep in touch with the outside world there is a telex and fax and a daily paper of choice.

Close your eyes and think of Porthaut Sheets, pate de foie gras, Tatinger Blanc de Blanc, the late summer gentle winds off the sea in Provence and its fields of colorful flowers and you then will envision Le Hamak.

This is where they held the 1979 Summit - need I say more?

GETTING MARRIED?

You will need the following documents in order to get married at La Hamak:
- birth certificate (or copy with raised seal)
- certificate of good conduct (including certification of "single status")
- residency card (one of the couple must have resided on the island at least one month)
- medical certificate (including blood test) issued within 3 months of marriage
- French translation of English language documents.

A "Bulletin de Marriage" and "Livret de Famille" are delivered at the ceremony. No fee is involved.

For more information contact:
Hotel Hamak
97118 Saint-Francois
Guadeloupe, French West Indies.
Telephone: (590) 88.59.99
Telefax: (590) 88.41.92
Telex: 919753 GL

Jamaica

Half Moon Golf, Tennis & Beach Club
"An Island Within an Island"

Wendy Canning Church

A 10 minute drive from Sangster International Airport, yet light years away, one finds the **Half Moon Golf, Tennis and Beach Club** on 400 secluded acres. Beautifully fashioned in colonial architecture, she rests with her vantagepoint a silver sand beach, the Caribbean as backdrop, Half Moon Golf, Tennis & Beach Club proudly prevails as it has for over some 40 years as one of the best Resorts/Hotels in the world.

I visited Half Moon with my parents as a teenager. Still having fond memories of our joyful family holiday at this fashionable haven, you can imagine my curiosity as to how and if it had changed since its opening in 1954 with only 30 guest rooms and 17 villas.

It is interesting to note that throughout this qualitative property's life, Heinz Simonitsch has been at the helm. Knowing the Half Moon of yesterday and becoming reacquainted with her today, the guest will appreciate this gentleman's continuing high standard of professionalism.

Half Moon has received the AAA, Four Diamonds and Golden Fork Awards for its elegant standards and impeccable service. It is a member of Elegant Resorts International and Elegant Resorts of Jamaica.

After the devastating hurricane of 1988 the property's occupancy and activities have been expanded, making it a complete resort, which one might say is an understatement when speaking of Half Moon. It truly is an island within an island.

Half Moon Hotel Villa, Jamaica by Wendy Canning Church

Today, the world traveler can choose from one of the attractive, newly appointed 50 rooms, 170 suites, 23 royal suites, or 20 villas. The villas are situated along picturesque East Bay amidst lush tropical gardens and border the Wetland Nature Reserve.

Accommodations are air conditioned, with TV, mini-bar, direct dial telephone, splendid bathrooms, 110v electrical outlets, in-room safe, and are embellished by balconies or patios, with an ocean and/or garden view. All are tastefully decorated and a guest would not be surprised to see them in the latest edition of *Architectural Digest*.

A nursery has been established, thus the Hotel is now self-sufficient in its plants, cut flowers and fresh herb requirements. It maintains a full time landscaping crew of 57

Located behind the nursery are the herb and vegetable gardens. All produce is used in food preparation by the kitchen for each of their superb restaurants: Seagrape Terrace (Jamaican/International), IL Giardino (Italian), Sugar Mill (Jamaican/ International), Croquet Bar (Light Snacks), La Baguette (Snack counter & bar), Lychee Garden (Chinese), Sakura (Oriental), Cedar Bar (Light meals/Afternoon tea), 19th Hole (Light Snacks), Royal Stocks (Pub and Eatery), and Jamaican Restaurant (Taste of Jamaica). The cuisine is delicious, always presented beautifully and served with both warmth and professionalism.

We commend Half Moon for these and other ongoing methods of working in tandem for the quests' enjoyment whilst still preserving nature's faultless surroundings.

The Resort's land and sea activities are numerous. One can select from an impressive menu served by a professional staff. The Clubhouse, an imposing structure embellished by cultivated vegetation, sits high on a bluff. The 18-hole golf course has received a face-lift, is beautifully maintained, and has now been officially rated by the U.S.G.A.

There are 13 tennis courts (7 lit), 4 squash courts, 3 swimming pools, a full range of water sports, horseback riding, fitness center, aerobics, sauna, Jacuzzi, and an 18 hole putting course.

The Children's Activity Center features a duck pond, swimming pool, sand boxes, swings, a horse shoe court, and tennis courts. Indulge your child in an interesting array of planned daily activities expertly guided by a Guest Services Coordinator. Activities are planned based on three age groups: 3-7 years, 7-12 years, and 12-14 years. A nanny service will be provided for parents requesting individual service at a nominal fee.

In fact you really never have to leave the property. On premises there is a bank, duty-free shopping, commissary, pharmacy, designer boutiques, dentist, doctor, lawyer, and a conference center.

The conference facilities can accommodate up to 300 persons for a banquet and 514 for theater-style seating. I cannot think of a more superb setting to mix business with a post holiday.

The Half Moon Wedding Package includes: Marriage Officer; Best Man, Maid of Honor/Witness; Bouquet of flowers; Jamaican Wedding Cake; Bottle of Champagne; Professional Video; roll of 36 pictures and negatives; and an Elegant Horse Drawn Carriage Tour of the property. **Be sure to check the Jamaican Tourist Authority regulations for any documents that you need to produce before marrying.**

THE SPA: BODY WORKS

"At Half Moon we realize the importance of a strong body, holistic spirit and mind. The perfect way to spend a relaxing vacation and gain a new lease on life."

The Spa at Half Moon is designed to stress pampering and well being of body and mind. Here, spa guests can begin a personalized regime designed to suit their needs.

Spa cuisine is delicious. Tantalize your taste buds with fresh fruits - bananas, pineapples, mangoes, etc., or start the morning off with a scrumptious "New Beginnings" breakfast, which ranges from egg white omelet stuffed with a medley of blanched Jamaican vegetables to enjoying a selection of herbal teas.

The spa offers a selection of advanced Nautilus equipment along with Lifeower, Lifesstride, Lifecycle and Recumbent Lifecycle machines. Aerobic exercise ranges from low-impact classes and stretch and tone up sessions to power workouts. After an invigorating workout, sample an assortment of natural fruit juices at the juice and snack bar located at the Oleander Terrace a.k.a. "La Baguette". This provides an excellent way to "cool down".

Dinner allows you to select individual items to suit your pleasure or be adventurous and choose the Table d'hôte menu which brings together a superb combination of items selected by Executive Chef, Roger Wiles. You may also consult with Chef Wiles if you have any other special dietary needs.

Located at the Hibiscus Pool, Body Works is owned by Sheila Gray, one of the most knowledgeable ladies I have ever met in her field.

Her staff is expertly trained and treatments include Body Massage, Facials, Aromatherapy, Contour Wrap, Sea Algae Wrap, Lymph Drainage Wrap, Body Scrub, Manicure, and Pedicure.

SCUBA DIVING & SNORKELING

The scuba diving center is on premises. Dives are offered to suit every level of experience. Three of my favorites were minutes from the shore.

Colony Reef, at a depth of 48 feet one can view a jungle of coral rising from the sea floor in a plethora of shapes and sizes (pillar, grooved brain, butter print, ribbon, ivory brush, sheet, and elliptical) in the crystalline waters. There were no large fish but the waters were teeming with reef fish (blue, shy, and indigo hamlet, yellowhead and creole wrasse, red bank, stoplight, and blue parrotfish, and schools of squirrelfish and a number of small grouper).

Holiday Inn, is a nice reef dive, which slopes off to a sandy bottom. Tiny shrimp, juveniles and blue tang, pork fish, yellowtang snapper, sergeant major, and banded butterfly fish populated the turquoise waters, dashing in and out of the reef whose backdrop was exceptionally scenic due to the interesting configuration of the barrel coral.

My favorite dive was **Half Moon Reef**. We dived at 40 feet maximum and had wonderful light from above to explore the comely setting. We encountered starfish, spiny lobsters hidden between the crevices. Barracuda swam blatantly with us as if to let us know, lest we forgot, that this was indeed their kingdom. Reef squid, coral, spiny spider crab, bristle and plume worm, Venus and common sea fan along with bright red and orange wall sponges lent wonderful color to their haunt.

There is a snorkeling boat that will take clients to nearby reefs to enjoy the colorful variety offshore. And in addition to their regular published rates for diving, they also offer a series of special packages for your pleasure.

Their **Adventure Packages** are designed to not only offer you the finest dive sites in Montego Bay, but also to introduce you to a little of the culture. Several of these adventures stretch over 2 or 3 days, so you will get to know your fellow divers, divemasters and instructors fairly well. They strive to offer a safe, well-rounded experience complimented with a smile.

- One-day trips that cover the entire Montego Bay Marine Park.
- Special night dives that explore "The Old Man's Head" and end with a delicious fish feast—cooked Jamaican Style.
- Two tank dives that explore all the reefs they cover.
- A unique program for divers and their non-diving companion—designed to allow them to share in this wonderful underwater world.
- An ongoing search dive for the source of the "Devil's Kitchen" that includes a tour of the Great House - Rose Hall - where it was said that the wicked Mistress, Annie Palmer, used to go to the waters known as Devil's Kitchen and cleanse. There is a purported fresh water spring under the sea.

I found the entire staff at the center to be well-trained and to have a love of the sea, giving each diver the attention needed both above and beneath the water, making every trip a pleasurable one.

When making reservations inquire about the different package plans offered guests. Most include a "sleep-around" program with other hotels. A "dine-around" plan is also available except for those residing in the villas.

For more information contact:

Half Moon
P.O. Box 80
Montego Bay, Jamaica, W.I
Telephone: 809-953-2211
Reservations: 809-953-2615
Telefax: 809-953-2731

Martinique

Les Trois Ilets

The Bakoua Hotel

Wendy Canning Church

The Bakoua Hotel is located in the northern Caribbean on Les Trois Ilets. Its grounds are awash in color nestled between towering palm trees, intertwined with plantings of mango, guava, papaya, and banana. Hibiscus, magnolia, and oleander complete this setting which exudes an ambiance of serenity prevalent throughout the property. I found the Bakoua to be an excellent choice. Within its grounds one could completely relax while at the same time it was a convenient drive to the scuba diving and snorkeling centers.

Guests have a choice of one of three wings that are perched on a hillside overlooking the harbor to view the white water of the boats' wake as they travel to and fro, or accommodations directly on the beach.

Hotel Bakoua courtesy of Elizabeth A. Walsh, Laura Davidson Public Relations

Be sure to ask for Room 229 overlooking the sea in the middle wing, or directly on the beach request the Vanille Suite at the far corner whose windows face both the harbor on one side and sea on the other as does its patio. Both are away from the buzz of activity on the beach, or Room 134 above Vanille, which also has a lovely balcony with the identical view as the Vanille.

Children are welcome, as is your dog weighing 5 kg or under at extra charge. Baby-sitting can be arranged.

The air-conditioned guest wings are separated into rooms with twin beds or double beds and have balconies. Rooms with double beds are tastefully furnished in French floral chintz with good-sized bath, French toiletries and fluffy bathrobes. All rooms have TV, direct dial phone, minibar, and safety deposit box.

Beach accommodations are in two-tiered buildings and have the same amenities as those in the wings. The upper floor has balconies, and the lower rooms have patios surrounded by pots of flaming bright red hibiscus and a lattice screen between allowing for privacy.

ACTIVITIES

The water sports club provides the following activities: pedal boats, water skiing and sea scooters (extra charge), windsurf and sunfish, canoes-kayak, deep-sea fishing (extra charge), two tennis courts with lighting, and volleyball.

The following can be arranged by the hotel: golf (extra charge) - 18 hole golf course, free shuttle service from the hotel, horseback riding center (free transfer from the hotel), cross-country biking, squash, gymnastics, body-building, dancing, yoga, modern jazz, and miniature golf.

A powder blue, Olympic-sized pool sits at the hillsides' edge. Here one can swim, sun, take a drink or have luncheon.

There is also a boutique and flower shop on the premises.

Hotel Sofitel Bakoua
97229 Trois Ilets, Martinique
Tel: (596) 66.02.02
Fax: (596) 66.00.41

BEACHES

All beaches in Martinique are public. At hotels one can pay for a beach chair and spend the day. Most hotel beaches are topless, while at public ones ladies tend to cover up.

The Bakoua beach is divided into 3 sections, with one for the guests only, which is furnished with chairs and straw huts. A beach monitor is also on hand to serve refreshing drinks, reserve your hut or change your beach towel. You can swim to the Coco Bar and have a drink.

DINING

The open-air **Le Chateaubriand** restaurant with sweeping views of the mirror-like water beyond serves a buffet breakfast to satisfy any nationality's taste in an attractive ambiance. Candlelight dinners are also offered here. One can enjoy European as well as Creole delights.

Creole cuisine is a skillful mixture of flavors both in taste and color. Before hand they offer: accras, stuffed crab, colombos, blaffs, as well as lobsters, sea urchins and other seafood. Not to mention the famous punch cocktail or an aged rum for after dinner.

For a more relaxed atmosphere guests may choose **Le Jardin Tropical.**

Theme Evenings include Grands Ballets de la Martinique, limbo dancing, and Creole and French music. For night owls "Le Grommier" bar and club features a wide range of cocktails.

AREAS OF INTEREST

Make a point of visiting some of the fine sights in Martinique: Dames **Des Tropiques** includes a full day aboard a 260 foot schooner headed for la Pointe des Negres, Rocher du Diamant then back to Grande Anse. Spend a half-day aboard a glass-bottomed submarine vision boat at the **Sea Aquarium**, discovering the ocean bed around Trois Ilets, Cap Salomon and Anse d'Arlet. Go on a guided tour of **Fort-de-France** and learn the city's legendary heritage and see unusual faces. The ferry to Fort-de-France is just 5 minutes away at the marina.

Take a plane trip over the beautiful **Grenadine Islands.** Visit **North Creole** via an air-conditioned coach trip visiting Sacre-Coeur, the Balata gardens, Mount Pelee, Saint-Pierre and the ruins, a rum distillery and plantations. Take an air-conditioned coach trip to the south, visiting La Pagerie, Anses d'Arlet, Rocher du Diamant, a distillery and the south coast beaches.

The Indian Ocean

Mauritius

Le Touessrok Hotel

"Utter Perfection"

Wendy Canning Church

Le Touessrok is a luxurious tranquil paradise splendid enough to please any sybarite. It is a unique luxury resort situated on the east coast of Mauritius (one hour from the airport) surrounded by an archipelago of tropical islands sheltered by coral reefs. After a $58 million renovation it reopened with a new look and a new manager, Phillippe M. E. Requim (a charming Frenchman with an Asian hotel background-an unbeatable combination).

Wherever you stand in Le Touessrok, you have a view of the ocean.

All accommodations form a circular pattern around the island. On the mainland are two wings. The Hibiscus wing within which is the Royal Suite and the Coral wing. These are stretched out amongst private beaches on either side. **My favorite suites are those situated on the Ile aux Lievres, reached by a footbridge from the public areas of the hotel.**

All rooms have: electronic safe, mini-bar, hair dryer, remote control color television and a four channel video system (English, French, German and Italian), radio and taped music (classical, pop and easy listening), direct dial telephone, individually controlled air-conditioning, en suite bathroom with a tub and shower, a lounge with sliding doors opening onto a private balcony with an ocean view, and all are superbly appointed in a pale palette of peach, sand and green.

Restaurants at the hotel serve beautifully presented cuisine. Begin with a cool drink at the Le Sega bar, overlooking the larger of two swimming pools reached by stepping-stones. Afterward, savor a romantic dinner at Gianno - the hotel's intimate and highly acclaimed Italian restaurant. During the meal, strolling minstrels complete the ambiance. Les Paillotes (a la carte restaurant) is relaxed and informal, overlooking the Lagoon and the swimming pool. La Passerelle (main dining room with 400 seats) serves Mauritian gastronomy, a breakfast buffet or dinner.

Le Touessrok Courtesy of Le Touessrok

Afternoon tea is served daily. There is 24-hour room service.

On the mainland, an array of activities is available: 4 floodlit tennis courts, petanque, volleyball, football and a pool. A smaller pool is suitable on Ile aux Lievres. At the hotel you'll find paddleboats, canoes and windsurfers. **Snorkeling and trips in a glass bottom boat are included.**

There is a Young Pirates Club for children between the ages of 4 and 12 that is open throughout the year and is supervised by an experienced hostess and offers and action packed entertainment program.

The Corsair Club is for teenagers and operates mainly during holiday periods.

Heliconia Games Room is situated near reception. It has two half-sized pool tables, table tennis, and facilities for other indoor games.

Other amenities include: Sauna, massage, beauty care, Pouncing Jewelers, China-town, Nectarine-clothing, The Beach Shop for beachwear, Le Touessrok Gift Collection and the Drugstore for books, magazines and general refreshments, hairdressing salon, baby-sitting clinic, horse-riding, florist, airport transfers, car hire and excursions.

Golf at **Le Saint Geran Hotel** is a 20-minute drive from Le Touessrok. Free shuttle bus and equipment is available.

ILE AUX CERFS

There are free aquatic sports on Ile aux Cerfs. Here one finds Hobbie cats, laser sails, windsurfers, paddleboats, canoes, water-skiing, **snorkeling** and trips in a glass bottom boat. Also available on Isle aux Cerfs are parasailing, **pirogues for snorkeling at the reef,** fishing and trips to the waterfall, deep-sea fishing, scuba diving and sailing cruises.

Paul and Virginie is a restaurant famous for seafood on Ile aux Cerfs and was named after a legendary couple who were thwarted in love. It is open-air dining and is most romantic.

Take luncheon at **La Chaumiere**, which gets its name from the thatched umbrellas that shelter each table (A chaumiere is a wooden structure covered by palm thatch).

This open-air restaurant is built into the surrounding trees and rocks and is much like dining in your own private tree house. Sip chilled white wine and sample some of the mouthwatering Mauritian delicacies for which this restaurant is famed.

Lor Brizan, a charming bar on the beach serves wicked pre-lunch cocktails. Should you wish, snacks and drinks can be served to you on the beach.

ILLOT MANGENIE

Open at night on request for special functions such as Pirate Evenings, Tropical Island Evenings and Creole, Ilot Mangenie is a private desert island five minutes from the hotel.

Ilot Mangenie is exclusively for the use of Le Touessrok guests and is the perfect hideaway for those in search of tranquility. Frequent boat service transports hotel guests to and from the island.

Luncheon arrives by boat complete with Man Friday and one can sample succulent lobster and chilled white wine. There are 350 acres of filao trees but seldom more than 60 people.

The only permanent residents in the 100-acre virgin forest are shy oriental deer that gave the island its name, and giant tortoises, some of which are over 200 years old. A variety of exotic birds are also to be found. Wander away from the main beaches and you will find stretches of coral sand that are completely deserted.

THE SCUBA DIVING AND SNORKELING

The east coast of Mauritius offers adventurous and challenging diving. Here one will not find the mellow dives of Flic and Flac, but rather deeper dives and stronger currents. The trade off is that the diver is favored with the pelagics as well as varied species of reef fish. **Snorkelers usually join the boats to Ile aux Cerfs or Illot Mangerie.**

Pierre Sport Dive Ltd. has in-house scuba and snorkeling facilities at the hotel. The dive boats are comfortable with canopy, captain and a ratio of one guide to four divers. Certification cards and logbooks are required. **The service is excellent and safety is a top priority.**

I only spent four nights at Le Touessrok after my trip to the Comoros. If you count the no dive regulations because of arrival and departure times, this really cut into the diving I was able to do.

FLAG ISLAND

For less experienced divers the lagoon is a wonderful spot. **Snorkelers are welcomed to join in many mellow dives.** At a maximum depth of 18 meters we got one hour out of a tank and saw a multitude of sea life that is ever present in the Indian Ocean.

A free descent brought us to the first reef off Flag Island. A sandy bottom provided a perfect blanket for the different colored sea horses, a honeycomb moray hiding in the reef, puffer fish, sea worm, and a huge sea cucumber.

Passing over to the second reef: **Big Rock** juvenile angel fish greeted us along with needlefish, yellow tail barracuda, semi-circle angel fish, orange spotted emperors, titan triggerfish and dusky batfish.

THE PASS

After our entry we descended to the beautiful landscape of coral encrusted walls. Schools of shark and large carp swam along with us at a depth of 90 feet. Swift currents carried us. We ascended slowly with bicolor parrotfish, squid, Moorish idols, imperial angelfish, and trumpfish and giant wrasse. The free ascent allowed us to gas off slowly as we watched schools of fish in varying sizes sway to the rhythm of the seas.

On my return, I will plan to spend a week with Pierre and his marvelous staff and dive, dive, dive, for what I saw impressed me. On all outings the seas were high, but the captain handled the boat skillfully and our guide made sure entry and exit was smooth on all the dives.

Le Touessrok Hotel: "Utter Perfection-Above and Beneath Its Waters"
Le Touessrok Hotel
Trou dëeau Douce

SCUBA AND SNORKELING FACILITIES QUESTIONNAIRE

NAME **Pierre Sports Diving Ltd**
ADDRESS **Le Touessrok Hotel & Ile - Aux - Cerfs**
Trou D'eau Douce, Mauritius
CONTACT **Anthony B Pierre**
TITLE **Chief Instructor**
TELEPHONE **(230) 419 2451** FAX **(230) 419 2025**

CAPITOL: **Port - Louis**
POPULATION: **1.3 Million**
CURRENCY: **Rupee**
AIRLINES: **Air Mauritius**
VISA/PASSPORT? **Yes**

GOVERNMENT: **Democracy**
LANGUAGE: **Kreol, English, French**
ELECTRICITY: **220v**
DEPARTURE TAX? **RS 100**
PROOF OF CITIZENSHIP? **Yes**

YOUR FACILITY IS QUALIFIED AS: **Resort**
BUISINESS HOURS: **8:30am - 4:00pm**
CERTIFYING AGENCIES: **PADI, C.M.A.S. & V.E.T.L.**
LOG BOOK REQUIRED? **Yes**
EQUIPMENT: **Rentals, Airfills**
PRIMARY LINE OF EQUIPMENT: **Spirotechnique**
PHOTOGRAPHIC EQUIPMENT:

CHARTER/DIVE BOAT AVAILABLE? **Yes**
COAST GUARD APPROVED? **Yes**
SHIP TO SHORE? **Yes** RADAR **No**
DIVE MASTER/INSTRUCTOR ABOARD? **Yes**

DIVER CAPACITY **14 & 10**
CAPTAIN LICENSE? **No**

DIVING & SNORKELING: **Salt**
TYPE OF DIVING/SNORKELING IN AREA? **Wall, Wreck, Reef**
DIVING/SNORKELING IN YOUR AREA IS BEST SUITED: **Beginner, Intermediate & Advanced**
BEST TIME OF YEAR FOR DIVING/SNORKELING: **Oct - Apr**
TEMPERATURE: NOV-APRIL **27-30 C** MAY-OCT: **20-27 C**
VISIBILITY: DIVING **20+ FT** SNORKELING:

PACKAGES AVAILABLE: **Dive**
ACCOMMODATIONS NEARBY: **Hotel, Home Rentals**
ACCOMMODATIONS RATES: **Expensive, Moderate**
RESTAURANTS NEARBY: **Expensive, Moderate**
YOUR AREA IS: **Quiet With Activities**
LOCAL ACTIVITY/NIGHTLIFE: . **Disco, Pubs & Casino**
CAR NEEDED TO EXPLORE AREA? **Yes**
DUTY FREE SHOPPING? **Yes**

LOCAL EMERGENCY SERVICES:
COASTGUARD **Op. Room**
TELEPHONE: **208-8317/2122770**
CALLSIGNS: **(Air Rescue)- 637 3889**

NEAREST HYPERBARIC TREATMENT FACILITY:
AUTHORITY: **Special Mobile Force**
LOCATION: **Vacoas**
TELEPHONE: **686-1011**

LOCAL DIVING DOCTOR:
NAME: **Serge Maurice, Dr. Ramloll**
LOCATION: **Georgetown QBournes**
TELEPHONE: **454-8053**

Mauritius
Tel 230-419-2451
Fax 230- 419-2020

Air Mauritius
U.S. Tel 800-537-1182
U.S. Fax 201-871-6983

Indian Ocean

Mauritius

Paradise Cove Hotel

Anse Laurie

Flawless

Wendy Canning Church

On my second visit to Mauritius the first stop was at the lovely Paradise Cove Hotel situated in the far north of the island at Anse Laurie. Our twelve-hour flight on Air Mauritius from London brought us to the hotel late in the morning. The service is impeccable. Mauritians take pride in their work no matter how simple the task may be.

In the early 1990's, Jean Marc Harel conceived the idea of developing a resort hotel at Anse La Raie that would be consistent with the philosophies of conservation yet enable vacationers to relax comfortably in a setting of great natural beauty.

The original Mauritian architect was Mr. Maurice Giraud. Building materials used in the construction were local volcanic rocks, straw, etc. The hotel opened with 64 rooms. **Paradise Cove was selected to be the first hotel in the Indian Ocean to display the plaque of Excellence of the Small Luxury Hotels "S.L.H." of the world, and in 1995 became a member of The Relais and Chateau Hotel Group.**

The air-conditioned rooms all have private balconies or terraces views over the secluded cove and coconut-planted beach. They are set in one or two-story bungalow-style buildings, spacious, elegant, fully equipped with telephone, minibar and music system, private bathroom with separate bath and shower as well as a TV/video system. Interconnecting rooms are also available for families.

In September 1993 and 1994, the Paradise Cove won the first prize "Fleurir Maurice." The gardens are a place of great contemplation and relaxation.

The entire complex is embraced by a palm-fringed cove with hidden inlets. A guest can have absolute privacy and quiet on their own piece of white talcum beach.

Opposite the cove a beautiful rock garden interspersed with a munificent array of blooming flowers leads to yet another beach and the boathouse, a vast lagoon protected by a coral reef.

A full range of water sports are available, including options of a day charter on a yacht, as well as scuba-diving with fully-qualified instructors (CMAS and VETL).

Hindu Offerings by Wendy Canning Church

367

The restaurants LaCocoteraie and LaBelle Creole and main public areas overlook the lagoon. **Cuisine is wonderful and beautifully presented.** Emphasis is on international gourmet dishes and Mauritian cuisine. Do not miss their Mauritian festival dinner. It is truly memorable. Room service is available. Breakfast arrives with a daily paper. Picnics are wonderful and fun to take on outings.

The hotel offers a range of facilities: boutique and gift shop, daily entertainment, game room with billiard table, same day laundry service, swimming pool, travel agent and car hire desks, full equipped boathouse, deep sea fishing, and diving center.

THE SCUBA DIVING AND SNORKELING

Mauritius is known to divers worldwide, bringing to mind rich images of colorful coral reefs, dramatic underwater features and clear calm waters. Paradise Cove Hotel is a diver's dream-come-true, with its exclusive location offering diving sites of remarkable contrast just minutes away by boat.

Cap Divers services the hotel guests and owner Karl Heinz, and his partner Marie-Christine will take you for a sheltered dive just off Grand-Baie or across the ocean to the wild untouched diving spots around the northern islets. **At Paradise Cove good diving is possible year round.**

We dived in Mauritius in late October. On our previous visit we covered La Piroque at Flic and Flac. This location is different diving than you will find up north.

Here the seas are less sheltered. There are also small islands off Paradise Cove with deep walls and reefs. I found the diving more challenging and exciting, in the sense that the dives were deeper, the sea rougher, and the underwater terrain offered a wider variety of the big fish.

We dived with owner Karl and no more than six divers. Karl believes in small groups. He is an excellent guide, warm and affable and quite knowledgeable about the sea.

Whale Rock (38m) Grand Baie (10-20m) Round Island, Flat Island (20m). Pigeon Rock (15-20m) and Coin de Mere (10-25m) are adventuresome dive sites to suit all levels under the proper sea conditions.

One of our favorite dives was at **Perey Bere** outer reef. On this outing we had a mixed level of divers. This was a nice mellow-shallow dive. We were able to get 64 minutes of bottom time. As we cruised along the sandy bottom making our way up the reef we felt like kids in a candy store. It was impossible to keep track of all the marine life around us.

CORAL GARDENS

Situated on the outer reef of the north wall, this comely reef dive is a must. At a maximum depth of 51 feet, divers drift along with the current and emperor angelfish, honeycomb groupers, yellowtail lyretail, schools of bluestrip snappers, clownfish, spotted trumpet fish, goldsaddle goatfish, blue spotted stingray interspersed with anemones in a rainbow of color.

COIN DE MER

Again this site is situated on the outer reef which means strong currents and a drift dive. Because of our shallow depth we had over an hour to enjoy all the diversified flora and fauna. The fish: checker board wrasse, blue-striped snapper, sea goldies, small peacock flounder, convict tang, shadow soldier fish, shrimp, spotfin, squirrel fish, schools of clown fish all came so close to us they almost touched our masks. We swam along the sandy bottom where gaping crevices in the reef showed hiding moray eels whilst the diminutive reef fish swam in and out of small openings. At one point two large rays raised from the sandy bottom as in lift off for orbit. **A dive to request.** It exemplifies the abundance of healthy sea life, is suitable for all experience levels and one gets lots of bottom time to delight in it all.

Karl Heinz-Berger rates high marks for his entire center; sensitivity to the sea, sage knowledge of it and safety first.

With Heinz you will be in good hands. We feel very comfortable recommending he and Marie Christine for safe and enjoyable dives.

Snorkelers are welcome on board. Whenever you go to Mauritius don't miss diving with Cap Divers.

AND WHEN YOU COME UP FOR AIR
While in Mauritius we used the services of White Sand Tours. Because we spend so much time photographing, it is always better for us to hire a car with driver.

White Sands has a tour desk at Paradise Cove. We book our driver for the entire stay so he could transfer us and deliver us to Sir Seewoosagur Ramgoolam International Airport and take us on special tours of the island. **We cannot recommend their service highly enough. Not only are their staff safe drivers, but have also been trained as histori-cal guides.** White Sand Tours' guides, hostesses, and representatives are multilingual and converse freely in English, French, German, Italian, Spanish and Japanese.

White Sand Tours
IBL Tourism Division
M1 Motorway
Port St. Louis, Mauritius
Tel. 208-5424 Fax 230-208-8524

We took the full day Romance of the South Tour. This tour is designed to show you the very best that Mauritius has to offer including the most spectacular scenery on the island. The order of the itinerary does vary according to where you are staying but high-lights of the day include a visit to Trou aux Cerfs, the crater of an extinct volcano, and a trip south into the hills to visit the sacred lake of grand Bassin, the Black River Gorges, the forests of Plaine Champagne and a part of the Central Plateau. **At Chamarel, well off the beaten track, you can see waterfalls and the unique seven colored earth.** This tour really does offer you the chance of travelling into the heart of the island and discovering some more of the magic of Mauritius. It includes lunch at wonderful Varangue sur Morne restaurant.

Our stay was delightful and we felt totally replenished to continue our further dis-covery of Mauritius. Days were filled with sun, scuba diving, tours, wonderful cuisine and a great old brandy after dinner at Le Bar with moon, stars and candlelight for illu-mination. Returning to our charming room our beds were turned down and we slipped under the covers waiting another blissful day in paradise.

Paradise Cove would make an ideal spot for that special honeymoon or anniversary. It is for the guest who truly wants a perfect setting, perfect service, and perfect food in a little slice of paradise - *Paradise Cove: Sheer Paradise*

Paradise Cove Hotel
Anse Laurie
Mauritius
Tel. 230-262-7983
Fax 230-262-7736

Philippines

Samal Island
Pearl Farm Beach Resort

Lynn Funkhouser

Pearl Farm Beach Resort is an exquisite tropical treasure and world class beach resort. It is located on Samal Island and, as its name suggests, it was a pearl farm until 1990. Designed by a very gifted Filipino architect, Pearl Farm features a gorgeous free-form swimming pool that appears to spill into the ocean, a lagoon with a charming bridge and

NAME   **The Cap Divers LTD.**
ADDRESS   **Paradise Cove Hotel - Anse La Raie**
              Mauritius
CONTACT   **Karl - Heinz Berger**
TITLE   **Diving Instructor**
TELEPHONE **230-2837890**   FAX   **837890**

CAPITOL: **Port - Louis**   GOVERNMENT: **Democracy**
POPULATION: **1,200,000**   LANGUAGE: **French, English**
CURRENCY: **Rupee**   ELECTRICITY: **220v**
AIRLINES: **Air Mauritius**   DEPARTURE TAX **RS 100**
VISA/PASSPORT **Yes**   PROOF OF CITIZENSHIP? **Yes**

YOUR FACILITY IS QUALIFIED AS: **Scuba Center**
BUISINESS HOURS: **9:00am**
CERTIFYING AGENCIES: **CMAS/VETL German**
LOG BOOK REQUIRED?   **Yes**
EQUIPMENT: **Rentals**
PRIMARY LINE OF EQUIPMENT: **ScubaPro**
PHOTOGRAPHIC EQUIPMENT: **Video**

CHARTER/DIVE BOAT AVAILABLE?   **Yes**   DIVER CAPACITY   **8**
COAST GUARD APPROVED?   **Yes**   CAPTAIN LICENSE? **Yes**
SHIP TO SHORE?   **LORAN ? No**   RADAR? **No**
DIVE MASTER/INSTRUCTOR ABOARD? **Yes, Both**

DIVING & SNORKELING: **Salt**
TYPE OF DIVING/SNORKELING IN AREA?   **Wall, Wreck, Cave**
DIVING/SNORKELING IN YOUR AREA IS BEST SUITED FOR: **Beginner, Intermediate & Advanced**
BEST TIME OF YEAR FOR DIVING/SNORKELING:
TEMPERATURE: NOV-APRIL   **27-28 F**   MAY-OCT: **20-25 F**
VISIBILITY: DIVING   **60 FT**   SNORKELING:

PACKAGES AVAILABLE: **Dive**
ACCOMMODATIONS NEARBY: **Hotel**
ACCOMMODATIONS RATES: **Moderate**
RESTAURANTS NEARBY: **Inexpensive**
LOCAL ACTIVITY/NIGHTLIFE: **Restaurant, Disco**
CAR NEEDED TO EXPLORE AREA?   **Yes**
DUTY FREE SHOPPING?   **Yes**

LOCAL EMERGENCY SERVICES: NEAREST HYPERBARIC TREATMENT FACILITY
COASTGUARD **OP Room**   AUTHORITY: **Special Mobile Force**
TELEPHONE: **208-8317/212 2770**   LOCATION: **Vacoas**
CALLSIGNS: **Air Rescue/637-3889**   TELEPHONE: **686 1011**

LOCAL DIVING DOCTOR:
NAME: **Serge Maurice**
LOCATION: **Georgetown Qbornes**
TELEPHONE: **454-8053**

Pearl Farm by Lynn Funkhouser

a waterfall, tennis courts surrounded by wonderful foliage, and a two story bar for a beautiful view (or photo) of it all. Nothing is left to chance. When I was there, sand was barged in and four workers were sifting all of it through screens. There is a large children's playground, a jeepney to tour the grounds, a game and reading room, a boutique, a woman in native dress demonstrating the area's intricate weaving, musical groups, and even a cockatoo to entertain guests.

The gardens and landscaping are spectacular! This is lush tropical vegetation right off a high budget Hollywood movie set. Just walking to your room is a visual and aromatic delight. Almost every palm tree has orchids, ferns, or bromeliads growing on it. The furniture is made in a carpentry shop on the premises. Their own flower plantation provides the flowers for spectacular arrangements, some of them 20 feet tall. Their fruit plantation provides all the delicious Philippine fruits. They raise their beef and chicken and aquaculture the fish served there. Needless to say the food is excellent. Buffets are works of art (and save some time, if you can tear yourself away from all this to go diving). 160 employees attend to your every need.

To reach the Pearl Farm Beach Resort take Philippine Airlines (PAL) airbus service from the new Manila Domestic Airport to Davao City, Mindanao Island, which is a 90-minute flight. From there transfer to a bus or taxi to the Davao Insular Hotel and then take a 40-minute banca ride to Samal Island. Accommodations include 19 Samal Houses, which are built over the water, 17 longhouse rooms, 2 longhouse suites, and 6 two story superior Samal suites to choose from. All are air-conditioned and well appointed.

A great asset is the temperate climate, which is favorable all year. **Even during the rainy season or typhoon season elsewhere, diving is fine here.** If you love reef fish, an extraordinary number of invertebrates, and nice corals, **you will really enjoy the diving.** If you crave big fish and high intensity diving. Pearl Farm still may hold your interest because the diving is wonderful and the resort is so magnificent. **The lack of large fish points to overfishing,** but the hard and soft corals are healthy and beautiful. **When large fish are removed from an area the imbalance that is created is extremely interesting, because invertebrates that are rare or small in other areas aren't being preyed upon as much so they are here in great abundance.** The reefs are now being protected, so they can only get even better.

Diving is done from very large, comfortable, new bancas (boats). Night dives are spectacular with Spanish dancers, pleurobranchs, fluorescent orange anemones covered with shrimp, crocodile fish, many lionfish, cuttlefish, octopus, squid, beautiful soft corals, and fabulous backgrounds to enhance your photographs. The most abundant anemonefish is the maroon or spinecheek anemonefish, but others are found also. Not far from shore are two wrecks in 70' to 140' depths. Even snorkeling in front of the Samal houses in interesting.

For those of you who want big fish, Mushroom Rock is the best site for diving with schools of barracudas, jacks, snappers, and possibly a tuna or two. It is located on the south point of the island and has strong currents.

Pearl Farm Beach Resort would be an excellent choice for a honeymoon, or a place to bring a non-diving partner, or even hold a company incentive reward program week. Sun bathing on the white sand beaches, swimming in the ocean or fabulous pool, waterskiing, windsurfing, playing tennis, fishing, and game room activities are all possibilities. Wave runners and speedboats are also available. Optional tours to Davao City, a banana plantation, orchid farms, fruit markets, island hopping, village walking, golf, and a casino are offered. Picturesque Mount Apo overlooks Davao and can be hiked or climbed. The endangered Philippine monkey-eating eagle breeding and conservation station is located at the base of Mount Apo and this tour is also offered at the resort. **Shopping is good and some of the best handicrafts in the country come from this area. The Pearl Farm Beach Resort is a real gem!**

Pearl Farm
Davao City
Mindanao Island, Phillipines

French West Indies

St. BARTH'S

Hotel Carl Gustaf

Wendy Canning Church

After a pleasant flight to Saint Martin and on to Saint Barthelemy. Your plane will hardly have touched down at the quaint Gustavia Airport when your assigned driver from the Carl Gustaf whisks you into the lofty Gustavia hillside where the hotel is located.

Built in 1991, the Carl Gustaf overlooks the charming town of Gustavia, which was declared a free port, and made capital of the island in 1875. Named for Sweden's King Gustaf, the Hotel opened in 1991. To say it has a spectacular view of the harbor and the sea is an understatement!

View from Honeymoon Suitre Hotel Carl Gustoff by Wendy Canning Church

In a refreshing lush green setting, each suite provides extensive living space (860 sq. ft for single suites, 1180 sq. ft. for doubles). Two telephones, two stereos, two televisions, a fax machine and several ceiling fans are standard. The sitting area opens on to your private patio through glass doors. Each suite has a king-size bed, and the bathroom has a double sink vanity. A compact kitchen is hidden in a corner. **Be sure to request the Honeymoon Suite, which sets atop the hotel overlooking the bay. The lovely expanse of the patio has an enormous whirlpool where you can sip champagne and celebrate special occasions, or request Suite 40, the Stina Suite that accommodates up to 4 people.** The cuisine is an outstanding combination of Creole and Gallic classics. The restaurant with its panoramic view has its candlelight supplemented by a romantic glow from the lighted buoys in the bay. The vintage wine list is superb.

From the port of Gustavia, take a sail on board the *Carl Gustaf* and enjoy a spot of sunbathing out on the blue ocean. **A 46-foot luxury cabin cruiser, the *Carl Gustaf*, waits your beckoning to discover the beaches and coves from the sea or to head for one of the nearby islands with enchanting names. (Pain de Sucre, Coco, Tortue, Bonhome).** You can enjoy an unforgettable meal on board, or have a picnic lunch on Saint Martin or a swim on the deserted island of Pinel.

The *Carl Gustaf* also offers deep sea fishing and half day excursions: Round trip of Saint-Barths, Colombier Beach, Fourchue island, snorkeling in turquoise waters, or quick shopping in Saint-Martin

The pleasant and competent staff of the Carl Gustaf is available to satisfy your every need. They can arrange anything from tennis to horseback riding, or if you feel the need, French lessons. Grand Galet beach, which is excellent for shelling, is less than 100 yards away.

The Carl Gustaf is the finest example of what French hotels have to offer for the honeymoon or anniversary stay.

Hotel Carl Gustaf
Rue Des Normands
Gustavia
97133 Saint-Barthelemy
French West Indies
800 346 5358
Tel: (590) 27 82 83
Fax: (590) 27 82 37

St. Lucia

Jalousie Hilton Plantation Resort and Spa

Wendy Canning Church

Jalousie Hilton Plantation Resort and Spa, a hillside retreat 50 minutes from Hewanorra Airport, is in every sense an oasis from the madding crowds. This oasis is truly a thing of alluring beauty with an ambiance that allows the guest to become reacquainted with their mind and body—feeling the balance of ying and yang.

Jalousie is nestled between Petit and Gros Piton on 325 acres on the southwestern coast, 20 minutes from the town of Soufriere. The flowered hillsides are ablaze with wild patches of color. Dense and luxuriant rain forests lead the hiker by natural springs, spectacular banana trees and dramatic waterfalls.

Its 115 private one-bedroom cottages, suites and Sugar Mill rooms are scattered across the base slopes of Les Pitons Mountains. **(Ask for cottage 906).** Decorated with furnishings of carved and inlaid woods, tile floors and native straw carpeting, each room features a private verandah, air-conditioning, ceiling fans, remote control TV with satellite reception, refrigerated service bar, coffee machine, in-room safe, direct-dial tele-

Jalousie Hilton Plantation Resort and SPA courtesy of Jalousie Hilton Plantation

phone, AM/FM clock radio and hairdryer. Cottage suites have a private plunge pool and stocked mini bar. The electricity is 220V/50 cycle with British three prong wall sockets. The marble tile baths are large with fluffy towels, bathrobe and herbal toiletries. Vaulted ceilings give each room a feeling of space and coolness.

Jalousie has its own extensive vegetable and fruit garden. Its fish are caught right on the property or delivered fresh from local fishermen. Guests may dine al fresco on seafood and Creole specialties at the seaside **Pier Restaurant** or enjoy stately surroundings and views of Anse des Pitons Bay by moonlight from the **Greathouse Plantation Room**. More casual offerings can be found at **The Verandah**, which features a breakfast buffet in a pleasant courtyard setting and **The Bayside Bar and Grill** for sandwiches, salads, meats and fresh fish grilled to order. There are also four bars and lounges on the property including a juice bar at the spa and an intimate **Jwen Se Munla** ("meet the people") bar.

After dinner one might retire to the Greathouse furnished in tasteful colonial antiques to play a board game or read. A peaceful pool deck provides a quiet place for guests to gather on the rambling Greathouse lawn, which slopes gently to a shimmering volcanic sand beach and the clear blue sea. Meal plans are available.

Waterfront activities dominate day life with swimming, snorkeling, sunfish and catamaran sailing, windsurfing, aquacycling, water-skiing, kayaking and shore scuba diving. Equipment and instruction are readily available and included. There are squash and tennis courts, which are lit for night play. There is a vast network of hiking trails on Jalousie's grounds and in the adjacent hillsides. There is also children's program with daily resort and beach activities.

Open-water scuba diving, deep-sea fishing and horseback riding are offered at an additional charge.

The **Jalousie Golf Facility** is set between the two Piton Mountains overlooking the resort, providing dramatic views and fresh sea breezes. The scenic countryside also makes this a unique and captivating golf experience for any golfer. A pro shop is available to outfit players with clubs, bags and pull-carts. Clothing, balls and tees are available for sale.

THE SPA

The information binder began with these words: "Welcome to the Spa at Jalousie Hilton Plantation. Now is the time to relax and unwind. Spend some time with us and we'll provide you with the time and atmosphere in which to de-stress, re-tune and gear-up for an enjoyable St. Lucian holiday."

I arrived at the Spa in the category of your typical 20th century executive. I would dive in the morning and have spa treatments in the afternoon. The Spa is run on a personalized and highly professional basis. It can be rated up there with the Golden Door, a 5-star spa; I have had the pleasure of visiting many times.

At Jalousie Hilton Plantation Resort you are entitled to enjoy the following free of charge: Men's and Women's sauna, jacuzzi, cold plunge pool, a full range of exercise equipment, stretch classes, pool classes, fitness classes, walks and non-alcoholic fruit drinks at the Sunsplash Deck.

Guests with energy for additional complimentary activities can play squash or swing into action on four Plexicushion tennis courts. Qualified instructors are on hand to maximize the effectiveness of workouts for guests at every fitness level, offering personal supervision of programs for inch loss, cardiovascular fitness, weight training, muscle stretch, flexibility and toning. If you wish for personalized training, just ask. There are two types of personal training, a take home exercise program, and body composition analysis.

Facials include French facials, aroma facials, men's facials, purifying facials and back treatment, and mini facial. Massages include two types of Swedish massage, two types of anti-stress massage, two types of deep tissue massage, aromatherapy massage, and aromatherapy scalp massage.

Spa revitalizing treatment, body polish, paraffin body treatment, seaweed body compression wrap, top to toe bronzing, and top up bronzing are among the deluxe treatments offered.

Body treatments consist of hydrotherapy, paraffin body treatment, seaweed body masque, seaweed anti-stress treatment, seaweed sports pack, seaweed-localized pack, Vichy shower, and seaweed scalp treatment.

Hands and feet may be treated with manicure, manicure without polish, French manicure, pedicure, pedicure without polish, change of polish, hand masque, foot masque, hand and foot masque, mitt hydration (hands), mitt hydration (feet), and mitt hydration (hands and feet).

Eyelash tinting, and eyebrow tinting,and eyebrow shaping all are offered. Waxing is also available.

I took advantage of the a la carte services and left the resort feeling ten years younger. The warm and highly trained staff are to be commended for their degree of professionalism and warmth. The staff is superbly trained and takes great pride in practicing the philosophy of Jalousie Hilton Plantation Spa. Jalousie Spa is the ideal retreat for travelers seeking a luxurious hideaway for rejuvenation, pampering and soothing the spirit.

THE SCUBA DIVING & SNORKELING

There is excellent snorkeling right off Jalousie's Beach. A snorkeling trail has been roped off especially for snorkelers. Here you will sample teems of sea life inhabiting pristine, shallow water reefs in a safe, confined environment.

Certified divers must present proof of certification. Don't forget your logbook, many scuba centers are asking to see it. A certification program is available at Jalousie primarily as a completion course for guests with previous dive experience.

Directly beneath St. Lucia's fabled landmark, The Pitons, there is an underwater kingdom of superlative beauty. Here you will find a dreamlike outpost with sea creatures in one of the healthiest habitats I have yet to dive!

Since Jalousie has been designated a national marine park, divers and snorkelers may not touch or disturb the underwater environment to insure the preservation of its unadulterated marine life. No gloves may be worn when diving in St. Lucia.

There are eleven dive sites to choose from. The following are some of my favorites:

LANDSLIDE

Landslide, just 2 minutes from Jalousie by boat, is a vertical fringe reef right off Petit Piton. Piles of coral have grown one atop each other, over time and sea life has taken advantage of it. Since this is a drift dive, we leisurely floated as the topography unfolded and delighted us. Layered massive ledges of sheet coral jutted out. Almost every reef fish was seen in its juvenile stage since June is the time they are present here.

A number of species of damselfish came into view. Being the most aggressive species of fish in the sea, it is lucky they are small—allowing the diver to get close. Bristle worm, arrow crab, spiny lobster, plumb worm, Venus sea fan, black coral with purple and melon vase sponges growing between their branches, sea rod, sea whip, bright red and yellow sponge, along with deep fuchsia sponge made **this a superb dive!**

FATASTASIA

Fatastasia is located off North Soufriere. **Aptly named, this dive spot with munificent coral walls, ledges and valleys, is likened to a fantasy world.** Entering this realm of luxuriant topography, the diver will find dense areas filled with gorgonias, black coral and white telesto. At the core of this are fields of corals, green mountainous star, solitary dish, larger flower, lobed star, brown mountainous star, and bespeckled lobed star, purple leaf, ivory tube, and sheet. The entire reef was rife with the juveniles. **Request this dive!**

MALGARE TOU

Malgare Tou was my last and most unforgettable dive with Jalousie. If you did no other dive but this one with Jalousie your visit would be well worth it. The current was at a nice steady clip as we drifted along, inspecting crevices between the variety of corals and peaking into the reams of barrel sponges.

A large barracuda glided along moving its rocket like shimmering silver body as if it were master of the seas. Melon colored vase sponges with touches of soft lavender grew out from the reef. The dense black coral resembled the lush vegetation of the rain forest. Deep fuchsia, fiery orange and bright yellow lemon sponges all played their part in the dramatic scene. As if this were not enough, a tiny damselfish dressed in sequins swam out of a multi-shaped deep brown barrel sponge.

AREAS OF INTEREST

Sightseeing options in the area include the world's only drive-in volcano, Sulfur Springs, Diamond Falls, Diamond Botanical Gardens and rain forest tour at Fond St. Jacques. (See "The Helen of West Indies" story in our St. Lucia Forward.).

For more information contact:
Jalousie Hilton Plantation Resort & Spa
P.O. Box 251
Soufriere, St. Lucia, W.I.
Telephone: 809-459-7666
Facsimile: 809-459-7667

Saint Martin

Privilege Resort and Spa

"Come and Experience Your Dream"

Wendy Canning Church

On one of the prettiest sites in the Caribbean sits the Privilege Resort and Spa, with incredible vistas overlooking the turquoise waters of a natural Caribbean cove on the French side of St. Martin. One of the beaches on this cove has private access for Privilege Resort guests only. Located in Anse Marcel, Privilege is less than 25 minutes from the Princess Juliana International Airport.

The stylish hotel with its elegant Creole architecture offers privacy and seclusion within lush tropical vegetation and 40 spacious luxury rooms and suites. Each has a king size bed and a pullout sofa bed, remote control air-conditioning, ceiling fan, mini bar, room safe, color television and telephone. They have large marble bathrooms with 220v current plugs for American 110v. All rooms have a private balcony with a fabulous panoramic view.

Utopique at Le Privilege Resort and Spa courtesy of Wimco

Breakfast is served in your room or on the terrace at the swimming pool. You will enjoy gourmet French and Italian cuisine in their three restaurants. The Grill, located at the top of the hill and Gourmet Panoramic Restaurants offer divine tasting French specialties, Creole delicacies or light selections, or you may decide to dine at their third restaurant at the marina below La Louisianne.

If the spa is not enough, other activities available on the program include 6 tennis courts, 4 squash courts, 2 racquetball courts and 2 swimming pools, gymnastics, aerobic dance and body building classes.

At the front desk you can arrange horseback riding, water-skiing, wave runners, jet skiing, deep sea fishing, scuba diving, golf at Mullet Bay and day trips to the neighboring islands of St. Barths, Fourcave, Anguills, Tintmarrs, Pinel, Saba and Scilley Cay. There are a dozen Virgin Islands within a range of 20 miles.

There are 10 casinos on the island and 300 restaurants, bars and nightclubs. Privilege provides a free shuttle to the local casino as well as, on request, service to both capital cities of Marigot and Philipsburg.

Sylvie Milio is the affable and highly efficient General Manager of Privilege and is on hand to satisfy your needs. If you want to relax, play, get pampered and healthy this is the place for you.

There are a number of packages available: Honeymoon, Health Spa and Discovery.

THE BALNEOTHERAPY SPA

The Spa gives a complete and restful impression. The Spa will help you discover the well being of spirit and body. It has all of the latest equipment and most important, a well-trained and experienced professional staff. The services include: messages, Shiatsu, lymphatic drainage, anti-cellulite messages, slimming cure, anti-stress cure, tonic cure, hydrojet, seaweed body mask, individual water jet bath, aigotherapy, steam room and esthetic beauty treatments.

The staff at the spa is highly professional. One is truly pampered yet just as importantly a guest is involved and guided through an individually tailored program to achieve your optimal balance between body and sprit -come and experience your dream, a new awakening and balance of spirit, mind and body.

For more information contact:
West Indies Management Company
P.O. Box 1461 Newport, RI 02840
Tel: 401-849-8012

Fax: 401-847-6290
Paris Numero Vert: 05 90 16 20
London Free Phone: 0-800-89-8318

Grenadines

Palm Island

Palm Island Beach club

Wendy Canning Church and Coleman F. Church 3rd

Lying 1,600 miles southwest of Miami and 35 miles between St. Vincent and Grenada, the Grenadines stretch like a jade necklace on an azure sea at the southern end of the Caribbean. No one really knows the number of islands, cays, inlets and rocky outcrops.

It is believed that the first inhabitants were the peaceful Arawaks arriving in 900 B.C. from South America in wooden boats. They lived by farming and fishing. The ambitious, warlike Caribs drove them out in the 17th century. The French invaded in 1719, driving out the Caribs, establishing a permanent settlement. These islands and St. Vincent (referred to by the natives as the mainland) changed hands frequently from then on between the French and English.

Sugar was king in the 18th century and so was Britain. The English had no use for the black Caribs and sent them to Honduras, importing Portuguese and natives from the East Indies to work the lucrative plantations.

Today, the political power of the Grenadines is split between the independent nation state of Grenada with Petit St. Vincent and Carriacou under its leadership, and the remaining islands governed by St. Vincent who also gained independence in 1979.

Most of the islands remain unfamiliar to all but the most seasoned, adventuresome traveler or avid sailor who speak their names in whispers: St. Vincent, Grenada, Mustique, Bequia, Canouan, Mayreau, Petit St. Vincent, Carib, Union, Palm Island and Ronda for fear they will become thriving gentrified vacation centers.

The Grenadines are not easily accessible, but are unquestionably well worth the extra traveling time. Upon arrival the voyager will not be weary, but rather refreshed by a retreat of silver sand beaches, underwater gardens, shimmering crystalline waters, safe anchorages, superb unpolluted air, solitude, serenity, and safety.

Each island evokes its unique culture, yet offers accommodations in small elegant hotels of understated elegance and hospitality. Although secluded, one will find all the amenities and activities they would in a livelier spot, yet in an aura of relaxed hospitality and grace.

Because of their proximity to the equator, year-round temperatures fluctuate slightly between 75 and 85 degrees. The coolest months are from November to February, the drier months December to June, and the wet season July to November.

Out For A Dive by Wendy Canning Church

378

English is the native language, but one will also hear lilting patois spoken between the natives. The currency is Eastern Caribbean dollar.

Air Mustique flies to these islands from Barbados. Their private charters can be arranged from other islands. A valid passport is needed to enter.

PALM ISLAND BEACH CLUB

Where the warm Caribbean meets the Atlantic in the Southern Grenadines, Palm Island welcomes world-weary travelers to the secluded and unique **Palm Island Beach Club.**

To reach Palm Island you fly to Barbados (we flew **American Airlines**), where you connect with **Mustique Airways** twin engine charter that takes you to **Union Island.** After clearing customs, a golf cart delivers you to the Anchorage Yacht Club dock and Palm Island Beach Club launch for your ten-minute journey to the little isle of paradise.

The casually elegant Palm Island Beach Club is family operated and staffed by some of the friendliest people in the Grenadines. It becomes your private paradise where the warmth of the tropical climate is matched by the warmth of the staff. How many places are there in the world where you can sleep while gentle sea breezes dance through your cottage, whose doors you <u>never</u> **lock?**

In the private island's gentle embrace, natural beauty, serenity, informality and old-fashioned hospitality combine to refresh and reinvigorate those who sojourn here. **Adventurer and author John Caldwell, his artist wife, Mary, and sons Johnny and Roger, sailed around the world on a homemade yacht to find the tropical 130-acre paradise of sea, sand, sun, and sailing that is Palm Island. And for more than a quarter century they have entertained guests in exceedingly high, but easy going style.**

Rates include beachfront accommodations, three meals, four o'clock tea with fresh pastries served on your private patio, room service, laundry service, airport transfers, weekly punch party, tennis and water sports (except scuba).

The Beach Club's 24 roomy cottages are just a coconut throw from the Caribbean's awesome, crystalline and colorful waters...deep ocean blue to bright turquoise.

Simple but tasteful cottages are decorated in cool pastel covered rattan furnishings accented by natural woven straw rugs. Armoires with ample storage, and a refrigerator and coffee/tea maker are a thoughtful inclusion. **Request cottage 19 or 20 for complete privacy.**

Guests may request king or twin beds when booking. Three walls of wooden Jalousie windows catch the intoxicating breezes. Most of the accommodations have a well-shielded stone shower outside which can be entered from the bath or patio. The cottage slate patios extend into the sand with sea beyond.

There are also rental apartments and villas on the island. The larger villas accommodate family and friends who are traveling together. Personal cooks and maids are available.

Staple foods, drinks, fresh herbs, wines, liquors, notions, pharmaceuticals, candy bars, etc. are available at the Halfway Mart (Halfway from Kingstown, St. Vincent to St. George's, Grenada).

The cuisine is beautifully presented, delicious and plentiful. Breakfast and luncheon are buffet style, while dinner is continental, served to guests at candlelit tables overlooking the sea and twinkling lights of Union Island. Dinner music is provided by the gentle lapping of the waves and sounds of silence. **It doesn't get more romantic than this!**

Prince, the chef, has been there for 25+ years. Fresh fish is his specialty, with lobster twice weekly, and now and then a Creole surprise. Fresh fruit and vegetables are in abundance from nearby St. Vincent. A ship's bell is rung to announce meals.

In season there is a **Fish and Steak Barbecue** on Saturdays with calypso music and a "jump up" for those who can make it to the dance floor. Tuesday is the **Manager's Punch Party** at owner John and Mary Caldwell's home. Wednesday is a **Fish and Chicken Barbecue** with calypso music.

If you wish to dine out or have a night on the town, you can go over to Union Island for French cuisine at the **Anchorage Yacht Club** or local fare at the **Sunny Grenadines** or the **Clifton Beach Hotels.**

A soft white sand beach rings the 130-acre private island. You can reach any part of the beach by strolling under clear warm skies along Highway 90, which is a _ mile walking trail John built around the island and called "The road to health, fitness and longevity."

A multitude of watersports is offered: swimming, day sailing to the **Tobago Cays** and other nearby islands on the private yacht, a wonderland of snorkeling and scuba diving on acres of coral gardens, windsurfing or sailing their sunfish.

Tucked away in a small cottage in the middle of the visual odyssey, a gentle Italian lady will perform specialized body treatment by appointment.

Before arriving, I contracted an extremely bad flu. Adriana Dember, in two days, brought me back to life. Adriana is an experienced professional masseuse from Trieste in Northern Italy. Her massages combine essential oils and reflexology. Aquatic gymnastics are also available.

For reservations contact:
Ralph Locke Islands
P.O. Box 492477
Los Angelas, CA 90049 USA
Tel: 1-800-223-1108
Fax: 1-310-440-4220
Toll Free from UK 0-800-894-057
Air Mustique
795 Franklin Ave.
Franklin Lakes, NJ 07417
1-800-526-4789

THE SCUBA DIVING & SNORKELING

There are two dive operations located on Union Island. Each will pick divers up and take guests to dive and snorkel sites around the island and as far as Tobago Cays.

While the dive sites nearest the hotel and Union Island are pleasant; we felt there was too much boat traffic to be diving here in shallow waters.

A half-hour away, Tobago Cays offers wonderful diving. The visibility on all three of our trips there was unlimited. The corals and fish life are abundant and varied. **The diving and snorkeling in this area is first rate.**

Grenadines Dive on Union Island is owned and operated by Glenroy Adams. He offers dive/snorkel tours, instruction, and rendezvous with yachts anywhere in the Grenadines. His specialty is the Tobago Cays. For more information call (809) 458-8138, fax (809) 458-8122, or use VHF 16/68.

Some of our favorite dives in the area were **Mayreau Garden, World's End Reef, Egg Reef,** and *Purina*, a wreck off Mayreau Island.

Snorkelers are welcome on the boat. The sites that divers dive are also suitable for snorkelers.

TOBAGO CAYS

The Northern end is larger and deeper than the eastern end and offers the best and safest diving. **Currents can be strong at times, so it is best to check each site for suitable conditions.**

On our dives here we saw nurse shark, schools of big grouper and your garden-variety fish chart reef fish.

THE PURINA

The wreck of the *H. M. S. Purina* lies in 40 feet of water off the island of Mayreau. A British gunboat, it hit the reef and sunk in 1918. Over time, healthy corals and sponges have called the *Purina* home. We saw the largest boxfish ever. The wreck is rife with reef fish.

West Indies

Windward Islands

St. Vincent

Young Island Resort

Wendy Canning Church

Young Island is a visual odyssey under clear warm skies. You feel a bit like Katherine Hepburn and Humphrey Bogart boarding the *African Queen* style ferry that delivers you to the 35 acre triangular shaped island resort 200 yards or five minutes from the southern coast of St. Vincent.

Is it the unfettered beauty of this holiday haunt capped by the crystal seas that surround it or perhaps the relaxed hospitality with five star cuisine and service provided by the warm and gentle staff that guarantees so many returning guests? Add to this an array of activities offered to keep the most energetic guest happy or the solitude (sounds of silence) that satisfies those seeking to replenish and rebalance their being and you have a complete picture of Young Island.

Tradition tells us that Chatoyer, the mighty Carib Chief, saw a black charger belonging to Sir William Young, the British Governor at the time. He greatly admired the horse and wished to own him. "If you desire it, its yours" said Sir William to the Chief. Chatoyer gratefully accepted the horse in exchange for an island-Youngs Island.

It later became known as Young Island.

Vincentian owners Vidal Browne and Dr. Frederick Ballantyne along with **General Manager Bianca Williams see that this ship sails on tranquil seas and a guest's request is satisfied immediately.**

Thirty cottages awash in island color both inside and out are sprinkled across the hillside, (home to lizards, parrots, peacocks and tritt tree frogs that happily live among the profusion of flora and fancifully colored foliage) down to the underwater gardens and cream colored beach below. All cottages have a refrigerator, wall safe, ceiling fans, king bed (twins on request), open air showers and private patios. Luxury suites have a bedroom, sitting room and large terrace; (some have private plunge pools). Deluxe larger rooms have a sitting area within the bedroom, and a very large private patio. Superior cottages are nearest the beach, shoreline or low on the hillside. All accommodations have ocean views. A hand laundry is available for personal items.

All meals are served in open air thatched roofed dining areas and you always have a view of the water. Dinner is a five-course meal five nights a week, excepting Wednesday (local buffet dinner) and Saturday (barbecue and buffet).

The cuisine is a mix of international and national with emphasis on the freshest of prime meats, fresh fruits and vegetables. There is an extensive, excellent wine list.

Don't miss the Friday evening Manager's cocktail party at Rock Fort (Fort Duvernette). A local stringband plays and afterward on Young Island at dinner. They have steelband music on Barbecue night (Saturday), and in high season a band plays on Wednesday evenings.

Fort Duvernette aglow for General Managers Weekly Feté. Courtesy of Young Island Resort Weekly.

Before luncheon swim up to the Coconut Bar where drinks are served in guess what? Coconuts! Dress at dinner is casually elegant. Barefoot is the fashion during the day.

Room service is available for breakfast. Picnic baskets may be ordered in advance for trips off island.

Babysitting can be arranged. The tour desk will happily book a car for you and suggest sites/tours of interest.

Watersports. Beach attendants are qualified windsurfing instructors and arrangements for lessons can be with them. Snorkeling equipment, Sunfish and windsurfers are available with the resort's compliments. One day's notice is enough to ensure a ride in the glass bottom boat. Sail away for a day, a week or a month on one of the club's four crewed private yachts that are available for charter.

Scuba Diving/Snorkeling. Diving in the waters of St. Vincent is like diving in a huge well-stocked aquarium. Clear, unspoiled waters provide an enormous range of diving conditions; many dive sites are within 20 yards of shore. Dive St. Vincent and Fantasea Tours offer dive sites to suit any level of experience. The front office will assist you in contacting them.

Or just lie in a hammock and finish the book that you promised yourself you would finish.

There is a boutique across the water called The Dock Shop.

Editors Note:
We stayed in cottage #9, which is at the south end of the resort. It was directly on the bay and had a large patio for sunning and a covered area for reading with private steps to our own beach. Cottages #29 and #30 are set high on the hillside and have spectacular ocean views from very large terraces with comfortable seating areas They have comely bedrooms and baths with outdoor showers.

Please see forward on St. Vincent for scuba diving and snorkeling
Young Island is a visual odyssey under clear warm skies.

U.S.A and Canada Reservations
Ralph Locke Islands, Inc.
P.O. Box 492477
Los Angeles, CA 90049-8477
Toll Free U.S. and Canada 1-800-223-1108
Fax (310) 440-4220
Toll Free UK 0-800-894-4220

Turkey

Istanbul

The Ciragan Palace

Wendy Canning Church

My room overlooked the Bosphorus and to my right I had a wonderful view of the Palace. Yes the Palace! As their brochure states, the hotel is linked to the historical Ciragan Palace,. A Palace worthy of the world of Scheherazade, brilliant white marble facade, classic Ottoman architecture, international flair, Ciragan pronounced Shi-ra-gan is Turkish for "torches". For torches once illuminated the Palace so extravagantly that they gave its name Ciragan Palace, "Palace of The Torches."

I arrived at The Ciragan Palace very late in the evening. But despite the hour, all at the front desk greeted me in a very warm and friendly manner with just the right air of professionalism, living up to the five star Kempinski Hotel chain standards.

The Ciragan Palace hotel dates back to the 16th century and was destroyed many times. Completely refurbished in the 1990's, it gives a handful of guests all the luxurious modern amenities while at the same time keeping its historical integrity. Downstairs

Cirogen Palace Hotel by Wendy Canning Church

you will find a grand ballroom and conference rooms. Upstairs there is a handful of luxurious suites. Adjacent to the Palace is the new hotel with 322 guestrooms and 15 suites, all with balconies and many with superb views of the Bosphorus.

While I was there, the King and Queen of Jordan stayed at the Palace. I was fortunate enough to have a tour of the private apartments: understated elegance, modern amenities in a historical setting. Could a traveler ask for more?

General Manager, Willi Dietz, runs a tight ship with white glove inspection by his staff. The Publican Relations Manager, sees that both royalty and guest alike have their stay perfectly orchestrated, whether for banquet, conference, or vacation.

Every service one could ask for is available, 24-hour room service, valet, hairdresser, Turkish bath, shopping gallery, a casino, business service, and wonderful small and large restaurants serving fine cuisine and vintage wines. **This is a perfect way to begin or end your trip to Turkey by staying even for a short while in a symbol of its century old history and being pampered like a Sultan! The only word I can think of is indulgence. Do indulge yourself for one night or many nights - whatever your pocketbook can allow.**

In the morning before you depart, awaken early, as the sun is rising over the Bosphorus. Take in both the view of the Asian and European sides. Don your swim suit and go to the large beautiful pool which looks as if it's waters run right into the sea. Have a leisurely breakfast beside the pool among the exquisite plantings. Know that at that moment your being is both in the past and in the present.

Then promise yourself, "One day I will return."

For more information contact:
Ciragan Palace Hotel
Kempinski Istanbul
Ciragan Caddesi 84
Besiktas 80700 Istanbul, Turkey
Telephone 011.90.212.258 33.77
Telefax 011.90.212.259 66.87

Thailand

THE ORIENTAL, BANGKOK

Wendy Canning Church

Lodgings range from five-star hotels to bungalows, guesthouses, houseboats, hostels and beachside huts. For years however, I had read and heard from friends about the first class service and amenities of The Oriental, Bangkok. Many find it to be the best hotel in the world. Thus, I vowed if I were ever in Thailand, I would surely treat myself and stay there.

I arrived at 3 a.m. in the morning after a 26 hour flight from Boston, another hour at the airport filling out papers for my lost luggage that had been sent to England, and then a 45 minute trip from the airport. I must say I was a harried, almost comatose, individual.

The Oriental Hotel, Bangkok courtesy of The Oriental Hotel

Approaching the front desk I was greeted warmly by an elegant young gentleman. As he showed me to my room, I mentioned something to him about the airlines losing my luggage and having nothing to wear. He turned to me saying, I will inform housekeeping. This all went over my head, considering the hour and my dilemma.

We entered my room and after giving me a brief tour, he bowed and wished me a pleasant stay.

Not more than 5 minutes later there was a light rap at my door. Opening it, I saw a man standing there holding a straw, flat basket lined in white linen. The contents were a new jade green satin nightgown, hairbrush, baby powder, and panty hose.

None of these items ever appeared on my bill. What grace, what thoughtfulness, and such a warm gesture for a weary traveler! I now understand why travel critics and my friends think it the best hotel in the world.

The Oriental is on Silom Street with the Chao Phya River on one side and surrounded by flowering gardens on the other. The business district and shopping are nearby.

The 339 guestrooms and 34 suites are decorated in Thai fashion, with every modern amenity a seasoned traveler would expect. **Exotic orchids decorate the bedroom and bath. A different tropical fruit is delivered to your room each day with a little card explaining its region; Rose Apple or Water Apple (Eugenia Acquaea) is grown on a broad evergreen shade tree native to South East Asia.** The taste differs according to variety and it is often eaten in Thailand with a salt, sugar and chili dip. This fruit is harvested throughout the year in Petchburi.

In the marble bathroom you will find Thai bath salts along with an assortment of toiletries and fluffy robes and slippers for each guest. A silver carafe of cold water is always filled. **At the writing table is stationary with the Hotel's letterhead at the top and the guest's name engraved at the bottom.**

All rooms include color satellite television, in-house movies, radio and in-house music programs, refrigerator, mini-bar, telephones with direct international dialing, and a safe. There is butler service for each room, 24-hour room service and a daily newspaper.

One can choose from 10 restaurants and bars. **The Normandie** offers French cuisine. **The China House** across the street offers Classic Cantonese. **Lord Jim's** has seafood and international cuisine. **The Verandah** serves Thai and international cuisine. **The Terrace** offers steak and seafood barbecues. If you're craving pizza or Italian food go to **Ciao**. **Rim Naam Terrace** is another good Thai restaurant. **Sala Rim Naam** is a Thai restaurant that also has Thai dancers. **The Bamboo Bar** is the place to go for international entertainment. Try **Authors' Lounge** for afternoon tea.

Two swimming pools, the world famous Thai Cooking School and Thai Culture Program, the Spa, Oriental Sport Center, and tennis and squash are all just across the river. Conference facilities are also available.

The hotel offers air-conditioned river express service along with helicopter service to and from the airport.

Their brochure states, Recent years have seen The Oriental achieve it apotheosis as one of the world's finest hotels; a fact attested to by a broad spectrum of international authorities. I now have firsthand experience and attest to this. **General Manager, Kurt Wachtveitl, and his staff are to be commended for their high standard of service in an ambiance of beauty, grace and gentility.**

For more information contact:
The Oriental
48 Oriental Avenue
Bangkok 10500, Thailand
Telephone 2360400, 2360420
Facsimile (662) 2361937-9
Telex 82997 ORIENTAL TH

Thailand

Bangkok

The Sukhothai

Wendy Canning Church

In ancient Sukhothai (the first Thai capital, 13th - 14 century) a gentle, charming people developed an intricate societal system, where architectural splendor abounded and gracious service and devotion to duty was a way of life. Today, under the keen eye of Resident Manager, Peter Schnyder, and his corporate staff, The Sukhothai Bangkok offers a charm and grace reminiscent of a time long ago.

Located along Embassy Row on South Sathorn Road, the service and decor of The Sukhothai Hotel are a reflection of the most gracious Thai traditions. An island of beauty and serenity is discovered beyond its palm-lined driveway, surrounded by six acres of exotic flowering gardens and ponds laden with exquisite water lilies in every hue. The lobby, with its sleek modern decor of subtle grandeur blends in perfect harmony with the ancient Thai artifacts that adorn it. This is the perfect balance of Ying and Yang.

This same feeling is carried out in the public rooms and in each of the 226 rooms including 80 suites. An example of the personal touch found in one's room was a melange of exotic fruits that welcomed each guest atop the minibar on an ancient faux black pedestal. Adjacent is a fingerbowl with an orchid floating gingerly atop. Splendorous bathrooms are mirror-accented with oversized baths, a separate shower and toilet, luxurious toiletries, hairdryer, bathrobes, telephone, bottled water, fresh potpourri, and a beautiful garland of exotic flowers adorns the side of the tub.

The Sukhothai Hotel, Bangkok courtesy of The Sukhothai Hotel

Additional amenities include large closets, individually controlled air conditioning, IDD, provision for facsimile, color television, CNN news service, radio, mini bar, refrigerator, same day laundry and dry-cleaning, and personal safe. **Each guest has his or her own butler. There is 24-hour room service. Management has seen that every visitor will have a sense of welcome, elegance, serenity, and luxuriant privacy.**

Gourmets arrive from all over the city to enjoy dining facilities at The Sukhothai Bangkok: **The Celadon** is one of the most authentic traditional Thai restaurants in the city. **La Noppamas** has a beautiful dining room serving a blend of Eastern and Western dishes. The **Noppamas Bar** is an intimate venue for pre and after dinner drinks. **The Terrazzo** offers open-air dining with Italian dishes. **The Colonnade** provides a relaxing atmosphere for light meals, snacks and a wide range of beverages with daily entertainment. Lobby salons are the perfect setting for a quick refreshing drink, afternoon tea, cocktails or business gatherings.

The Sukhothai maintains close ties with Bangkok's finest golf clubs. On-site leisure facilities include a fully equipped Health Centre with gymnasium, sauna and massage, a 25-meter swimming pool, two squash courts and tennis courts.

A state-of-the-art business center caters to groups and individuals. Banquet facilities cater from 40 to 300 guests.

For more information contact:
The Sukhothai Bangkok
13/3 South Sathorn Road
Bangkok 10120, Thailand
Tel: (66-2) 287 0222
Fax: (66-2) 287 4980

Sailing a Sampling of the Windward Islands

The Star Clipper
The Number One Romantic Cruise

Wendy Canning Church

The brochure states: "The very notion of rigid itineraries is foreign to Star Clippers. In contrast to crowded cruise ships, your nimble clipper ship is free to follow the allure of fine sailing weather. To go where others can not follow. To explore pristine harbors and secret places known only to local yachtsmen. And being a sailing ship, she leaves each anchorage as clean and unspoiled as she found it."

There she was, this beautiful maiden of elegance and grace, beckoning to us like Circe to join her on another voyage. The *Star Clipper* is 360 feet long; making it the largest clipper ship ever built. A replica of the "Greyhounds of the Seas", she is the newest, tallest and fastest of the "tall ships". Yet despite her size, her tasteful design and ambiance makes one feel they are cruising on a yacht.

She carries 180 passengers and a crew of 70. There are 90 air conditioned cabins most with private marble bathrooms, wall-to-wall carpeting, wall safe, multi-channel radio, television, telephone, reading lamps, dressing tables, mirror and wardrobe, 110 volt outlet and a hairdryer.

Star Clipper at Sunset by Wendy Canning Church

There is a dining salon, piano lounge, bars, library and ample deck space for the two swimming pools, deck chairs and stretch-out areas.

This is not a ship designed for children because of the rigging, nor does she have access for the handicapped.

Each of the staffs takes a great pride in the ship. They want to know if even the slightest detail does not come up to the high standards that they have set. There is even a hot line aboard for passengers who need assistance with anything from a battery for their camera to a leaky faucet.

On Star Clipper the guest is always right even if they are wrong.

DAY ONE

As we boarded, Captain Juergen Mueller Cyran and crew welcomed and embraced us as old friends. A steel band played, rum punch was handed around, and delicious hors d'oeuvres served on top deck. This tone of warmth and tasteful style continued throughout the sailing.

Dinner was superb and beautifully presented with an emphasis on healthy fresh foods. The excellent wine list complemented the cuisine (at surprisingly low prices). After dinner we joined others on the upper deck. Sipping champagne, we watched the lights of Barbados glittering like diamonds as the ship slipped out of the harbor.

Billowing sails hoisted, cruising with the moon to light her path, her course was set for Tobago, our first port of call.

Tobago Rays by Lois Hatcher

DAY TWO - TOBAGO

Each morning began with the Captain's "story time" regarding the day's activities and our current destination. The week long sailing encompassed stops at historic islands, tours of these islands, trips to the beach (with all sorts of grown-up water toys), **excellent snorkeling and, of course, scuba diving.**

Scuba divers should not expect the kind of dive schedule that one would have on a liveaboard. The ship usually sails at night, which limits night diving and because it arrives at destinations at different times, there cannot be a fixed diving schedule. "Schedules" are dictated by the winds, which are always subject to change. This type of itinerary proves to be refreshing, because it lends itself to a balanced, yet unregimented vacation, rather than having to be at a certain place each day at a designated time.

You can count on crystal clear visibility, the comfort and camaraderie of diving in small groups, exploring enchanted dive sites, and some of the most dazzling underwater topography you've ever seen.

Our first port of call was Tobago. As the ship dropped anchor in the small harbor of Scarborough, one could glimpse the bottle green vegetation reaching high into the hills and spilling down into the bay whose small houses, awash in palettes of pastels, sat at water's edge.

Tobago, and its sister island, Trinidad, shaped like a Cuban cigar, form the independent republic of Trinidad-Tobago. No two sisters could be more different. Tobagans are directly descended from African slaves brought to farm the sugar plantations of this supreme British Crown Colony. On the other hand, Trinidad is a mixture of many races.

When sugar was no longer king, Tobago fell on hard times in 1884, and in 1889 it was made a ward of Trinidad. Even today there is what one might call a rift between the two islands.

Snorkeling tours in glass bottom boats are arranged to nearby Buccoo Reef. Here you will find a varied repository of reef fish. Spectacular underwater gardens will be found comprising brain, table, finger and plate coral. Manta rays are seen there often along with all the bantam marine life.

Divers usually take a car to the other side of the island, and then a native Captain takes you to the dive site in 10 minutes. We however, opted to go by boat. The waters were a bit choppy, but it was a treat to see the winsome beauty of Tobago from the sea.

We dived off **Little Tobago**; a 450-acre bird sanctuary also called "Bird of Paradise".

We chose to do a drift dive since the currents were very strong. We rolled over into the gossamer waters that unveiled an eye boggling assortment of sea life—silver salmon, barracuda, elegant French and Emperor angelfish, schools of black durgeon, large multi-colored spotlight parrotfish, peacock flounder, trunkfish, and shoals of smaller reef fish.

Swimming along the reef, we found the flora to be just as captivating and bristling as the fish life, tall staghorn, layered sheet coral and huge brain coral, sea rod, purple and venue sea fan, red wall sponge and the brightest of mustard colored tube sponge. The barrel sponges were particularly impressive as they were twisted in numerous different shapes almost as if a potter had formed them on his wheel.

Suddenly our guide spotted an Atlantic Manta ray. It was immense, yet glided above like a ballerina in *Giselle*. This was my first sighting of a Manta, hence the highlight of my dive. It was worth the entire week's voyage to see it. This is a site not to be missed!

TOBAGO AREAS OF INTEREST

We toured the charming small town. Shopping is not top on one's list here, but we did spot a local artisan's wares, lovely artwork made from the Calabash shell on the front walls of his house. The Calabash is an inedible fruit. The artisan cuts out the center and paints the shells to make masks, pocketbooks, etc.

Weathered West Indian style stores and the small restaurant had a winsome charm. Nearby, a cricket match was taking place with an enthusiastic audience (including my husband).

One will find picture-perfect beaches southeast of Scarborough. **Pigeon Point** is one of the comeliest. They have rooms to change in and a small restaurant.

Driving towards the Caribbean side you will see the Trinidad-Tobago residence of the President at **Fort William**. Traveling on you will come to the larger city of **Speyside** with restaurants and shops.

DAY THREE - GRENADA

Anchoring off St. George's, the capital of Grenada, early Monday morning. Three dives were planned at **Molinaire**, one in the morning, afternoon, and a night dive.

Only ten minutes from the ship, this is a mellow reef dive that is perfect for all levels of divers and snorkelers. The waters are unadulterated and the fringe reef (wall reef) tops out at 30 feet.

We did both the morning and afternoon dive, so we could cover the entire area and acquaint ourselves with it for the night dive.

Descending to the sandy bottom we navigated down the valleys like highways between the sites. Fish life is smaller here but plentiful. Pufferfish, butterfly fish, French angelfish, spotted moray eel and an octopus were a sampling of what we saw. I call this reef "fish in love" for never have I seen so many fish swim in pairs.

GRENADA AREAS OF INTEREST

The shops in **Georgetown** carry a variety of duty-free goods from cashmere to perfume. Visit the lively **open-air market** for straw goods and, of course, spices.

Two-mile **Grand Anse Beach** has a spot for every sun worshipper.

At **Gouyave** (formerly Charlotte Town), you will find the primary **spice factory**.

Dougaldston Estate is a working plantation, and one of the main growers and exporters of nutmeg and cocoa.

Grenville is the second largest town in Grenada. It has its own **spice factory** and an **outdoor market**.

In the north are **Sauteurs** and **Morne des Sauteurs** (Leaper's Hill). East of here is **Levera Bay** an idyllic spot to swim. This is where Columbus is said to have seen the island in 1498.

When returning to St. George's beware of the hairpin turns in the road taking you through tropical rainforests and past gorges of stunning beauty. Visit **Grand Etang National Park** along the way. Its extinct volcano, 549 meters (1,800 feet) high, cradles a beautiful lake of 13 acres.

DAY FOUR - CARRIACOU

We dropped anchor the next day between Carriacou and Sandy Island. In the morning we visited the small town. The island's population is 8,000. **Here there are over 100 rum shops, but only one gas station.**

One can sense the serenity that has lasted since the first settlers arrived. Its people keep very much to themselves. They were indifferent to our visit and we had the feeling they would just as soon be left to their daily routine of fishing. Some say voodoo is still practiced here.

We hired a taxi and toured the area, catching glimpses of the ruins of former sugar plantations. There were wonderful pristine beaches.

Do visit the **museum in Hillsborough**, its capital, on the western shores. **This area is home to artist Canute Caliste, who has gained a well-earned reputation for his primitive native paintings.** He is almost blind, but continues his work. Ask a taxi driver to take you to his gallery. His works are for sale and on display in his small native shop next to his home on the outskirts of town.

SANDY ISLAND

After visiting the town, **we spent a delightful day scuba diving and snorkeling**, and devouring a resplendent barbecue picnic.

There is a nice reef off Sandy Island that bottoms at 60 feet. Here you will see all species of reef fish and a thriving underwater kingdom.

DAY FIVE - BEQUIA

Bequia is situated between St. Vincent on its north nine miles away and Mustique seven miles south. Its population of 4,874 speaks English. The winter temperatures range from 65 - 85 degrees and in summer between 75 - 95 degrees.

The Caribs occupied Bequia as warring factions fought for power on other islands. In 1675, *The Palmira*, a slave ship, sank off Bequia. Many Africans survived and they became known as Black Caribs. Bequia continued to retain her independence from the British, French, Spanish, and Dutch until the 18th century. A treaty in 1762 gave Bequia to England but in 1779 it was given to France until finally with the Treaty of Versailles it was again given back to the English. In 1979 Bequia gained independence under the British Commonwealth, today administered by Prime Minister Rt. Honorable J.E. Mitchell.

Bequia has become a little livelier since the airport was built, but it still remains a haven for yachties. Boat building continues to thrive.

There are many beaches of alluring beauty on Bequia. At the southern end of **Admiralty Bay** on the leeward side are **Princess Margaret Beach** and **Lower Bay**. On the northern side is **Friendship Bay**. On the southern side of the island you will find **Spring Bay**. **All of these beaches offer superb snorkeling.**

The two dives offered in Bequia were at **Devil's Table** off Moon Hole and **Devil's Cape**, both on the west side. Both of these were drift dives because of the currents.

At Devil's Table, we dropped down to 50 feet off a vertical coral wall. Swimming out from this is a web of tunnels and crevices. Further along, one reaches the vertical coral wall, making a truly interesting dive. Along with the common reef fish, we saw lobster, a spotted moray eel, healthy hard and soft coral, and a good-sized stingray.

At Devil's Cape we saw a wondrous variety of reef fish. A stingray and many eels call the site home. The visibility was excellent.

BEQUIA AREAS OF INTEREST

The shopping area is in the capital, **Port Elizabeth.** We found almost anything a visitor might need on its one long rear street—lovely boutiques, restaurants, the bank, customs, the post office, and even the police station. Colorful beach wraps can be found at **Solanders.**

Especially recommended are the **Bequia Bookshop** and the **Crab Hole Boutique** that had not only the loveliest selection of clothing and native craft, but also its owners could not have been more hospitable.

Stop for a cool drink at the **Fragipani Restaurant**.

DAY SIX - ST. LUCIA

St. Lucia, the largest of the English speaking windwards, was the last stop on our itinerary. She is a melange of wondrous sights from her coastline of secluded, silver sand beaches, to her hills of thick jungle vegetation scented with perfumed flowers in a kaleidoscope of color. The towering Pitons seem to brush the clouds and slip into its magical, clear waters, which are alive with sea creatures.

It was not until the mid-17th century that the French were able to drive out the fierce Caribs and set up a colony on St. Lucia. The French influence is still seen today. English is the official language, but its 150,000 natives speak patois.

The British longed to add this prosperous and beautiful island to their pocketbook of colonies and throughout the 17th and 18th centuries continued to make a bid for her. Alas, all efforts failed and in 1802 with the Treaty of Versailles, St. Lucia remained French.

The 19th century saw her change her political seat after Napoleon fell to the British. Her large plantations of cotton, coffee, sugar, and coconut contented not only the British landowners, but also the St. Lucia government. Slaves gained their freedom, and the 20th century brought St. Lucia full circle to independence.

We dived in the **Marine Reserve** where it is necessary to hire a local guide, because the entire area around the Pitons is a Marine Reserve. Our dive site, the **4 Pitons**, was comprised of conical shaped reefs that began at 15 feet and descended to 80 feet. It was mind boggling to see so many varieties of invertebrates, chromatic and healthy. We viewed a wealth of black coral throughout the dive. The barrel sponges grew in every shape and size.

Sea Horse by Peter Jackson

There is excellent snorkeling at Grand Anse, Castries, and Rodney Rock Beach.

ST. LUCIA AREAS OF INTEREST

Although the St. Lucia government has built new roads, many have hair-raising turns, but do be brave and hire a car or taxi and tour this gem that sits atop a volcano.

From the **Governor's Residence** you will have a majestic view of St. Lucia's lush scenery, the Pitons, and Castries. This Victorian era building also houses a small museum.

The northern road is the best on the island. **Driving through its emerald hills you will find some wonderful beaches: Vigie Beach, Cros Islet, and Choe Beach.**

A museum, as well as a bird sanctuary, are found on **Pigeon Island**, a National Park linked by road to the main island. It is a repository of wild life with the ever-present scent of wild jungle flowers.

If you do nothing else, a must on the south of the island is the Soufriere Volcano.

In the town of **Soufriere** you will find a wonderful **open-air market** abuzz with activity. The shopping arcade is built in typical West Indian style. St. Lucia is not a shopping mecca, but local artisans make lovely baskets, hats and placemats of straw. This is a good spot for photographs.

Duty-free shops at the hotels carry designer clothes, cosmetics and perfumes.

Try a Piton, the local beer.

HOMEWARD BOUND

That evening, the Captain hosted a dinner for his guests. The crew had spoiled us extravagantly each day, but that night their special efforts created an evening that would stand up to any 5-star restaurant. Champagne was passed around and he toasted us with the most charming and warmest sentiments.

By day the *Star Clipper* takes you to worlds yet unknown, entertains you, delights you, and aims to stretch your minds and feed your souls. At night she lull you to sleep, her bow cutting sharply through the blue seas. **On this voyage she did not disappoint to enchant, pamper and seduce us, so that even before it was time to say goodbye, we discussed a future date and itinerary to sail her again. The Star Clipper** is Rated the Number 1 Romantic Cruise. We concur!

For more information contact:
Star Clippers
4101 Salzedo Avenue
Coral Gables, Florida 33146, USA
Phone: 1-800-442-0553 USA
Phone: 305-442-0553
Fax: 305-442-1611

BIOGRAPHIES OF AUTHORS
AND PHOTOGRAPHERS

Instructor **Rod Abbotson** has been diving since 1979 and since 1984 in a professional capacity. He operated his own dive base in Sardinia (Mediterranean) for 8 years. Rod loves to impart his enthusiasm and knowledge to other divers, particularly novice divers.

Gill Balchin is responsible for the overall operations of Seastar Watersports as well as manager of the Alcazar Hotel. Diving is one of the few relaxations's he enjoys. Gill has been living in Jordan for the last 15 years and has a wealth of information to give any visitor and advice on what to see and do in Jordan to make the most of their holiday.

Carol Boone, a native of Austin, Texas, began her fascination with photography at age twelve. She has traveled extensively since then, capturing images throughout the world.

Carol graduated in 1982 from the University of Texas with a B.S. in Communications, and studied photography at Brooks Photographic Art Institute in Santa Barbara. She has been in numerous publications on photography, diving science, nature and travel. She has also had exhibits in Austin, Santa Barbara, Aspen and Houston.

Today, Carol has her own portrait business in Austin, and travels to photograph the sea. She has photographed in the Caribbean, Hawaii, California, New Guinea, Australia, Micronesia, the Red Sea and Suborn Islands.

Tom Boyd is president of Rockfish Productions, Inc., a California video/film production company that produces environmentally themed documentaries. Rockfish recently completed a mini-documentary on the Florida Manatee.

Orville S. Carman is 39 years old and has been in the Navy since high school, spending most of his time overseas. He is a U.S. Navy Mineman and part of the Military Police/Customs operation. He received his Open Water certification in 1987, but has not been able to do much diving lately due to the distance to the only legal site for foreigners to dive. However, he has had the chance to go snorkeling on Crete with the Greek EOD, a bomb disposal unit, and found a 200-pound W.W.II naval gun shell.

Richard H. Cassens was born and reared in Glen Cove, Long Island, New York. Growing up within six blocks of the sound, his water experience started as soon as he could walk. At the age of ten, with mask, snorkel and fins, Richard discovered that with a spear he could get eels hiding in the grass. In 1959, at age 14, he made his first scuba dive and loved it. The visibility was 10 feet, and the bottom was sand, but he still loved that dive.

After completing his degree in 1974, Richard signed on with the U.S. Peace Corps. Finding himself in Jamaica, W.I., where the waters are warm and clear, he resumed free diving. Upon returning to the U.S., Richard received his diving certification. Then in 1983 he completed the NAUI instructor's certification course. Since then Richard has certified over 350 new divers and over 50 advanced divers. Richard also received a U.S. Coast Guard Captains License (100 ton).

After leaving his position as Senior Industrial Engineer, General Dynamics, Convair Division, Richard started America II, Scuba Diving Charters in Mission Bay, San Diego. He is currently a Scuba Diving Charter Boat Captain on America II out of Mission Bay, San Diego, California.

Andy Cobb introduced me to my first dive with hundreds of sharks on Aliwal Shoal at a site called "The Cathedral". The dive was magical and taught me that these enormous creatures of the sea are more to be respected than feared.

Andy, with his partner, **Jane**, specialize in professional, personalized, safe, eco-oriented adventures. As a SATOUR registered field guide, he can put a diving/snorkeling, non-diver and game park safari together for small groups in Natal, tours of the Natal battlefields, staying in a Zulu kraal, or a walking safari in the Cape or Transvaal.

Andy formed the Kenya Diving Association in order to self regulate the diving industry in Kenya. A great cheek even though he had crossed over to being a NAUI Advanced Diver (now Master Diver). The mix of commercial, resort diving and amateur divers in the association was unique. The association likewise had an excellent relationship with the Kenya Navy. In fact the association was able to commission the Kenya Navy Recompression Chamber and provide a manning roster with qualified chamber operators, should anyone in the diving community require recompression.

Andy moved to South Africa in early 1981, where he became a NAUI Scuba Instructor and served the South African Police Diving Unit for eight years. During this time he pioneered diving on Aliwal Shoal, off the south coast of Kwazulu/Natal in the Indian Ocean.

Steve Curtis arrived in Kenya from Zimbabwe 11 years ago. Having dived a great deal with the Military in Rhodesia, Steve decided to make his deep love of the water into a career by pursuing the sport of Scuba Diving.

Steve's thorough briefings are legendary, as is his caring attitude to both new and experienced divers. Where the boats go each day depends on an assessment of the conditions, with good visibility and no currents a top priority. Customers' request for specific dive sites are honored when possible.

One of Steve's pet projects is the conservation of the reefs. He voluntarily trained members of the Kenya Wildlife Service (a Government organization set up to control and protect the Parks and Reserves in Kenya) to PADI Open Water Diver Status in order that they may "police" and protect the reefs more efficiently.

Cherry Dobbins, who is a British diver and qualified instructor, has many years' experience diving around Cyprus. She runs Cydive, Ltd. a well-established British Sub-Aqua Club and PADI school.

Stephen John Dye's diving qualifications: Royal Navy ships diver, H.S.E. Part III commercial diver, British Sub Aqua Club dive leader. Experienced in Naval diving, civil engineering diving, and sports diving.

Current occupation: Robert Gordon's Institute of Technology Survival School. Involved with training offshore workers in the oil industry. Training includes free-fall lifeboat abandonment, fire fighting, underwater helicopter escape, in water survival techniques.

Raymond Elman is an artist and writer living in Truro, Massachusetts on Cape Cod. He has written travel pieces for various newspapers and magazines and is the author of *A Critical Guide to Cross-Country Ski Areas*, published by Viking/Penguin. He has also published and edited several art magazines. Mr. Elman's paintings, prints, and drawings have been widely exhibited, beginning with his first exhibit in Provincetown in 1971. His work hangs in many US embassies around the world, and in several museums. He is also deeply involved with computer-based communications and is the president of Streamline Communications, Inc. of Boston.

Lynn Funkhouser is an internationally published photographer, author, lecturer, environmentalist, andventuress, and leader in dive travel. She specializes in underwater, nature, travel, and environmental images.

Her dramatic photos have been published in calendars, ads, and major magazines, notably in "Audubon", "Animals", "International Wildlife", "Time" and "National Geographic". Lynn is committed to making a difference on this planet through her images and lectures. She serves as Vice President of the International Marinelife Alliance, USA and as an Advisory Director to Ocean Voice International, Canada.

Lynn was honored to receive the 1994 SEASPACE/PADI Environmental Awareness Award "for her continuing efforts promoting reef preservation in the Philippines and around the world." She leads several trips a year to the Philippines.

If you wish to contact her, you can call her at 312 467 4340, or E-mail at Lynn-Funkhouser@compuserve.com.

Martha Watkins Gilkes is a free lance photojournalist, an underwater photographer, and a professional underwater model based on Antigua. A scuba diving instructor through PADI for 18 years, she owns and operates her own scuba diving business, Fanta-Sea Island Divers, on Antigua. She has lived in the Caribbean for 20 years and has dived throughout the entire Caribbean region. She has served as the President of the Barbados based Eastern Caribbean Safe Diving Association for the past 13 years and also serves as the Diving Liaison Officer for the Historical and Archeological Society of Antigua.

Jane and Richard Goulston are NAUI, ACUC, and TDI instructors that are actively teaching in the Northeast. Jane is the founder of Sea Scuba, and teaches adapted aquatics for Easter Seals. She is also a co-instructor for the MIT scuba program. Jane is an artist in her spare time and sculpts, while Richard is an Engineer in the biotech industry.

Bruce Hastings, a NAUI instructor, has been diving for over 20 years. He has dived extensively around the outer islands of Boston Harbor and the New England north shore, but now prefers the warmer southern waters and tries to make several trips to the Bahamas and Caribbean yearly.

Lois Hatcher has been active in diving since 1982 when she learned how to dive off the frigid coast of western Canada. Since her first dive she was hooked and went on to become a PADI instructor. She has worked in Southern California, Canada, Thailand and Australia.

As the amount of dives she logged grew in number, so did her interest in Underwater Photography. She now resides in Grand Cayman where she owns a sucessful underwater photo/video shop and spends her days snapping pictures, teaching photo classes and shooting videos for visitors to the island.

Willie Hewitt was born in Barbados, but moved to New Zealand in 1974 at age 11 where he became open water certified at age 16, and then became a PADI OWSI in 1988. Since then Willie has successfully completed nine specialty rating, including Underwater Photography, and now is a PADI IDC Staff Instructor.

He started Underwater Photography in 1989. Returning to Barbados later that same year, Willie continues to indulge in his hobby. He has taken photos in New Zealand, St. Lucia and Grenada.

Willie's photos have been published, but at the moment he mainly takes photos for personal enjoyment. He spends most of his energies owning and managing the scuba centers at Sandy Lane and Cobblers' Cove, plus servicing scuba divers on the west coast of Barbados.

Bill Hull is a former teacher and researcher of children's thinking. He continues to explore these interests by studying his own learning of physical skills, especially ice dancing and table tennis. He lives in Cambridge, Mass.

Joan Iaconetti is a freelance writer/photographer, based in Manhattan and in the Caribbean during the winter months. Her diving travel articles have appeared in *Travel & Leisure, Caribbean Travel & Life* and *New Woman*, and she covered the Caymans and the Grenadines for *Fodor's Caribbean Guidebooks*.

Mike Innis began diving in 1958 for the U.S. Navy. He holds certifications from PADI, NAUI, NACD, IANTD, PSA, and TDI, and is a certified cavern, cave and extended range diver. Mike's been taking underwater pictures, both still and video, for the last 12 years, and has had his work published in several different diving periodicals. He retired from IBM Corporation after 30 years of service, and now finally has the time to dive almost as much as he wants to.

Don Lanman is a PADI rescue level diver with over 27 years of diving experience. He has logged hundreds of dives around the world, including: Hong Kong, Truk Lagoon, Honolulu, Maui, Kona, Bahamas, Netherlands Antilles, Bimini, Cabo San Lucas, Puerto Vallarta, Cozumel, Grand Cayman, Australia, Florida, Nevada, Ohio, Arizona, New Mexico, Texas and California. Don owns a Direct Response Advertising Agency in Sausalito, California with a focus on the travel industry.

Alan Marquardt is an experienced and published underwater photographer and videographer, guide and a superb one at that. He is the owner of South Side Scuba in Bermuda.

Donna Marchetti is a free-lance writer from Cleveland, Ohio. Her articles on travel, diving, and other topics have appeared in the New York Times, Los Angeles Times, Cleveland Plain Dealer, Scuba Times, Rodale's Scuba Diving and many other publications. She is a contributing writer for North Coast Sports, a sports and outdoors recreation newspaper based in Cleveland. An avid diver, she has dived in Dominica, Puerto Rico, Cozumel, St. Kitts, Florida, New England, California, Palau, Rota, and the Great Lakes. Her favorite close-to-home dive spot is the Niagara River.

Glen Mullin San Francisco, CA USA Certification date: 1986 experience in Monterey California diving, Pacific Northwest, Caribbean, GBR, Australia, Indonesia, Hawaii.

Simon Nelson has 17 years of diving experience and has dived in Ireland, the United Kingdom, the Meditteranean, Kenya, the Red Sea and the Caribbean. With his wife, also a keen diver, they run a small dive shop and marine chandlery. After 7 years working around the world as an engineer they settled in West Cork six years ago to indulge their passion for scuba diving and to provide facilities for others wishing to enjoy the wonders of this beautiful corner of a beautiful county.

Jeffrey Ray Noordhoek is originally from Nebraska. Jeffrey now lives in Chicago. He enjoys hunting, fishing, and the performing arts.

Captain Victor Organ started diving in 1965 at the age of 14 in Palm Beach, Florida. Holds certifications from NAUI, SSI, PADI and is currently an Instructor Trainer for PDIC and IDEA. Over the last 26 years he has logged over 1,800 dives of which 1,600 were made in the Red Sea.

Other diving locations and experience include the Atlantic off the Florida Coast and Keys, St. Croix, USVI, Mediterranean Sea from Cyprus and Italy, Seychelles in the Indian Ocean, Sea of Siam off Thailand, China Sea and Zulu Sea in the Philippines, Hawaii in the South Pacific and altitude and ice diving in the Flaming Gorge, Wyoming.

He has written several articles for local dive club news letters and has had pictures featured in Ahlam Wahsalam, Saudia's flight magazine, the Wild Life Book of Saudi Arabia and numerous advertising layouts for local hotels and companies.

Chris Politopoulos is the diving instructor (PADI & NAUI) and owner of the diving center, Lucky Scuba Divers. His diving experience includes being in an Underwater Destruction Team as an officer of the Greek Navy for ten years, 1970-1980.

Karen Rodriguez: I was born in Pampa, Texas, and am an Air Force brat, having traveled all over the world I eventually got to Cali, Colombia with my Colombian husband. I learned to dive in Cali and became a Fedecas instructor five years ago. I am also a PADI and NAUI instructor. For the past seven years I have organized live-aboard trips to the Pacific Coast using anything I could get my hands on as long as it would float. A year and a half ago my partner, Harold Botero, also a NAUI instructor, and I bought a typical Colombian banana boat. It floated, but just barely! We have redone the hull and put in navigational equipment for safety. We provide clean sheets and fresh water to bathe in from a faucet, good food, and wonderful diving.

Beginning writing at age seven, owning his first printing press at nine, **Bill Roe** was inspired by his grandfather, both a writer and a deckhand aboard the classic windjammers in the pre-turn of the century Merchant Marine.

Being raised around the fishing pier in Deerfield Beach, FL in the late fifties, Bill strengthened his bond with the sea, and learned to SCUBA dive in 1962.

In the early eighties, Bill began writing features and reviews for Florida Scuba News, a Florida Dive Magazine. His travels for the Magazine have taken him throughout the Keys a dozen times each year. Bill expressed happiness when offered the chance to share "his Keys" with our readers.

In March of 1994 **Louise Seddon** became suddenly ill and passed away in a tiny hospital in her beloved Roatan. She was on a diving/photography excursion, of course.

Born in Murphysboro, Tennessee, Louise chose to become an educator; her sister, Rae, went on to become a doctor and an astronaut.

In 1978, **Steve Simonsen** helped open the first dive shop in Boulder, Colorado. In 1979, he bacame a NAUI instructor. He first began using a Nikonos II in Cozumel, Mexico. Steve traveled to exotic destinations such as Moorea in French Polynesia, the Red Sea in Egypt, Martinique in the French West Indies, Cancun and Playa Blanca in Mexico.

Paul Snowman has been scuba diving since 1979 and has completed over 1,000 dives. He has a First-Class Diver Rating from the N.Z. Underwater Association. He is also a C.M.A.S. 4 Star Diver and N.A.U.I. Openwater II.

With over 30 years experience as a hunter in Northern woods, first with a firearm, then with a camera, **Ron Streeter** learned that being close to nature, and understanding it, was the only way to photograph it.

Ron made an easy transition to U/W photography back in 1985. Since then, he averages 300 dives a year in search for the perfect shot.

Shooting literally thousands of slides annually as he travels the Keys and the Caribbean, Ron processes each one himself to achieve control of the quality of his work.

Ron uses housed cameras, with a combination of strobes he mixes and matches to get proper light for his photos. Drawing from his long time "real job" as an Electronic Engineer, he often finds himself on the phone to various manufacturers, discussing improvements to these devices.

With thousands of slides on file already, Ron has become his own "stock house", and is in the process of forming one, in conjunction with several other South Florida photographers.

If you have need for some quality underwater shots, or wish to discuss an assignment either topside or below, call him in Ft. Lauderdale at 305-561-8879.

Mark Strickland has had a close relationship with the sea since an early age. Growing up in Florida, he has worked many years as an ocean lifeguard, boat captain, and diving instuctor. After living in the Virgin Islands and Australia, Mark headed to Phuket, Thailand where he has been based for the last 8 years. Rarely setting foot on dry land, Mark spends most of his time among the islands and reefs of the Andaman Sea, serving as a cruise director/photo pro on Fantasea Divers' live-aboard dive boat, M/V Fantasea.

Mark's photos and articles have appeared in Magazines and books around the world, including Asian Diver, Action Asia, Ocean Realm, Discover Diving, Scuba Times, Trilogy, UWF, Sawasdee, Tauchen, Sub, Sportdiving, Sport Diver and many others. He is also the principle author and photographer for Asian Diver's latest book SCUBA GUIDE THAILAND.

Mark operates his own stock photo/video library, OCEANIC IMPRESSIONS, P.O. Box 22 Patong Beach, Phuket 83150, Thailand, Tel: (66-76 340-309.)

Charlene Taylor lives in a small Texas town, an hour's drive north of Dallas. In 1982, a NAUI dive instructor, Susan Lucas, taught her to dive and since then she has advanced to the level of Assistant Instructor. She takes pictures with a Canon EOS 650 in an Ikelite housing and loves every minute underwater

She is a Justice of the Peace Court Clerk in Denison, Texas, a certified NAUI Asst. Instructor, and has been to Cozumel three times, the Florida Keys, Belize (Isla Mia live-aboard) and Roatan twice.

Kurt Turner: He grew up in Northern New York State, where he survived several early near drowning accidents. Initial underwater experiences include snorkeling and an attempt at building an underwater breathing apparatus to retrieve soda pop bottles from beneath piers and docks. He joined the Navy in 1960 and was introduced to their style of diving in 1964. After 8 years of service he settled in Los Angeles for 20 years, he is a graduate of Pepperdine University.

Presently, he lives in Florida where he is active in the diving community. He holds numerous diving certifications including instructor cards from NAUI and YMCA.

Al J. Venter has been diving for a quarter of a century from the South China Sea to the Caribbean, including the Indian Ocean, Red Sea, the Meditterranean and most of Africa and the Atlantic Islands (Cape Verde, Sao Tome, etc.)

Al is an author, publisher, journalist, and documentary film maker. He has made 33 films on African and island states, and others on the wars in Afghanistan, El Salvador, Middle East (including Lebanon and Beirut), Israel, Biafran, Ethiopia, Portugal, Rhodesia, and Angola. He has also produced an underwater film entitled "The Witch Hunters".

His main preoccupations include diving, writing and highlighting potential ecological disasters.

Instructor **Elja E. Vries** has been diving since 1984 and since 1993 in a professional capacity. She is a marine biologist. Her knowledge of the uniqueness of the ecological niche that is the Gulf of Aqaba is an added plus for divers.

What Readers Said About Aqua Expeditions Volume I:

"No diver worth his weight belt could fail to be thrilled upon finding a copy of Aqua Expeditions global travel guide."
Boston Herald, Adventure Getaways by Ric Bourie

"On behalf of the Ministry of Tourism of Turkey please accept our deep appreciation and thanks for the wonderful chapter on Turkey in Aqua Expeditions. We were very impressed not only by the detailed presentation of all the related information but also with the amount of research you had to make to create such a wonderful and stimulating piece on Turkey. You have contributed a great deal to the promotion of Turkey, a country which values her rich heritage and historical treasures."
Leyla Ozhan, Director, Turkish Tourist Office

Congratulations! You have produced a splendid book.
Ian Carlton, Retired Director, Waterstones Booksellers

I've been diving for 20 years all over the world. I love your book, Aqua Expeditions. I am exposing it to my dive friends and professional organizations.
Annette Spaulding, Bellows Falls, VT

I see it as one-of-a-kind. While most other books we carry on dive locations target where to dive in a specific part of the world, your book covers a multitude of places. It is well written. Congratulations on the fantastic job!
Best Publishing Company, Jim Joiner, Director

Your most interesting book should be catalogued promptly for the Athenaeum's collections. In particuler the section on Mauritius caught my eye and envy.
Library of the Boston Athenaeum
Rodney Armstrong, Director and Librarian

My ambitious goal is to be certified as an instructor. My dream inspired by Wendy Canning Church's Aqua Expeditions.
Michael J. Flynn

Top sub-aqua expert and writer Wendy Canning Church has rated Bermuda a diving and snorkeling paradise in her international bible for divers. It's now distributed worldwide.
Raymond Hainey, The Royal Gazette, Bermuda

"Each dive center or live-aboard listed holds the highest of safety standards, and the resorts/hotels selected deliver the quality they advertise."
DEMA Daily Reporter, Underwater USA

Each location entry describes underwater features, conditions, and wildlife, and offers an expert assessment of onshore resources. Special sections cover "Honeymoon" dives for couples looking for an unforgettable vacation.

Aqua Expeditions is without question the most comprehensive guide to local and exotic diving locations. The rating of accommodations and dining facilities is an incomparable asset.
Smoki Bacon and Richard Concannon,
Co-hosts T.V. Show: On The Town

You will find information about exotic places that is just about impossible to find anywhere else. Ever read an article on the underwater statue of Christ in the harbor in Portofino, Italy? Or the submerged caves off the coast of Kenya? ...The book is illustrated throughout by gorgeous color photographs taken both underwater and above.
Outdoor Adventures, Donna Marchetti

A description of some of the best dive sites, and technical details regarding facilities.
John Bantin, "Diver" Magazine, Great Britain

Have you always wanted to try scuba diving, but were absolutely clueless as to where to begin? Check Aqua Expeditions: A Global Travel Guide for the Scuba Diver and Snorkeler provides detailed information on dive sites and boat/resort operators located all over the world.
Rachel Grumman, Dare To Be You, New Woman Magazine

Have bought your book Aqua Expeditions which I find an excellent tool for people like me that heavily travel and enjoy diving.
Demetrios Stratos, Greece

Going by the book: Before your next dive trip, pick up a copy of Wendy Canning Church's Aqua Expeditions. It's full of detailed information on safe, licensed dive sites all over the world.
Sports Traveler

Aqua Expeditions, Great!!!
Martha Franklin

Not only "hot spots" but "hideaways" – all over the world. It also provides insights into cultures, history and even topside excursions.
Caribbean Compass

You did a great job on the book! My best for the future.
Douglas Triggs, Attorney at Law

The book reads like a personal journal, a novel and in parts it is poetry!
Gloria Nemerowiz, President Pine Manor College